C000292502

Atlas contents

Scale 1:190,000 or 3 miles to 1 inch

Map pages	inside front cover

Route planning	**II–XVI**
Route planner	II–V
London district	VI–VII
Road safety cameras	VIII
Tourist sites with satnav friendly postcodes	IX
Caravan and camping sites in Britain	X–XI
Traffic signs and road markings	XII–XIII
Channel hopping	XIV–XV
Ferries to Ireland and the Isle of Man	XVI

Atlas symbols	1

Road maps 1:190,000 scale	2–112
Channel Islands 1:135,000 scale	6–7
Isle of Man 1:190,000 scale	60
Skye & The Small Isles 1:340,000 scale	100
Western Isles 1:703,000 scale	106
Orkney and Shetland Islands 1:709,000 scale	106

Ferry ports

Aberdeen Harbour	99	Harwich Int. Port	23	Pembroke Dock	XVI
Calais	XV	Heysham Harbour	XVI	Plymouth, Port of	XIV
Channel Tunnel	13	Holyhead Harbour	XVI	Poole, Port of	XIV
Dover, Port of	XV	Liverpool Docks	XVI	Port of Tyne	77
Fishguard Harbour	XVI	Newhaven Harbour	XV	Portsmouth Harbour	XV

Restricted junctions	113

Ireland road maps 1:1 million scale	114–115

Town plans

Aberdeen	99	Great Yarmouth	51	Nottingham	120
Aberystwyth	32	Harrogate	118	Oxford	120
Bath	116	Inverness	118	Peterborough	121
Birmingham	116	Ipswich	119	Plymouth	121
Blackpool	116	Kingston upon Hull	119	Portsmouth	121
Bradford	116	Leeds	119	Salisbury	121
Bristol	116	Leicester	119	Sheffield	121
Cambridge	116	Lincoln	119	Southampton	121
Canterbury	117	Liverpool	54	Southend-on-Sea	23
Cardiff	117	Llandudno	53	Stratford-	
Chester	117	LONDON	119	upon-Avon	122
Coventry	117	Manchester	120	Sunderland	71
Derby	117	Middlesbrough	71	Swansea	122
Dundee	117	Milton Keynes	120	Swindon	122
Durham	118	Newcastle		Wolverhampton	122
Edinburgh	118	upon Tyne	120	Worcester	122
Exeter	118	Newquay	3	York	122
Glasgow	118	Norwich	120		

Index to place names	123–144
County, administrative area map	123

Distances and journey times	inside back cover

25th edition June 2015

© AA Media Limited 2015

Original edition printed 1991.

Cartography:
All cartography in this atlas edited, designed and produced by the Mapping Services Department of AA Publishing (A05305).

This atlas contains Ordnance Survey data © Crown copyright and database right 2015

This atlas is based upon Crown Copyright and is reproduced with the permission of Land & Property Services under delegated authority from the Controller of Her Majesty's Stationery Office, © Crown copyright and database right 2015. PMLPA No. 100497.

© Ordnance Survey Ireland/Government of Ireland. Copyright Permit No. MP000115.

Publisher's Notes:
Published by AA Publishing (a trading name of AA Media Limited, whose registered office is Fanum House, Basing View, Basingstoke, Hampshire RG21 4EA, UK. Registered number 06112600).

All rights reserved. No part of this publication may be reproduced, stored in a retrieval system, or transmitted in any form or by any means – electronic, mechanical, photocopying, recording or otherwise – unless the permission of the publisher has been given beforehand.

ISBN: 978 0 7495 7682 0 (spiral bound)
ISBN: 978 0 7495 7681 3 (paperback)

A CIP catalogue record for this book is available from The British Library.

Disclaimer:
The contents of this atlas are believed to be correct at the time of the latest revision, it will not contain any subsequent amended, new or temporary information including diversions and traffic control or enforcement systems. The publishers cannot be held responsible or liable for any loss or damage occasioned to any person acting or refraining from action as a result of any use or reliance on material in this atlas, nor for any errors, omissions or changes in such material. This does not affect your statutory rights.

The publishers would welcome information to correct any errors or omissions and to keep this atlas up to date. Please write to the Atlas Editor, AA Publishing, The Automobile Association, Fanum House, Basing View, Basingstoke, Hampshire RG21 4EA, UK.
E-mail: roadatlasfeedback@theaa.com

Acknowledgements:
AA Publishing would like to thank the following for their assistance in producing this atlas:

RoadPilot mobile Information on fixed speed camera locations provided by and © 2015 RoadPilot Ltd.

Crematoria data provided by the Cremation Society of Great Britain. Cadw, English Heritage, Forestry Commission, Historic Scotland, Johnsons, National Trust and National Trust for Scotland, RSPB, The Wildlife Trust, Scottish Natural Heritage, Natural England, The Countryside Council for Wales (road maps).

Road signs are © Crown Copyright 2015. Reproduced under the terms of the Open Government Licence.

Printer:
Printed in Italy by Canale & C. S.p.A.

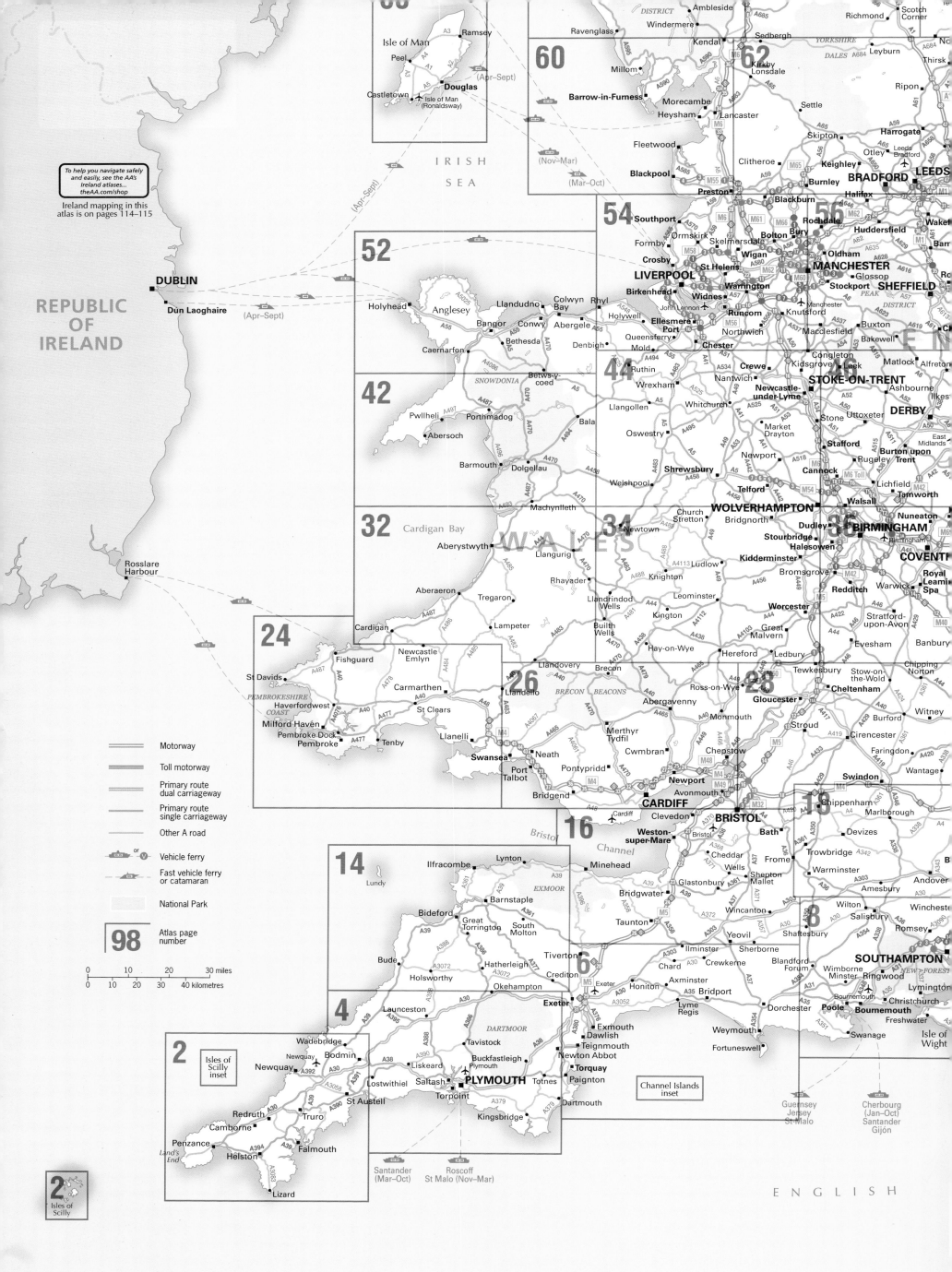

Route planner

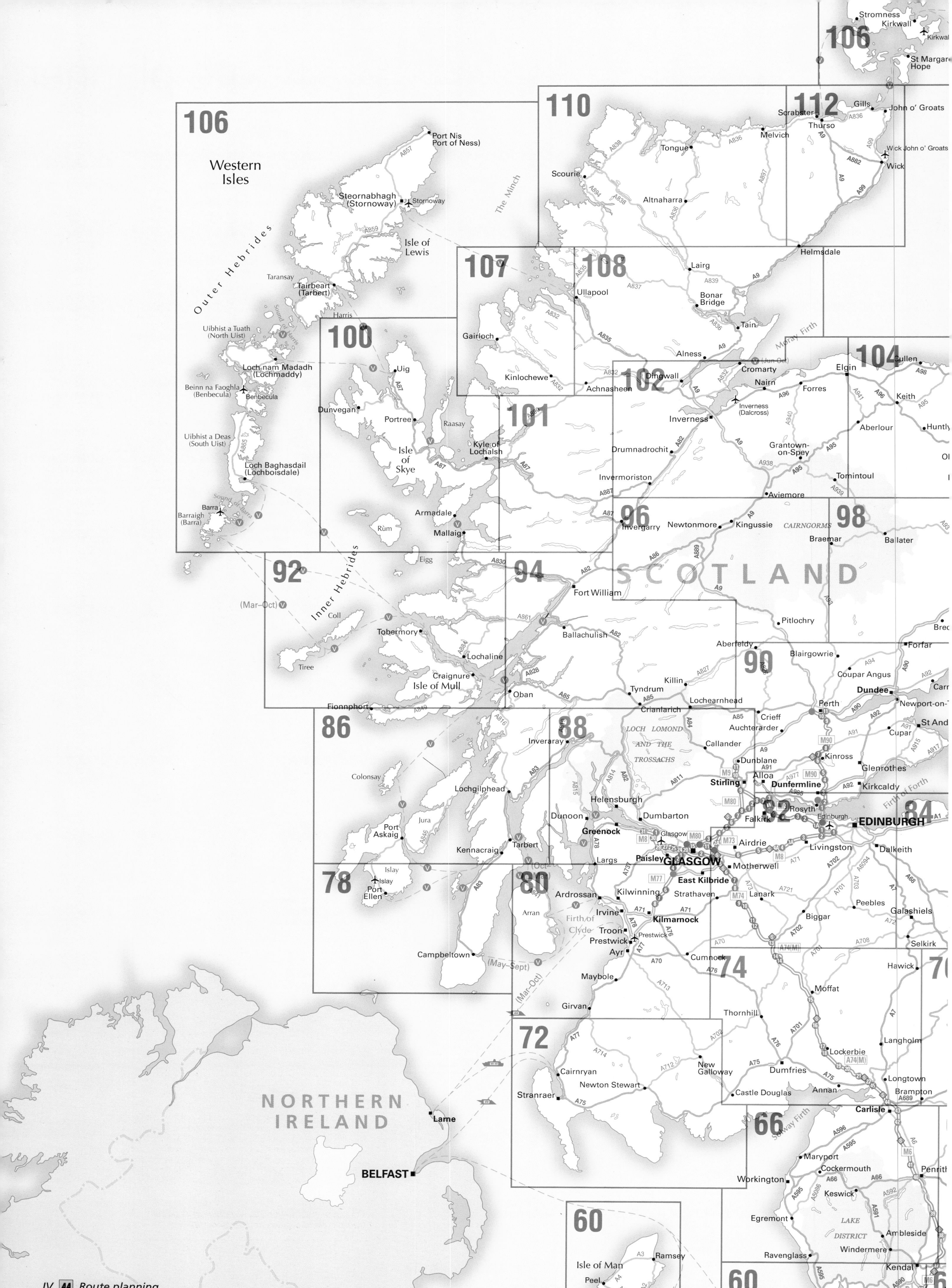

106

110

106

112

Western
Isles

Port Nis
Port of Ness)

Stromness
Kirkwall
Kirkwall

St Margar
Hope

Gills
John o' Groats

Scrabster
Thurso
Melvich

Wick John o' Groats

Scourie
Tongue
Altnaharra

Wick

Outer Hebrides

Steornabhagh
(Stornoway)
Stornoway

Isle of
Lewis

The Minch

107

108

104

Lairg

Ullapool

Bonar
Bridge

Elgin
Cullen

Keith

Taransay
Tairbeart
(Tarbert)

Harris

Gairloch

Tain

Forres

Aberlour

Huntly

Ol

Uibhist a Tuath
(North Uist)

100

Kinlochewe

Achnasheen

102

Dingwall
Cromarty
Nairn

Grantown-
on-Spey

Loch nam Madadh
(Lochmaddy)

Uig

Inverness
(Dalcross)

Beinn na Faoghla
(Benbecula)
Benbecula

Dunvegan

Portree

Raasay

101

Drumnadrochit

Inverness

Tomintoul

Uibhist a Deas
(South Uist)

Isle
of
Skye

Kyle of
Lochalsh

Invermoriston

Aviemore

Loch Baghasdail
(Lochboisdale)

96

Invergarry
Newtonmore
Kingussie

CAIRNGORMS

Barra

Armadale

Braemar

Ballater

Barraigh
(Barra)

Mallaig

SCOTLAND

Rùm

Eigg

94

Fort William

Pitlochry

Bred

92

Coll

Inner Hebrides

Ballachulish

Aberfeldy

Blairgowrie

Forfar

(Mar–Oct)

Tobermory

Lochaline

Killin

90

Coupar Angus

Carr

Tiree

Isle of Mull

Craignure

Oban

Tyndrum

Lochearnhead

Crianlarich

Crieff

Auchterarder

Perth

Dundee

Newport-on-

St And

Cupar

Fionnphort

86

88

Inveraray

LOCH LOMOND
AND THE
TROSSACHS

Callander

Dunblane

Kinross

Glenrothes

Colonsay

Lochgilphead

Helensburgh

Stirling

Alloa

Dunfermline

Kirkcaldy

Jura

Dunoon

Dumbarton

Rosyth

EDINBURGH

84

Port
Askaig

Kennacraig
Tarbert

Greenock

Glasgow

Airdrie

Livingston

Dalkeith

Largs

Paisley
GLASGOW

Motherwell

78

Islay

80

Ardrossan

Kilwinning

East Kilbride

Strathaven
Lanark

Peebles

Galashiels

70

Port
Ellen

Arran

Firth of
Clyde

Irvine

Troon
Prestwick
Ayr

Kilmarnock

Cumnock

Biggar

Selkirk

Hawick

Campbeltown

(May–Sept)

Maybole

Thornhill

Moffat

72

(Mar–Oct)

Girvan

Langholm

Cairnryan

New
Galloway

Dumfries

Lockerbie

Longtown
Brampton

Stranraer

Newton Stewart

Castle Douglas

Annan

Carlisle

66

**NORTHERN
IRELAND**

Larne

Maryport
Cockermouth

Pentri

Workington

Keswick

BELFAST

60

Isle of Man
Peel

Ramsey

Egremont

LAKE
DISTRICT

Ambleside

Ravenglass

Windermere

(Apr–Sept)

60

Millom

Kendal

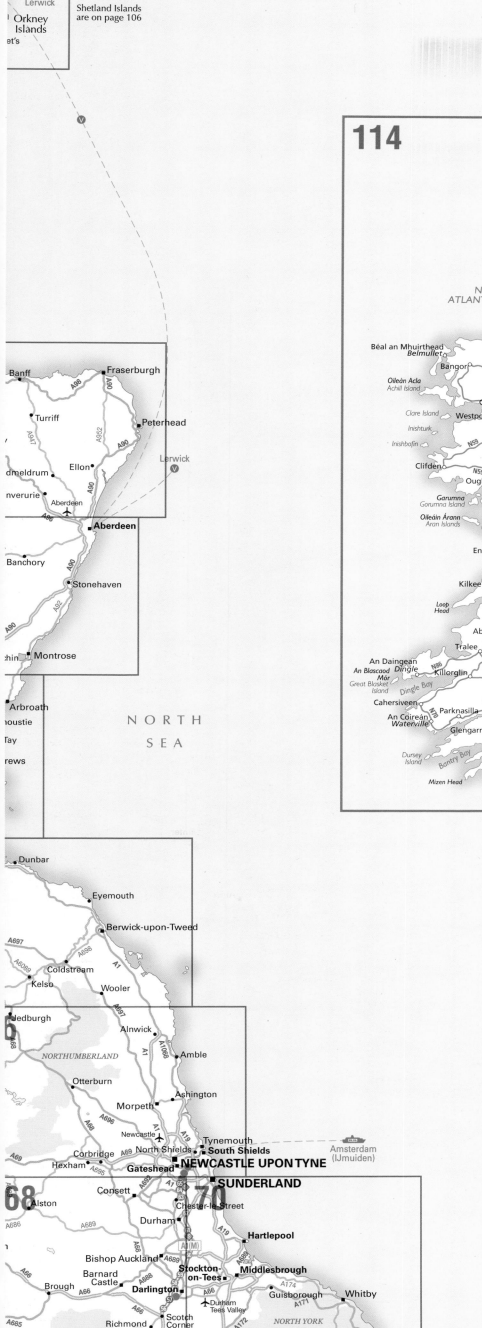

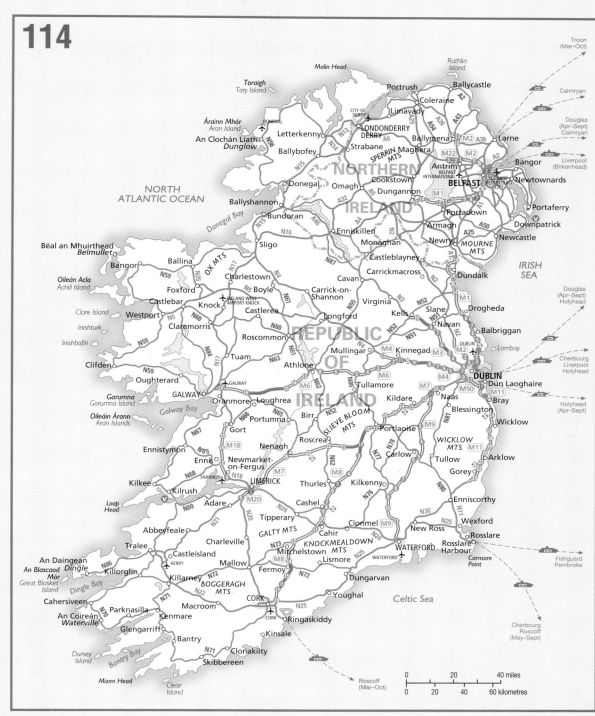

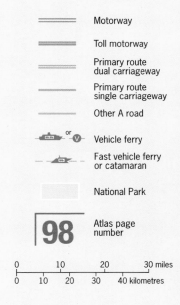

	Motorway
	Toll motorway
	Primary route dual carriageway
	Primary route single carriageway
	Other A road
	Vehicle ferry
	Fast vehicle ferry or catamaran
	National Park
98	Atlas page number

| 0 | 10 | 20 | 30 miles |
| 0 | 10 | 20 | 30 | 40 kilometres |

EMERGENCY DIVERSION ROUTES

In an emergency it may be necessary to close a section of motorway or other main road to traffic, so a temporary sign may advise drivers to follow a diversion route. To help drivers navigate the route, black symbols on yellow patches may be permanently displayed on existing direction signs, including motorway signs. Symbols may also be used on separate signs with yellow backgrounds.

For further information see www.highways.gov.uk, trafficscotland.org and traffic-wales.com

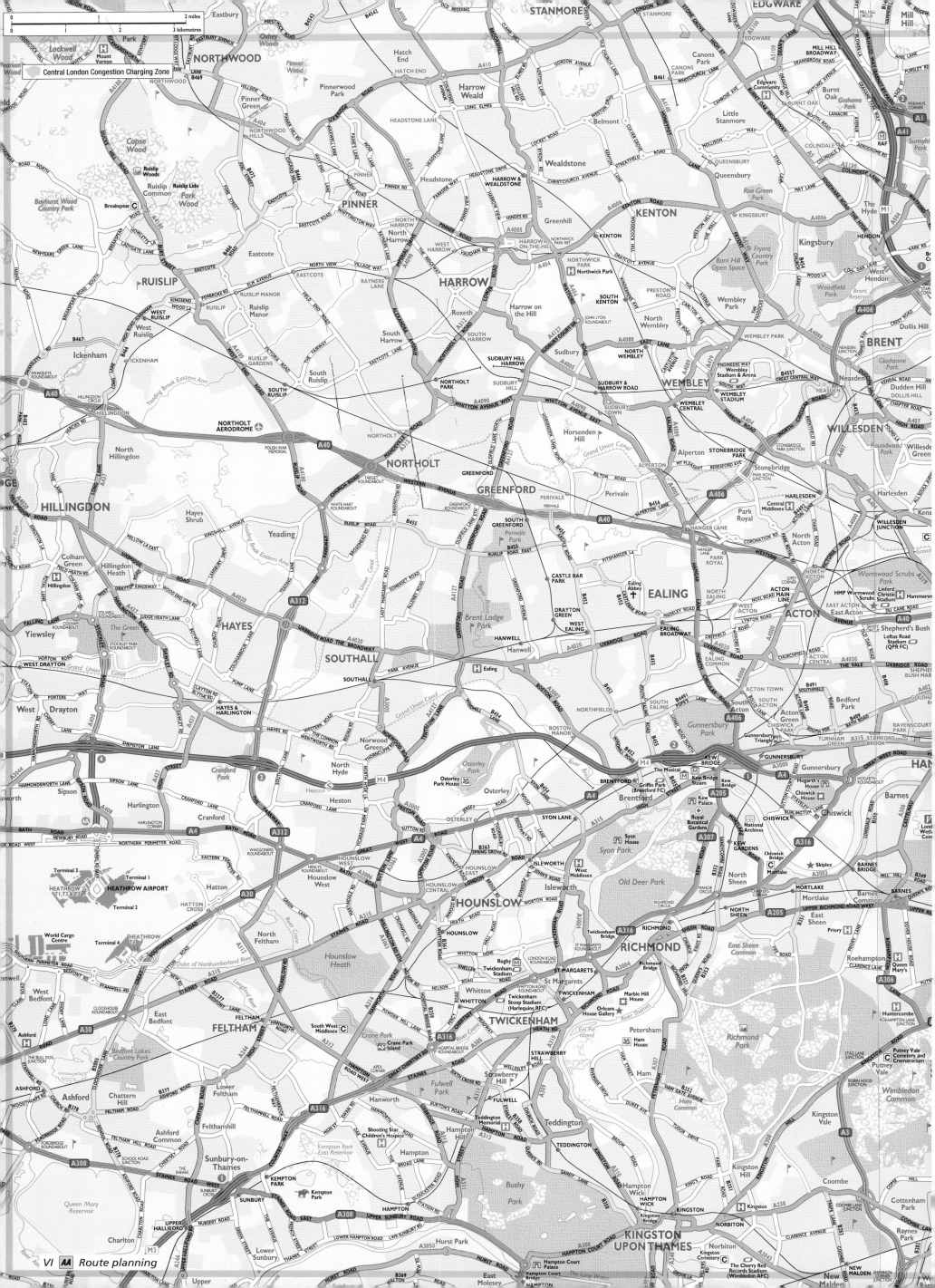

Road safety cameras

First, the advice you would expect from the AA - we advise drivers to always follow the signed speed limits - breaking the speed limit is illegal and can cost lives.

Both the AA and the Government believe that safety cameras ('speed cameras') should be operated within a transparent system. By providing information relating to road safety and speed hotspots, the AA believes that the driver is better placed to be aware of speed limits and can ensure adherence to them, thus making the roads safer for all users.

Most fixed cameras are installed at accident 'black spots' where four or more fatal or serious road collisions have occurred over the previous three years. It is the policy of both the police and the Department for Transport to make the location of cameras as well known as possible. By showing camera locations in this atlas the AA is identifying the places where extra care should be taken while driving. Speeding is illegal and dangerous and you MUST keep within the speed limit at all times.

Gatso™

Truvelo™

SPECS™

Traffipax™

There are currently more than 3,000 fixed cameras in Britain and the road mapping in this atlas identifies their on-the-road locations.

Mobile cameras are also deployed at other sites where speed is perceived to be a problem and mobile enforcement often takes place at the fixed camera sites shown on the maps in this atlas. Additionally, regular police enforcement can take place on any road.

Speed Limits	Built up areas*	Single carriageways	Dual carriageways	Motorways
Types of vehicle	MPH (km/h)	MPH (km/h)	MPH (km/h)	MPH (km/h)
Cars & motorcycles (including car derived vans up to 2 tonnes maximum laden weight)	30 (48)	60 (96)	70 (112)	70 (112)
Cars towing caravans or trailers (including car derived vans and motorcycles)	30 (48)	50 (80)	60 (96)	60 (96)
Buses, coaches and minibuses (not exceeding 12 metres (39 feet) in overall length)	30 (48)	50 (80)	60 (96)	70 (112)
Goods vehicles (not exceeding 7.5 tonnes maximum laden weight)	30 (48)	50 (80)	60 (96)	70+ (112)
Goods vehicles (exceeding 7.5 tonnes maximum laden weight)	30 (48)	40‡ (64)	50§ (80)	60 (96)

* The 30mph (48km/h) limit usually applies to all traffic on all roads with street lighting unless signs show otherwise.

† 60mph (96km/h) if articulated or towing a trailer.

‡ May increase to 50mph (80km/h) in April 2015. Check www.gov.uk to confirm

§ May increase to 60mph (96km/h) in April 2015. Check www.gov.uk to confirm

This symbol is used on the mapping to identify **individual** camera locations - with speed limits (mph)

This symbol is used on the mapping to identify **multiple** cameras on the same stretch of road - with speed limits (mph)

This symbol is used on the mapping to highlight SPECS™ camera systems which calculate your **average speed** along a stretch of road between two or more sets of cameras - with speed limits (mph)

Read this before you use the atlas

Safety cameras and speed limits
The fixed camera symbols on the mapping show the maximum speed in mph that applies to that particular stretch of road and above which the camera is set to activate. The actual road speed limit however will vary for different vehicle types and you must ensure that you drive within the speed limit for your particular class of vehicle at all times.

The chart left details the speed limits applying to the different classes. Don't forget that mobile enforcement can take account of vehicle class at any designated site.

Camera locations
1 The camera locations were correct at the time of finalising the information to go to press.

2 Camera locations are approximate due to limitations in the scale of the road mapping used in this atlas.

3 In towns and urban areas camera locations are shown only on roads that appear on the road maps in this atlas.

4 Where two or more cameras appear close together, a special symbol is used to indicate multiple cameras on the same stretch of road.

5 Our symbols do not indicate the direction in which cameras point.

6 On the mapping we symbolise more than 3,000 fixed camera locations. Mobile laser device locations, roadwork cameras and 'fixed red light' cameras cannot be shown.

Tourist sites with satnav friendly postcodes

ENGLAND

- Acorn Bank Garden CA10 1SP Cumb 68 D7
- Aldborough Roman Site YO51 9ES N York 63 U6
- Alfriston Clergy House BN26 5TL E Susx 11 S10
- Alton Towers ST10 4DB Staffs 46 E5
- Anglesey Abbey CB25 9EJ Cambs 39 R8
- Anne Hathaway's Cottage CV37 9HH Warwks 36 G10
- Antony House PL11 2QA Cnwll 5 L9
- Appuldurcombe House PO38 3EW IoW 9 Q13
- Apsley House W1J 7NT Gt Lon 21 N7
- Arlington Court EX31 4LP Devon 15 P4
- Ascott LU7 0PS Bucks 30 J8
- Ashby-de-la-Zouch Castle LE65 1BR Leics 47 L10
- Athelhampton House & Gardens DT2 7LG Dorset 7 U6
- Attingham Park SY4 4TP Shrops 45 M11
- Audley End House & Gardens CB11 4JF Essex 39 R13
- Avebury Manor & Garden SN8 1RF Wilts 18 G6
- Baconsthorpe Castle NR25 6LN Norfk 50 K6
- Baddesley Clinton Hall B93 0DQ Warwks 36 H6
- Bamburgh Castle NE69 7DF Nthumb 85 T11
- Barnard Castle DL12 8PR Dur 69 M9
- Barrington Court TA19 0NQ Somset 17 L13
- Basildon Park RG8 9NR W Berk 19 T5
- Bateman's TN19 7DS E Susx 12 C11
- Battle of Britain Memorial Flight Visitor Centre LN4 4SY Lincs 48 K2
- Beamish Museum DH9 0RG Dur 69 R2
- Beatrix Potter Gallery LA22 0NS Cumb 67 N13
- Beaulieu SO42 7ZN Hants 9 M8
- Belton House NG32 2LS Lincs 48 D6
- Belvoir Castle NG32 1PE Leics 48 B7
- Bembridge Windmill PO35 5SQ IoW 9 S11
- Beningbrough Hall & Gardens YO30 1DD N York 64 C8
- Benthall Hall TF12 5RX Shrops 45 Q13
- Berkeley Castle GL13 9PJ Gloucs 28 C8
- Berrington Hall HR6 0DW Herefs 35 M8
- Berry Pomeroy Castle TQ9 6LJ Devon 5 U8
- Beth Chatto Gardens CO7 7DB Essex 23 Q3
- Biddulph Grange Garden ST8 7SD Staffs 45 U2
- Bishop's Waltham Palace SO32 1DH Hants 9 Q5
- Blackpool Zoo FY3 8PP Bpool 61 Q12
- Blenheim Palace OX20 1PX Oxon 29 T4
- Blickling Estate NR11 6NF Norfk 51 L8
- Blue John Cavern S33 8WA Derbys 56 H10
- Bodiam Castle TN32 5UA E Susx 12 E10
- Bolsover Castle S44 6PR Derbys 57 Q12
- Boscobel House ST19 9AR Staffs 45 T12
- Bovington Tank Museum BH20 6JG Dorset 8 A11
- Bowes Castle DL12 9LD Dur 69 L10
- Bradford Industrial Museum BD2 3HP W Yorks 63 P13
- Bradley Manor TQ12 6BN Devon 5 U6
- Bramber Castle BN44 3WW W Susx 10 K8
- Brinkburn Priory NE65 8AR Nthumb 77 N6
- Bristol Zoo Gardens BS8 3HA Bristl 27 V13
- British Library NW1 2DB Gt Lon 21 N6
- British Museum WC1B 3DG Gt Lon 21 N6
- Brockhampton Estate WR6 5TB Herefs 35 Q9
- Brough Castle CA17 4EJ Cumb 68 G10
- Buckfast Abbey TQ11 0EE Devon 5 S7
- Buckingham Palace SW1A 1AA Gt Lon 21 N7
- Buckland Abbey PL20 6EY Devon 5 M7
- Buscot Park SN7 8BU Oxon 29 P8
- Byland Abbey YO61 4BD N York 64 C4
- Cadbury World B30 2LU Birm 36 D4
- Calke Abbey DE73 7LE Derbys 47 L9
- Canons Ashby House NN11 3SD Nhants 37 Q10
- Canterbury Cathedral CT1 2EH Kent 13 N4
- Carisbrooke Castle PO30 1XY IoW 9 P11
- Carlyle's House SW3 5HL Gt Lon 21 N7
- Castle Drogo EX6 6PB Devon 5 S2
- Castle Howard YO60 7DA N York 64 G5
- Castle Rising Castle PE31 6AH Norfk 49 U9
- Charlecote Park CV35 9ER Warwks 36 J9
- Chartwell TN16 1PS Kent 21 S12
- Chastleton House GL56 0SU Oxon 29 P2
- Chatsworth DE45 1PP Derbys 57 L12
- Chedworth Roman Villa GL54 3LJ Gloucs 29 L5
- Chessington World of Adventures KT9 2NE Gt Lon 21 L10
- Chester Cathedral CH1 2HU Ches W 54 K13
- Chester Zoo CH2 1EU Ches W 54 K12
- Chesters Roman Fort NE46 4EU Nthumb 76 J11
- Chiswick House W4 2RP Gt Lon 21 M7
- Chysauster Ancient Village TR20 8XA Cnwll 2 D10
- Claremont Landscape Garden KT10 9JG Surrey 20 K10
- Claydon House MK18 2EY Bucks 30 F7
- Cleeve Abbey TA23 0PS Somset 16 D8
- Clevedon Court BS21 6QU N Som 17 M2
- Cliveden SL6 0JA Bucks 20 F5
- Clouds Hill BH20 7NQ Dorset 7 V6
- Clumber Park S80 3AZ Notts 57 T12
- Colchester Zoo CO3 0SL Essex 23 N3
- Coleridge Cottage TA5 1NQ Somset 16 G9
- Coleton Fishacre TQ6 0EQ Devon 6 B14
- Compton Castle TQ3 1TA Devon 5 V8
- Conisbrough Castle DN12 3BU Donc 57 R7
- Corbridge Roman Town NE45 5NT Nthumb 76 K13
- Corfe Castle BH20 5EZ Dorset 8 D12
- Corsham Court SN13 0BZ Wilts 18 C6
- Cotehele PL12 6TA Cnwll 5 L7
- Coughton Court B49 5JA Warwks 36 E8
- Courts Garden BA14 6RR Wilts 18 C8
- Cragside NE65 7PX Nthumb 77 M5
- Crealy Great Adventure Park EX5 1DR Devon 6 D6
- Crich Tramway Village DE4 5DP Derbys 46 K2
- Croft Castle HR6 9PW Herefs 34 K7
- Croome Park WR8 9JS Worcs 35 U12
- Deddington Castle OX15 0TE Oxon 29 U1
- Didcot Railway Centre OX11 7NJ Oxon 19 R2
- Dover Castle CT16 1HU Kent 13 R7
- Drayton Manor Theme Park B78 3SA Staffs 46 G13
- Dudmaston Estate WV15 6QN Shrops 35 R3
- Dunham Massey WA14 4SJ Traffd 55 R9
- Dunstanburgh Castle NE66 3TT Nthumb 77 R1
- Dunster Castle TA24 6SL Somset 16 C8
- Durham Cathedral DH1 3EH Dur 69 S4
- Dyrham Park SN14 8HY S Glos 28 D12
- East Riddlesden Hall BD20 5EL Brad 63 M11
- Eden Project PL24 2SG Cnwll 3 R6
- Eltham Palace & Gardens SE9 5QE Gt Lon 21 R8
- Emmetts Garden TN14 6BA Kent 21 S12
- Exmoor Zoo EX31 4SG Devon 15 Q4
- Farleigh Hungerford Castle BA2 7RS Somset 18 B9
- Farnborough Hall OX17 1DU Warwks 37 M11
- Felbrigg Hall NR11 8PR Norfk 51 L6
- Fenton House & Garden NW3 6SP Gt Lon 21 N5
- Finch Foundry EX20 2NW Devon 5 Q2
- Finchale Priory DH1 5SH Dur 69 S3
- Fishbourne Roman Palace PO19 3QR W Susx 10 C9
- Flamingo Land YO17 6UX N York 64 H4
- Forde Abbey TA20 4LU Somset 7 L3
- Fountains Abbey & Studley Royal HG4 3DY N York 63 R6
- Gawthorpe Hall BB12 8UA Lancs 62 G13
- Gisborough Priory TS14 6HG R & Cl 70 K9
- Glendurgan Garden TR11 5JZ Cnwll 2 K11
- Goodrich Castle HR9 6HY Herefs 28 A4
- Great Chalfield Manor & Garden SN12 8NH Wilts 18 C8
- Great Coxwell Barn SN7 7LZ Oxon 29 Q9
- Greenway TQ5 0ES Devon 5 V10
- Haddon Hall DE45 1LA Derbys 56 K13
- Hailes Abbey GL54 5PB Gloucs 28 L1
- Ham House & Garden TW10 7RS Gt Lon 21 L8
- Hampton Court Palace KT8 9AU Gt Lon 21 L9
- Hanbury Hall WR9 7EA Worcs 36 B8
- Hardwick Hall S44 5QJ Derbys 57 Q14
- Hardy's Cottage DT2 8QJ Dorset 7 T6
- Hare Hill SK10 4PY Ches E 56 C11
- Hatchlands Park GU4 7RT Surrey 20 J12
- Heale Gardens SP4 6NU Wilts 18 H13
- Helmsley Castle YO62 5AB N York 64 E3
- Hereford Cathedral HR1 2NG Herefs 35 M13
- Hergest Croft Gardens HR5 3EG Herefs 34 G9
- Hever Castle & Gardens TN8 7NG Kent 21 S13
- Hidcote Manor Garden GL55 6LR Gloucs 36 G12
- Hill Top LA22 0LF Cumb 67 N13
- Hinton Ampner SO24 0LA Hants 9 R3
- Holkham Hall NR23 1AB Norfk 50 E5
- Housesteads Roman Fort NE47 6NN Nthumb 76 F12
- Howletts Wild Animal Park CT4 5EL Kent 13 N4
- Hughenden Manor HP14 4LA Bucks 20 E3
- Hurst Castle SO41 0TP Hants 9 L11
- Hylands House & Park CM2 8WQ Essex 22 G7
- Ickworth IP29 5QE Suffk 40 D8
- Ightham Mote TN15 0NT Kent 21 U12
- Ironbridge Gorge Museums TF8 7DQ Wrekin 45 Q13
- Kedleston Hall DE22 5JH Derbys 46 K5
- Kenilworth Castle & Elizabethan Garden CV8 1NE Warwks 36 J6
- Kenwood House NW3 7JR Gt Lon 21 N5
- Killerton EX5 3LE Devon 6 C4
- King John's Hunting Lodge BS26 2AP Somset 17 M6
- Kingston Lacy BH21 4EA Dorset 8 D8
- Kirby Hall NN17 3EN Nhants 38 D2
- Knightshayes Court EX16 7RQ Devon 16 C13
- Knole House TN13 1HU Kent 21 T12
- Knowsley Safari Park L34 4AN Knows 55 L8
- Lacock Abbey SN15 2LG Wilts 18 D7
- Lamb House TN31 7ES E Susx 12 H11
- Lanhydrock House PL30 5AD Cnwll 3 R4
- Launceston Castle PL15 7DR Cnwll 4 J4
- Leeds Castle ME17 1PB Kent 12 F5
- Legoland SL4 4AY W&M 20 F8
- Lindisfarne Castle TD15 2SH Nthumb 85 S10
- Lindisfarne Priory TD15 2RX Nthumb 85 S10
- Little Moreton Hall CW12 4SD Ches E 45 T2
- Liverpool Cathedral L1 7AZ Lpool 54 J9
- Longleat BA12 7NW Wilts 18 B12
- Losely Park GU3 1HS Surrey 20 G13
- Lost Gardens of Heligan PL26 6EN Cnwll 3 P7
- Ludgershall Castle SP11 9QR Wilts 19 L10
- Lydford Castle EX20 4BH Devon 5 N4
- Lyme Park, House & Garden SK12 2NX Ches E 56 E10
- Lytes Cary Manor TA11 7HU Somset 17 P11
- Lyveden New Bield PE8 5AT Nhants 38 E3
- Maiden Castle DT2 9PP Dorset 7 S7
- Mapledurham RG4 7TR Oxon 19 U5
- Marble Hill House TW1 2NL Gt Lon 21 L8
- Marwell Wildlife SO21 1JH Hants 9 Q4
- Melford Hall CO10 9AA Suffk 40 E11
- Merseyside Maritime Museum L3 4AQ Lpool 54 H9
- Minster Lovell Hall OX29 0RR Oxon 29 R5
- Mompesson House SP1 2EL Wilts 8 G3
- Monk Bretton Priory S71 5QD Barns 57 N5
- Montacute House TA15 6XP Somset 17 N13
- Morwellham Quay PL19 8JL Devon 5 L7
- Moseley Old Hall WV10 7HY Staffs 46 B13
- Mottisfont SO51 0LP Hants 9 L3
- Mottistone Manor Garden PO30 4ED IoW 9 N12
- Mount Grace Priory DL6 3JG N York 70 F13
- National Gallery WC2N 5DN Gt Lon 21 N6
- National Maritime Museum SE10 9NF Gt Lon 21 Q7
- National Motorcycle Museum B92 0ED Solhll 36 H4
- National Portrait Gallery WC2H 0HE Gt Lon 21 N6
- National Railway Museum YO26 4XJ York 64 D9
- National Space Centre LE4 5NS C Leic 47 Q12
- Natural History Museum SW7 5BD Gt Lon 21 N7
- Needles Old Battery PO39 0JH IoW 8 K12
- Nene Valley Railway PE8 6LR Cambs 38 H1
- Netley Abbey SO31 5FB Hants 9 P7
- Newark Air Museum NG24 2NY Notts 48 B2
- Newtown Old Town Hall PO30 4PA IoW 9 N10
- North Leigh Roman Villa OX29 6QB Oxon 29 S4
- Norwich Cathedral NR1 4DH Norfk 51 M12
- Nostell Priory WF4 1QE Wakefd 57 P3
- Nunnington Hall YO62 5UY N York 64 F4
- Nymans RH17 6EB W Susx 11 M5
- Old Royal Naval College SE10 9NN Gt Lon 21 Q7
- Old Sarum SP1 3SD Wilts 8 G2
- Old Wardour Castle SP3 6RR Wilts 8 C3
- Oliver Cromwell's House CB7 4HF Cambs 39 R4
- Orford Castle IP12 2ND Suffk 41 R10
- Ormesby Hall TS3 0SR R & Cl 70 H9
- Osborne House PO32 6JX IoW 9 Q9
- Osterley Park & House TW7 4RB Gt Lon 20 K7
- Overbeck's TQ8 8LW Devon 5 S13
- Oxburgh Hall PE33 9PS Norfk 50 B13
- Packwood House B94 6AT Warwks 36 G6
- Paignton Zoo TQ4 7EU Torbay 6 A13
- Paycocke's CO6 1NS Essex 22 K3
- Peckover House & Garden PE13 1JR Cambs 49 Q12
- Pendennis Castle TR11 4LP Cnwll 3 L10
- Petworth House & Park GU28 0AE W Susx 10 F6
- Pevensey Castle BN24 5LE E Susx 11 U10
- Peveril Castle S33 8WQ Derbys 56 J10
- Polesden Lacey RH5 6BD Surrey 20 K12
- Portland Castle DT5 1AZ Dorset 7 S10
- Portsmouth Historic Dockyard PO1 3LJ C Port 9 S8
- Powderham Castle EX6 8JQ Devon 6 C8
- Prior Park Landscape Garden BA2 5AH BaNES 17 U4
- Prudhoe Castle NE42 6NA Nthumb 77 M13
- Quarry Bank Mill SK9 4LA Ches E 55 T10
- Quebec House TN16 1TD Kent 21 R12
- Ramsey Abbey Gatehouse PE17 1DH Cambs 39 L3
- Reculver Towers & Roman Fort CT6 6SU Kent 13 P2
- Red House DA6 8JF Gt Lon 21 S7
- Restormel Castle PL22 0EE Cnwll 4 E8
- Richborough Roman Fort CT13 9JW Kent 13 R3
- Richmond Castle DL10 4QW N York 69 Q12
- Roche Abbey S66 8NW Rothm 57 R9
- Rochester Castle ME1 1SW Medway 12 D2
- Rockbourne Roman Villa SP6 3PG Hants 8 G5
- Roman Baths & Pump Room BA1 1LZ BaNES 17 U4
- Royal Botanic Gardens, Kew TW9 3AB Gt Lon 21 L7
- Royal Observatory Greenwich SE10 8XJ Gt Lon 21 Q7
- Rufford Old Hall L40 1SG Lancs 55 L3
- Runnymede SL4 2JJ W & M 20 G8
- Rushton Triangular Lodge NN14 1RP Nhants 38 B4
- Rycote Chapel OX9 2PA Oxon 30 E12
- St Leonard's Tower ME19 6PE Kent 12 C4
- St Michael's Mount TR17 0HT Cnwll 2 E11
- St Paul's Cathedral EC4M 8AD Gt Lon 21 P6
- Salisbury Cathedral SP1 2EJ Wilts 8 G3
- Saltram PL7 1UH C Plym 5 N9
- Sandham Memorial Chapel RG20 9JT Hants 19 Q8
- Sandringham House & Grounds PE35 6EH Norfk 49 U8
- Saxtead Green Post Mill IP13 9QQ Suffk 41 N8
- Scarborough Castle YO11 1HY N York 65 P2
- Science Museum SW7 2DD Gt Lon 21 N7
- Scotney Castle TN3 8JN Kent 12 C8
- Shaw's Corner AL6 9BX Herts 31 Q9
- Sheffield Park & Garden TN22 3QX E Susx 11 Q6
- Sherborne Old Castle DT9 3SA Dorset 17 R13
- Sissinghurst Castle Garden TN17 2AB Kent 12 F8
- Slimbridge Wetland Centre GL2 7BT Gloucs 28 D6
- Sizergh Castle & Garden LA8 8AE Cumb 61 T2
- Smallhythe Place TN30 7NG Kent 12 G10
- Snowshill Manor & Garden WR12 7JU Gloucs 36 E14
- Souter Lighthouse SR6 7NH S Tyne 77 U13
- Speke Hall, Garden & Estate L24 1XD Lpool 54 K10
- Spinnaker Tower PO1 3TT C Port 9 S9
- Stokesay Castle SY7 9AH Shrops 34 K4
- Stonehenge SP4 7DE Wilts 18 H12
- Stourhead BA12 6QD Wilts 17 U10
- Stowe Landscape Gardens MK18 5EQ Bucks 30 E5
- Sudbury Hall DE6 5HT Derbys 46 G7
- Sulgrave Manor OX17 2SD Nhants 37 Q11
- Sunnycroft TF1 2DR Wrekin 45 Q11
- Sutton Hoo IP12 3DJ Suffk 41 N11
- Sutton House E9 6JQ Gt Lon 21 Q5
- Tate Britain SW1P 4RG Gt Lon 21 N7
- Tate Liverpool L3 4BB Lpool 54 H9
- Tate Modern SE1 9TG Gt Lon 21 P6
- Tattershall Castle LN4 4LR Lincs 48 K2
- Tatton Park WA16 6QN Ches E 55 R10
- The Lowry M50 3AZ Salfd 55 T7
- The Vyne RG24 9HL Hants 19 T9
- The Weir HR4 7QF Herefs 34 K12
- Thornton Abbey & Gatehouse DN39 6TU N Linc 58 K3
- Thorpe Park KT16 8PN Surrey 20 H9
- Tilbury Fort RM18 7NR Thurr 22 G12
- Tintagel Castle PL34 0HE Cnwll 4 C3
- Tintinhull Garden BA22 8PZ Somset 17 P13
- Totnes Castle TQ9 5NU Devon 5 U8
- Tower of London EC3N 4AB Gt Lon 21 P6
- Townend LA23 1LB Cumb 67 P12
- Treasurer's House YO1 7JL York 64 E9
- Trelissick Garden TR3 6QL Cnwll 3 L9
- Trengwainton Garden TR20 8RZ Cnwll 2 C10
- Trerice TR8 4PG Cnwll 3 L5
- Twycross Zoo CV9 3PX Leics 46 K12
- Upnor Castle ME2 4XG Medway 22 J13
- Uppark House & Garden GU31 5QR W Susx 10 B7
- Upton House & Garden OX15 6HT Warwks 37 L11
- Victoria & Albert Museum SW7 2RL Gt Lon 21 N7
- Waddesdon Manor HP18 0JH Bucks 30 F9
- Wakehurst Place RH17 6TN W Susx 11 N4
- Wall Roman Site WS14 0AW Staffs 46 E12
- Wallington NE61 4AR Nthumb 77 L9
- Walmer Castle & Gardens CT14 7LJ Kent 13 S6
- Warkworth Castle & Hermitage NE65 0UJ Nthumb 77 Q4
- Warner Bros Studio Tour WD25 7LS Herts 31 N12
- Warwick Castle CV34 4QU Warwks 36 J8
- Washington Old Hall NE38 7LE Sundld 70 D1
- Waterperry Gardens OX33 1LG Oxon 30 D11
- Weeting Castle IP27 0RQ Norfk 40 C3
- Wenlock Priory TF13 6HS Shrops 45 P13
- West Midland Safari Park DY12 1LF Worcs 35 T5
- West Wycombe Park HP14 3AJ Bucks 20 D4
- Westbury Court Garden GL14 1PD Gloucs 28 D5
- Westminster Abbey SW1P 3PA Gt Lon 21 N7
- Westonbirt Arboretum GL8 8QS Gloucs 28 G9
- Westwood Manor BA15 2AF Wilts 18 B9
- Whitby Abbey YO22 4JT N York 71 R10
- Wightwick Manor & Gardens WV6 8EE Wolves 45 U14
- Wimpole Estate SG8 0BW Cambs 39 M10
- Winchester Cathedral SO23 9LS Hants 9 P3
- Winchester City Mill SO23 0EJ Hants 9 P3
- Windsor Castle SL4 1NJ W & M 20 G7
- Winkworth Arboretum GU8 4AD Surrey 10 F2
- Wisley RHS Garden GU23 6QB Surrey 20 J11
- Woburn Safari Park MK17 9QN Beds C 31 L6
- Wookey Hole Caves BA5 1BA Somset 17 P7
- Woolsthorpe Manor NG33 5PD Lincs 48 D9
- Wordsworth House CA13 9RX Cumb 66 H6
- Wrest Park MK45 4HR Beds C 31 N5
- Wroxeter Roman City SY5 6PR Shrops 45 N12
- WWT Arundel Wetland Centre BN18 9PB W Susx 10 G9
- Yarmouth Castle PO41 0PB IoW 9 M11
- York Minster YO1 7HH York 64 E9
- ZSL London Zoo NW1 4RY Gt Lon 21 N6
- ZSL Whipsnade Zoo LU6 2LF Beds C 31 M9

SCOTLAND

- Aberdour Castle KY3 0SL Fife 83 N1
- Alloa Tower FK10 1PP Clacks 90 C13
- Angus Folk Museum DD8 1RT Angus 91 N2
- Arbroath Abbey DD11 1EG Angus 91 T3
- Arduaine Garden PA34 4XQ Ag & B 87 P3
- Bachelors' Club KA5 5RB S Ayrs 81 N7
- Balmoral Castle Grounds AB35 5TB Abers 98 D5
- Balvenie Castle AB55 4DH Moray 104 C7
- Bannockburn Heritage Centre FK7 0LJ Stirlg 89 S7
- Blackness Castle EH49 7NH Falk 83 L2
- Blair Castle PH18 5TL P & K 97 P10
- Bothwell Castle G71 8BL S Lans 82 C7
- Branklyn Garden PH2 7BB P & K 90 H7
- Brodick Castle, Garden & Country Park KA27 8HY N Ayrs 80 E5
- Brodie Castle IV36 2TE Moray 103 Q4
- Broughton House & Garden DG6 4JX D & G 73 R9
- Burleigh Castle KY13 9GG P & K 90 H11
- Burrell Collection G43 1AT C Glas 89 N13
- Caerlaverock Castle DG1 4RU D & G 74 K12
- Cardoness Castle DG7 2EH D & G 73 P8
- Carnassarie Castle PA31 8RQ Ag & B 87 Q5
- Castle Campbell & Garden FK14 7PP Clacks 90 E12
- Castle Fraser, Garden & Estate AB51 7LD Abers 105 L13
- Castle Kennedy & Gardens DG9 8BX D & G 72 E7
- Castle Menzies PH15 2JD P & K 90 B2
- Corgarff Castle AB36 8YP Abers 98 D2
- Craigievar Castle AB33 8JF Abers 98 K2
- Craigmillar Castle EH16 4SY C Edin 83 Q4
- Crarae Garden PA32 8YA Ag & B 87 T6
- Crathes Castle & Garden AB31 5QJ Abers 99 N4
- Crichton Castle EH37 5XA Mdloth 83 S6
- Crossraguel Abbey KA19 8HQ S Ayrs 80 K11
- Culloden Battlefield IV2 5EU Highld 102 K6
- Culross Palace KY12 8JH Fife 82 J1
- Culzean Castle & Country Park KA19 8LE S Ayrs 80 J10
- Dallas Dhu Distillery IV36 2RR Moray 103 R4
- David Livingstone Centre G72 9BY S Lans 82 C7
- Dirleton Castle & Garden EH39 5ER E Loth 84 E2
- Doune Castle FK16 6EA Stirlg 89 R5
- Drum Castle, Garden & Estate AB31 5EY Abers 99 P3
- Dryburgh Abbey TD6 0RQ Border 84 F12
- Duff House AB45 3SX Abers 104 K3
- Dumbarton Castle G82 1JJ W Duns 88 J11
- Dundrennan Abbey DG6 4QH D & G 73 S10
- Dunnottar Castle AB39 2TL Abers 99 R7
- Dunstaffnage Castle PA37 1PZ Ag & B 94 B12
- Edinburgh Castle EH1 2NG C Edin 83 Q4
- Edinburgh Zoo EH12 6TS C Edin 83 P4
- Edzell Castle & Garden DD9 7UE Angus 98 K10
- Eilean Donan Castle IV40 8DX Highld 101 M6
- Elgin Cathedral IV30 1HU Moray 103 V3
- Falkirk Wheel FK1 4RS Falk 82 G2
- Falkland Palace & Garden KY15 7BU Fife 91 L10
- Fort George IV2 7TE Highld 103 L4
- Fyvie Castle AB53 8JS Abers 105 M8
- Georgian House EH2 4DR C Edin 83 P4
- Gladstone's Land EH1 2NT C Edin 83 Q4
- Glamis Castle DD8 1RJ Angus 91 N2
- Glasgow Botanic Gardens G12 0UE C Glas 89 N12
- Glasgow Cathedral G4 0QZ C Glas 89 P12
- Glasgow Science Centre G51 1EA C Glas 89 N12
- Glen Grant Distillery AB38 7BS Moray 104 B6
- Glenluce Abbey DG8 0AF D & G 72 F8
- Greenbank Garden G76 8RB E Rens 81 R1
- Haddo House AB41 7EQ Abers 105 P9
- Harmony Garden TD6 9LJ Border 84 E12
- Hermitage Castle TD9 0LU Border 75 U6
- Highland Wildlife Park PH21 1NL Highld 97 N3
- Hill House G84 9AJ Ag & B 88 G9
- Hill of Tarvit Mansionhouse & Garden KY15 5PB Fife 91 N9
- Holmwood G44 3YG C Glas 89 N14
- House of Dun DD10 9LQ Angus 99 M12
- House of the Binns EH49 7NA W Loth 83 L3
- Hunterian Museum G12 8QQ C Glas 89 N12
- Huntingtower Castle PH1 3JL P & K 90 G7
- Huntly Castle AB54 4SH Abers 104 G7
- Hutchesons' Hall G1 1EJ C Glas 89 N12
- Inchmahome Priory FK8 3RA Stirlg 89 N5
- Inveresk Lodge Garden EH21 7TE E Loth 83 R4
- Inverewe Garden & Estate IV22 2LG Highld 107 Q8
- Inverlochy Castle PH33 6SN Highld 94 G3
- Kellie Castle & Garden KY10 2RF Fife 91 R10
- Kildrummy Castle AB33 8RA Abers 104 F12
- Killiecrankie Visitor Centre PH16 5LG P & K 97 Q11
- Leith Hall Garden & Estate AB54 4NQ Abers 104 G10
- Linlithgow Palace EH49 7AL W Loth 82 K3
- Lochleven Castle KY13 8UF P & K 90 H11
- Logan Botanic Garden DG9 9ND D & G 72 D11
- Malleny Garden EH14 7AF C Edin 83 N5
- Melrose Abbey TD6 9LG Border 84 E12
- National Museum of Scotland EH1 1JF C Edin 83 Q4
- Newark Castle PA14 5NH Inver 88 H11
- Palace of Holyroodhouse EH8 8DX C Edin 83 Q4
- Pitmedden Garden AB41 7PD Abers 105 P10
- Preston Mill EH40 3DS E Loth 84 F3
- Priorwood Garden TD6 9PX Border 84 E12
- Robert Smail's Printing Works EH44 6HA Border 83 R11
- Rothesay Castle PA20 0DA Ag & B 88 C13
- Royal Botanic Garden Edinburgh EH3 5LR C Edin 83 P3
- Royal Yacht Britannia EH6 6JJ C Edin 83 Q3
- St Andrews Aquarium KY16 9AS Fife 91 R8
- Scone Palace PH2 6BD P & K 90 H6
- Smailholm Tower TD5 7PG Border 84 G12
- Souter Johnnie's Cottage KA19 8HY S Ayrs 80 J11
- Stirling Castle FK8 1EJ Stirlg 89 S7
- Sweetheart Abbey DG2 8BU D & G 74 J12
- Tantallon Castle EH39 5PN E Loth 84 F1
- Tenement House G3 6QN C Glas 89 N12
- Threave Castle DG7 1TJ D & G 74 D13
- Threave Garden DG7 1RX D & G 74 E13
- Tolquhon Castle AB41 7LP Abers 105 P10
- Traquair House EH44 6PW Border 83 R11
- Urquhart Castle IV63 6XJ Highld 102 F10
- Weaver's Cottage PA10 2JG Rens 88 K13
- Whithorn Priory & Museum DG8 8PY D & G 73 L11

WALES

- Aberconwy House LL32 8AY Conwy 53 N7
- Aberdulais Tin Works & Waterfall SA10 8EU Neath 26 D8
- Beaumaris Castle LL58 8AP IoA 52 K7
- Big Pit: National Coal Museum NP4 9XP Torfn 27 N6
- Bodnant Garden LL28 5RE Conwy 53 P8
- Caerleon Roman Fortress & Baths NP18 1AE Newpt 27 Q9
- Caernarfon Castle LL55 2AY Gwynd 52 G10
- Caldicot Castle & Country Park NP26 4HU Mons 27 T10
- Cardiff Castle CF10 3RB Cardif 27 M12
- Castell Coch CF15 7JS Cardif 27 L11
- Chirk Castle LL14 5AF Wrexhm 44 G6
- Colby Woodland Garden SA67 8PP Pembks 25 L9
- Conwy Castle LL32 8AY Conwy 53 N7
- Criccieth Castle LL52 0DP Gwynd 42 K6
- Dinefwr Park & Castle SA19 6RT Carmth 25 V6
- Dolaucothi Gold Mines SA19 8US Carmth 33 N12
- Erddig LL13 0YT Wrexhm 44 H4
- Ffestiniog Railway LL49 9NF Gwynd 43 N5
- Harlech Castle LL46 2YH Gwynd 43 L7
- Llanerchaeron SA48 8DG Cerdgn 32 J8
- National Showcaves Centre for Wales SA9 1GJ Powys 26 E4
- Penrhyn Castle LL57 4HT Gwynd 52 K8
- Plas Newydd LL61 6DQ IoA 52 H9
- Plas yn Rhiw LL53 8AB Gwynd 42 D8
- Portmeirion LL48 6ER Gwynd 43 L6
- Powis Castle & Garden SY21 8RF Powys 44 F12
- Raglan Castle NP15 2BT Mons 27 S6
- Sygun Copper Mine LL55 4NE Gwynd 43 M4
- Tintern Abbey NP16 6SE Mons 27 U7
- Tudor Merchant's House SA70 7BX Pembks 24 K10
- Tŷ Mawr Wybrnant LL25 0HJ Conwy 43 Q3
- Valle Crucis Abbey LL20 8DD Denbgs 44 F5

Caravan and camping sites in Britain

These pages list the top 300 AA-inspected Caravan and Camping (C & C) sites in the Pennant rating scheme. **Five Pennant Premier sites are shown in green,** Four Pennant sites are shown in blue.
Listings include addresses, telephone numbers and websites together with page and grid references to locate the sites in the atlas. The total number of touring pitches is also included for each site, together with the type of pitch available.
The following abbreviations are used: **C = Caravan CV = Campervan T = Tent**

To find out more about the AA's Pennant rating scheme and other rated caravan and camping sites not included on these pages please visit ***theAA.com***

ENGLAND

Alders Caravan Park
Home Farm, Alne, York
YO61 1RY
Tel: 01347 838722 64 C6
alderscaravanpark.co.uk
Total Pitches: 87 (C, CV & T)

Andrewshayes Holiday Park
Dalwood, Axminster
EX13 7DY
Tel: 01404 831225 6 H5
andrewshayes.co.uk
Total Pitches: 150 (C, CV & T)

Apple Tree Park C & C Site
A38, Claypits, Stonehouse
GL10 3AL
Tel: 01452 742362 75 T13
appletreepark.co.uk
Total Pitches: 65 (C, CV & T)

Appuldurcombe Gardens Holiday Park
Appuldurcombe Road, Wroxall, Isle of Wight
PO38 3EP
Tel: 01983 852597 9 Q12
appuldurcombegardens.co.uk
Total Pitches: 130 (C, CV & T)

Arrow Bank Holiday Park
Nun House Farm, Eardisland, Leominster
HR6 9BG
Tel: 01544 388312 34 K9
arrowbank.co.uk
Total Pitches: 38 (C, CV & T)

Atlantic Bays Holiday Park
St Merryn, Padstow
PL28 8PY
Tel: 01841 520855 3 M2
atlanticbaysholidaypark.co.uk
Total Pitches: 70 (C, CV & T)

Ayr Holiday Park
St Ives, Cornwall
TR26 1EJ
Tel: 01736 795855 2 E8
ayrholidaypark.co.uk
Total Pitches: 40 (C, CV & T)

Back of Beyond Touring Park
234 Ringwood Rd, St Leonards, Dorset
BH24 2SB
Tel: 01202 876968 8 F8
backofbeyondtouringpark.co.uk
Total Pitches: 80 (C, CV & T)

Bagwell Farm Touring Park
Knights in the Bottom, Chickerell, Weymouth
DT3 4EA
Tel: 01305 782575 7 R8
bagwellfarm.co.uk
Total Pitches: 320 (C, CV & T)

Bardsea Leisure Park
Priory Road, Ulverston
LA12 9QE
Tel: 01229 584712 61 P4
bardsealeisure.co.uk
Total Pitches: 83 (C & CV)

Barn Farm Campsite
Barn Farm, Birchover, Matlock
DE4 2BL
Tel: 01629 650245 46 H1
barnfarmcamping.com
Total Pitches: 50 (C, CV & T)

Barnstones C & C Site
Great Bourton, Banbury
OX17 1QU
Tel: 01295 750289 37 N12
Total Pitches: 49 (C, CV & T)

Bath Chew Valley Caravan Park
Ham Lane, Bishop Sutton
BS39 5TZ
Tel: 01275 332127 17 Q5
bathchewvalley.co.uk
Total Pitches: 45 (C, CV & T)

Bay View Holiday Park
Bolton le Sands, Carnforth
LA5 9TN
Tel: 01524 701508 61 T6
holgates.co.uk
Total Pitches: 100 (C, CV & T)

Beaconsfield Farm Caravan Park
Battlefield, Shrewsbury
SY4 4AA
Tel: 01939 210370 45 M10
beaconsfield-farm.co.uk
Total Pitches: 60 (C & CV)

Beech Croft Farm
Beech Croft, Blackwell in the Peak, Buxton
SK17 9TQ
Tel: 01298 85330 56 H12
beechcroftfarm.co.uk
Total Pitches: 30 (C, CV & T)

Bellingham C & C Club Site
Brown Rigg, Bellingham
NE48 2JY
Tel: 01434 220175 76 G9
campingandcaravanningclub.co.uk/bellingham
Total Pitches: 64 (C, CV & T)

Beverley Parks C & C Park
Goodrington Road, Paignton
TQ4 7JE
Tel: 01803 661979 6 A13
beverley-holidays.co.uk
Total Pitches: 172 (C, CV & T)

Bingham Grange Touring & Camping Park
Melplash, Bridport
DT6 3TT
Tel: 01308 488234 7 N5
binghamgrange.co.uk
Total Pitches: 150 (C, CV & T)

Blackmore Vale C & C Park
Sherborne Causeway, Shaftesbury
SP7 9PX
Tel: 01747 851523 8 A4
blackmorevalecaravanpark.co.uk
Total Pitches: 16 (C, CV & T)

Blue Rose Caravan Country Park
Star Carr Lane, Brandesburton
YO25 8RU
Tel: 01964 543366 65 Q10
bluerosepark.com
Total Pitches: 58 (C & CV)

Bo Peep Farm Caravan Park
Bo Peep Farm, Aynho Road, Adderbury, Banbury
OX17 3NP
Tel: 01295 810605 37 N14
bo-peep.co.uk
Total Pitches: 104 (C, CV & T)

Briarfields Motel & Touring Park
Gloucester Road, Cheltenham
GL51 0SX
Tel: 01242 235324 28 H3
briarfields.net
Total Pitches: 72 (C, CV & T)

Broadhembury C & C Park
Steeds Lane, Kingsnorth, Ashford
TN26 1NQ
Tel: 01233 620859 12 K8
broadhembury.co.uk
Total Pitches: 110 (C, CV & T)

Brokerswood Country Park
Brokerswood, Westbury
BA13 4EH
Tel: 01373 822238 18 B10
brokerswoodcountrypark.co.uk
Total Pitches: 69 (C, CV & T)

Budemeadows Touring Park
Widemouth Bay, Bude
EX23 0NA
Tel: 01288 361646 14 F12
budemeadows.com
Total Pitches: 145 (C, CV & T)

Burrowhayes Farm C & C Site & Riding Stables
West Luccombe, Porlock, Minehead
TA24 8HT
Tel: 01643 862463 16 B7
burrowhayes.co.uk
Total Pitches: 120 (C, CV & T)

Burton Constable Holiday Park & Arboretum
Old Lodges, Sproatley, Hull
HU11 4LJ
Tel: 01964 562508 65 R12
burtonconstable.co.uk
Total Pitches: 140 (C, CV & T)

Cakes & Ale
Abbey Lane, Theberton, Leiston
IP16 4TE
Tel: 01728 831655 41 R8
cakesandale.co.uk
Total Pitches: 55 (C, CV & T)

Calloose C & C Park
Leedstown, Hayle
TR27 5ET
Tel: 01736 850431 2 F10
calloose.co.uk
Total Pitches: 109 (C, CV & T)

Camping Caradon Touring Park
Trelawne, Looe
PL13 2NA
Tel: 01503 272388 4 G10
campingcaradon.co.uk
Total Pitches: 75 (C, CV & T)

Capesthorne Hall
Congleton Road, Siddington, Macclesfield
SK11 9JY
Tel: 01625 861221 55 T12
capesthorne.com
Total Pitches: 50 (C & CV)

Carlton Meres Country Park
Rendham Road, Carlton, Saxmundham
IP17 2QP
Tel: 01728 603344 41 Q7
carlton-meres.co.uk
Total Pitches: 96 (C, CV & T)

Carlyon Bay C & C Park
Bethesda, Cypress Avenue, Carlyon Bay
PL25 3RE
Tel: 01726 812735 3 R6
carlyonbay.net
Total Pitches: 180 (C, CV & T)

Carnevas Holiday Park & Farm Cottages
Carnevas Farm, St Merryn
PL28 8PN
Tel: 01841 520230 3 M2
carnevasholidaypark.co.uk
Total Pitches: 195 (C, CV & T)

Carnon Downs C & C Park
Carnon Downs, Truro
TR3 6JJ
Tel: 01872 862283 3 L8
carnon-downs-caravanpark.co.uk
Total Pitches: 150 (C, CV & T)

Carvynick Country Club
Summercourt, Newquay
TR8 5AF
Tel: 01872 510716 3 M5
carvynick.co.uk
Total Pitches: 47 (C & CV)

Castlerigg Hall C & C Park
Castlerigg Hall, Keswick
CA12 4TE
Tel: 017687 74499 67 L8
castlerigg.co.uk
Total Pitches: 48 (C, CV & T)

Cayton Village Caravan Park
Mill Lane, Cayton Bay, Scarborough
YO11 3NN
Tel: 01723 583171 65 P3
caytontouring.co.uk
Total Pitches: 310 (C, CV & T)

Cheddar Bridge Touring Park
Draycott Rd, Cheddar
BS27 3RJ
Tel: 01934 743048 17 N6
cheddarbridge.co.uk
Total Pitches: 45 (C, CV & T)

Cheddar Mendip Heights C & C Club Site
Townsend, Priddy, Wells
BA5 3BP
Tel: 01749 870241 17 P6
campingandcaravanningclub.co.uk/cheddar
Total Pitches: 90 (C, CV & T)

Chiverton Park
East Hill, Blackwater
TR4 8HS
Tel: 01872 560667 2 J7
chivertonpark.co.uk
Total Pitches: 12 (C, CV & T)

Church Farm C & C Park
The Bungalow, Church Farm, High Street, Sixpenny Handley, Salisbury
SP5 5ND
Tel: 01725 552563 8 D5
churchfarmcandcpark.co.uk
Total Pitches: 35 (C, CV & T)

Chy Carne Holiday Park
Kuggar, Ruan Minor, Helston
TR12 7LX
Tel: 01326 290200 2 J13
chycarne.co.uk
Total Pitches: 30 (C, CV & T)

Claylands Caravan Park
Cabus, Garstang
PR3 1AJ
Tel: 01524 791242 61 T10
claylands.com
Total Pitches: 30 (C, CV & T)

Clippesby Hall
Hall Lane, Clippesby, Great Yarmouth
NR29 3BL
Tel: 01493 367800 51 R11
clippesby.com
Total Pitches: 120 (C, CV & T)

Cofton Country Holidays
Starcross, Dawlish
EX6 8RP
Tel: 01626 890111 6 C8
coftonholidays.co.uk
Total Pitches: 450 (C, CV & T)

Coombe Touring Park
Race Plain, Netherhampton, Salisbury
SP2 8PN
Tel: 01722 328451 8 F3
coombecaravanpark.co.uk
Total Pitches: 50 (C, CV & T)

Corfe Castle C & C Club Site
Bucknowle, Wareham
BH20 5PQ
Tel: 01929 480280 8 C12
campingandcaravanningclub.co.uk/corfecastle
Total Pitches: 80 (C, CV & T)

Cornish Farm Touring Park
Shoreditch, Taunton
TA3 7BS
Tel: 01823 327746 16 H12
cornishfarm.com
Total Pitches: 50 (C, CV & T)

Cosawes Park
Perranarworthal, Truro
TR3 7QS
Tel: 01872 863724 2 K9
cosawestouringandcamping.co.uk
Total Pitches: 59 (C, CV & T)

Cote Ghyll C & C Park
Osmotherley, Northallerton
DL6 3AH
Tel: 01609 883425 70 G13
coteghyll.com
Total Pitches: 77 (C, CV & T)

Cotswold View Touring Park
Enstone Road, Charlbury
OX7 3JH
Tel: 01608 810314 29 S3
cotswoldview.co.uk
Total Pitches: 125 (C, CV & T)

Country View Holiday Park
Sand Road, Sand Bay, Weston-super-Mare
BS22 9UJ
Tel: 01934 627595 16 K4
cvhp.co.uk
Total Pitches: 190 (C, CV & T)

Cove C & C Park
Ullswater, Watermillock
CA11 0LS
Tel: 017684 86549 67 P8
cove-park.co.uk
Total Pitches: 50 (C, CV & T)

Crealy Meadows C & C Park
Sidmouth Road, Clyst St Mary, Exeter
EX5 1DR
Tel: 01395 234888 6 D6
crealymeadows.co.uk
Total Pitches: 120 (C, CV & T)

Crows Nest Caravan Park
Gristhorpe, Filey
YO14 9PS
Tel: 01723 582206 65 P3
crowsnestcaravanpark.com
Total Pitches: 49 (C, CV & T)

Dell Touring Park
Beyton Road, Thurston, Bury St Edmunds
IP31 3RB
Tel: 01359 270121 40 F8
thedellcaravanpark.co.uk
Total Pitches: 50 (C, CV & T)

Diamond Farm C & C Park
Islip Road, Bletchingdon
OX5 3DR
Tel: 01869 350909 30 B9
diamondpark.co.uk
Total Pitches: 37 (C, CV & T)

Dibles Park
Dibles Road, Warsash, Southampton
SO31 9SA
Tel: 01489 575232 9 Q7
diblespark.co.uk
Total Pitches: 14 (C, CV & T)

Dolbeare Park C & C
St Ive Road, Landrake, Saltash
PL12 5AF
Tel: 01752 851332 4 K8
dolbeare.co.uk
Total Pitches: 60 (C, CV & T)

Dornafield
Dornafield Farm, Two Mile Oak, Newton Abbot
TQ12 6DD
Tel: 01803 812732 5 U7
dornafield.com
Total Pitches: 135 (C, CV & T)

East Fleet Farm Touring Park
Chickerell, Weymouth
DT3 4DW
Tel: 01305 785768 7 R9
eastfleet.co.uk
Total Pitches: 400 (C, CV & T)

Eden Valley Holiday Park
Lanlivery, Nr Lostwithiel
PL30 5BU
Tel: 01208 872277 3 R5
edenvalleyholidaypark.co.uk
Total Pitches: 56 (C, CV & T)

Eskdale C & C Club Site
Boot, Holmrook
CA19 1TH
Tel: 019467 23253 66 J12
campingandcaravanningclub.co.uk/eskdale
Total Pitches: 100 (CV & T)

Exe Valley Caravan Site
Mill House, Bridgetown, Dulverton
TA22 9JR
Tel: 01643 851432 16 B10
exevalleycamping.co.uk
Total Pitches: 48 (C, CV & T)

Fernwood Caravan Park
Lyneal, Ellesmere
SY12 0QF
Tel: 01948 710221 45 L7
fernwoodpark.co.uk
Total Pitches: 60 (C & CV)

Fields End Water Caravan Park & Fishery
Benwick Road, Doddington, March
PE15 0TY
Tel: 01354 740199 39 N2
fieldsendcaravans.co.uk
Total Pitches: 52 (C, CV & T)

Fishpool Farm Caravan Park
Fishpool Road, Delamere, Northwich
CW8 2HP
Tel: 01606 883970 55 N13
fishpoolfarmcaravanpark.co.uk
Total Pitches: 50 (C, CV & T)

Flusco Wood
Flusco, Penrith
CA11 0JB
Tel: 017684 80020 67 Q7
fluscowood.co.uk
Total Pitches: 36 (C & CV)

Globe Vale Holiday Park
Radnor, Redruth
TR16 4BH
Tel: 01209 891183 2 J8
globevale.co.uk
Total Pitches: 138 (C, CV & T)

Golden Cap Holiday Park
Seatown, Chideock, Bridport
DT6 6JX
Tel: 01308 422139 7 M6
wdlh.co.uk
Total Pitches: 108 (C, CV & T)

Golden Square Touring Caravan Park
Oswaldkirk, Helmsley
YO62 5YQ
Tel: 01439 788269 64 E4
goldensquarecaravanpark.com
Total Pitches: 129 (C, CV & T)

Golden Valley C & C Park
Coach Road, Ripley
DE55 4ES
Tel: 01773 513881 47 M3
goldenvalleycaravanpark.co.uk
Total Pitches: 45 (C, CV & T)

Goosewood Caravan Park
Sutton-on-the-Forest, York
YO61 1ET
Tel: 01347 810829 64 D7
flowerofmay.com
Total Pitches: 100 (C & CV)

Green Acres Caravan Park
High Knells, Houghton, Carlisle
CA6 4JW
Tel: 01228 675418 75 T13
caravanpark-cumbria.com
Total Pitches: 30 (C, CV & T)

Greenacres Touring Park
Haywards Lane, Chelston, Wellington
TA21 9PH
Tel: 01823 652844 16 G12
greenacres-wellington.co.uk
Total Pitches: 40 (C & CV)

Greenhill Farm C & C Park
Greenhill Farm, New Road, Landford, Salisbury
SP5 2AZ
Tel: 01794 324117 8 K5
greenhillholidays.co.uk
Total Pitches: 160 (C, CV & T)

Greenhill Leisure Park
Greenhill Farm, Station Road, Bletchingdon, Oxford
OX5 3BQ
Tel: 01869 351600 29 U4
greenhill-leisure-park.co.uk
Total Pitches: 92 (C, CV & T)

Grouse Hill Caravan Park
Flask Bungalow Farm, Fylingdales, Robin Hood's Bay
YO22 4QH
Tel: 01947 880543 71 R12
grousehill.co.uk
Total Pitches: 175 (C, CV & T)

Gunvenna Caravan Park
St Minver, Wadebridge
PL27 6QN
Tel: 01208 862405 4 B5
gunvenna.co.uk
Total Pitches: 75 (C, CV & T)

Gwithian Farm Campsite
Gwithian Farm, Gwithian, Hayle
TR27 5BX
Tel: 01736 753127 2 F8
gwithianfarm.co.uk
Total Pitches: 87 (C, CV & T)

Harbury Fields
Harbury Fields Farm, Harbury, Nr Leamington Spa
CV33 9JN
Tel: 01926 612457 37 L8
harburyfields.co.uk
Total Pitches: 59 (C & CV)

Heathfield Farm Camping
Heathfield Road, Freshwater, Isle of Wight
PO40 9SH
Tel: 01983 407822 9 L11
heathfieldcamping.co.uk
Total Pitches: 60 (C, CV & T)

Heathland Beach Caravan Park
London Road, Kessingland
NR33 7PJ
Tel: 01502 740337 41 T3
heathlandbeach.co.uk
Total Pitches: 63 (C, CV & T)

Hele Valley Holiday Park
Hele Bay, Ilfracombe
EX34 9RD
Tel: 01271 862460 15 M3
helevalley.co.uk
Total Pitches: 55 (C, CV & T)

Hendra Holiday Park
Newquay
TR8 4NY
Tel: 01637 875778 3 L4
hendra-holidays.com
Total Pitches: 548 (C, CV & T)

Herding Hill Farm
Shield Hill, Haltwhistle
NE49 9NW
Tel: 01434 320175 76 E13
herdinghillfarm.co.uk
Total Pitches: 44 (C, CV & T)

Hidden Valley Park
West Down, Braunton, Ilfracombe
EX34 8NU
Tel: 01271 813837 15 M4
hiddenvalleypark.com
Total Pitches: 100 (C, CV & T)

Highfield Farm Touring Park
Long Road, Comberton, Cambridge
CB23 7DG
Tel: 01223 262308 39 N9
highfieldfarmtouringpark.co.uk
Total Pitches: 120 (C, CV & T)

Highlands End Holiday Park
Eype, Bridport, Dorset
DT6 6AR
Tel: 01308 422139 7 N6
wdlh.co.uk
Total Pitches: 195 (C, CV & T)

Hill Cottage Farm C & C Park
Sandleheath Road, Alderholt, Fordingbridge
SP6 3EG
Tel: 01425 650513 8 G6
hillcottagefarmcampingandcaravanpark.co.uk
Total Pitches: 95 (C, CV & T)

Hill Farm Caravan Park
Branches Lane, Sherfield English, Romsey
SO51 6FH
Tel: 01794 340402 8 K4
hillfarmpark.com
Total Pitches: 100 (C, CV & T)

Hill of Oaks & Blakeholme
Windermere
LA12 8NR
Tel: 015395 31578 61 R2
hillofoaks.co.uk
Total Pitches: 43 (C & CV)

Hillside Caravan Park
Canvas Farm, Moor Road, Thirsk
YO7 4BR
Tel: 01845 537349 63 U2
hillsidecaravanpark.co.uk
Total Pitches: 35 (C & CV)

Hollins Farm C & C
Far Arnside, Carnforth
LA5 0SL
Tel: 01524 701508 61 S4
holgates.co.uk
Total Pitches: 12 (C, CV & T)

Homing Park
Church Lane, Seasalter, Whitstable
CT5 4BU
Tel: 01227 771777 13 L3
homingpark.co.uk
Total Pitches: 43 (C, CV & T)

Honeybridge Park
Honeybridge Lane, Dial Post, Horsham
RH13 8NX
Tel: 01403 710923 10 K7
honeybridgepark.co.uk
Total Pitches: 130 (C, CV & T)

Hurley Riverside Park
Park Office, Hurley, Nr Maidenhead
SL6 5NE
Tel: 01628 824493 20 D6
hurleyriversidepark.co.uk
Total Pitches: 200 (C, CV & T)

Hylton Caravan Park
Eden Street, Silloth
CA7 4AY
Tel: 016973 31707 66 H2
stanwix.com
Total Pitches: 90 (C, CV & T)

Jacobs Mount Caravan Park
Jacobs Mount, Stepney Road, Scarborough
YO12 5NL
Tel: 01723 361178 65 N2
jacobsmount.com
Total Pitches: 156 (C, CV & T)

Jasmine Caravan Park
Cross Lane, Snainton, Scarborough
YO13 9BE
Tel: 01723 859240 65 L3
jasminepark.co.uk
Total Pitches: 68 (C, CV & T)

Juliot's Well Holiday Park
Camelford, Cornwall
PL32 9RF
Tel: 01840 213302 4 D4
juliotswell.com
Total Pitches: 39 (C, CV & T)

Kenneggy Cove Holiday Park
Higher Kenneggy, Rosudgeon, Penzance
TR20 9AU
Tel: 01736 763453 2 F11
kenneggycove.co.uk
Total Pitches: 45 (C, CV & T)

King's Lynn C & C Park
New Road, North Runcton, King's Lynn
PE33 0RA
Tel: 01553 840004 49 T10
kl-cc.co.uk
Total Pitches: 150 (C, CV & T)

Kneps Farm Holiday Park
River Road, Stanah, Thornton-Cleveleys, Blackpool
FY5 5LR
Tel: 01253 823632 61 R11
knepsfarm.co.uk
Total Pitches: 40 (C & CV)

Ladycross Plantation Caravan Park
Egton, Whitby
YO21 1UA
Tel: 01947 895502 71 P11
ladycrossplantation.co.uk
Total Pitches: 130 (C, CV & T)

Lady's Mile Holiday Park
Dawlish, Devon
EX7 0LX
Tel: 01626 863411 6 C9
ladysmile.co.uk
Total Pitches: 570 (C, CV & T)

Lamb Cottage Caravan Park
Dalefords Lane, Whitegate, Northwich
CW8 2BN
Tel: 01606 882302 55 P13
lambcottage.co.uk
Total Pitches: 45 (C & CV)

Langstone Manor C & C Park
Moortown, Tavistock
PL19 9JZ
Tel: 01822 613371 5 N6
langstone-manor.co.uk
Total Pitches: 40 (C, CV & T)

Lebberston Touring Park
Filey Road, Lebberston, Scarborough
YO11 3PE
Tel: 01723 585723 65 P3
lebberstontouring.co.uk
Total Pitches: 125 (C & CV)

Lee Valley C & C Park
Meridian Way, Edmonton, London
N9 0AR
Tel: 020 8803 6900 21 Q4
visitleevalley.org.uk
Total Pitches: 100 (C, CV & T)

Lee Valley Campsite
Sewardstone Road, Chingford, London
E4 7RA
Tel: 020 8529 5689 21 Q3
visitleevalley.org.uk
Total Pitches: 81 (C, CV & T)

Lickpenny Caravan Site
Lickpenny Lane, Tansley, Matlock
DE4 5GF
Tel: 01629 583040 46 K2
lickpennycaravanpark.co.uk
Total Pitches: 80 (C & CV)

Lime Tree Park
Dukes Drive, Buxton
SK17 9RP
Tel: 01298 22988 56 G12
limetreeparkbuxton.co.uk
Total Pitches: 106 (C, CV & T)

Lincoln Farm Park Oxfordshire
High Street, Standlake
OX29 7RH
Tel: 01865 300239 29 S7
lincolnfarmpark.co.uk
Total Pitches: 90 (C, CV & T)

Little Cotton Caravan Park
Little Cotton, Dartmouth
TQ6 0LB
Tel: 01803 832558 5 V10
littlecotton.co.uk
Total Pitches: 95 (C, CV & T)

Little Lakeland Caravan Park
Wortwell, Harleston
IP20 0EL
Tel: 01986 788646 41 N3
littlelakeland.co.uk
Total Pitches: 38 (C, CV & T)

Long Acres Touring Park
Station Road, Old Leake, Boston
PE22 9RF
Tel: 01205 871555 49 N3
longacres-caravanpark.co.uk
Total Pitches: 40 (C, CV & T)

Long Hazel Park
High Street, Sparkford, Yeovil
BA22 7JH
Tel: 01963 440002 17 R11
longhazelpark.co.uk
Total Pitches: 50 (C, CV & T)

Longnor Wood Holiday Park
Newtown, Longnor, Nr Buxton
SK17 0NG
Tel: 01298 83648 56 G14
longnorwood.co.uk
Total Pitches: 47 (C, CV & T)

Lower Polladras Touring Park
Carleen, Breage, Helston
TR13 9NX
Tel: 01736 762220 2 G10
lower-polladras.co.uk
Total Pitches: 39 (C, CV & T)

Lowther Holiday Park
Eamont Bridge, Penrith
CA10 2JB
Tel: 01768 863631 67 R7
lowther-holidaypark.co.uk
Total Pitches: 180 (C, CV & T)

Lytton Lawn Touring Park
Lymore Lane, Milford on Sea
SO41 0TX
Tel: 01590 648331 8 K10
shorefield.co.uk
Total Pitches: 136 (C, CV & T)

Manor Wood Country Caravan Park
Manor Wood, Coddington, Chester
CH3 9EN
Tel: 01829 782990 45 L2
cheshire-caravan-sites.co.uk
Total Pitches: 45 (C, CV & T)

Meadowbank Holidays
Stour Way, Christchurch
BH23 2PQ
Tel: 01202 483597 8 G10
meadowbank-holidays.co.uk
Total Pitches: 41 (C & CV)

Merley Court
Merley, Wimborne Minster
BH21 3AA
Tel: 01590 648331 8 E9
shorefield.co.uk
Total Pitches: 160 (C, CV & T)

Middlewood Farm Holiday Park
Middlewood Lane, Fylingthorpe, Robin Hood's Bay, Whitby
YO22 4UF
Tel: 01947 880414 71 R12
middlewoodfarm.com
Total Pitches: 100 (C, CV & T)

Minnows Touring Park
Holbrook Lane, Sampford Peverell
EX16 7EN
Tel: 01884 821770 16 D13
minnowstouringpark.co.uk
Total Pitches: 59 (C, CV & T)

Moon & Sixpence
Newbourn Road, Waldringfield, Woodbridge
IP12 4PP
Tel: 01473 736650 41 N11
moonandsixpence.eu
Total Pitches: 50 (C & CV)

Moss Wood Caravan Park
Crimbles Lane, Cockerham
LA2 0ES
Tel: 01524 791041 61 T10
mosswood.co.uk
Total Pitches: 25 (C, CV & T)

Naburn Lock Caravan Park
Naburn
YO19 4RU
Tel: 01904 728697 64 E10
naburnlock.co.uk
Total Pitches: 100 (C, CV & T)

Newberry Valley Park
Woodlands, Combe Martin
EX34 0AT
Tel: 01271 882334 15 N3
newberryvalleypark.co.uk
Total Pitches: 110 (C, CV & T)

Newhaven Caravan & Camping Park
Newhaven, Nr Buxton
SK17 0DT
Tel: 01298 84300 46 G2
newhavencaravanpark.co.uk
Total Pitches: 125 (C, CV & T)

Newlands C & C Park
Charmouth, Bridport
DT6 6RB
Tel: 01297 560259 7 L6
newlandsholidays.co.uk
Total Pitches: 240 (C, CV & T)

Newperran Holiday Park
Rejerrah, Newquay
TR8 5QJ
Tel: 01872 572407 2 K6
newperran.co.uk
Total Pitches: 357 (C, CV & T)

Ninham Country Holidays
Ninham, Shanklin, Isle of Wight
PO37 7PL
Tel: 01983 864243 9 R12
ninham-holidays.co.uk
Total Pitches: 150 (C, CV & T)

North Morte Farm C & C Park
North Morte Road, Mortehoe, Woolacombe
EX34 7EG
Tel: 01271 870381 15 L3
northmortefarm.co.uk
Total Pitches: 180 (C, CV & T)

Northam Farm Caravan & Touring Park
Brean, Burnham-on-Sea
TA8 2SE
Tel: 01278 751244 16 K5
northamfarm.co.uk
Total Pitches: 350 (C, CV & T)

Oakdown Country Holiday Park
Gatedown Lane, Sidmouth
EX10 0PT
Tel: 01297 680387 6 G6
oakdown.co.uk
Total Pitches: 150 (C, CV & T)

Oathill Farm Touring and Camping Site
Oathill, Crewkerne
TA18 8PZ
Tel: 01460 30234 7 M3
oathillfarmleisure.co.uk
Total Pitches: 13 (C, CV & T)

Old Hall Caravan Park
Capernwray, Carnforth
LA6 1AD
Tel: 01524 733276 61 U5
oldhallcaravanpark.co.uk
Total Pitches: 38 (C & CV)

Orchard Park
Frampton Lane, Hubbert's Bridge, Boston
PE20 3QU
Tel: 01205 290328 49 L5
orchardpark.co.uk
Total Pitches: 87 (C, CV & T)

Ord House Country Park
East Ord, Berwick-upon-Tweed
TD15 2NS
Tel: 01289 305288 85 P8
ordhouse.co.uk
Total Pitches: 79 (C, CV & T)

Oxon Hall Touring Park
Welshpool Road, Shrewsbury
SY3 5FB
Tel: 01743 340868 45 L11
morris-leisure.co.uk
Total Pitches: 105 (C, CV & T)

Padstow Touring Park
Padstow
PL28 8LE
Tel: 01841 532061 3 N2
padstowtouringpark.co.uk
Total Pitches: 150 (C, CV & T)

Park Cliffe Camping & Caravan Estate
Birks Road, Tower Wood, Windermere
LA23 3PG
Tel: 01539 531344 61 R1
parkcliffe.co.uk
Total Pitches: 60 (C, CV & T)

Parkers Farm Holiday Park
Higher Mead Farm, Ashburton, Devon
TQ13 7LJ
Tel: 01364 654869 5 T6
parkersfarmholidays.co.uk
Total Pitches: 100 (C, CV & T)

Parkland C & C Site
Sorley Green Cross, Kingsbridge
TQ7 4AF
Tel: 01548 852723 5 S11
parklandsite.co.uk
Total Pitches: 100 (C, CV & T)

Pear Tree Holiday Park
Organford Road, Holton Heath, Organford, Poole
BH16 6LA
Tel: 01202 622434 8 C10
peartreepark.co.uk
Total Pitches: 154 (C, CV & T)

Penrose Holiday Park
Goonhavern, Truro
TR4 9QF
Tel: 01872 573185 2 K6
penroseholidaypark.com
Total Pitches: 110 (C, CV & T)

Pentire Haven Holiday Park
Stibb Road, Kilkhampton, Bude
EX23 9QY
Tel: 01288 321601 14 F10
pentirehaven.co.uk
Total Pitches: 120 (C, CV & T)

Piccadilly Caravan Park
Folly Lane West, Lacock
SN15 2LP
Tel: 01249 730260 18 D7
piccadillylacock.co.uk
Total Pitches: 41 (C, CV & T)

Pilgrims Way C & C Park
Church Green Road, Fishtoft, Boston
PE21 0QY
Tel: 01205 366646 49 N5
pilgrimsway-caravanandcamping.com
Total Pitches: 22 (C, CV & T)

Polmanter Touring Park
Halsetown, St Ives
TR26 3LX
Tel: 01736 795640 2 E9
polmanter.com
Total Pitches: 270 (C, CV & T)

Porlock Caravan Park
Porlock, Minehead
TA24 8ND
Tel: 01643 862269 15 U3
porlockcaravanpark.co.uk
Total Pitches: 40 (C, CV & T)

Porthtowan Tourist Park
Mile Hill, Porthtowan, Truro
TR4 8TY
Tel: 01209 890256 2 H7
porthtowantouristpark.co.uk
Total Pitches: 80 (C, CV & T)

Quantock Orchard Caravan Park
Flaxpool, Crowcombe, Taunton
TA4 4AW
Tel: 01984 618618 16 F9
quantock-orchard.co.uk
Total Pitches: 60 (C, CV & T)

Ranch Caravan Park
Station Road, Honeybourne, Evesham
WR11 7PR
Tel: 01386 830744 36 F12
ranch.co.uk
Total Pitches: 120 (C & CV)

Ripley Caravan Park
Knaresborough Road, Ripley, Harrogate
HG3 3AU
Tel: 01423 770050 63 R7
ripleycaravanpark.com
Total Pitches: 100 (C, CV & T)

River Dart Country Park
Holne Park, Ashburton
TQ13 7NP
Tel: 01364 652511 5 S7
riverdart.co.uk
Total Pitches: 170 (C, CV & T)

River Valley Holiday Park
London Apprentice, St Austell
PL26 7AP
Tel: 01726 73533 3 Q6
rivervalleyholidaypark.co.uk
Total Pitches: 45 (C, CV & T)

Riverside C & C Park
Marsh Lane, North Molton Road, South Molton
EX36 3HQ
Tel: 01769 579269 15 R7
exmoorriverside.co.uk
Total Pitches: 54 (C, CV & T)

Riverside Caravan Park
High Bentham, Lancaster
LA2 7FJ
Tel: 015242 61272 62 D6
riversidecaravanpark.co.uk
Total Pitches: 61 (C & CV)

Riverside Caravan Park
Leigham Manor Drive, Marsh Mills, Plymouth
PL6 8LL
Tel: 01752 344122 5 N9
riversidecaravanpark.com
Total Pitches: 259 (C, CV & T)

Riverside Meadows Country Caravan Park
Ure Bank Top, Ripon
HG4 1JD
Tel: 01765 602964 63 S5
flowerofmay.com
Total Pitches: 80 (C, CV & T)

Rose Farm Touring & Camping Park
Stepshort, Belton, Nr Great Yarmouth
NR31 9JS
Tel: 01493 780896 51 S13
rosefarmtouringpark.co.uk
Total Pitches: 145 (C, CV & T)

Ross Park
Park Hill Farm, Ipplepen, Newton Abbot
TQ12 5TT
Tel: 01803 812983 5 U7
rossparkcaravanpark.co.uk
Total Pitches: 110 (C, CV & T)

Rudding Holiday Park
Follifoot, Harrogate
HG3 1JH
Tel: 01423 870439 63 S9
ruddingholidaypark.co.uk
Total Pitches: 141 (C, CV & T)

Rutland C & C
Park Lane, Greetham, Oakham
LE15 7FN
Tel: 01572 813520 48 D11
rutlandcaravanandcamping.co.uk
Total Pitches: 130 (C, CV & T)

St Helens Caravan Park
Wykeham, Scarborough
YO13 9QD
Tel: 01723 862771 65 M3
sthelenscaravanpark.co.uk
Total Pitches: 250 (C, CV & T)

St Mabyn Holiday Park
Longstone Road, St Mabyn, Wadebridge
PL30 3BY
Tel: 01208 841677 3 R2
stmabynholidaypark.co.uk
Total Pitches: 120 (C, CV & T)

Sandy Balls Holiday Village
Sandy Balls Estate Ltd, Godshill, Fordingbridge
SP6 2JZ
Tel: 0844 693 1336 8 H6
sandyballs.co.uk
Total Pitches: 225 (C, CV & T)

Seaview International Holiday Park
Boswinger, Mevagissey
PL26 6LL
Tel: 01726 843425 3 P8
seaviewinternational.com
Total Pitches: 201 (C, CV & T)

Severn Gorge Park
Bridgnorth Road, Tweedale, Telford
TF7 4JB
Tel: 01952 684789 45 R12
severngorgepark.co.uk
Total Pitches: 12 (C & CV)

Shamba Holidays
230 Ringwood Road, St Leonards, Ringwood
BH24 2SB
Tel: 01202 873302 8 G8
shambaholidays.co.uk
Total Pitches: 150 (C, CV & T)

Shaw Hall Holiday Park
Smithy Lane, Scarisbrick, Ormskirk
L40 8HJ
Tel: 01704 840298 54 J4
shawhall.co.uk
Total Pitches: 37 (C, CV & T)

Shrubbery Touring Park
Rousdon, Lyme Regis
DT7 3XW
Tel: 01297 442227 6 J6
shrubberypark.co.uk
Total Pitches: 120 (C, CV & T)

Silverbow Park
Perranwell, Goonhavern
TR4 9NX
Tel: 01872 572347 2 K6
chycor.co.uk/parks/silverbow
Total Pitches: 90 (C, CV & T)

Silverdale Caravan Park
Middlebarrow Plain, Cove Road, Silverdale, Nr Carnforth
LA5 0SH
Tel: 01524 701508 61 T4
holgates.co.uk
Total Pitches: 80 (C, CV & T)

Skelwith Fold Caravan Park
Ambleside, Cumbria
LA22 0HX
Tel: 015394 32277 67 N12
skelwith.com
Total Pitches: 150 (C & CV)

Somers Wood Caravan Park
Somers Road, Meriden
CV7 7PL
Tel: 01676 522978 36 H4
somerswood.co.uk
Total Pitches: 48 (C & CV)

South Lytchett Manor C & C Park
Dorchester Road, Lytchett Minster, Poole
BH16 6JB
Tel: 01202 622577 8 D10
southlytchettmanor.co.uk
Total Pitches: 150 (C, CV & T)

South Meadows Caravan Park
South Road, Belford
NE70 7DP
Tel: 01668 213326 85 S12
southmeadows.co.uk
Total Pitches: 120 (C, CV & T)

Southfork Caravan Park
Parrett Works, Martock
TA12 6AE
Tel: 01935 825661 17 M13
southforkcaravans.co.uk
Total Pitches: 27 (C, CV & T)

Springfield Holiday Park
Tedburn St Mary, Exeter
EX6 6EW
Tel: 01647 24242 5 U2
springfieldholidaypark.co.uk
Total Pitches: 48 (C, CV & T)

Stanmore Hall Touring Park
Stourbridge Road, Bridgnorth
WV15 6DT
Tel: 01746 761761 35 R2
morris-leisure.co.uk
Total Pitches: 129 (C, CV & T)

Stowford Farm Meadows
Berry Down, Combe Martin
EX34 0PW
Tel: 01271 882476 15 N4
stowford.co.uk
Total Pitches: 700 (C, CV & T)

Stroud Hill Park
Fen Road, Pidley
PE28 3DE
Tel: 01487 741333 39 M5
stroudhillpark.co.uk
Total Pitches: 60 (C, CV & T)

Sumners Ponds Fishery & Campsite
Chapel Road, Barns Green, Horsham
RH13 0PR
Tel: 01403 732539 10 J5
sumnersponds.co.uk
Total Pitches: 86 (C, CV & T)

Sun Valley Resort
Pentewan Road, St Austell
PL26 6DJ
Tel: 01726 843266 3 Q7
sunvalleyresort.co.uk
Total Pitches: 29 (C, CV & T)

Swiss Farm Touring & Camping
Marlow Road, Henley-on-Thames
RG9 2HY
Tel: 01491 573419 20 C6
swissfarmcamping.co.uk
Total Pitches: 140 (C, CV & T)

Tanner Farm Touring C & C Park
Tanner Farm, Goudhurst Road, Marden
TN12 9ND
Tel: 01622 832399 12 D7
tannerfarmpark.co.uk
Total Pitches: 100 (C, CV & T)

Tattershall Lakes Country Park
Sleaford Road, Tattershall
LN4 4LR
Tel: 01526 348800 48 K2
tattershall-lakes.com
Total Pitches: 186 (C, CV & T)

Tehidy Holiday Park
Harris Mill, Illogan, Portreath
TR16 4JQ
Tel: 01209 216489 2 H8
tehidy.co.uk
Total Pitches: 18 (C, CV & T)

Teversal C & C Club Site
Silverhill Lane, Teversal
NG17 3JJ
Tel: 01623 551838 47 N1
campingandcaravanningclub.co.uk/teversal
Total Pitches: 126 (C, CV & T)

The Inside Park
Down House Estate, Blandford Forum
DT11 9AD
Tel: 01258 453719 8 B8
theinsidepark.co.uk
Total Pitches: 125 (C, CV & T)

The Laurels Holiday Park
Padstow Road, Whitecross, Wadebridge
PL27 7JQ
Tel: 01209 313474 3 P2
thelaurelsholidaypark.co.uk
Total Pitches: 30 (C, CV & T)

The Old Brick Kilns
Little Barney Lane, Barney, Fakenham
NR21 0NL
Tel: 01328 878305 50 H7
old-brick-kilns.co.uk
Total Pitches: 65 (C, CV & T)

The Old Oaks Touring Park
Wick Farm, Wick, Glastonbury
BA6 8JS
Tel: 01458 831437 17 P9
theoldoaks.co.uk
Total Pitches: 98 (C, CV & T)

The Orchards Holiday Caravan Park
Main Road, Newbridge, Yarmouth, Isle of Wight
PO41 0TS
Tel: 01983 531331 9 N11
orchards-holiday-park.co.uk
Total Pitches: 160 (C, CV & T)

The Quiet Site
Ullswater, Watermillock
CA11 0LS
Tel: 07768 727016 67 P8
thequietsite.co.uk
Total Pitches: 100 (C, CV & T)

Tollgate Farm C & C Park
Budnick Hill, Perranporth
TR6 0AD
Tel: 01872 572130 2 K6
tollgatefarm.co.uk
Total Pitches: 102 (C, CV & T)

Townsend Touring Park
Townsend Farm, Pembridge, Leominster
HR6 9HB
Tel: 01544 388527 34 J9
townsendfarm.co.uk
Total Pitches: 60 (C, CV & T)

Treago Farm Caravan Site
Crantock, Newquay
TR8 5QS
Tel: 01637 830277 2 K4
treagofarm.co.uk
Total Pitches: 90 (C, CV & T)

Trencreek Holiday Park
Hillcrest, Higher Trencreek, Newquay
TR8 4NS
Tel: 01637 874210 3 L4
trencreekholidaypark.co.uk
Total Pitches: 194 (C, CV & T)

Trethem Mill Touring Park
St Just-in-Roseland, Nr St Mawes, Truro
TR2 5JF
Tel: 01872 580504 3 M9
trethem.com
Total Pitches: 84 (C, CV & T)

Trevalgan Touring Park
Trevalgan, St Ives
TR26 3BJ
Tel: 01736 791892 2 D9
trevalgantouringpark.co.uk
Total Pitches: 120 (C, CV & T)

Trevarth Holiday Park
Blackwater, Truro
TR4 8HR
Tel: 01872 560266 2 J7
trevarth.co.uk
Total Pitches: 30 (C, CV & T)

Trevella Tourist Park
Crantock, Newquay
TR8 5EW
Tel: 01637 830308 3 L5
trevella.co.uk
Total Pitches: 171 (C, CV & T)

Trevornick Holiday Park
Holywell Bay, Newquay
TR8 5PW
Tel: 01637 830531 2 K5
trevornick.co.uk
Total Pitches: 688 (C, CV & T)

Troutbeck C & C Club Site
Hutton Moor End, Troutbeck, Penrith
CA11 0SX
Tel: 017687 79149 67 N7
campingandcaravanningclub.co.uk/troutbeck
Total Pitches: 54 (C, CV & T)

Truro C & C Park
Truro
TR4 8QN
Tel: 01872 560274 2 K7
trurocaravanandcampingpark.co.uk
Total Pitches: 51 (C, CV & T)

Tudor C & C
Shepherds Patch, Slimbridge, Gloucester
GL2 7BP
Tel: 01453 890483 28 D7
tudorcaravanpark.com
Total Pitches: 75 (C, CV & T)

Two Mills Touring Park
Yarmouth Road, North Walsham
NR28 9NA
Tel: 01692 405829 51 N8
twomills.co.uk
Total Pitches: 81 (C, CV & T)

Ulwell Cottage Caravan Park
Ulwell Cottage, Ulwell, Swanage
BH19 3DG
Tel: 01929 422823 8 E12
ulwellcottagepark.co.uk
Total Pitches: 77 (C, CV & T)

Vale of Pickering Caravan Park
Carr House Farm, Allerston, Pickering
YO18 7PQ
Tel: 01723 859280 64 K3
valeofpickering.co.uk
Total Pitches: 120 (C, CV & T)

Wagtail Country Park
Cliff Lane, Marston, Grantham
NG32 2HU
Tel: 01400 251955 48 C5
wagtailcountrypark.co.uk
Total Pitches: 76 (C & CV)

Warcombe Farm C & C Park
Station Road, Mortehoe
EX34 7EJ
Tel: 01271 870690 15 L3
warcombefarm.co.uk
Total Pitches: 250 (C, CV & T)

Wareham Forest Tourist Park
North Trigon, Wareham
BH20 7NZ
Tel: 01929 551393 8 B10
warehamforest.co.uk
Total Pitches: 200 (C, CV & T)

Watergate Bay Touring Park
Watergate Bay, Tregurrian
TR8 4AD
Tel: 01637 860387 3 L4
watergatebaytouringpark.co.uk
Total Pitches: 171 (C, CV & T)

Waterrow Touring Park
Wiveliscombe, Taunton
TA4 2AZ
Tel: 01984 623464 16 E11
waterrowpark.co.uk
Total Pitches: 45 (C, CV & T)

Waters Edge Caravan Park
Crooklands, Nr Kendal
LA7 7NN
Tel: 015395 67708 61 U3
watersedgecaravanpark.co.uk
Total Pitches: 26 (C, CV & T)

Wayfarers C & C Park
Relubbus Lane, St Hilary, Penzance
TR20 9EF
Tel: 01736 763326 2 F10
wayfarerspark.co.uk
Total Pitches: 32 (C, CV & T)

Wells Holiday Park
Haybridge, Wells
BA5 1AJ
Tel: 01749 676869 17 P7
wellsholidaypark.co.uk
Total Pitches: 72 (C, CV & T)

Westwood Caravan Park
Old Felixstowe Road, Bucklesham, Ipswich
IP10 0BN
Tel: 01473 659637 41 N12
westwoodcaravanpark.co.uk
Total Pitches: 100 (C, CV & T)

Wheathill Touring Park
Wheathill, Bridgnorth
WV16 6QT
Tel: 01584 823456 35 P4
wheathillpark.co.uk
Total Pitches: 25 (C & CV)

Whitefield Forest Touring Park
Brading Road, Ryde, Isle of Wight
PO33 1QL
Tel: 01983 617069 9 S11
whitefieldforest.co.uk
Total Pitches: 90 (C, CV & T)

Widdicombe Farm Touring Park
Marldon, Paignton
TQ3 1ST
Tel: 01803 558325 5 V8
widdicombefarm.co.uk
Total Pitches: 180 (C, CV & T)

Widemouth Fields C & C Park
Park Farm, Poundstock, Bude
EX23 0NA
Tel: 01288 361351 14 F12
widemouthbaytouring.co.uk
Total Pitches: 156 (C, CV & T)

Wild Rose Park
Ormside, Appleby-in-Westmorland
CA16 6EJ
Tel: 017683 51077 68 E9
wildrose.co.uk
Total Pitches: 226 (C & CV)

Wilksworth Farm Caravan Park
Cranborne Road, Wimborne Minster
BH21 4HW
Tel: 01202 885467 8 E8
wilksworthfarmcaravanpark.co.uk
Total Pitches: 85 (C, CV & T)

Wood Farm C & C Park
Axminster Road, Charmouth
DT6 6BT
Tel: 01297 560697 7 L6
woodfarm.co.uk
Total Pitches: 175 (C, CV & T)

Wooda Farm Holiday Park
Poughill, Bude
EX23 9HJ
Tel: 01288 352069 14 F11
wooda.co.uk
Total Pitches: 200 (C, CV & T)

Woodclose Caravan Park
High Casterton, Kirkby Lonsdale
LA6 2SE
Tel: 01524 271597 62 C4
woodclosepark.com
Total Pitches: 29 (C, CV & T)

Woodhall Country Park
Stixwold Road, Woodhall Spa
LN10 6UJ
Tel: 01526 353710 59 L14
woodhallcountrypark.co.uk
Total Pitches: 115 (C, CV & T)

Woodland Springs Adult Touring Park
Venton, Drewsteignton
EX6 6PG
Tel: 01647 231695 5 R2
woodlandsprings.co.uk
Total Pitches: 81 (C, CV & T)

Woodlands Grove C & C Park
Blackawton, Dartmouth
TQ9 7DQ
Tel: 01803 712598 5 U10
woodlands-caravanpark.com
Total Pitches: 350 (C, CV & T)

Woodovis Park
Gulworthy, Tavistock
PL19 8NY
Tel: 01822 832968 5 L6
woodovis.com
Total Pitches: 50 (C, CV & T)

Yeatheridge Farm Caravan Park
East Worlington, Crediton
EX17 4TN
Tel: 01884 860330 15 S10
yeatheridge.co.uk
Total Pitches: 103 (C, CV & T)

Zeacombe House Caravan Park
Blackerton Cross, East Anstey, Tiverton
EX16 9JU
Tel: 01398 341279 15 U8
zeacombeadultretreat.co.uk
Total Pitches: 50 (C, CV & T)

SCOTLAND

Beecraigs C & C Site
Beecraigs Country Park, The Visitor Centre, Linlithgow
EH49 6PL
Tel: 01506 844516 82 K4
beecraigs.com
Total Pitches: 36 (C, CV & T)

Blair Castle Caravan Park
Blair Atholl, Pitlochry
PH18 5SR
Tel: 01796 481263 97 P10
blaircastlecaravanpark.co.uk
Total Pitches: 226 (C, CV & T)

Brighouse Bay Holiday Park
Brighouse Bay, Borgue, Kirkcudbright
DG6 4TS
Tel: 01557 870267 73 Q10
gillespie-leisure.co.uk
Total Pitches: 190 (C, CV & T)

Cairnsmill Holiday Park
Largo Road, St Andrews
KY16 8NN
Tel: 01334 473604 91 Q9
cairnsmill.co.uk
Total Pitches: 62 (C, CV & T)

Castle Cary Holiday Park
Creetown, Newton Stewart
DG8 7DQ
Tel: 01671 820264 73 M8
castlecary-caravans.com
Total Pitches: 50 (C, CV & T)

Craigtoun Meadows Holiday Park
Mount Melville, St Andrews
KY16 8PQ
Tel: 01334 475959 91 Q8
craigtounmeadows.co.uk
Total Pitches: 57 (C, CV & T)

Drum Mohr Caravan Park
Levenhall, Musselburgh
EH21 8JS
Tel: 0131 665 6867 83 S4
drummohr.org
Total Pitches: 120 (C, CV & T)

Gart Caravan Park
The Gart, Callander
FK17 8LE
Tel: 01877 330002 89 P4
theholidaypark.co.uk
Total Pitches: 128 (C & CV)

Glenearly Caravan Park
Dalbeattie
DG5 4NE
Tel: 01556 611393 74 F13
glenearlycaravanpark.co.uk
Total Pitches: 39 (C, CV & T)

Glen Nevis C & C Park
Glen Nevis, Fort William
PH33 6SX
Tel: 01397 702191 94 G4
glen-nevis.co.uk
Total Pitches: 380 (C, CV & T)

Hoddom Castle Caravan Park
Hoddom, Lockerbie
DG11 1AS
Tel: 01576 300251 75 N11
hoddomcastle.co.uk
Total Pitches: 200 (C, CV & T)

Huntly Castle Caravan Park
The Meadow, Huntly
AB54 4UJ
Tel: 01466 794999 104 G7
huntlycastle.co.uk
Total Pitches: 90 (C, CV & T)

Invercoe C & C Park
Glencoe, Ballachulish
PH49 4HP
Tel: 01855 811210 94 F7
invercoe.co.uk
Total Pitches: 60 (C, CV & T)

Linnhe Lochside Holidays
Corpach, Fort William
PH33 7NL
Tel: 01397 772376 94 F3
linnhe-lochside-holidays.co.uk
Total Pitches: 85 (C, CV & T)

Loch Ken Holiday Park
Parton, Castle Douglas
DG7 3NE
Tel: 01644 470282 73 R5
lochkenholidaypark.co.uk
Total Pitches: 40 (C, CV & T)

Lomond Woods Holiday Park
Old Luss Road, Balloch, Loch Lomond
G83 8QP
Tel: 01389 755000 88 J9
holiday-parks.co.uk
Total Pitches: 100 (C & CV)

Milton of Fonab Caravan Park
Bridge Road, Pitlochry
PH16 5NA
Tel: 01796 472882 97 Q12
fonab.co.uk
Total Pitches: 154 (C, CV & T)

River Tilt Caravan Park
Blair Atholl, Pitlochry
PH18 5TE
Tel: 01796 481467 97 P10
rivertilt.co.uk
Total Pitches: 30 (C, CV & T)

Sands of Luce Holiday Park
Sands of Luce, Sandhead, Stranraer
DG9 9JN
Tel: 01776 830456 94 G8
sandsofluceholidaypark.co.uk
Total Pitches: 100 (C, CV & T)

Seaward Caravan Park
Dhoon Bay, Kirkudbright
DG6 4TJ
Tel: 01557 870267 73 R10
gillespie-leisure.co.uk
Total Pitches: 25 (C, CV & T)

Shieling Holidays
Craignure, Isle of Mull
PA65 6AY
Tel: 01680 812496 93 S11
shielingholidays.co.uk
Total Pitches: 90 (C, CV & T)

Silver Sands Leisure Park
Covesea, West Beach, Lossiemouth
IV31 6SP
Tel: 01343 813262 103 V1
silver-sands.co.uk
Total Pitches: 140 (C, CV & T)

Skye C & C Club Site
Loch Greshornish, Borve, Arnisort, Edinbane, Isle of Skye
IV51 9PS
Tel: 01470 582230 100 c4
campingandcaravanningclub.co.uk/skye
Total Pitches: 105 (C, CV & T)

Thurston Manor Leisure Park
Innerwick, Dunbar
EH42 1SA
Tel: 01368 840643 84 J4
thurstonmanor.co.uk
Total Pitches: 120 (C, CV & T)

Trossachs Holiday Park
Aberfoyle
FK8 3SA
Tel: 01877 382614 89 M6
trossachsholidays.co.uk
Total Pitches: 66 (C, CV & T)

Witches Craig C & C Park
Blairlogie, Stirling
FK9 5PX
Tel: 01786 474947 89 T6
witchescraig.co.uk
Total Pitches: 60 (C, CV & T)

WALES

Barcdy Touring C & C Park
Talsarnau
LL47 6YG
Tel: 01766 770736 43 M6
barcdy.co.uk
Total Pitches: 80 (C, CV & T)

Bodnant Caravan Park
Nebo Road, Llanrwst, Conwy Valley
LL26 0SD
Tel: 01492 640248 53 P10
bodnant-caravan-park.co.uk
Total Pitches: 54 (C, CV & T)

Bron Derw Touring Caravan Park
Llanrwst
LL26 0YT
Tel: 01492 640494 53 N10
bronderw-wales.co.uk
Total Pitches: 48 (C & CV)

Bron-Y-Wendon Caravan Park
Wern Road, Llanddulas, Colwyn Bay
LL22 8HG
Tel: 01492 512903 53 R7
northwales-holidays.co.uk
Total Pitches: 130 (C & CV)

Caerfai Bay Caravan & Tent Park
Caerfai Bay, St Davids, Haverfordwest
SA62 6QT
Tel: 01437 720274 24 C6
caerfaibay.co.uk
Total Pitches: 106 (C, CV & T)

Cenarth Falls Holiday Park
Cenarth, Newcastle Emlyn
SA38 9JS
Tel: 01239 710345 32 E12
cenarth-holipark.co.uk
Total Pitches: 30 (C, CV & T)

Daisy Bank Caravan Park
Snead, Churchstoke
SY15 6EB
Tel: 01588 620471 34 H2
daisy-bank.co.uk
Total Pitches: 80 (C, CV & T)

Dinlle Caravan Park
Dinas Dinlle, Caernarfon
LL54 5TW
Tel: 01286 830324 52 F11
thornleyleisure.co.uk
Total Pitches: 175 (C, CV & T)

Disserth C & C Park
Disserth, Howey, Llandrindod Wells
LD1 6NL
Tel: 01597 860277 34 B9
disserth.biz
Total Pitches: 30 (C, CV & T)

Eisteddfa
Eisteddfa Lodge, Pentrefelin, Criccieth
LL52 0PT
Tel: 01766 522696 42 K6
eisteddfapark.co.uk
Total Pitches: 100 (C, CV & T)

Erwlon C & C Park
Brecon Road, Llandovery
SA20 0RD
Tel: 01550 721021 33 Q14
erwlon.co.uk
Total Pitches: 75 (C, CV & T)

Fforest Fields C & C Park
Hundred House, Builth Wells
LD1 5RT
Tel: 01982 570406 34 D10
fforestfields.co.uk
Total Pitches: 80 (C, CV & T)

Hendre Mynach Touring C & C Park
Llanaber Road, Barmouth
LL42 1YR
Tel: 01341 280262 43 M10
hendremynach.co.uk
Total Pitches: 240 (C, CV & T)

Home Farm Caravan Park
Marian-Glas, Isle of Anglesey
LL73 8PH
Tel: 01248 410614 52 G6
homefarm-anglesey.co.uk
Total Pitches: 102 (C, CV & T)

Hunters Hamlet Caravan Park
Sirior Goch Farm, Betws-yn-Rhos, Abergele
LL22 8PL
Tel: 01745 832237 53 R8
huntershamlet.co.uk
Total Pitches: 30 (C & CV)

Islawrffordd Caravan Park
Tal-y-bont, Barmouth
LL43 2AQ
Tel: 01341 247269 43 L9
islawrffordd.co.uk
Total Pitches: 105 (C, CV & T)

Llys Derwen C & C Site
Ffordd Bryngwyn, Llanrug, Caernarfon
LL55 4RD
Tel: 01286 673322 52 H10
llysderwen.co.uk
Total Pitches: 20 (C, CV & T)

Moelfryn C & C Park
Ty-Cefn, Pant-y-Bwlch, Newcastle Emlyn
SA38 9JE
Tel: 01559 371231 25 P3
moelfryncaravanpark.co.uk
Total Pitches: 25 (C, CV & T)

Pencelli Castle C & C Park
Pencelli, Brecon
LD3 7LX
Tel: 01874 665451 26 K3
pencelli-castle.com
Total Pitches: 80 (C, CV & T)

Penisar Mynydd Caravan Park
Caerwys Road, Rhuallt, St Asaph
LL17 0TY
Tel: 01745 582227 54 C11
penisarmynydd.co.uk
Total Pitches: 71 (C, CV & T)

Plas Farm Caravan Park
Betws-yn-Rhos, Abergele
LL22 8AU
Tel: 01492 680254 53 Q8
plasfarmcaravanpark.co.uk
Total Pitches: 54 (C, CV & T)

Plassey Holiday Park
The Plassey, Eyton, Wrexham
LL13 0SP
Tel: 01978 780277 44 J4
plassey.com
Total Pitches: 90 (C, CV & T)

Pont Kemys C & C Park
Chainbridge, Abergavenny
NP7 9DS
Tel: 01873 880688 27 Q6
pontkemys.com
Total Pitches: 65 (C, CV & T)

River View Touring Park
The Dingle, Llanedi, Pontarddulais
SA4 0FH
Tel: 01269 844876 25 U9
riverviewtouringpark.com
Total Pitches: 60 (C, CV & T)

Riverside Camping
Seiont Nurseries, Pont Rug, Caernarfon
LL55 2BB
Tel: 01286 678781 52 H10
riversidecamping.co.uk
Total Pitches: 73 (C, CV & T)

St David's Park
Red Wharf Bay, Pentraeth, Isle of Anglesey
LL75 8RJ
Tel: 01248 852341 52 H6
stdavidspark.com
Total Pitches: 45 (C, CV & T)

The Little Yurt Meadow
Bay Tree Barns, Mill Road, Bronington
SY13 3HJ
Tel: 01948 780136 45 L6
thelittleyurtmeadow.co.uk
Total Pitches: 3 (T)

Trawsdir Touring C & C Park
Llanaber, Barmouth
LL42 1RR
Tel: 01341 280999 43 L10
barmouthholidays.co.uk
Total Pitches: 70 (C, CV & T)

Trefalun Park
Devonshire Drive, St Florence, Tenby
SA70 8RD
Tel: 01646 651514 24 J10
trefalunpark.co.uk
Total Pitches: 90 (C, CV & T)

Tyddyn Isaf Caravan Park
Lligwy Bay, Dulas, Isle of Anglesey
LL70 9PQ
Tel: 01248 410203 52 G5
tyddynisaf.co.uk
Total Pitches: 80 (C, CV & T)

Wernddu Caravan Park
Old Ross Road, Abergavenny
NP7 8NG
Tel: 01873 856223 27 Q4
wernddu-golf-club.co.uk
Total Pitches: 70 (C, CV & T)

CHANNEL ISLANDS

Beuvelande Camp Site
Beuvelande, St Martin, Jersey
JE3 6EZ
Tel: 01534 853575 7 e2
campingjersey.com
Total Pitches: 150 (C, CV & T)

Fauxquets Valley Campsite
Castel, Guernsey
GY5 7QL
Tel: 01481 255460 6 d3
fauxquets.co.uk
Total Pitches: 120 (C, CV & T)

Rozel Camping Park
Summerville Farm, St Martin, Jersey
JE3 6AX
Tel: 01534 855200 7 f2
rozelcamping.co.uk
Total Pitches: 100 (C, CV & T)

Traffic signs and road markings

Traffic signs

Signs giving orders

**Signs with red circles are mostly prohibitive.
Plates below signs qualify their message.**

 Entry to 20mph zone

 End of 20mph zone

 Maximum speed

 National speed limit applies

 School crossing patrol

Stop and give way

Give way to traffic on major road

Manually operated temporary STOP and GO signs

No entry for vehicular traffic

No vehicles except bicycles being pushed

No cycling

No motor vehicles

No buses (over 8 passenger seats)

No overtaking

No towed caravans

No vehicles carrying explosives

No vehicle or combination of vehicles over length shown

No vehicles over height shown

No vehicles over width shown

Give priority to vehicles from opposite direction

No right turn

No left turn

No U-turns

No goods vehicles over maximum gross weight shown (in tonnes) except for loading and unloading

 WEAK BRIDGE No vehicles over maximum gross weight shown (in tonnes)

Parking restricted to permit holders

No stopping during period indicated except for buses

No stopping during times shown except for as long as necessary to set down or pick up passengers

No waiting

No stopping (Clearway)

Signs with blue circles but no red border mostly give positive instruction.

Ahead only

Turn left ahead (right if symbol reversed)

Turn left (right if symbol reversed)

Keep left (right if symbol reversed)

Vehicles may pass either side to reach same destination

Mini-roundabout (roundabout circulation – give way to vehicles from the immediate right)

Route to be used by pedal cycles only

Segregated pedal cycle and pedestrian route

Minimum speed

End of minimum speed

Buses and cycles only

Trams only

Pedestrian crossing point over tramway

One-way traffic (note: compare circular 'Ahead only' sign)

With-flow bus and cycle lane

Contraflow bus lane

With-flow pedal cycle lane

Note: The signs shown in this road atlas are those most commonly in use and are not all drawn to the same scale. In Scotland and Wales bilingual versions of some signs are used, showing both English and Gaelic or Welsh spellings. Some older designs of signs may still be seen on the roads. A comprehensive explanation of the signing system illustrating the vast majority of road signs can be found in the AA's handbook *Know Your Road Signs*. Where there is a reference to a rule number, this refers to *The Highway Code*, which is detailed in the AA's guide. Both of these publications are on sale at theaa.com/shop and booksellers.

Warning signs

Mostly triangular

Distance to 'STOP' line ahead

Dual carriageway ends

Road narrows on right (left if symbol reversed)

Road narrows on both sides

Distance to 'Give Way' line ahead

Crossroads

Junction on bend ahead

T-junction with priority over vehicles from the right

Staggered junction

Traffic merging from left ahead

The priority through route is indicated by the broader line.

Double bend first to left (symbol may be reversed)

Bend to right (or left if symbol reversed)

Roundabout

Uneven road

Plate below some signs

Two-way traffic crosses one-way road

Two-way traffic straight ahead

Opening or swing bridge ahead

Low-flying aircraft or sudden aircraft noise

Falling or fallen rocks

Traffic signals not in use

Traffic signals

Slippery road

Steep hill downwards

Steep hill upwards

Gradients may be shown as a ratio i.e. 20% = 1:5

Tunnel ahead

Trams crossing ahead

Level crossing with barrier or gate ahead

Level crossing without barrier or gate ahead

Level crossing without barrier

School crossing patrol ahead (some signs have amber lights which flash when crossings are in use)

Frail (or blind or disabled if shown) pedestrians likely to cross road ahead

Pedestrians in road ahead

Zebra crossing

Overhead electric cable; plate indicates maximum height of vehicles which can pass safely

Available width of headroom indicated

Sharp deviation of route to left (or right if chevrons reversed)

Light signals ahead at level crossing, airfield or bridge

Miniature warning lights at level crossings

Cattle

Wild animals

Wild horses or ponies

Accompanied horses or ponies

Cycle route ahead

Risk of ice

Traffic queues likely ahead

Distance over which road humps extend

Hidden dip

Soft verges

Side winds

Hump bridge

Ford

Worded warning sign

Quayside or river bank

Risk of grounding

Direction signs

Mostly rectangular

Signs on motorways – blue backgrounds

 At a junction leading directly into a motorway (junction number may be shown on a black background)

 On approaches to junctions (junction number on black background)

 Route confirmatory sign after junction

 Downward pointing arrows mean 'Get in lane' The left-hand lane leads to a different destination from the other lanes.

 The panel with the inclined arrow indicates the destinations which can be reached by leaving the motorway at the next junction

Signs on primary routes - green backgrounds

 On approaches to junctions

 At the junction

 Route confirmatory sign after junction

 On approaches to junctions

On approach to a junction in Wales (bilingual)

Blue panels indicate that the motorway starts at the junction ahead. Motorways shown in brackets can also be reached along the route indicated. White panels indicate local or non-primary routes leading from the junction ahead. Brown panels indicate the route to tourist attractions. The name of the junction may be shown at the top of the sign. The aircraft symbol indicates the route to an airport. A symbol may be included to warn of a hazard or restriction along that route.

Primary route forming part of a ring road

R

Signs on non-primary and local routes - black borders

 On approaches to junctions

At the junction

Direction to toilets with access for the disabled

Green panels indicate that the primary route starts at the junction ahead. Route numbers on a blue background show the direction to a motorway. Route numbers on a green background show the direction to a primary route.

Other direction signs

 Picnic site

 Ancient monument in the care of English Heritage

 Direction to a car park

 Zoo — Tourist attraction

 Direction to camping and caravan site

 Advisory route for lorries

 Route for pedal cycles forming part of a network

 Recommended route for pedal cycles to place shown

  Route for pedestrians

Emergency diversion routes

 Symbols showing emergency diversion route for motorway and other main road traffic

Diversion route

In an emergency it may be necessary to close a section of motorway or other main road to traffic, so a temporary sign may advise drivers to follow a diversion route. To help drivers navigate the route, black symbols on yellow patches may be permanently displayed on existing direction signs, including motorway signs. Symbols may also be used on separate signs with yellow backgrounds.

For further information see highways.gov.uk, trafficscotland.org and traffic-wales.com

Information signs

All rectangular

Entrance to controlled parking zone

Entrance to congestion charging zone

Greater London Low Emission Zone (LEZ)

Advance warning of restriction or prohibition ahead

Parking place for solo motorcycles

With-flow bus lane ahead which pedal cycles and taxis may also use

Lane designated for use by high occupancy vehicles (HOV) – see rule 142

Vehicles permitted to use an HOV lane ahead

End of motorway

Start of motorway and point from which motorway regulations apply

Appropriate traffic lanes at junction ahead

Traffic on the main carriageway coming from right has priority over joining traffic

Additional traffic joining from left ahead. Traffic on main carriageway has priority over joining traffic from right hand lane of slip road.

Traffic in right hand lane of slip road joining the main carriageway has priority over left hand lane

'Countdown' markers at exit from motorway (each bar represents 100 yards to the exit). Green-backed markers may be used on primary routes and white-backed markers with black bars on other routes. At approaches to concealed level crossings white-backed markers with red bars may be used. Although these will be erected at equal distances the bars do not represent 100 yard intervals.

GOOD FOOD
Puddleworth services

Motorway service area sign showing the operator's name

Traffic has priority over oncoming traffic

Hospital ahead with Accident and Emergency facilities

Tourist information point

No through road for vehicles

Recommended route for pedal cycles

Home Zone Entry*

Area in which cameras are used to enforce traffic regulations

Bus lane

Bus lane on road at junction ahead

*Home Zone Entry – You are entering an area where people could be using the whole street for a range of activities. You should drive slowly and carefully and be prepared to stop to allow people time to move out of the way.

Roadworks signs

Road works

Loose chippings

SLOW WET TAR

Temporary hazard at roadworks

800 yards

Temporary lane closure (the number and position of arrows and red bars may be varied according to lanes open and closed)

Slow-moving or stationary works vehicle blocking a traffic lane. Pass in the direction shown by the arrow.

Mandatory speed limit ahead

Delays possible until Sept
1 mile

Roadworks 1 mile ahead

Sorry for any delay
End

End of roadworks and any temporary restrictions including speed limits

800 yds

Signs used on the back of slow-moving or stationary works vehicle warning of a lane closed ahead by a works vehicle. There are no cones on the road.

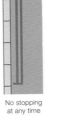
450 yds

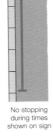
800 yards

Lane restrictions at roadworks ahead

STAY IN LANE
Max speed 30

One lane crossover at contraflow roadworks

Road markings

Across the carriageway

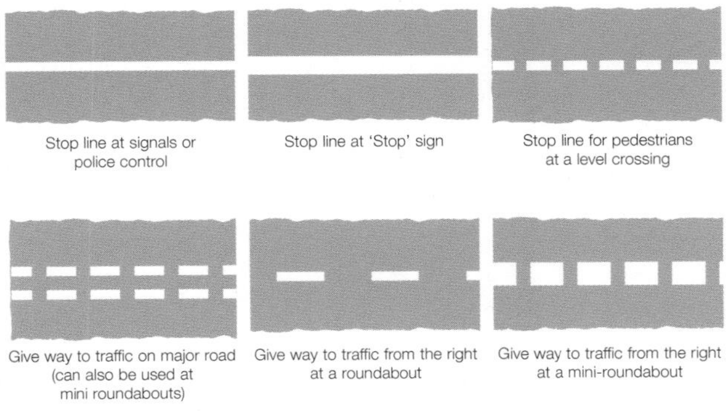

Stop line at signals or police control

Stop line at 'Stop' sign

Stop line for pedestrians at a level crossing

Give way to traffic on major road (can also be used at mini roundabouts)

Give way to traffic from the right at a roundabout

Give way to traffic from the right at a mini-roundabout

Along the carriageway

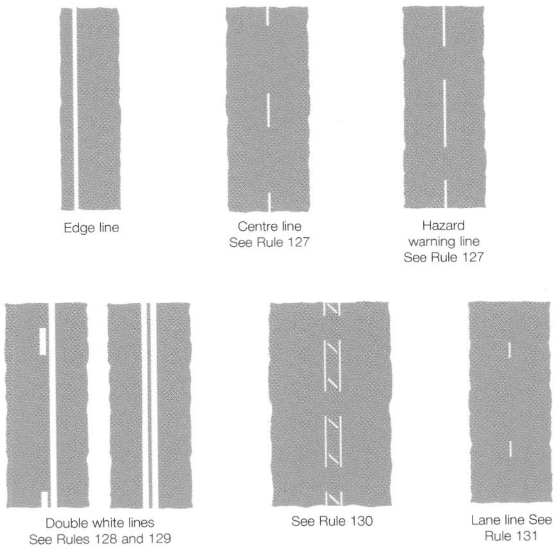

Edge line

Centre line See Rule 127

Hazard warning line See Rule 127

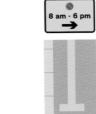

Double white lines See Rules 128 and 129

See Rule 130

Lane line See Rule 131

Along the edge of the carriageway

Waiting restrictions

Waiting restrictions indicated by yellow lines apply to the carriageway, pavement and verge. You may stop to load or unload (unless there are also loading restrictions as described below) or while passengers board or alight. Double yellow lines mean no waiting at any time, unless there are signs that specifically indicate seasonal restrictions. The times at which the restrictions apply for other road markings are shown on nearby plates or on entry signs to controlled parking zones. If no days are shown on the signs, the restrictions are in force every day including Sundays and Bank Holidays. White bay markings and upright signs (see below) indicate where parking is allowed.

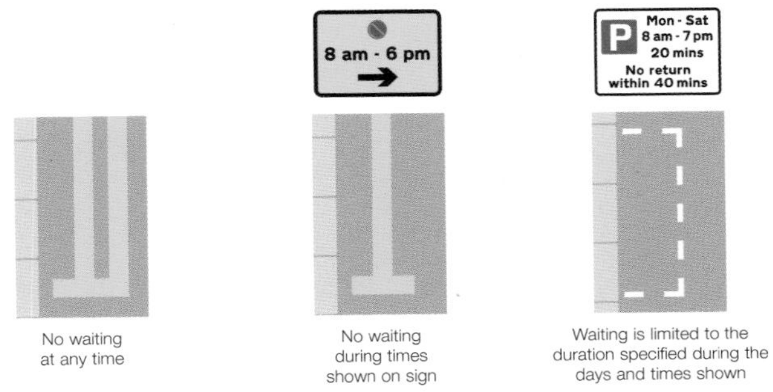

No waiting at any time

8 am – 6 pm

No waiting during times shown on sign

Mon - Sat 8 am-7pm 20 mins No return within 40 mins

Waiting is limited to the duration specified during the days and times shown

Red Route stopping controls

Red lines are used on some roads instead of yellow lines. In London the double and single red lines used on Red Routes indicate that stopping to park, load/unload or to board and alight from a vehicle (except for a licensed taxi or if you hold a Blue Badge) is prohibited. The red lines apply to the carriageway, pavement and verge. The times that the red line prohibitions apply are shown on nearby signs, but the double red line ALWAYS means no stopping at any time. On Red Routes you may stop to park, load/unload in specially marked boxes and adjacent signs specify the times and purposes and duration allowed. A box MARKED IN RED indicates that it may only be available for the purpose specified for part of the day (e.g. between busy peak periods). A box MARKED IN WHITE means that it is available throughout the day.

RED AND SINGLE YELLOW LINES CAN ONLY GIVE A GUIDE TO THE RESTRICTIONS AND CONTROLS IN FORCE AND SIGNS, NEARBY OR AT A ZONE ENTRY, MUST BE CONSULTED.

RED ROUTE No stopping at any time

No stopping at any time

RED ROUTE No stopping Mon - Sat 7am - 7pm

No stopping during times shown on sign

RED ROUTE P Mon - Sat 7am - 7pm No return within 2 hours

Parking is limited to the duration specified during the days and times shown

RED ROUTE No loading Mon - Sat 7am - 7pm Except 10am - 4pm loading max 20 mins

Only loading may take place at the times shown for up to a maximum duration of 20 mins

On the kerb or at the edge of the carriageway

Loading restrictions on roads other than Red Routes

Yellow marks on the kerb or at the edge of the carriageway indicate that loading or unloading is prohibited at the times shown on the nearby black and white plates. You may stop while passengers board or alight. If no days are indicated on the signs the restrictions are in force every day including Sundays and Bank Holidays.

ALWAYS CHECK THE TIMES SHOWN ON THE PLATES.

Lengths of road reserved for vehicles loading and unloading are indicated by a white 'bay' marking with the words 'Loading Only' and a sign with the white on blue 'trolley' symbol. This sign also shows whether loading and unloading is restricted to goods vehicles and the times at which the bay can be used. If no times or days are shown it may be used at any time. Vehicles may not park here if they are not loading or unloading.

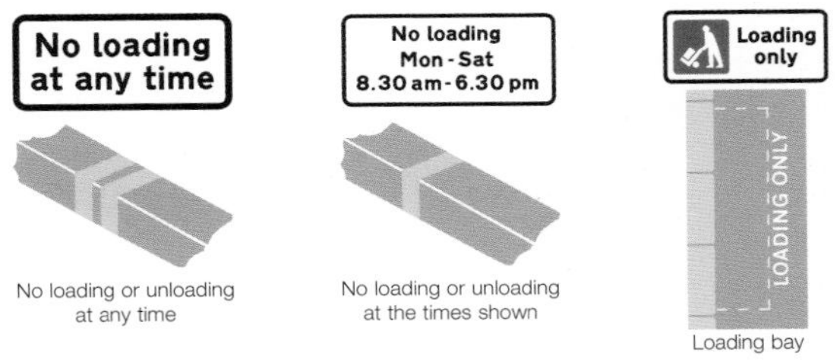

No loading at any time

No loading or unloading at any time

No loading Mon - Sat 8.30 am- 6.30 pm

No loading or unloading at the times shown

Loading only

Loading bay

Other road markings

SCHOOL — KEEP — CLEAR

Keep entrance clear of stationary vehicles, even if picking up or setting down children

Warning of 'Give Way' just ahead

Parking space reserved for vehicles named

BUS STOP

See Rule 243

BUS LANE

See Rule 141

Box junction - See Rule 174

KEEP CLEAR

Do not block that part of the carriageway indicated

CITY A3 YORK ST

Indication of traffic lanes

Light signals controlling traffic

Traffic Light Signals

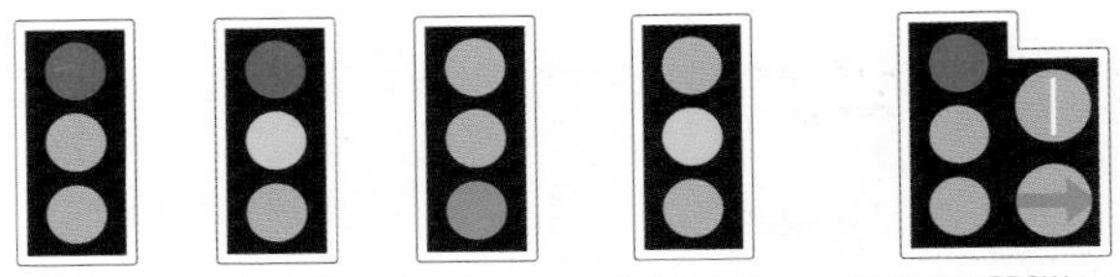

RED means 'Stop'. Wait behind the stop line on the carriageway.

RED AND AMBER also means 'Stop'. Do not pass through or start until GREEN shows.

GREEN means you may go on if the way is clear. Take special care if you intend to turn left or right and give way to pedestrians who are crossing.

AMBER means 'Stop' at the stop line. You may go on only if the AMBER appears after you have crossed the stop line or are so close to it that to pull up might cause an accident.

A GREEN ARROW may be provided in addition to the full green signal if movement in a certain direction is allowed before or after the full green phase. If the way is clear you may go but only in the direction shown by the arrow. You may do this whatever other lights may be showing. White light signals may be provided for trams.

Flashing red lights

Alternately flashing red lights mean YOU MUST STOP

At level crossings, lifting bridges, airfields, fire stations, etc.

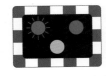

Motorway signals

You MUST NOT proceed further in this lane

Change lane

Reduced visibility ahead

Lane ahead closed

Temporary maximum speed advised and information message

Leave motorway at next exit

Temporary maximum speed advised

End of restriction

Lane control signals

Green arrow – lane available to traffic facing the sign
Red crosses – lane closed to traffic facing the sign
White diagonal arrow – change lanes in direction shown

Channel hopping

For business or pleasure, hopping on a ferry across to France, Belgium or the Channel Islands has never been easier.

The vehicle ferry routes shown on this map give you all the options, together with detailed port plans to help you navigate to and from the ferry terminals. Simply choose your preferred route, not forgetting the fast sailings; then check the colour-coded table for ferry operators, crossing times and contact details.

Bon voyage!

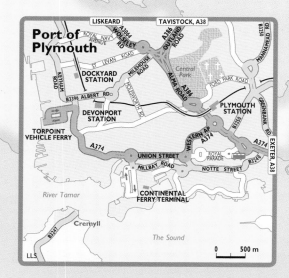

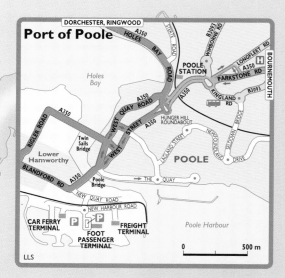

Fast ferry

Conventional ferry

ENGLISH CHANNEL FERRY CROSSINGS AND OPERATORS

From	To	Journey Time	Operator	Telephone	Website
Dover	Calais	1 hr 30 mins	DFDS Seaways	0871 522 9955	dfdsseaways.co.uk
Dover	Calais	1 hr 30 mins	My Ferry Link	0844 248 2100	myferrylink.com
Dover	Calais	1 hr 30 mins	P&O Ferries	0871 664 2020	poferries.com
Dover	Dunkerque	2 hrs	DFDS Seaways	0871 522 9955	dfdsseaways.co.uk
Folkestone	Calais (Coquelles)	35 mins	Eurotunnel	0844 335 3535	eurotunnel.com
Newhaven	Dieppe	4 hrs	DFDS Seaways	0871 522 9955	dfdsseaways.co.uk
Plymouth	Roscoff	6–8 hrs	Brittany Ferries	0871 244 0744	brittany-ferries.co.uk
Plymouth	St-Malo	10 hrs 15 mins (Nov–Mar)	Brittany Ferries	0871 244 0744	brittany-ferries.co.uk
Poole	Cherbourg	4 hrs 15 mins (Jan–Oct)	Brittany Ferries	0871 244 0744	brittany-ferries.co.uk
Poole	Guernsey	3 hrs	Condor Ferries	0845 609 1024	condorferries.co.uk
Poole	Jersey	4 hrs 30 mins	Condor Ferries	0845 609 1024	condorferries.co.uk
Poole	St-Malo	7–12 hrs (via Channel Is.)	Condor Ferries	0845 609 1024	condorferries.co.uk
Portsmouth	Caen (Ouistreham)	6–7 hrs	Brittany Ferries	0871 244 0744	brittany-ferries.co.uk
Portsmouth	Cherbourg	3 hrs (May–Sept)	Brittany Ferries	0871 244 0744	brittany-ferries.co.uk
Portsmouth	Guernsey	7 hrs	Condor Ferries	0845 609 1024	condorferries.co.uk
Portsmouth	Jersey	8–11 hrs	Condor Ferries	0845 609 1024	condorferries.co.uk
Portsmouth	Le Havre	3 hrs 45 mins (May–Sept)	Brittany Ferries	0871 244 0744	brittany-ferries.co.uk
Portsmouth	Le Havre	8 hrs (Mar–Oct)	Brittany Ferries	0871 244 0744	brittany-ferries.co.uk
Portsmouth	St-Malo	9–11 hrs	Brittany Ferries	0871 244 0744	brittany-ferries.co.uk

Ferry services listed are provided as a guide only and are liable to change at short notice.

Please check sailings before planning your journey.

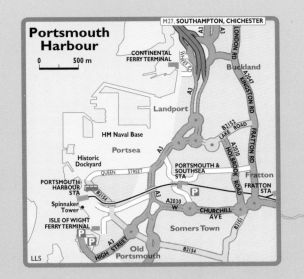

Portsmouth Harbour

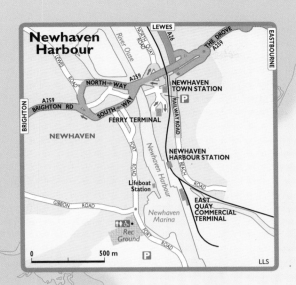

Newhaven Harbour

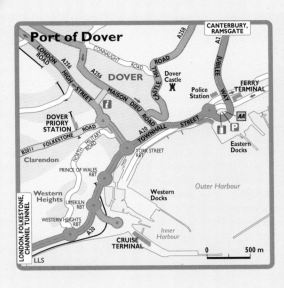

Port of Dover

C H A N N E L

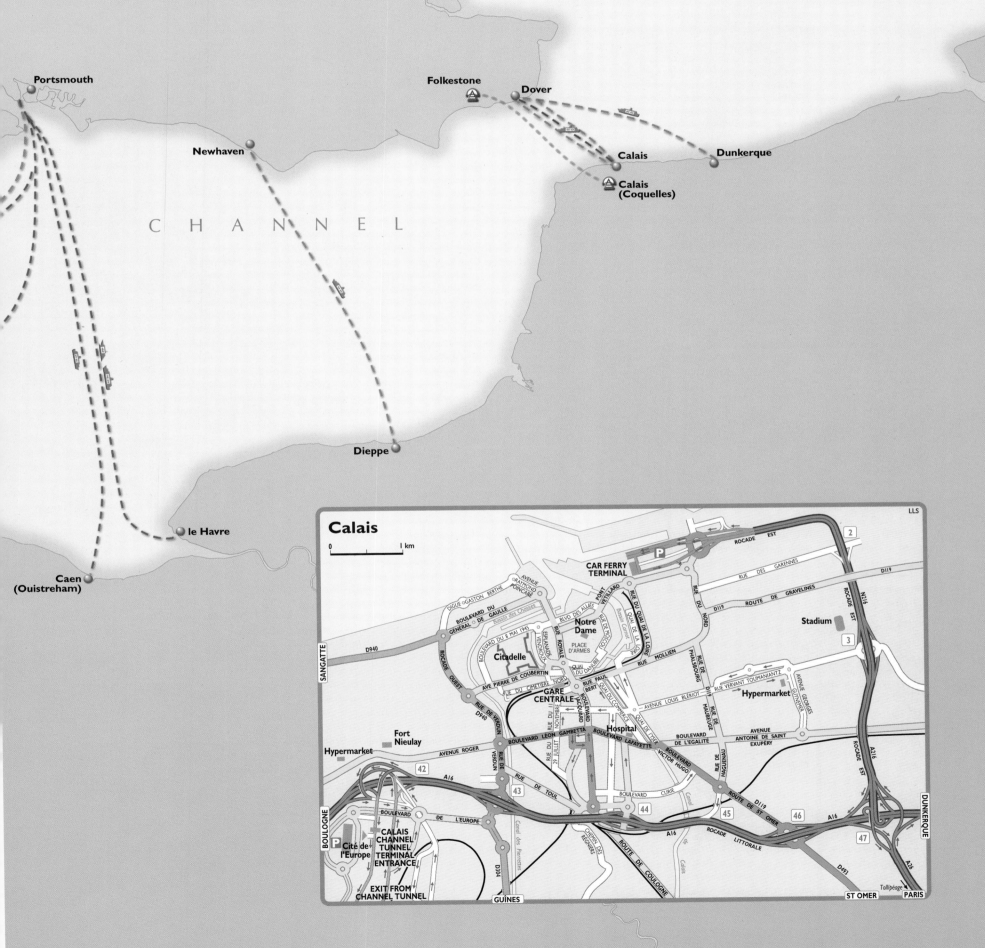

Calais

Ferries to Ireland and the Isle of Man

With so many sea crossings to Ireland and the Isle of Man this map will
help you make the right choice.

The vehicle ferry routes shown on this map give you all the options,
together with detailed port plans to help you navigate to and from
the ferry terminals. Simply choose your preferred route, not forgetting
the fast sailings; then check the colour-coded table for ferry operators,
crossing times and contact details.

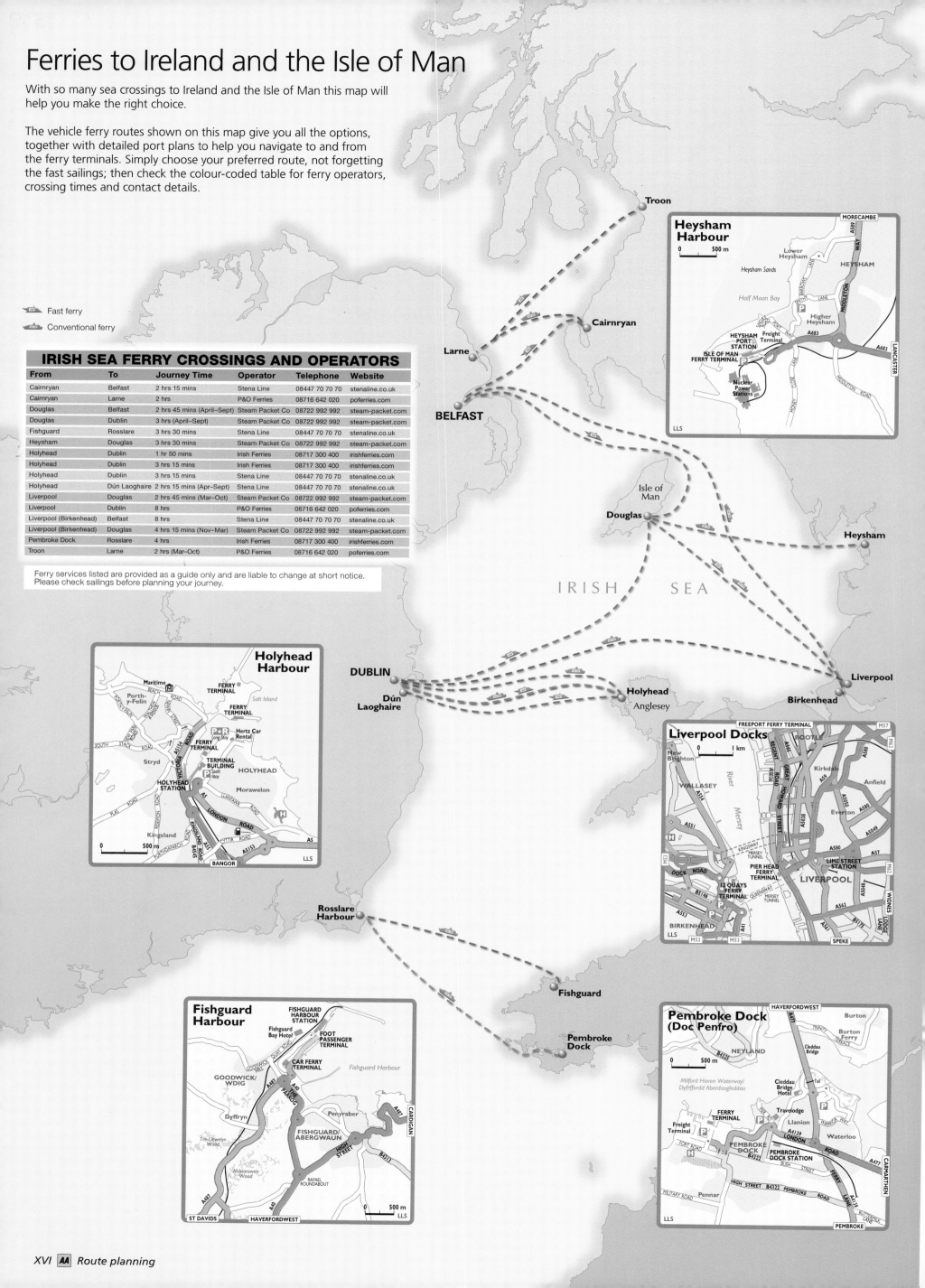

Fast ferry

Conventional ferry

IRISH SEA FERRY CROSSINGS AND OPERATORS

From	To	Journey Time	Operator	Telephone	Website
Cairnryan	Belfast	2 hrs 15 mins	Stena Line	08447 70 70 70	stenaline.co.uk
Cairnryan	Larne	2 hrs	P&O Ferries	08716 642 020	poferries.com
Douglas	Belfast	2 hrs 45 mins (April–Sept)	Steam Packet Co	08722 992 992	steam-packet.com
Douglas	Dublin	3 hrs (April–Sept)	Steam Packet Co	08722 992 992	steam-packet.com
Fishguard	Rosslare	3 hrs 30 mins	Stena Line	08447 70 70 70	stenaline.co.uk
Heysham	Douglas	3 hrs 30 mins	Steam Packet Co	08722 992 992	steam-packet.com
Holyhead	Dublin	1 hr 50 mins	Irish Ferries	08717 300 400	irishferries.com
Holyhead	Dublin	3 hrs 15 mins	Irish Ferries	08717 300 400	irishferries.com
Holyhead	Dublin	3 hrs 15 mins	Stena Line	08447 70 70 70	stenaline.co.uk
Holyhead	Dún Laoghaire	2 hrs 15 mins (Apr–Sept)	Stena Line	08447 70 70 70	stenaline.co.uk
Liverpool	Douglas	2 hrs 45 mins (Mar–Oct)	Steam Packet Co	08722 992 992	steam-packet.com
Liverpool	Dublin	8 hrs	P&O Ferries	08716 642 020	poferries.com
Liverpool (Birkenhead)	Belfast	8 hrs	Stena Line	08447 70 70 70	stenaline.co.uk
Liverpool (Birkenhead)	Douglas	4 hrs 15 mins (Nov–Mar)	Steam Packet Co	08722 992 992	steam-packet.com
Pembroke Dock	Rosslare	4 hrs	Irish Ferries	08717 300 400	irishferries.com
Troon	Larne	2 hrs (Mar–Oct)	P&O Ferries	08716 642 020	poferries.com

Ferry services listed are provided as a guide only and are liable to change at short notice.
Please check sailings before planning your journey.

Atlas symbols

Motoring information

M4	Motorway with number	3	Restricted primary route junctions		Narrow primary/other A/B road with passing places (Scotland)		Railway line, in tunnel	30	Safety camera site (fixed location) with speed limit in mph
Toll	Toll motorway with toll station	S	Primary route service area		Road under construction/ approved		Railway station and level crossing	50	Section of road with two or more fixed safety cameras, with speed limit in mph
6	Motorway junction with and without number	BATH	Primary route destination		Road tunnel		Tourist railway	40 40	Average speed (SPECS™) camera system with speed limit in mph
5	Restricted motorway junctions	A1123	Other A road single/ dual carriageway	Toll	Road toll, steep gradient (arrows point downhill)		City, town, village or other built-up area	V	Fixed safety camera site with variable speed limit
Fleet S	Motorway service area	B2070	B road single/ dual carriageway	5	Distance in miles between symbols		Airport, heliport	P·R	Park and Ride (at least 6 days per week)
	Motorway and junction under construction		Minor road more than 4 metres wide, less than 4 metres wide	or V	Vehicle ferry	H	24-hour Accident & Emergency hospital	628 637 Lecht Summit	Height in metres, mountain pass
A3	Primary route single/ dual carriageway		Roundabout		Fast vehicle ferry or catamaran	C	Crematorium		National boundary
11	Primary route junction with and without number		Interchange/junction	F	International freight terminal		Sandy beach		County, administrative boundary

Touring information   To avoid disappointment, check opening times before visiting

	Scenic Route	M	Museum or art gallery		Aquarium		Steam railway centre		National Trust for Scotland property
i	Tourist Information Centre		Industrial interest	RSPB	RSPB site		Cave		English Heritage site
i	Tourist Information Centre (seasonal)		Aqueduct or viaduct		National Nature Reserve (England, Scotland, Wales)		Windmill, monument		Historic Scotland site
V	Visitor or heritage centre		Garden		Wildlife Trust reserve		Golf course (AA listed)		Cadw (Welsh heritage) site
	Picnic site		Arboretum		Local nature reserve		County cricket ground	★	Other place of interest
	Caravan site (AA inspected)		Vineyard		Forest drive		Rugby Union national stadium		Boxed symbols indicate attractions within urban areas
	Camping site (AA inspected)		Country park		National trail		International athletics stadium		World Heritage Site (UNESCO)
	Caravan & camping site (AA inspected)		Agricultural showground		Viewpoint		Horse racing, show jumping		National Park
	Abbey, cathedral or priory		Theme park		Hill-fort		Motor-racing circuit		National Scenic Area (Scotland)
	Ruined abbey, cathedral or priory		Farm or animal centre		Roman antiquity		Air show venue		Forest Park
	Castle		Zoological or wildlife collection		Prehistoric monument		Ski slope (natural, artificial)		Heritage coast
	Historic house or building		Bird collection	1066	Battle site with year		National Trust property		Major shopping centre

Town plans

2	Motorway and junction		Railway station		Toilet, with facilities for the less able	i	Tourist Information Centre	†	Abbey, chapel, church
	Primary road single/ dual carriageway		Tramway		Building of interest	V	Visitor or heritage centre		Synagogue
	A road single/ dual carriageway		London Underground station		Ruined building		Post Office		Mosque
	B road single/ dual carriageway		London Overground station		City wall		Public library		Golf course
	Local road single/ dual carriageway		Rail interchange		Cliff lift		Shopping centre		Racecourse
	Other road single/dual carriageway, minor road		Docklands Light Railway (DLR) station		Cliff escarpment		Shopmobility		Nature reserve
	One-way, gated/ closed road	o	Light rapid transit system station		River/canal, lake		Theatre or performing arts centre		Aquarium
	Restricted access		Airport, heliport		Lock, weir		Cinema		World Heritage Site (UNESCO)
	Pedestrian area	R	Railair terminal		Park/sports ground/ open space	M	Museum		English Heritage site
	Footpath	P+	Park and Ride (at least 6 days per week)		Cemetery		Castle		Historic Scotland site
	Road under construction	P	Car park		Woodland		Castle mound		Cadw (Welsh heritage) site
	Road tunnel		Bus/coach station		Built-up area	•	Monument, statue		National Trust site
	Level crossing	H H	24-hour Accident & Emergency hospital, other hospital		Beach		Viewpoint		National Trust for Scotland site

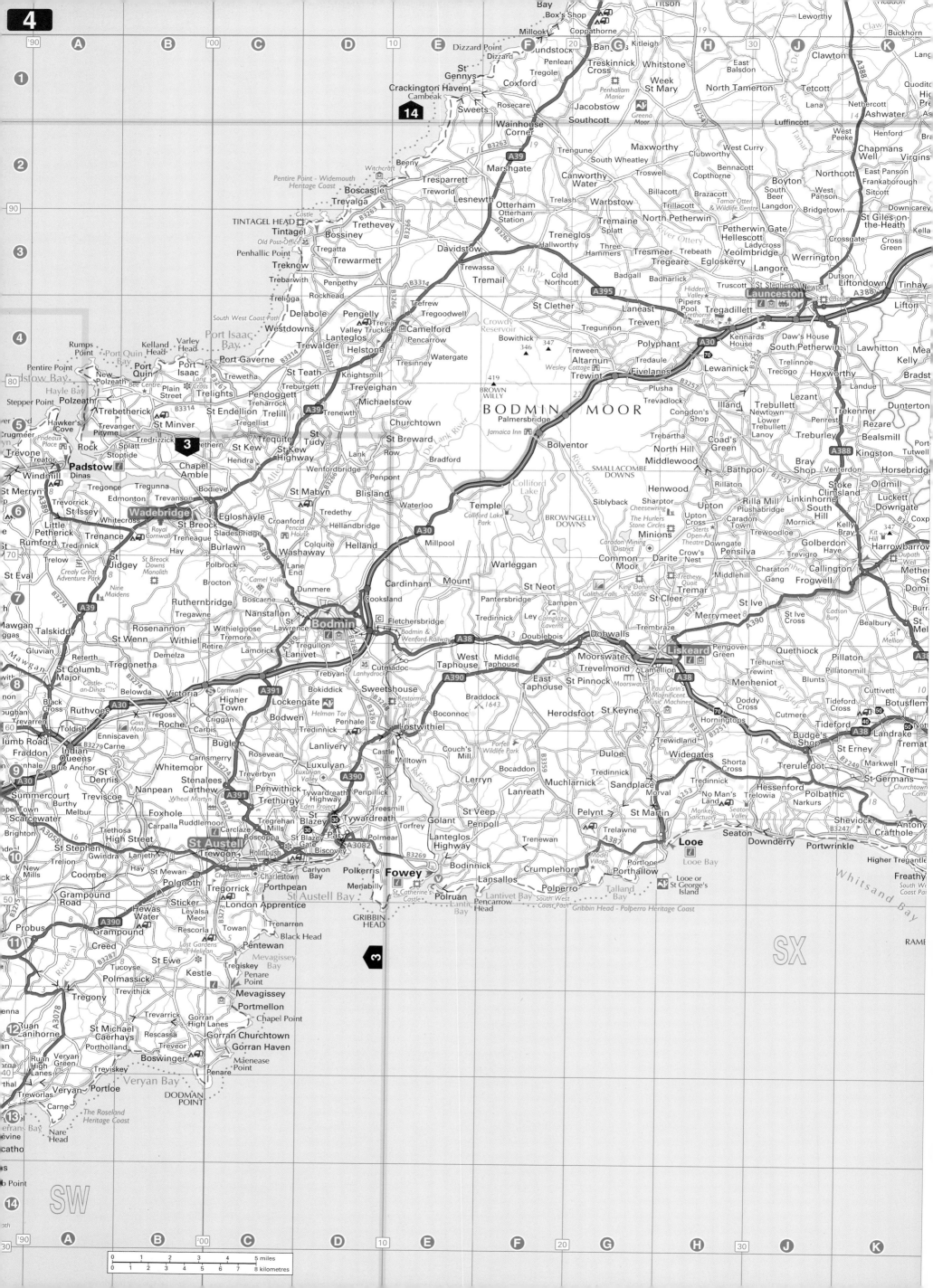

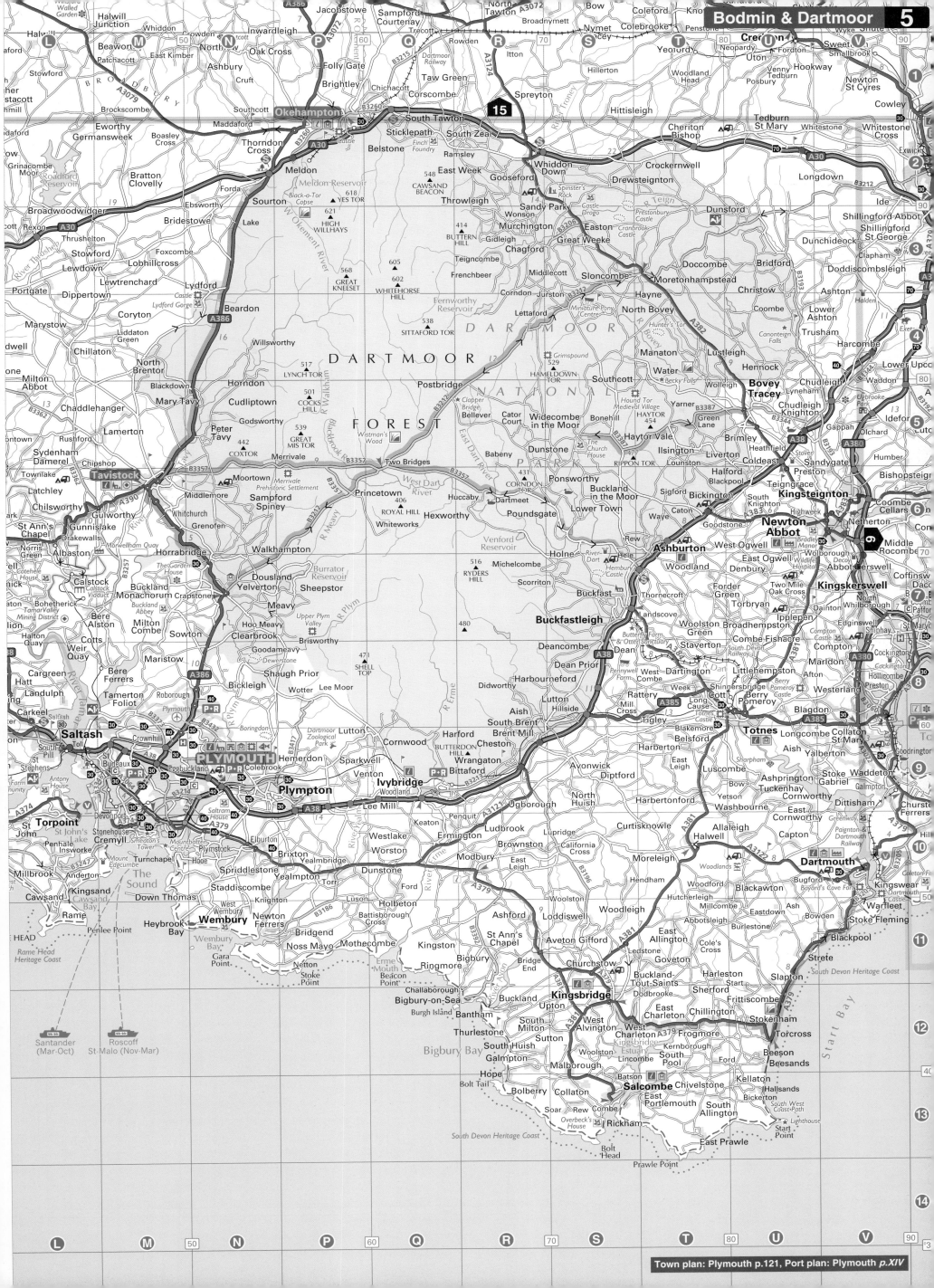

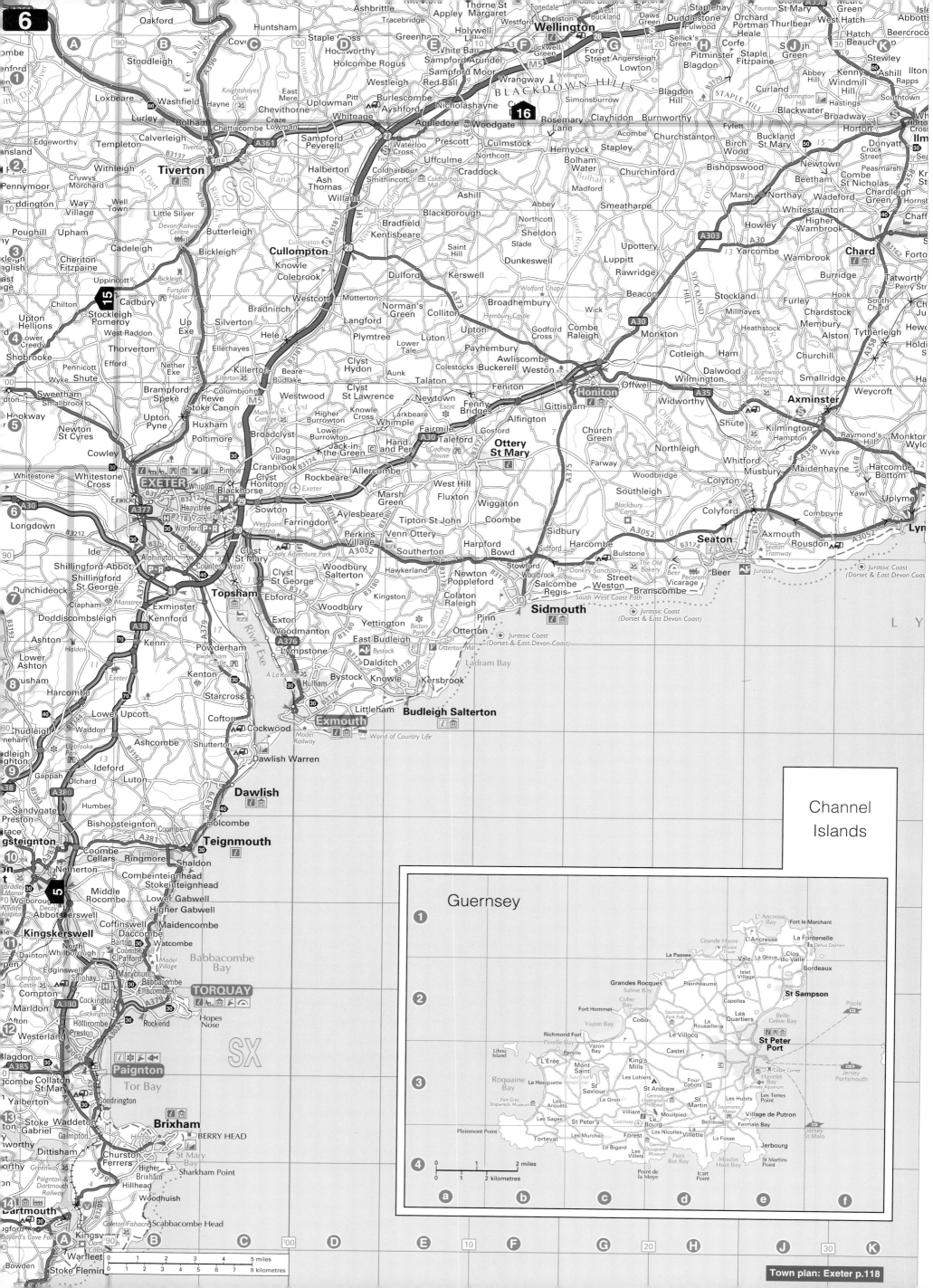

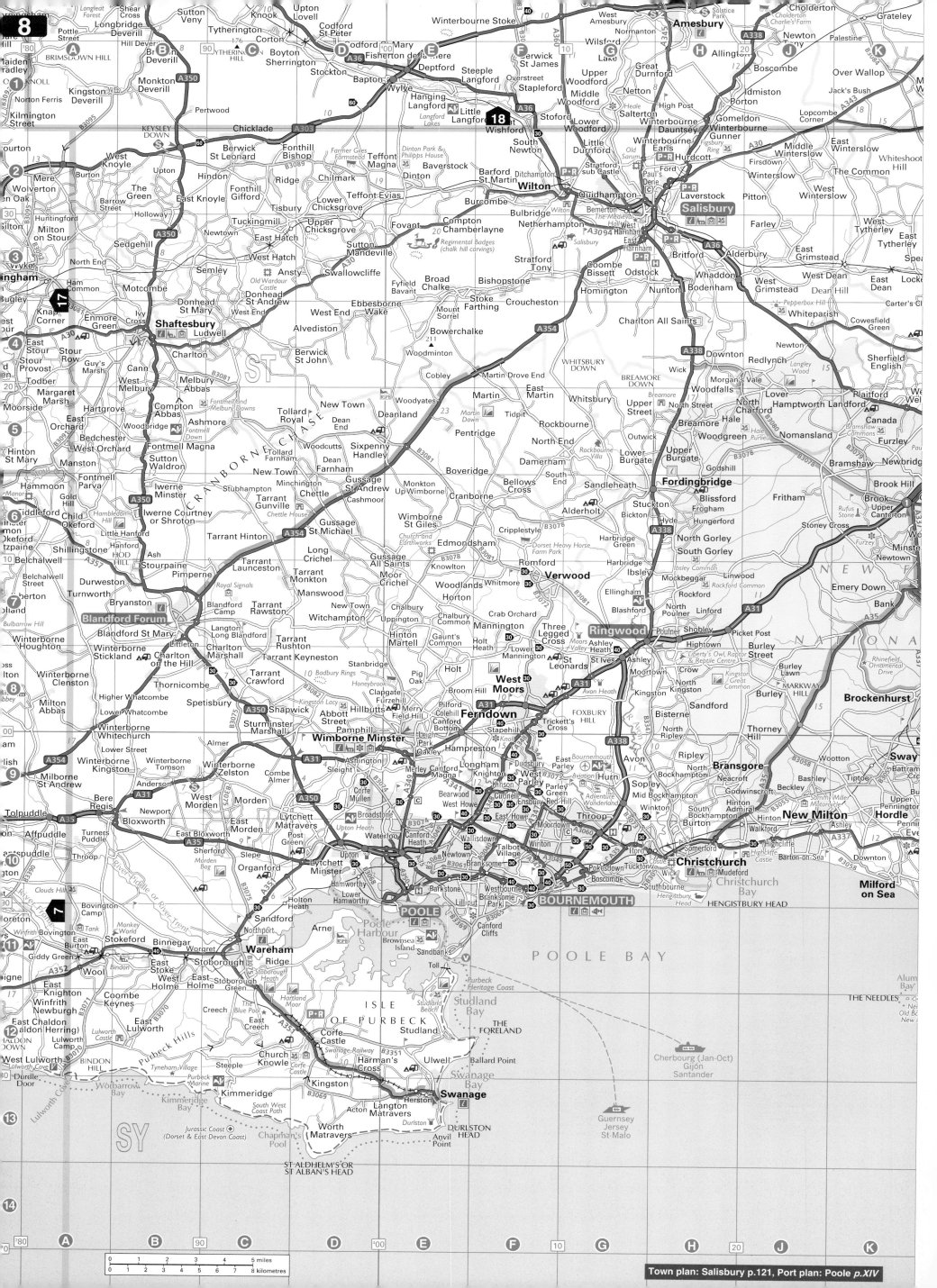

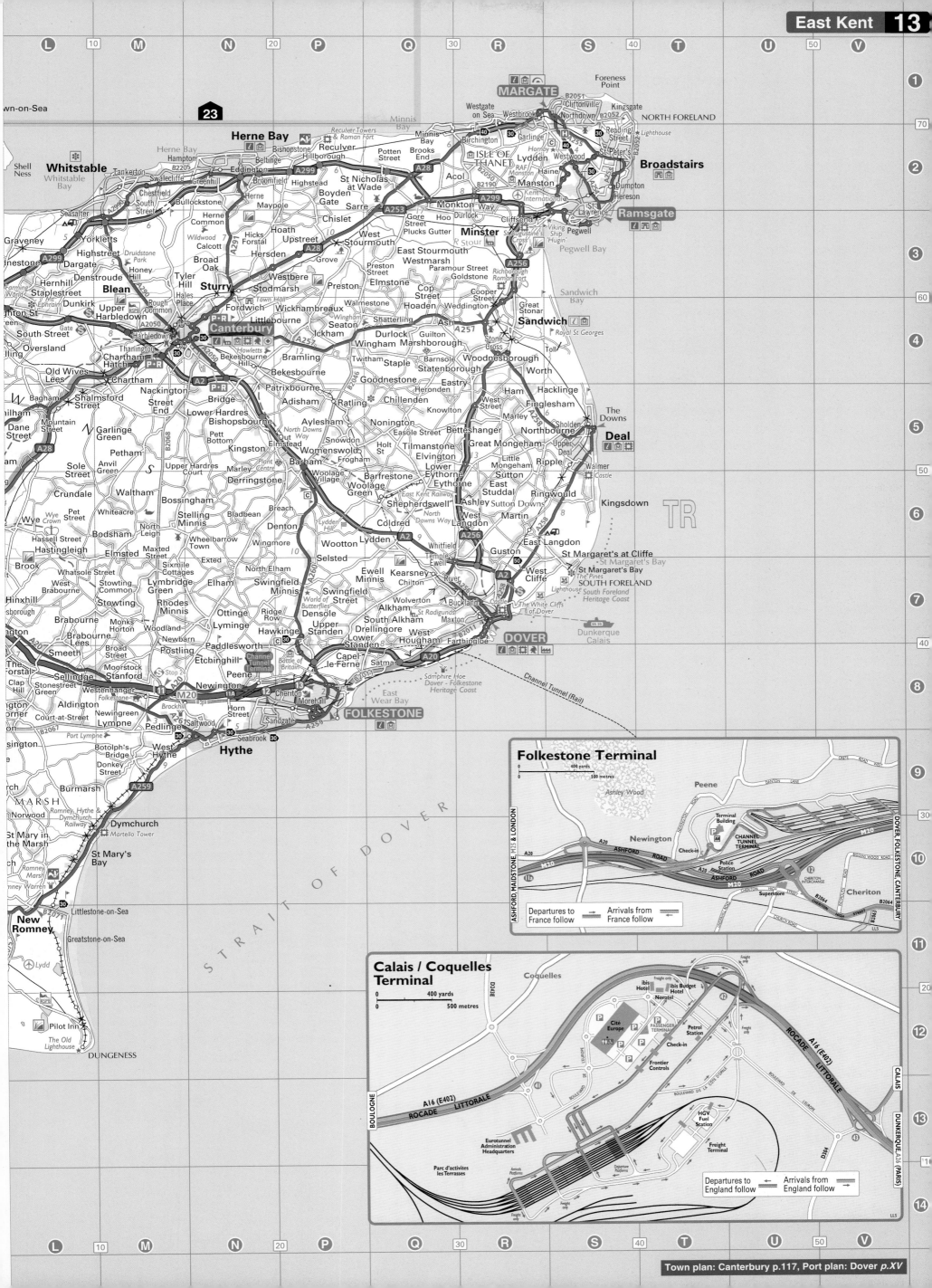

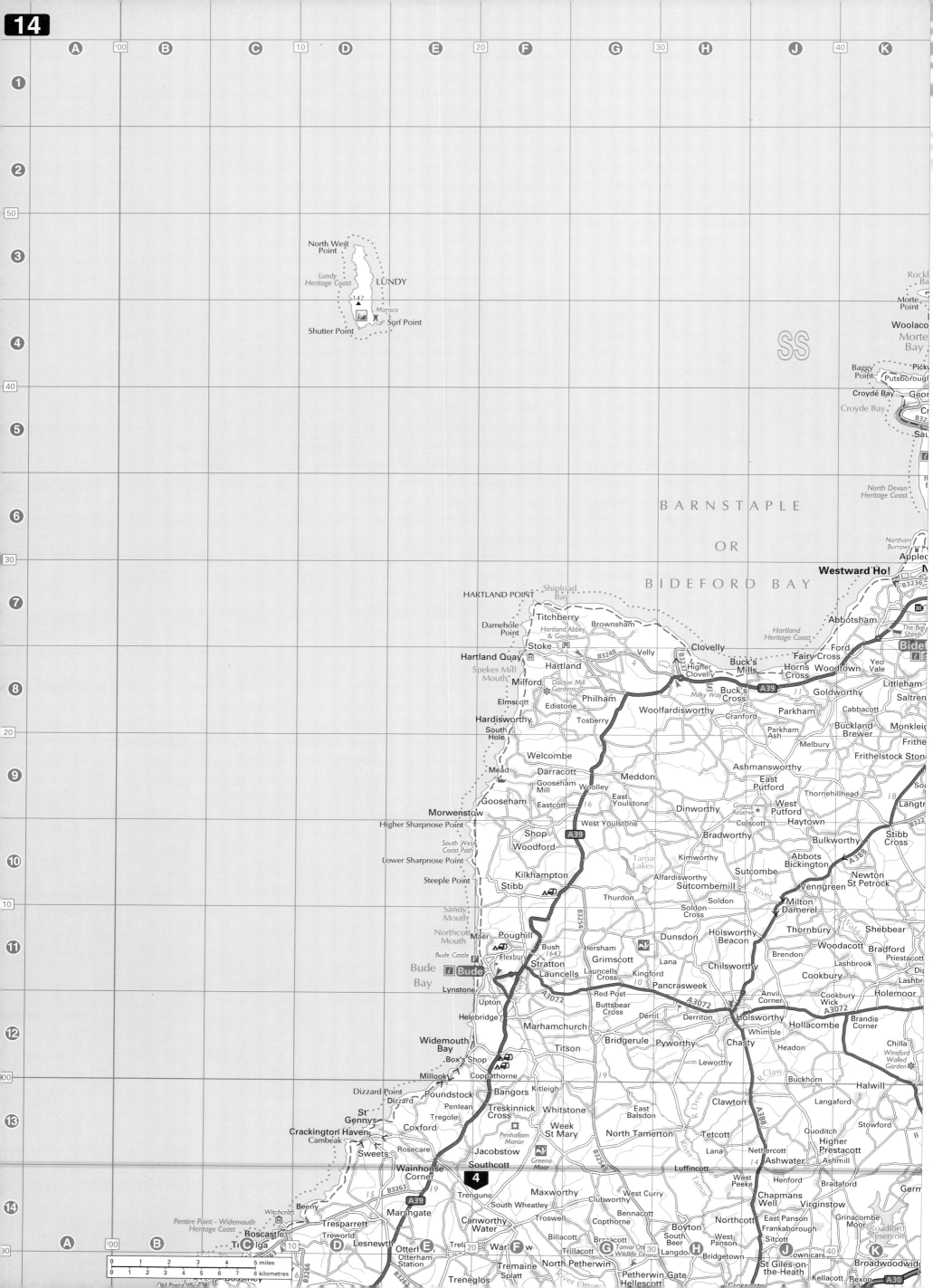

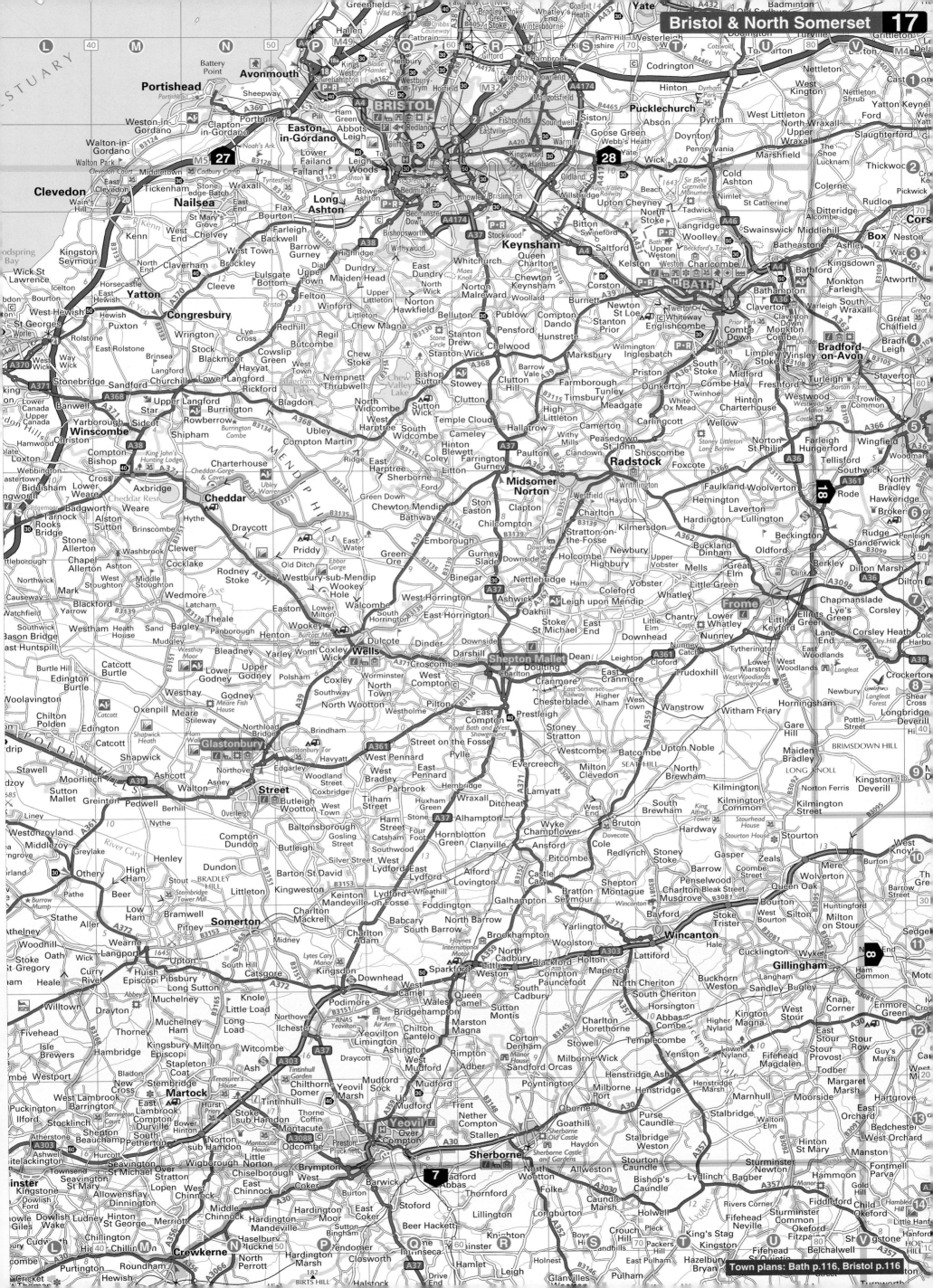

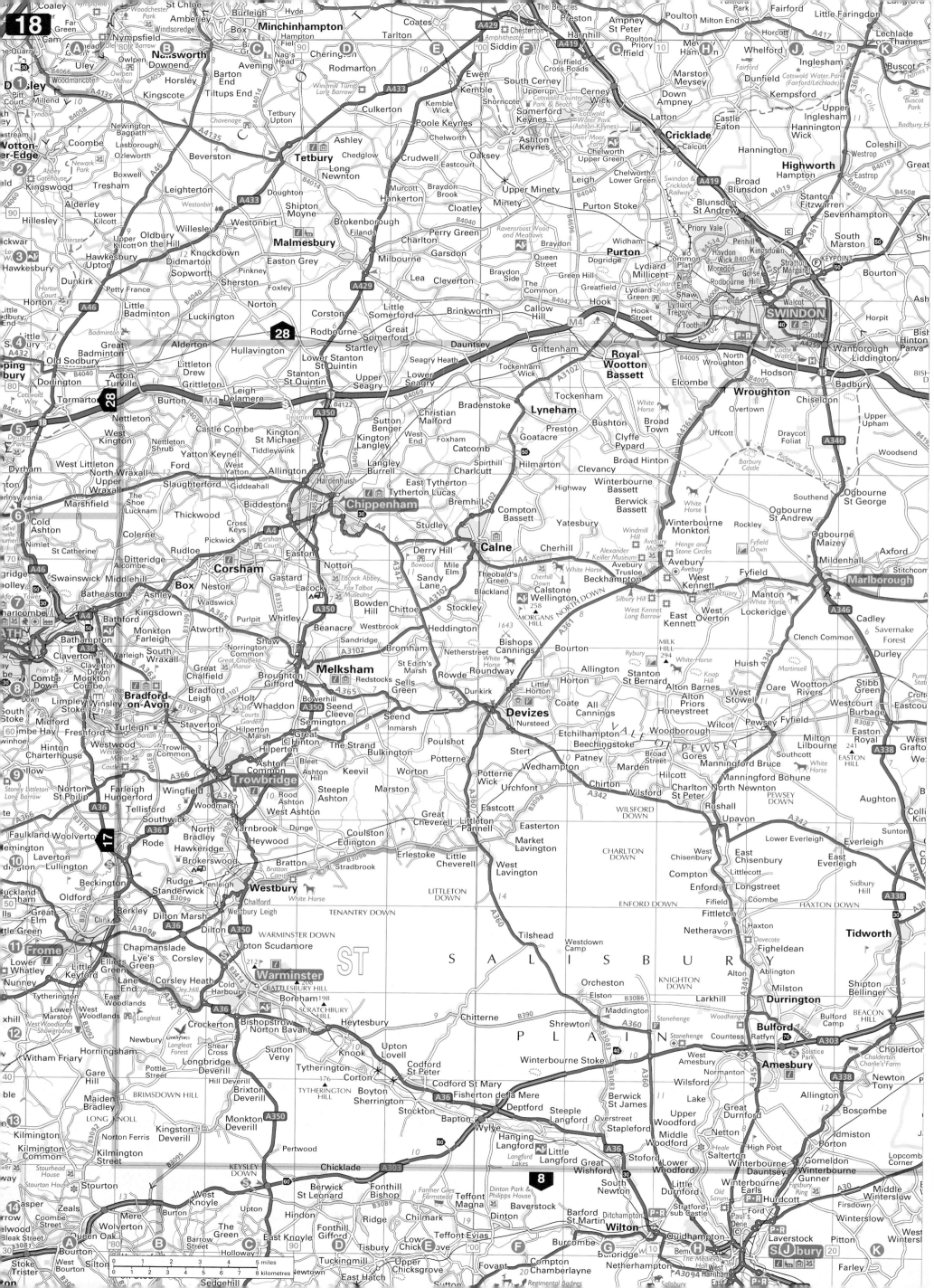

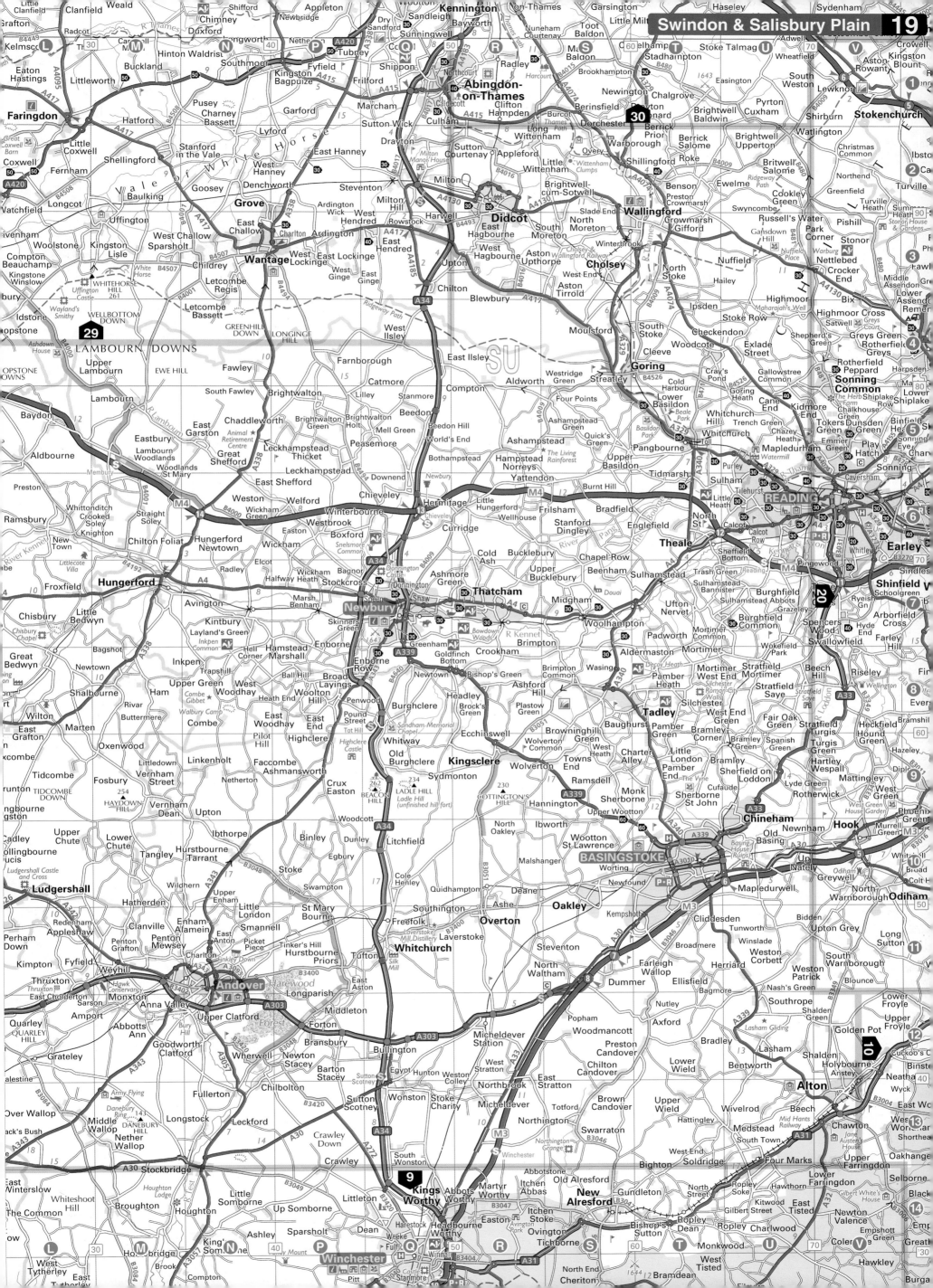

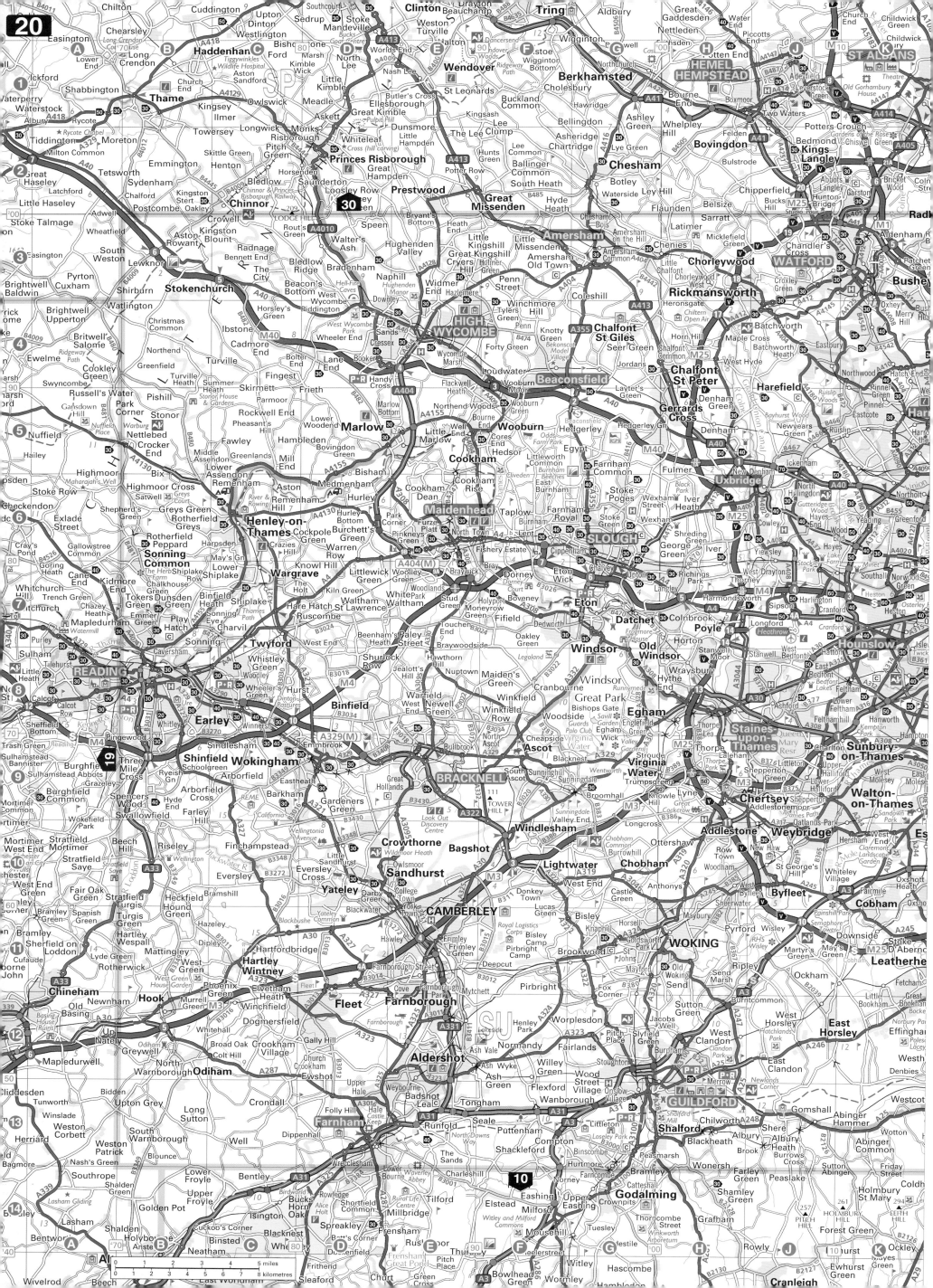

Harwich International Port

HARWICH INTERNATIONAL STATION
PASSENGER & CRUISE TERMINAL
CAR FERRY TERMINAL
CONTAINER TERMINAL
Parkeston
Harwich Industrial Estate
Superstore
PARKESTON ROUNDABOUT
ST NICHOLAS ROUNDABOUT
Dovercourt
Upper Dovercourt
A136
A120
0   400 m

Southend-on-Sea

LONDON, BASILDON
HM Customs & Excise
Museum & Planetarium
SOUTHEND VICTORIA STATION
Superstore
The Victoria
South Essex College
Travelodge
Leisure Centre
University of Essex
South Essex College
SOUTHEND CENTRAL STATION
County Court
Salvation Army
Uni of Essex
Naval & Military Club
Royal Hotel
The Royals
St John's
Palace Hotel
Victoria Statue
Porters Civic House
Porters Grange School
Sacred Heart Sch
Kingdom Hall
All Saints
SOUTHCHURCH ROAD
QUEENSWAY
SHOEBURYNESS
SOUTHCHURCH AVENUE
Kursaal Entertainment Centre
SeaLife Adventure
ESPLANADE
MARINE PARADE
0   200 m

Key place names on main map:

Nayland, Holbrook, Chelmondiston, Trimley Lower Street, Shotley, Ferry, Walton, Felixstowe, Harwich, Colchester, Manningtree, Mistley, Ramsey, Dovercourt, Hoek van Holland Esbjerg, Pennyhole Bay, Landguard Fort, Landguard Point

Marks Tey, Tiptree, Wivenhoe, Brightlingsea, West Mersea, MERSEA ISLAND, Walton on the Naze, The Naze, Frinton-on-Sea, Kirby Cross, CLACTON-ON-SEA, Jaywick, St Osyth, Holland-on-Sea, Point Clear

Maldon, Heybridge, Goldhanger, Tollesbury, Bradwell-on-Sea, Bradwell Waterside, River Blackwater, Southminster, Burnham-on-Crouch, Tillingham, Dengie, Mayland, Steeple, Asheldham

Ashingdon, Rochford, FOULNESS ISLAND, Courtsend, Churchend, Wallasea Island, Paglesham, Great Wakering, Shoeburyness, North Shoebury, SOUTHEND-ON-SEA, Westcliff-on-Sea, Prittlewell, Southchurch, Thorpe Bay, Shoebury Ness, ESTUARY

Sheerness, Thamesport, Minster, ISLE OF SHEPPEY, Queenborough, Halfway Houses, Eastchurch, Leysdown-on-Sea, Warden Point, Mud Row, Sittingbourne, Elmley Island, Isle of Harty, Shell Ness, Whitstable, Whitstable Bay, Tankerton, Herne Bay, Reculver, Beltinge, Swalecliffe, Chestfield, Seasalter, MARGATE, Westgate on Sea, Westbrook, ISLE OF THANET, Birchington, Manston, Acol, St Nicholas at Wade, Sarre, Minster

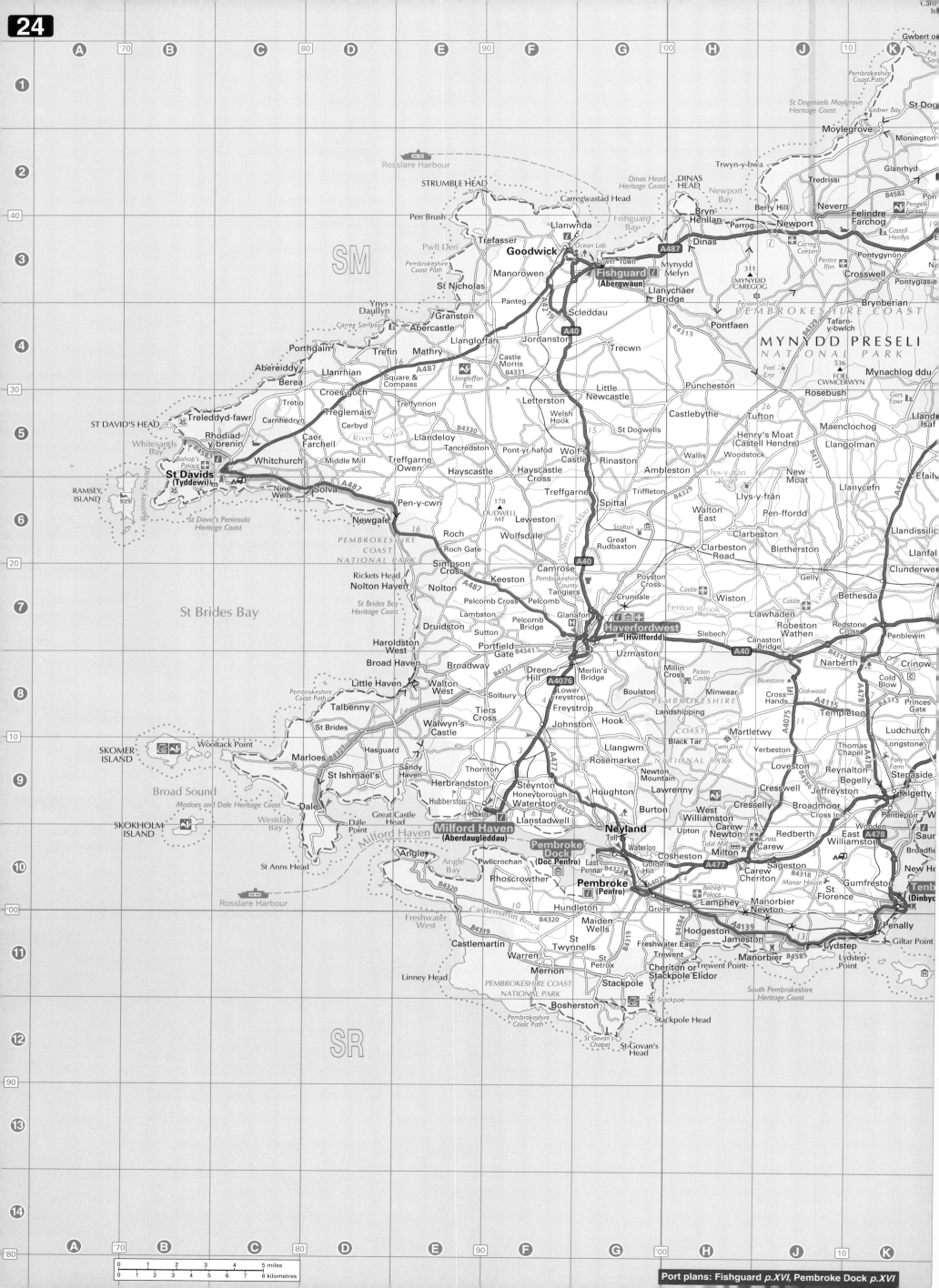

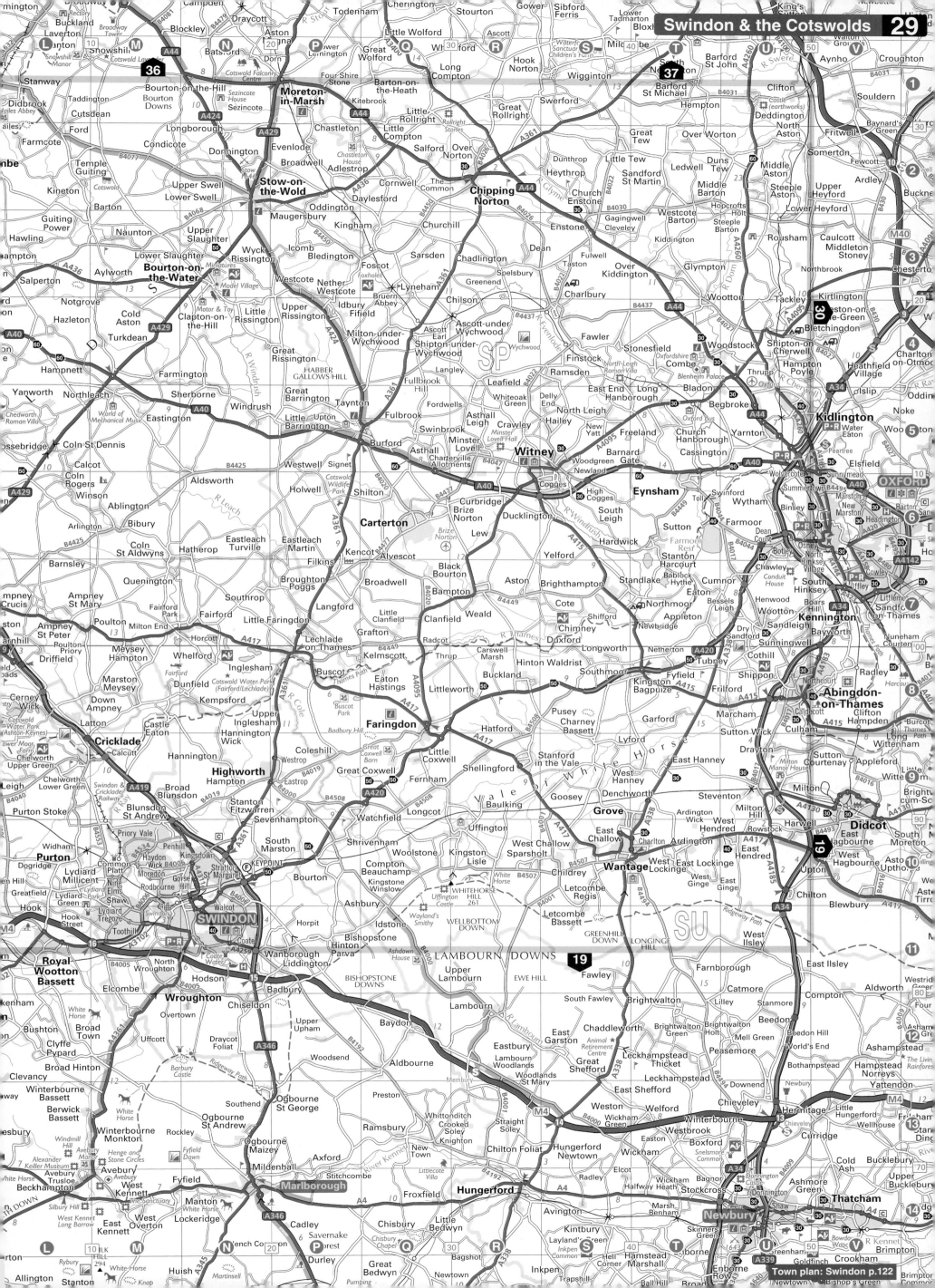

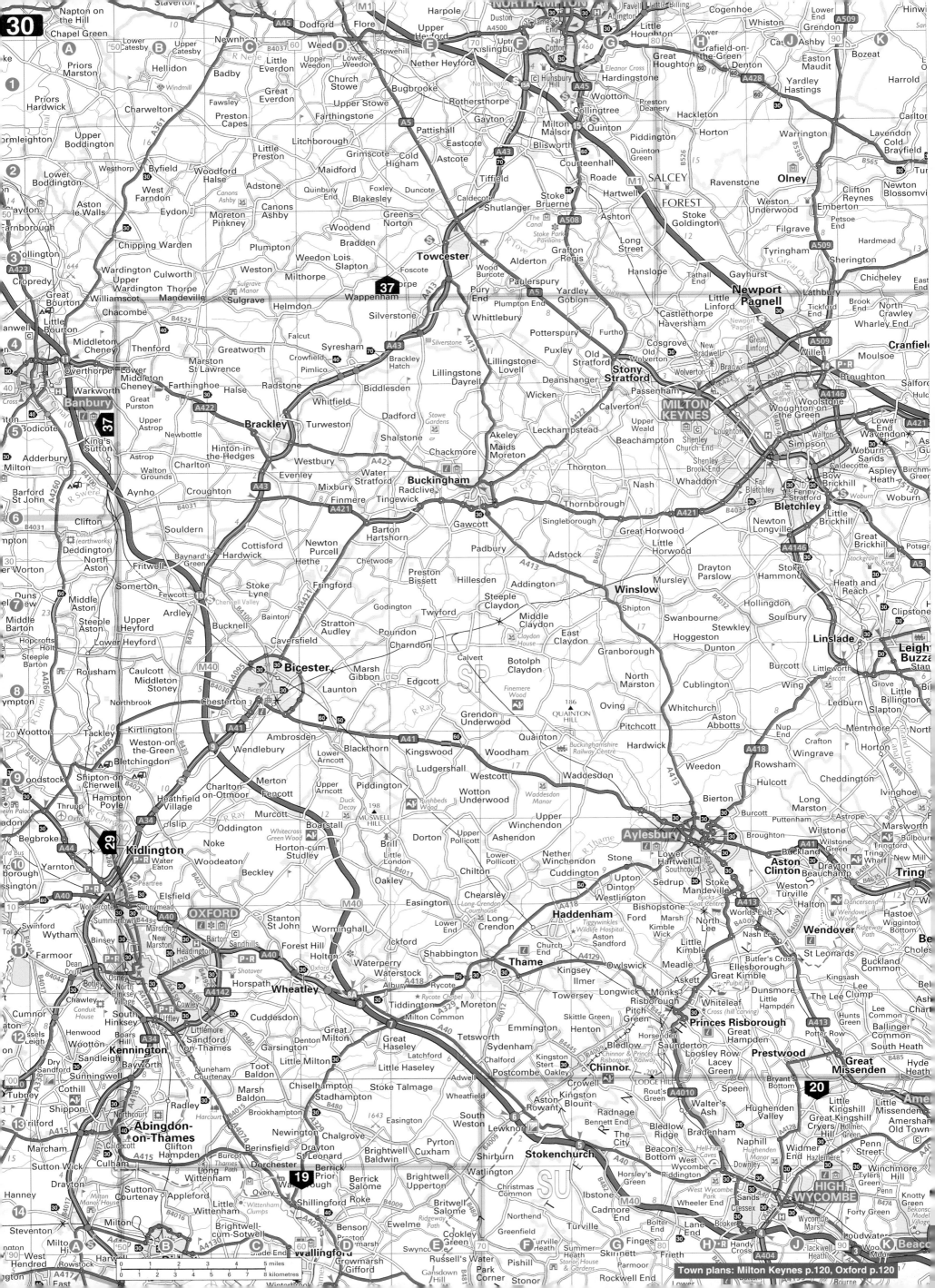

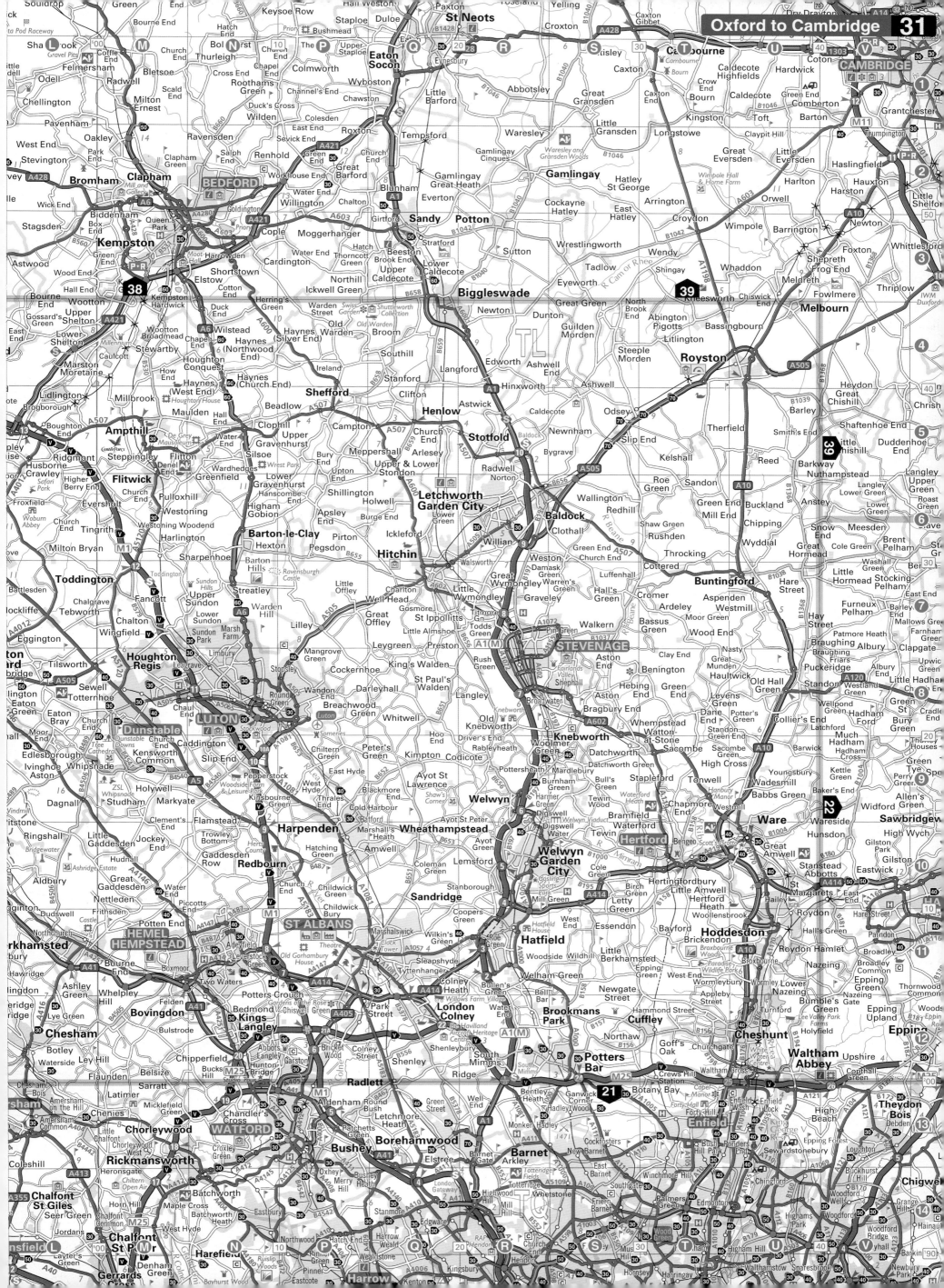

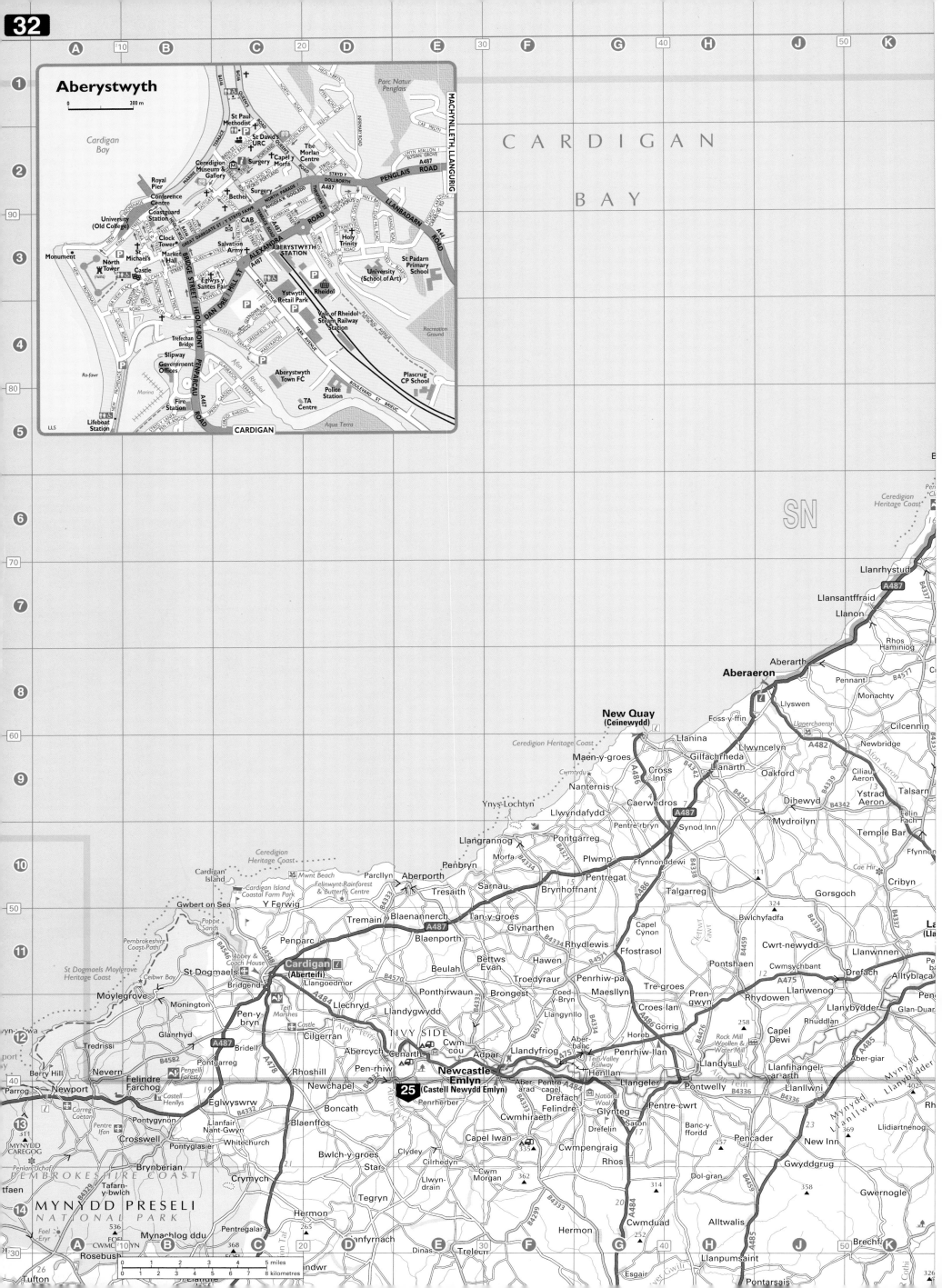

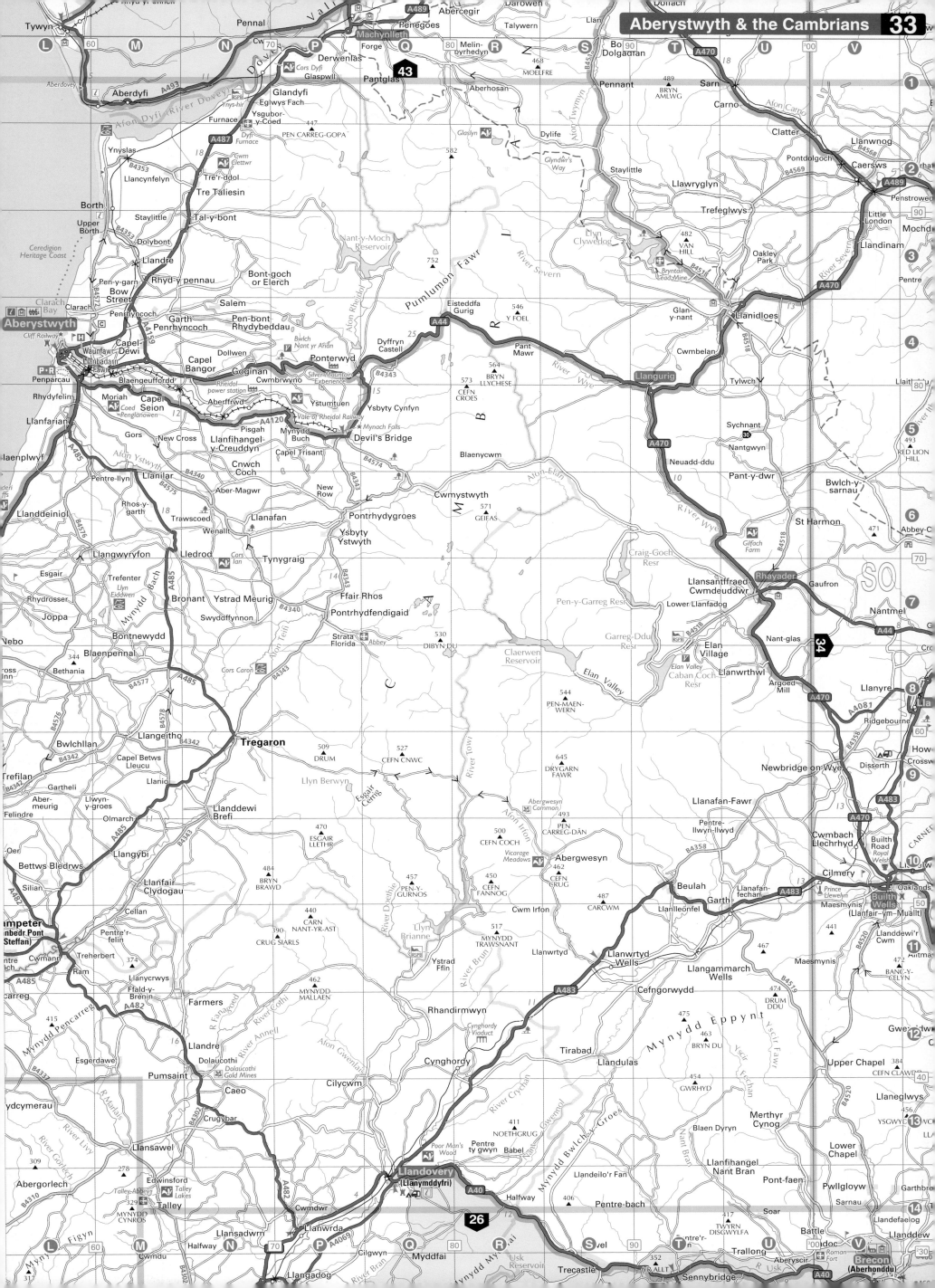

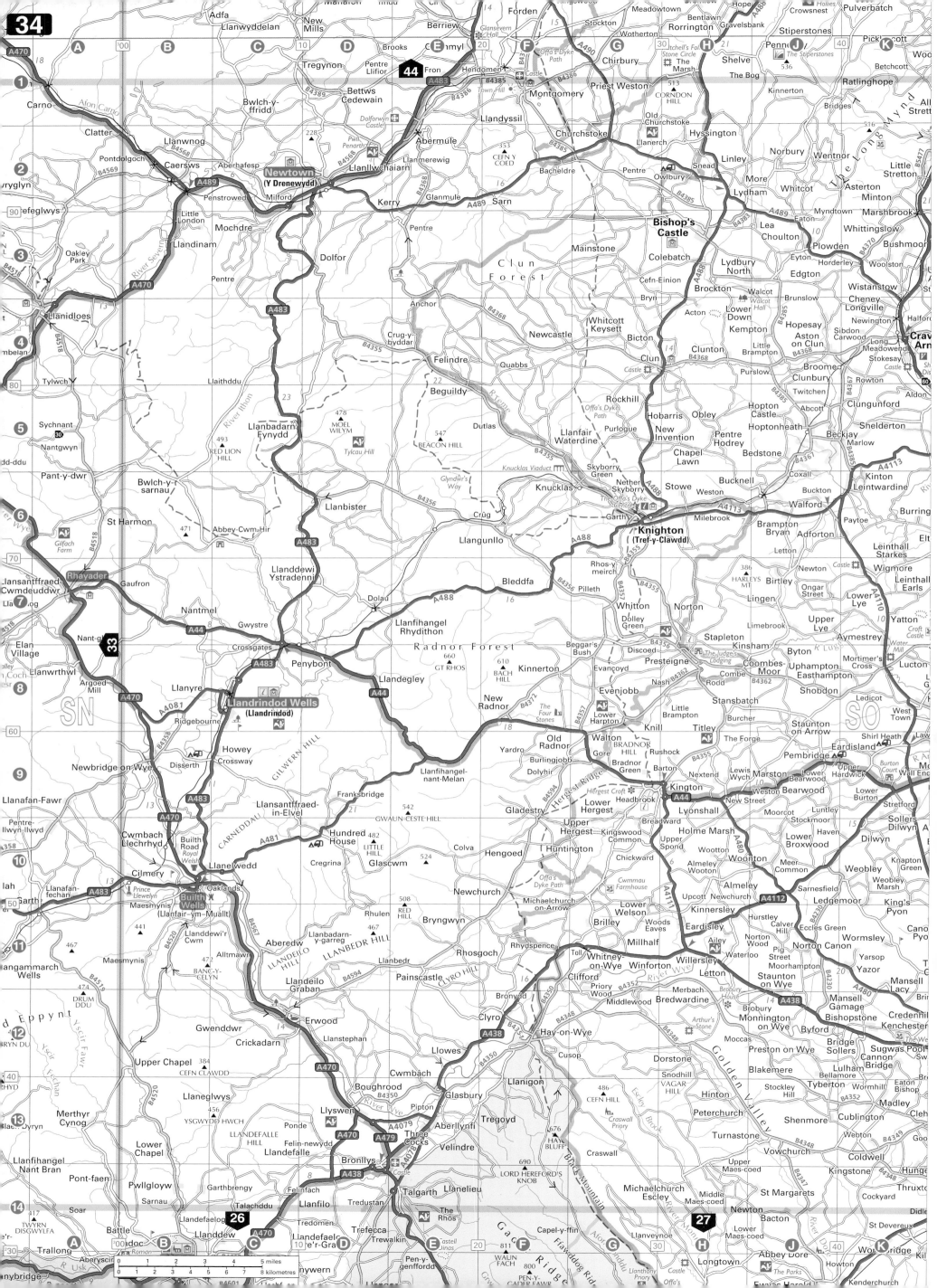

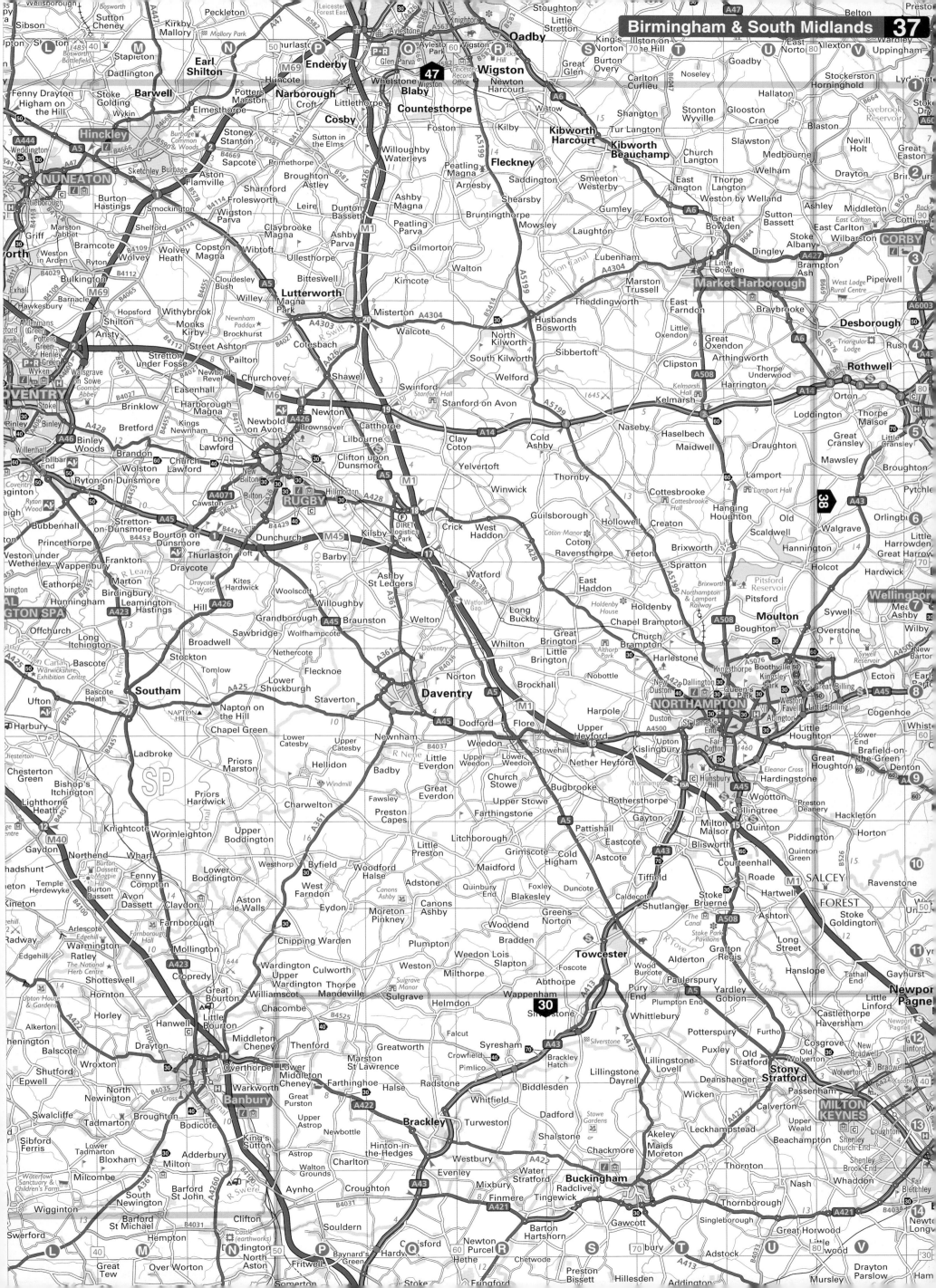

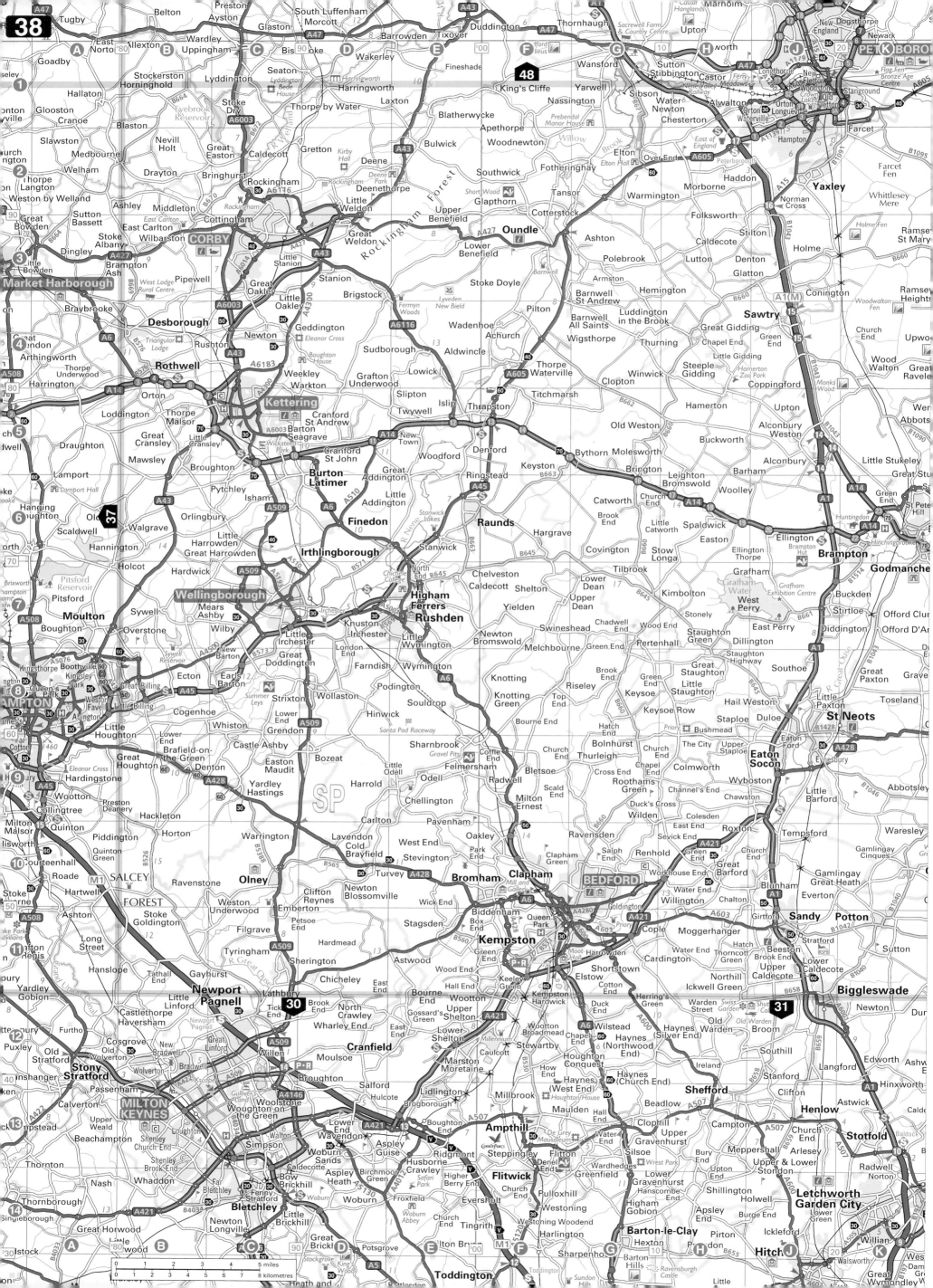

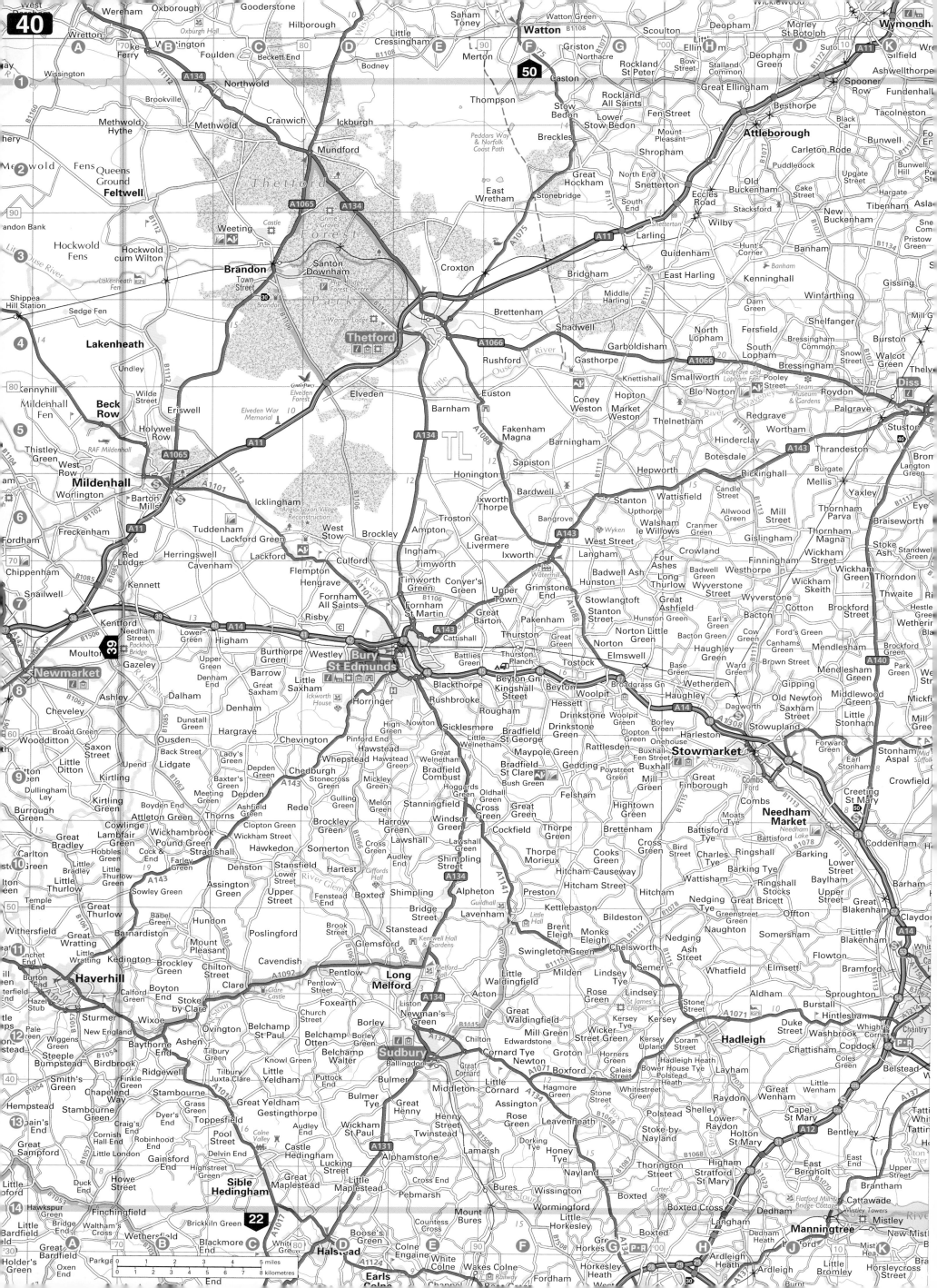

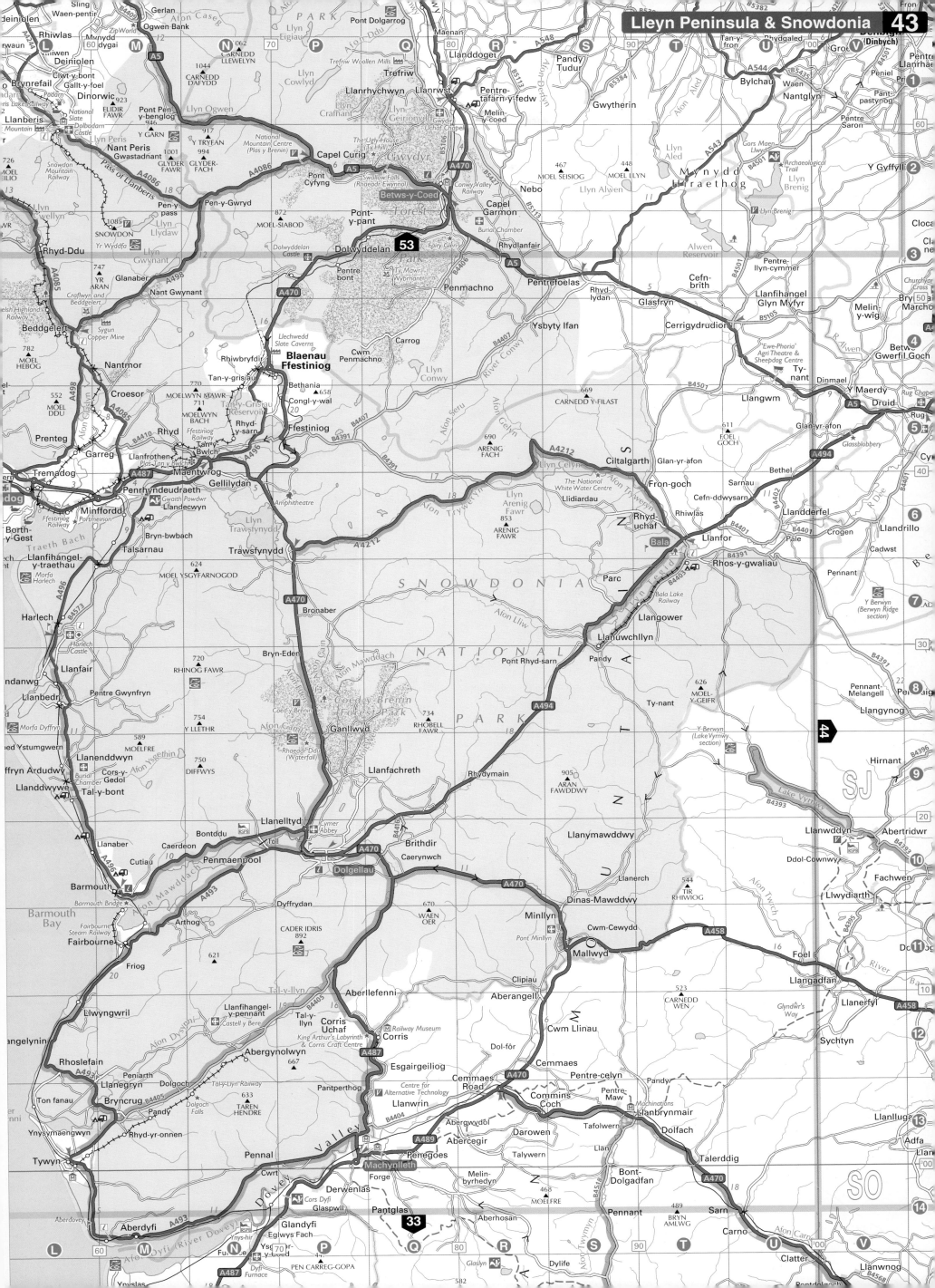

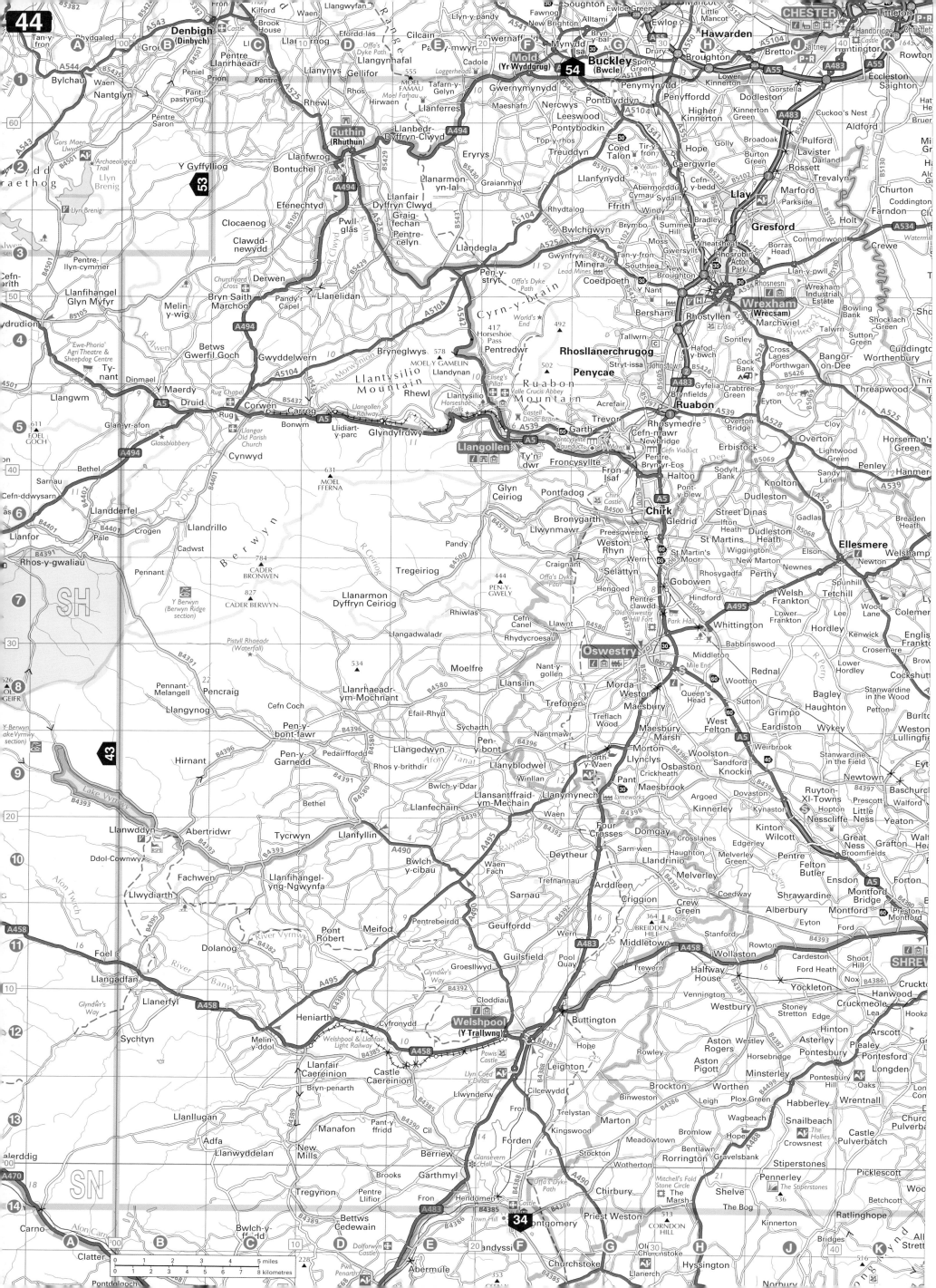

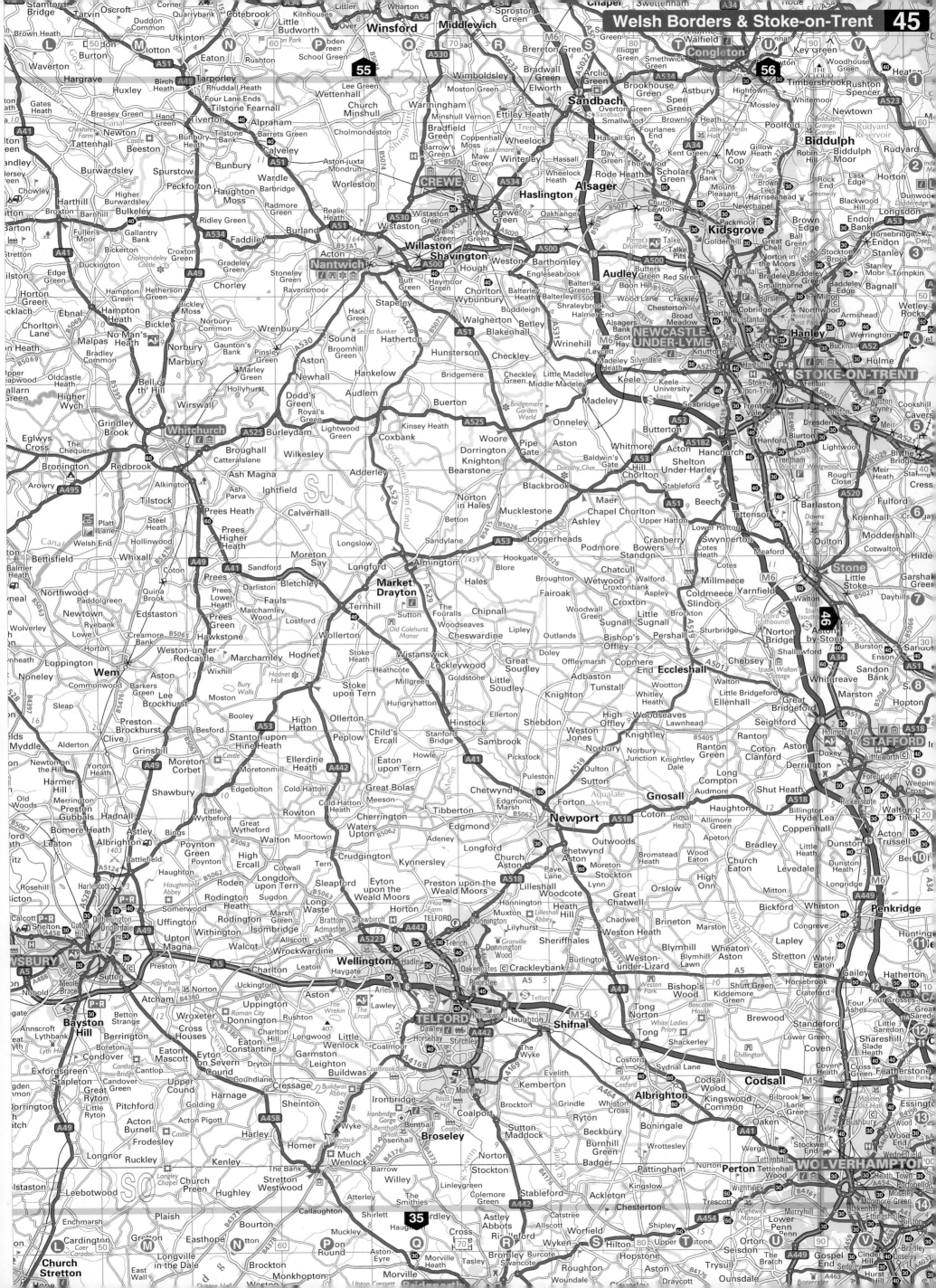

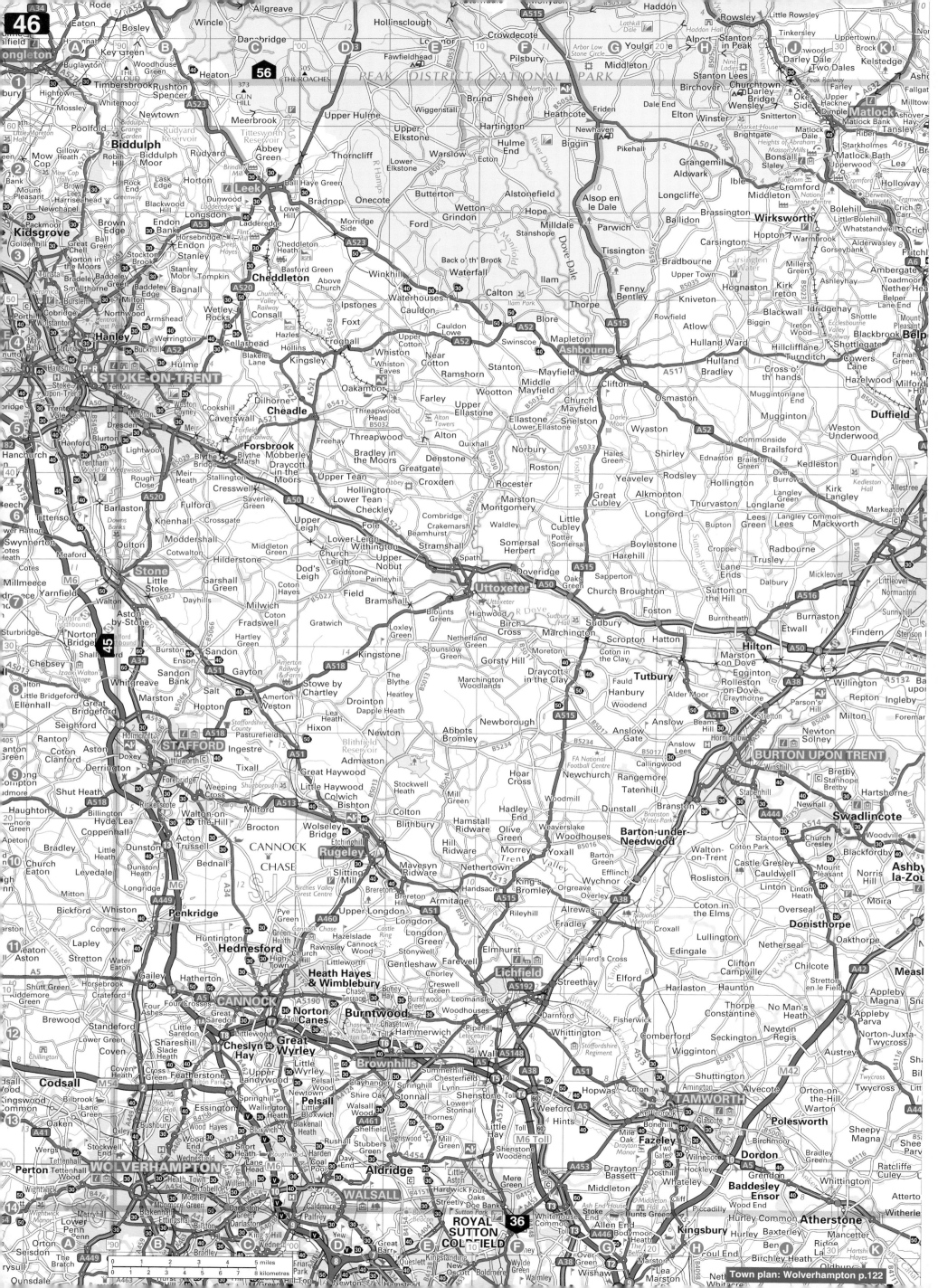

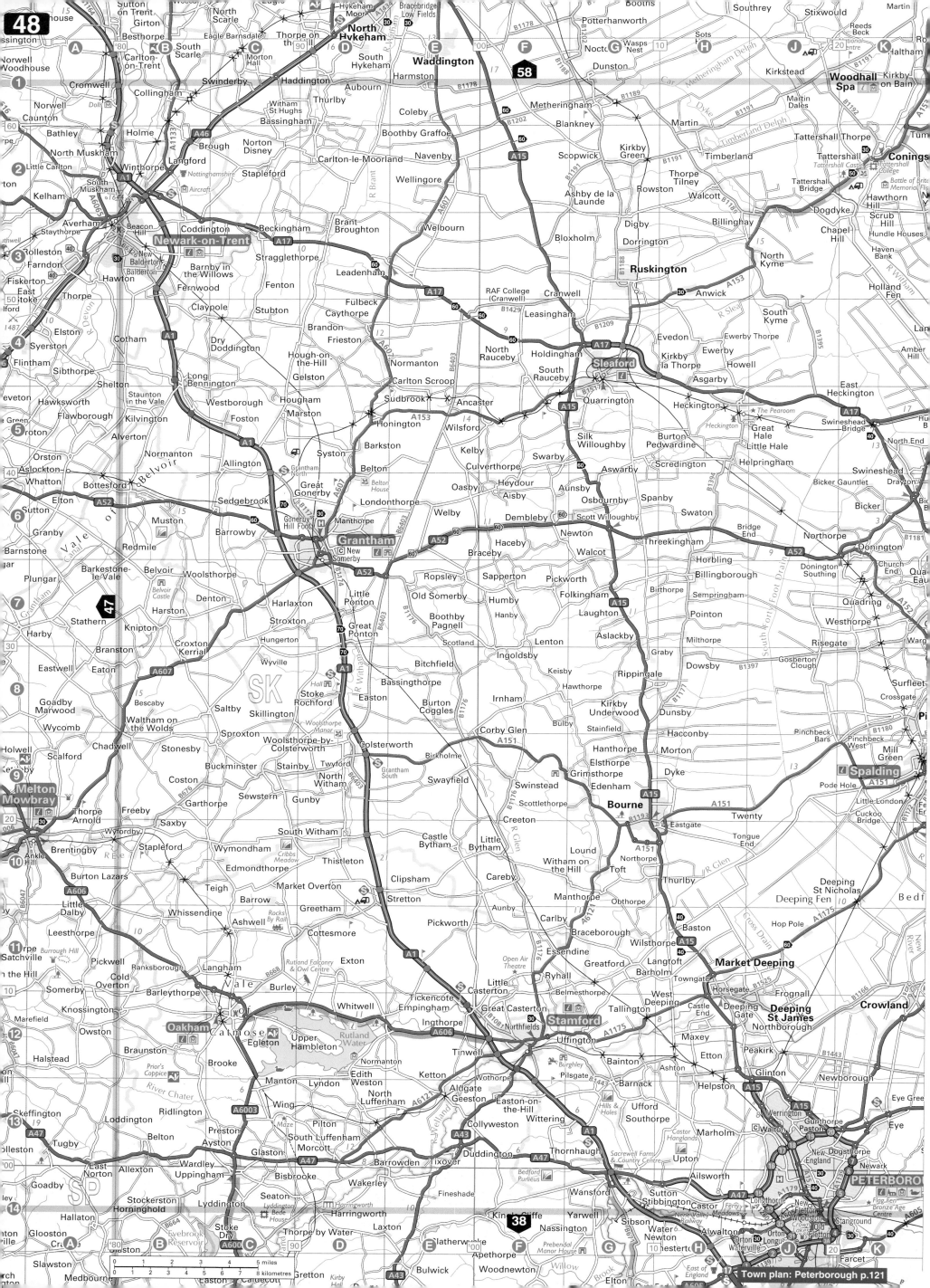

THE WASH

Great Yarmouth (inset town plan)

NORWICH   CAISTER
LOWESTOFT

200 m

TG

TM

THE BROADS

NORWICH

GREAT YARMOUTH

Cromer
West Runton
East Runton
Overstrand
Sidestrand
Northrepps
Trimingham
Mundesley
Lower Street
Paston
Knapton
Bacton
Walcott
Happisburgh
Eccles on Sea
Hempstead
Sea Palling
Waxham
Whimpwell Green
Horsey
Winterton-on-Sea
Hemsby
Scratby
California
Caister-on-Sea
West Caister
Great Yarmouth
Gorleston-on-Sea
Belton
Browston Green
Hopton on Sea
Corton

Aylsham
North Walsham
Stalham
Hickling
Ludham
Acle
Brundall
NORWICH
Hellesdon
Drayton

Llandudno

Saltcoats
Ravenglass
Roman Bath House
Newbiggin
Hycemoor
Selker Bay
Hyton
Annaside
Gutterby Spa

SC

NX

Isle of Man

0 1 2 3 4 5 miles
0 1 2 3 4 5 6 7 8 kilometres

POINT OF AYRE

Ayres
Rue Point
Port Cranstal
The Lhen
Cranstal
Cronk y Bing
A10
A19
B6
A16
A17
Bride
Andreas
A9
A10
Shellag Point
Jurby Head
Jurby
A14
B3
Sandygate
B14
Regaby
A13
St Jude's
Ballachurry Fort
The Grove
Ramsey Bay
The Cronk
Closg
Sartfield
Sulby
B14
Ramsey (Rhumsaa)
Ballaugh
A3
Churchtown
B16
A3
Manx Electric Railway
Port e Vullen
Orrisdale
Cronk Sumark
Glen Auldyn
Dreemskerry
A15
Ancient Crosses
Maughold
Orrisdale Head
ISLE OF
NORTH BARRULE
Maughold Head
Ravensdale
A14
Ballafayle
Ballajora
Kirk Michael
MAN
561
Corrany
Cashtal yn Ard
Cooildarry
Block Eary
488
620 SNAEFELL
462
Glen Mona
Barregarrow
Sulby Reservoir
SLIEAU LHEAN
A4
A3
The Bungalow
Snaefell Mountain Railway
Dhoon Bay
Knocksharry
B10
545
BEINN Y PHOTT
Great Laxey Wheel
Peel Castle
Cronk-y-Voddy
Laxey
St Patrick's Isle
487
King Orry's Grave
Peel (Purt ny-hinshey)
COLDEN
Millennium Way
Ballaleannagh
Old Laxey
Laxey Head
Contrary Head
A20
Corrins Folly
Tynwald Hill
479
SLIEAU RUY
Creg ny Baa
B20
Cloven Stones
Patrick
A30
A1
Laxey Bay
St John's
Greeba
Baldwin
A18
Baldrine
Manx Electric Railway
Waterfall
Glen Maye
A23
Crosby
Glen Vine
A1
Clay Head
Lower Foxdale
Strang
Onchan (Kiondroghad)
Dalby
Foxdale
Eairy
Union Mills
Norse Houses
Groudle Glen Railway
Niarbyl
A24
Onchan Head
Cronkbourne
Niarbyl Bay
Round Table
483
A27
SOUTH BARRULE
Dalby Mountain
437
Braaid
Brough Fort
DOUGLAS (DOOLISH)
Belfast
CRONK NY ARREY LAA
B39
Closeclark
St Marks
A2
Douglas Head
Heysham
Ballamodha
Millennium Way
A5
Liverpool
Fleshwick Bay
A36
Grenaby
A26
Santon
A25
A37
Ballakilpheric
Ballabeg
Rushen Abbey
Isle of Man Steam Railway
Port Soderick
Milners Tower
Ballafesson
Colby
Santon Head
Bradda Head
A7
Cronk ny Merriu
Dublin
Birkenhead
Port Erin
Ballasalla
A5
Howe
A31
Derbyhaven
Isle of Man (Ronaldsway)
Castletown
Port St Mary
B53
Cregneash
Close ny Chollagh
Hango Hill
Scarlett
Scarlett Point
SC
The Sound
Meayll Circle
Castletown Bay
Calf Sound
Silverdale Glen
Herring Tower
Spanish Head
Dreswick Point
CALF OF MAN
Caigher Point

▽ Manx Heritage site

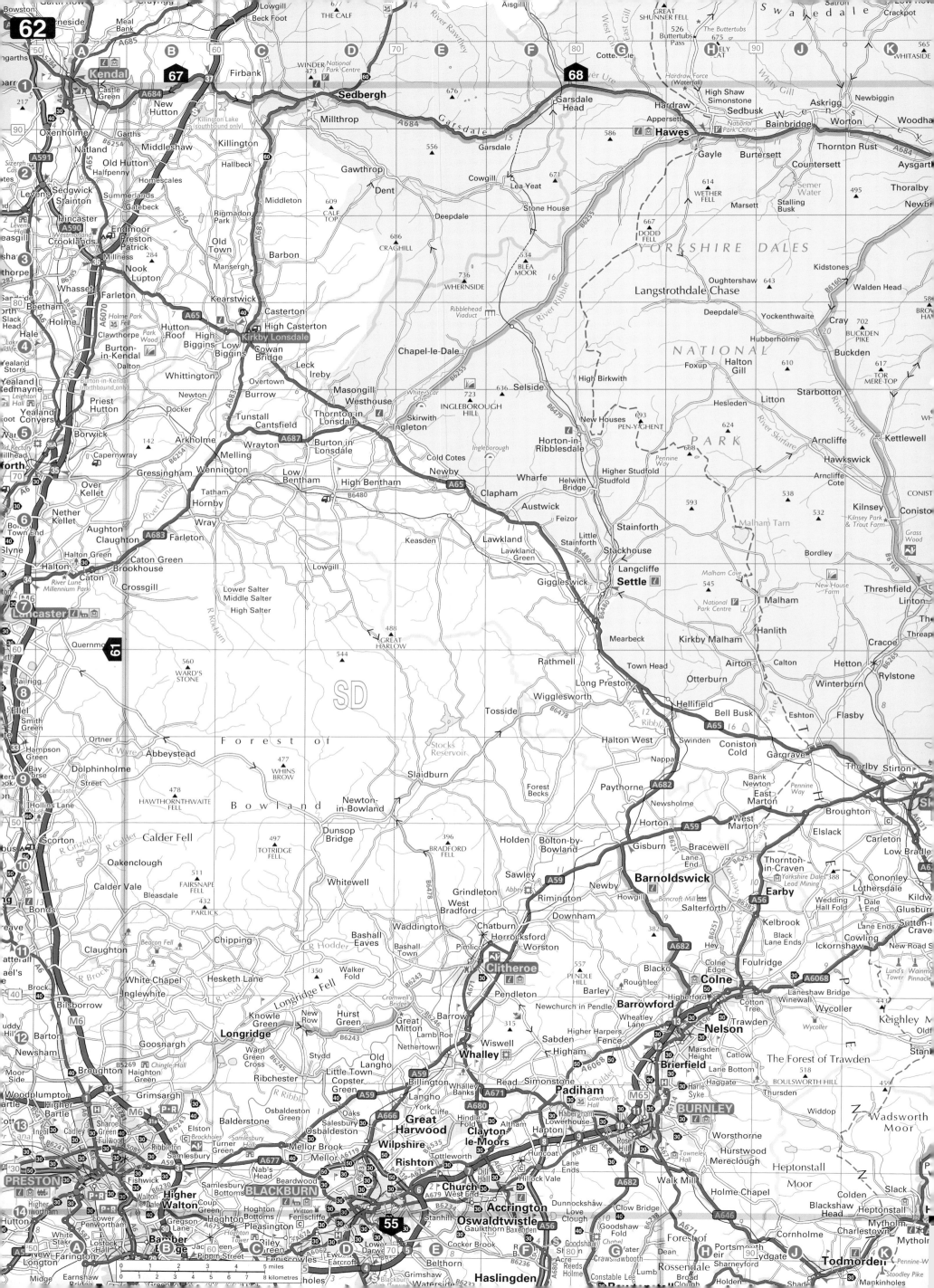

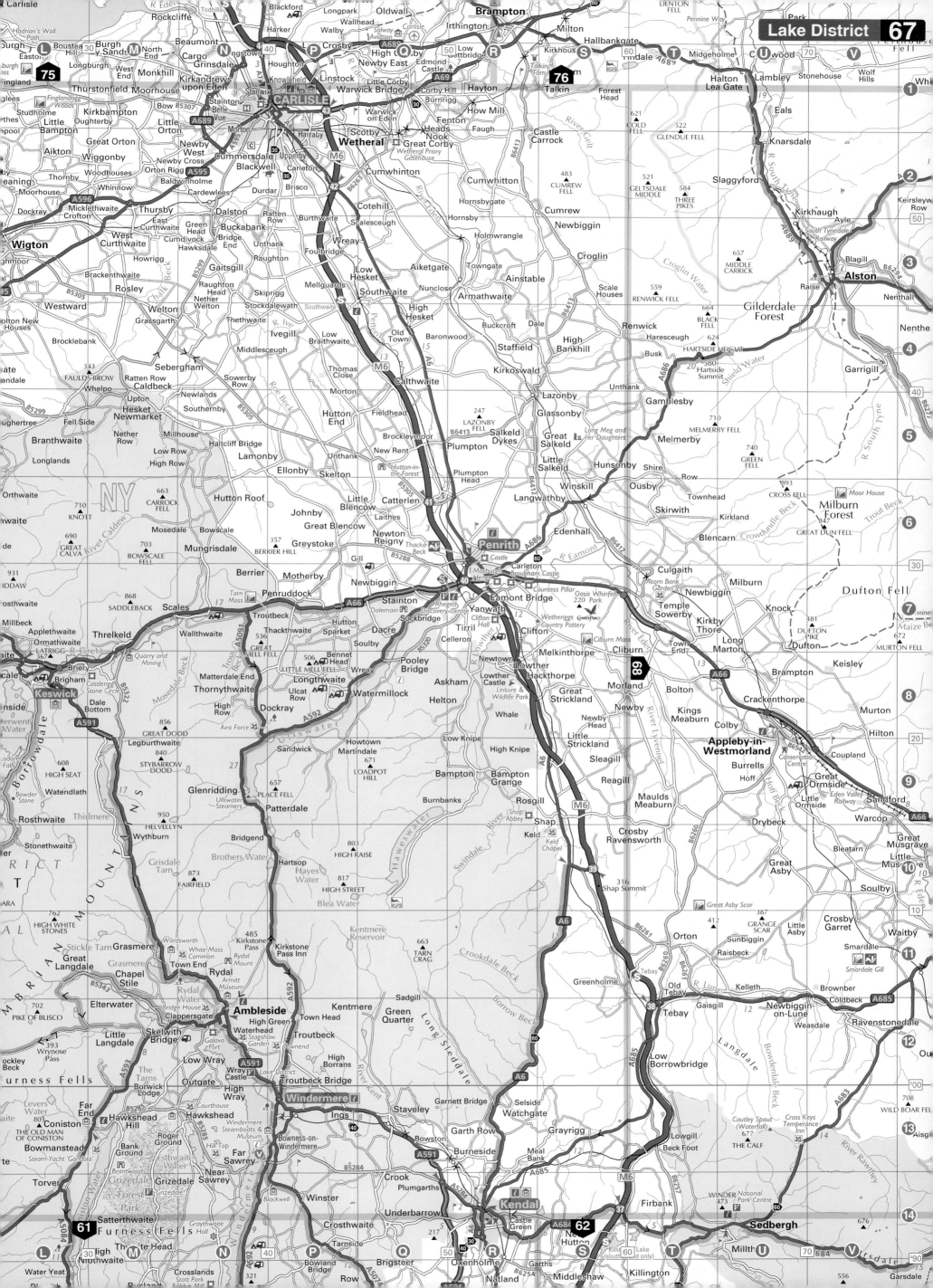

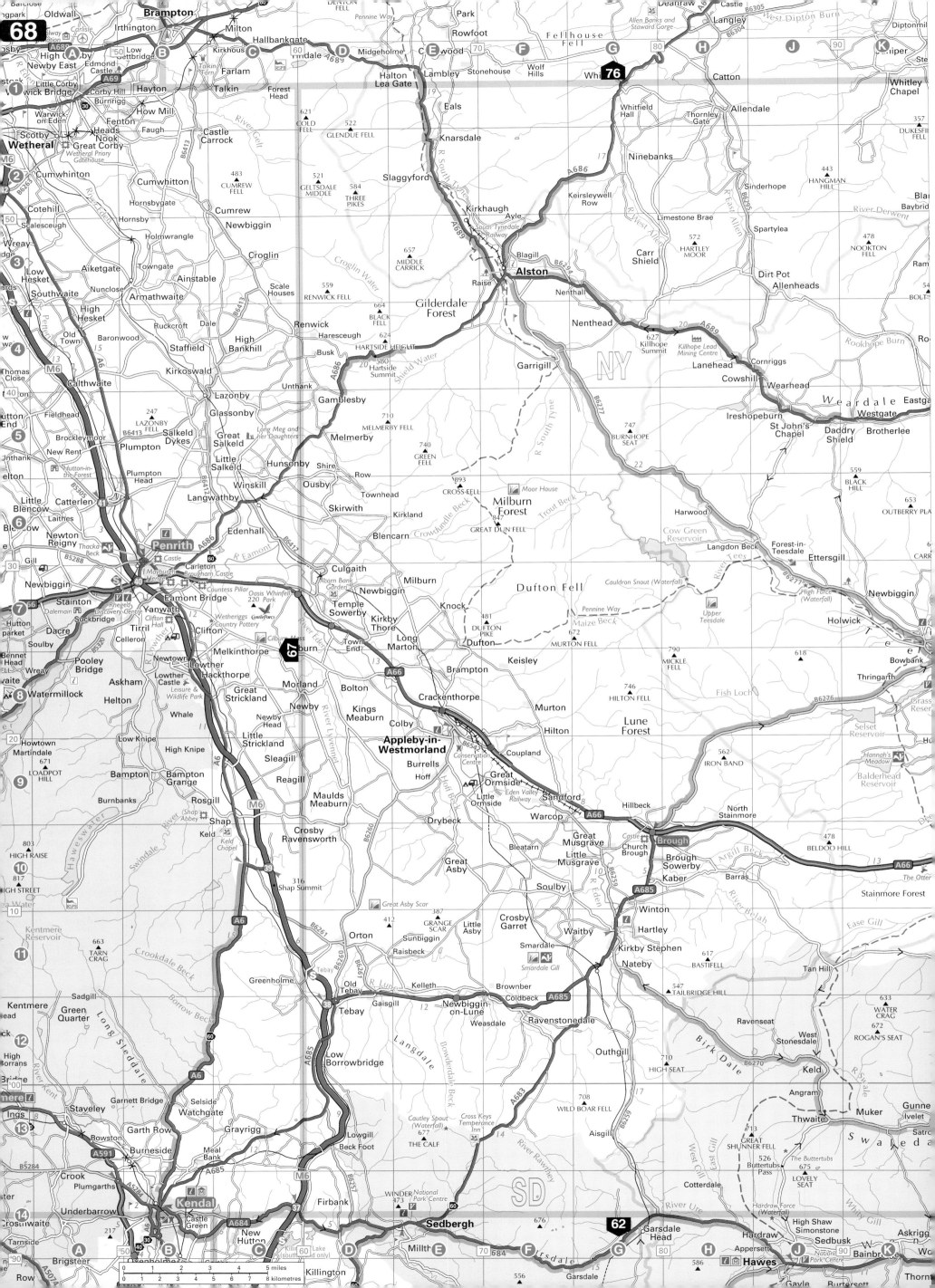

Sunderland

SOUTH SHIELDS

M Metro station

GATESHEAD, NEWCASTLE

River Wear

Wearmouth Bridge

Echo 24

Superstore
TRIMDON STREET

Superstore

A183

LIVINGSTONE RD
Police
Station
Empire
Mag Ct
HMRC

ST MARY'S WAY

WEST WEAR STREET

St Mary's

Sunniside
Leisure

Bowling
Alley

SANS STREET

Surgery

Fire
Station

St Mark's

Sunderland
Minster

Crowtree
Leisure
Centre

SUNDERLAND
STATION

CHESTER-LE-STREET

University of
Sunderland
(City Campus)

The Bridges

Travelodge

Arts
Centre

County
Court

Surgery

Surgery

Hudson
Road
School

Halls of
Residence
(UOS)

University of
Sunderland

CHESTER ROAD

BURN PARK ROAD

Transport
Interchange

Sunderland
Museum &
Winter
Gardens

Mowbray
Gardens

Statue

Royalty

STOCKTON ROAD

West
Park

War
Memorial

Civic Centre
& Register
Office

Kingdom
Hall

PEEL ST

SALEM RD

Burn Park

St Anthony's
Girls' School

St
George's

PARK ROAD

Statue

Masonic
Hall

Thornhill
Park School

Argyle House
School

Thornbeck
College

Sunderland
High School

DURHAM

TEESSIDE, (A19)

Middlesbrough

A178
TRANSPORTER BRIDGE

Police
HQ

BRIDGE STREET W

MIDDLESBROUGH
STATION

Middlesbrough
College

METZ BRIDGE
ROAD

MARSH ROAD

STATION STREET

RIVERSIDE PARK ROAD

A66

WILSON STREET

Hill Street

Dundas

Town
Hall

Thistle
Hotel

Leisure
Park

TEESPORT

Superstore

Empire

Cleveland
Centre

Council
Offices

Register
Office

Combined
Court
Centre

Cannon Park
Ind Est

NEWPORT ROAD

Travelodge

All Saints

Mag
Ct

MIMA
Art Gallery

STOCKTON

HEYWOOD STREET

Newport
Primary
School

Teesside
University

Surgery

Abingdon
Primary
School

Newport South
Business Park

Sikh
Temple

Salvation
Army

Teesside
University

Christadelphian
Hall

Ayresome
Primary
School

Ayresome
Gardens

Teesside
University

Teesside
University

Archibald
Primary School

AYRESOME STREET

Surgery

Meml

Meml

Albert
Park

St Joseph's
RC Primary
School

Sacred Heart
RC Primary
School

Dorman

Fountain

Surgery
Ambulance
Station

RC Church
of the
Sacred Heart

Boathouse

Fire
Station

STOKESLEY

Saltburn-
by-the-
Sea

Saltburn Smugglers

New Brotton

Carlin How

Skinningrove

Hummersea Scar

Brotton

Skelton

New
Skelton

North
Skelton

Kilton

Upton

Boulby

Staithes

Heritage Centre

Loftus

Dalehouse

Easington

Port Mulgrave

North Yorkshire and
Cleveland Heritage Coast

Lingdale

Kilton
Thorpe

Liverton
Mines

Hinderwell

Newton
Mulgrave

Runswick
Bay

Woodhill

Liverton

Handale

Roxby

Borrowby

Runswick

Kettleness

Stanghow

A171

Moorsholm

Scaling

B1266

Ellerby

Goldsborough

Overdale
Wyke

Gerrick

Scaling Dam

Mickleby

A174

Lythe

Sandsend

Sandsend
Wyke

West
Barnby

East
Barnby

Raithwaite

Sandsend

Ugthorpe

Dunsley

Newholm

Whitby

Abbey

Saltwick
Bay

Danby

Stonegate

Hutton
Mulgrave

Ruswarp

Stainsacre

The Moors
Centre

301

Castleton

Ainthorpe

Lealholm

Lealholm
Side

Aislaby

Briggswath

Sneaton

High Hawsker

Westerdale

The
Green

Egton

Sleights

Ugglebarnby

Low
Hawsker

River Esk

Esk Dale

Iburndale

Sneatonthorpe

Ness Point or
North Cheek

Danby Bottom

Glaisdale

Grosmont

Robin Hood's Bay

Street

Egton Bridge

Key Green

Littlebeck

Raw

Fylingthorpe

Robin
Hood's Bay

NORTH YORK MOORS

Beck Hole

B1416

Old Peak or
South Cheek

326
PIKE HILL

Goathland

Ravenscar

369

A171

NATIONAL PARK

North Yorkshire
Moors Railway

292

Staintondale

Shire Horse Centre

Hayburn
Wyke

TA

Church
Houses

Rosedale

Wheeldale
Roman Road

Eller Beck

Hackness

Cloughton
Newlands

Low
Bell End

Thorgill

Newtondale
Forest Drive

Harwood
Dale

Cloughton
Wyke

Low Mill

Rosedale Abbey

Stape

THE YORK MOORS

NORTH RIDING

Hole of
Horcum

Cromer Point

Cloughton

Hartoft End

290

River Seven

Farndale

Bridestones
(Rock Formation)

Bickley

Broxa

Silpho

Burniston

Cleveland Way

A165

Gillam

Lastingham

Newton
Rawcliffe

Levisham

Dalby
Forest Drive

Toll

Landale
Rigg

Hackness

Wrench
Green

Suffield

Scalby

Scarborough

admoor

Hutton-
le-Hole

Spaunton

Lockton

Appleton-

Cawthorn

Cropton

239

Everley

Castle

64

65

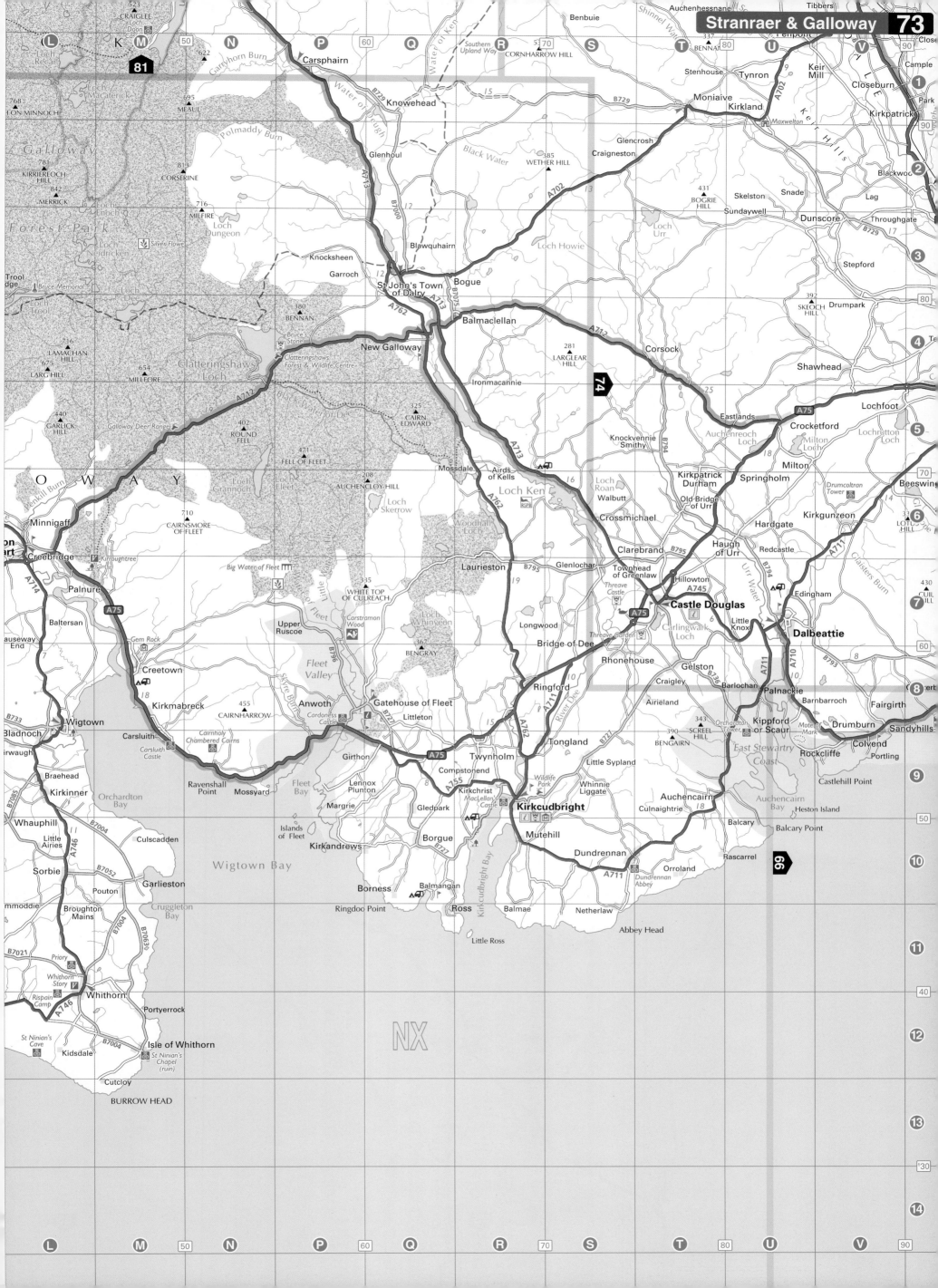

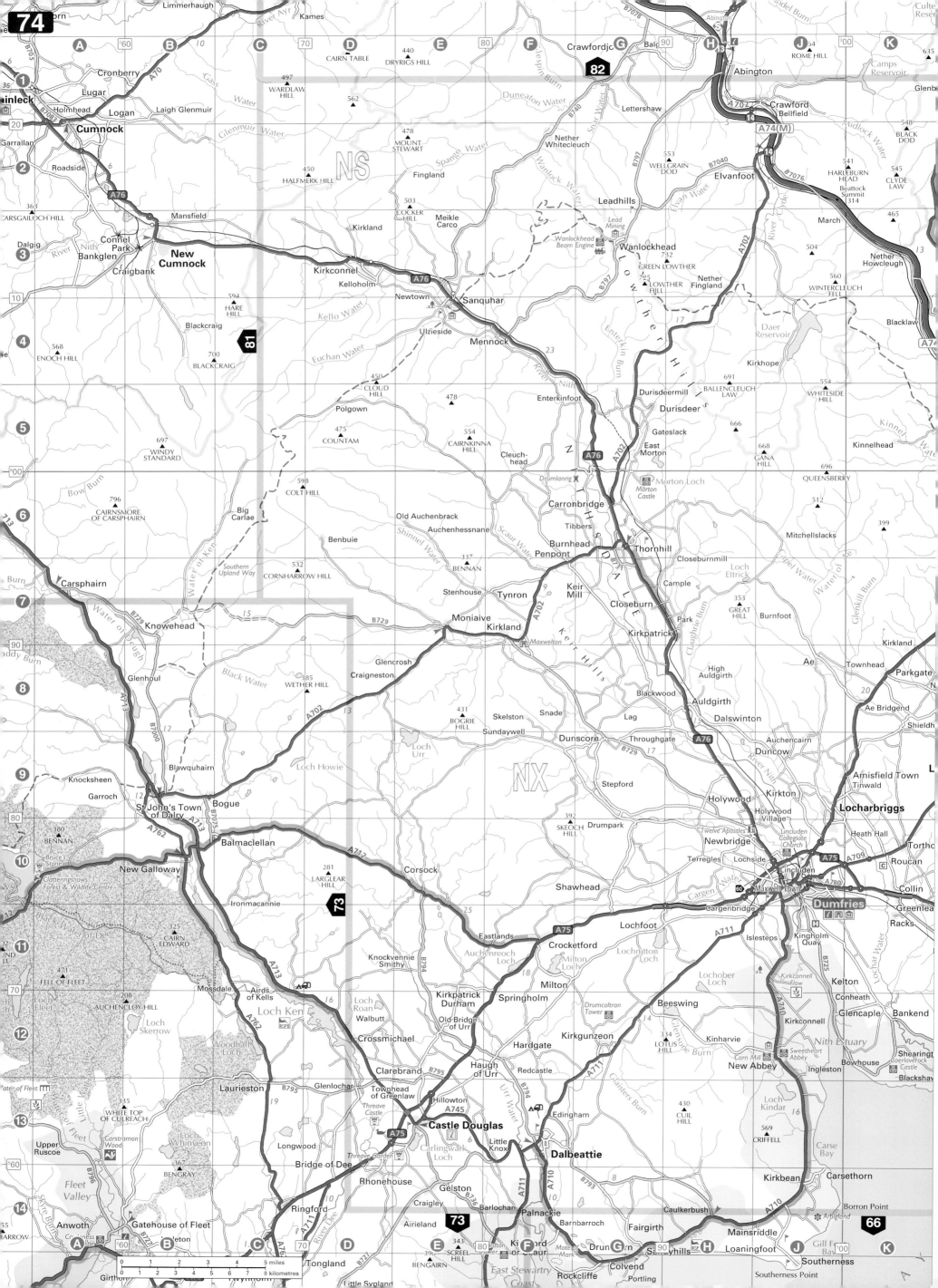

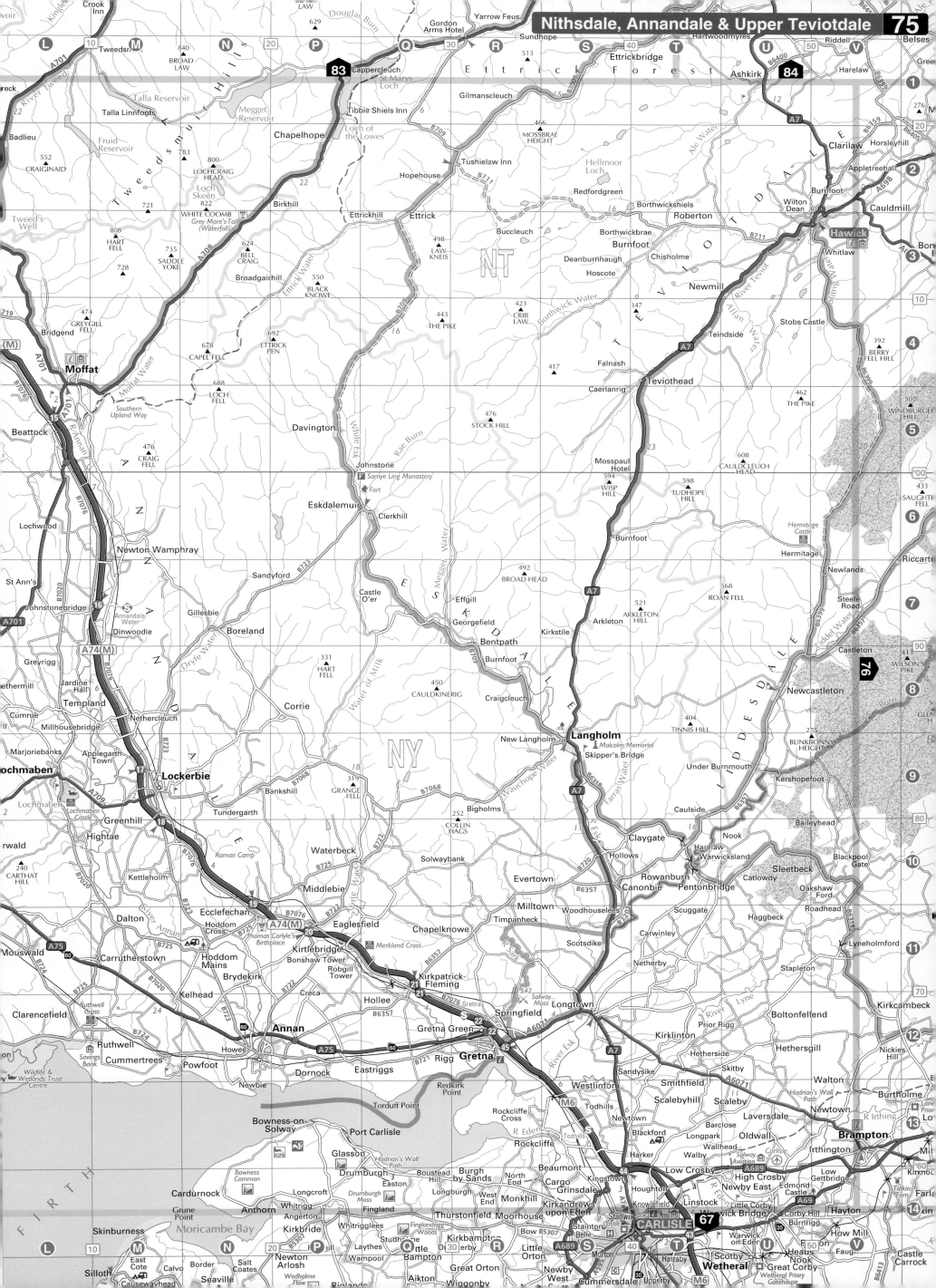

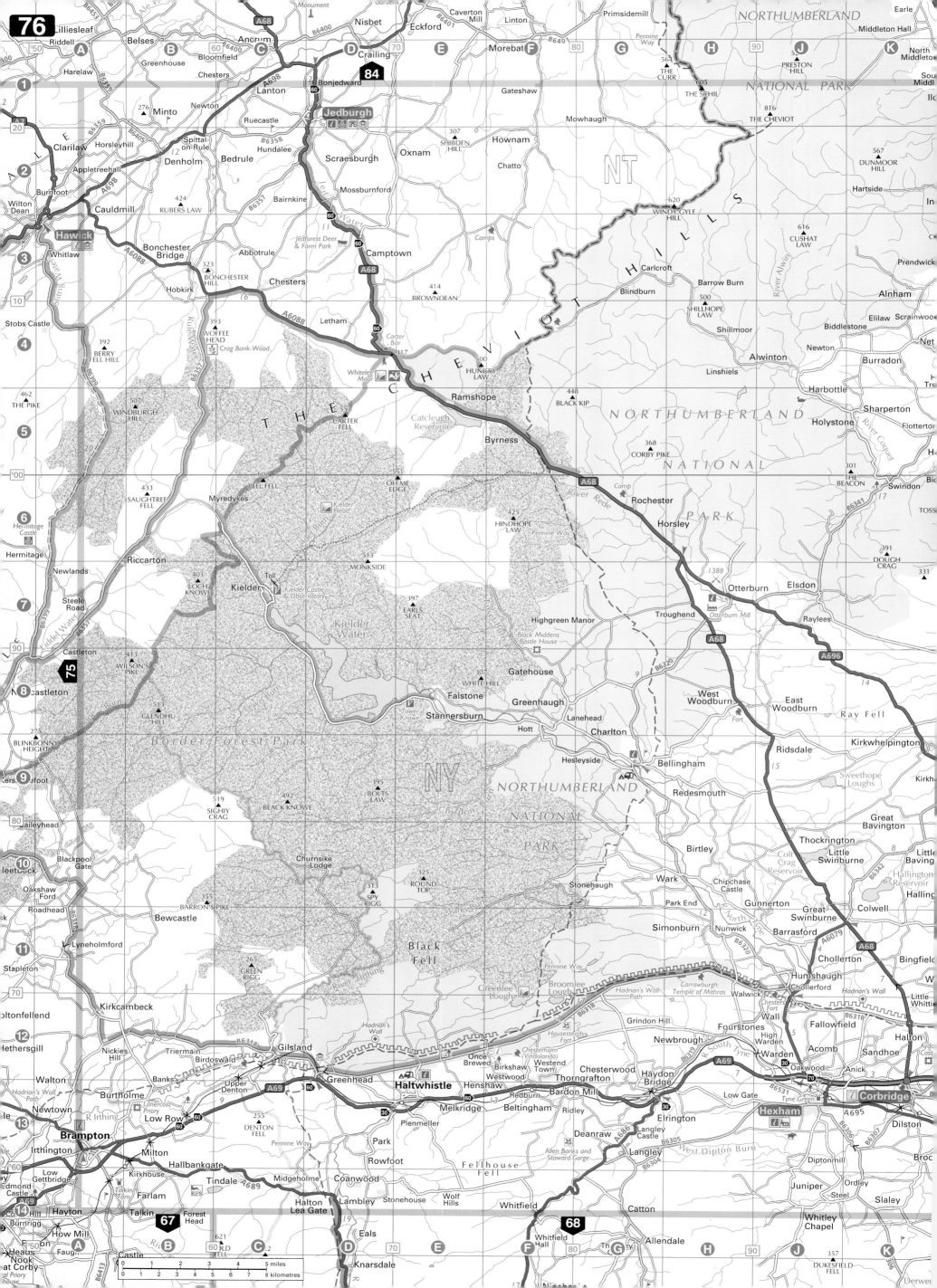

Port of Tyne

Town plan: Newcastle upon Tyne p.120

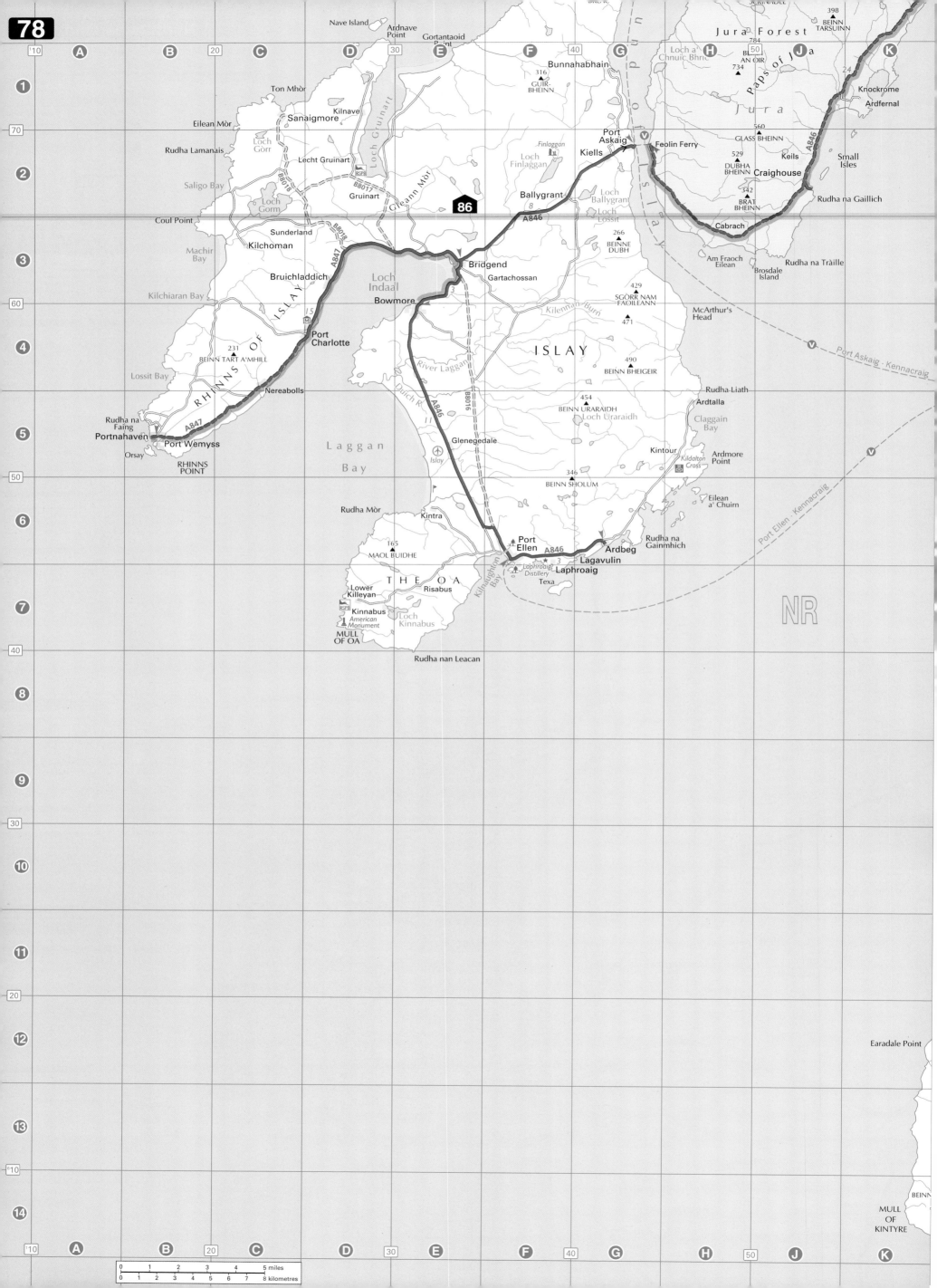

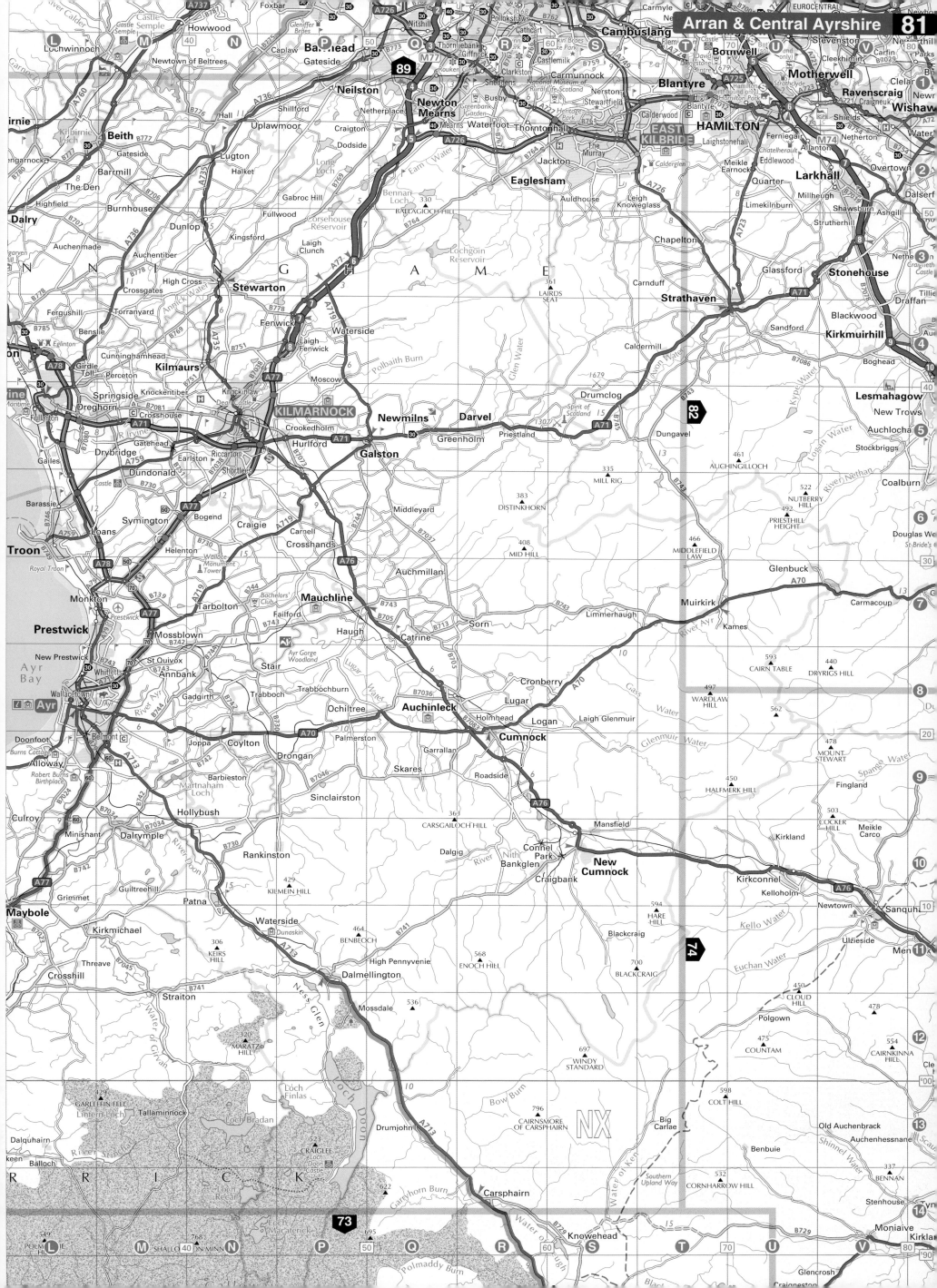

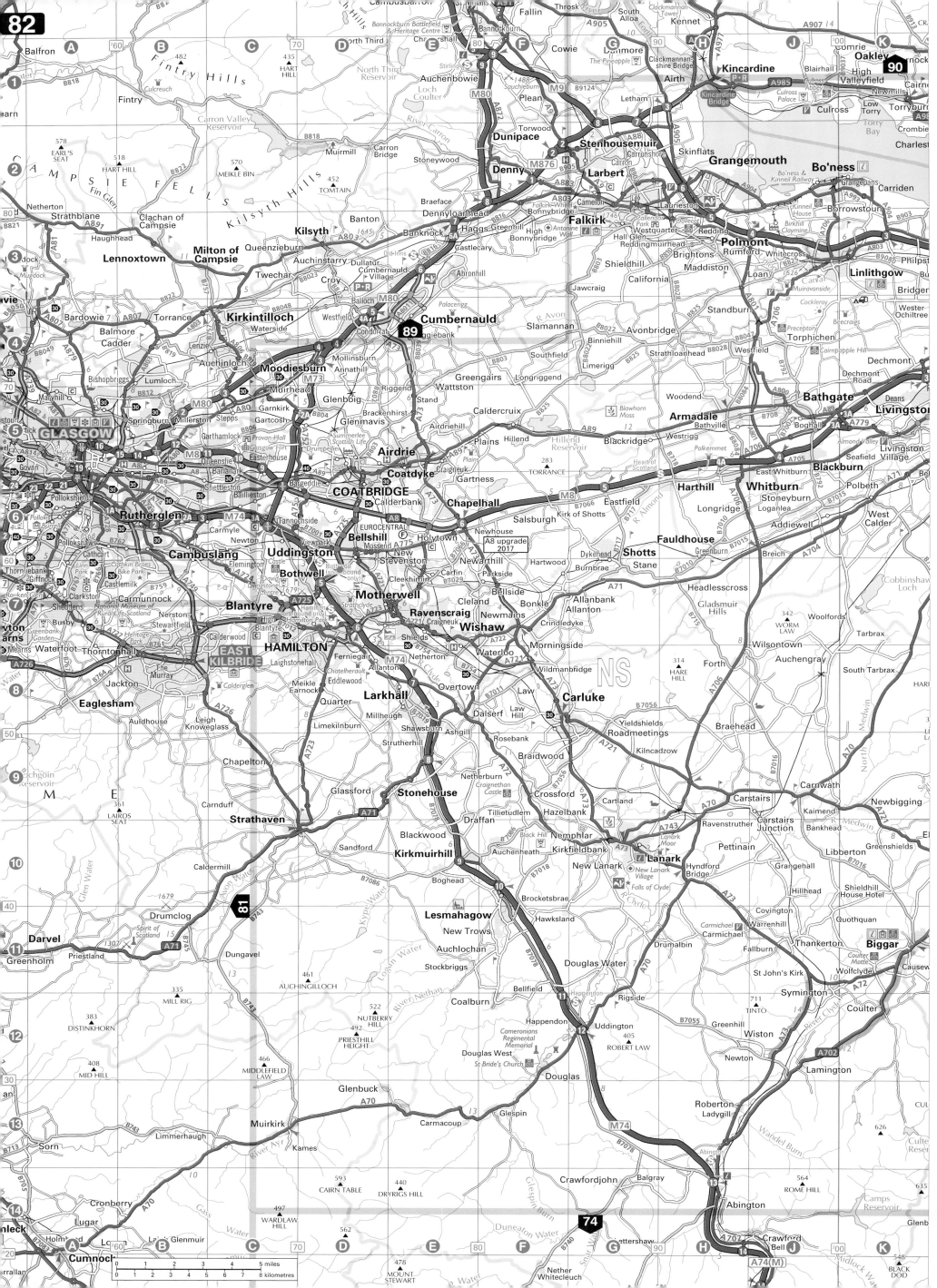

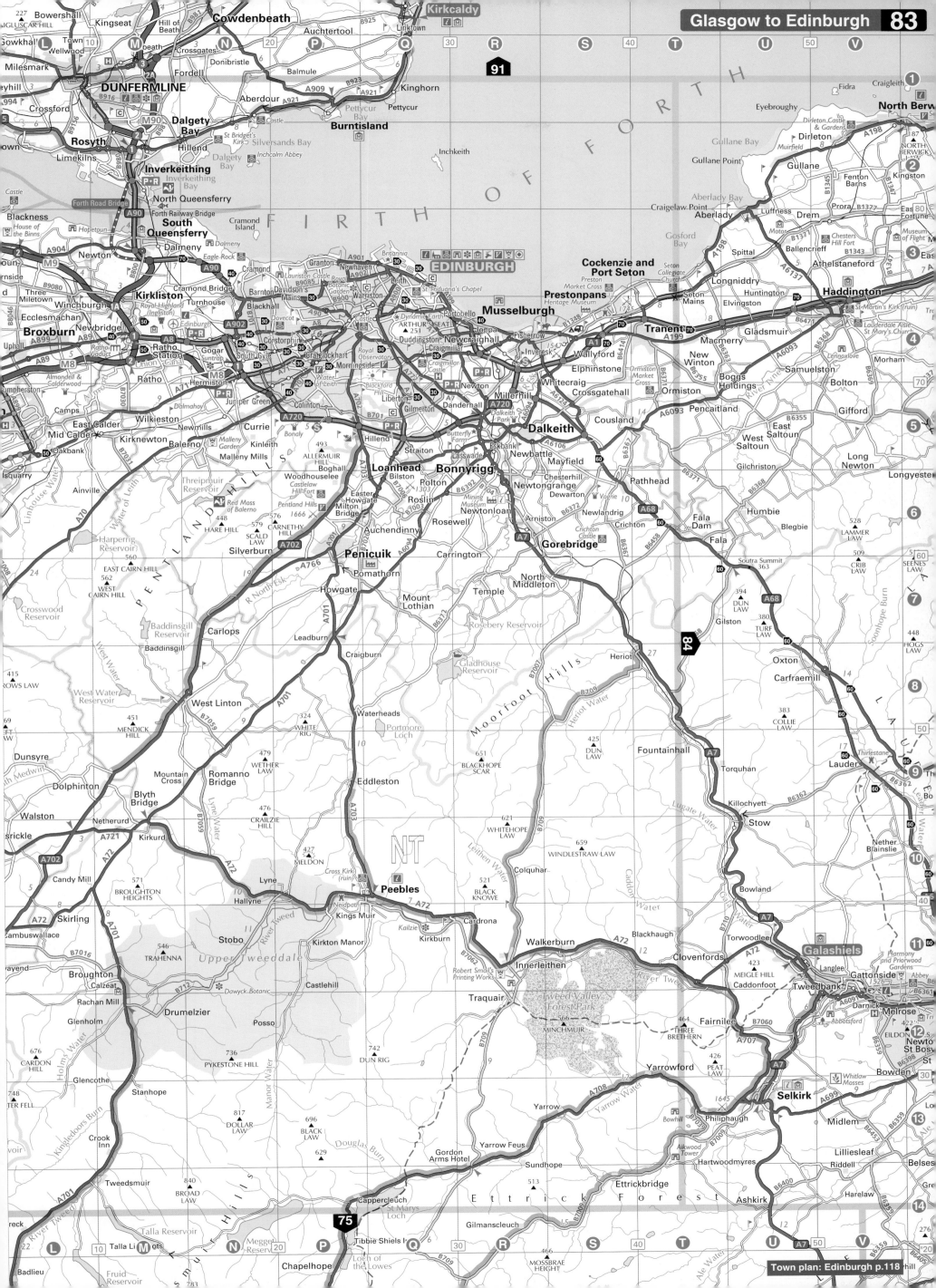

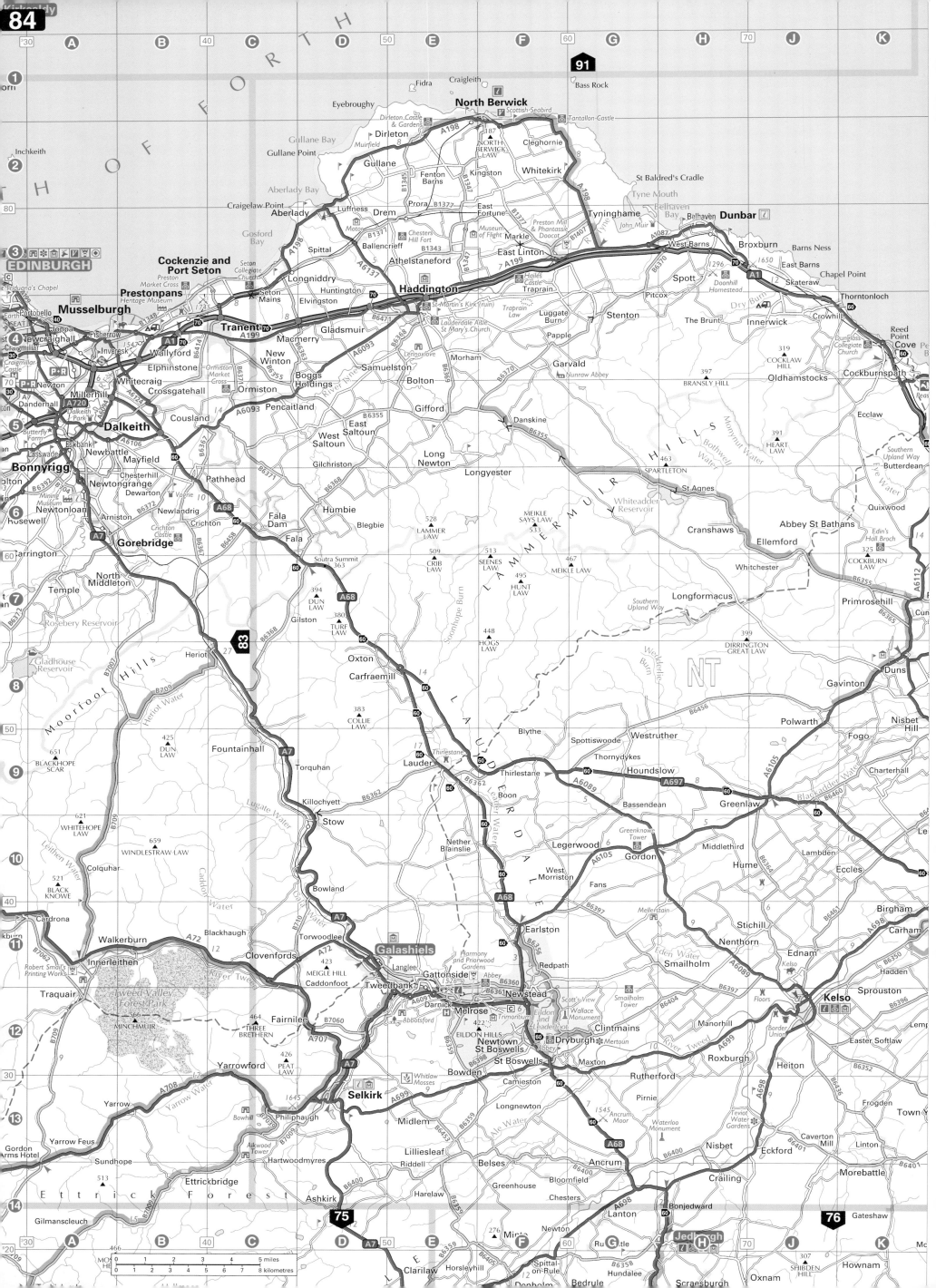

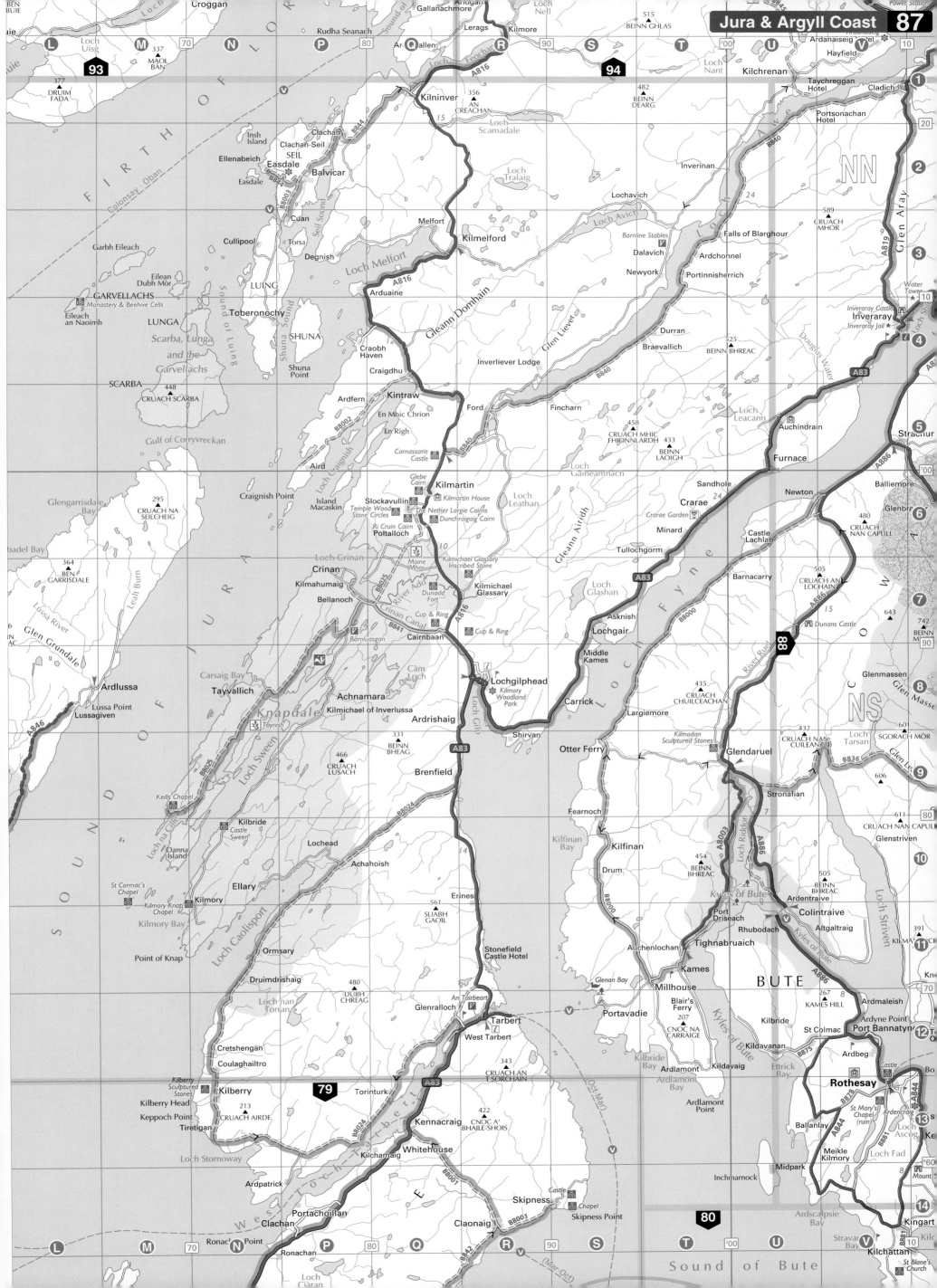

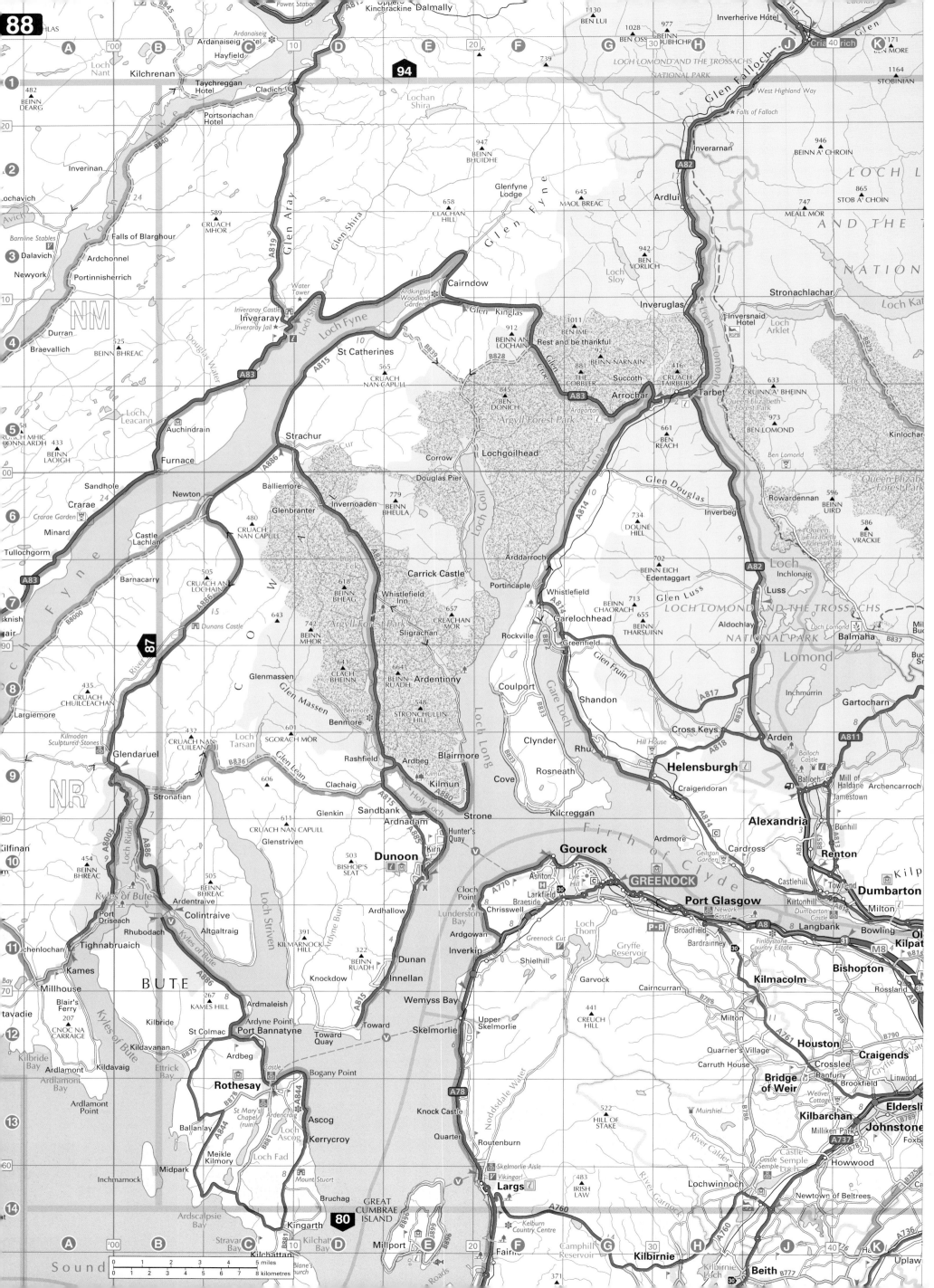

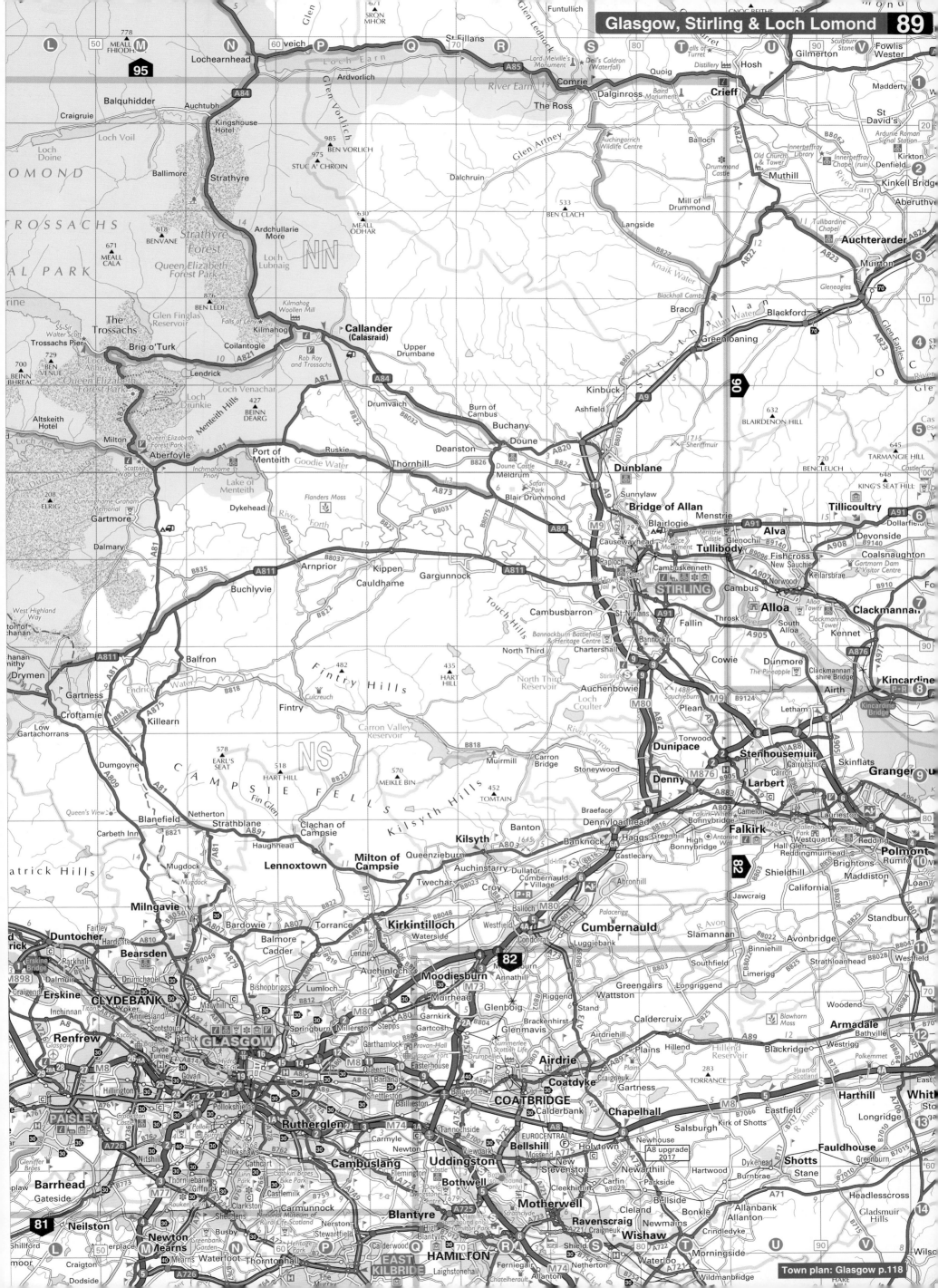

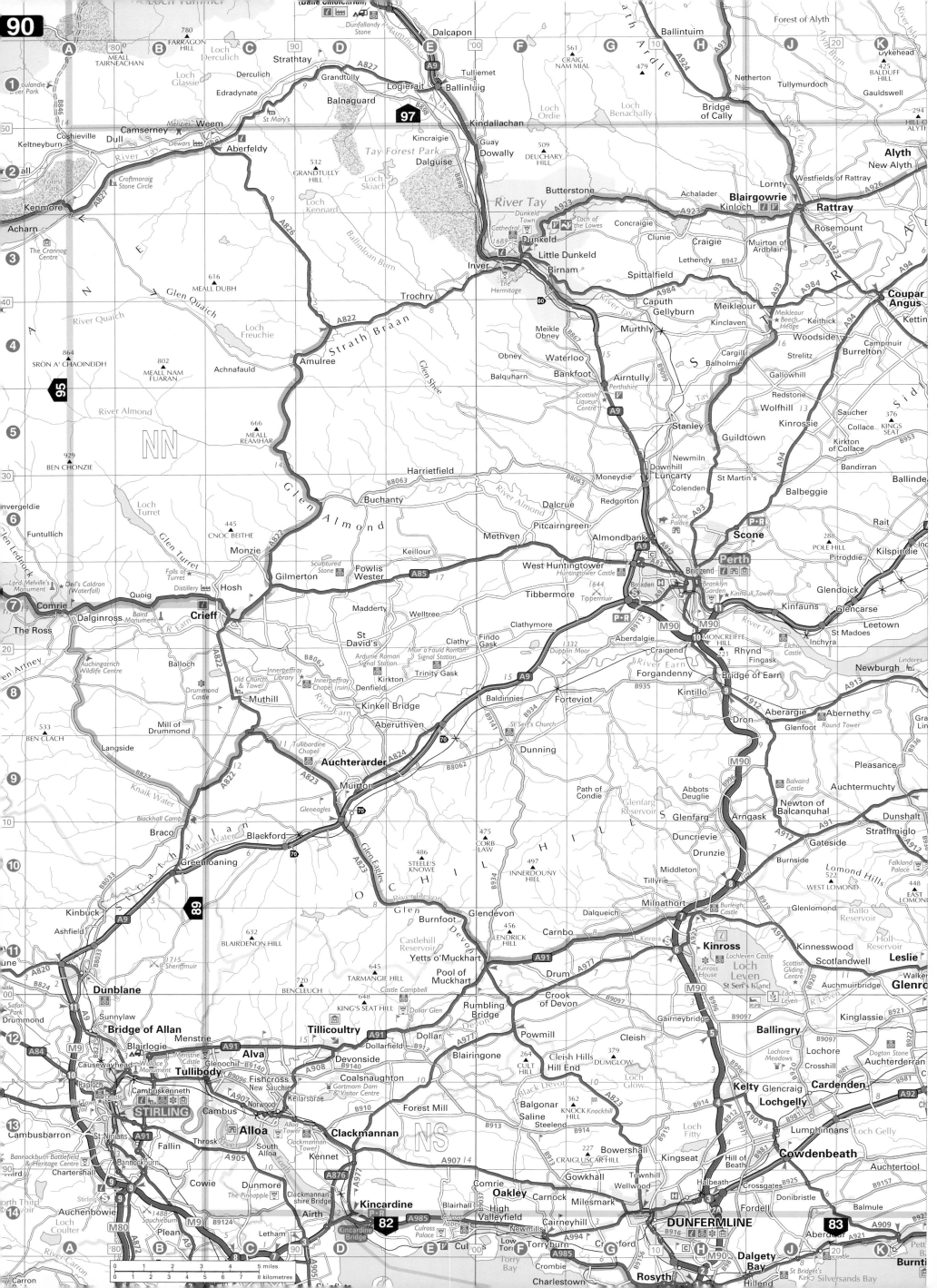

NL

COLL

Rudha nam Meirleach

The Small

Eilean nan Each

Eilean Mòr
Rudha Mòr
Rudha Sgor-innis
Bousd
Sorisdale
Bagh a Chaisteil (Castlebay)
Loch Baghasdail (Lochboisdale)

Ardnan Po

Arnabost
Grishipoll
Clabhach
Loch Cliad
Cliad Bay
B8072
B8071
Coll, Oban
Quinish

Hogh Bay
Ballyhaugh
Arinagour
B8070
Totronald
Coll
Acha
Feall Bay
Arileod
Uig
Eilean Ornsay
Caliach Point
Calgary
Calgary Point
Crossapol Bay
Rudha Fàsachd
Calgary Bay
Treshnish Point
Ensay
CÀRN

Bagh a Chaisteil (Castlebay)
Gunna
(Mar-Oct)
Loch Breachacha
Rudh' a' Chaoil
Burg

Rudha Port Bhiosd
Clachan Mor
Balephetrish Bay
Caoles
B8069
Rudha Dubh
Fladda
Loch Bhasapoll
B8068
Ruaig
Lunga
Haugh Bay
Ballevullin
Cornoigmore
Kenovay
Gott Bay
Loch
Kilkenneth
B8068
Tiree
Scarinish
TRESHNISH ISLES
Gometra
Moss
Heylipoll
B8065
Middleton
Crossapoll
TIREE
Barrapoll
B8065
Hynish Bay
Loch a Phuill
B8067
Balemartine
Bac Mòr or Dutchmans Cap
UL
Rinn Thorbhais
Mannel
Bac Beag
Balephuill Bay
Hynish

Staffa
Fingal's Cave
Little Colonsay
Loch na Keal, Isle of Mull

Rudha nan Cearc
IONA
Iona Abbey & Nunnery
Baile Mòr
Kintra
MacLean's Cross
Fionnphort
(Mar-Oct)
Aridhglas
Loch na Lathaich
St Columba Exhibition Centre
86
Bunessan
Soa Island
ROSS OF MULL
Erraid
Ardchiavaig

0 1 2 3 4 5 miles
0 1 2 3 4 5 6 7 8 kilometres

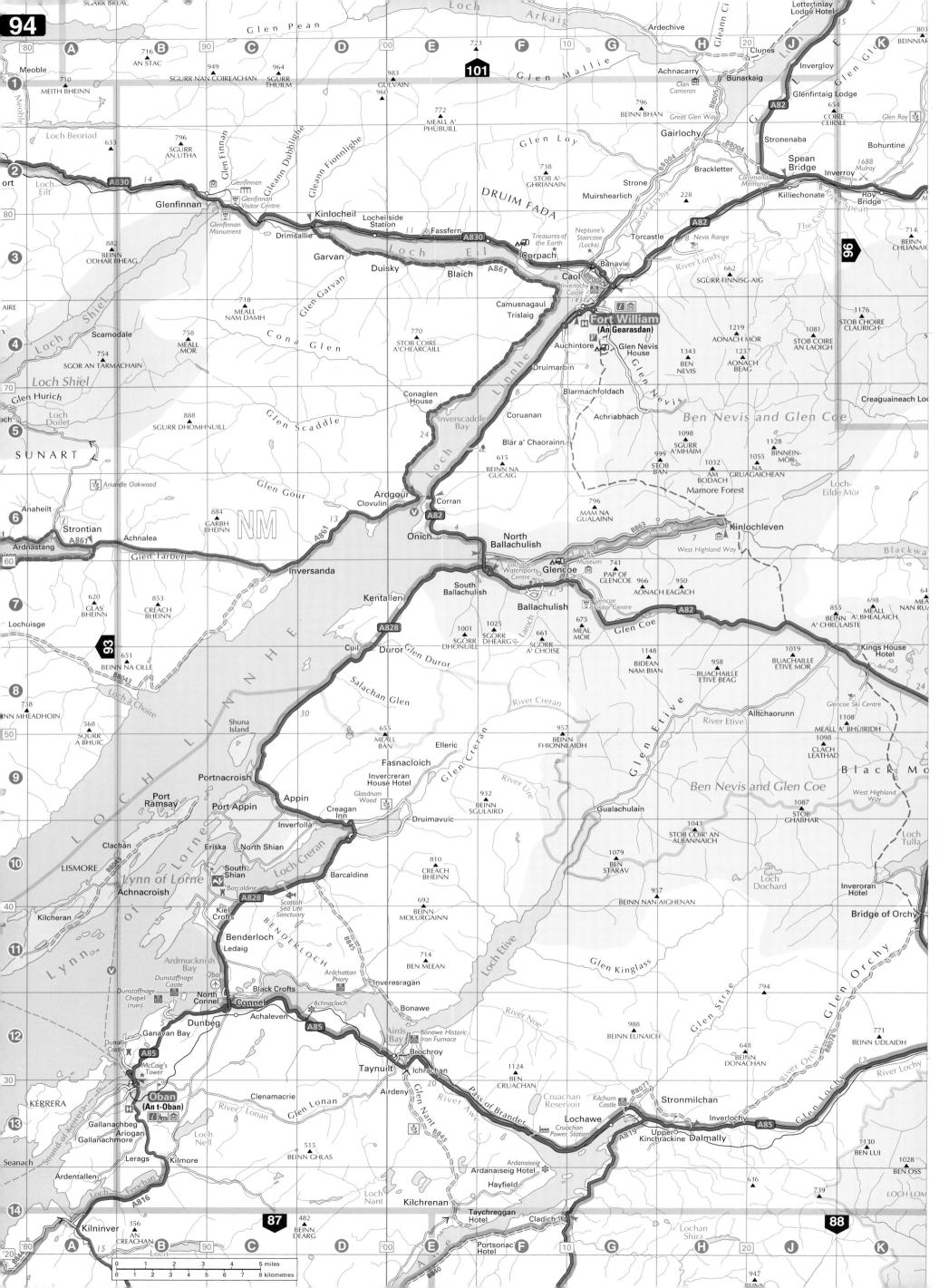

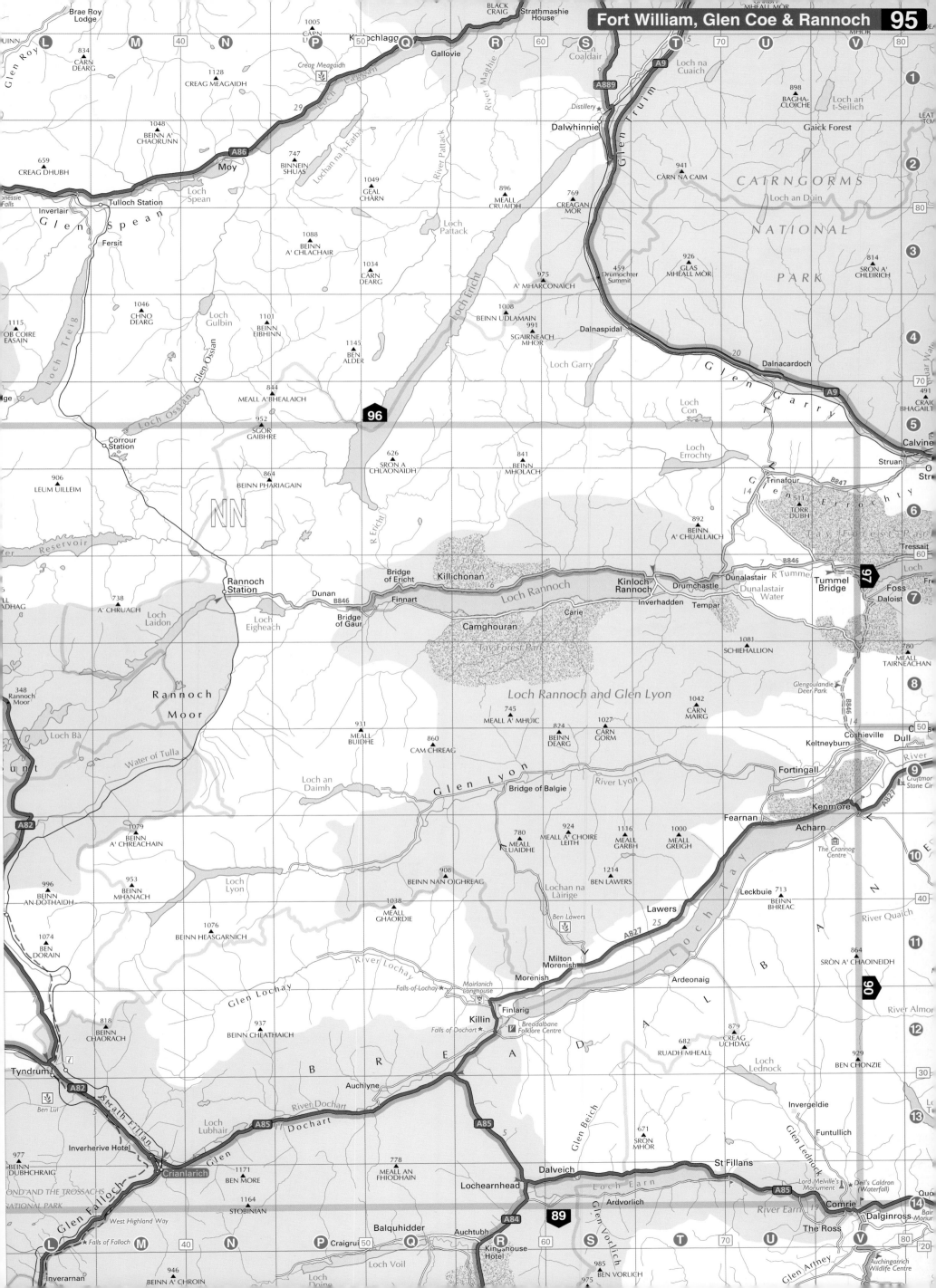

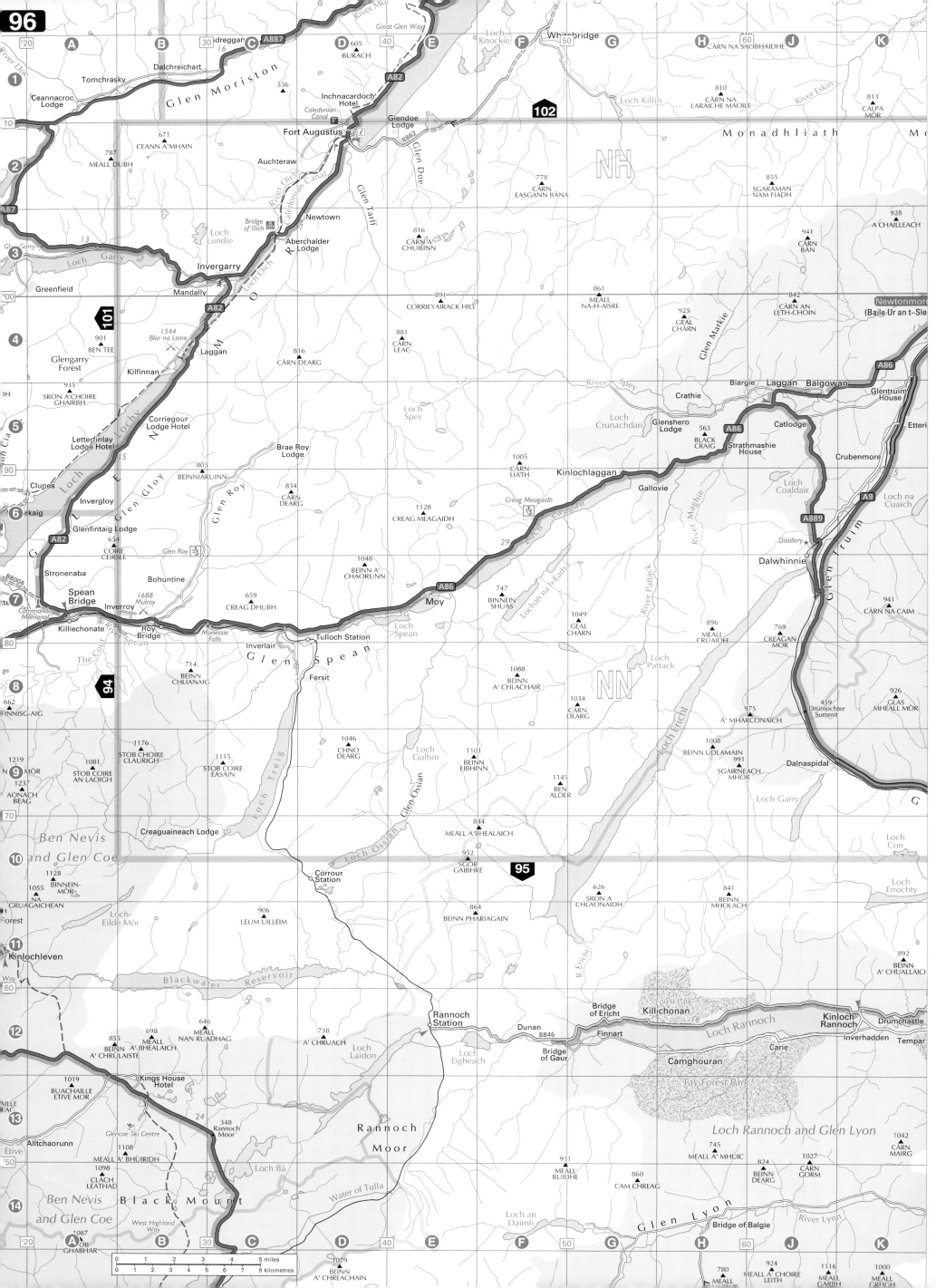

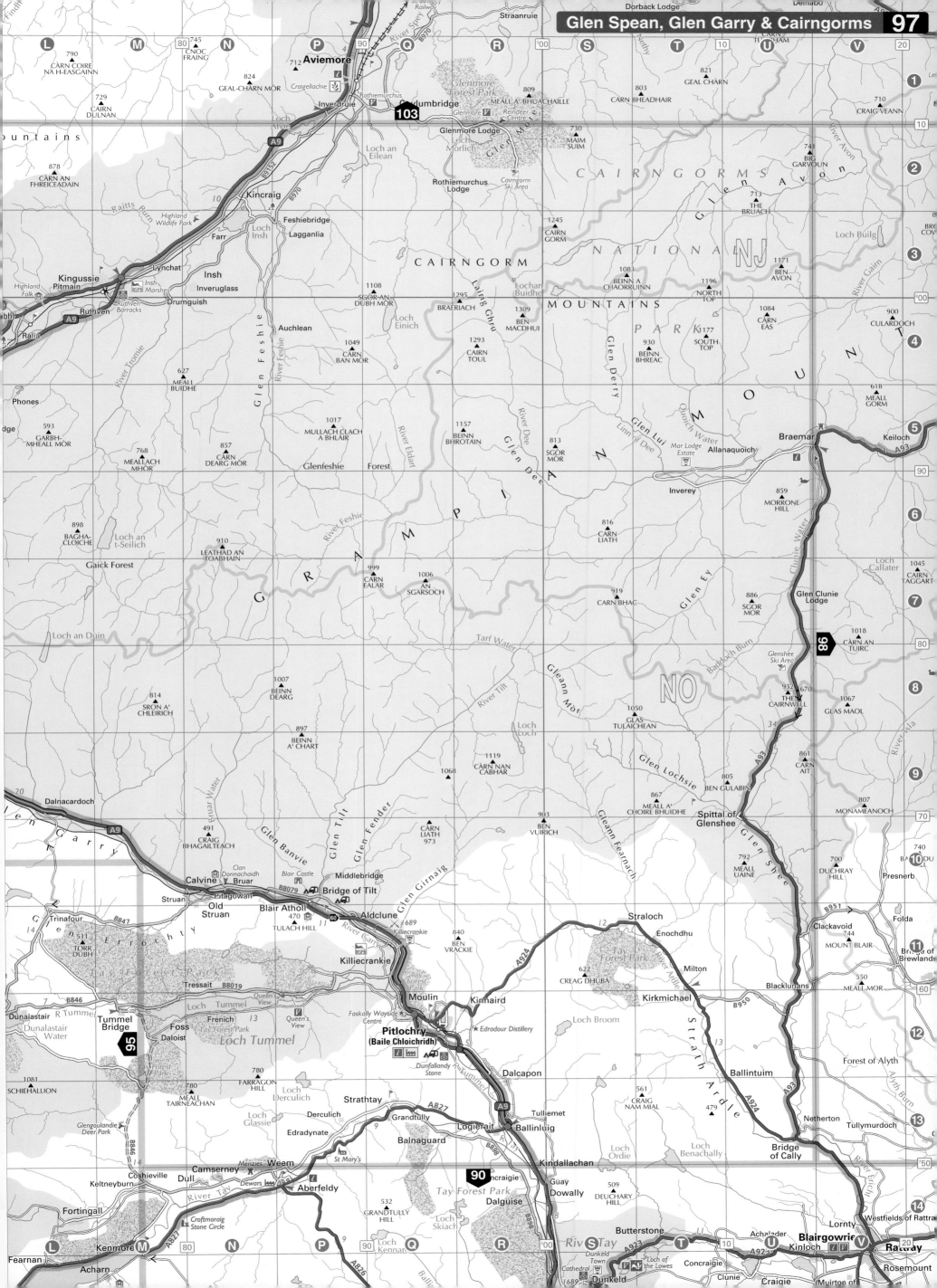

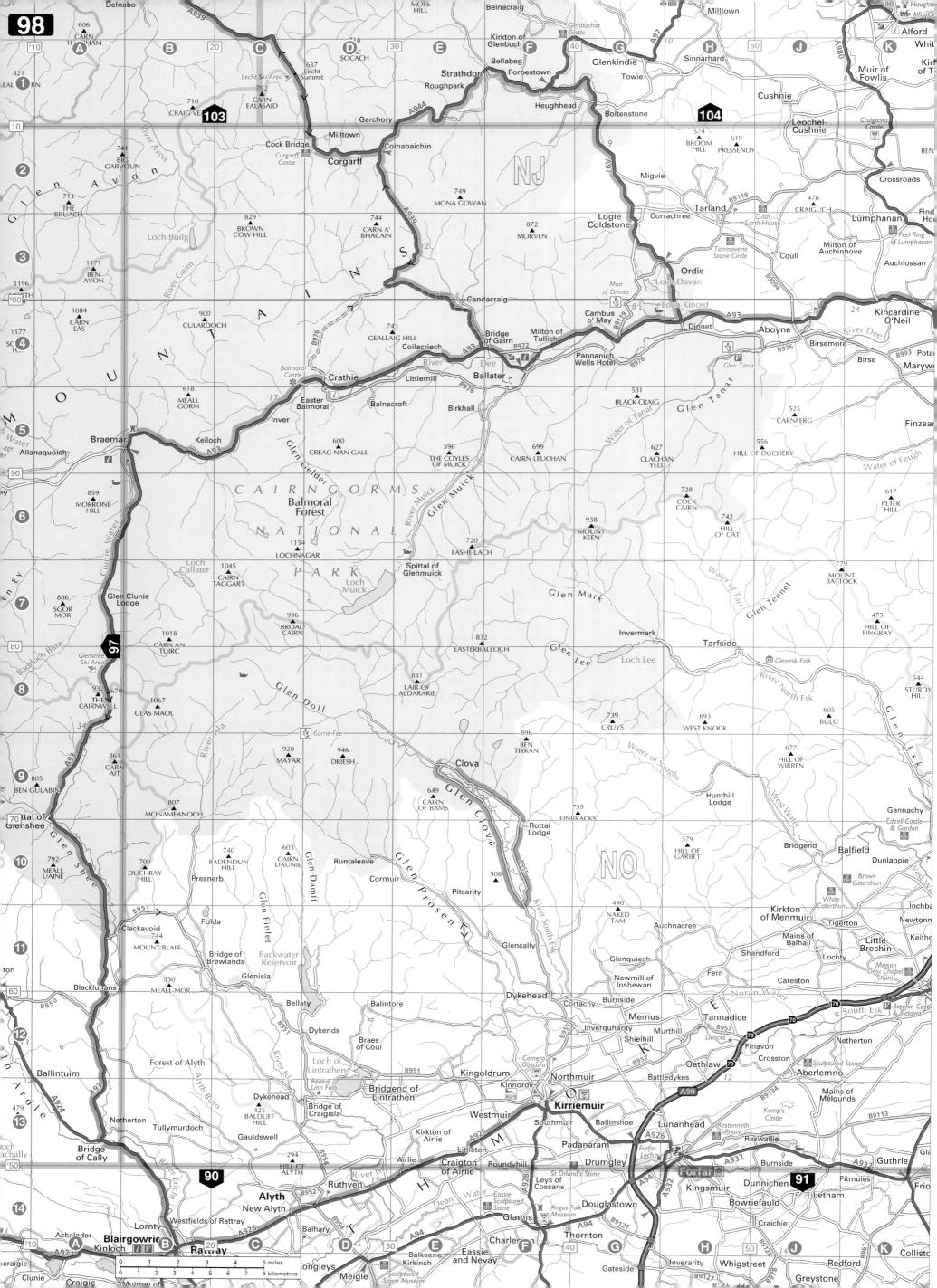

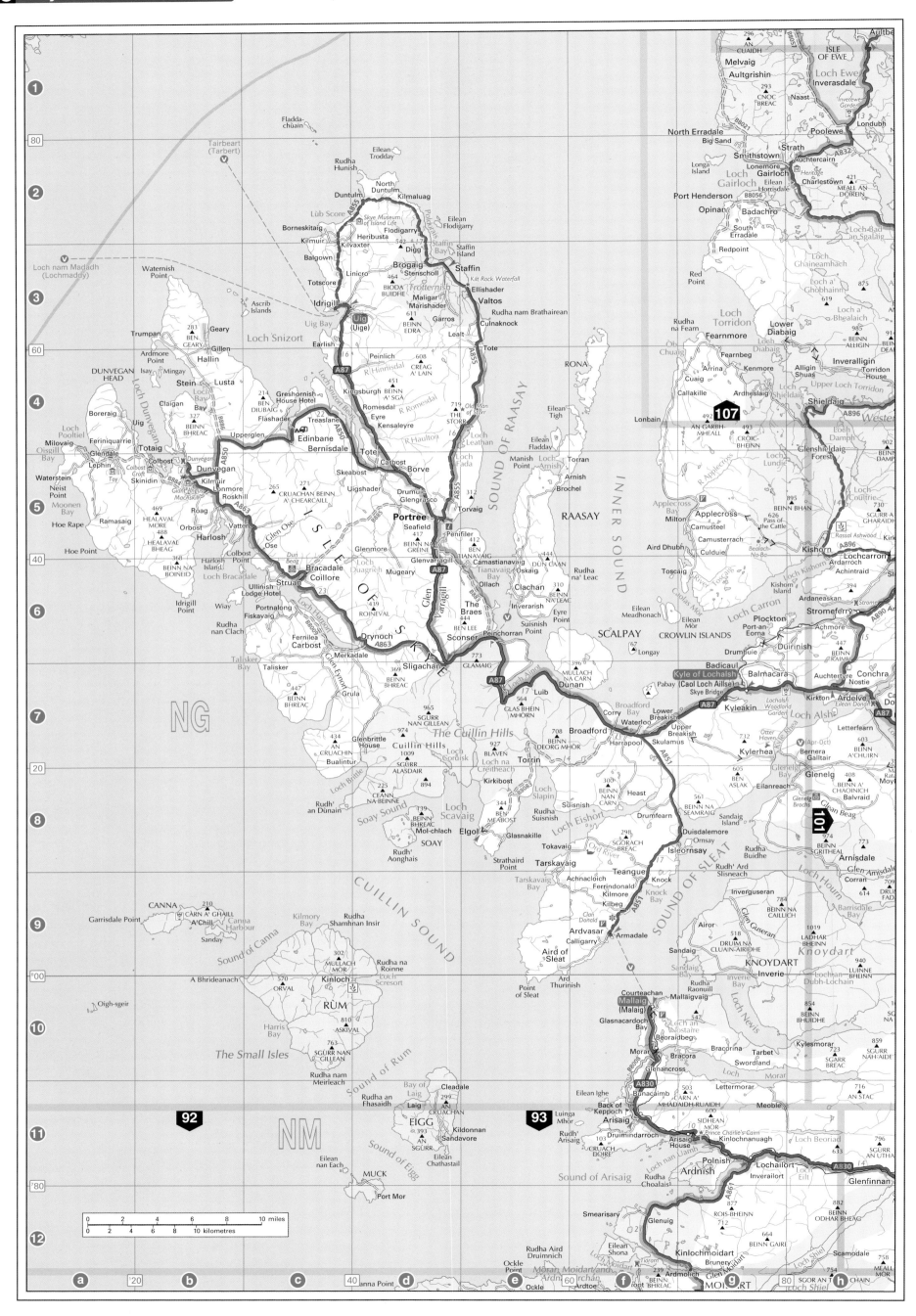

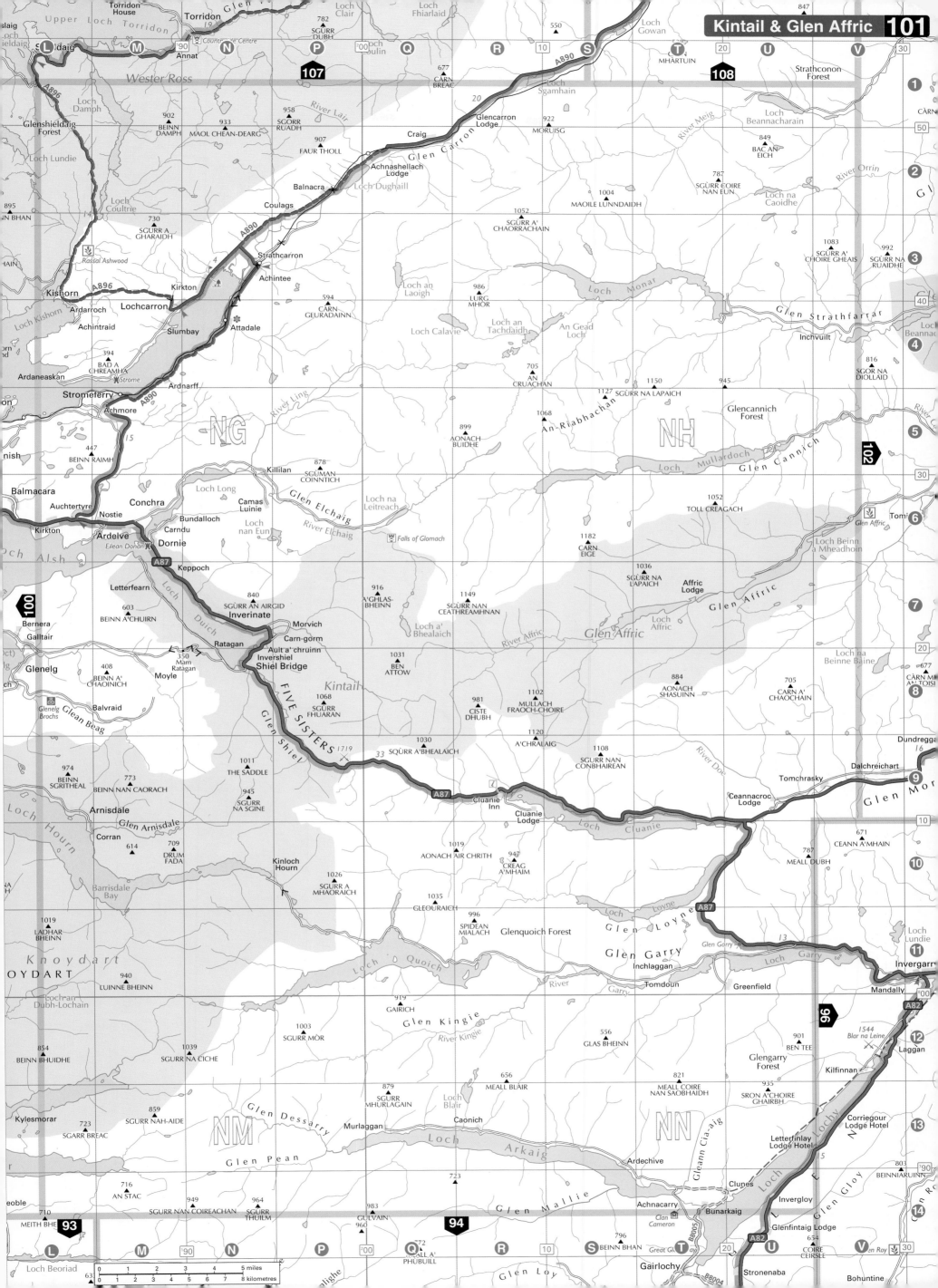

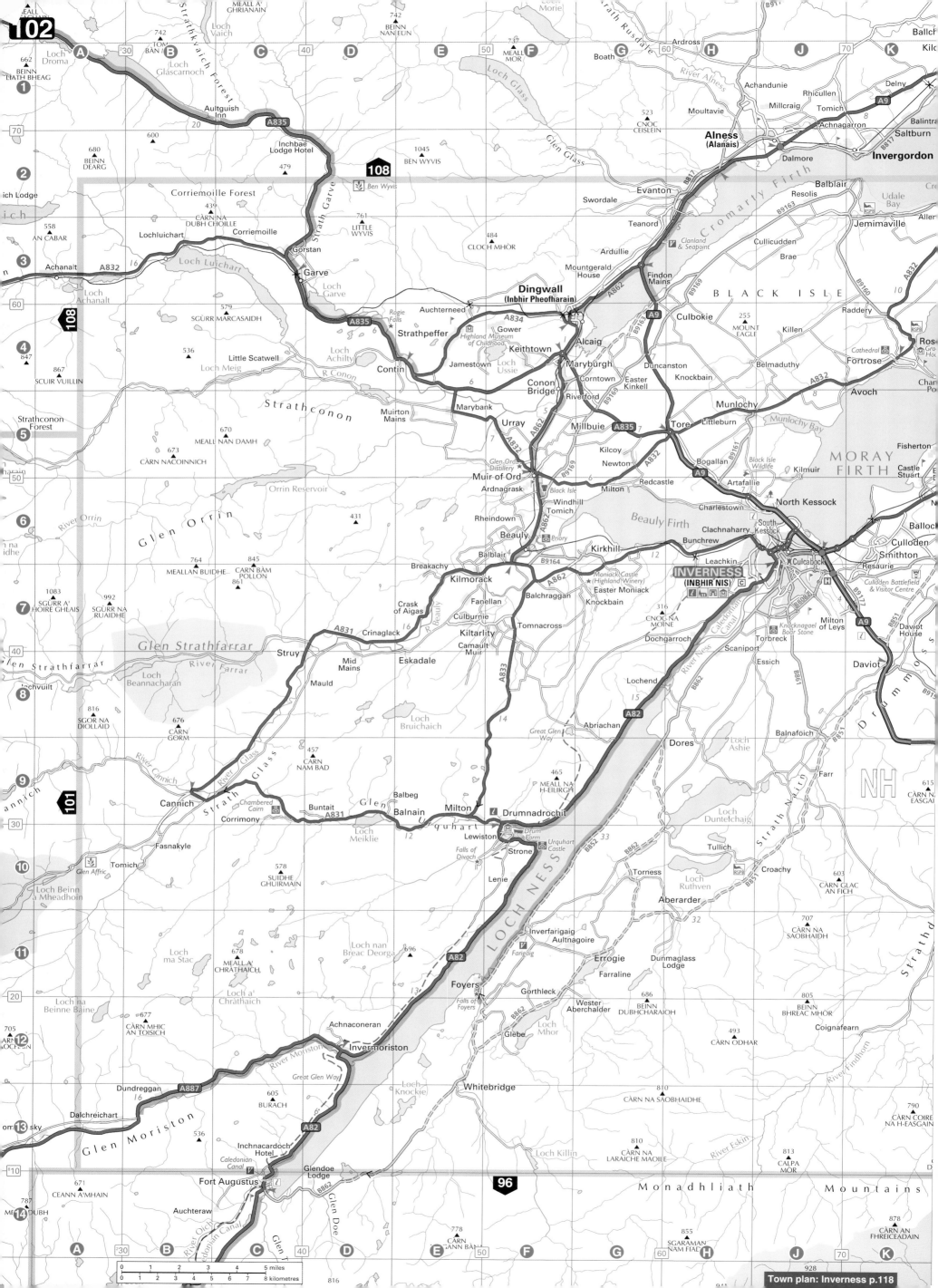

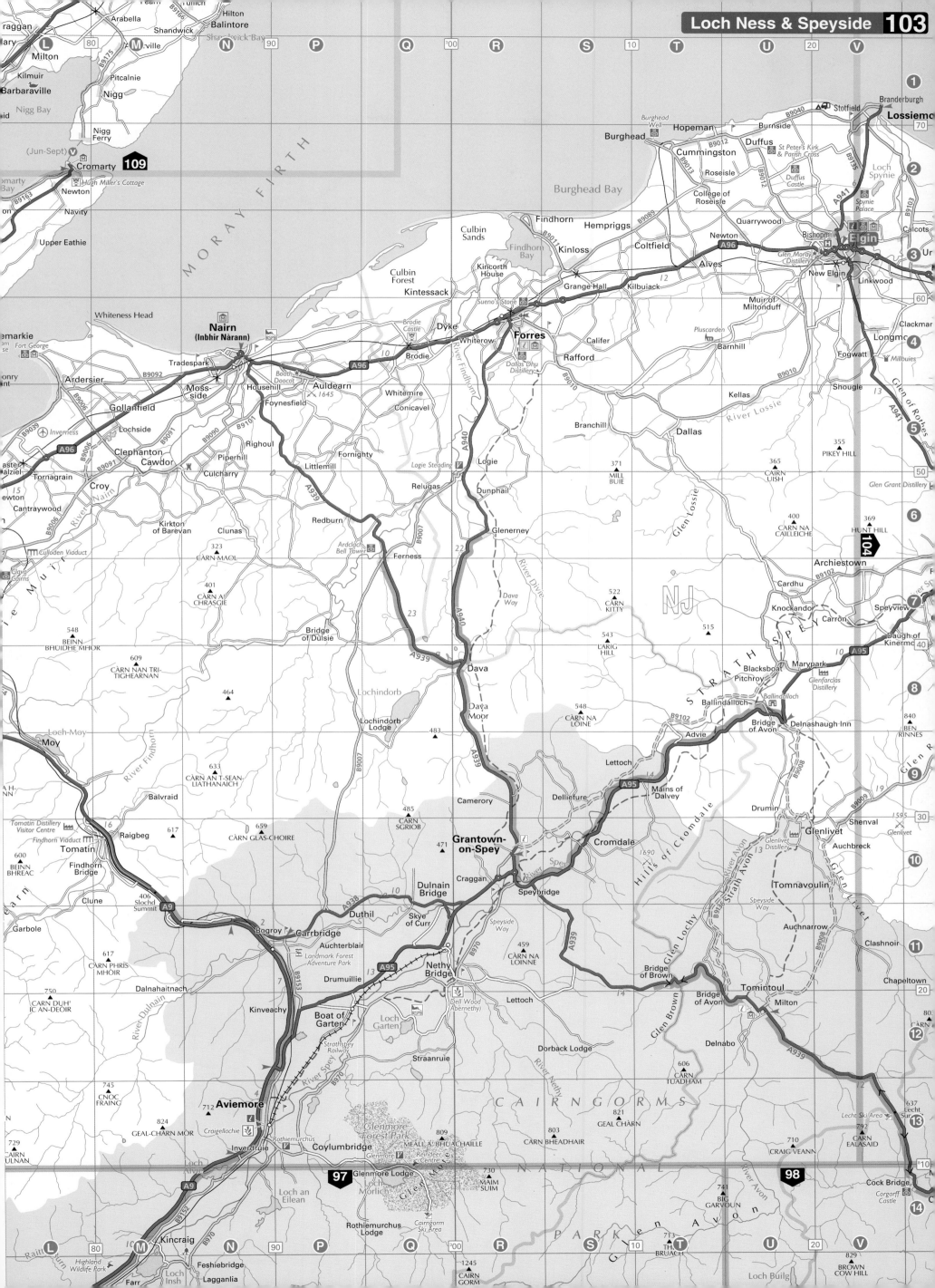

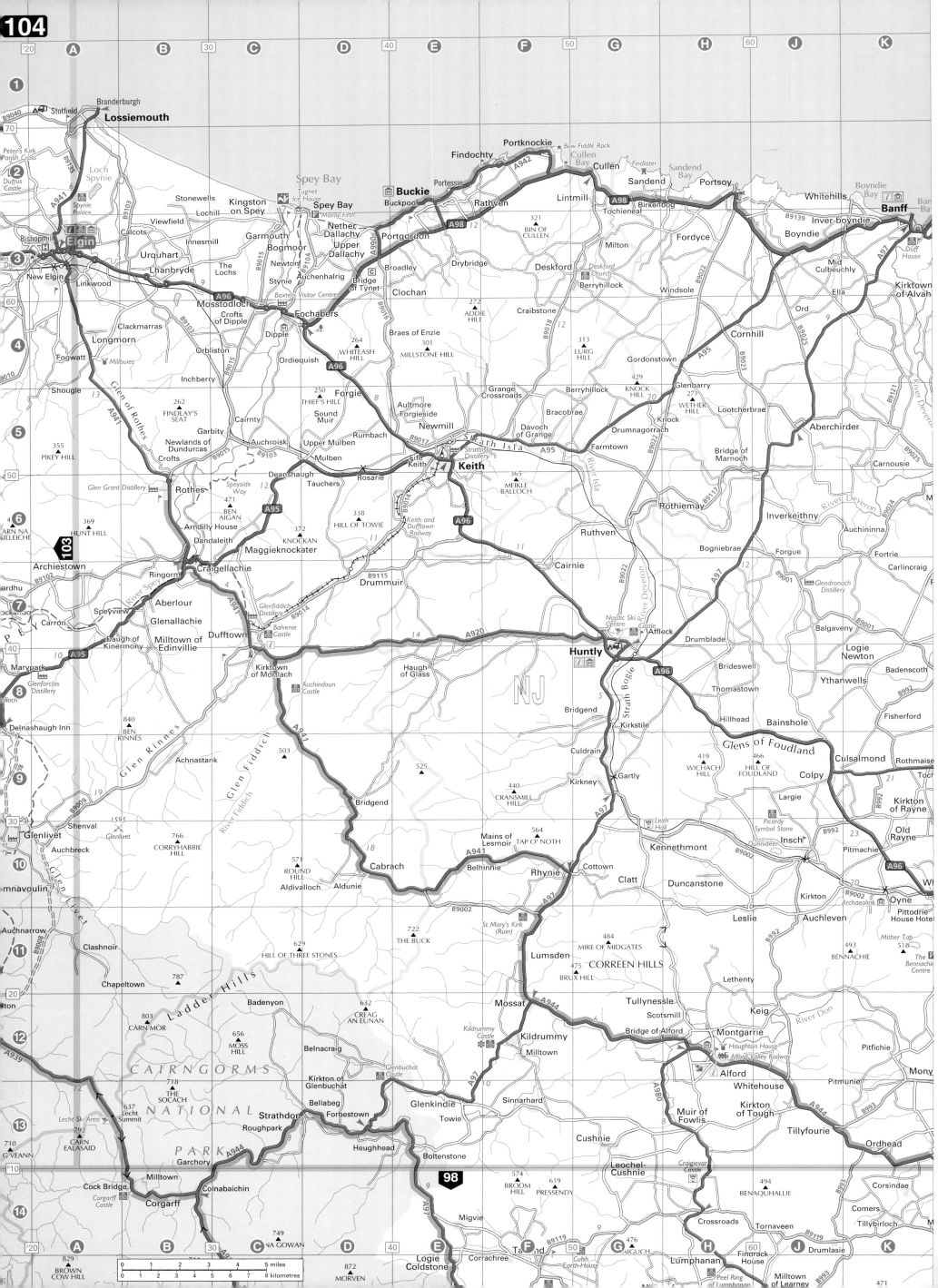

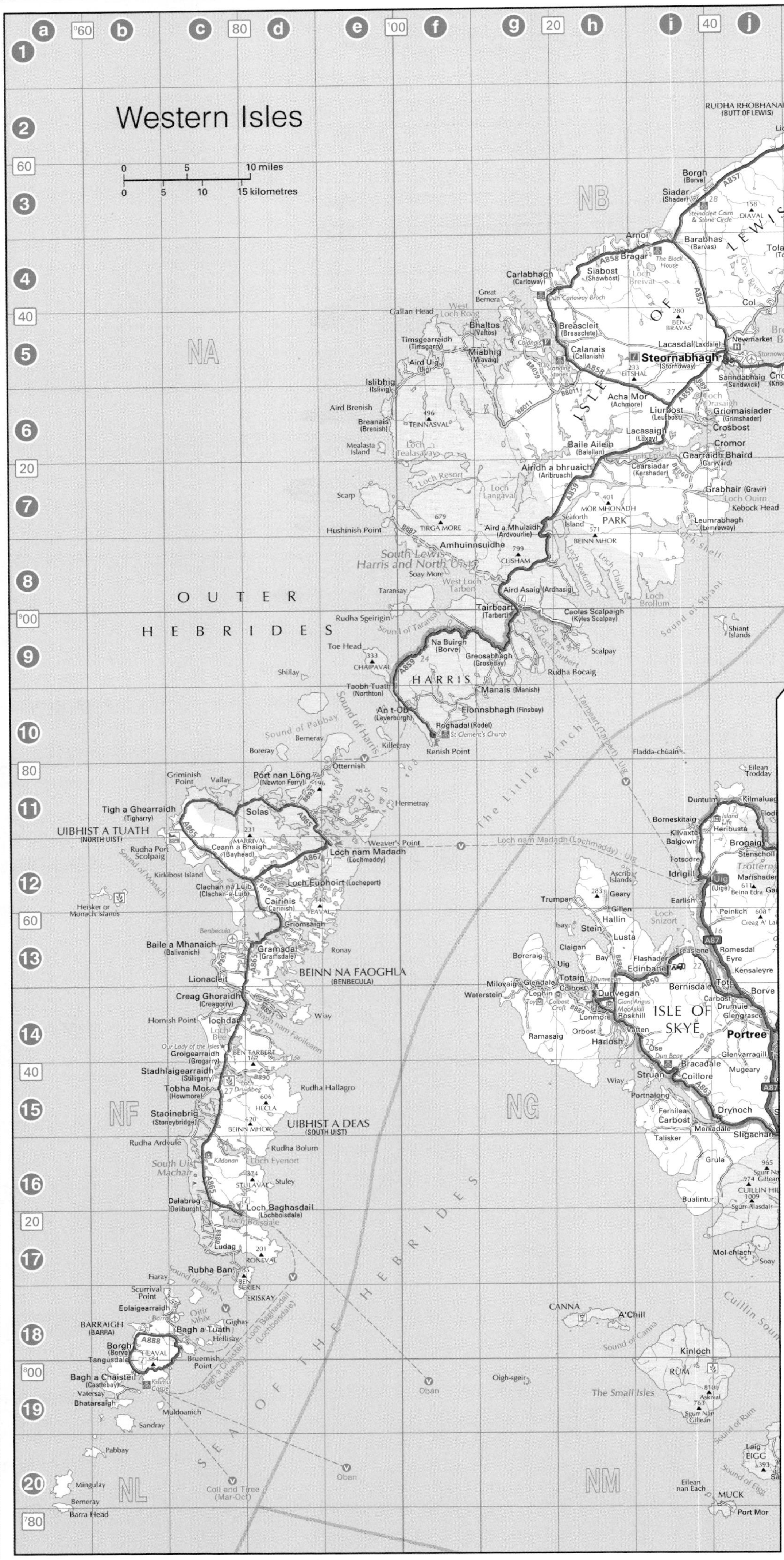

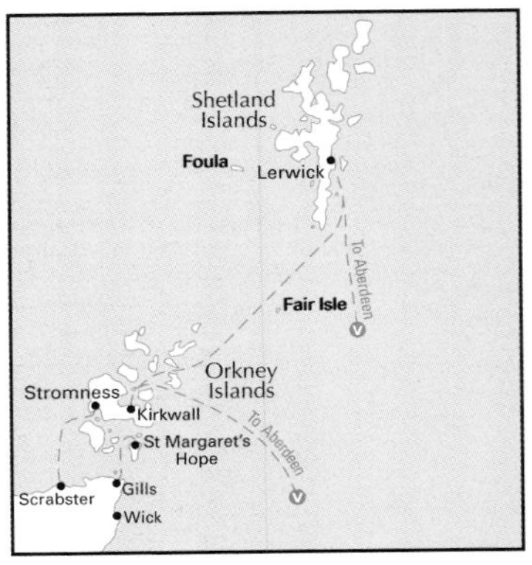

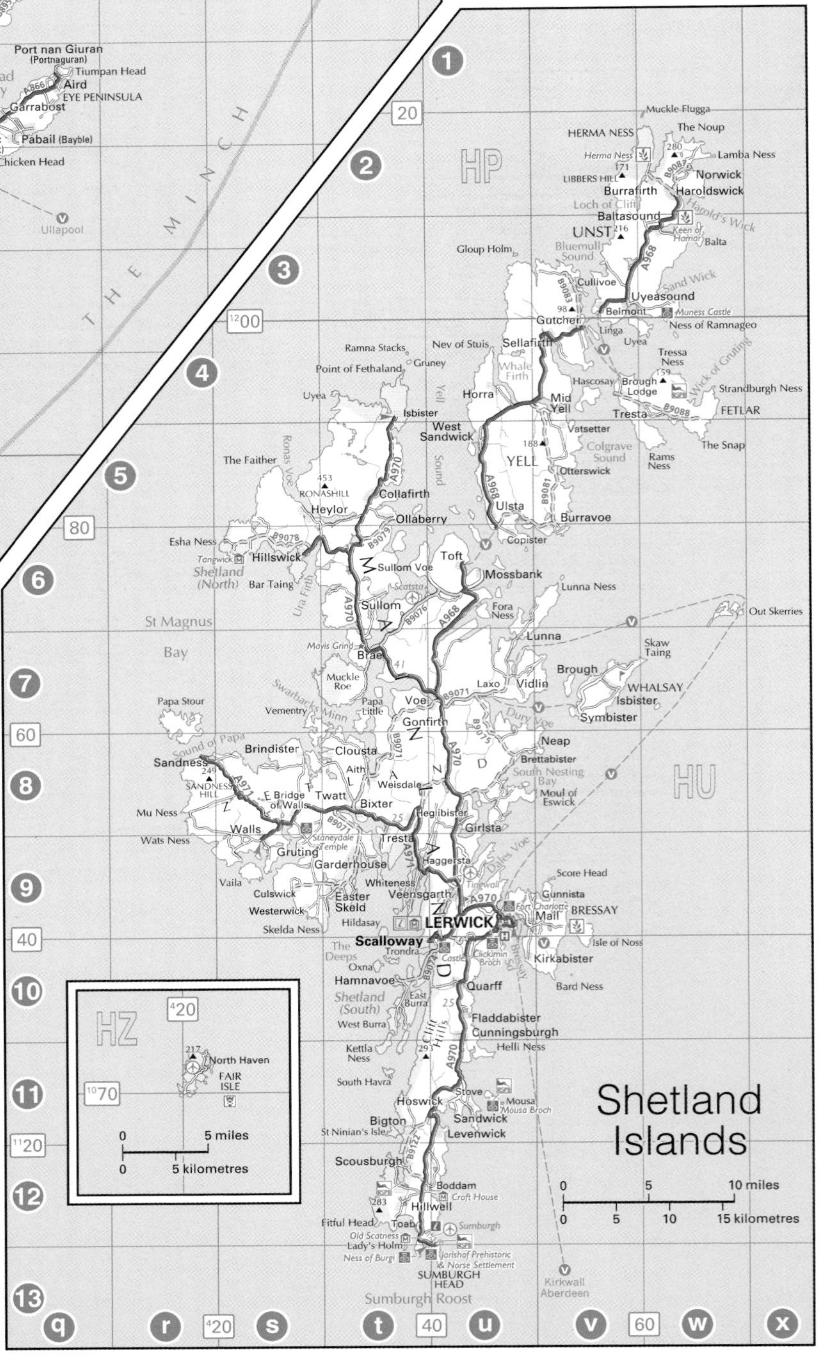

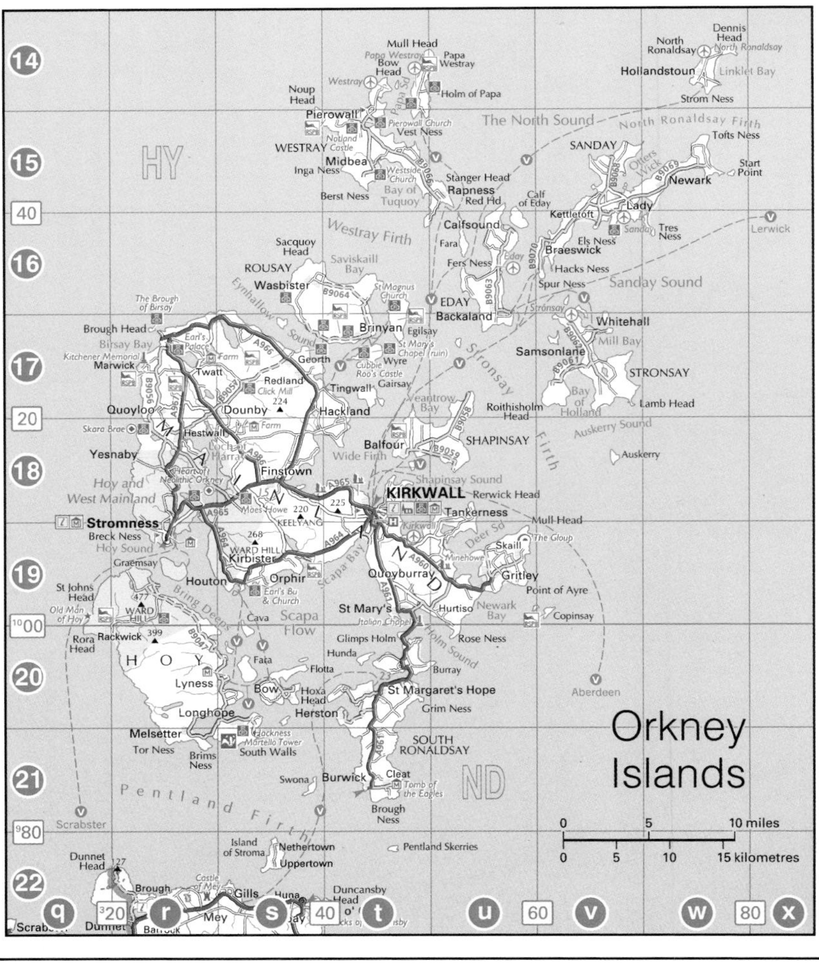

Western Isles

Isle of Lewis

NB

NA

OUTER

HEBRIDES

Steornabhagh (Stornoway)

HARRIS

South Lewis, Harris and North Uist

NF

NG

Isle of Skye

Portree

UIBHIST A TUATH (NORTH UIST)

BEINN NA FAOGHLA (BENBECULA)

UIBHIST A DEAS (SOUTH UIST)

BARRAIGH (BARRA)

NL

NM

The Small Isles

SEA OF THE HEBRIDES

SOUND OF THE HEBRIDES

Shetland Islands

HP

HU

HZ

FAIR ISLE

LERWICK

SCALLOWAY

YELL

UNST

FETLAR

Orkney Islands

HY

ND

KIRKWALL

Stromness

WESTRAY

SANDAY

STRONSAY

EDAY

ROUSAY

HOY

SOUTH RONALDSAY

FERRY SERVICES

Western Isles

Lewis is linked by ferry to the mainland at Ullapool, with daily sailings. There are ferry services from Harris (Tairbeart) and North Uist (Loch nam Madadh) to Uig on Skye. Harris and North Uist are connected by a ferry service between An t-Ob (Leverburgh) and Berneray, and then by causeway to Otternish. South Uist and Barra are served by ferry services from Oban, and a ferry service operates between Eriskay and Barra, and another causeway links South Uist to Eriskay.

Berneray, North Uist, Benbecula, South Uist and Eriskay are all connected by causeways.

Shetland Islands

The main service is from Aberdeen on the mainland to the island port of Lerwick. A service from Kirkwall (Orkney) to Lerwick is also available. Shetland Islands Council operates an inter-island car ferry service.

Orkney Islands

The main service is from Scrabster on the Caithness coast to Stromness and there is a further service from Gills (Caithness) to St Margaret's Hope on South Ronaldsay. A service from Aberdeen to Kirkwall provides a link to Shetland at Lerwick. Inter-island car ferry services are also operated (advance reservations recommended).

NC

NB

NG

NH

Wester Ross

COIGACH

BEINN EIGHE

Glen Torridon

Glen Docherty

Places and features:

Soyea Island
Loch Inver
Lochinver
Inverkirkaig
River Kirkaig
Fionn Loch
SUILVEN 732
Enard Bay
Eilean Mòr
Rhu Coigach
Rubha Mòr
Reiff
Achnahaird
Altandhu
Loch Sionascaig
CUL MO
Eilean Mullagrach
Isle Ristol
Polbain
Loch Osgaig
Badentarbet
STAC POLLAIDH 612
SUMMER ISLES
Achiltibuie
CUL BEAG 769
Loch Lurgainn
Glas-leac Mòr
Tanera Beg
Badentarbat Bay
Polglass
Ben Mor Coigach
Steornabhagh (Stornoway)
Tanera Mòr
Horse Island
Horse Sound
Achduart
BEN MORE COIGACH 652
Culnacraig
Glas-leac Beag
Eilean Dubh
Priest Island
Leac Dhonn
Cailleach Head
Isle Martin
Strathcanaird
Strath Canaird
Greenstone Point
Rudha Beag
Ardmair
Mellon Udrigle
Stattic Point
Scoraig
Annat Bay
Morefield
GRUINARD ISLAND
Rhireavach
BEINN GHOBHLACH 635
Ullapool (Ulapul)
Foura
Cove
Laide
Gruinard Bay
Badluarach
Little Loch Broom
A832
Rudha Reidh
Mellon Charles
Ormiscaig
Gruinard
Badralloch
Badcaul
AN CUAIDH 296
Aultbea
A832
SAIL MHOR 764
Ardessie
Camusnagaul
Melvaig
ISLE OF EWE
Loch Ewe
Gruinard River
Dundonnell
32
Ardindrean
Aultgrishin
CREAG-MHEAL BEAG 347
Lochan Gaineamhaich
Inverasdale
CNOC BREAC 293
Loch Fada
Let
Naast
AN TEALLACH 1062
Inverewe Garden
13
MEALL NA MEINE 250
BEINN A' CHAISGEIN BEAG 681
Loch na Sealga
CARN BHIORAIN 507
Crofto
North Erradale
Poolewe
Londubh
BEINN DEARG MHOR 906
Big Sand
Fionn Loch
Wester Ross
Strath
A832
Dubh Loch
Smithstown
Auchtercairn
BEINN AIRIDH CHARR 791
MEALL AN T-SITHE 601
Longa Island
Lonemore
Heritage
Loch a' Bhraoin
Loch Gairloch
Gairloch
Charlestown
MEALL AN DOIREIN 421
Maree
SGURRBAN 974
MULLACH COIRE MHIC FHEARCHAIR 1019
Eilean Horrisdale
BEINN LAIR 859
Lochan Fada
A' CHAILLEACH 999
Port Henderson
B8056
Loch Bad an Sgalaig
Loch Garbhaig
Badachro
Opinan
Loch Maree Hotel
Letterewe
South Erradale
Talladale
A832
SLIOCH 981
Redpoint
Maree
Loch Ghaineamhach
Kinlochewe Forest
BEINN NAN RAMH 711
Red Point
Loch na A-Oidhche
BEINN A' MHUINIDH 680
Loch a' Ghobhainn
BAOSBHEINN 875
Kinlochewe
BEINN AN EOIN 855
FIONN BHEINN 933
Rudha na Fearn
Loch a' Bhealaich
Fearnmore
BEINN BHREAC 619
724
Loch Torridon
Beinn Eighe
Incheril
Fearnbeg
Ob Chuaig
Lower Diabaig
BEINN ALLIGIN 985
RUADH-STAC MOR 1009
Kinlochewe
Arrina
Loch Diabaig
BEINN DEARG 914
972
Kenmore
Cuaig
Inveralligin
LIATHACH 1053
1024
Allt Docherty
Callakille
Allagin Shuas
Torridon House
SGURR DUBH 782
Torridon
Loch Clair
Loch a' Chroisg
Ardheslaig
Upper Loch Torridon
A896
Loch Fhiarlaid
Loch Gowa
Loch Shieldaig
Countryside Centre
Annat
Loch Coulin
Lonbain
AN GARBH-MHEALL 492
Shieldaig
550
CARN BREAC 677
CROIC-BHEINN 493
Wester Ross
Loch Sgamhain
Glenshieldaig Forest
A896
Loch Damph
SGORR RUADH 902
MAOL CHEAN-DEARG 958
River Lair
Glen Docherty
A890
BEINN DAMPH
SGORR RUADH 907
MORUISG
Craig
Carron

0 1 2 3 4 5 miles
0 1 2 3 4 5 6 7 8 kilometres

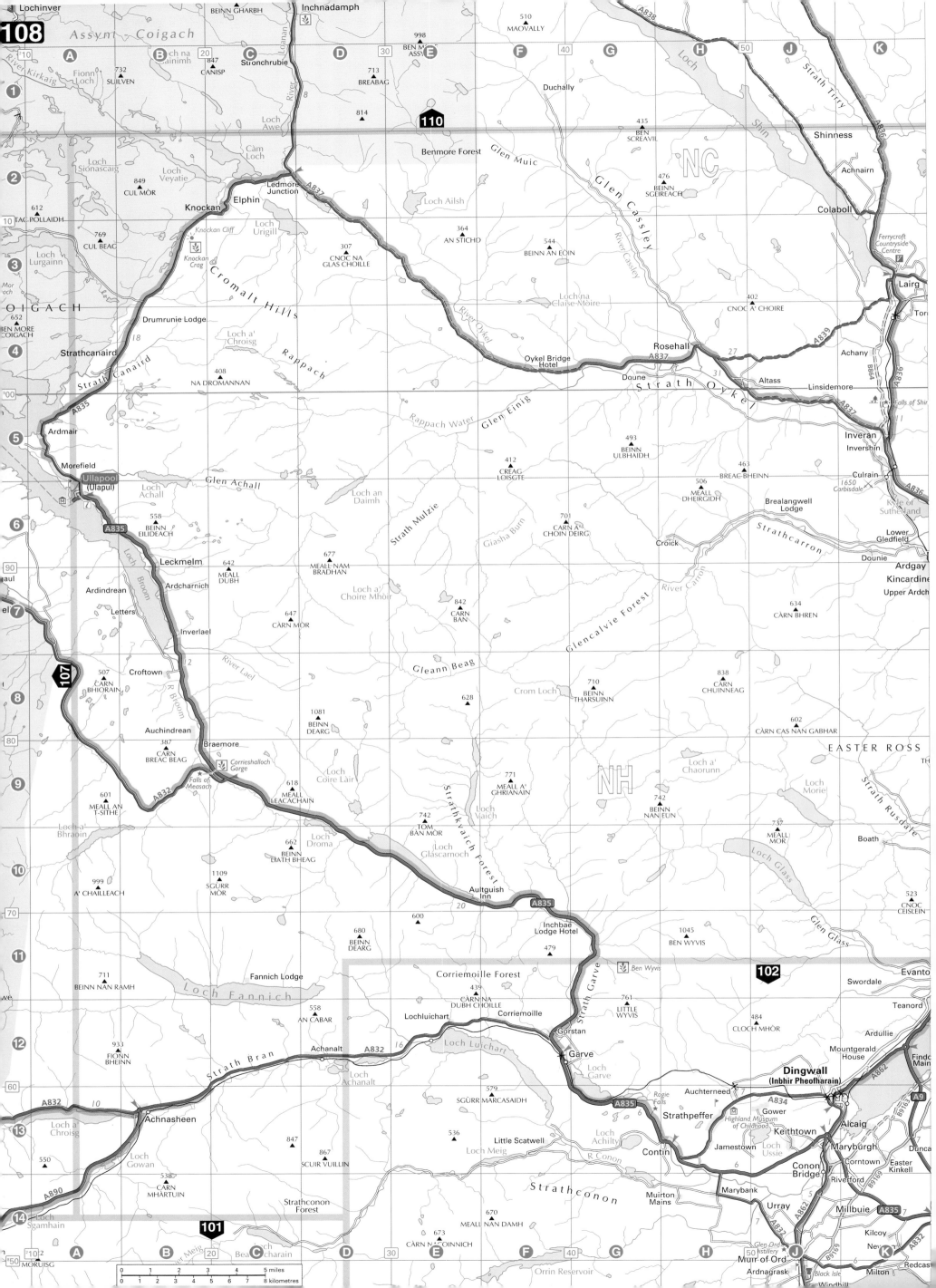

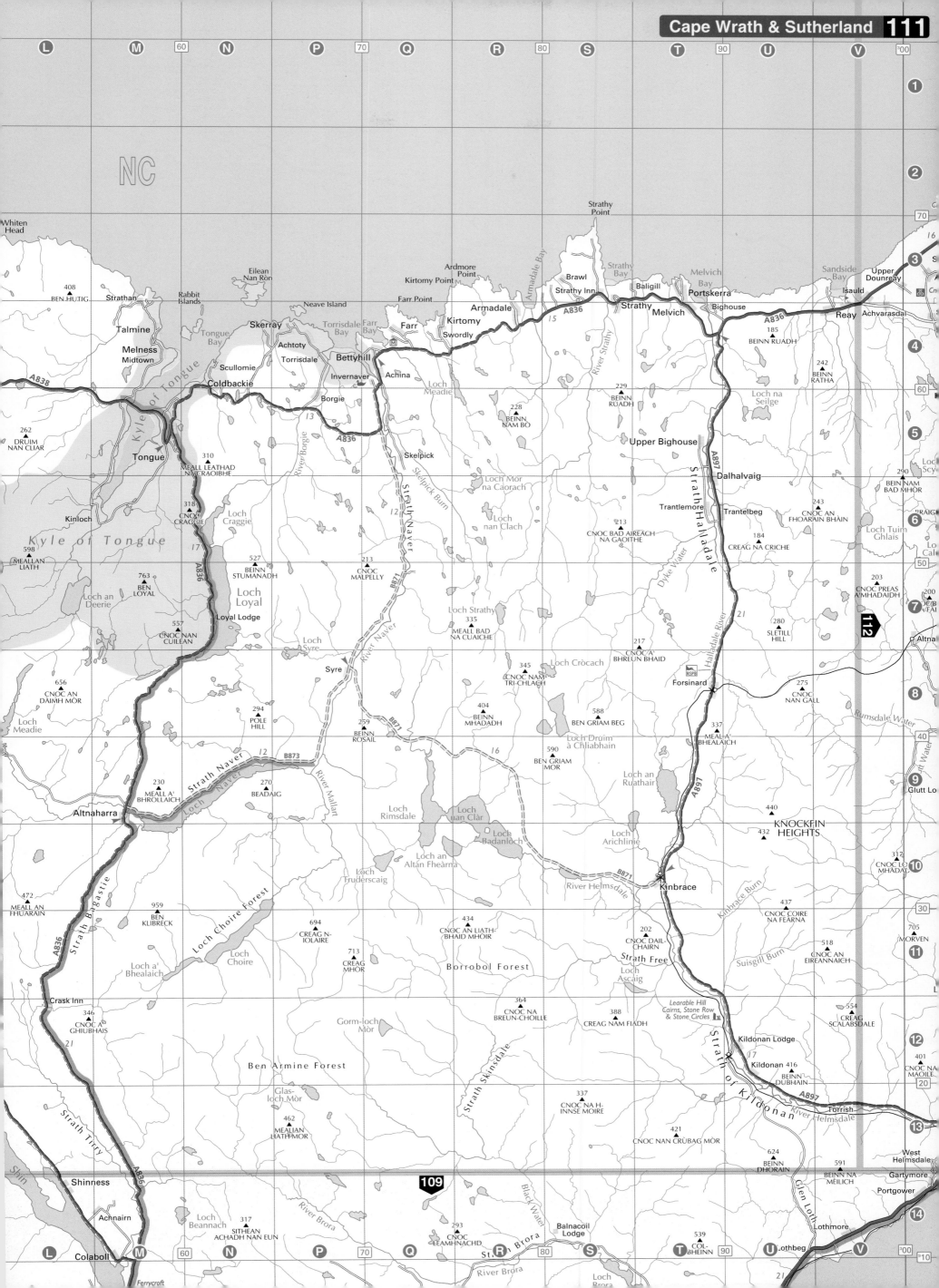

NC

Whiten Head

408 ▲ BEN HUTIG
Strathan

Talmine

Melness
Midtown

A838

262 ▲ DRUIM NAN CLIAR

Tongue

Kinloch

Kyle of Tongue

598 ▲ MEALLAN LIATH

763 ▲ BEN LOYAL

Loch an Deerie

Rabbit Islands

Eilean Nan Ròn

Tongue Bay

Skerray

Achtoty

Scullomie

Torrisdale

Coldbackie

Borgie

310 ▲ MEALL LEATHAD NA CRAOIBHE

318 ▲ CNOC CRAGGIE

Loch Craggie

527 ▲ BEINN STUMANADH

Loyal Lodge

557 ▲ CNOC NAN CUILEAN

Loch Loyal

Neave Island

Torrisdale Bay

Farr Bay

Farr Point

Bettyhill

Invernaver

Achina

Kyle of Tongue

A836

River Borgie

Strath Naver

Skelpick

Skelpick Burn

213 ▲ CNOC MALPELLY

Loch Syre

Syre

River Naver

Loch Meadie

Ardmore Point

Kirtomy Point

Farr

Kirtomy

Swordly

Loch Mòr na Caorach

Loch nan Clach

Armadale Bay

Brawl

Strathy Inn

Armadale

A836

15

228 ▲ BEINN NAM BÒ

229 ▲ BEINN RUADH

Upper Bighouse

213 CNOC BAD AIREACH NA GAOITHE

Loch Strathy

335 ▲ MEALL BAD NA CUAICHE

345 ▲ CNOC NAM TRI-CHLACH

Strathy Point

River Strathy

Baligill

Strathy Bay

Strathy

Melvich

Melvich Bay

Bighouse

Portskerra

A836

185 ▲ BEINN RUADH

Sandside Bay

Isauld

Upper Dounreay

Reay

Achvarasdal

290 ▲ BEINN NAM BAD MHOR

Loch na Seilge

Strath Halladale

Dalhalvaig

Trantlemore

Trantelbeg

A897

243 ▲ CNOC AN FHOARAIN BHÀIN

184 ▲ CREAG NA CRICHE

217 ▲ CNOC A' BHREUN BHAID

Forsinard

Dyke Water

242 ▲ BEINN RATHA

Loch Tuim Ghlais

203 ▲ CNOC PREAS A'MHADAIDH

280 ▲ SLETILL HILL

112

275 ▲ CNOC NAN GALL

337 ▲ MEALL A' BHEALAICH

Rumsdale Water

294 ▲ POLE HILL

259 ▲ BEINN ROSAIL

B871

404 ▲ BEINN MHADADH

588 ▲ BEN GRIAM BEG

590 ▲ BEN GRIAM MOR

Loch Druim à Chliabhain

656 ▲ CNOC AN DÀIMH MÒR

Loch Meadie

Strath Naver

B873

230 ▲ MEALL A' BHROLLAICH

270 ▲ BEADAIG

Altnaharra

River Mallart

Loch Rimsdale

Loch nan Clàr

Loch Badanloch

Loch an Altàn Fheàrna

Loch Arichlinie

Loch an Ruathair

440

432

KNOCKFIN HEIGHTS

Halladale River

A891

472 ▲ MEALL AN FHUARAIN

959 ▲ BEN KLIBRECK

Loch Choire Forest

Loch Choire

Loch a' Bhealaich

Strath Bagastie

A836

Crask Inn

346 ▲ CNOC A' GHIUBHAIS

Ben Armine Forest

Strath Tirry

Shinness

694 ▲ CREAG N-IOLAIRE

713 ▲ CREAG MHÒR

Glas-loch Mòr

462 ▲ MEALIAN LIATH-MÒR

Gorm-loch Mòr

Loch Truderscaig

River Helmsdale

Kinbrace

434 ▲ CNOC AN LIATH-BHAID MHOIR

364 ▲ CNOC NA BREUN-CHOILLE

Borrobol Forest

Strath Skinsdale

337 ▲ CNOC NA H-INNSE MOIRE

421 ▲ CNOC NAN CRÙBAG MÒR

B871

202 ▲ CNOC DAIL-CHAIRN

Strath Free

Loch Ascaig

388 ▲ CREAG NAM FIADH

Learable Hill Cairns, Stone Row & Stone Circles

Kildonan Lodge

Kildonan

416 ▲ BEINN DUBHAIN

A897

Strath of Kildonan

River Helmsdale

437 ▲ CNOC COIRE NA FEARNA

Suisgill Burn

Kinbrace Burn

518 ▲ CNOC AN EIREANNAICH

705 ▲ MORVEN

554 ▲ CREAG SCALABSDALE

624 ▲ BEINN DHORAIN

591 ▲ BEINN NA MEILICH

Torrish

West Helmsdale

Gartymore

Portgower

Glen Loth

Lothmore

317 ▲ CNOC LO MHADAL

401 ▲ CNOC NA MAOILE

109

Achnairn

317 ▲ SITHEAN ACHADH NAN EUN

Loch Beannach

River Brora

293 ▲ CNOC LEAMHNACHD

Black Water

Balnacoil Lodge

St R Brora

539 ▲ COL-BHEINN

Colaboll

Ferrycroft

River Brora

Loch Brora

Shin

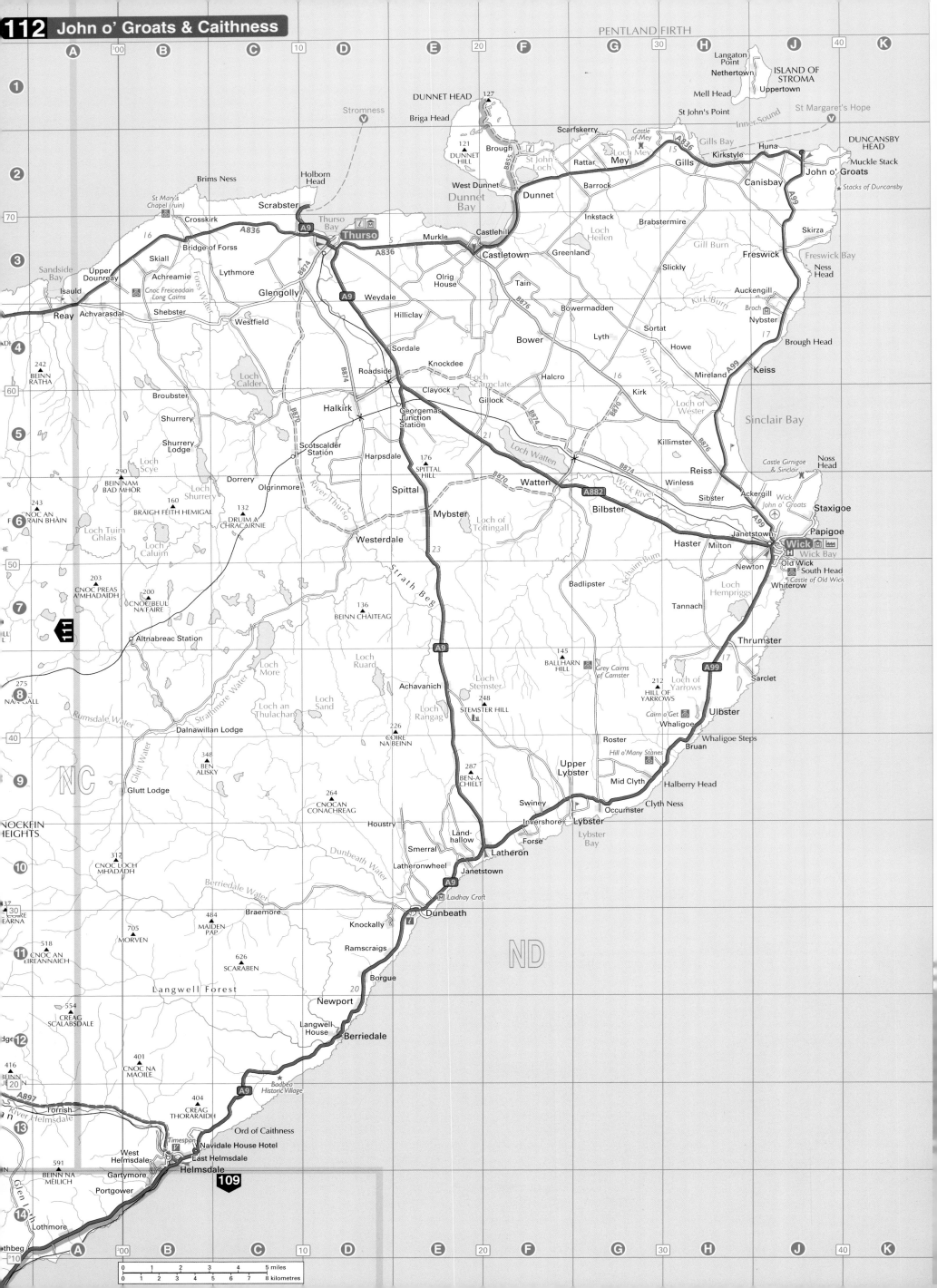

Restricted junctions

Motorway and Primary Route junctions which have access or exit restrictions are shown on the map pages thus:

M1 London - Leeds

Junction	Northbound	Southbound
2	Access only from A1 *(northbound)*	Exit only to A1 *(southbound)*
4	Access only from A41 *(northbound)*	Exit only to A41 *(southbound)*
6A	Access only from M25 (no link from A405)	Exit only to M25 (no link from A405)
7	Access only from A414	Exit only to A414
17	Exit only to M45	Access only from M45
19	Exit only to M6 *(northbound)*	Access only from M6
21A	Exit only, no access	Access only, no exit
23A	Access only from A42	No restriction
24A	Access only, no exit	Exit only, no access
35A	Exit only, no access	Access only, no exit
43	Exit only to M621	Access only from M621
48	Exit only to A1(M) *(northbound)*	Access only from A1(M) *(southbound)*

M2 Rochester - Faversham

Junction	Westbound	Eastbound
1	No exit to A2 *(eastbound)*	No access from A2 *(westbound)*

M3 Sunbury - Southampton

Junction	Northeastbound	Southwestbound
8	Access only from A303, no exit	Exit only to A303, no access
10	Exit only, no access	Access only, no exit
14	Access from M27 only, no exit	No access to M27 *(westbound)*

M4 London - South Wales

Junction	Westbound	Eastbound
1	Access only from A4 *(westbound)*	Exit only to A4 *(eastbound)*
21	Exit only to M48	Access only from M48
23	Access only from M48	Exit only to M48
25	Exit only, no access	Access only, no exit
25A	Exit only, no access	Access only, no exit
29	Exit only to A48(M)	Access only from A48(M)
38	Exit only, no access	No restriction
39	Access only, no exit	No access or exit

M5 Birmingham - Exeter

Junction	Northeastbound	Southwestbound
10	Access only, no exit	Exit only, no access
11A	Access only from A417 *(westbound)*	Exit only to A417 *(eastbound)*
18A	Exit only to M49	Access only from M49
18	Exit only, no access	Access only, no exit

M6 Toll Motorway

Junction	Northwestbound	Southeastbound
T1	Access only, no exit	No access or exit
T2	No access or exit	Exit only, no access
T3	Staggered junction, follow signs - access only from A38 *(northbound)*	Staggered junction, follow signs - access only from A38 *(southbound)*
T5	Access only, no exit	Exit only to A5148 *(northbound)*, no access
T7	Exit only, no access	Access only, no exit
T8	Exit only, no access	Access only, no exit

M6 Rugby - Carlisle

Junction	Northbound	Southbound
3A	Exit only to M6 Toll	Access only from M6 Toll
4A	Access only from M42 *(southbound)*	Exit only to M42
5	Exit only, no access	Access only, no exit
10A	Exit only to M54	Access only from M54
11A	Access only from M6 Toll	Exit only to M6 Toll
with M56 (jct 20A)	No restriction	Access only from M56 *(eastbound)*
20	Access only, no exit	No restriction
24	Access only, no exit	Exit only, no access
25	Exit only, no access	Access only, no exit
29	No direct access, use adjacent slip road to jct 29A	No direct exit, use adjacent slip road from jct 29A
29A	Access only, no exit	Exit only, no access
30	Access only from M61	Exit only to M61
31A	Exit only, no access	Access only, no exit
45	Exit only, no access	Access only, no exit

M8 Edinburgh - Bishopton

Junction	Westbound	Eastbound
8	No access from M73 *(southbound)* or from A8 *(eastbound)* & A89	No exit to M73 *(northbound)* or to A8 *(westbound)* & A89
9	Access only, no exit	Exit only, no access
13	Access only from M80 *(southbound)*	Exit only to M80 *(northbound)*
14	Access only, no exit	Exit only, no access
16	Exit only to A804	Access only from A879
17	Exit only to A82	No restriction
18	Access only from A82 *(eastbound)*	Exit only to A814
19	No access from A814 *(westbound)*	Exit only to A814 *(westbound)*
20	Exit only, no access	Access only, no exit
21	Access only, no exit	Exit only to A8
22	Exit only to M77 *(southbound)*	Access only from M77 *(northbound)*
23	Exit only to B768	Access only from B768
25	No access or exit from or to A8	No access or exit from or to A8
25A	Exit only, no access	Access only, no exit
28	Exit only, no access	Access only, no exit
28A	Exit only to A737	Access only from A737

M9 Edinburgh - Dunblane

Junction	Northwestbound	Southeastbound
2	Access only, no exit	Exit only, no access
3	Exit only, no access	Access only, no exit
6	Access only, no exit	Exit only to A905
8	Exit only to M876 *(southwestbound)*	Access only from M876 *(northeastbound)*

M11 London - Cambridge

Junction	Northbound	Southbound
4	Access only from A406 *(eastbound)*	Exit only to A406
5	Exit only, no access	Access only, no exit
9	Exit only to A11	Access only from A11
13	Exit only, no access	Access only, no exit
14	Exit only, no access	Access only, no exit

M20 Swanley - Folkestone

Junction	Northwestbound	Southeastbound
2	Staggered junction; follow signs - access only	Staggered junction; follow signs - exit only
3	Exit only to M26 *(westbound)*	Access only from M26 *(eastbound)*
5	Access only from A20	For access follow signs - exit only to A20
6	No restriction	For exit follow signs
11A	Access only, no exit	Exit only, no access

M23 Hooley - Crawley

Junction	Northbound	Southbound
7	Exit only to A23 *(northbound)*	Access only from A23 *(southbound)*
10A	Access only, no exit	Exit only, no access

M25 London Orbital Motorway

Junction	Clockwise	Anticlockwise
1B	No direct access, use slip road to Jct 2. Exit only	Access only, no exit
5	No exit to M26 *(eastbound)*	No access from M26
19	Exit only, no access	Access only, no exit
21	Access only from M1 *(southbound)*. Exit only to M1 *(northbound)*	Access only from M1 *(southbound)*. Exit only to M1 *(northbound)*
31	No exit (use slip road via jct 30), access only	No access (use slip road via jct 30), exit only

M26 Sevenoaks - Wrotham

Junction	Westbound	Eastbound
with M25 (jct 5)	Exit only to clockwise M25 *(westbound)*	Access only from anticlockwise M25 *(eastbound)*
with M20 (jct 3)	Access only from M20 *(northwestbound)*	Exit only to M20 *(southeastbound)*

M27 Cadnam - Portsmouth

Junction	Westbound	Eastbound
4	Staggered junction; follow signs - access only from M3 *(southbound)*. Exit only to M3 *(northbound)*	Staggered junction; follow signs - access only from M3 *(southbound)*. Exit only to M3 *(northbound)*
10	Exit only, no access	Access only, no exit
12	Staggered junction; follow signs - exit only to M275 *(southbound)*	Staggered junction; follow signs - access only from M275 *(northbound)*

M40 London - Birmingham

Junction	Northwestbound	Southeastbound
3	Exit only, no access	Access only, no exit
7	Exit only, no access	Access only, no exit
8	Exit only to M40/A40	Access only from M40/A40
13	Exit only, no access	Access only, no exit
14	Access only, no exit	Exit only, no access
16	Access only, no exit	Exit only, no access

M42 Bromsgrove - Measham

Junction	Northeastbound	Southwestbound
1	Access only, no exit	Exit only, no access
7	Exit only to M6 *(northwestbound)*	Access only from M6 *(northwestbound)*
7A	Exit only to M6 *(southeastbound)*	No access or exit
8	Access only from M6 *(southeastbound)*	Exit only to M6 *(northwestbound)*

M45 Coventry - M1

Junction	Westbound	Eastbound
Dunchurch (unnumbered)	Access only from A45	Exit only, no access
with M1 (jct 17)	Access only from M1 *(northbound)*	Exit only to M1 *(southbound)*

M53 Mersey Tunnel - Chester

Junction	Northbound	Southbound
11	Access only from M56 *(westbound)*. Exit only to M56 *(eastbound)*	Access only from M56 *(westbound)*. Exit only to M56 *(eastbound)*

M54 Telford

Junction	Westbound	Eastbound
with M6 (jct 10A)	Access only from M6 *(northbound)*	Exit only to M6 *(southbound)*

M56 North Cheshire

Junction	Westbound	Eastbound
1	Access only from M60 *(westbound)*	Exit only to M60 *(eastbound)* & A34 *(northbound)*
2	Exit only, no access	Access only, no exit
3	Access only, no exit	Exit only, no access
4	Exit only, no access	Access only, no exit
7	Exit only, no access	No restriction
8	Access only, no exit	No access or exit
15	Exit only to M53	Access only from M53
16	No access or exit	No restriction

M57 Liverpool Outer Ring Road

Junction	Northwestbound	Southeastbound
3	Access only, no exit	Exit only, no access
5	Access only from A580 *(westbound)*	Exit only, no access

M58 Liverpool - Wigan

Junction	Westbound	Eastbound
1	Exit only, no access	Access only, no exit

M60 Manchester Orbital

Junction	Clockwise	Anticlockwise
2	Access only, no exit	Exit only, no access
3	No access from M56	Access only from A34 *(northbound)*
4	Access only from A34 *(northbound)*. Exit only to M56	Access only from M56 *(eastbound)*. Exit only to A34 *(southbound)*
5	Access and exit only from and to A5103 *(northbound)*	Access and exit only from and to A5103 *(southbound)*
7	No direct access, use slip road to jct 8. Exit only to A56	Access only from A56. No exit - use jct 8
14	Access from A580 *(eastbound)*	Exit only to A580 *(westbound)*
16	Access only, no exit	Exit only, no access
20	Exit only, no access	Access only, no exit
22	No restriction	Exit only, no access
25	Exit only, no access	No restriction
26	No restriction	Exit only, no access
27	Access only, no exit	Exit only, no access

M61 Manchester - Preston

Junction	Northwestbound	Southeastbound
3	No access or exit	Exit only, no access
with M6 (jct 30)	Exit only to M6 *(northbound)*	Access only from M6 *(southbound)*

M62 Liverpool - Kingston upon Hull

Junction	Westbound	Eastbound
23	Access only, no exit	Exit only, no access
32A	No access to A1(M) (southbound)	No restriction

M65 Preston - Colne

Junction	Northeastbound	Southwestbound
9	Exit only, no access	Access only, no exit
11	Access only, no exit	Exit only, no access

M66 Bury

Junction	Northbound	Southbound
with A56	Exit only to A56 *(northbound)*	Access only from A56 *(southbound)*
1	Exit only, no access	Access only, no exit

M67 Hyde Bypass

Junction	Westbound	Eastbound
1	Access only, no exit	Exit only, no access
2	Exit only, no access	Access only, no exit
3	Exit only, no access	No restriction

M69 Coventry - Leicester

Junction	Northbound	Southbound
2	Access only, no exit	Exit only, no access

M73 East of Glasgow

Junction	Northbound	Southbound
2	No access from or exit to A89. No access from M8 *(eastbound)*	No access from or exit to A89. No exit to M8 *(westbound)*

M74 and A74(M) Glasgow - Gretna

Junction	Northbound	Southbound
3	Exit only, no access	Access only, no exit
3A	Access only, no exit	Exit only, no access
7	Access only, no exit	Exit only, no access
9	No access or exit	Exit only, no access
10	No restrictions	Access only, no exit
11	Access only, no exit	Exit only, no access
12	Exit only, no access	Access only, no exit
18	Exit only, no access	Access only, no exit

M77 South of Glasgow

Junction	Northbound	Southbound
with M8 (jct 22)	No exit to M8 *(westbound)*	No access from M8 *(eastbound)*
4	Access only, no exit	Exit only, no access
6	Access only, no exit	Exit only, no access
7	Access only, no exit	No restriction

M80 Glasgow - Stirling

Junction	Northbound	Southbound
4A	Exit only, no access	Access only, no exit
6A	Access only, no exit	Exit only, no access
8	Exit only to M876 *(northeastbound)*	Access only from M876 *(southwestbound)*

M90 Forth Road Bridge - Perth

Junction	Northbound	Southbound
2A	Exit only to A92 *(eastbound)*	Access only from A92 *(westbound)*
7	Access only, no exit	Exit only, no access
8	Exit only, no access	Access only, no exit
10	No access from A912. No exit to A912 *(southbound)*	No access from A912 *(northbound)*. No exit to A912

M180 Doncaster - Grimsby

Junction	Westbound	Eastbound
1	Access only, no exit	Exit only, no access

M606 Bradford Spur

Junction	Northbound	Southbound
2	Exit only, no access	No restriction

M621 Leeds - M1

Junction	Clockwise	Anticlockwise
2A	Access only, no exit	Exit only, no access
4	No exit or access	No restriction
5	Access only, no exit	Exit only, no access
6	Exit only, no access	Access only, no exit
with M1 (jct 43)	Exit only to M1 *(southbound)*	Access only from M1 *(northbound)*

M876 Bonnybridge - Kincardine Bridge

Junction	Northeastbound	Southwestbound
with M80 (jct 5)	Access only from M80 *(northbound)*	Exit only to M80 *(southbound)*
with M9 (jct 8)	Exit only to M9 *(eastbound)*	Access only from M9 *(westbound)*

A1(M) South Mimms - Baldock

Junction	Northbound	Southbound
2	Exit only, no access	Access only, no exit
3	No restriction	Exit only, no access
5	Access only, no exit	No access or exit

A1(M) Pontefract - Bedale

Junction	Northbound	Southbound
41	No access to M62 *(eastbound)*	No restriction
43	Access only from M1 *(northbound)*	Exit only to M1 *(southbound)*

A1(M) Scotch Corner - Newcastle upon Tyne

Junction	Northbound	Southbound
57	Exit only to A66(M) *(eastbound)*	Access only from A66(M) *(westbound)*
65	No access. Exit only to A194(M) & A1 *(northbound)*	No exit. Access only from A194(M) & A1 *(southbound)*

A3(M) Horndean - Havant

Junction	Northbound	Southbound
1	Access only from A3	Exit only to A3
4	Exit only, no access	Access only, no exit

A48(M) Cardiff Spur

Junction	Westbound	Eastbound
29	Access only from M4 *(westbound)*	Exit only to M4 *(eastbound)*
29A	Exit only to A48 *(westbound)*	Access only from A48 *(eastbound)*

A66(M) Darlington Spur

Junction	Westbound	Eastbound
with A1(M) (jct 57)	Exit only to A1(M) *(southbound)*	Access only from A1(M) *(northbound)*

A194(M) Newcastle upon Tyne

Junction	Northbound	Southbound
with A1(M) (jct 65)	Access only from A1(M) *(northbound)*	Exit only to A1(M) *(southbound)*

A12 M25 - Ipswich

Junction	Northeastbound	Southwestbound
13	Access only, no exit	No restriction
14	Exit only, no access	Access only, no exit
20A	Exit only, no access	Access only, no exit
20B	Access only, no exit	Exit only, no access
21	No restriction	Access only, no exit
23	Exit only, no access	Access only, no exit
24	Access only, no exit	Exit only, no access
27	Exit only, no access	Access only, no exit
Dedham & Stratford St Mary (unnumbered)	Exit only	Access only

A14 M1 - Felixstowe

Junction	Westbound	Eastbound
with M1/M6 (jct19)	Exit only to M6 and M1 *(northbound)*	Access only from M6 and M1 *(southbound)*
4	Exit only, no access	Access only, no exit
31	Access only from A1307	Exit only, to A1307
34	Access only, no exit	Exit only, no access
36	Exit only to A11 Access only from A1303	Access only from A11
38	Access only from A11	Exit only to A11
39	Exit only, no access	Access only, no exit
61	Access only, no exit	Exit only, no access

A55 Holyhead - Chester

Junction	Westbound	Eastbound
8A	Exit only, no access	Access only, no exit
23A	Access only, no exit	Exit only, no access
24A	Exit only, no access	No access or exit
33A	Exit only, no access	No access or exit
33B	Exit only, no access	Access only, no exit
37	Exit only to A5104	Access only from A5104

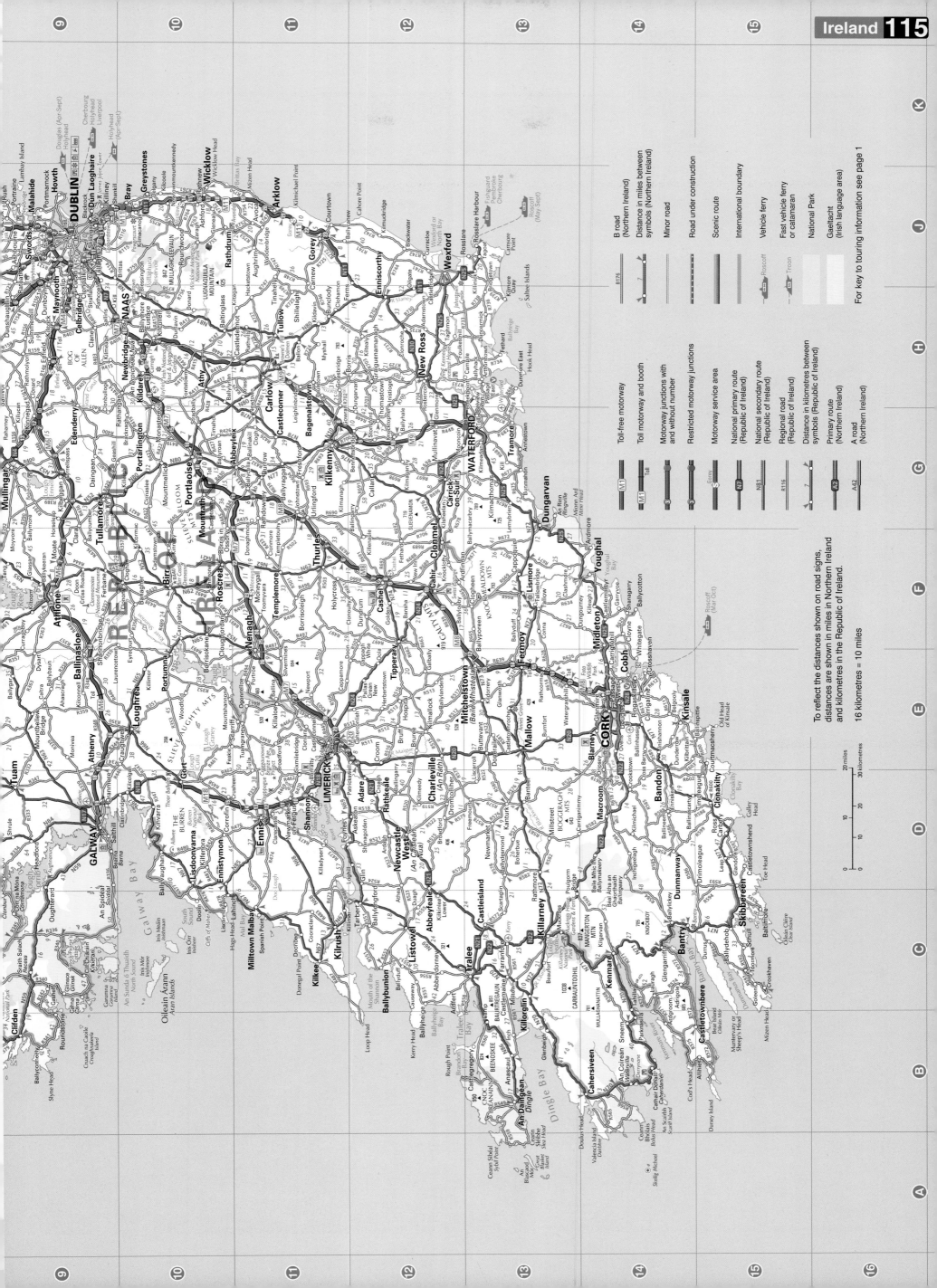

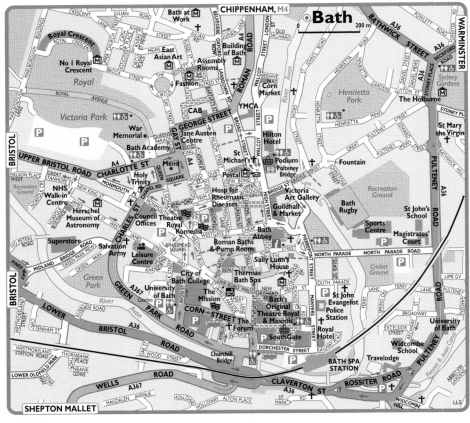

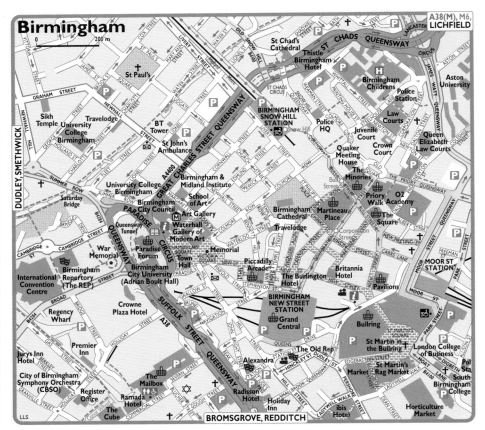

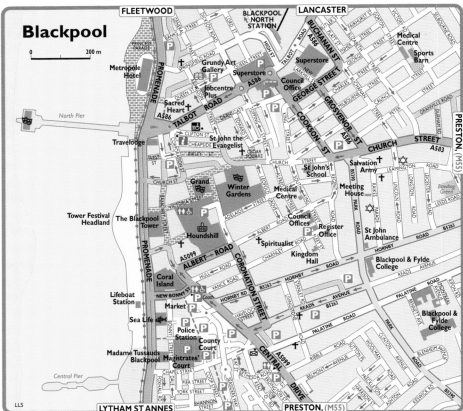

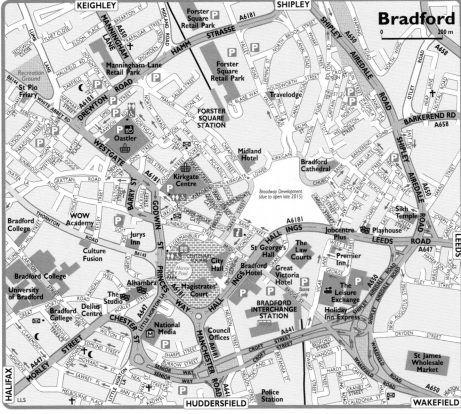

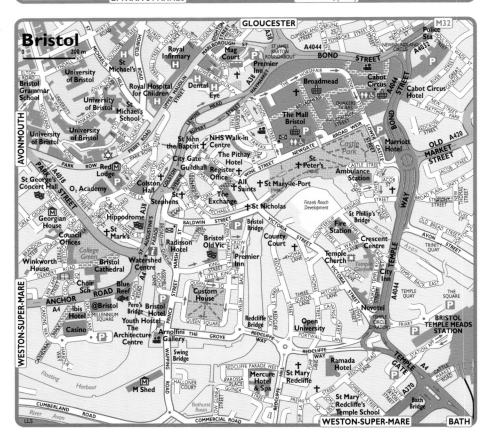

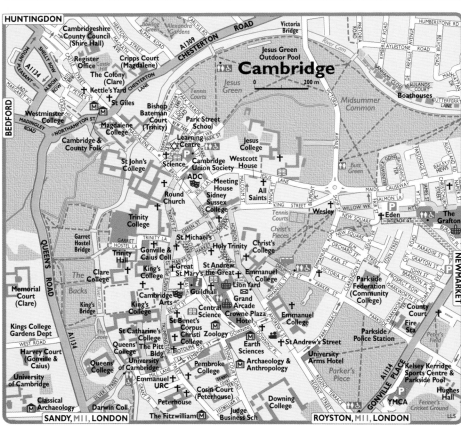

Canterbury
Cardiff

Chester
Coventry

Derby
Dundee

117

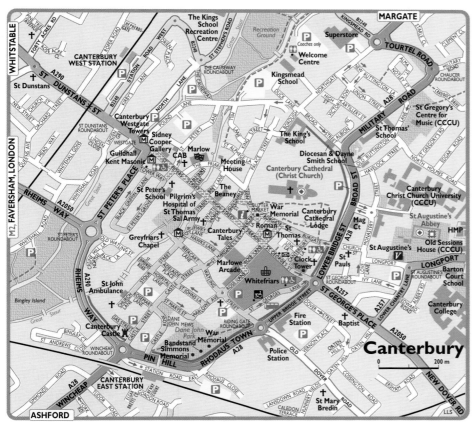

Canterbury

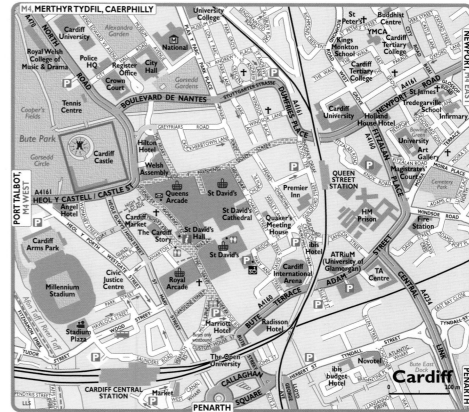

Cardiff

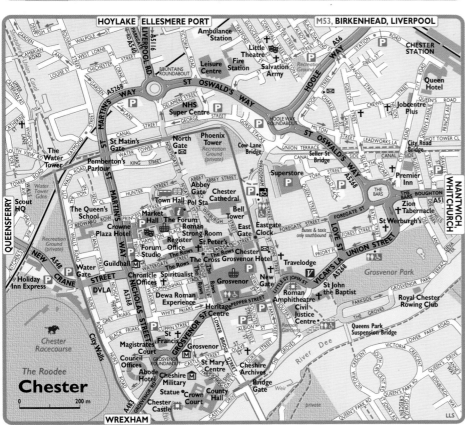

Chester

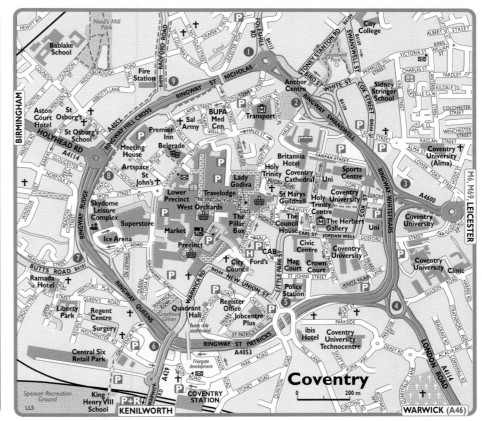

Coventry

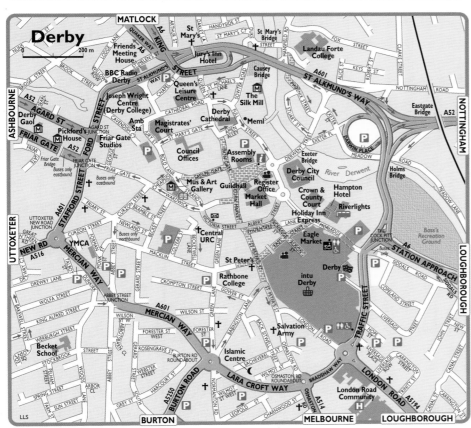

Derby

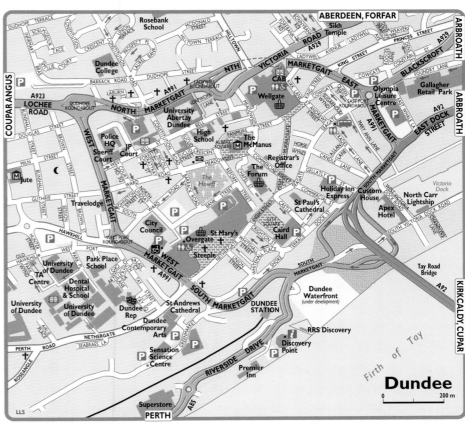

Dundee

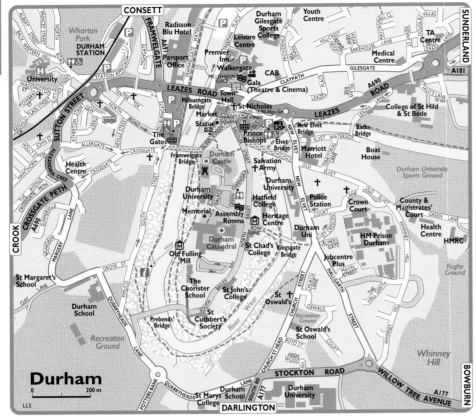

Durham

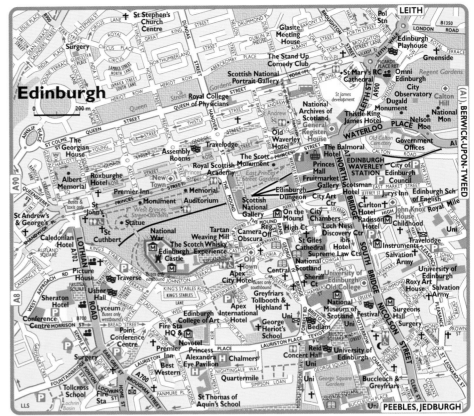

Edinburgh

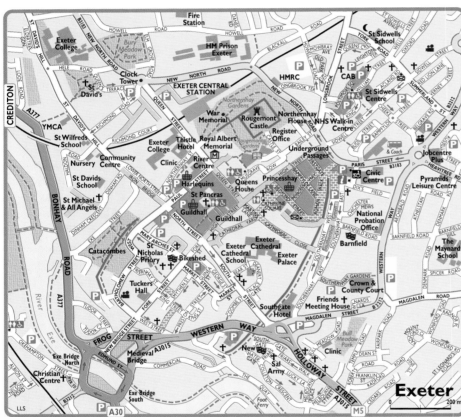

Exeter

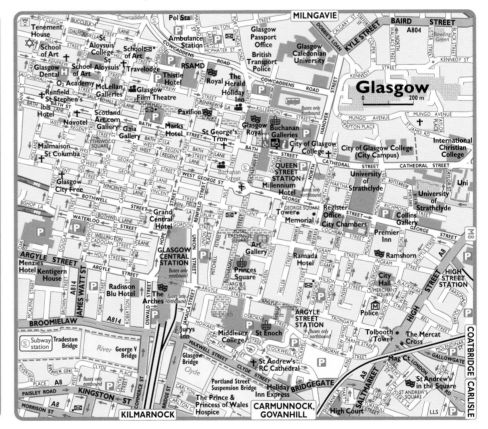

Glasgow

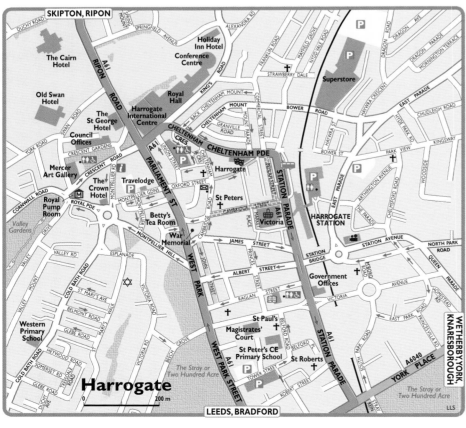

Harrogate

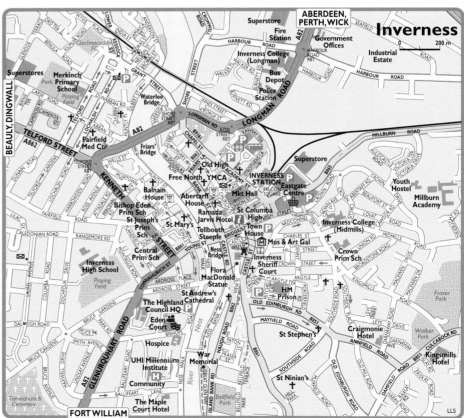

Inverness

Ipswich
Kingston upon Hull

Leeds
Leicester

Lincoln
London

119

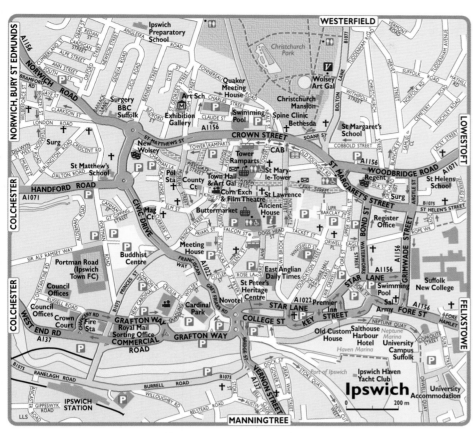

Ipswich

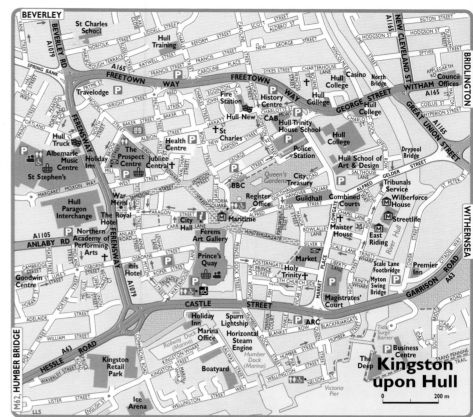

Kingston upon Hull

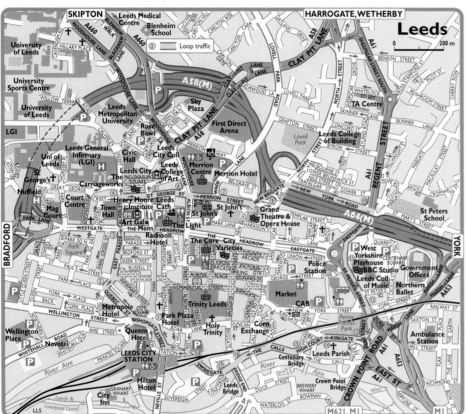

Leeds

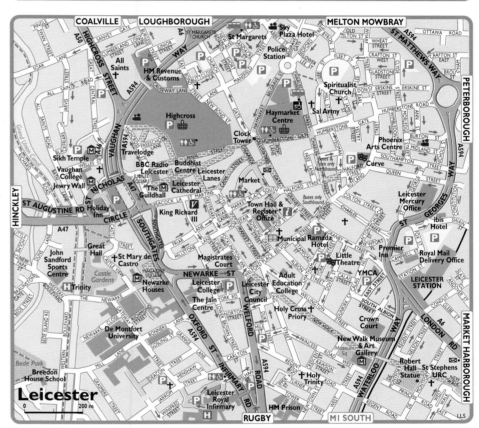

Leicester

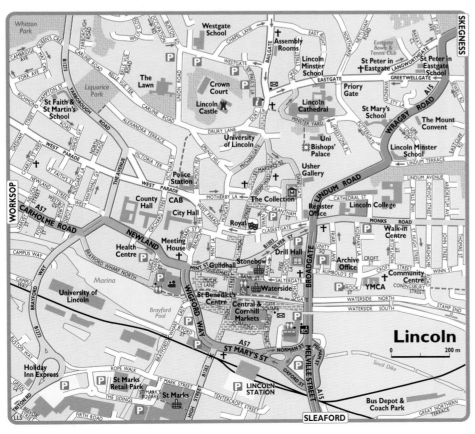

Lincoln

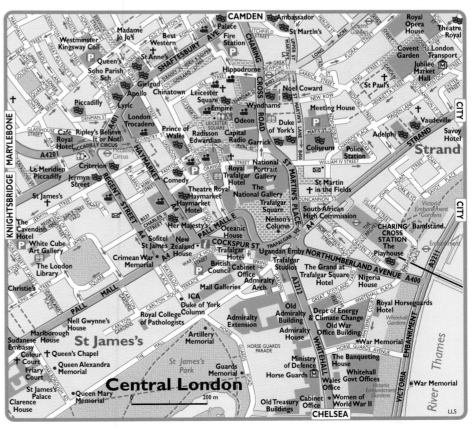

Central London

120 Manchester
Milton Keynes

Newcastle upon Tyne
Norwich

Nottingham
Oxford

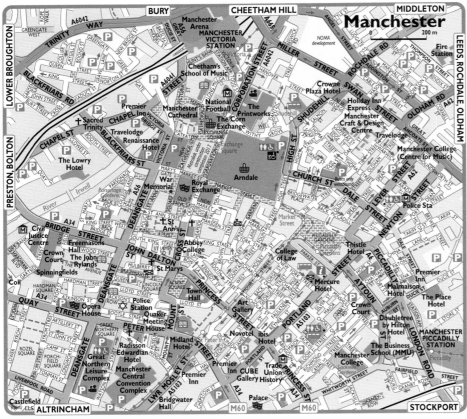

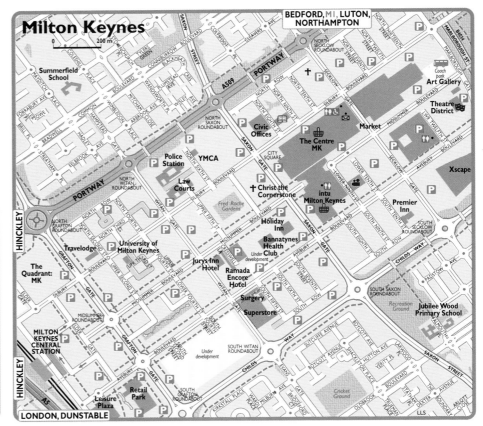

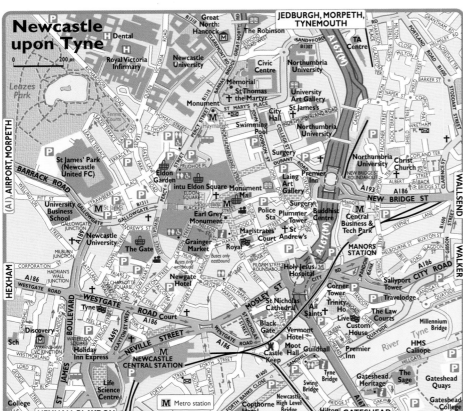

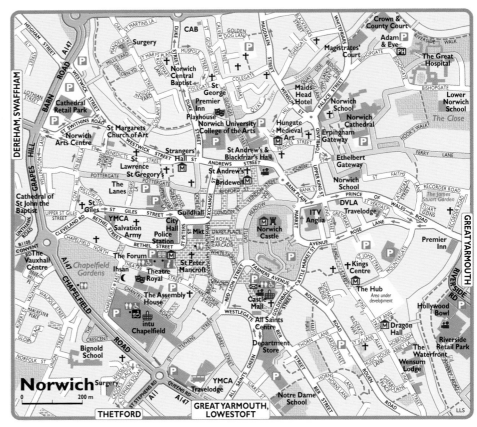

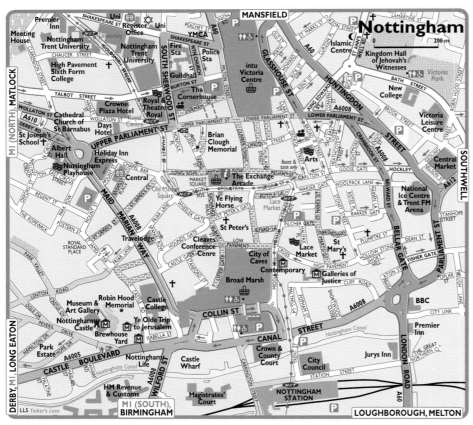

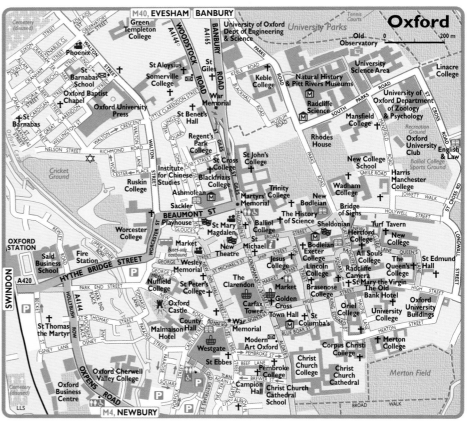

Peterborough
Plymouth

Portsmouth
Salisbury

Sheffield
Southampton 121

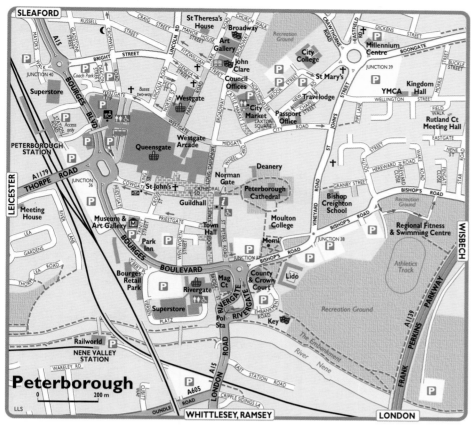

Peterborough

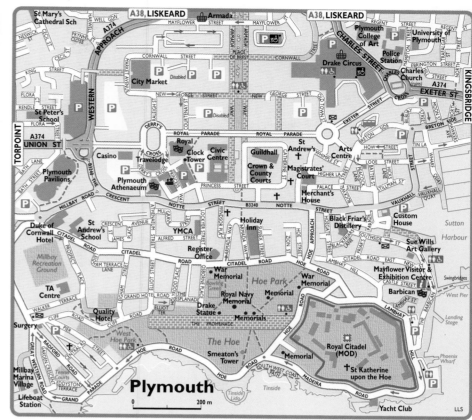

Plymouth

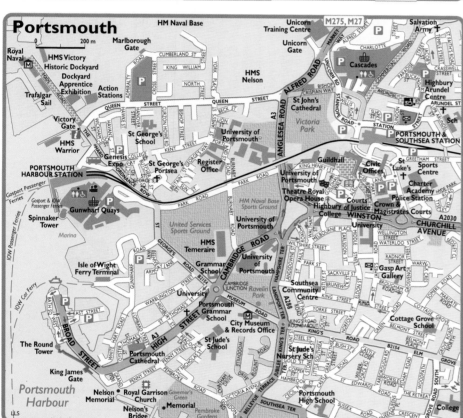

Portsmouth

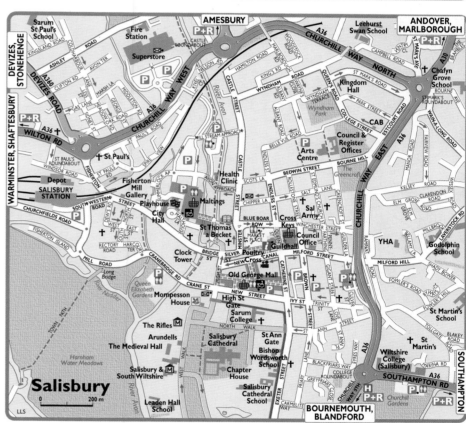

Salisbury

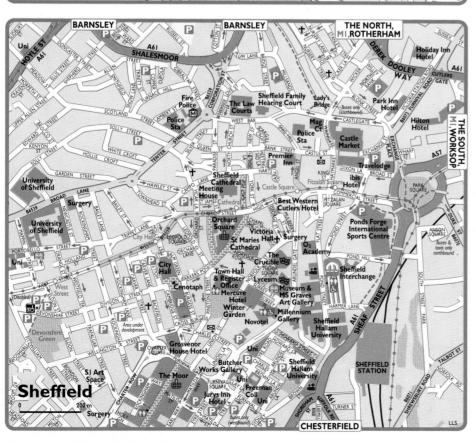

Sheffield

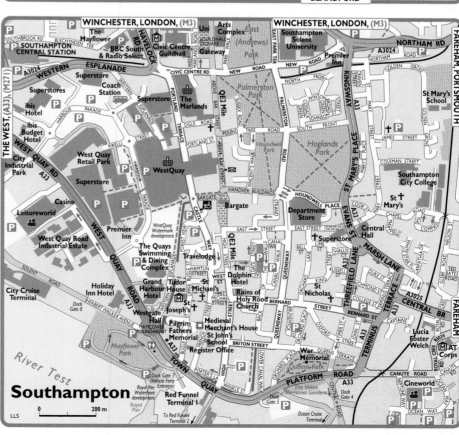

Southampton

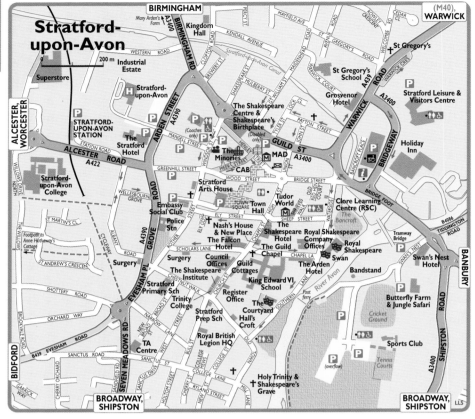

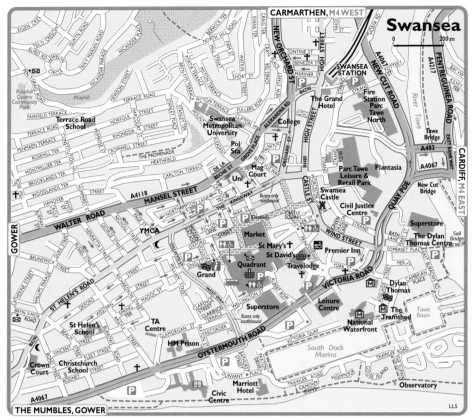

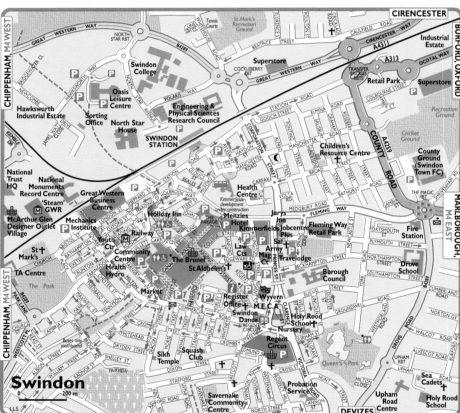

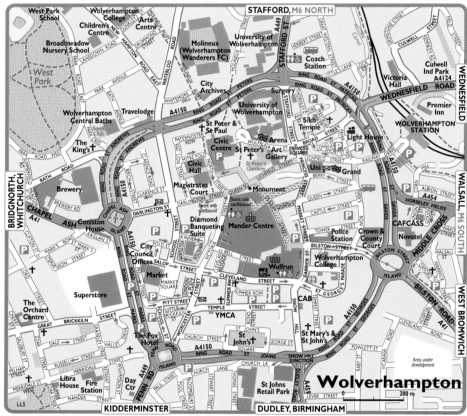

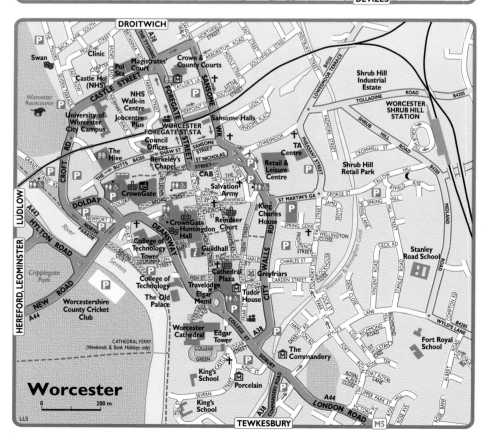

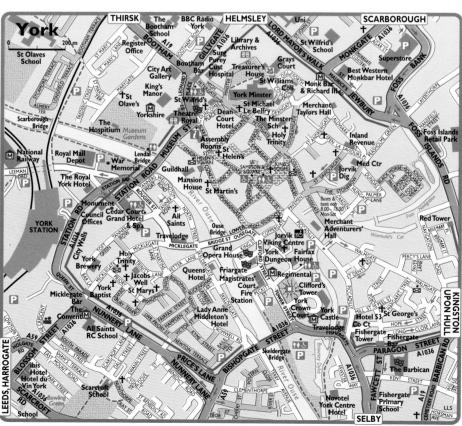

Index to place names

This index lists places appearing in the main-map section of the atlas in alphabetical order. The reference following each name gives the atlas page number and grid reference of the square in which the place appears. The map shows counties, unitary authorities and administrative areas, together with a list of the abbreviated name forms used in the index. The top 100 places of tourist interest are indexed in **red**, World Heritage sites in **green**, motorway service areas in **blue**, airports in blue *italic* and National Parks in green *italic*.

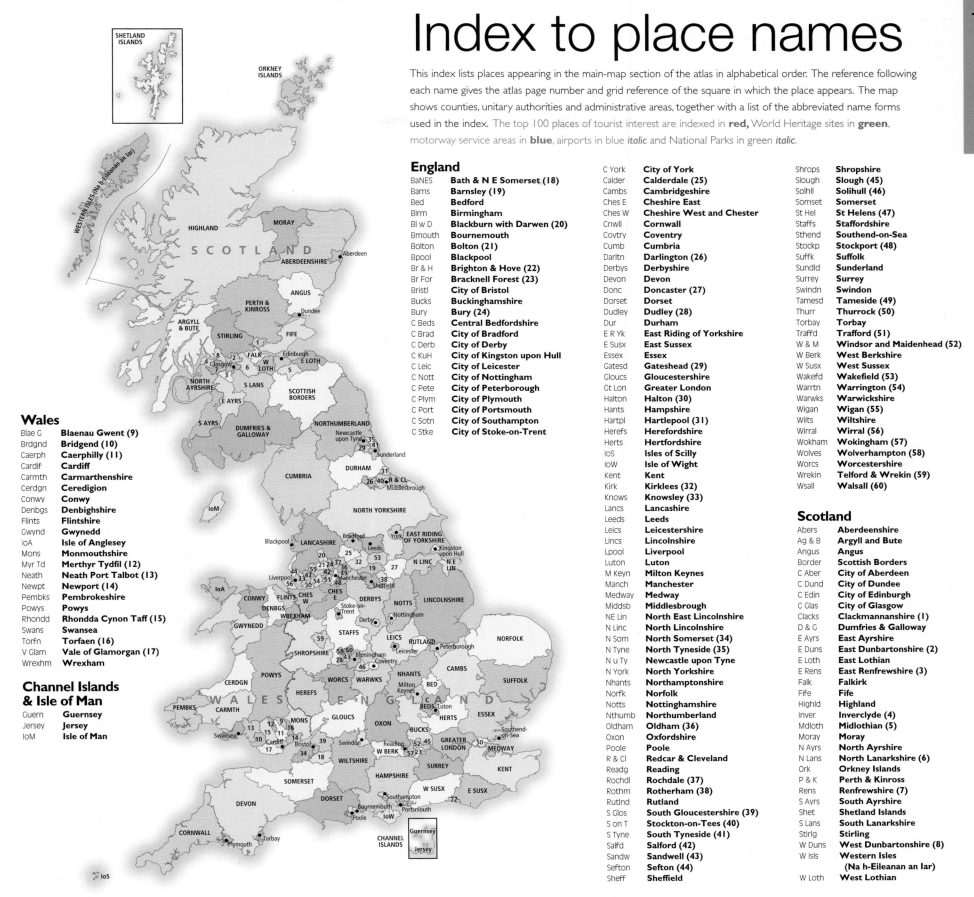

Wales

Blae G	**Blaenau Gwent (9)**
Brdgnd	**Bridgend (10)**
Caerph	**Caerphilly (11)**
Cardif	**Cardiff**
Carmth	**Carmarthenshire**
Cerdgn	**Ceredigion**
Conwy	**Conwy**
Denbgs	**Denbighshire**
Flints	**Flintshire**
Gwynd	**Gwynedd**
IoA	**Isle of Anglesey**
Mons	**Monmouthshire**
Myr Td	**Merthyr Tydfil (12)**
Neath	**Neath Port Talbot (13)**
Newpt	**Newport (14)**
Pembks	**Pembrokeshire**
Powys	**Powys**
Rhondd	**Rhondda Cynon Taff (15)**
Swans	**Swansea**
Torfn	**Torfaen (16)**
V Glam	**Vale of Glamorgan (17)**
Wrexhm	**Wrexham**

Channel Islands & Isle of Man

Guern	**Guernsey**
Jersey	**Jersey**
IoM	**Isle of Man**

England

BaNES	**Bath & N E Somerset (18)**
Barns	**Barnsley (19)**
Bed	**Bedford**
Birm	**Birmingham**
Bl w D	**Blackburn with Darwen (20)**
Bmouth	**Bournemouth**
Bolton	**Bolton (21)**
Bpool	**Blackpool**
Br & H	**Brighton & Hove (22)**
Br For	**Bracknell Forest (23)**
Bristl	**City of Bristol**
Bucks	**Buckinghamshire**
Bury	**Bury (24)**
C Beds	**Central Bedfordshire**
C Brad	**City of Bradford**
C Derb	**City of Derby**
C KuH	**City of Kingston upon Hull**
C Leic	**City of Leicester**
C Nott	**City of Nottingham**
C Pete	**City of Peterborough**
C Plym	**City of Plymouth**
C Port	**City of Portsmouth**
C Sotn	**City of Southampton**
C Stke	**City of Stoke-on-Trent**
C York	**City of York**
Calder	**Calderdale (25)**
Cambs	**Cambridgeshire**
Ches E	**Cheshire East**
Ches W	**Cheshire West and Chester**
Cnwll	**Cornwall**
Covtry	**Coventry**
Cumb	**Cumbria**
Darltn	**Darlington (26)**
Derbys	**Derbyshire**
Devon	**Devon**
Donc	**Doncaster (27)**
Dorset	**Dorset**
Dudley	**Dudley (28)**
Dur	**Durham**
E R Yk	**East Riding of Yorkshire**
E Susx	**East Sussex**
Essex	**Essex**
Gatesd	**Gateshead (29)**
Gloucs	**Gloucestershire**
Gt Lon	**Greater London**
Halton	**Halton (30)**
Hants	**Hampshire**
Hartpl	**Hartlepool (31)**
Herefs	**Herefordshire**
Herts	**Hertfordshire**
IoS	**Isles of Scilly**
IoW	**Isle of Wight**
Kent	**Kent**
Kirk	**Kirklees (32)**
Knows	**Knowsley (33)**
Lancs	**Lancashire**
Leeds	**Leeds**
Leics	**Leicestershire**
Lincs	**Lincolnshire**
Lpool	**Liverpool**
Luton	**Luton**
M Keyn	**Milton Keynes**
Manch	**Manchester**
Medway	**Medway**
Middsb	**Middlesbrough**
NE Lin	**North East Lincolnshire**
N Linc	**North Lincolnshire**
N Som	**North Somerset (34)**
N Tyne	**North Tyneside (35)**
N u Ty	**Newcastle upon Tyne**
N York	**North Yorkshire**
Nhants	**Northamptonshire**
Norfk	**Norfolk**
Notts	**Nottinghamshire**
Nthumb	**Northumberland**
Oldham	**Oldham (36)**
Oxon	**Oxfordshire**
Poole	**Poole**
R & Cl	**Redcar & Cleveland**
Readg	**Reading**
Rochdl	**Rochdale (37)**
Rothm	**Rotherham (38)**
Rutlnd	**Rutland**
S Glos	**South Gloucestershire (39)**
S on T	**Stockton-on-Tees (40)**
S Tyne	**South Tyneside (41)**
Salfd	**Salford (42)**
Sandw	**Sandwell (43)**
Sefton	**Sefton (44)**
Sheff	**Sheffield**
Shrops	**Shropshire**
Slough	**Slough (45)**
Solhll	**Solihull (46)**
Somset	**Somerset**
St Hel	**St Helens (47)**
Staffs	**Staffordshire**
Sthend	**Southend-on-Sea**
Stockp	**Stockport (48)**
Suffk	**Suffolk**
Sundld	**Sunderland**
Surrey	**Surrey**
Swindn	**Swindon**
Tamesd	**Tameside (49)**
Thurr	**Thurrock (50)**
Torbay	**Torbay**
Traffd	**Trafford (51)**
W & M	**Windsor and Maidenhead (52)**
W Berk	**West Berkshire**
W Susx	**West Sussex**
Wakefd	**Wakefield (53)**
Warrtn	**Warrington (54)**
Warwks	**Warwickshire**
Wigan	**Wigan (55)**
Wilts	**Wiltshire**
Wirral	**Wirral (56)**
Wokham	**Wokingham (57)**
Wolves	**Wolverhampton (58)**
Worcs	**Worcestershire**
Wrekin	**Telford & Wrekin (59)**
Wsall	**Walsall (60)**

Scotland

Abers	**Aberdeenshire**
Ag & B	**Argyll and Bute**
Angus	**Angus**
Border	**Scottish Borders**
C Aber	**City of Aberdeen**
C Dund	**City of Dundee**
C Edin	**City of Edinburgh**
C Glas	**City of Glasgow**
Clacks	**Clackmannanshire (1)**
D & G	**Dumfries & Galloway**
E Ayrs	**East Ayrshire**
E Duns	**East Dunbartonshire (2)**
E Loth	**East Lothian**
E Rens	**East Renfrewshire (3)**
Falk	**Falkirk**
Fife	**Fife**
Highld	**Highland**
Inver	**Inverclyde (4)**
Mdloth	**Midlothian (5)**
Moray	**Moray**
N Ayrs	**North Ayrshire**
N Lans	**North Lanarkshire (6)**
Ork	**Orkney Islands**
P & K	**Perth & Kinross**
Rens	**Renfrewshire (7)**
S Ayrs	**South Ayrshire**
Shet	**Shetland Islands**
S Lans	**South Lanarkshire**
Stirlg	**Stirling**
W Duns	**West Dunbartonshire (8)**
W Isls	**Western Isles (Na h-Eileanan an Iar)**
W Loth	**West Lothian**

Using the National Grid

With an Ordnance Survey National Grid reference you can pinpoint anywhere in the country in this atlas. The blue grid lines which divide the main-map pages into 5km squares for ease of indexing also match the National Grid. A National Grid reference gives two letters and some figures. An example is how to find the summit of mount Snowdon using its 4-figure grid reference of **SH6154**.

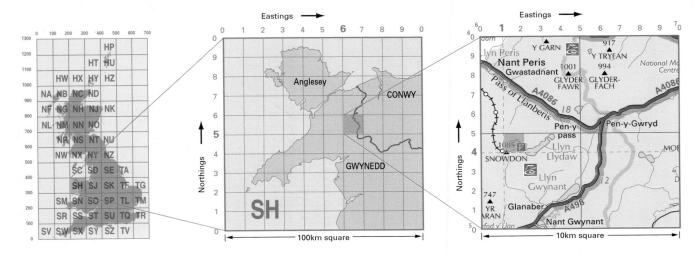

The letters **SH** indicate the 100km square of the National Grid in which Snowdon is located.

In a 4-figure grid reference the first two figures (eastings) are read along the map from left to right, the second two (northings) up the map. The figures **6** and **5**, the first and third figures of the Snowdon reference, indicate the 10km square within the **SH** square, lying above (north) and right (east) of the intersection of the vertical (easting) line **6** and horizontal (northing) line **5**.

The summit is finally pinpointed by figures **1** and **4** which locate a 1km square within the 10km square. At road atlas scales these grid lines are normally estimated by eye.

A

Abbas Combe Somset 17 T12
Abberley Worcs 35 S7
Abberley Common Worcs 35 R7
Abberton Essex 23 P4
Abberton Worcs 36 C10
Abberwick Nthumb 77 N3
Abbess Roding Essex 22 E5
Abbey Devon 6 F2
Abbey-Cwm-Hir Powys 34 C6
Abbeydale Sheff 57 M10
Abbey Dore Herefs 27 R1
Abbey Green Staffs 46 C2
Abbey Hill Somset 16 J13
Abbey St Bathans Border 84 K6
Abbeystead Lancs 62 B9
Abbey Town Cumb 66 J2
Abbey Village Lancs 55 P2
Abbey Wood Gt Lon 21 S7
Abbotrule Border 76 C3
Abbots Bickington Devon 14 J10
Abbots Bromley Staffs 46 E9
Abbotsbury Dorset 7 Q7
Abbot's Chair Derbys 56 F8
Abbots Deuglie P & K 90 H9
Abbotsham Devon 14 K7
Abbotskerswell Devon 5 V7
Abbots Langley Herts 31 N12
Abbotsleigh Devon 5 U11
Abbots Leigh N Som 27 U13
Abbotsley Cambs 38 K9
Abbots Morton Worcs 36 D9
Abbots Ripton Cambs 38 K5
Abbot's Salford Warwks 36 E10
Abbotstone Hants 9 R2
Abbotswood Hants 9 M4
Abbots Worthy Hants 9 P2
Abbotts Ann Hants 19 M12
Abbott Street Dorset 8 D8
Abcott Shrops 34 J5
Abdon Shrops 35 N3
Abenhall Gloucs 28 C4
Aberaeron Cerdgn 32 J8
Aberaman Rhondd 26 J7
Aberangell Gwynd 43 R11
Aber-arad Carmth 32 F12
Aberarder Highld 102 H10
Aberargie P & K 90 J8
Aberarth Cerdgn 32 J8
Aberavon Neath 26 C10
Aber-banc Cerdgn 32 G12
Aberbargoed Caerph 27 M7
Aberbeeg Blae G 27 N7
Abercanaid Myr Td 26 K7
Abercarn Caerph 27 N9
Abercastle Pembks 24 E4
Abercegir Powys 43 R13
Aberchalder Lodge Highld 96 C3
Aberchirder Abers 104 J5
Aber Clydach Powys 27 L3
Abercraf Powys 26 E5
Abercregan Neath 26 E8
Abercwmboi Rhondd 26 J8
Abercych Pembks 32 D12
Abercynon Rhondd 26 K9
Aberdalgie P & K 90 G7
Aberdare Rhondd 26 J7
Aberdaron Gwynd 42 C8
Aberdeen C Aber 99 S2
Aberdeen Airport C Aber 105 P13
Aberdeen Crematorium C Aber 99 R2
Aberdesach Gwynd 42 H3
Aberdour Fife 83 N1
Aberdulais Neath 26 D8
Aberdyfi Gwynd 33 M1
Aberedw Powys 34 C11
Abereiddy Pembks 24 C4
Abererch Gwynd 42 G6
Aberfan Myr Td 26 K7
Aberfeldy P & K 90 C2
Aberffraw IoA 52 E9
Aberffrwd Cerdgn 33 N5
Aberford Leeds 63 U12
Aberfoyle Stirlg 89 M5
Abergarw Brdgnd 26 G11
Abergarwed Neath 26 E7
Abergavenny Mons 27 P5
Abergele Conwy 53 R7
Aber-giar Carmth 32 K12
Abergorlech Carmth 25 U4
Abergwesyn Powys 33 S10
Abergwili Carmth 25 R6
Abergwydol Powys 43 Q13
Abergwynfi Neath 26 F8
Abergwyngregyn Gwynd 53 L8
Abergynolwyn Gwynd 43 N12
Aberhafesp Powys 34 C2
Aberhosan Powys 33 R1
Aberkenfig Brdgnd 26 F11
Aberlady E Loth 84 D3
Aberlemno Angus 98 J12
Aberllefenni Gwynd 43 Q12
Aberllynfi Powys 34 E13
Aberlour Moray 104 B7
Aber-Magwr Cerdgn 33 N6
Aber-meurig Cerdgn 33 L9
Abermorddu Flints 44 H2
Abermule Powys 34 E2
Abernant Carmth 25 P6
Aber-nant Rhondd 26 J7
Abernethy P & K 90 J8
Abernyte P & K 91 L5
Aberporth Cerdgn 32 E10
Abersoch Gwynd 42 F8
Abersychan Torfn 27 P7
Aberthin V Glam 26 J13
Abertillery Blae G 27 N7
Abertridwr Caerph 27 L10
Abertridwr Powys 44 B10
Abertysswg Caerph 27 L6
Aberuthven P & K 90 E8
Aberyscir Powys 26 H2
Aberystwyth Cerdgn 33 L4
Aberystwyth Crematorium Cerdgn 33 M4
Abingdon-on-Thames Oxon 29 U8
Abinger Common Surrey 20 K13
Abinger Hammer Surrey 20 J13
Abington Nhants 37 U8
Abington S Lans 82 H14
Abington Pigotts Cambs 31 T4
Abington Services S Lans 82 H14
Abingworth W Susx 10 J7
Ab Kettleby Leics 47 T9
Ab Lench Worcs 36 D10
Ablington Gloucs 29 M6
Ablington Wilts 18 J11
Abney Derbys 56 J10
Above Church Staffs 46 D3
Aboyne Abers 98 J4
Abram Wigan 55 P6
Abriachan Highld 102 G8
Abridge Essex 21 S3
Abronhill N Lans 89 S10
Abson S Glos 28 D13
Abthorpe Nhants 37 R11
Aby Lincs 59 R11
Acaster Malbis C York 64 D10
Acaster Selby N York 64 D11
Accrington Lancs 62 F14
Accrington Crematorium Lancs 62 F14
Acha Ag & B 92 F8
Achahoish Ag & B 87 P10
Achalader P & K 90 H2
Achaleven Ag & B 94 C12
Acha Mor W Isls 106 i6
Achanalt Highld 108 D12
Achandunie Highld 109 L10
Achany Highld 108 K4
Acharacle Highld 93 R5
Acharn Highld 93 S8
Acharn P & K 95 V10
Achavanich Highld 112 E8
Achduart Highld 107 T4
Achfary Highld 110 F9
A'Chill Highld 100 b9
Achiltibuie Highld 107 T3
Achina Highld 111 Q4
Achinhoan Ag & B 79 P12
Achintee Highld 101 N3
Achintraid Highld 101 L4
Achmelvich Highld 110 B12
Achmore Highld 101 M5
Achmore W Isls 106 i6
Achnacarnin Highld 110 A10
Achnacarry Highld 101 T14
Achnacloich Highld 100 e9
Achnaconeran Highld 102 D12
Achnacroish Ag & B 94 B10
Achnadrish House Ag & B 93 M8
Achnafauld P & K 90 C4
Achnagarron Highld 109 M10
Achnaha Highld 93 M5
Achnahaird Highld 107 T2
Achnairn Highld 108 K2
Achnalea Highld 94 B6
Achnamara Ag & B 87 P8
Achnasheen Highld 108 B13
Achnashellach Lodge Highld 101 Q2
Achnastank Moray 104 B9
Achosnich Highld 93 L5
Achranich Highld 93 S9
Achreamie Highld 112 B3
Achriabhach Highld 94 G5
Achriesgill Highld 110 F6
Achtoty Highld 111 P4
Achurch Nhants 38 F4
Achvaich Highld 109 N6
Achvarasdal Highld 112 A4
Ackergill Highld 112 J6
Acklam Middsb 70 G9
Acklam N York 64 H7
Ackleton Shrops 45 S14
Acklington Nthumb 77 Q5
Ackton Wakefd 57 P2
Ackworth Moor Top Wakefd 57 P3
Acle Norfk 51 R11
Acock's Green Birm 36 F4
Acol Kent 13 R2
Acomb C York 64 D9
Acomb Nthumb 76 J12
Acombe Somset 6 G2
Aconbury Herefs 35 M14
Acre Lancs 55 S2
Acrefair Wrexhm 44 G5
Acton Ches E 45 P3
Acton Dorset 8 D13
Acton Gt Lon 21 M6
Acton Shrops 34 H4
Acton Staffs 45 T5
Acton Suffk 40 E11
Acton Worcs 35 T7
Acton Beauchamp Herefs 35 Q10
Acton Bridge Ches W 55 N11
Acton Burnell Shrops 45 M13
Acton Green Herefs 35 Q10
Acton Park Wrexhm 44 H3
Acton Pigott Shrops 45 M13
Acton Round Shrops 35 P1
Acton Scott Shrops 35 L3
Acton Trussell Staffs 46 B10
Acton Turville S Glos 18 B4
Adbaston Staffs 45 S8
Adber Dorset 17 Q12
Adbolton Notts 47 Q6
Adderbury Oxon 37 N13
Adderley Shrops 45 Q6
Adderstone Nthumb 85 S12
Addiewell W Loth 82 J6
Addingham C Brad 63 M10
Addington Bucks 30 F7
Addington Gt Lon 21 Q10
Addington Kent 12 C4
Addiscombe Gt Lon 21 P9
Addlestone Surrey 20 J10
Addlestonemoor Surrey 20 J9
Addlethorpe Lincs 59 T13
Adeney Wrekin 45 Q10
Adeyfield Herts 31 N11
Adfa Powys 44 C13
Adforton Herefs 34 K6
Adisham Kent 13 P5
Adlestrop Gloucs 29 P2
Adlingfleet E R Yk 58 D2
Adlington Ches E 56 D10
Adlington Lancs 55 P4
Admaston Staffs 46 D9
Admaston Wrekin 45 P11
Admington Warwks 36 H11
Adpar Cerdgn 32 F12
Adsborough Somset 16 J11
Adscombe Somset 16 G9
Adstock Bucks 30 F7
Adstone Nhants 37 Q10
Adswood Stockp 56 C9
Adversane W Susx 10 H6
Advie Highld 103 T9
Adwalton Leeds 63 Q14
Adwell Oxon 30 E13
Adwick Le Street Donc 57 R5
Adwick upon Dearne Donc 57 Q6
Ae D & G 74 J8
Ae Bridgend D & G 74 K8
Afan Forest Park Neath 26 F8
Affetside Bury 55 S4
Affleck Abers 104 H7
Affpuddle Dorset 7 V6
Affric Lodge Highld 101 T7
Afon-wen Flints 54 D12
Afton Devon 5 U8
Afton IoW 9 L11
Agecroft Crematorium Salfd 55 T6
Agglethorpe N York 63 M2
Aigburth Lpool 54 J9
Aike E R Yk 65 N10
Aiketgate Cumb 67 Q3
Aikhead Cumb 66 K3
Aikton Cumb 67 L2
Ailby Lincs 59 R11
Ailey Herefs 34 H11
Ailsworth C Pete 48 H14
Ainderby Quernhow N York 63 S3
Ainderby Steeple N York 63 S1
Aingers Green Essex 23 R3
Ainsdale Sefton 54 H4
Ainsdale-on-Sea Sefton 54 G4
Ainstable Cumb 67 R3
Ainsworth Bury 55 S4
Ainthorpe N York 71 M11
Aintree Sefton 54 J7
Ainville W Loth 83 M6
Aird Ag & B 87 P5
Aird D & G 72 D7
Aird W Isls 106 k5
Aird a Mhulaidh W Isls 106 g7
Aird Asaig W Isls 106 g8
Aird Dhubh Highld 100 g5
Airdeny Ag & B 94 D13
Aird of Kinloch Ag & B 93 N13
Aird of Sleat Highld 100 e9
Airdrie N Lans 82 E5
Airdriehill N Lans 82 E5
Airds of Kells D & G 73 R5
Aird Uig W Isls 106 f5
Airidh a bhruaich W Isls 106 h7
Airieland D & G 73 T8
Airlie Angus 98 E13
Airmyn E R Yk 58 B2
Airntully P & K 90 G4
Airor Highld 100 g9
Airth Falk 82 H1
Airton N York 62 J8
Aisby Lincs 48 F6
Aisby Lincs 58 E8
Aisgill Cumb 68 G13
Aish Devon 5 R8
Aish Devon 5 U9
Aisholt Somset 16 G9
Aiskew N York 63 R2
Aislaby N York 64 H2
Aislaby N York 71 Q11
Aislaby S on T 70 F10
Aisthorpe Lincs 58 F10
Aith Shet 106 t8
Akeld Nthumb 85 P13
Akeley Bucks 30 F5
Akenham Suffk 40 K11
Albaston Cnwll 5 L6
Alberbury Shrops 44 J11
Albourne W Susx 11 M7
Albourne Green W Susx 11 M7
Albrighton Shrops 45 L10
Albrighton Shrops 45 T13
Alburgh Norfk 41 N3
Albury Herts 22 B3
Albury Oxon 30 E11
Albury Surrey 20 H13
Albury End Herts 22 B3
Albury Heath Surrey 20 J13
Alby Hill Norfk 51 L7
Alcaig Highld 102 G4
Alcaston Shrops 35 L3
Alcester Warwks 36 E9
Alcester Lane End Birm 36 E4
Alciston E Susx 11 S9
Alcombe Somset 16 C7
Alcombe Wilts 18 B7
Alconbury Cambs 38 J5
Alconbury Weston Cambs 38 J5
Aldborough N York 63 U6
Aldborough Norfk 51 L7
Aldbourne Wilts 19 L5
Aldbrough E R Yk 65 S12
Aldbrough St John N York 69 R10
Aldbury Herts 31 L10
Aldcliffe Lancs 61 T7
Aldclune P & K 97 P11
Aldeburgh Suffk 41 S9
Aldeby Norfk 41 R2
Aldenham Herts 20 K3
Alderbury Wilts 8 H3
Aldercar Derbys 47 M4
Alderford Norfk 50 K10
Alderholt Dorset 8 G6
Alderley Gloucs 28 E9
Alderley Edge Ches E 55 T11
Aldermans Green Covtry 37 L4
Aldermaston W Berk 19 S7
Alderminster Warwks 36 H11
Alder Moor Staffs 46 H8
Aldersey Green Ches W 45 L2
Aldershot Hants 20 E12
Alderton Gloucs 36 D14
Alderton Nhants 37 T11
Alderton Shrops 45 L9
Alderton Suffk 41 P12
Alderton Wilts 28 F11
Alderwasley Derbys 46 K3
Aldfield N York 63 R6
Aldford Ches W 44 K2
Aldgate Rutlnd 48 E13
Aldham Essex 23 M2
Aldham Suffk 40 J11
Aldingbourne W Susx 10 E9
Aldingham Cumb 61 P5
Aldington Kent 13 L8
Aldington Worcs 36 E12
Aldington Corner Kent 13 L8
Aldivalloch Moray 104 D10
Aldochlay Ag & B 88 J7
Aldon Shrops 34 K5
Aldoth Cumb 66 H3
Aldreth Cambs 39 P6
Aldridge Wsall 46 E13
Aldringham Suffk 41 R8
Aldro N York 64 J7
Aldsworth Gloucs 29 N6
Aldsworth W Susx 10 B9
Aldunie Moray 104 D10
Aldwark Derbys 46 H2
Aldwark N York 64 B7
Aldwick W Susx 10 E11
Aldwincle Nhants 38 F4
Aldworth W Berk 19 S5
Alexandria W Duns 88 J10
Aley Somset 16 G9
Alfardisworthy Devon 14 G10
Alfington Devon 6 F5
Alfold Surrey 10 G4
Alfold Bars W Susx 10 G4
Alfold Crossways Surrey 10 G3
Alford Abers 104 H12
Alford Lincs 59 S11
Alford Somset 17 R10
Alford Crematorium Lincs 59 R11
Alfreton Derbys 47 M2
Alfrick Worcs 35 R10
Alfrick Pound Worcs 35 R10
Alfriston E Susx 11 S10
Algarkirk Lincs 49 L6
Alhampton Somset 17 R10
Alkborough N Linc 58 E2
Alkerton Gloucs 28 E6
Alkerton Oxon 37 L12
Alkham Kent 13 Q7
Alkington Shrops 45 M6
Alkmonton Derbys 46 G6
Allaleigh Devon 5 U10
Allanaquoich Abers 97 U5
Allanbank N Lans 82 F7
Allanton Border 85 M8
Allanton N Lans 82 F7
Allanton S Lans 82 D8
Allaston Gloucs 28 B7
Allbrook Hants 9 P4
All Cannings Wilts 18 G8
Allendale Nthumb 68 H1
Allen End Warwks 36 G1
Allenheads Nthumb 68 J3
Allensford Dur 69 N2
Allen's Green Herts 22 C4
Allensmore Herefs 35 L13
Allenton C Derb 47 L7
Aller Devon 15 S7
Aller Somset 17 M11
Allerby Cumb 66 G5
Allercombe Devon 6 D6
Allerford Somset 16 B7
Allerston N York 64 K3
Allerthorpe E R Yk 64 H10
Allerton C Brad 63 N13
Allerton Highld 103 L2
Allerton Lpool 54 J9
Allerton Bywater Leeds 63 U14
Allerton Mauleverer N York 63 U8
Allesley Covtry 36 K4
Allestree C Derb 46 K6
Allet Common Cnwll 2 K7
Allexton Leics 48 B13
Allgreave Ches E 56 E13
Allhallows Medway 22 K12
Allhallows-on-Sea Medway 22 K12
Alligin Shuas Highld 107 P13
Allimore Green Staffs 45 U10
Allington Dorset 7 N6
Allington Kent 12 E4
Allington Lincs 48 C5
Allington Wilts 18 C5
Allington Wilts 18 G8
Allington Wilts 18 K13
Allithwaite Cumb 61 R4
Alloa Clacks 90 C13
Allonby Cumb 66 G4
Allostock Ches W 55 R12
Alloway S Ayrs 81 L9
Allowenshay Somset 7 L2
All Saints South Elmham Suffk 41 P4
Allscott Shrops 35 R1
Allscott Wrekin 45 P11
All Stretton Shrops 35 L1
Alltami Flints 54 G13
Alltchaorunn Highld 94 H8
Alltmawr Powys 34 C11
Alltwalis Carmth 25 R4
Alltwen Neath 26 C7
Alltyblaca Cerdgn 32 K11
Allweston Dorset 7 S2
Allwood Green Suffk 40 H6
Almeley Herefs 34 H10
Almeley Wooton Herefs 34 H10
Almer Dorset 8 C9
Almholme Donc 57 S5
Almington Staffs 45 R7
Almodington W Susx 10 C11
Almondbank P & K 90 G6
Almondbury Kirk 56 J4
Almondsbury S Glos 28 B11
Alne N York 64 B6
Alness Highld 109 M11
Alnham Nthumb 76 K3
Alnmouth Nthumb 77 Q3
Alnwick Nthumb 77 P3
Alperton Gt Lon 21 L6
Alphamstone Essex 40 E13
Alpheton Suffk 40 E10
Alphington Devon 6 B6
Alpington Norfk 51 N13
Alport Derbys 56 K14
Alpraham Ches E 45 N2
Alresford Essex 23 Q3
Alrewas Staffs 46 G11
Alsager Ches E 45 S2
Alsagers Bank Staffs 45 S4
Alsop en le Dale Derbys 46 G3
Alston Cumb 68 F3
Alston Devon 6 K4
Alstone Gloucs 36 C14
Alstone Somset 16 K7
Alstonefield Staffs 46 F2
Alston Sutton Somset 17 M6
Alswear Devon 15 R8
Alt Oldham 56 D6
Altandhu Highld 107 S2
Altarnun Cnwll 4 G4
Altass Highld 108 J4
Altcreich Ag & B 93 R11
Altgaltraig Ag & B 88 B11
Altham Lancs 62 F13
Althorne Essex 23 M8
Althorpe N Linc 58 D5
Altnabreac Station Highld 112 B7
Altnaharra Highld 111 M9
Altofts Wakefd 57 N2
Alton Derbys 57 N14
Alton Hants 19 V13
Alton Staffs 46 E5
Alton Wilts 18 J11
Alton Barnes Wilts 18 H8
Alton Pancras Dorset 7 T4
Alton Priors Wilts 18 H8
Alton Towers Staffs 46 E5
Altrincham Traffd 55 S9
Altrincham Crematorium Traffd 55 R9
Altskeith Hotel Stirlg 89 L5
Alva Clacks 90 C12
Alvanley Ches W 55 L12
Alvaston C Derb 47 L7
Alvechurch Worcs 36 D6
Alvecote Warwks 46 H13
Alvediston Wilts 8 D4
Alveley Shrops 35 S4
Alverdiscott Devon 15 M7
Alverstoke Hants 9 S9
Alverstone IoW 9 R11
Alverthorpe Wakefd 57 M2
Alverton Notts 47 U5
Alves Moray 103 T3
Alvescot Oxon 29 Q7
Alveston S Glos 28 B10
Alveston Warwks 36 H9
Alvingham Lincs 59 Q8
Alvington Gloucs 28 B7
Alwalton C Pete 38 H1
Alwinton Nthumb 76 J4
Alwoodley Leeds 63 R11
Alwoodley Gates Leeds 63 S11
Alyth P & K 90 K2
Ambergate Derbys 46 K3
Amber Hill Lincs 48 K4
Amberley Gloucs 28 G7
Amberley W Susx 10 G8
Amber Row Derbys 47 L2
Amberstone E Susx 11 T8
Amble Nthumb 77 R5
Amblecote Dudley 35 U3
Ambler Thorn C Brad 63 M14
Ambleside Cumb 67 N12
Ambleston Pembks 24 H5
Ambrosden Oxon 30 D9
Amcotts N Linc 58 E4
America Cambs 39 P5
Amersham Bucks 20 G3
Amersham Common Bucks 20 G3
Amersham Old Town Bucks 20 G3
Amersham on the Hill Bucks 20 G3
Amerton Staffs 46 C8
Amerton Railway & Farm Staffs 46 C8
Amesbury Wilts 18 J12
Amhuinnsuidhe W Isls 106 f8
Amington Staffs 46 H13
Amisfield Town D & G 74 K9
Amlwch IoA 52 F4
Ammanford Carmth 26 A5
Amotherby N York 64 G5
Ampfield Hants 9 N4
Ampleforth N York 64 D4
Ampney Crucis Gloucs 29 L7
Ampney St Mary Gloucs 29 L7
Ampney St Peter Gloucs 29 L7
Amport Hants 19 M12
Ampthill C Beds 31 M5
Ampton Suffk 40 E6
Amroth Pembks 25 L9
Amulree P & K 90 C4
Amwell Herts 31 Q10
Anaheilt Highld 93 U6
Ancaster Lincs 48 E5
Anchor Shrops 34 E3
Ancroft Nthumb 85 P9
Ancrum Border 84 G14
Ancton W Susx 10 F10
Anderby Lincs 59 T11
Andersea Somset 16 K10
Andersfield Somset 16 H10
Anderson Dorset 8 B9
Anderton Ches W 55 P11
Anderton Cnwll 5 L10
Andover Hants 19 N11
Andoversford Gloucs 28 K4
Andreas IoM 60 g3
Anelog Gwynd 42 C8
Anerley Gt Lon 21 P9
Anfield Lpool 54 J8
Anfield Crematorium Lpool 54 J8
Angarrack Cnwll 2 F9
Angarrick Cnwll 2 K9
Angelbank Shrops 35 N5
Angersleigh Somset 16 G13
Angerton Cumb 66 K1
Angle Pembks 24 E10
Anglesey IoA 52 F6
Anglesey Abbey Cambs 39 R8
Angmering W Susx 10 H10
Angram N York 64 C10
Angram N York 68 J13
Angrouse Cnwll 2 H13
Anick Nthumb 76 J12
Ankerville Highld 109 Q10
Ankle Hill Leics 47 U10
Anlaby E R Yk 65 N14
Anmer Norfk 50 B8
Anmore Hants 9 T6
Annan D & G 75 N12
Annandale Water Services D & G 75 M7
Annaside Cumb 60 K2
Annat Highld 107 Q14
Annathill N Lans 82 D4
Anna Valley Hants 19 N12
Annbank S Ayrs 81 N8
Anne Hathaway's Cottage Warwks 36 G10
Annesley Notts 47 P3
Annesley Woodhouse Notts 47 N3
Annfield Plain Dur 69 Q2
Anniesland C Glas 89 M12
Annitsford N Tyne 77 R11
Annscroft Shrops 45 L12
Ansdell Lancs 61 Q14
Ansford Somset 17 R10
Ansley Warwks 36 K2
Anslow Staffs 46 H8
Anslow Gate Staffs 46 G9
Anslow Lees Staffs 46 H9
Ansteadbrook Surrey 10 E4
Anstey Hants 10 A2
Anstey Herts 39 P14
Anstey Leics 47 Q12
Anstruther Fife 91 S11
Ansty W Susx 11 M6
Ansty Warwks 37 M4
Ansty Wilts 8 D3
Ansty Cross Dorset 7 U4
Anthill Common Hants 9 S6
Anthonys Surrey 20 H10
Anthorn Cumb 75 N14
Antingham Norfk 51 N7
An t-Ob W Isls 106 f10
Antonine Wall Falk 89 T10
Anton's Gowt Lincs 49 M4
Antony Cnwll 5 L10
Antrobus Ches W 55 P11
Anvil Corner Devon 14 J12
Anvil Green Kent 13 M6
Anwick Lincs 48 H3
Anwoth D & G 73 P8
Aperfield Gt Lon 21 R11
Apes Dale Worcs 36 C6
Apethorpe Nhants 38 F1
Apeton Staffs 45 U10
Apley Lincs 58 K11
Apperknowle Derbys 57 N11
Apperley Gloucs 28 G2
Apperley Bridge C Brad 63 P12
Apperley Dene Nthumb 77 M14
Appersett N York 62 H1
Appin Ag & B 94 C9
Appleby N Linc 58 G4
Appleby-in-Westmorland Cumb 68 E8
Appleby Magna Leics 46 K12
Appleby Parva Leics 46 K12
Appleby Street Herts 31 T12
Applecross Highld 100 g5
Appledore Devon 6 E2
Appledore Devon 15 L6
Appledore Kent 12 J10
Appledore Heath Kent 12 J9
Appleford Oxon 19 R2
Applegarth Town D & G 75 M9
Applehaigh Wakefd 57 N4
Appleshaw Hants 19 M11
Applethwaite Cumb 67 L7
Appleton Halton 55 M9
Appleton Oxon 29 T7
Appleton Warrtn 55 P10
Appleton-le-Moors N York 64 G2
Appleton-le-Street N York 64 G5
Appleton Roebuck N York 64 D11
Appleton Thorn Warrtn 55 P10
Appleton Wiske N York 70 E12
Appletreehall Border 75 V2
Appletreewick N York 63 M7
Appley Somset 16 E12
Appley Bridge Lancs 55 M5
Apse Heath IoW 9 R12
Apsley End C Beds 31 P6
Apuldram W Susx 10 C10
Arabella Highld 109 Q9
Arbirlot Angus 91 T3
Arboll Highld 109 R8
Arborfield Wokham 20 C9
Arborfield Cross Wokham 20 C9
Arbourthorne Sheff 57 N9
Arbroath Angus 91 T3
Arbuthnott Abers 99 P8
Arcadia Kent 12 G8
Archddu Carmth 25 R10
Archdeacon Newton Darltn 69 S9
Archencarroch W Duns 88 K9
Archiestown Moray 104 A7
Archirondel Jersey 7 f2
Arclid Green Ches E 45 S1
Ardallie Abers 105 S8
Ardanaiseig Hotel Ag & B 94 F14
Ardaneaskan Highld 101 L4
Ardarroch Highld 101 L4
Ardbeg Ag & B 78 G6
Ardbeg Ag & B 88 C12
Ardbeg Ag & B 88 E9
Ardcharnich Highld 108 B7
Ardchiavaig Ag & B 86 F2
Ardchonnel Ag & B 87 T3
Ardchullarie More Stirlg 89 N3
Arddarroch Ag & B 88 F7
Arddleen Powys 44 G10
Ardechive Highld 101 S13
Ardeer N Ayrs 80 K4
Ardeley Herts 31 T7
Ardelve Highld 101 M6
Arden Ag & B 88 J9
Ardens Grafton Warwks 36 F10
Ardentallen Ag & B 93 U14
Ardentinny Ag & B 88 E8
Ardentraive Ag & B 88 B11
Ardeonaig Stirlg 95 T11
Ardersier Highld 103 L5
Ardessie Highld 107 U7
Ardfern Ag & B 87 Q5
Ardfernal Ag & B 86 K11
Ardgay Highld 108 K6
Ardgour Highld 94 E6
Ardgowan Inver 88 F11
Ardhallow Ag & B 88 E11
Ardhasig W Isls 106 g8
Ardheslaig Highld 107 N13
Ardindrean Highld 108 B7
Ardingly W Susx 11 N5
Ardington Oxon 29 T10
Ardington Wick Oxon 29 T10
Ardlamont Ag & B 87 T12
Ardleigh Essex 23 Q2
Ardleigh Heath Essex 23 P1
Ardler P & K 91 L3
Ardley Oxon 30 B7
Ardley End Essex 22 D5
Ardlui Ag & B 88 H2
Ardlussa Ag & B 87 L8
Ardmair Highld 107 V5
Ardmaleish Ag & B 88 C12
Ardminish Ag & B 79 L6
Ardmolich Highld 93 S4
Ardmore Ag & B 88 H10
Ardmore Highld 109 N7
Ardnadam Ag & B 88 E9
Ardnagrask Highld 102 F6
Ardnarff Highld 101 M4
Ardnastang Highld 93 U6
Ardpatrick Ag & B 79 P4
Ardrishaig Ag & B 87 R8
Ardross Highld 109 L10
Ardrossan N Ayrs 80 J4
Ardsley Barns 57 N5
Ardsley East Leeds 57 M1
Ardslignish Highld 93 P6
Ardtalla Ag & B 78 H5
Ardtoe Highld 93 Q4
Arduaine Ag & B 87 P3
Ardullie Highld 102 G3
Ardvasar Highld 100 f9
Ardvorlich P & K 95 S14
Ardvourlie W Isls 106 g7
Ardwell D & G 72 E10
Ardwick Manch 56 C7
Areley Kings Worcs 35 S6
Arevegaig Highld 93 R5
Arford Hants 10 C3
Arglam E R Yk 64 H12
Argoed Caerph 27 M8
Argoed Shrops 44 H9
Argoed Mill Powys 33 U8
Argos Hill E Susx 11 T5
Argyll Forest Park Ag & B 88 F5
Aribruach W Isls 106 h7
Aridhglas Ag & B 92 J14
Arileod Ag & B 92 F8
Arinagour Ag & B 92 G7
Ariogan Ag & B 94 B13
Arisaig Highld 93 R1
Arisaig House Highld 93 R2
Arkendale N York 63 T7
Arkesden Essex 39 Q14
Arkholme Lancs 62 B5
Arkleby Cumb 66 H5
Arkleton D & G 75 S7
Arkle Town N York 69 M12
Arkley Gt Lon 21 M3
Arksey Donc 57 S5
Arkwright Town Derbys 57 P12
Arle Gloucs 28 H3
Arlecdon Cumb 66 F9
Arlescote Warwks 37 L11
Arlesey C Beds 31 Q5
Arleston Wrekin 45 Q11
Arley Ches E 55 Q10
Arley Warwks 36 J2
Arlingham Gloucs 28 D5
Arlington Devon 15 P4
Arlington E Susx 11 S9
Arlington Gloucs 29 M6
Arlington Beccott Devon 15 P4
Armadale Highld 100 f9
Armadale Highld 111 R4
Armadale W Loth 82 H5
Armaside Cumb 66 J7
Armathwaite Cumb 67 R3
Arminghall Norfk 51 N13
Armitage Staffs 46 E10
Armitage Bridge Kirk 56 H4
Armley Leeds 63 R13
Armscote Warwks 36 H12
Armshead Staffs 46 B4
Armston Nhants 38 G3
Armthorpe Donc 57 T6
Arnabost Ag & B 92 G6
Arnaby Cumb 61 M3
Arncliffe N York 62 J5
Arncliffe Cote N York 62 J5
Arncroach Fife 91 R10
Arndilly House Moray 104 B6
Arne Dorset 8 D11
Arnesby Leics 37 R2
Arngask P & K 90 H9
Arnisdale Highld 101 L9
Arnish Highld 100 e5
Arniston Mdloth 83 R6
Arnol W Isls 106 i4
Arnold E R Yk 65 Q11
Arnold Notts 47 Q4
Arnprior Stirlg 89 P7
Arnside Cumb 61 T4
Aros Ag & B 93 P9
Arowry Wrexhm 45 L6
Arrad Foot Cumb 61 Q3
Arram E R Yk 65 N11
Arran N Ayrs 79 S8
Arrathorne N York 69 R14
Arreton IoW 9 Q11
Arrina Highld 107 M13
Arrington Cambs 39 M10
Arrochar Ag & B 88 G5
Arrow Warwks 36 E9
Arrowfield Top Worcs 36 D6
Arscott Shrops 44 K12
Artafallie Highld 102 H6
Arthington Leeds 63 R11
Arthingworth Nhants 37 U4
Arthog Gwynd 43 M11
Arthrath Abers 105 R8
Arthursdale Leeds 63 T12
Artrochie Abers 105 S9
Arundel W Susx 10 G9
Asby Cumb 66 G8
Ascog Ag & B 88 D13
Ascot W & M 20 F9
Ascott Warwks 36 K14
Ascott Earl Oxon 29 R4
Ascott-under-Wychwood Oxon 29 R4
Asenby N York 63 T4
Asfordby Leics 47 T10
Asfordby Hill Leics 47 T10
Asgarby Lincs 48 H4
Asgarby Lincs 59 P13
Ash Devon 5 U11
Ash Devon 15 M11
Ash Dorset 8 B6
Ash Kent 12 B3
Ash Kent 13 Q4
Ash Somset 16 J12
Ash Somset 17 N12
Ash Surrey 20 F12
Ashampstead W Berk 19 S5
Ashampstead Green W Berk 19 S5
Ashbocking Suffk 41 L10
Ashbourne Derbys 46 G4
Ashbrittle Somset 16 E12
Ashburnham Place E Susx 12 C13
Ashburton Devon 5 T6
Ashbury Devon 15 M13
Ashbury Oxon 29 Q10
Ashby N Linc 58 E5
Ashby by Partney Lincs 59 R13
Ashby cum Fenby NE Lin 59 N6
Ashby de la Launde Lincs 48 G2
Ashby-de-la-Zouch Leics 47 L10
Ashby Folville Leics 47 T11
Ashby Magna Leics 37 Q2
Ashby Parva Leics 37 P3
Ashby Puerorum Lincs 59 P12
Ashby St Ledgers Nhants 37 Q7
Ashby St Mary Norfk 51 P13
Ashchurch Gloucs 36 B14
Ashcombe Devon 6 B9
Ashcombe N Som 16 K4
Ashcott Somset 17 M9
Ashdon Essex 39 S12
Ashe Hants 19 R10
Asheldham Essex 23 N7
Ashen Essex 40 B12
Ashendon Bucks 30 F10
Asheridge Bucks 30 K12
Ashfield Hants 9 M5
Ashfield Herefs 28 A3
Ashfield Stirlg 89 S5
Ashfield cum Thorpe Suffk 41 M8
Ashfield Green Suffk 40 C9
Ashfield Green Suffk 41 N6
Ashfold Crossways W Susx 11 L5
Ashford Devon 5 R11
Ashford Devon 15 M5
Ashford Kent 12 K7
Ashford Surrey 20 J8
Ashford Bowdler Shrops 35 M6
Ashford Carbonell Shrops 35 M6
Ashford Hill Hants 19 S8
Ashford in the Water Derbys 56 J13
Ashgill S Lans 82 E8
Ash Green Surrey 20 F13
Ash Green Warwks 36 K4
Ashill Devon 6 E2
Ashill Norfk 50 E13
Ashill Somset 16 K13
Ashingdon Essex 23 L9
Ashington Nthumb 77 R8
Ashington Poole 8 E9
Ashington Somset 17 Q12
Ashington W Susx 10 J7
Ashkirk Border 75 U1
Ashlett Hants 9 P8
Ashleworth Gloucs 28 F2
Ashleworth Quay Gloucs 28 F2
Ashley Cambs 39 U8
Ashley Ches E 55 S10
Ashley Devon 15 Q10
Ashley Dorset 8 G8
Ashley Gloucs 28 H9
Ashley Hants 8 K9
Ashley Hants 9 M2
Ashley Kent 13 R6
Ashley Nhants 37 U2
Ashley Staffs 45 S6
Ashley Wilts 18 B7
Ashley Green Bucks 31 L11
Ashleyhay Derbys 46 J3
Ashley Heath Dorset 8 G8
Ashley Moor Herefs 35 L7
Ash Magna Shrops 45 N6
Ashmansworth Hants 19 P9
Ashmansworthy Devon 14 H9
Ashmead Green Gloucs 28 E8
Ashmill Devon 14 J13
Ash Mill Devon 15 S8
Ashmore Dorset 8 C5
Ashmore Green W Berk 19 R7
Ashorne Warwks 36 K9
Ashover Derbys 57 M14
Ashover Hay Derbys 46 K1
Ashow Warwks 36 K6
Ash Parva Shrops 45 N6
Ashperton Herefs 35 P12
Ashprington Devon 5 U9
Ash Priors Somset 16 G11
Ashreigney Devon 15 P10
Ash Street Suffk 40 H11
Ashtead Surrey 21 L11
Ash Thomas Devon 6 D2
Ashton C Pete 48 H12
Ashton Ches W 55 M13
Ashton Cnwll 2 G11
Ashton Devon 5 V4
Ashton Hants 9 Q5
Ashton Herefs 35 M8
Ashton Inver 88 F10
Ashton Nhants 37 U11
Ashton Nhants 38 G3
Ashton Somset 17 M7
Ashton Common Wilts 18 C9
Ashton Hill Wilts 18 D9
Ashton-in-Makerfield Wigan 55 N7
Ashton Keynes Wilts 28 K9
Ashton under Hill Worcs 36 C13
Ashton-under-Lyne Tamesd 56 D7
Ashton upon Mersey Traffd 55 S8
Ashurst Hants 9 L6
Ashurst Kent 11 S3
Ashurst Lancs 55 L5
Ashurst W Susx 10 K7
Ashurstwood W Susx 11 Q3
Ash Vale Surrey 20 E12
Ashwater Devon 14 J13
Ashwell Herts 31 S5
Ashwell Rutlnd 48 C11
Ashwell Somset 17 L13
Ashwell End Herts 31 S4
Ashwellthorpe Norfk 50 K14
Ashwick Somset 17 R7
Ashwicken Norfk 50 B10
Ashwood Staffs 35 U3
Askam in Furness Cumb 61 N4
Askern Donc 57 S4
Askerswell Dorset 7 P6
Askett Bucks 30 H11
Askham Cumb 67 R8
Askham Notts 58 B12
Askham Bryan C York 64 D10
Askham Richard C York 64 C10
Asknish Ag & B 87 S7
Askrigg N York 62 J1
Askwith N York 63 P10
Aslackby Lincs 48 G7
Aslacton Norfk 41 L2
Aslockton Notts 47 T6
Asney Somset 17 N9
Aspall Suffk 41 L8
Aspatria Cumb 66 H4
Aspenden Herts 31 U7
Aspenshaw Derbys 56 F9
Asperton Lincs 49 L6
Aspley Staffs 45 T7
Aspley Guise C Beds 30 K5
Aspley Heath C Beds 30 K6
Aspley Heath Warwks 36 E6
Aspull Wigan 55 P5
Aspull Common Wigan 55 P7
Asselby E R Yk 64 G14
Asserby Lincs 59 S11
Asserby Turn Lincs 59 S11
Assington Suffk 40 F13
Assington Green Suffk 40 C10
Astbury Ches E 45 T1
Astcote Nhants 37 S10
Asterby Lincs 59 N11
Asterley Shrops 44 J12
Asterton Shrops 34 J2
Asthall Oxon 29 Q5
Asthall Leigh Oxon 29 R5
Astle Highld 109 N6
Astley Shrops 45 M10
Astley Warwks 36 K3
Astley Wigan 55 R6
Astley Worcs 35 S7
Astley Abbots Shrops 35 R1
Astley Bridge Bolton 55 R4
Astley Cross Worcs 35 T7
Astley Green Wigan 55 R7
Aston Birm 36 E3
Aston Ches E 45 P4
Aston Ches W 55 N11
Aston Derbys 56 J10
Aston Flints 54 H13
Aston Herefs 35 L8
Aston Herts 31 S8
Aston Oxon 29 R7
Aston Rothm 57 Q9
Aston Shrops 35 T2
Aston Shrops 45 M8
Aston Staffs 45 S5
Aston Staffs 45 U9
Aston Wokham 20 C6
Aston Wrekin 45 P12
Aston Abbotts Bucks 30 H8
Aston Botterell Shrops 35 P4
Aston-by-Stone Staffs 46 B7
Aston Cantlow Warwks 36 F8
Aston Clinton Bucks 30 J10
Aston Crews Herefs 28 C3
Aston Cross Gloucs 36 B14
Aston End Herts 31 S8
Aston-Eyre Shrops 35 Q2
Aston Fields Worcs 36 C7
Aston Flamville Leics 37 N2
Aston Heath Ches W 55 N11
Aston Ingham Herefs 28 C3
Aston juxta Mondrum Ches E 45 P2
Aston le Walls Nhants 37 N10
Aston Magna Gloucs 36 G13
Aston Munslow Shrops 35 M3
Aston on Clun Shrops 34 J4
Aston Pigott Shrops 44 H12
Aston Rogers Shrops 44 H12
Aston Rowant Oxon 20 B3
Aston Sandford Bucks 30 G11
Aston Somerville Worcs 36 D13
Aston-sub-Edge Gloucs 36 F12
Aston Tirrold Oxon 19 S3
Aston-upon-Trent Derbys 47 M8
Aston Upthorpe Oxon 19 S3
Astrop Nhants 30 B5
Astrope Herts 30 J10
Astwick C Beds 31 R5
Astwith Derbys 57 P14
Astwood M Keyn 38 E11
Astwood Worcs 36 B7
Astwood Bank Worcs 36 D8
Aswarby Lincs 48 G6
Aswardby Lincs 59 Q12
Atcham Shrops 45 M12
Atch Lench Worcs 36 D10
Athelhampton Dorset 7 U6
Athelington Suffk 41 M6
Athelney Somset 16 K11
Athelstaneford E Loth 84 E3
Atherfield Green IoW 9 P13
Atherington Devon 15 N8
Atherington W Susx 10 G10
Atherstone Somset 17 L13
Atherstone Warwks 46 K14
Atherstone on Stour Warwks 36 H10
Atherton Wigan 55 Q6
Atley Hill N York 69 S12
Atlow Derbys 46 H4
Attadale Highld 101 N4
Attenborough Notts 47 P7
Atterby Lincs 58 G8
Attercliffe Sheff 57 N9
Atterley Shrops 45 P14
Atterton Leics 47 L14
Attingham Park Shrops 45 M12
Attleborough Norfk 40 H1
Attleborough Warwks 37 L2
Attlebridge Norfk 50 K10
Attleton Green Suffk 40 B10
Atwick E R Yk 65 R9
Atworth Wilts 18 C7
Auberrow Herefs 35 L11
Aubourn Lincs 58 F14
Auchbreck Moray 103 V10
Auchedly Abers 105 P9
Auchenblae Abers 99 N8
Auchenbowie Stirlg 89 S8
Auchencairn D & G 73 T9
Auchencairn D & G 74 J9
Auchencairn N Ayrs 80 E7
Auchencrow Border 85 M6
Auchendinny Mdloth 83 Q6
Auchengray S Lans 82 J8
Auchenhalrig Moray 104 D3
Auchenheath S Lans 82 F10
Auchenhessnane D & G 74 F6
Auchenlochan Ag & B 87 T11
Auchenmade N Ayrs 81 M3
Auchenmalg D & G 72 G9
Auchentiber N Ayrs 81 M3
Auchindrain Ag & B 88 B5
Auchindrean Highld 108 B8
Auchininna Abers 104 K6
Auchinleck E Ayrs 81 R8
Auchinloch N Lans 89 Q11
Auchinstarry N Lans 89 R10
Auchintore Highld 94 F4
Auchiries Abers 105 T8
Auchlean Highld 97 P4
Auchlee Abers 99 R4
Auchleven Abers 104 J11
Auchlochan S Lans 82 F11
Auchlossan Abers 98 K3
Auchlyne Stirlg 95 Q13
Auchmillan E Ayrs 81 Q7
Auchmithie Angus 91 U3
Auchmuirbridge Fife 90 K11
Auchnacree Angus 98 H11
Auchnagatt Abers 105 Q7
Auchnarrow Moray 103 V11
Auchnotteroch D & G 72 B7
Auchroisk Moray 104 C5
Auchterarder P & K 90 D9
Auchteraw Highld 96 D2
Auchterblair Highld 103 P11
Auchtercairn Highld 107 P9
Auchterderran Fife 90 K12
Auchterhouse Angus 91 M4
Auchterless Abers 105 L7
Auchtermuchty Fife 90 K9
Auchterneed Highld 102 E4
Auchtertool Fife 90 K13
Auchtertyre Highld 101 L6
Auchtubh Stirlg 89 N1
Auckengill Highld 112 J3
Auckley Donc 57 T6
Audenshaw Tamesd 56 D7
Audlem Ches E 45 Q5
Audley Staffs 45 S3
Audley End Essex 39 R13
Audley End Essex 40 D13
Audley End Suffk 40 E10
Audley End House & Gardens Essex 39 R13
Audmore Staffs 45 T9
Audnam Dudley 35 U3
Aughertree Cumb 67 L5
Aughton E R Yk 64 G12
Aughton Lancs 54 J5
Aughton Lancs 62 B6
Aughton Rothm 57 Q9
Aughton Wilts 18 K9
Aughton Park Lancs 54 K5
Auldearn Highld 103 P4
Aulden Herefs 35 L10
Auldgirth D & G 74 H8
Auldhouse S Lans 81 S2
Ault a' chruinn Highld 101 N7
Aultbea Highld 107 Q7
Aultgrishin Highld 107 M7
Aultguish Inn Highld 108 F10
Ault Hucknall Derbys 57 Q13
Aultmore Moray 104 E5
Aultnagoire Highld 102 F11
Aultnamain Inn Highld 109 M8
Aunby Lincs 48 F11
Aunk Devon 6 D4
Aunsby Lincs 48 F6
Aust S Glos 28 A10
Austendike Lincs 49 L9
Austerfield Donc 57 U8
Austerlands Oldham 56 E5
Austhorpe Leeds 63 T13
Austonley Kirk 56 H5
Austrey Warwks 46 J12
Austwick N York 62 F6
Authorpe Lincs 59 Q10
Authorpe Row Lincs 59 T12
Avebury Wilts 18 H7
Avebury Wilts 18 H7
Avebury Trusloe Wilts 18 G7
Aveley Thurr 22 E11
Avening Gloucs 28 G8
Averham Notts 47 U3
Aveton Gifford Devon 5 R11
Aviemore Highld 103 N13
Avington W Berk 19 N7
Avoch Highld 102 K4
Avon Hants 8 G9
Avonbridge Falk 82 H4
Avon Dassett Warwks 37 M10
Avonmouth Bristl 27 U12
Avonwick Devon 5 S9
Awbridge Hants 9 L4
Awkley S Glos 28 A10
Awliscombe Devon 6 F4
Awre Gloucs 28 D6
Awsworth Notts 47 N5
Axborough Worcs 35 U5
Axbridge Somset 17 M6
Axford Hants 19 T12
Axford Wilts 18 K6
Axminster Devon 6 J5
Axmouth Devon 6 J6
Axton Flints 54 D10
Aycliffe Dur 69 S8
Aydon Nthumb 77 L12
Aylburton Gloucs 28 B7
Ayle Nthumb 68 F3
Aylesbeare Devon 6 D6
Aylesbury Bucks 30 H10
Aylesby NE Lin 59 M5
Aylesford Kent 12 D4
Aylesham Kent 13 P5
Aylestone C Leic 47 Q13
Aylestone Park C Leic 47 Q13
Aylmerton Norfk 51 L6
Aylsham Norfk 51 L8
Aylton Herefs 35 Q13
Aylworth Gloucs 29 M3
Aymestrey Herefs 34 K7
Aynho Nhants 30 B6
Ayot Green Herts 31 R10
Ayot St Lawrence Herts 31 Q9
Ayot St Peter Herts 31 R9
Ayr S Ayrs 81 L8
Aysgarth N York 63 L2
Ayshford Devon 16 D13
Ayside Cumb 61 R3
Ayston Rutlnd 48 C13
Aythorpe Roding Essex 22 E4
Ayton Border 85 N6
Azerley N York 63 R5

B

Babbacombe Torbay 6 B11
Babbington Notts 47 N5
Babbinswood Shrops 44 H8
Babbs Green Herts 31 U9
Babcary Somset 17 Q11
Babel Carmth 33 R13
Babel Green Suffk 40 B11
Babell Flints 54 E12
Babeny Devon 5 R5
Bablock Hythe Oxon 29 T7
Babraham Cambs 39 R10
Babworth Notts 57 U10
Bachau IoA 52 F6
Bache Shrops 35 L4
Bacheldre Powys 34 F2
Bachelor's Bump E Susx 12 F13
Backaland Ork 106 u16
Backbarrow Cumb 61 R3
Backe Carmth 25 N7
Backfolds Abers 105 S5
Backford Ches W 54 J12
Backford Cross Ches W 54 J12
Backies Highld 109 Q4
Back of Keppoch Highld 100 f11
Back o' th' Brook Staffs 46 E3
Back Street Suffk 40 B9
Backwell N Som 17 N3
Backworth N Tyne 77 S11
Bacon's End Solhll 36 G3
Baconsthorpe Norfk 50 K6
Bacton Herefs 27 R1
Bacton Norfk 51 P7
Bacton Suffk 40 J7
Bacton Green Suffk 40 H7
Bacup Lancs 56 C2
Badachro Highld 107 N10
Badbury Swindn 18 J4
Badby Nhants 37 Q9
Badcall Highld 110 D8
Badcall Highld 110 E5
Badcaul Highld 107 T6
Baddeley Edge C Stke 46 B3
Baddeley Green C Stke 46 B3
Baddesley Clinton Warwks 36 H6
Baddesley Ensor Warwks 46 J14
Baddidarrach Highld 110 B12
Baddinsgill Border 83 M8
Badenscoth Abers 104 K8
Badentarbet Highld 107 T3
Badenyon Abers 104 C12
Badgall Cnwll 4 G3
Badgeney Cambs 39 P1
Badger Shrops 45 S14
Badger's Cross Cnwll 2 D10
Badgers Mount Kent 21 S10
Badgeworth Gloucs 28 H4
Badgworth Somset 17 L6
Badharlick Cnwll 4 H3
Badicaul Highld 100 g7
Badingham Suffk 41 P7
Badlesmere Kent 12 K5
Badlieu Border 75 L2
Badlipster Highld 112 F7
Badluarach Highld 107 S6
Badninish Highld 109 P6
Badrallach Highld 107 U6
Badsey Worcs 36 E12
Badshot Lea Surrey 20 E13
Badsworth Wakefd 57 Q4
Badwell Ash Suffk 40 G7
Badwell Green Suffk 40 H7
Bagber Dorset 7 U2
Bagby N York 64 B3
Bag Enderby Lincs 59 Q12
Bagendon Gloucs 28 K6
Bagginswood Shrops 35 Q4
Baggrow Cumb 66 J4
Bagh a Chaisteil W Isls 106 b19
Bagham Kent 13 L5
Bagh a Tuath W Isls 106 c18
Bagillt Flints 54 F11
Baginton Warwks 36 K6
Baglan Neath 26 C9
Bagley Leeds 63 Q12
Bagley Shrops 44 K8
Bagley Somset 17 N7
Bagmore Hants 19 U12
Bagnall Staffs 46 B3
Bagnor W Berk 19 Q7
Bagshot Surrey 20 F10
Bagshot Wilts 19 M7
Bagstone S Glos 28 C10
Bagthorpe Notts 47 N3
Bagworth Leics 47 M12
Bagwy Llydiart Herefs 27 S2
Baildon C Brad 63 P12
Baildon Green C Brad 63 N12
Baile Ailein W Isls 106 h6
Baile a Mhanaich W Isls 106 c13
Baile Mor Ag & B 92 H14
Bailey Green Hants 9 T3
Baileyhead Cumb 75 V10
Bailiff Bridge Calder 56 H1
Baillieston C Glas 82 C6
Bailrigg Lancs 61 T8
Bainbridge N York 62 J1
Bainshole Abers 104 J8
Bainton C Pete 48 G12
Bainton E R Yk 65 M9
Bainton Oxon 30 C7
Baintown Fife 91 N11
Bairnkine Border 76 D2
Baker's End Herts 31 U9
Baker Street Thurr 22 F11
Bakewell Derbys 56 K13
Bala Gwynd 43 T6
Balallan W Isls 106 h6
Balbeg Highld 102 D9
Balbeggie P & K 90 J6
Balblair Highld 102 F6
Balblair Highld 102 K2
Balby Donc 57 S6
Balcary D & G 73 U10
Balchraggan Highld 102 F7
Balchreick Highld 110 D4
Balcombe W Susx 11 N4
Balcombe Lane W Susx 11 N4
Balcomie Links Fife 91 T10
Baldersby N York 63 T4
Baldersby St James N York 63 T4
Balderstone Lancs 62 C13
Balderstone Rochdl 56 D4
Balderton Notts 48 B3
Baldhu Cnwll 2 K8
Baldinnie Fife 91 P9
Baldinnies P & K 90 F8
Baldock Herts 31 R6
Baldock Services Herts 31 R5
Baldovie C Dund 91 Q5
Baldrine IoM 60 g6
Baldslow E Susx 12 F13
Baldwin IoM 60 f6
Baldwinholme Cumb 67 M2
Baldwin's Gate Staffs 45 S6
Baldwin's Hill W Susx 11 P3
Bale Norfk 50 H6
Baledgarno P & K 91 L5
Balemartine Ag & B 92 B10
Balerno C Edin 83 N5
Balfarg Fife 91 L11
Balfield Angus 98 J10
Balfour Ork 106 t18
Balfron Stirlg 89 M8
Balgaveny Abers 104 K7
Balgonar Fife 90 F13
Balgowan D & G 72 E11
Balgowan Highld 96 J5
Balgown Highld 100 c3
Balgracie D & G 72 B7
Balgray S Lans 82 G14
Balham Gt Lon 21 N8
Balhary P & K 91 L2
Balholmie P & K 90 H4
Baligill Highld 111 T3
Balintore Angus 98 D12
Balintore Highld 109 R9
Balintraid Highld 109 N10
Balivanich W Isls 106 c13
Balk N York 64 B3
Balkeerie Angus 91 M3
Balkholme E R Yk 64 H14
Ballabeg IoM 60 d8
Ballachulish Highld 94 F7
Ballafesson IoM 60 c8
Ballajora IoM 60 h4
Ballakilpheric IoM 60 c8
Ballamodha IoM 60 d8
Ballanlay Ag & B 88 B13
Ballantrae S Ayrs 72 D3
Ballards Gore Essex 23 M9
Ballards Green Warwks 36 J2
Ballasalla IoM 60 d8
Ballater Abers 98 F4
Ballaugh IoM 60 e4
Ballchraggan Highld 109 P9
Ballencrieff E Loth 84 D3
Ballevullin Ag & B 92 B9
Ball Green C Stke 45 U3
Ball Haye Green Staffs 46 C2
Ball Hill Hants 19 P8
Ballidon Derbys 46 H3
Balliekine N Ayrs 79 R8
Balliemore Ag & B 88 D6
Balligmorrie S Ayrs 72 G1
Ballimore Stirlg 89 M2
Ballindalloch Moray 103 U8
Ballindean P & K 91 L6
Ballingdon Suffk 40 E12
Ballinger Common Bucks 30 K12
Ballingham Herefs 28 A1
Ballingry Fife 90 J12
Ballinluig P & K 97 R13
Ballinshoe Angus 98 G13
Ballintuim P & K 97 U12
Balloch Highld 102 K6
Balloch N Lans 89 R11
Balloch P & K 89 T2
Balloch S Ayrs 81 L13
Balloch W Duns 88 J9
Balls Cross W Susx 10 F5
Balls Green E Susx 11 R3
Ball's Green Gloucs 28 G8
Ballygown Ag & B 93 L10
Ballygrant Ag & B 86 F12
Ballyhaugh Ag & B 92 F7
Balmacara Highld 100 h7
Balmaclellan D & G 73 R4
Balmae D & G 73 R11
Balmaha Stirlg 88 K7
Balmalcolm Fife 91 M10
Balmangan D & G 73 Q10
Balmedie Abers 105 R12
Balmer Heath Shrops 44 K7
Balmerino Fife 91 N7
Balmerlawn Hants 9 L8
Balmichael N Ayrs 79 S9
Balmore E Duns 89 N11
Balmuchy Highld 109 R9
Balmule Fife 90 K14
Balmullo Fife 91 P7
Balnacoil Lodge Highld 109 Q2
Balnacra Highld 101 P2
Balnacroft Abers 98 D5
Balnafoich Highld 102 J8
Balnaguard P & K 97 Q13
Balnahard Ag & B 86 G6
Balnahard Ag & B 93 M12
Balnain Highld 102 D9
Balnakeil Highld 110 H3
Balne N York 57 S3

Balquharn - Borley Green 125

Balquharn P & K 90 F4
Balquhidder Stirlg 89 M1
Balsall Common Solhll 36 H5
Balsall Heath Birm 36 E4
Balsall Street Solhll 36 H5
Balscote Oxon 37 L12
Balsham Cambs 39 S10
Baltasound Shet 106 w3
Balterley Staffs 45 S3
Balterley Green Staffs 45 S3
Balterley Heath Staffs 45 R3
Baltersan D & G 73 L7
Baltonsborough Somset 17 P10
Balvicar Ag & B 87 P2
Balvraid Highld 101 L8
Balvraid Highld 103 M9
Balwest Cnwll 2 F10
Bamber Bridge Lancs 55 N1
Bamber's Green Essex 22 E3
Bamburgh Nthumb 85 T12
Bamburgh Castle Nthumb 85 T11
Bamford Derbys 56 K10
Bamford Rochdl 56 C4
Bampton Cumb 67 R9
Bampton Devon 16 C12
Bampton Oxon 29 R7
Bampton Grange Cumb 67 R9
Banavie Highld 94 G3
Banbury Oxon 37 N12
Banbury Crematorium Oxon 37 N12
Bancffosfelen Carmth 25 S8
Banchory Abers 99 M4
Banchory-Devenick Abers 99 S3
Bancycapel Carmth 25 R8
Bancyfelin Carmth 25 P7
Banc-y-ffordd Carmth 25 R3
Bandirran P & K 90 K5
Bandrake Head Cumb 61 Q2
Banff Abers 104 K3
Bangor Gwynd 52 J8
Bangor Crematorium Gwynd 52 J8
Bangor-on-Dee Wrexhm 44 J4
Bangors Cnwll 14 F13
Bangor's Green Lancs 54 J5
Bangrove Suffk 40 F6
Banham Norfk 40 J3
Bank Hants 8 K7
Bankend D & G 74 K12
Bankfoot P & K 90 G4
Bankglen E Ayrs 81 R10
Bank Ground Cumb 67 M13
Bankhead C Aber 99 S2
Bankhead S Lans 82 J10
Bank Newton N York 62 J9
Banknock Falk 89 S10
Banks Cumb 76 B13
Banks Lancs 54 J2
Banks Green Worcs 36 C7
Bankshill D & G 75 N9
Bank Street Worcs 35 P8
Bank Top Calder 56 H2
Bank Top Lancs 55 M5
Banningham Norfk 51 M8
Bannister Green Essex 22 G3
Bannockburn Stirlg 89 T7
Banstead Surrey 21 N11
Bantham Devon 5 R12
Banton N Lans 89 R10
Banwell N Som 17 L5
Bapchild Kent 12 H3
Bapton Wilts 18 E13
Barabhas W Isls 106 i4
Barassie S Ayrs 81 L6
Barbaraville Highld 109 N10
Barber Booth Derbys 56 H10
Barber Green Cumb 61 R3
Barbieston S Ayrs 81 N9
Barbon Cumb 62 C3
Barbridge Ches E 45 P2
Barbrook Devon 15 R3
Barby Nhants 37 P6
Barcaldine Ag & B 94 D10
Barcheston Warwks 36 J13
Barclose Cumb 75 T13
Barcombe E Susx 11 Q8
Barcombe Cross E Susx 11 Q7
Barcroft C Brad 63 L12
Barden N York 69 P14
Barden Park Kent 21 U13
Bardfield End Green Essex 22 F1
Bardfield Saling Essex 22 G2
Bardney Lincs 58 K13
Bardon Leics 47 M11
Bardon Mill Nthumb 76 F13
Bardowie E Duns 89 N11
Bardown E Susx 12 C10
Bardrainney Inver 88 H11
Bardsea Cumb 61 Q5
Bardsey Leeds 63 T11
Bardsey Island Gwynd 42 B9
Bardsley Oldham 56 D6
Bardwell Suffk 40 F6
Bare Lancs 61 T7
Bareppa Cnwll 2 K11
Barfad D & G 72 J6
Barford Norfk 50 K12
Barford Warwks 36 J8
Barford St John Oxon 37 M14
Barford St Martin Wilts 8 F2
Barford St Michael Oxon 37 M14
Barfrestone Kent 13 Q5
Bargate Derbys 47 L4
Bargeddie N Lans 82 C6
Bargoed Caerph 27 M8
Bargrennan D & G 72 K4
Barham Cambs 38 H5
Barham Kent 13 P5
Barham Suffk 40 K10
Barham Crematorium Kent 13 P6
Bar Hill Cambs 39 N8
Barholm Lincs 48 G11
Barkby Leics 47 R12
Barkby Thorpe Leics 47 R12
Barkers Green Shrops 45 M8
Barkestone-le-Vale Leics 47 U7
Barkham Wokham 20 C9
Barking Gt Lon 21 R6
Barking Suffk 40 J10
Barkingside Gt Lon 21 R5
Barking Tye Suffk 40 J10
Barkisland Calder 56 G3
Barkla Shop Cnwll 2 J6
Barkston Lincs 48 D5
Barkston Ash N York 64 B12
Barkway Herts 31 U5
Barlanark C Glas 89 Q13
Barlaston Staffs 45 U6
Barlavington W Susx 10 F7
Barlborough Derbys 57 Q11
Barlby N York 64 E13
Barlestone Leics 47 M12
Barley Herts 39 P13
Barley Lancs 62 G11
Barleycroft End Herts 22 B2
Barley Hole Rothm 57 N7
Barleythorpe Rutlnd 48 B12
Barling Essex 23 M10
Barlings Lincs 58 J12
Barlochan D & G 73 U8
Barlow Derbys 57 M12
Barlow Gatesd 77 P13
Barlow N York 64 E14
Barmby Moor E R Yk 64 H10
Barmby on the Marsh E R Yk 64 F14
Barmer Norfk 50 D7
Barming Heath Kent 12 D4
Barmollack Ag & B 79 Q7
Barmouth Gwynd 43 M10
Barmpton Darltn 70 D9
Barmston E R Yk 65 R8
Barnaby Green Suffk 41 S4
Barnacarry Ag & B 87 U7
Barnack C Pete 48 G12
Barnacle Warwks 37 L4
Barnard Castle Dur 69 N9
Barnard Gate Oxon 29 T5
Barnardiston Suffk 40 B11
Barnbarroch D & G 66 B1
Barnburgh Donc 57 Q6
Barnby Suffk 41 S3
Barnby Dun Donc 57 T5
Barnby in the Willows Notts 48 C3
Barnby Moor Notts 57 U10
Barncorkrie D & G 72 D12
Barnehurst Gt Lon 21 S7
Barnes Gt Lon 21 M7
Barnes Street Kent 12 B6
Barnet Gt Lon 21 M3
Barnetby le Wold N Linc 58 J5
Barnet Gate Gt Lon 21 M3
Barney Norfk 50 G7
Barnham Suffk 40 E5
Barnham W Susx 10 F10
Barnham Broom Norfk 50 J12
Barnhead Angus 99 M12
Barnhill C Dund 91 Q5
Barnhill Ches W 45 L3
Barnhill Moray 103 T4
Barnhills D & G 72 B5
Barningham Dur 69 N10
Barningham Suffk 40 G5
Barnoldby le Beck NE Lin 59 M6
Barnoldswick Lancs 62 H10
Barnsdale Bar Donc 57 R4
Barns Green W Susx 10 J5
Barnsley Barns 57 M5
Barnsley Gloucs 29 L7
Barnsley Crematorium Barns 57 N5
Barnsole Kent 13 Q4
Barnstaple Devon 15 N6
Barnston Essex 22 F4
Barnston Wirral 54 G10
Barnstone Notts 47 T6
Barnt Green Worcs 36 D6
Barnton C Edin 83 N4
Barnton Ches W 55 P12
Barnwell All Saints Nhants 38 F4
Barnwell St Andrew Nhants 38 G4
Barnwood Gloucs 28 G4
Baron's Cross Herefs 35 L9
Baronwood Cumb 67 R4
Barr S Ayrs 80 K14
Barra W Isls 106 b18
Barra Airport W Isls 106 c18
Barrachan D & G 72 K10
Barraigh W Isls 106 b18
Barrapoll Ag & B 92 A10
Barras Cumb 68 H10
Barrasford Nthumb 76 J11
Barregarrow IoM 60 e5
Barrets Green Ches E 45 N2
Barrhead E Rens 89 L14
Barrhill S Ayrs 72 G3
Barrington Cambs 39 N11
Barrington Somset 17 L13
Barripper Cnwll 2 G9
Barrmill N Ayrs 81 M2
Barrock Highld 112 G2
Barrow Gloucs 28 G3
Barrow Lancs 62 E12
Barrow Rutlnd 48 C10
Barrow Shrops 45 Q13
Barrow Somset 17 T10
Barrow Suffk 40 C8
Barroway Drove Norfk 49 S13
Barrow Bridge Bolton 55 Q4
Barrow Burn Nthumb 76 H3
Barrowby Lincs 48 C6
Barrowden Rutlnd 48 D13
Barrowford Lancs 62 H12
Barrow Gurney N Som 17 P3
Barrow Haven N Linc 58 J2
Barrow Hill Derbys 57 P11
Barrow-in-Furness Cumb 61 N6
Barrow Island Cumb 61 M6
Barrow Nook Lancs 54 K6
Barrow's Green Ches E 45 Q2
Barrow Street Wilts 8 A2
Barrow-upon-Humber N Linc 58 J2
Barrow upon Soar Leics 47 Q10
Barrow upon Trent Derbys 47 L8
Barrow Vale BaNES 17 R4
Barry Angus 91 R5
Barry V Glam 16 F3
Barry Island V Glam 16 F3
Barsby Leics 47 S11
Barsham Suffk 41 Q3
Barston Solhll 36 H5
Bartestree Herefs 35 N12
Barthol Chapel Abers 105 N9
Bartholomew Green Essex 22 H3
Barthomley Ches E 45 S3
Bartley Hants 9 L6
Bartley Green Birm 36 D4
Bartlow Cambs 39 S11
Barton Cambs 39 P9
Barton Ches W 44 K3
Barton Gloucs 29 L2
Barton Herefs 34 G9
Barton Lancs 54 J5
Barton Lancs 61 U12
Barton N York 69 R11
Barton Oxon 30 C11
Barton Torbay 6 B11
Barton Warwks 36 F10
Barton Bendish Norfk 50 B12
Barton End Gloucs 28 F8
Barton Green Staffs 46 G10
Barton Hartshorn Bucks 30 D6
Barton Hill N York 64 G7
Barton in Fabis Notts 47 P7
Barton in the Beans Leics 47 L12
Barton-le-Clay C Beds 31 N6
Barton-le-Street N York 64 G5
Barton-le-Willows N York 64 G7
Barton Mills Suffk 40 B6
Barton-on-Sea Hants 8 J10
Barton-on-the-Heath Warwks 36 J14
Barton St David Somset 17 P10
Barton Seagrave Nhants 38 C5
Barton Stacey Hants 19 P12
Barton Town Devon 15 Q4
Barton Turf Norfk 51 Q9
Barton-under-Needwood Staffs 46 G10
Barton-upon-Humber N Linc 58 H2
Barton upon Irwell Salfd 55 S7
Barton Waterside N Linc 58 H2
Barugh Barns 57 M5
Barugh Green Barns 57 M5
Barvas W Isls 106 i4
Barway Cambs 39 S5
Barwell Leics 37 M1
Barwick Devon 15 N11
Barwick Herts 31 U9
Barwick Somset 7 Q2
Barwick in Elmet Leeds 63 U12
Baschurch Shrops 44 K9
Bascote Warwks 37 M8
Bascote Heath Warwks 37 L8
Base Green Suffk 40 H8
Basford Green Staffs 46 C3
Bashall Eaves Lancs 62 D11
Bashall Town Lancs 62 E11
Bashley Hants 8 J9
Basildon Essex 22 H10
Basildon & District Crematorium Essex 22 J10
Basingstoke Hants 19 T10
Basingstoke Crematorium Hants 19 S11
Baslow Derbys 57 L12
Bason Bridge Somset 16 K7
Bassaleg Newpt 27 P10
Bassendean Border 84 G9
Bassenthwaite Cumb 66 K6
Bassett C Sotn 9 N5
Bassingbourn Cambs 31 T4
Bassingfield Notts 47 R6
Bassingham Lincs 48 D2
Bassingthorpe Lincs 48 E8
Bassus Green Herts 31 T7
Basted Kent 12 B4
Baston Lincs 48 H11
Bastwick Norfk 51 R10
Batch Somset 16 K5
Batchworth Herts 20 J4
Batchworth Heath Herts 20 J4
Batcombe Dorset 7 R4
Batcombe Somset 17 S9
Bate Heath Ches E 55 Q11
Batford Herts 31 P9
Bath BaNES 17 T4
Bathampton BaNES 17 U3
Bath, City of BaNES 17 U4
Bathealton Somset 16 E12
Batheaston BaNES 17 U3
Bathford BaNES 17 U3
Bathgate W Loth 82 J5
Bathley Notts 47 U2
Bathpool Cnwll 4 H6
Bathpool Somset 16 J11
Bath Side Essex 23 U1
Bathville W Loth 82 H5
Bathway Somset 17 Q6
Batley Kirk 56 K2
Batsford Gloucs 36 G14
Batson Devon 5 S13
Battersby N York 70 J11
Battersea Gt Lon 21 N7
Battisborough Cross Devon 5 P11
Battisford Suffk 40 J10
Battisford Tye Suffk 40 H10
Battle E Susx 12 E12
Battle Powys 26 J1
Battleborough Somset 16 K6
Battledown Gloucs 28 J3
Battledykes Angus 98 H12
Battlefield Shrops 45 M10
Battlesbridge Essex 22 J9
Battlesden C Beds 31 L7
Battleton Somset 16 B11
Battlies Green Suffk 40 F8
Battramsley Cross Hants 9 L9
Batt's Corner Hants 10 C2
Baughton Worcs 35 U12
Baughurst Hants 19 S8
Baulds Abers 99 L5
Baulking Oxon 29 R9
Baumber Lincs 59 M12
Baunton Gloucs 28 K7
Baveney Wood Shrops 35 Q5
Baverstock Wilts 8 E2
Bawburgh Norfk 51 L12
Bawdeswell Norfk 50 H9
Bawdrip Somset 16 K9
Bawdsey Suffk 41 P12
Bawsey Norfk 49 U9
Bawtry Donc 57 T8
Baxenden Lancs 55 S1
Baxterley Warwks 36 J1
Baxter's Green Suffk 40 C9
Bay Highld 100 b4
Bayble W Isls 106 k5
Baybridge Hants 9 Q4
Baybridge Nthumb 69 L2
Baycliff Cumb 61 P5
Baydon Wilts 19 L5
Bayford Herts 31 T11
Bayford Somset 17 T11
Bayhead W Isls 106 c12
Bay Horse Lancs 61 T9
Bayley's Hill Kent 21 T12
Baylham Suffk 40 K10
Baynard's Green Oxon 30 B7
Baysdale Abbey N York 70 K11
Baysham Herefs 27 V2
Bayston Hill Shrops 45 L12
Baythorne End Essex 40 B12
Bayton Worcs 35 Q6
Bayton Common Worcs 35 R6
Bayworth Oxon 29 U7
Beach S Glos 17 T2
Beachampton Bucks 30 G5
Beachamwell Norfk 50 C12
Beachley Gloucs 27 V9
Beachy Head E Susx 11 T11
Beacon Devon 6 G3
Beacon End Essex 23 N3
Beacon Hill E Susx 11 S4
Beacon Hill Kent 12 F9
Beacon Hill Notts 48 B3
Beacon Hill Surrey 10 D3
Beacon's Bottom Bucks 20 C3
Beaconsfield Bucks 20 F4
Beaconsfield Services Bucks 20 G5
Beadlam N York 64 F3
Beadlow C Beds 31 P5
Beadnell Nthumb 85 U13
Beaford Devon 15 N9
Beal N York 57 R1
Beal Nthumb 85 R10
Bealbury Cnwll 4 K7
Bealsmill Cnwll 4 K5
Beam Hill Staffs 46 H8
Beamhurst Staffs 46 E6
Beaminster Dorset 7 N4
Beamish Dur 69 R2
Beamish Museum Dur 69 R2
Beamsley N York 63 M9
Bean Kent 22 E13
Beanacre Wilts 18 D7
Beanley Nthumb 77 M2
Beardon Devon 5 N4
Beardwood Bl w D 62 D14
Beare Devon 6 C4
Beare Green Surrey 10 K2
Bearley Warwks 36 G8
Bearley Cross Warwks 36 G8
Bearpark Dur 69 R4
Bearsden E Duns 89 M11
Bearsted Kent 12 F4
Bearstone Shrops 45 R6
Bearwood Birm 36 D3
Bearwood Herefs 34 J9
Bearwood Poole 8 E9
Beattock D & G 75 L5
Beauchamp Roding Essex 22 E6
Beauchief Sheff 57 M10
Beaudesert Warwks 36 G7
Beaufort Blae G 27 M5
Beaulieu Hants 9 M8
Beaulieu Road Station Hants 9 L7
Beauly Highld 102 F6
Beaumaris IoA 52 K7
Beaumaris Castle IoA 52 K7
Beaumont Cumb 75 R14
Beaumont Essex 23 S3
Beaumont Jersey 7 c3
Beaumont Hill Darltn 69 S9
Beausale Warwks 36 H6
Beauworth Hants 9 R3
Beaworthy Devon 15 L13
Beazley End Essex 22 H2
Bebington Wirral 54 H10
Bebside Nthumb 77 R9
Beccles Suffk 41 R3
Becconsall Lancs 55 L2
Beckbury Shrops 45 S13
Beckenham Gt Lon 21 Q9
Beckenham Crematorium Gt Lon 21 Q9
Beckermet Cumb 66 F11
Beckett End Norfk 50 C14
Beckfoot Cumb 61 M2
Beckfoot Cumb 66 G3
Beckfoot Cumb 66 J12
Beck Foot Cumb 68 D13
Beckford Worcs 36 C13
Beckhampton Wilts 18 G7
Beck Hole N York 71 P12
Beckingham Lincs 48 C3
Beckingham Notts 58 C9
Beckington Somset 18 B10
Beckjay Shrops 34 J5
Beckley E Susx 12 G11
Beckley Hants 8 J9
Beckley Oxon 30 C10
Beck Row Suffk 39 U5
Becks C Brad 63 L10
Beck Side Cumb 61 N3
Beck Side Cumb 61 R3
Beckton Gt Lon 21 R6
Beckwithshaw N York 63 R9
Becontree Gt Lon 21 S5
Becquet Vincent Jersey 7 d2
Bedale N York 63 R2
Bedburn Dur 69 N6
Bedchester Dorset 8 B5
Beddau Rhondd 26 K10
Beddgelert Gwynd 43 L4
Beddingham E Susx 11 Q9
Beddington Gt Lon 21 P9
Beddington Corner Gt Lon 21 N9
Bedfield Suffk 41 M7
Bedfield Little Green Suffk 41 M7
Bedford Bed 38 F11
Bedford Crematorium Bed 38 G10
Bedgebury Cross Kent 12 D9
Bedham W Susx 10 G6
Bedhampton Hants 9 U7
Bedingfield Suffk 41 L7
Bedingfield Green Suffk 41 L7
Bedlam N York 63 R7
Bedlington Nthumb 77 R9
Bedlinog Myr Td 26 K7
Bedminster Bristl 17 Q2
Bedminster Down Bristl 17 Q2
Bedmond Herts 31 N12
Bednall Staffs 46 C10
Bedrule Border 76 C2
Bedstone Shrops 34 J5
Bedwas Caerph 27 M10
Bedwellty Caerph 27 M7
Bedworth Warwks 37 L3
Bedworth Woodlands Warwks 36 K3
Beeby Leics 47 S12
Beech Hants 19 U13
Beech Staffs 45 U6
Beech Hill W Berk 19 U8
Beechingstoke Wilts 18 G9
Beedon W Berk 19 Q5
Beedon Hill W Berk 19 Q5
Beeford E R Yk 65 Q9
Beeley Derbys 57 L13
Beelsby NE Lin 59 M6
Beenham W Berk 19 S7
Beenham's Heath W & M 20 D7
Beeny Cnwll 4 E2
Beer Devon 6 H7
Beer Somset 17 M10
Beercrocombe Somset 16 K12
Beer Hackett Dorset 7 R2
Beesands Devon 5 U12
Beesby Lincs 59 S10
Beeson Devon 5 U12
Beeston C Beds 38 J11
Beeston Ches W 45 M2
Beeston Leeds 63 R13
Beeston Norfk 50 F10
Beeston Notts 47 P6
Beeston Regis Norfk 51 L5
Beeswing D & G 74 G12
Beetham Cumb 61 T4
Beetham Somset 6 J2
Beetley Norfk 50 G10
Began Cardif 27 N11
Begbroke Oxon 29 U5
Begdale Cambs 49 Q12
Begelly Pembks 24 K9
Beggarington Hill Leeds 57 L2
Beggar's Bush Powys 34 G8
Beguildy Powys 34 E5
Beighton Norfk 51 Q12
Beighton Sheff 57 P10
Beinn Na Faoghla W Isls 106 d13
Beith N Ayrs 81 M2
Bekesbourne Kent 13 N4
Bekesbourne Hill Kent 13 N4
Belaugh Norfk 51 N10
Belbroughton Worcs 36 B5
Belchalwell Dorset 7 U3
Belchalwell Street Dorset 7 U3
Belchamp Otten Essex 40 D12
Belchamp St Paul Essex 40 C12
Belchamp Walter Essex 40 D12
Belchford Lincs 59 N11
Belford Nthumb 85 S12
Belgrave C Leic 47 Q12
Belhaven E Loth 84 H3
Belhelvie Abers 105 Q12
Belhinnie Abers 104 F10
Bellabeg Abers 104 D13
Bellamore Herefs 34 J12
Bellanoch Ag & B 87 P7
Bellasize E R Yk 64 J14
Bellaty Angus 98 C12
Bell Bar Herts 31 S11
Bell Busk N York 62 J8
Belleau Lincs 59 R11
Bell End Worcs 36 B5
Bellerby N York 69 P14
Bellever Devon 5 R5
Belle Vue Cumb 67 N1
Belle Vue Wakefd 57 M3
Bellfield S Lans 74 J1
Bellfield S Lans 82 F12
Bell Heath Worcs 36 B5
Bell Hill Hants 9 U4
Bellingdon Bucks 30 K11
Bellingham Nthumb 76 G9
Belloch Ag & B 79 M8
Bellochantuy Ag & B 79 M9
Bell o' th' Hill Ches W 45 M4
Bellows Cross Dorset 8 F6
Bells Cross Suffk 41 L10
Bellshill N Lans 82 D6
Bellshill Nthumb 85 S12
Bellside N Lans 82 F7
Bellsquarry W Loth 82 K5
Bells Yew Green E Susx 11 U3
Belluton BaNES 17 R4
Belmaduthy Highld 102 H4
Belmesthorpe Rutlnd 48 F11
Belmont Bl w D 55 Q3
Belmont Gt Lon 21 N10
Belmont S Ayrs 81 L9
Belmont Shet 106 v3
Belnacraig Abers 104 D12
Belowda Cnwll 3 P4
Belper Derbys 46 K4
Belper Lane End Derbys 46 K4
Belph Derbys 57 R11
Belsay Nthumb 77 M10
Belses Border 84 F13
Belsford Devon 5 T9
Belsize Herts 31 M12
Belstead Suffk 40 K12
Belstone Devon 5 Q2
Belthorn Lancs 55 R2
Beltinge Kent 13 N2
Beltingham Nthumb 76 F13
Beltoft N Linc 58 D5
Belton Leics 47 M9
Belton Lincs 48 D6
Belton N Linc 58 C5
Belton Norfk 51 S13
Belton Rutlnd 48 B13
Belton House Lincs 48 D6
Beltring Kent 12 C6
Belvedere Gt Lon 21 S7
Belvoir Leics 48 B7
Bembridge IoW 9 S11
Bemerton Wilts 8 G2
Bempton E R Yk 65 R5
Benacre Suffk 41 T4
Benbecula W Isls 106 d13
Benbecula Airport W Isls 106 c13
Benbuie D & G 74 D6
Benderloch Ag & B 94 C11
Benenden Kent 12 F9
Benfieldside Dur 69 N2
Bengates Norfk 51 P8
Bengeo Herts 31 T10
Bengeworth Worcs 36 D12
Benhall Green Suffk 41 Q8
Benhall Street Suffk 41 Q8
Benholm Abers 99 Q10
Beningbrough N York 64 C8
Benington Herts 31 S8
Benington Lincs 49 N4
Benington Sea End Lincs 49 P4
Benllech IoA 52 H6
Benmore Ag & B 88 D8
Bennacott Cnwll 4 H2
Bennan N Ayrs 80 D8
Bennet Head Cumb 67 P8
Bennetland E R Yk 64 J14
Bennett End Bucks 20 C3
Ben Nevis Highld 94 H4
Benniworth Lincs 59 M10
Benover Kent 12 D6
Ben Rhydding C Brad 63 N10
Benslie N Ayrs 81 L4
Benson Oxon 19 T2
Bentfield Green Essex 22 D2
Benthall Shrops 45 Q13
Bentham Gloucs 28 H4
Benthoul C Aber 99 Q3
Bentlawn Shrops 44 H13
Bentley Donc 57 S5
Bentley E R Yk 65 N12
Bentley Hants 10 B2
Bentley Suffk 40 K13
Bentley Warwks 36 J1
Bentley Crematorium Essex 22 E8
Bentley Heath Herts 21 N3
Bentley Heath Solhll 36 G5
Benton Devon 15 Q5
Bentpath D & G 75 R7
Bentwichen Devon 15 R6
Bentworth Hants 19 U12
Benvie Angus 91 M5
Benville Dorset 7 P4
Benwick Cambs 39 M2
Beoley Worcs 36 E7
Beoraidbeg Highld 100 f10
Bepton W Susx 10 D7
Berden Essex 22 C2
Berea Pembks 24 C4
Bere Alston Devon 5 L7
Bere Ferrers Devon 5 M8
Berepper Cnwll 2 H12
Bere Regis Dorset 8 A10
Bergh Apton Norfk 51 P13
Berhill Somset 17 M9
Berinsfield Oxon 30 C13
Berkeley Gloucs 28 C8
Berkeley Heath Gloucs 28 C8
Berkeley Road Gloucs 28 D7
Berkhamsted Herts 31 L11
Berkley Somset 18 B11
Berkswell Solhll 36 H5
Bermondsey Gt Lon 21 P7
Bermuda Warwks 37 L3
Bernera Highld 100 h7
Bernisdale Highld 100 d4
Berrick Prior Oxon 19 T2
Berrick Salome Oxon 19 T2
Berriedale Highld 112 D12
Berrier Cumb 67 N7
Berriew Powys 44 E13
Berrington Nthumb 85 Q10
Berrington Shrops 45 M12
Berrington Worcs 35 N7
Berrington Green Worcs 35 N7
Berrow Somset 16 J6
Berrow Worcs 35 S14
Berrow Green Worcs 35 R9
Berry Brow Kirk 56 H4
Berry Cross Devon 15 L10
Berry Down Cross Devon 15 N4
Berry Hill Gloucs 27 V5
Berry Hill Pembks 24 J2
Berryhillock Moray 104 G3
Berryhillock Moray 104 G5
Berrynarbor Devon 15 N3
Berry Pomeroy Devon 5 U8
Berry's Green Gt Lon 21 R11
Bersham Wrexhm 44 H4
Berthengam Flints 54 D11
Berwick E Susx 11 S9
Berwick Bassett Wilts 18 G6
Berwick Hill Nthumb 77 P10
Berwick St James Wilts 18 G13
Berwick St John Wilts 8 C4
Berwick St Leonard Wilts 8 C2
Berwick-upon-Tweed Nthumb 85 P8
Bescaby Leics 48 B8
Bescar Lancs 54 J4
Besford Shrops 45 N8
Besford Worcs 36 B12
Bessacarr Donc 57 T6
Bessels Leigh Oxon 29 U7
Besses o' th' Barn Bury 55 T5
Bessingby E R Yk 65 R6
Bessingham Norfk 51 L6
Bestbeech Hill E Susx 11 U4
Besthorpe Norfk 40 J1
Besthorpe Notts 58 D14
Bestwood Village Notts 47 Q4
Beswick E R Yk 65 N10
Betchcott Shrops 44 K14
Betchworth Surrey 21 M12
Bethania Cerdgn 33 L8
Bethania Gwynd 43 P5
Bethel Gwynd 43 U6
Bethel Gwynd 52 H9
Bethel IoA 52 E8
Bethel Powys 44 D9
Bethersden Kent 12 H7
Bethesda Gwynd 52 K9
Bethesda Pembks 24 J7
Bethlehem Carmth 26 B2
Bethnal Green Gt Lon 21 P6
Betley Staffs 45 S4
Betsham Kent 22 F13
Betteshanger Kent 13 R5
Bettiscombe Dorset 7 L4
Bettisfield Wrexhm 45 L6
Betton Shrops 45 Q6
Betton Strange Shrops 45 M12
Bettws Newpt 27 P9
Bettws Bledrws Cerdgn 33 L10
Bettws Cedewain Powys 34 D1
Bettws Evan Cerdgn 32 F11
Bettws-Newydd Mons 27 R6
Bettyhill Highld 111 Q4
Betws Brdgnd 26 G10
Betws Carmth 26 A5
Betws Garmon Gwynd 52 H11
Betws Gwerfil Goch Denbgs 44 B4
Betws-y-Coed Conwy 53 N11
Betws-yn-Rhos Conwy 53 R8
Beulah Cerdgn 32 E11
Beulah Powys 33 T10
Bevendean Br & H 11 N9
Bevercotes Notts 57 U12
Beverley E R Yk 65 N12
Beverston Gloucs 28 G9
Bevington Gloucs 28 C8
Bewaldeth Cumb 66 K6
Bewcastle Cumb 76 B11
Bewdley Worcs 35 S5
Bewerley N York 63 P6
Bewholme E R Yk 65 R10
Bewlbridge Kent 12 C9
Bexhill E Susx 12 D14
Bexley Gt Lon 21 S8
Bexleyheath Gt Lon 21 S7
Bexleyhill W Susx 10 E5
Bexon Kent 12 G4
Bexwell Norfk 49 T13
Beyton Suffk 40 F8
Beyton Green Suffk 40 F8
Bhaltos W Isls 106 f5
Bhatarsaigh W Isls 106 b19
Bibstone S Glos 28 C9
Bibury Gloucs 29 M6
Bicester Oxon 30 C8
Bickenhill Solhll 36 G4
Bicker Lincs 48 K6
Bicker Bar Lincs 48 K6
Bicker Gauntlet Lincs 48 K6
Bickershaw Wigan 55 P6
Bickerstaffe Lancs 54 K6
Bickerton Ches E 45 M3
Bickerton Devon 5 U13
Bickerton N York 64 B9
Bickerton Nthumb 76 K5
Bickford Staffs 45 U11
Bickington Devon 5 U6
Bickington Devon 15 M6
Bickleigh Devon 5 N8
Bickleigh Devon 6 B3
Bickleton Devon 15 M6
Bickley Ches W 45 M4
Bickley Gt Lon 21 R9
Bickley N York 65 L1
Bickley Worcs 35 P6
Bickley Moss Ches W 45 M4
Bicknacre Essex 22 J7
Bicknoller Somset 16 F9
Bicknor Kent 12 G4
Bickton Hants 8 G6
Bicton Herefs 35 L8
Bicton Shrops 34 G4
Bicton Shrops 44 K10
Bidborough Kent 11 T2
Bidden Hants 20 B13
Biddenden Kent 12 G8
Biddenden Green Kent 12 G7
Biddenham Bed 38 F10
Biddestone Wilts 18 C6
Biddisham Somset 17 L6
Biddlesden Bucks 30 D5
Biddlestone Nthumb 76 K4
Biddulph Staffs 45 U2
Biddulph Moor Staffs 46 B2
Bideford Devon 15 L7
Bidford-on-Avon Warwks 36 F10
Bidston Wirral 54 G8
Bielby E R Yk 64 H11
Bieldside C Aber 99 R3
Bierley IoW 9 Q13
Bierton Bucks 30 H9
Big Balcraig D & G 72 K11
Bigbury Devon 5 R11
Bigbury-on-Sea Devon 5 R12
Bigby Lincs 58 J5
Big Carlae D & G 81 T13
Biggar Cumb 61 M6
Biggar S Lans 82 K11
Biggin Derbys 46 G2
Biggin Derbys 46 J4
Biggin N York 64 C13
Biggin Hill Gt Lon 21 R11
Biggin Hill Airport Gt Lon 21 R10
Biggleswade C Beds 31 Q4
Bigholms D & G 75 R9
Bighouse Highld 111 T4
Bighton Hants 9 S2
Biglands Cumb 67 L2
Bignor W Susx 10 F8
Bigrigg Cumb 66 F10
Big Sand Highld 107 N9
Bigton Shet 106 t11
Bilborough C Nott 47 P5
Bilbrook Somset 16 D8
Bilbrook Staffs 45 U13
Bilbrough N York 64 C10
Bilbster Highld 112 G6
Bildershaw Dur 69 R8
Bildeston Suffk 40 G11
Billacott Cnwll 4 H2
Billericay Essex 22 G9
Billesdon Leics 47 T13
Billesley Warwks 36 F9
Billingborough Lincs 48 H7
Billinge St Hel 55 M6
Billingford Norfk 41 L5
Billingford Norfk 50 H9
Billingham S on T 70 G8
Billinghay Lincs 48 J3
Billingley Barns 57 P6
Billingshurst W Susx 10 H5
Billingsley Shrops 35 R4
Billington C Beds 30 K8
Billington Lancs 62 E12
Billington Staffs 45 U9
Billockby Norfk 51 R11
Billy Row Dur 69 Q5
Bilsborrow Lancs 61 U12
Bilsby Lincs 59 S11
Bilsham W Susx 10 F10
Bilsington Kent 12 K9
Bilsthorpe Notts 47 R1
Bilsthorpe Moor Notts 47 S1
Bilston Mdloth 83 Q6
Bilston Wolves 36 C1
Bilstone Leics 47 L12
Bilting Kent 13 L6
Bilton E R Yk 65 R13
Bilton N York 63 S8
Bilton N York 64 B10
Bilton Nthumb 77 Q3
Bilton Warwks 37 N6
Bilton Banks Nthumb 77 Q3
Binbrook Lincs 59 M8
Binchester Blocks Dur 69 R6
Bincombe Dorset 7 S8
Binegar Somset 17 R7
Bines Green W Susx 10 K7
Binfield Br For 20 D8
Binfield Heath Oxon 20 B7
Bingfield Nthumb 76 K11
Bingham Notts 47 T6
Bingham's Melcombe Dorset 7 U4
Bingley C Brad 63 N12
Bings Shrops 45 M10
Binham Norfk 50 G6
Binley Covtry 37 L5
Binley Hants 19 P10
Binley Woods Warwks 37 L5
Binnegar Dorset 8 B11
Binniehill Falk 82 G4
Binscombe Surrey 20 G13
Binsey Oxon 29 U6
Binstead IoW 9 R10
Binsted Hants 10 B2
Binsted W Susx 10 F9
Binton Warwks 36 F10
Bintree Norfk 50 H9
Binweston Shrops 44 H13
Birch Essex 23 M4
Birch Rochdl 56 C5
Bircham Newton Norfk 50 C7
Bircham Tofts Norfk 50 C7
Birchanger Essex 22 D3
Birchanger Green Services Essex 22 D3
Birch Cross Staffs 46 F7
Birchencliffe Kirk 56 H3
Bircher Herefs 35 L7
Birchfield Birm 36 E2
Birch Green Essex 23 M4
Birch Green Herts 31 S10
Birch Green Worcs 35 U11
Birchgrove Cardif 27 M12
Birchgrove Swans 26 C8
Birchgrove W Susx 11 Q5
Birch Heath Ches W 45 M1
Birch Hill Ches W 55 M12
Birchington Kent 13 R2
Birchley Heath Warwks 36 J2
Birchmoor Warwks 46 J13
Birchmoor Green C Beds 31 L6
Birchover Derbys 46 H1
Birch Services Rochdl 55 T5
Birch Vale Derbys 56 F9
Birchwood Lincs 58 F13
Birch Wood Somset 6 H2
Birchwood Warrtn 55 Q8
Bircotes Notts 57 T8
Birdbrook Essex 40 B12
Birdforth N York 64 B4
Birdham W Susx 10 C10
Birdingbury Warwks 37 M7
Birdlip Gloucs 28 H5
Birdoswald Cumb 76 C12
Birdsall N York 64 J6
Birds Edge Kirk 56 K5
Birds Green Essex 22 E6
Birdsgreen Shrops 35 S3
Birdsmoorgate Dorset 7 L4
Bird Street Suffk 40 H10
Birdwell Barns 57 M6
Birdwood Gloucs 28 D4
Birgham Border 84 K11
Birichin Highld 109 P6
Birkacre Lancs 55 N4
Birkby N York 70 D12
Birkdale Sefton 54 H4
Birkenbog Abers 104 G2
Birkenhead Wirral 54 H9
Birkenhills Abers 105 L6
Birkenshaw Kirk 63 Q14
Birkhall Abers 98 E5
Birkhill Angus 91 N5
Birkhill D & G 75 P2
Birkholme Lincs 48 E9
Birkin N York 57 R1
Birks Leeds 57 L1
Birkshaw Nthumb 76 F12
Birley Herefs 35 L10
Birley Carr Sheff 57 M8
Birling Kent 12 C3
Birling Nthumb 77 Q4
Birling Gap E Susx 11 T11
Birlingham Worcs 36 B12
Birmingham Birm 36 E3
Birmingham Airport Solhll 36 G4
Birnam P & K 90 F3
Birness Abers 105 R9
Birse Abers 98 K4
Birsemore Abers 98 J4
Birstall Kirk 56 K1
Birstall Leics 47 Q12
Birstwith N York 63 Q8
Birthorpe Lincs 48 H7
Birtley Gatesd 69 S1
Birtley Herefs 34 J7
Birtley Nthumb 76 H10
Birtley Crematorium Gatesd 69 S1
Birts Street Worcs 35 S13
Bisbrooke Rutlnd 48 C14
Biscathorpe Lincs 59 M10
Biscovey Cnwll 3 R6
Bisham W & M 20 D5
Bishampton Worcs 36 C10
Bish Mill Devon 15 R7
Bishop Auckland Dur 69 R7
Bishopbridge Lincs 58 H8
Bishopbriggs E Duns 89 P11
Bishop Burton E R Yk 65 M12
Bishop Middleham Dur 70 D6
Bishopmill Moray 103 V3
Bishop Monkton N York 63 S6
Bishop Norton Lincs 58 G8
Bishopsbourne Kent 13 N5
Bishops Cannings Wilts 18 F8
Bishop's Castle Shrops 34 H3
Bishop's Caundle Dorset 7 S2
Bishop's Cleeve Gloucs 28 J2
Bishop's Frome Herefs 35 Q11
Bishops Gate Surrey 20 G8
Bishop's Green Essex 22 F4
Bishop's Green Hants 19 R8
Bishops Hull Somset 16 H12
Bishop's Itchington Warwks 37 L9
Bishops Lydeard Somset 16 G11
Bishop's Norton Gloucs 28 F3
Bishop's Nympton Devon 15 S8
Bishop's Offley Staffs 45 S8
Bishop's Stortford Herts 22 C3
Bishop's Sutton Hants 9 S2
Bishop's Tachbrook Warwks 36 K8
Bishop's Tawton Devon 15 N7
Bishopsteignton Devon 6 B10
Bishopstoke Hants 9 P5
Bishopston Swans 25 U13
Bishopstone Bucks 30 H10
Bishopstone E Susx 11 R10
Bishopstone Herefs 34 K12
Bishopstone Kent 13 P2
Bishopstone Swindn 29 P11
Bishopstone Wilts 8 F3
Bishopstrow Wilts 18 C12
Bishop Sutton BaNES 17 Q5
Bishop's Waltham Hants 9 R5
Bishopswood Somset 6 J2
Bishop's Wood Staffs 45 T12
Bishopsworth Bristl 17 Q3
Bishop Thornton N York 63 R7
Bishopthorpe C York 64 D10
Bishopton Darltn 70 E8
Bishopton Rens 88 K11
Bishopton Warwks 36 G9
Bishop Wilton E R Yk 64 H8
Bishton Newpt 27 R10
Bishton Staffs 46 D9
Bisley Gloucs 28 H6
Bisley Surrey 20 G11
Bisley Camp Surrey 20 F11
Bispham Bpool 61 Q11
Bispham Green Lancs 55 L4
Bissoe Cnwll 2 K8
Bisterne Hants 8 G8
Bitchet Green Kent 21 U12
Bitchfield Lincs 48 E8
Bittadon Devon 15 M4
Bittaford Devon 5 R9
Bittering Norfk 50 F10
Bitterley Shrops 35 N5
Bitterne C Sotn 9 P6
Bitteswell Leics 37 P3
Bitton S Glos 17 S3
Bix Oxon 20 B6
Bixter Shet 106 t8
Blaby Leics 47 Q14
Blackadder Border 85 L8
Blackawton Devon 5 U10
Blackbeck Cumb 66 F11
Blackborough Devon 6 E3
Blackborough End Norfk 49 U10
Black Bourton Oxon 29 Q7
Blackboys E Susx 11 S6
Blackbrook Derbys 46 K4
Blackbrook St Hel 55 M7
Blackbrook Staffs 45 S6
Blackbrook Surrey 21 L13
Blackburn Abers 105 N13
Blackburn Bl w D 62 D14
Blackburn Rothm 57 N8
Blackburn W Loth 82 J5
Blackburn with Darwen Services Bl w D 55 Q2
Black Callerton N u Ty 77 P12
Black Car Norfk 40 J1
Black Corner W Susx 11 M3
Blackcraig E Ayrs 81 S11
Black Crofts Ag & B 94 C12
Black Cross Cnwll 3 N4
Blackden Heath Ches E 55 S12
Blackdog Abers 105 R13
Black Dog Devon 15 T11
Blackdown Devon 5 N5
Blackdown Dorset 7 L4
Blackdyke Cumb 66 H2
Blacker Barns 57 M5
Blacker Hill Barns 57 N6
Blackfen Gt Lon 21 S8
Blackfield Hants 9 N8
Blackford Cumb 75 S13
Blackford P & K 90 C10
Blackford Somset 17 M7
Blackford Somset 17 S11
Blackfordby Leics 46 K10
Blackgang IoW 9 P13
Blackhall C Edin 83 N3
Blackhall Dur 70 G5
Blackhall Colliery Dur 70 G5
Blackhall Mill Gatesd 69 P1
Blackhaugh Border 83 T11
Blackheath Essex 23 P3
Blackheath Gt Lon 21 Q7
Blackheath Sandw 36 C3
Blackheath Suffk 41 R6
Blackheath Surrey 20 H13
Black Heddon Nthumb 77 M10
Blackhill Abers 105 T4
Blackhill Abers 105 T7
Blackhill Dur 69 N2
Blackhill of Clackriach Abers 105 Q6
Blackhorse Devon 6 C6
Blackjack Lincs 49 L6
Blackland Wilts 18 F7
Black Lane Ends Lancs 62 J11
Blacklaw D & G 74 K4
Blackley Manch 56 C6
Blackley Crematorium Manch 55 T6
Blacklunans P & K 97 U11
Blackmarstone Herefs 35 M13
Blackmill Brdgnd 26 G10
Blackmoor Hants 10 B4
Black Moor Leeds 63 R12
Blackmoor N Som 17 N4
Blackmoorfoot Kirk 56 G4
Blackmore Essex 22 F7
Blackmore End Essex 22 H1
Blackmore End Herts 31 Q9
Blackness Falk 83 L3
Blacknest Hants 10 B2
Blacknest W & M 20 G9
Black Notley Essex 22 J3
Blacko Lancs 62 H11
Black Pill Swans 25 V12
Blackpool Bpool 61 Q12
Blackpool Devon 5 U6
Blackpool Devon 5 V11
Blackpool Gate Cumb 76 A10
Blackridge W Loth 82 G5
Blackrock Cnwll 2 H10
Blackrock Mons 27 N5
Blackrod Bolton 55 P4
Blacksboat Moray 103 U8
Blackshaw D & G 74 K12
Blackshaw Head Calder 62 K14
Blacksmith's Green Suffk 40 K7
Blacksnape Bl w D 55 R2
Blackstone W Susx 11 L7
Black Street Suffk 41 T3
Black Tar Pembks 24 G9
Blackthorn Oxon 30 D9
Blackthorpe Suffk 40 F8
Blacktoft E R Yk 58 D2
Blacktop C Aber 99 R3
Black Torrington Devon 15 L11
Blackwall Derbys 46 J4
Blackwater Cnwll 2 J7
Blackwater Hants 20 D11
Blackwater IoW 9 Q11
Blackwater Somset 16 J13
Blackwaterfoot N Ayrs 79 S10
Blackwell Cumb 67 P2
Blackwell Darltn 69 S10
Blackwell Derbys 47 M2
Blackwell Derbys 56 H12
Blackwell Warwks 36 H12
Blackwell Worcs 36 C6
Blackwellsend Green Gloucs 28 E2
Blackwood Caerph 27 M8
Blackwood D & G 74 H8
Blackwood S Lans 82 E10
Blackwood Hill Staffs 46 B2
Blacon Ches W 54 J13
Bladbean Kent 13 N6
Bladnoch D & G 73 L9
Bladon Oxon 29 U5
Bladon Somset 17 M12
Blaenannerch Cerdgn 32 D11
Blaenau Ffestiniog Gwynd 43 P4
Blaenavon Torfn 27 P6
Blaenavon Industrial Landscape Torfn 27 N6
Blaen Dyryn Powys 33 T13
Blaenffos Pembks 25 L3
Blaengarw Brdgnd 26 G9
Blaengeuffordd Cerdgn 33 M4
Blaengwrach Neath 26 F6
Blaengwynfi Neath 26 F8
Blaenllechau Rhondd 26 J8
Blaenpennal Cerdgn 33 M8
Blaenplwyf Cerdgn 33 L5
Blaenporth Cerdgn 32 E11
Blaenrhondda Rhondd 26 G8
Blaenwaun Carmth 25 M5
Blaen-y-Coed Carmth 25 P5
Blaen-y-cwm Blae G 27 L5
Blaenycwm Cerdgn 33 R5
Blaen-y-cwm Rhondd 26 G8
Blagdon N Som 17 P5
Blagdon Somset 16 H13
Blagdon Torbay 5 V8
Blagdon Hill Somset 16 H13
Blagill Cumb 68 F3
Blaguegate Lancs 55 L5
Blaich Highld 94 E3
Blain Highld 93 R5
Blaina Blae G 27 N6
Blair Atholl P & K 97 P10
Blair Drummond Stirlg 89 R6
Blairgowrie P & K 90 J2
Blairhall Fife 82 J1
Blairingone P & K 90 E12
Blairlogie Stirlg 89 T6
Blairmore Ag & B 88 E9
Blairmore Highld 110 D5
Blair's Ferry Ag & B 87 T12
Blaisdon Gloucs 28 D4
Blakebrook Worcs 35 T5
Blakedown Worcs 35 U5
Blake End Essex 22 H3
Blakeley Lane Staffs 46 C4
Blakemere Ches W 55 N12
Blakemere Herefs 34 J12
Blakemore Devon 5 T8
Blakenall Heath Wsall 46 D13
Blakeney Gloucs 28 C6
Blakeney Norfk 50 H5
Blakenhall Ches E 45 R4
Blakenhall Wolves 36 B1
Blakeshall Worcs 35 T4
Blakesley Nhants 37 R10
Blanchland Nthumb 69 L2
Blandford Camp Dorset 8 C7
Blandford Forum Dorset 8 B7
Blandford St Mary Dorset 8 B7
Bland Hill N York 63 Q9
Blanefield Stirlg 89 M10
Blankney Lincs 48 G1
Blantyre S Lans 82 C7
Blar a' Chaorainn Highld 94 G5
Blargie Highld 96 J5
Blarmachfoldach Highld 94 F5
Blashford Hants 8 H7
Blaston Leics 38 B1
Blatherwycke Nhants 38 E1
Blawith Cumb 61 P2
Blawquhairn D & G 73 Q3
Blaxhall Suffk 41 Q9
Blaxton Donc 57 U6
Blaydon Gatesd 77 P13
Bleadney Somset 17 N7
Bleadon N Som 16 K5
Bleak Street Somset 17 U10
Blean Kent 13 M3
Bleasby Lincs 58 K10
Bleasby Notts 47 T4
Bleasdale Lancs 62 B10
Bleatarn Cumb 68 F10
Bleathwood Herefs 35 N6
Blebocraigs Fife 91 P8
Bleddfa Powys 34 F7
Bledington Gloucs 29 P3
Bledlow Bucks 30 G12
Bledlow Ridge Bucks 20 C3
Bleet Wilts 18 C9
Blegbie E Loth 84 D6
Blencarn Cumb 68 D6
Blencogo Cumb 66 J3
Blendworth Hants 9 U6
Blenheim Palace Oxon 29 T4
Blennerhasset Cumb 66 J4
Bletchingdon Oxon 30 B9
Bletchingley Surrey 21 P12
Bletchley M Keyn 30 J6
Bletchley Shrops 45 P7
Bletherston Pembks 24 J6
Bletsoe Bed 38 F9
Blewbury Oxon 19 R3
Blickling Norfk 51 L8
Blidworth Notts 47 Q2
Blidworth Bottoms Notts 47 Q3
Blindburn Nthumb 76 G3
Blindcrake Cumb 66 H6
Blindley Heath Surrey 21 Q13
Blisland Cnwll 4 E6
Blissford Hants 8 H6
Bliss Gate Worcs 35 R6
Blisworth Nhants 37 T10
Blithbury Staffs 46 E10
Blitterlees Cumb 66 H2
Blockley Gloucs 36 G14
Blofield Norfk 51 P12
Blofield Heath Norfk 51 P11
Blo Norton Norfk 40 H5
Bloomfield Border 84 F14
Blore Staffs 45 R7
Blore Staffs 46 F4
Blounce Hants 20 B13
Blounts Green Staffs 46 E7
Blowick Sefton 54 J3
Bloxham Oxon 37 M13
Bloxholm Lincs 48 G3
Bloxwich Wsall 46 C13
Bloxworth Dorset 8 B10
Blubberhouses N York 63 P8
Blue Anchor Cnwll 3 N5
Blue Anchor Somset 16 D8
Blue Bell Hill Kent 12 D3
Blue John Cavern Derbys 56 H10
Blundellsands Sefton 54 H7
Blundeston Suffk 41 T1
Blunham C Beds 38 J10
Blunsdon St Andrew Swindn 29 M10
Bluntington Worcs 35 V6
Bluntisham Cambs 39 N6
Blunts Cnwll 4 J8
Blunts Green Warwks 36 F7
Blurton C Stke 45 U5
Blyborough Lincs 58 F8
Blyford Suffk 41 R5
Blymhill Staffs 45 T11
Blymhill Lawn Staffs 45 T11
Blyth Notts 57 T9
Blyth Nthumb 77 S9
Blyth Bridge Border 83 M9
Blythburgh Suffk 41 R5
Blyth Crematorium Nthumb 77 S9
Blythe Border 84 F9
Blythe Bridge Staffs 46 C5
Blythe End Warwks 36 H2
Blythe Marsh Staffs 46 C5
Blyton Lincs 58 E8
Boarhills Fife 91 S9
Boarhunt Hants 9 S7
Boarley Kent 12 E4
Boarsgreave Lancs 55 T2
Boarshead E Susx 11 S4
Boar's Head Wigan 55 N5
Boars Hill Oxon 29 U7
Boarstall Bucks 30 D10
Boasley Cross Devon 5 N2
Boath Highld 108 K10
Boat of Garten Highld 103 P12
Bobbing Kent 12 G2
Bobbington Staffs 35 T2
Bobbingworth Essex 22 D6
Bocaddon Cnwll 4 F9
Bocking Essex 22 J3
Bocking Churchstreet Essex 22 J2
Bockleton Worcs 35 N8
Boconnoc Cnwll 4 E8
Boddam Abers 105 U7
Boddam Shet 106 t12
Boddington Gloucs 28 G2
Bodedern IoA 52 D6
Bodelwyddan Denbgs 53 T7
Bodenham Herefs 35 M10
Bodenham Wilts 8 H3
Bodenham Moor Herefs 35 M10
Bodewryd IoA 52 F4
Bodfari Denbgs 54 C12
Bodffordd IoA 52 F7
Bodfuan Gwynd 42 F6
Bodham Norfk 50 K5
Bodiam E Susx 12 E10
Bodicote Oxon 37 N13
Bodieve Cnwll 3 P2
Bodinnick Cnwll 4 E10
Bodle Street Green E Susx 11 V8
Bodmin Cnwll 3 R3
Bodmin Moor Cnwll 4 F5
Bodney Norfk 50 D14
Bodorgan IoA 52 E9
Bodsham Kent 13 M6
Bodwen Cnwll 3 Q4
Bodymoor Heath Warwks 36 G1
Bogallan Highld 102 H5
Bogbrae Abers 105 S8
Bogend S Ayrs 81 N6
Boggs Holdings E Loth 84 C4
Boghall Mdloth 83 P5
Boghall W Loth 82 J5
Boghead S Lans 82 E10
Bogmoor Moray 104 D3
Bogmuir Abers 99 L9
Bogniebrae Abers 104 H6
Bognor Regis W Susx 10 E11
Bogroy Highld 103 P11
Bogue D & G 73 Q3
Bohetherick Cnwll 5 L7
Bohortha Cnwll 3 M10
Bohuntine Highld 96 B7
Bojewyan Cnwll 2 B10
Bokiddick Cnwll 3 R4
Bolam Dur 69 Q8
Bolam Nthumb 77 N9
Bolberry Devon 5 R13
Bold Heath St Hel 55 M9
Boldmere Birm 36 F2
Boldon Colliery S Tyne 77 S13
Boldre Hants 9 L9
Boldron Dur 69 M10
Bole Notts 58 C9
Bolehill Derbys 46 J2
Bole Hill Derbys 57 M12
Bolenowe Cnwll 2 H9
Bolham Devon 16 C13
Bolham Water Devon 6 G2
Bolingey Cnwll 2 K6
Bollington Ches E 56 D11
Bollington Cross Ches E 56 D11
Bollow Gloucs 28 D5
Bolney W Susx 11 M6
Bolnhurst Bed 38 G9
Bolshan Angus 99 L13
Bolsover Derbys 57 Q12
Bolster Moor Kirk 56 G3
Bolsterstone Sheff 57 L7
Boltby N York 64 B2
Boltenstone Abers 104 E13
Bolter End Bucks 20 C4
Bolton Bolton 55 R5
Bolton Cumb 68 D8
Bolton E Loth 84 E4
Bolton E R Yk 64 H9
Bolton Nthumb 77 N3
Bolton Abbey N York 63 M9
Bolton Bridge N York 63 M9
Bolton-by-Bowland Lancs 62 F10
Boltonfellend Cumb 75 U12
Boltongate Cumb 66 K4
Bolton le Sands Lancs 61 T6
Bolton Low Houses Cumb 66 K4
Bolton New Houses Cumb 66 K4
Bolton-on-Swale N York 69 S13
Bolton Percy N York 64 C11
Bolton Town End Lancs 61 T6
Bolton Upon Dearne Barns 57 Q6
Bolventor Cnwll 4 F5
Bomarsund Nthumb 77 R9
Bomere Heath Shrops 45 L10
Bonar Bridge Highld 109 L6
Bonawe Ag & B 94 E12
Bonby N Linc 58 H3
Boncath Pembks 25 M3
Bonchester Bridge Border 76 B3
Bonchurch IoW 9 R13
Bondleigh Devon 15 Q12
Bonds Lancs 61 T11
Bonehill Devon 5 S5
Bonehill Staffs 46 G13
Bo'ness Falk 82 K2
Boney Hay Staffs 46 D11
Bonhill W Duns 88 J10
Boningale Shrops 45 T13
Bonjedward Border 84 H14
Bonkle N Lans 82 F7
Bonnington Angus 91 S4
Bonnington Kent 13 L8
Bonnybank Fife 91 N11
Bonnybridge Falk 89 T10
Bonnykelly Abers 105 P5
Bonnyrigg Mdloth 83 R5
Bonnyton Angus 91 M4
Bonsall Derbys 46 J2
Bonshaw Tower D & G 75 P11
Bont Mons 27 R4
Bontddu Gwynd 43 N10
Bont-Dolgadfan Powys 43 S13
Bont-goch or Elerch Cerdgn 33 N3
Bonthorpe Lincs 59 S12
Bontnewydd Cerdgn 33 M7
Bontnewydd Gwynd 52 G11
Bontuchel Denbgs 44 C2
Bonvilston V Glam 26 K13
Bonwm Denbgs 44 D5
Bon-y-maen Swans 26 B8
Boode Devon 15 M5
Booker Bucks 20 D4
Booley Shrops 45 N8
Boon Border 84 F9
Boon Hill Staffs 45 T3
Boorley Green Hants 9 Q6
Boosbeck R & Cl 71 L9
Boose's Green Essex 22 K1
Boot Cumb 66 J12
Booth Calder 56 F1
Boothby Graffoe Lincs 48 E2
Boothby Pagnell Lincs 48 E7
Boothferry E R Yk 58 B1
Booth Green Ches E 56 D10
Boothstown Salfd 55 R6
Booth Town Calder 56 G1
Boothville Nhants 37 U8
Bootle Cumb 61 L2
Bootle Sefton 54 H7
Boots Green Ches W 55 S12
Boot Street Suffk 41 M11
Booze N York 69 M12
Boraston Shrops 35 P7
Bordeaux Guern 6 e2
Borden Kent 12 G3
Borden W Susx 10 C6
Border Cumb 66 J2
Border Forest Park 76 C9
Borders Crematorium Border 84 F12
Bordley N York 62 J6
Bordon Camp Hants 10 B3
Boreham Essex 22 J6
Boreham Wilts 18 C12
Boreham Street E Susx 11 V8
Borehamwood Herts 21 L3
Boreland D & G 75 N7
Boreraig Highld 100 a4
Boreton Shrops 45 M12
Borgh W Isls 106 b18
Borgh W Isls 106 j3
Borgie Highld 111 P5
Borgue D & G 73 Q10
Borgue Highld 112 D11
Borley Essex 40 D12
Borley Green Essex 40 D12

Borley Green Suffk....40 G8
Borneskitaig Highld....100 C2
Borness D & G....73 Q10
Boroughbridge N York....63 T6
Borough Green Kent....12 B4
Borras Head Wrexhm....44 J3
Borrowash Derbys....47 M7
Borrowby N York....64 B1
Borrowby N York....71 N9
Borrowstoun Falk....82 J2
Borstal Medway....12 D2
Borth Cerdgn....33 M2
Borthwickbrae Border....75 T3
Borthwickshiels Border....75 T2
Borth-y-Gest Gwynd....43 L6
Borve Highld....100 d6
Borve W Isls....106 b18
Borve W Isls....106 f9
Borve W Isls....106 j13
Borwick Lancs....61 U5
Borwick Lodge Cumb....67 M13
Borwick Rails Cumb....61 M4
Bosavern Cnwll....2 B10
Bosbury Herefs....35 Q12
Boscastle Cnwll....4 D2
Boscombe Bmouth....8 G10
Boscombe Wilts....18 K13
Boscoppa Cnwll....3 Q6
Bosham W Susx....10 C10
Bosham Hoe W Susx....10 C10
Bosherston Pembks....24 G12
Boskednan Cnwll....2 C10
Boskenna Cnwll....2 C12
Bosley Ches E....56 C13
Bossall N York....64 G7
Bossiney Cnwll....4 D3
Bossingham Kent....13 N6
Bossington Somset....15 U3
Bostock Green Ches W....55 Q13
Boston Lincs....49 M5

Boston Crematorium
Lincs....49 M4
Boston Spa Leeds....63 U10
Boswarthan Cnwll....2 C10
Boswinger Cnwll....3 P8
Botallack Cnwll....2 B10

Botany Bay Gt Lon....21 N3
Botcheston Leics....47 N13
Botesdale Suffk....40 H5
Bothal Nthumb....77 Q8
Bothampstead W Berk....19 R5
Bothamsall Notts....57 U12
Bothel Cumb....66 J5
Bothenhampton Dorset....7 N6
Bothwell S Lans....82 D7
Bothwell Services S Lans....82 D7
Botley Bucks....31 L12
Botley Hants....9 Q6
Botley Oxon....29 U6
Botolph Claydon Bucks....30 F8
Botolphs W Susx....10 K9
Botolph's Bridge Kent....13 M9
Bottesford Leics....48 B6
Bottesford N Linc....58 E5
Bottomcraig Fife....91 N7
Bottom of Hutton Lancs....55 L1
Bottom o' th' Moor
Bolton....55 Q4
Bottoms Calder....56 D2
Bottoms Cnwll....2 B12
Botts Green Warwks....36 H2
Botusfleming Cnwll....4 J8
Botwnnog Gwynd....42 E7
Bough Beech Kent....21 S13
Boughrood Powys....34 D13
Boughspring Gloucs....27 V8
Boughton Nhants....37 U7
Boughton Norfk....49 V13
Boughton Notts....57 U13
Boughton Aluph Kent....12 K6
Boughton End C Beds....31 L5
Boughton Green Kent....12 E5

Boughton Malherbe
Kent....12 G6
Boughton Monchelsea
Kent....12 E5
Boughton Street Kent....13 L4
Boulby R & Cl....71 N9
Boulder Clough Calder....56 F2
Bouldnor IoW....9 M11
Bouldon Shrops....35 M3
Boulmer Nthumb....77 R3
Boulston Pembks....24 G8
Boultham Lincs....58 G13
Bourn Cambs....39 M9
Bourne Lincs....48 G9
Bournebridge Essex....22 D9
Bournebrook Birm....36 D4
Bourne End C Beds....31 L4
Bourne End Bucks....20 E5
Bourne End C Beds....31 L4
Bournemouth Bmouth....8 F10
Bournemouth Airport
Dorset....8 G9
Bournemouth
Crematorium
Bmouth....8 G10
Bournes Green Gloucs....28 H7
Bournes Green Sthend....23 M10
Bournheath Worcs....36 C6
Bournmoor Dur....70 D2
Bournstream Gloucs....28 D9
Bournville Birm....36 D4
Bourton Dorset....17 U10
Bourton N Som....17 L4
Bourton Oxon....29 P10
Bourton Shrops....35 N1
Bourton Wilts....18 H8
Bourton on Dunsmore
Warwks....37 M6
Bourton-on-the-Hill
Gloucs....29 N1
Bourton-on-the-Water
Gloucs....29 N3
Bousd Ag & B....92 H6
Boustead Hill Cumb....67 Q14
Bouth Cumb....61 Q2
Bouthwaite N York....63 N5
Bouts Worcs....36 D9
Boveney Bucks....20 F7
Boveridge Dorset....8 F6
Bovey Tracey Devon....5 U5
Bovingdon Herts....31 M12
Bovingdon Green Bucks....20 D5
Bovinger Essex....22 D6
Bovington Dorset....8 A11
Bovington Camp Dorset....8 A11
Bow Cumb....67 N1
Bow Devon....15 R12
Bow Gt Lon....21 Q6
Bow W Isls....106 s20
Bowbank Dur....68 b14
Bow Brickhill M Keyn....30 K5
Bowbridge Gloucs....28 G6
Bowburn Dur....70 D5
Bowcombe IoW....9 P11
Bowd Devon....6 F6
Bowden Border....84 F12
Bowden Devon....5 U12
Bowden Hill Wilts....18 D7
Bowdon Traffd....55 S9
Bower Highld....112 F4
Bower Ashton Bristl....27 V2
Bowerchalke Wilts....8 E4
Bowerhill Wilts....18 D8
Bower Hinton Somset....17 N13
Bower House Tye Suffk....40 G12
Bowermadden Highld....112 F4
Bowers Staffs....45 T6
Bowers Gifford Essex....22 J10
Bowershall Fife....90 G13
Bower's Row Leeds....63 U14
Bowes Dur....69 M9
Bowgreave Lancs....61 T11
Bowhouse D & G....74 J11
Bowithick Cnwll....4 F4
Bowker's Green Lancs....54 K6
Bowland Bridge Cumb....61 R2
Bowley Herefs....35 M10
Bowley Town Surrey....10 E3
Bowlhead Green Surrey....10 E3
Bowling C Brad....63 P13
Bowling W Duns....88 K11
Bowling Bank Wrexhm....44 J4
Bowling Green Worcs....35 U10
Bowmanstead Cumb....61 P2
Bowmore Ag & B....78 E4
Bowness-on-Solway
Cumb....75 P13
Bowness-on-
Windermere Cumb....67 P13
Bow of Fife Fife....91 M9
Bowriefauld Angus....91 R2
Bowscale Cumb....67 N6
Bowsden Nthumb....85 P10
Bowston Cumb....67 Q13
Bow Street Cerdgn....33 M3
Bow Street Norfk....50 H14
Box Gloucs....28 G7
Box Wilts....18 B7
Boxbush Gloucs....28 D5
Boxbush Gloucs....28 D5
Box End Bed....38 G11
Boxford Suffk....40 G12
Boxford W Berk....19 P6
Boxgrove W Susx....10 E9
Box Hill Surrey....21 L12
Boxley Kent....12 E4

Boxmoor Herts....31 M11
Box's Shop Cnwll....14 F12
Boxted Essex....23 P1
Boxted Suffk....40 D10
Boxted Cross Essex....23 P1
Boxworth Cambs....39 M7
Boxworth End Cambs....39 M7
Boyden End Suffk....40 B9
Boyden Gate Kent....13 P2
Boylestone Derbys....46 G6
Boyndie Abers....104 J3
Boyndlie Abers....105 Q3
Boynton E R Yk....65 Q6
Boysack Angus....91 T2
Boys Hill Dorset....7 S2
Boythorpe Derbys....57 N13
Boyton Cnwll....4 J2
Boyton Suffk....41 Q11
Boyton Wilts....18 E13
Boyton Cross Essex....22 F6
Boyton End Suffk....40 B12
Bozeat Nhants....38 D9
Braaid IoM....60 e7
Brabling Green Suffk....41 M8
Brabourne Kent....13 M7
Brabourne Lees Kent....13 L7
Bracadale Highld....100 c6
Braceborough Lincs....48 G11
Bracebridge Lincs....58 G13
Bracebridge Low Fields
Lincs....58 G13
Braceby Lincs....48 F7
Bracewell Lancs....62 H10
Brackenfield Derbys....47 L2
Brackenhirst N Lans....82 D5
Brackenthwaite Cumb....67 L3
Brackenthwaite N York....63 R9
Bracklesham W Susx....10 C11
Brackletter Highld....94 H2
Brackley Nhants....30 C5
Brackley Hatch Nhants....30 D4
Bracknell Br For....20 E9
Braco P & K....89 T4
Bracobrae Moray....104 G5
Bracon Ash Norfk....51 L14
Bracorina Highld....100 g10
Bradaford Devon....4 K2
Bradbourne Derbys....46 G3
Bradbury Dur....70 D7
Bradda IoM....60 b8
Bradden Nhants....37 R11
Braddock Cnwll....4 E8
Bradeley C Stke....45 U3
Bradenham Bucks....20 D3
Bradenstoke Wilts....18 F5
Bradfield Devon....6 E4
Bradfield Essex....23 R1
Bradfield Norfk....51 N7
Bradfield Sheff....57 L8
Bradfield W Berk....19 T6
Bradfield Combust Suffk....40 E9
Bradfield Green Ches E....45 Q2
Bradfield Heath Essex....23 R2
Bradfield St Clare Suffk....40 E9
Bradfield St George
Suffk....40 F9
Bradford C Brad....63 P13
Bradford Cnwll....4 G4
Bradford Devon....14 K11
Bradford Nthumb....77 M10
Bradford Nthumb....85 T12
Bradford Abbas Dorset....7 R2
Bradford Leigh Wilts....18 B8
Bradford-on-Avon Wilts....18 B8
Bradford-on-Tone
Somset....16 G12
Bradford Peverell
Dorset....7 S6
Bradiford Devon....15 N6
Brading IoW....9 S11
Bradley Derbys....46 H4
Bradley Hants....19 T12
Bradley NE Lin....59 M5
Bradley Staffs....45 U10
Bradley Wolves....46 C1
Bradley Wrexhm....44 H3
Bradley Common
Ches W....45 M4
Bradley Green Somset....16 J9
Bradley Green Warwks....36 J13
Bradley Green Worcs....36 C8
Bradley in the Moors
Staffs....46 E5
Bradley Stoke S Glos....28 B11
Bradmore Notts....47 Q7
Bradney Somset....16 K9
Bradninch Devon....6 C4
Bradnop Staffs....46 E2
Bradpole Dorset....7 N6
Bradshaw Bolton....55 R4
Bradshaw Calder....63 M14
Bradshaw Kirk....56 H2
Bradstone Devon....4 K4
Bradwall Green Ches E....55 S14
Bradwell Derbys....56 J10
Bradwell Devon....15 M4
Bradwell Essex....22 K3
Bradwell M Keyn....30 J5
Bradwell Norfk....51 T13
Bradwell Crematorium
Staffs....45 U4
Bradwell-on-Sea Essex....23 P6
Bradwell Waterside
Essex....23 N6
Bradworthy Devon....14 H10
Brae Highld....102 J3
Brae Shet....106 t7
Braeface Falk....89 S9
Braehead Angus....99 M13
Braehead D & G....73 L9
Braehead S Lans....82 J9
Braemar Abers....98 B5
Braemore Highld....108 B9
Braemore Highld....112 C10
Brae Roy Lodge Highld....96 C5
Braeside Inver....88 F11
Braes of Coul Angus....98 D13
Braes of Enzie Moray....104 D4
Braeswick Ag & B....105 T4
Brafferton Darltn....69 S8
Brafferton N York....63 U6
Brafield-on-the-Green
Nhants....38 B9
Bragar W Isls....106 h4
Bragbury End Herts....31 S9
Braidwood S Lans....82 F9
Brailsford Derbys....46 J5
Brailsford Green Derbys....46 J5
Brain's Green Gloucs....28 C6
Braintree Essex....22 J3
Braiseworth Suffk....40 K6
Braishfield Hants....9 L3
Braithwaite C Brad....63 L11
Braithwaite Cumb....66 K8
Braithwaite N York....63 M14
Braithwell Donc....57 R8
Brakenhurst Wakefd....57 P3
Bramber W Susx....10 K8
Brambridge Hants....9 P4
Bramcote Notts....47 P6
Bramcote Crematorium
Notts....47 P6
Bramdean Hants....9 S3
Bramerton Norfk....51 N13
Bramfield Herts....31 S9
Bramfield Suffk....41 Q6
Bramford Suffk....40 K11
Bramhall Stockp....56 C10
Bramham Leeds....63 U11
Bramhope Leeds....63 R11
Bramley Hants....19 U9
Bramley Leeds....63 Q12
Bramley Rothm....57 Q8
Bramley Surrey....10 G2
Bramley Corner Hants....19 U9
Bramley Green Hants....19 U9
Bramley Head N York....63 M4
Bramling Kent....13 P4
Brampford Speke Devon....6 B5
Brampton Cambs....38 K6
Brampton Cumb....67 R4
Brampton Cumb....68 K8
Brampton Lincs....58 D11
Brampton Norfk....51 M8
Brampton Rothm....57 P5
Brampton Suffk....41 R4
Brampton Abbotts
Herefs....28 A3
Brampton Ash Nhants....37 U3
Brampton Bryan Herefs....34 J6
Brampton-en-le-
Morthen Rothm....57 Q9
Bramshall Staffs....46 D6
Bramshaw Hants....8 K5
Bramshill Hants....20 B9
Bramshott Hants....10 C4
Bramwell Somset....17 M11
Branault Highld....93 P4
Brancaster Norfk....50 C5
Brancaster Staithe
Norfk....50 C5
Brancepeth Dur....69 R5
Branchill Moray....103 R5
Brand End Lincs....49 N4
Branderburgh Moray....104 A1
Brandesburton E R Yk....65 Q10

Brandeston Suffk....41 M8
Brand Green Gloucs....28 D2
Brandis Corner Devon....14 K12
Brandiston Norfk....50 K9
Brandon Dur....69 R4
Brandon Lincs....48 D4
Brandon Nthumb....77 L2
Brandon Suffk....40 C3
Brandon Warwks....37 M5
Brandon Bank Norfk....39 T3
Brandon Creek Norfk....39 T1
Brandon Parva Norfk....50 K12
Brandsby N York....64 D5
Brandy Wharf Lincs....58 H7
Brane Cnwll....2 C11
Bran End Essex....22 G2
Branksome Poole....8 E10
Branksome Park Poole....8 F10
Bransbury Hants....19 P12
Bransby Lincs....58 E11
Branscombe Devon....6 G7
Bransford Worcs....35 S10
Bransgore Hants....8 H9
Branshill Clacks....90 C12
Branson's Cross Worcs....36 E6
Branston Leics....48 B8
Branston Lincs....58 H13
Branston Staffs....46 H9
Branston Booths Lincs....58 J13
Branstone IoW....9 R12
Brant Broughton Lincs....48 D2
Brantham Suffk....40 K14
Branthwaite Cumb....66 G8
Branthwaite Cumb....67 N4
Brantingham E R Yk....65 L14
Branton Donc....57 T6
Branton Nthumb....77 L2
Branton Green N York....63 U7
Branxton Nthumb....85 M11
Brassey Green Ches W....45 N1
Brassington Derbys....46 H3
Brasted Kent....21 S12
Brasted Chart Kent....21 S12
Brathens Abers....99 M4
Bratoft Lincs....59 S1
Brattleby Lincs....58 F10
Bratton Somset....16 B7
Bratton Wrekin....45 P11
Bratton Clovelly Devon....5 N2
Bratton Fleming Devon....15 P5
Bratton Seymour
Somset....17 S11
Braughing Herts....22 B2
Braughing Friars Herts....22 C2
Braunston Nhants....37 P7
Braunston Rutlnd....48 B12
Braunstone Leics....47 Q13
Braunton Devon....15 L5
Brawby N York....64 G4
Brawl Highld....111 S3
Braworth N York....70 H11
Bray W & M....20 F7
Braybrooke Nhants....37 U4
Braydon Wilts....28 J10
Braydon Side Wilts....28 J9
Brayford Devon....15 Q6
Bray Shop Cnwll....4 J6
Bray's Hill E Susx....12 C13
Braystones Cumb....66 F11
Braythorn N York....63 Q10
Brayton N York....64 E13
Braywick W & M....20 E7
Braywoodside W & M....20 E7
Brazacott Cnwll....4 H2
Breach Kent....12 F3
Breach Kent....13 N6
Breachwood Green
Herts....31 Q8
Breaden Heath Shrops....44 J6
Breadsall Derbys....47 L6
Breadstone Gloucs....28 D7
Breadward Herefs....34 G10
Breage Cnwll....2 G11
Breakachy Highld....102 E7
Breakspear
Crematorium Gt Lon....21 J5
Brealangwell Lodge
Highld....108 J6
Bream Gloucs....27 V6
Breamore Hants....8 H5
Bream Somset....16 K7
Breanais W Isls....106 e6
Brearley Calder....56 F1
Brearton N York....63 S7
Breascleit W Isls....106 h5
Breasclete W Isls....106 h5
Breaston Derbys....47 N7
Brechfa Carmth....25 T4
Brechin Angus....99 L11
Breckles Norfk....50 G1
Brecon Powys....26 J2
Brecon Beacons
National Park Powys....26 G1
Bredbury Stockp....56 D8
Brede E Susx....12 F12
Bredenbury Herefs....35 N9
Bredfield Suffk....41 N10
Bredgar Kent....12 G3
Bredhurst Kent....12 E3
Bredon Worcs....36 B12
Bredon's Hardwick
Worcs....36 B13
Bredon's Norton
Worcs....36 B12
Bredwardine Herefs....34 H12
Breedon on the Hill Leics....47 M9
Breich W Loth....82 J6
Breightmet Bolton....55 R5
Breighton E R Yk....64 G13
Breinton Herefs....35 L12
Breinton Common
Herefs....35 L12
Bremhill Wilts....18 E6
Bremridge Devon....15 P7
Brenchley Kent....12 C7
Brendon Devon....15 R3
Brendon Devon....14 K9
Brendon Hill Somset....16 D10
Brenfield Ag & B....87 Q10
Brenish W Isls....106 e6
Brenkley N u Ty....77 Q10
Brent Cross Gt Lon....21 N5
Brent Eleigh Suffk....40 F11
Brentford Gt Lon....21 L7
Brentingby Leics....47 U11
Brent Knoll Somset....16 K6
Brent Mill Devon....5 Q9
Brent Pelham Herts....22 C1
Brentwood Essex....22 E9
Brenzett Kent....12 K10
Brenzett Green Kent....12 K10
Brereton Staffs....46 D10
Brereton Green Ches E....55 S14
Brereton Heath Ches E....55 T13
Brereton Hill Staffs....46 D10
Bressay Shet....106 v9
Bressingham Norfk....40 K4
Bressingham Common
Norfk....40 K4
Bretby Derbys....46 J9
Bretby Crematorium
Derbys....46 J9
Bretford Warwks....37 M5
Bretforton Worcs....36 E12
Bretherdale Head Cumb....67 S11
Bretherton Lancs....55 L2
Brettabister Shet....106 u8
Brettenham Norfk....40 G3
Brettenham Suffk....40 G10
Bretton Flints....44 H1
Bretton Derbys....56 J11
Brewers End Essex....22 E3
Brewer Street Surrey....21 P12
Brewood Staffs....45 U11
Briantspuddle Dorset....7 V6
Brick End Essex....22 E2
Brickendon Herts....31 T11
Bricket Wood Herts....31 P12
Brick Houses Sheff....57 M9
Brickkiln Green Essex....22 H1
Bride IoM....60 g2
Bridekirk Cumb....66 H6
Bridell Pembks....32 C12
Bridestowe Devon....5 N3
Brideswell Abers....104 H8
Bridford Devon....5 U3
Bridge Kent....13 N5
Bridge End Bed....38 F10
Bridge End Cumb....66 K3
Bridge End Cumb....67 N5
Bridge End Devon....5 R11
Bridge End Dur....69 N4
Bridge End Essex....22 G1
Bridge End Lincs....48 H5
Bridge End Nthumb....76 J12
Bridgefoot Cumb....66 G7
Bridgefoot Angus....91 M5
Bridge Green Essex....39 Q13
Bridgehampton Somset....17 Q12
Bridge Hewick N York....63 S5
Bridgehill Dur....69 N2
Bridgemary Hants....9 R8
Bridgemere Ches E....45 R4
Bridgend Abers....104 G8
Bridgend Ag & B....87 L9
Bridgend Ag & B....79 N2
Bridgend Angus....98 K11
Bridgend Brdgnd....26 G11
Bridgend Cerdgn....32 C11
Bridgend Cumb....67 P10
Bridgend D & G....74 J6
Bridgend Devon....5 P11
Bridgend Fife....91 L9
Bridgend Moray....104 D7
Bridgend P & K....90 H7
Bridgend W Loth....82 K3

Bridgend of Lintrathen
Angus....98 D13
Bridge of Alford Abers....104 H12
Bridge of Allan Stirlg....89 S6
Bridge of Avon Moray....103 U11
Bridge of Avon Moray....103 U9
Bridge of Balgie P & K....95 R9
Bridge of Brewlands
Angus....98 C12
Bridge of Brown Highld....103 T11
Bridge of Cally P & K....97 U13
Bridge of Canny Abers....99 M4
Bridge of Craigisla
Angus....98 D13
Bridge of Dee D & G....74 D14
Bridge of Don C Aber....99 S2
Bridge of Dulsie Highld....103 P7
Bridge of Dye Abers....99 M6
Bridge of Earn P & K....90 H7
Bridge of Ericht P & K....95 P5
Bridge of Feugh Abers....99 N5
Bridge of Forss Highld....111 V3
Bridge of Gairn Abers....98 F4
Bridge of Gaur P & K....95 P5
Bridge of Marnoch
Abers....104 H5
Bridge of Orchy Ag & B....94 K11
Bridge of Tilt P & K....97 P10
Bridge of Tynet Moray....104 D3
Bridge of Walls Shet....106 r8
Bridge of Weir Rens....88 J12
Bridge Reeve Devon....15 Q10
Bridge Sollers Herefs....34 K12
Bridge Street Suffk....40 E11
Bridgetown Cnwll....4 J3
Bridgetown Somset....16 B10
Bridge Trafford Ches W....55 L12
Bridge Yate S Glos....28 C13
Bridgham Norfk....40 G3
Bridgnorth Shrops....35 R2
Bridgwater Somset....16 K10
Bridgwater Services
Somset....16 K10
Bridlington E R Yk....65 R7
Bridport Dorset....7 N6
Bridstow Herefs....28 A3
Brierfield Lancs....62 G12
Brierley Barns....57 P4
Brierley Herefs....35 L9
Brierley Gloucs....28 B4
Brierley Hill Dudley....36 B3
Brierton Hartpl....70 G6
Briery Cumb....67 L8
Brigg N Linc....58 H5
Briggate Norfk....51 P8
Briggswath N York....71 Q11
Brigham Cumb....66 G6
Brigham E R Yk....65 P9
Brighouse Calder....63 N14
Brighstone IoW....9 N12
Brightgate Derbys....46 J2
Brighthampton Oxon....29 S7
Brightholmlee Sheff....57 L7
Brightley Devon....15 P13
Brightling E Susx....12 C11
Brightlingsea Essex....23 Q4
Brighton Br & H....11 N10
Brighton le Sands Sefton....54 H7
Brightons Falk....82 H3
Brightwalton W Berk....19 P5
Brightwalton Holt
W Berk....19 P5
Brightwell Suffk....41 N12
Brightwell Baldwin
Oxon....30 B13
Brightwell-cum-Sotwell
Oxon....19 S2
Brightwell Upperton
Oxon....19 U2
Brignall Dur....69 N10
Brig o'Turk Stirlg....89 M4
Brigsley NE Lin....59 N6
Brigsteer Cumb....67 N2
Brigstock Nhants....38 E3
Brill Bucks....30 E10
Brill Cnwll....2 J11
Brilley Herefs....34 G11
Brimfield Herefs....35 M7
Brimfield Cross Herefs....35 M7
Brimington Derbys....57 P12
Brimley Devon....5 U5
Brimpsfield Gloucs....28 H4
Brimpton W Berk....19 S8
Brimpton Common
W Berk....19 S8
Brimscombe Gloucs....28 G7
Brimstage Wirral....54 H10
Brincliffe Sheff....57 M10
Brind E R Yk....64 G13
Brindham Somset....17 P8
Brindister Shet....106 s8
Brindle Lancs....55 P2
Brineton Staffs....45 T11
Bringhurst Leics....38 B1
Brington Cambs....38 H5
Briningham Norfk....50 H6
Brinkely Notts....47 T3
Brinkhill Lincs....59 Q12
Brinkley Cambs....39 T10
Brinklow Warwks....37 M5
Brinkworth Wilts....28 K10
Brinscall Lancs....55 P2
Brinscombe Somset....17 L6
Brinsea N Som....17 M4
Brinsley Notts....47 N4
Brinsop Herefs....34 K12
Brinsworth Rothm....57 P9
Brinton Norfk....50 H6
Brinyan Ork....106 t17
Brisco Cumb....67 P2
Brisley Norfk....50 G9
Brislington Bristl....28 A13
Brissenden Green Kent....12 H8
Bristol Bristl....27 V13
Bristol Airport N Som....17 P3
Bristol Zoo Gardens
Bristl....27 V13
Briston Norfk....50 J7
Brisworthy Devon....5 N7
Britannia Lancs....56 C2
Britford Wilts....8 H3
Brithdir Caerph....27 L7
Brithdir Gwynd....43 Q10
British Legion Village
Kent....12 D4
Briton Ferry Neath....26 C9
Britwell Salome Oxon....19 U2
Brixham Torbay....6 A14
Brixton Devon....5 N9
Brixton Gt Lon....21 P7
Brixton Deverill Wilts....18 C13
Brixworth Nhants....37 T6
Brize Norton Oxon....29 Q6
Brize Norton Airport
Oxon....29 Q6
Broad Alley Worcs....35 U7
Broad Blunsdon Swindn....29 M9
Broadbottom Tamesd....56 E8
Broadbridge W Susx....10 C9
Broadbridge Heath
W Susx....10 J4
Broad Campden Gloucs....36 G13
Broad Carr Calder....56 G3
Broad Chalke Wilts....8 F3
Broad Clough Lancs....56 C2
Broadclyst Devon....6 C5
Broadfield Inver....88 H11
Broadfield Pembks....24 K10
Broadford Highld....100 f7
Broad Ford Kent....12 D8
Broadford Bridge
W Susx....10 H6
Broadgairhill Border....75 N6
Broadgass Green Suffk....40 G8
Broad Green Cambs....39 U9
Broad Green Essex....23 L3
Broad Green Worcs....35 S10
Broad Haven Pembks....24 E8
Broadhaugh Border....85 N11
Broadheath Traffd....55 S9
Broadheath Worcs....35 Q7
Broadhembury Devon....6 F4
Broadhempston Devon....5 U7
Broad Hill Cambs....39 S5
Broad Hinton Wilts....18 H5
Broadholme Lincs....58 E11
Broadland Row E Susx....12 F12
Broadley Essex....22 B6
Broadley Lancs....56 C3
Broadley Moray....104 D4
Broadley Common Essex....22 B6
Broad Marston Worcs....36 F11
Broadmayne Dorset....7 U7
Broadmere Hants....19 T11
Broadmoor Pembks....24 J9
Broad Oak Carmth....25 U6
Broad Oak Cumb....66 K13
Broad Oak Dorset....7 L5
Broad Oak E Susx....12 C12
Broad Oak E Susx....12 F11
Broadoak Gloucs....28 C5
Broad Oak Hants....9 V4

Broad Oak Herefs....27 T3
Broad Oak Kent....13 N3
Broad Oak St Hel....55 M7
Broad Road Wrexhm....44 J2
Broad Road Suffk....41 N5
Broad's Green Essex....22 G5
Broadstairs Kent....13 S2
Broadstone Shrops....35 M3
Broadstone Poole....8 E9
Broad Street E Susx....12 G12
Broad Street Kent....12 G4
Broad Street Medway....22 J13
Broad Street Green
Essex....23 L6
Broad Town Wilts....18 G5
Broadwas Worcs....35 S9
Broadwater Herts....31 R8
Broadwater W Susx....10 K9
Broadwaters Worcs....35 U5
Broadway Carmth....25 L9
Broadway Pembks....24 E8
Broadway Somset....16 K13
Broadway Suffk....41 Q5
Broadway Worcs....36 E13
Broadwell Gloucs....28 A5
Broadwell Gloucs....29 Q2
Broadwell Oxon....29 Q7
Broadwell Warwks....37 N7
Broadwey Dorset....7 S8
Broadwindsor Dorset....7 M4
Broadwoodkelly Devon....15 P11
Broadwoodwidger
Devon....4 K3
Brobury Herefs....34 H12
Brochel Highld....100 e5
Brochroy Ag & B....94 E12
Brock Lancs....61 U11
Brockamin Worcs....35 S10
Brockbridge Hants....9 S5
Brockdish Norfk....41 M5
Brockencote Worcs....35 U6
Brockenhurst Hants....8 K8
Brocketsbrae S Lans....82 F11
Brockford Street Suffk....40 K7
Brockhall Nhants....37 R8
Brockham Surrey....21 L13
Brockhampton Gloucs....28 H2
Brockhampton Gloucs....28 K3
Brockhampton Hants....9 U8
Brockhampton Herefs....28 A1
Brockhampton Green
Dorset....7 T3
Brockholes Kirk....56 J4
Brockhurst Derbys....57 M14
Brockhurst Warwks....37 M4
Brocklebank Cumb....67 M4
Brocklesby Lincs....59 L5
Brockley N Som....17 N3
Brockley Suffk....40 D8
Brockley Green Suffk....40 D10
Brockley Green Suffk....40 C10
Brockmoor Dudley....36 B3
Brockscombe Devon....15 N13
Brock's Green Hants....19 R8
Brockton Shrops....35 N3
Brockton Shrops....44 J13
Brockton Shrops....45 R13
Brockton Shrops....45 R11
Brockton Staffs....45 T7
Brockweir Gloucs....27 U7
Brockwood Park Hants....9 S4
Brockworth Gloucs....28 G4
Brocton Cnwll....3 Q3
Brocton Staffs....46 C10
Brodick N Ayrs....80 E6
Brodie Moray....103 Q4
Brodsworth Donc....57 R5
Brogaig Highld....100 d3
Brogborough C Beds....31 L5
Brokenborough Wilts....28 H9
Broken Cross Ches E....56 C12
Broken Cross Ches W....55 Q12
Brokerswood Wilts....18 B10
Bromborough Wirral....54 H10
Brome Suffk....40 K5
Brome Street Suffk....41 L5
Bromeswell Suffk....41 P10
Bromfield Cumb....66 J3
Bromfield Shrops....35 L5
Bromford Birm....36 F2
Bromham Bed....38 F10
Bromham Wilts....18 E7
Bromley Barns....57 M7
Bromley Dudley....36 B3
Bromley Gt Lon....21 R9
Bromley Shrops....35 R1
Bromley Common
Gt Lon....21 R9
Bromley Cross Bolton....55 R4
Bromley Cross Essex....23 R2
Bromley Green Kent....12 J8
Bromlow Shrops....44 H13
Brompton Medway....12 E2
Brompton N York....64 K2
Brompton N York....71 N14
Brompton-by-Sawdon
N York....65 L3
Brompton-on-Swale
N York....69 R13
Brompton Ralph Somset....16 E10
Brompton Regis Somset....16 C10
Bromsash Herefs....28 B3
Bromsberrow Heath
Gloucs....35 R14
Bromsgrove Worcs....36 C6
Bromstead Heath Staffs....45 S10
Bromyard Herefs....35 Q9
Bromyard Downs Herefs....35 Q9
Bronaber Gwynd....43 R7
Bronant Cerdgn....33 M7
Broncroft Shrops....35 M3
Brongest Cerdgn....32 F11
Bronington Wrexhm....45 L6
Bronllys Powys....34 E14
Bronnant Cerdgn....33 M7
Bronwydd Carmth....25 R4
Bronydd Powys....34 F13
Bronygarth Shrops....44 G6
**Brook Carmth....25 N9
Brook Hants....8 K5
Brook Hants....9 L3
Brook IoW....9 M12
Brook Kent....13 L6
Brook Surrey....10 G2
Brook Surrey....10 F3
Brooke Norfk....51 P14
Brooke Rutlnd....48 B12
Brookenby Lincs....59 L8
Brook End C Beds....38 H6
Brook End Cambs....38 H5
Brook End M Keyn....38 D11
Brookfield Rens....88 K13
Brookhampton Somset....17 R11
Brookhampton Oxon....30 B11
Brook Hill Hants....8 K5
Brook House Hants....9 V4
Brookhouse Lancs....61 U7
Brookhouse Rothm....57 R9
Brookhouse Green
Ches E....45 T1
Brookhouses Derbys....56 E8
Brookland Kent....12 J11
Brooklands Traffd....55 S8
Brookmans Park Herts....31 S12
Brooks Powys....44 D14
Brooks End Kent....13 Q2
Brooks Green W Susx....10 J5
Brook Street Essex....22 E9
Brook Street Kent....12 J8
Brook Street Suffk....40 E12
Brook Street W Susx....11 N5
Brookthorpe Gloucs....28 F5
Brookville Norfk....50 B14
Brookwood Surrey....20 G11
Broom C Beds....31 Q4
Broom Warwks....36 E10
Broome Norfk....41 Q2
Broome Shrops....35 L4
Broome Worcs....35 U4
Broomedge Warrtn....55 R10
Broomer's Corner
W Susx....10 J6
Broomfield Essex....22 H5
Broomfield Kent....12 F4
Broomfield Kent....13 N3
Broomfield Somset....16 H10
Broomfields Shrops....44 K10
Broomfleet E R Yk....58 F1
Broom Green Norfk....50 G9
Broomhall Ches E....45 P4
Broomhaugh Nthumb....77 L13
Broom Hill Barns....57 P5
Broom Hill Donc....57 R6
Broomhill Dorset....8 F8
Broomhill Norfk....50 B13
Broom Hill Worcs....36 B5
Broomhill Nthumb....77 R5
Broompark Dur....69 R4
Broom's Green Gloucs....35 R13
Broomsthorpe Norfk....50 E8
Brotherlee Dur....68 K4
Brora Highld....109 S7

Broseley Shrops....45 Q13
Brotherhouse Bar Lincs....49 L11
Brotherlee Dur....68 K5
Brothertoft Lincs....49 M3
Brotherton N York....57 Q1
Brotton R & Cl....71 L9
Broubster Highld....112 B5
Brough Cumb....68 G10
Brough E R Yk....58 F1
Brough Highld....112 F2
Brough Notts....58 D2
Brough Shet....106 v7
Brough Shet....106 u5
Brough Lodge Shet....106 v4
Brough Sowerby Cumb....68 G10
Broughton Border....83 N11
Broughton Bucks....30 H10
Broughton Cambs....39 L5
Broughton Flints....54 H14
Broughton Hants....9 L2
Broughton Lancs....61 U13
Broughton M Keyn....30 J5
Broughton N Linc....58 G5
Broughton N York....62 K8
Broughton N York....64 G4
Broughton Nhants....38 B5
Broughton Oxon....37 M13
Broughton Salfd....55 T7
Broughton Staffs....45 S7
**Broughton V Glam....16 C2
Broughton Astley Leics....37 Q2
Broughton Beck Cumb....61 P3
Broughton Gifford Wilts....18 C8
Broughton Green Worcs....36 C8
Broughton Hackett
Worcs....36 B10
Broughton-in-Furness
Cumb....61 N2
Broughton Mains D & G....73 M10
Broughton Mills Cumb....61 N2
Broughton Moor Cumb....66 G6
Broughton Poggs Oxon....29 P7
Broughton Tower Cumb....61 N2
Broughty Ferry C Dund....91 Q5
Brow End Cumb....61 N5
Browland Shet....106 r8
Brown Candover Hants....19 S13
Brown Edge Lancs....54 J4
Brown Edge Staffs....46 B3
Brown Heath Ches W....54 K13
Brownhall Abers....105 P7
Brownhills Fife....91 R8
Brownhills Wsall....46 E12
Brownieside Nthumb....85 T14
Browninghill Green
Hants....19 S9
Brown Lees Staffs....45 U2
Brownlow Heath Ches E....45 U1
Brownrigg Cumb....66 F8
Brownrigg Cumb....66 K4
Brownsea Island Dorset....8 E11
Brownsham Devon....14 F7
Brown's Green Birm....36 E2
Brownsham Devon....14 F7
Brownston Devon....5 R10
Brown Street Suffk....40 K8
Brow-of-the-Hill Norfk....49 V10
Brownhill Green Norfk....51 S10
Broxa N York....65 L1
Broxbourne Herts....31 U11
Broxburn E Loth....84 H3
Broxburn W Loth....82 K4
Broxfield Nthumb....77 Q2
Broxted Essex....22 E2
Broxton Ches W....45 L3
Broxwood Herefs....34 K10
Broyle Side E Susx....11 Q8
Bruan Highld....112 H9
Bruar P & K....97 N10
Brucefield Highld....109 S7
Bruchag Ag & B....88 D14
Bruera Ches W....54 K14
Bruern Abbey Oxon....29 Q3
Bruichladdich Ag & B....78 D4
Bruisyard Suffk....41 P7
Bruisyard Street Suffk....41 P7
Brumby N Linc....58 E5
Brund Staffs....46 F1
Brundall Norfk....51 P12
Brundish Suffk....41 N7
Brundish Street Suffk....41 N6
Brunery Highld....93 S4
Brunslow Shrops....34 J3
Brunswick Village N u Ty....77 Q11
Bruntcliffe Leeds....57 L1
Brunthwaite C Brad....63 M10
Bruntingthorpe Leics....37 R3
Brunton Fife....91 M7
Brunton Nthumb....85 U14
Brunton Wilts....18 K9
Brushford Devon....15 Q11
Brushford Somset....16 B11
Bruton Somset....17 S10
Bryan's Green Worcs....35 U7
Bryanston Dorset....8 B7
Bryant's Bottom Bucks....20 E3
Brydekirk D & G....75 N11
Bryher IoS....2 b1
Brymbo Wrexhm....44 G3
Brympton Somset....17 P13
Bryn Carmth....25 T9
Bryn Ches W....55 P12
Bryn Neath....26 E8
Bryn Shrops....34 G3
Bryn Wigan....55 M6
Brynaman Carmth....26 C6
Brynberian Pembks....24 K2
Brynbryddan Neath....26 D9
Bryncae Rhondd....26 H10
Bryncethin Brdgnd....26 G10
Bryncir Gwynd....42 J5
Bryn-coch Neath....26 C8
Bryncroes Gwynd....42 E7
Bryncrug Gwynd....43 N12
Brynderwen Powys....44 D14
Bryn Du IoA....52 D7
Bryn-Eden Gwynd....43 P8
Bryneglwys Denbgs....44 E4
Brynfields Wrexhm....44 H5
Brynford Flints....54 D12
Bryn Gates Wigan....55 N6
Bryn Golau Rhondd....26 H9
Bryngwran IoA....52 E7
Bryngwyn Mons....27 R6
Bryngwyn Powys....34 E11
Bryn-Henllan Pembks....24 H3
Brynhoffnant Cerdgn....32 F10
Brynithel Blae G....27 N7
Brynmawr Blae G....27 M5
Bryn-mawr Gwynd....42 E7
Brynmenyn Brdgnd....26 G10
Brynmill Swans....26 A9
Brynna Rhondd....26 H10
Bryn-penarth Powys....44 D13
Brynrefail Gwynd....52 J9
Brynrefail IoA....52 G5
Brynsadler Rhondd....26 J10
Bryn Saith Marchog
Denbgs....44 C3
Brynsiencyn IoA....52 G8
Brynteg IoA....52 G6
Bryn-y-bal Flints....54 F13
Bryn-y-Maen Conwy....53 P7
Bryn-yr-Eos Wrexhm....44 G5
Bualintur Highld....100 d7
Buarth-draw Flints....54 E11
Bubbenhall Warwks....37 L6
Bubwith E R Yk....64 G12
Buccleuch Border....75 R5
Buchanan Smithy Stirlg....89 L9
Buchanhaven Abers....105 U5
Buchanty P & K....90 D6
Buchany Stirlg....89 R5
Buchlyvie Stirlg....89 N7
Buckabank Cumb....67 N3
Buckden Cambs....38 J8
Buckden N York....62 J4
Buckenham Norfk....51 Q13
Buckerell Devon....6 F4
Buckfast Devon....5 S8
Buckfastleigh Devon....5 S8
Buckhaven Fife....91 M12
Buckholt Mons....27 U4
Buckhorn Weston
Dorset....17 U12
Buckhurst Hill Essex....21 S4
Buckie Moray....104 E3
Buckingham Bucks....30 E6
Buckland Bucks....30 J10
Buckland Devon....5 R11
Buckland Gloucs....36 E13
Buckland Hants....9 L8
Buckland Herts....31 U6
Buckland Kent....13 R7
Buckland Oxon....29 R8
Buckland Surrey....21 M12
Buckland Brewer Devon....14 K8
Buckland Common
Bucks....30 K11
Buckland Dinham
Somset....17 U6
Buckland Filleigh Devon....15 L11
Buckland in the Moor
Devon....5 S6
Buckland Monachorum
Devon....5 M7
Buckland Newton
Dorset....7 S4
Buckland Ripers Dorset....7 S8
Buckland St Mary
Somset....6 J2

Buckland-Tout-Saints
Devon....5 S11
Bucklebury W Berk....19 S6
Bucklers Hard Hants....9 N9
Bucklesham Suffk....41 M12
Buckley Flints....54 G14
Buckley Green Warwks....36 G7
Bucklow Hill Ches E....55 R10
Buckminster Leics....48 C9
Bucknall C Stke....46 B4
Bucknall Lincs....58 K13
Bucknell Oxon....30 C7
Bucknell Shrops....34 J6
Buckpool Moray....104 E3
Bucksburn C Aber....99 R2
Buck's Cross Devon....14 H8
Buckshaw Village Lancs....55 N2
Bucks Green W Susx....10 H4
Bucks Hill Herts....31 N12
Bucks Horn Oak Hants....10 C2
Buck's Mills Devon....14 H8
Buckton E R Yk....65 R5
Buckton Herefs....34 J6
Buckton Nthumb....85 R11
Buckworth Cambs....38 H5
Budby Notts....57 T13
Buddileigh Staffs....45 S4
Bude Cnwll....14 F11
Budge's Shop Cnwll....4 J9
Budlake Devon....6 C5
Budle Nthumb....85 T11
Budleigh Salterton
Devon....6 E8
Budock Water Cnwll....2 K10
Buerton Ches E....45 Q5
Bugbrooke Nhants....37 S9
Bugford Devon....5 U10
Buglawton Ches E....56 C14
Bugle Cnwll....3 Q5
Bugthorpe E R Yk....64 H8
Buildwas Shrops....45 P13
Builth Road Powys....34 B9
Builth Wells Powys....34 B10
Bulbourne Herts....30 K10
Bulby Lincs....48 G8
Bulcote Notts....47 R5
Buldoo Highld....111 V3
Bulford Wilts....18 J12
Bulford Camp Wilts....18 J12
Bulkeley Ches E....45 M3
Bulkington Warwks....37 L3
Bulkington Wilts....18 D9
Bulkworthy Devon....14 J9
Bullamoor N York....70 E14
Bull Bay IoA....52 F3
Bullbridge Derbys....47 L3
Bullbrook Br For....20 E9
Bullen's Green Herts....31 R11
Bulley Gloucs....28 E4
Bullgill Cumb....66 G5
Bullinghope Herefs....35 M13
Bullington Hants....19 R12
Bullington Lincs....58 J11
Bull's Green Herts....31 S10
Bull's Green Norfk....51 R14
Bulmer Essex....40 D12
Bulmer N York....64 F6
Bulmer Tye Essex....40 D13
Bulphan Thurr....22 F10
Bulstone Devon....6 G7
Bulstrode Herts....31 N12
Bulverhythe E Susx....12 E14
Bulwark Abers....105 Q6
Bulwell C Nott....47 P5
Bulwick Nhants....48 E14
Bumble's Green Essex....22 B6
Bunacaimb Highld....100 f11
Bunarkaig Highld....101 M14
Bunbury Ches E....45 N2
Bunbury Heath Ches E....45 N2
Bunchrew Highld....102 H6
Bundalloch Highld....101 M6
Bunessan Ag & B....86 F1
Bungay Suffk....41 Q3
Bunker's Hill Lincs....49 L2
Bunnahabhain Ag & B....78 G3
Bunny Notts....47 Q8
Buntait Highld....102 D7
Buntingford Herts....31 U7
Bunwell Norfk....40 K2
Bunwell Street Norfk....40 K1
Burbage Derbys....56 F12
Burbage Leics....37 N2
Burbage Wilts....18 K8
Burchett's Green W & M....20 D6
Burcombe Wilts....8 F2
Burcot Oxon....19 S2
Burcot Worcs....36 C6
Burcote Shrops....45 R13
Burcott Bucks....30 H8
Burdale N York....64 K7
Bures Essex....40 F13
Burford Oxon....29 Q5
Burford Shrops....35 N7
Burg Ag & B....92 K9
Burgate Suffk....40 J5
Burgates Hants....10 B4
Burge End Herts....31 P6
Burgess Hill W Susx....11 M6
Burgh Suffk....41 M10
Burgh by Sands Cumb....75 R14
Burgh Castle Norfk....51 S13
Burghclere Hants....19 Q8
Burghead Moray....103 U2
Burghfield W Berk....19 U7
Burghfield Common
W Berk....19 U7
Burgh Heath Surrey....21 N11
Burghill Herefs....35 L12
Burgh Island Devon....5 R11
Burgh le Marsh Lincs....59 S13
Burghnext Norfk....51 M9
Burgh next Aylsham
Norfk....51 M8
Burgh on Bain Lincs....59 L9
Burgh St Margaret Norfk....51 S11
Burgh St Peter Norfk....41 S1
Burghwallis Donc....57 R4
Burham Kent....12 D3
Buriton Hants....9 U4
Burland Ches E....45 P3
Burlawn Cnwll....3 P2
Burleigh Gloucs....28 G7
Burlescombe Devon....6 E2
Burleston Dorset....7 U5
Burlestone Devon....5 U11
Burley Hants....8 J8
Burley Rutlnd....48 B11
Burley Shrops....35 L2
Burley in Wharfedale
C Brad....63 P10
Burley Lawn Hants....8 J8
Burley Street Hants....8 J8
Burley Wood Head
C Brad....63 P10
Burlingham Green Norfk....51 Q11
Burlingjobb Powys....34 G9
Burlington Shrops....45 S11
Burlton Shrops....45 L8
Burmarsh Kent....13 M9
Burmington Warwks....36 J13
Burn N York....57 T1
Burnage Manch....56 C8
Burnaston Derbys....46 J7
Burnbanks Cumb....67 R9
Burnbrae N Lans....82 F7
Burncross Sheff....57 M7
Burndell W Susx....10 F9
Burnden Bolton....55 R5
Burnedge Rochdl....56 D4
Burneside Cumb....67 R12
Burneston N York....63 S2
Burnett BaNES....17 S3
Burnfoot Border....75 T3
Burnfoot Border....75 S5
Burnfoot D & G....74 H5
Burnfoot D & G....75 P10
Burnfoot P & K....90 D9
Burnham Bucks....20 F6
Burnham N Linc....58 J3
Burnham Deepdale
Norfk....50 D5
Burnham Green Herts....31 S9
Burnham Market Norfk....50 D5
Burnham Norton Norfk....50 D5
Burnham-on-Crouch
Essex....23 M7
Burnham-on-Sea
Somset....16 K7
Burnham Overy Norfk....50 D5
Burnham Overy Staithe
Norfk....50 D5
Burnham Thorpe Norfk....50 E5
Burnhaven Abers....105 U6
Burnhead D & G....74 F6
Burnhervie Abers....105 L13
Burnhill Green Staffs....45 S13
Burnhope Dur....69 Q3
Burnhouse N Ayrs....81 M2
Burniston N York....65 N2
Burnley Lancs....62 G13

Burnley Crematorium
Lancs....62 G13
Burnmouth Border....85 P6
Burn Naze Lancs....61 Q11
Burn of Cambus Stirlg....89 R5
Burnopfield Dur....69 Q1
Burnsall N York....63 M7
Burnside Angus....98 G12
Burnside Angus....98 J13
Burnside Fife....90 J10
Burnside Moray....103 V5
Burnside W Loth....83 L3
Burnside of Duntrune
Angus....91 P5
Burntcommon Surrey....20 H12
Burntheath Derbys....46 H7
Burnt Heath Essex....23 Q3
Burnt Hill W Berk....19 S6
Burnthouse Cnwll....2 K10
Burntisland Fife....83 P1
Burnt Oak E Susx....11 S5
Burntwood Staffs....46 E12
Burntwood Green Staffs....46 E12
Burnt Yates N York....63 R7
Burnworthy Somset....16 H13
Burpham Surrey....20 H12
Burpham W Susx....10 G9
Burradon Nthumb....76 K4
Burradon N Tyne....77 R11
Burrafirth Shet....106 w1
Burras Cnwll....2 H10
Burravoe Shet....106 v5
Burrells Cumb....68 E9
Burrelton P & K....90 J4
Burridge Devon....15 N5
Burridge Hants....9 Q6
Burrill N York....63 R2
Burringham N Linc....58 D5
Burrington Devon....15 P9
Burrington Herefs....34 K6
Burrington N Som....17 N5
Burrough End Cambs....39 T9
Burrough Green Cambs....39 T9
Burrough on the Hill
Leics....47 U11
Burrow Lancs....62 C5
Burrow Somset....16 B8
Burrow Bridge Somset....17 L10
Burrowhill Surrey....20 G10
Burrows Cross Surrey....20 J13
Burry Swans....25 S12
Burry Green Swans....25 S12
Burry Port Carmth....25 R10
Burscough Lancs....54 K4
Burscough Bridge Lancs....54 K3
Bursea E R Yk....64 H13
Burshill E R Yk....65 P10
Bursledon Hants....9 P7
Burslem C Stke....45 U4
Burstall Suffk....40 J12
Burstock Dorset....7 M4
Burston Norfk....40 K3
Burston Staffs....46 B7
Burstow Surrey....11 N2
Burstwick E R Yk....65 S14
Burtersett N York....62 H2
Burthorpe Green Suffk....40 C8
Burthwaite Cumb....67 P3
Burthy Cnwll....3 N5
Burtle Somset....17 L8
Burtoft Lincs....49 L6
Burton BCP....8 H10
Burton Ches W....54 H11
Burton Ches W....55 M14
Burton Dorset....7 V6
Burton Nthumb....85 T11
Burton Pembks....24 G9
Burton Somset....16 G8
Burton Wilts....18 B5
Burton Wilts....17 V10
Burton Agnes E R Yk....65 Q7
Burton Bradstock
Dorset....7 N7
Burton Coggles Lincs....48 E8
Burton Dassett Warwks....37 L10
Burton End Essex....22 D2
Burton End Suffk....40 B11
Burton Fleming E R Yk....65 Q5
Burton Green Warwks....36 J5
Burton Green Wrexhm....44 H2
Burton Hastings Warwks....37 M3
Burton-in-Kendal Cumb....61 U4
Burton-in-Kendal
Services Cumb....61 U4
Burton in Lonsdale
N York....62 D5
Burton Joyce Notts....47 R5
Burton Latimer Nhants....38 D5
Burton Lazars Leics....47 U10
Burton Leonard N York....63 S7
Burton on the Wolds
Leics....47 Q9
Burton Overy Leics....47 S14
Burton Pedwardine
Lincs....48 H5
Burton Pidsea E R Yk....65 S13
Burton Salmon N York....57 Q1
Burton's Green Essex....22 K2
Burton upon Stather
N Linc....58 E3
Burton upon Trent Staffs....46 H9
Burton Waters Lincs....58 F12
Burtonwood Warrtn....55 N8
Burtonwood Services
Warrtn....55 N8
Burwardsley Ches W....45 M2
Burwarton Shrops....35 P4
Burwash E Susx....12 C11
Burwash Common E Susx....12 B11
Burwash Weald E Susx....12 B11
Burwell Cambs....39 S8
Burwell Lincs....59 Q11
Burwen IoA....52 F3
Burwick Ork....106 t21
Bury Bury....55 S4
Bury Cambs....39 L4
Bury Somset....16 C11
Bury W Susx....10 G8
Bury End C Beds....31 N5
Bury Green Herts....22 C3
Bury St Edmunds Suffk....40 E8
Burythorpe N York....64 H7
Busbridge Surrey....10 F2
Busby E Rens....81 R2
Buscot Oxon....29 P8
Bush Abers....99 P9
Bush Cnwll....14 F11
Bushbury Wolves....46 B13
Bushby Leics....47 S13
Bushey Herts....31 N13
Bushey Heath Herts....31 N13
Bush Hill Park Gt Lon....21 P3
Bushley Worcs....35 U13
Bushley Green Worcs....35 U13
Bushmoor Shrops....34 K3
Bushton Wilts....18 G5
Bussage Gloucs....28 G7
Bussex Somset....16 K10
Butcher's Cross E Susx....11 S5
Butcombe N Som....17 P4
Bute Ag & B....88 D13
Butleigh Somset....17 P10
Butleigh Wootton
Somset....17 P9
Butler's Cross Bucks....30 H11
Butlers Marston Warwks....37 L11
Butley Suffk....41 Q10
Butley High Corner Suffk....41 Q11
Butterambe N York....64 F8
Buttercrambe N York....64 F8
Butterdean Border....84 K7
Butterknowle Dur....69 P7
Butterleigh Devon....6 C3
Buttermere Cumb....66 K9
Buttermere Wilts....19 M8
Buttershaw C Brad....63 N14
Butterstone P & K....90 F2
Butterton Staffs....46 E2
Butterton Staffs....45 U4
Butterwick Dur....70 E6
Butterwick Lincs....49 N4
Butterwick N York....64 K5
Butterwick N York....65 L6
Butt Green Ches E....45 Q3
Buttington Powys....44 F12
Buttonoak Shrops....35 R5
Buttonbridge Shrops....35 R5
Buttsash Hants....9 N7
Butt's Green Essex....22 H7
Buttsbear Cross Cnwll....14 G12
Buxhall Suffk....40 H9
Buxhall Fen Street Suffk....40 H9
Buxted E Susx....11 R5
Buxton Derbys....56 F12
Buxton Norfk....51 M9
Buxton Heath Norfk....51 L9
Bwlch Powys....27 M3

Bwlchgwyn Wrexhm 44 G3
Bwlchllan Cerdgn 33 L9
Bwlchnewydd Carmth 25 Q6
Bwlchtocyn Gwynd 42 F8
Bwlch-y-cibau Powys 44 E10
Bwlch-y-Ddar Powys 44 E9
Bwlchyfadfa Cerdgn 32 H11
Bwlch-y-ffridd Powys 34 C1
Bwlch-y-groes Pembks 25 M3
Bwlchymyrdd Swans 25 U11
Bwlch-y-sarnau Powys 34 B6
Byermoor Gatesd 69 Q1
Byers Green Dur 69 R6
Byfield Nhants 37 P10
Byfleet Surrey 20 J10
Byford Herefs 34 J12
Bygrave Herts 31 S5
Byker N u Ty 77 R13
Byland Abbey N York 64 C4
Bylchau Conwy 53 S10
Byley Ches W 55 R13
Bynea Carmth 25 T11
Byrness Nthumb 76 F5
Bystock Devon 6 D8
Bythorn Cambs 38 G5
Byton Herefs 34 J8
Bywell Nthumb 77 L13
Byworth W Susx 10 F6

C

Cabbacott Devon 14 K8
Cabourne Lincs 58 K6
Cabrach Ag & B 78 H3
Cabrach Moray 104 D10
Cabus Lancs 61 T10
Cackle Street E Susx 11 R5
Cackle Street E Susx 12 C12
Cackle Street E Susx 12 F12
Cadbury Devon 6 B3
Cadbury Barton Devon 15 Q9
Cadbury World Birm 36 D4
Cadder E Duns 89 P11
Caddington C Beds 31 N9
Caddonfoot Border 84 D11
Cadeby Donc 57 R6
Cadeby Leics 47 M13
Cadeleigh Devon 6 B3
Cade Street E Susx 11 U6
Cadgwith Cnwll 2 J14
Cadham Fife 91 L11
Cadishead Salfd 55 R8
Cadle Swans 25 V11
Cadley Lancs 61 U13
Cadley Wilts 18 K10
Cadley Wilts 18 K7
Cadmore End Bucks 20 C4
Cadnam Hants 9 L6
Cadney N Linc 58 H6
Cadole Flints 54 F14
Cadoxton V Glam 16 F3
Cadoxton Juxta-Neath Neath 26 D8
Cadwst Denbgs 44 B6
Caeathro Gwynd 52 H10
Caehopkin Powys 26 E5
Caenby Lincs 58 G9
Caeo Carmth 33 N12
Caerau Brdgnd 26 F9
Caerau Cardif 27 L12
Cae'r-bont Powys 26 E5
Cae'r bryn Carmth 25 U8
Caerdeon Gwynd 43 N10
Caer Farchell Pembks 24 C5
Caergeiliog IoA 52 D7
Caergwrle Flints 44 H2
Caerhun Conwy 53 N8
Caerlanrig Border 75 S5
Caerleon Newpt 27 Q9
Caernarfon Gwynd 52 G10
Caernarfon Castle Gwynd 52 G10
Caerphilly Caerph 27 M10
Caersws Powys 34 B2
Caerwedros Cerdgn 32 G9
Caerwent Mons 27 T9
Caerwys Flints 54 D12
Caerynwch Gwynd 43 Q10
Caggle Street Mons 27 R4
Caim IoA 52 K6
Cairinis W Isls 106 d12
Cairnbaan Ag & B 87 Q7
Cairnbulg Abers 105 S2
Cairncross Border 85 M6
Cairncurran Inver 88 H11
Cairndow Ag & B 88 E3
Cairneyhill Fife 82 K1
Cairngarroch D & G 72 D10
Cairngorms National Park 97 T3
Cairnie Abers 104 F7
Cairnorrie Abers 105 P7
Cairnryan D & G 72 D6
Cairnty Moray 104 C5
Caister-on-Sea Norfk 51 T11
Caistor Lincs 58 K6
Caistor St Edmund Norfk 51 M13
Cakebole Worcs 35 U6
Cake Street Norfk 40 J2
Calais Street Suffk 40 G13
Calanais W Isls 106 h5
Calbourne IoW 9 N11
Calceby Lincs 59 Q11
Calcot Flints 54 E12
Calcot Gloucs 29 L5
Calcot W Berk 19 U6
Calcot Row W Berk 19 U6
Calcots Moray 104 B3
Calcott Kent 13 N3
Calcott Shrops 44 K11
Calcutt N York 63 S8
Calcutt Wilts 29 M9
Caldbeck Cumb 67 M4
Caldbergh N York 63 M2
Caldecote Cambs 38 H3
Caldecote Cambs 39 M9
Caldecote Herts 31 R5
Caldecote Nhants 37 S10
Caldecote Highfields Cambs 39 N9
Caldecott Nhants 38 E7
Caldecott Oxon 29 U8
Caldecott Rutlnd 38 C2
Caldecotte M Keyn 30 J5
Calder Cumb 66 F12
Calderbank N Lans 82 E6
Calder Bridge Cumb 66 F11
Calderbrook Rochdl 56 D3
Caldercruix N Lans 82 F5
Calder Grove Wakefd 57 M3
Caldermill S Lans 81 T4
Caldermore Rochdl 56 D3
Calder Vale Lancs 61 U10
Calderwood S Lans 81 T1
Caldey Island Pembks 24 K11
Caldicot Mons 27 T10
Caldmore Wsall 46 D14
Caldwell N York 69 Q10
Caldy Wirral 54 F9
Caledfwlch Carmth 26 B2
Calenick Cnwll 3 L8
Calf of Man IoM 60 b9
Calford Green Suffk 40 B11
Calfsound Ork 106 u16
Calgary Ag & B 92 K8
Califer Moray 103 S4
California Falk 82 H3
California Norfk 51 T10
California Cross Devon 5 S10
Calke Derbys 47 L9
Calke Abbey Derbys 47 L9
Callakille Highld 107 L13
Callander Stirlg 89 P4
Callanish W Isls 106 h5
Callaughton Shrops 45 P14
Callestick Cnwll 2 K6
Calligarry Highld 100 f9
Callington Cnwll 4 K7
Callingwood Staffs 46 G9
Callow Herefs 35 L14
Callow End Worcs 35 T10
Callow Hill Wilts 28 K11
Callow Hill Worcs 35 R6
Callow Hill Worcs 36 D8
Callows Grave Worcs 35 N7
Calmore Hants 9 L6
Calmsden Gloucs 28 K6
Calne Wilts 18 E6
Calow Derbys 57 P12
Calshot Hants 9 P8
Calstock Cnwll 5 L7
Calstone Wellington Wilts 18 F7
Calthorpe Norfk 51 L7
Calthorpe Street Norfk 51 R8
Calthwaite Cumb 67 Q4
Calton N York 62 J8
Calton Staffs 46 F4
Calveley Ches E 45 N2
Calver Derbys 56 K12
Calverhall Shrops 45 P6
Calver Hill Herefs 34 J11
Calverleigh Devon 6 B2
Calverley Leeds 63 Q12
Calver Sough Derbys 56 K12
Calvert Bucks 30 E8
Calverton M Keyn 30 G5
Calverton Notts 47 R4
Calvine P & K 97 N10
Calvo Cumb 66 H2
Calzeat Border 83 M11
Cam Gloucs 28 E8
Camasachoirce Highld 93 T6
Camasine Highld 93 T6
Camas Luinie Highld 101 N6
Camastianavaig Highld 100 e6
Camault Muir Highld 102 F7
Camber E Susx 12 J12
Camberley Surrey 20 E10
Camberwell Gt Lon 21 P7
Camblesforth N York 57 T1
Cambo Nthumb 77 L8
Cambois Nthumb 77 S9
Camborne Cnwll 2 G8
Camborne and Redruth Mining District Cnwll 2 G8
Cambourne Cambs 39 M9
Cambridge Cambs 39 Q9
Cambridge Gloucs 28 D7
Cambridge Airport Cambs 39 Q9
Cambridge City Crematorium Cambs 39 N8
Cambrose Cnwll 2 H7
Cambus Clacks 90 C13
Cambusavie Platform Highld 109 P5
Cambusbarron Stirlg 89 S7
Cambuskenneth Stirlg 89 T7
Cambuslang S Lans 89 P13
Cambus o' May Abers 98 G4
Cambuswallace S Lans 82 K11
Camden Town Gt Lon 21 N6
Cameley BaNES 17 R5
Camelford Cnwll 4 E4
Camelon Falk 82 G2
Camerory Highld 103 R9
Camer's Green Worcs 35 S13
Camerton BaNES 17 S5
Camerton Cumb 66 F6
Camghouran P & K 95 R7
Camieston Border 84 F12
Cammachmore Abers 99 S4
Cammeringham Lincs 58 F10
Camore Highld 109 P7
Campbeltown Ag & B 79 N11
Campbeltown Airport Ag & B 79 M11
Camperdown N Tyne 77 R11
Cample D & G 74 G7
Campmuir P & K 90 K4
Camps W Loth 83 L5
Campsall Donc 57 R4
Campsea Ash Suffk 41 P9
Camps End Cambs 39 T12
Campton C Beds 31 P5
Camptown Border 76 D3
Camrose Pembks 24 F6
Camserney P & K 90 B2
Camusnagaul Highld 94 F4
Camusnagaul Highld 107 U7
Camusteel Highld 100 g5
Camusterrach Highld 100 g5
Canada Hants 8 K5
Canal Foot Cumb 61 Q4
Canaston Bridge Pembks 24 J7
Candacraig Abers 98 E4
Candlesby Lincs 59 S13
Candle Street Suffk 40 H6
Candover Green Shrops 45 M12
Candy Mill Border 83 L10
Cane End Oxon 19 U5
Canewdon Essex 23 M9
Canford Bottom Dorset 8 E8
Canford Cliffs Poole 8 F11
Canford Crematorium Bristl 27 V12
Canford Heath Poole 8 E10
Canford Magna Poole 8 E9
Canhams Green Suffk 40 J7
Canisbay Highld 112 H2
Canklow Rothm 57 P8
Canley Covtry 36 K5
Canley Crematorium Covtry 36 K5
Cann Dorset 8 B4
Canna Highld 100 b9
Cannich Highld 102 B9
Cannington Somset 16 J9
Canning Town Gt Lon 21 R6
Cannock Staffs 46 C11
Cannock Chase Staffs 46 C10
Cannock Wood Staffs 46 D11
Cannon Bridge Herefs 34 K12
Canonbie D & G 75 S10
Canon Frome Herefs 35 P12
Canon Pyon Herefs 35 L11
Canons Ashby Nhants 37 Q10
Canonstown Cnwll 2 E9
Canterbury Kent 13 M4
Canterbury Cathedral Kent 13 N4
Cantley Norfk 51 Q13
Cantlop Shrops 45 M12
Canton Cardif 27 M12
Cantraywood Highld 103 L6
Cantsfield Lancs 62 C5
Canvey Island Essex 22 J11
Canwick Lincs 58 G13
Canworthy Water Cnwll 4 G2
Caol Highld 94 G3
Caolas Scalpaigh W Isls 106 h9
Caoles Ag & B 92 D9
Caonich Highld 101 R13
Capel Kent 12 B7
Capel Surrey 10 K2
Capel Bangor Cerdgn 33 N4
Capel Betws Lleucu Cerdgn 33 M9
Capel Coch IoA 52 G6
Capel Curig Conwy 53 M11
Capel Cynon Cerdgn 32 G11
Capel Dewi Carmth 25 S6
Capel Dewi Cerdgn 32 J12
Capel-Dewi Cerdgn 33 M4
Capel Garmon Conwy 53 P11
Capel Green Suffk 41 Q11
Capel Gwyn Carmth 25 S6
Capel Gwyn IoA 52 D7
Capel Gwynfe Carmth 26 C3
Capel Hendre Carmth 25 U8
Capel Isaac Carmth 25 U5
Capel Iwan Carmth 25 N3
Capel le Ferne Kent 13 Q8
Capelles Guern 6 d2
Capel Llanilltern Cardif 26 K12
Capel Mawr IoA 52 F8
Capel Parc IoA 52 F5
Capel St Andrew Suffk 41 Q11
Capel St Mary Suffk 40 J13
Capel Seion Cerdgn 33 M5
Capel Trisant Cerdgn 33 P5
Capeluchaf Gwynd 42 H4
Capelulo Conwy 53 M7
Capel-y-ffin Powys 27 P1
Capel-y-graig Gwynd 52 H9
Capenhurst Ches W 54 J12
Capernwray Lancs 61 U5
Capheaton Nthumb 77 L9
Caplaw E Rens 88 K14
Capon's Green Suffk 41 N7
Cappercleuch Border 83 P14
Capstone Medway 12 E2
Capton Devon 5 U10
Capton Somset 16 E9
Caputh P & K 90 G3
Caradon Mining District Cnwll 4 G6
Caradon Town Cnwll 4 H6
Carbeth Inn Stirlg 89 M10
Carbis Cnwll 3 Q5
Carbis Bay Cnwll 2 E9
Carbost Highld 100 c6
Carbost Highld 100 d5
Carbrook Sheff 57 N9
Carbrooke Norfk 50 F13
Carburton Notts 57 T12
Carclaze Cnwll 3 Q6
Car Colston Notts 47 T5
Carcroft Donc 57 R5
Cardenden Fife 90 K12
Cardeston Shrops 44 J11
Cardewlees Cumb 67 N2
Cardhu Moray 103 U7
Cardiff Cardif 27 M12
Cardiff Airport V Glam 16 E3
Cardiff Gate Services Cardif 27 N11
Cardiff West Services Cardif 26 K12
Cardigan Cerdgn 32 C11
Cardinal's Green Cambs 39 T11
Cardington Bed 38 G11
Cardington Shrops 35 M1
Cardinham Cnwll 4 E7
Cardrain D & G 72 E13
Cardrona Border 83 R11
Cardross Ag & B 88 H10
Cardross Crematorium Ag & B 88 H10
Cardryne D & G 72 E13
Cardurnock Cumb 75 N14
Careby Lincs 48 F10
Careston Angus 98 J11
Carew Pembks 24 H10
Carew Cheriton Pembks 24 H10
Carew Newton Pembks 24 H10
Carey Herefs 27 V1
Carfin N Lans 82 E7
Carfraemill Border 84 E8
Cargate Green Norfk 51 Q11
Cargenbridge D & G 74 J10
Cargill P & K 90 J4
Cargo Cumb 75 S14
Cargreen Cnwll 5 L8
Cargurrel Cnwll 3 M9
Carham Nthumb 84 K11
Carhampton Somset 16 D8
Carharrack Cnwll 2 J8
Carie P & K 95 S7
Carinish W Isls 106 d12
Carisbrooke IoW 9 P11
Cark Cumb 61 R4
Carkeel Cnwll 5 L8
Carlabhagh W Isls 106 h4
Carland Cross Cnwll 3 M6
Carlbury Darltn 69 R9
Carlby Lincs 48 F11
Carlcroft Nthumb 76 G3
Carlecotes Barns 56 J6
Carleen Cnwll 2 G10
Carlesmoor N York 63 Q5
Carleton Cumb 66 F11
Carleton Cumb 67 P2
Carleton Cumb 67 R7
Carleton Lancs 61 Q12
Carleton N York 62 K10
Carleton Wakefd 57 Q2
Carleton Crematorium Bpool 61 Q12
Carleton Forehoe Norfk 50 J12
Carleton Rode Norfk 40 K2
Carleton St Peter Norfk 51 P13
Carlidnack Cnwll 2 K11
Carlincraig Abers 104 K7
Carlingcott BaNES 17 S5
Carlin How R & Cl 71 M9
Carlisle Cumb 67 N1
Carlisle Airport Cumb 75 U13
Carlisle Crematorium Cumb 67 N2
Carloggas Cnwll 3 M3
Carlops Border 83 N7
Carloway W Isls 106 h4
Carlton Barns 57 N4
Carlton Bed 38 E9
Carlton Cambs 39 T10
Carlton Leeds 57 M1
Carlton Leics 47 L13
Carlton N York 57 T2
Carlton N York 63 M3
Carlton N York 64 E2
Carlton Notts 47 R5
Carlton S on T 70 E8
Carlton Suffk 41 Q8
Carlton Colville Suffk 41 T3
Carlton Curlieu Leics 37 S1
Carlton Green Cambs 39 T10
Carlton Husthwaite N York 64 B4
Carlton-in-Cleveland N York 70 H12
Carlton in Lindrick Notts 57 S10
Carlton-le-Moorland Lincs 48 D2
Carlton Miniott N York 63 T3
Carlton-on-Trent Notts 58 C14
Carlton Scroop Lincs 48 D4
Carluke S Lans 82 F8
Carlyon Bay Cnwll 3 R6
Carmacoup S Lans 82 E13
Carmarthen Carmth 25 R6
Carmel Carmth 25 U7
Carmel Flints 54 E11
Carmel Gwynd 52 G12
Carmichael S Lans 82 H11
Carmountside Crematorium C Stke 46 B4
Carmunnock C Glas 89 N14
Carmyle C Glas 89 P13
Carmyllie Angus 91 R3
Carnaby E R Yk 65 Q6
Carnbee Fife 91 R10
Carnbo P & K 90 G11
Carn Brea Cnwll 2 H8
Carnbrogie Abers 105 P10
Carndu Highld 101 M6
Carnduff S Lans 81 T3
Carne Cnwll 2 K12
Carne Cnwll 3 N9
Carne Cnwll 3 P5
Carnell E Ayrs 81 P6
Carnewas Cnwll 3 M3
Carnforth Lancs 61 T5
Carn-gorm Highld 101 P7
Carnhedryn Pembks 24 D5
Carnhell Green Cnwll 2 G9
Carnie Abers 99 Q2
Carnkie Cnwll 2 H8
Carnkie Cnwll 2 J10
Carnkiet Cnwll 2 K6
Carno Powys 33 U1
Carnock Fife 90 F14
Carnon Downs Cnwll 2 K8
Carnousie Abers 104 K5
Carnoustie Angus 91 S5
Carnsmerry Cnwll 3 Q5
Carnwath S Lans 82 J9
Carnyorth Cnwll 2 B10
Carol Green Solhll 36 J5
Carpalla Cnwll 3 P6
Carperby N York 63 L2
Carr Rothm 57 R8
Carradale Ag & B 79 Q8
Carrbridge Highld 103 P11
Carrbrook Tamesd 56 E6
Carrefour Jersey 7 c2
Carreglefn IoA 52 E5
Carr Gate Wakefd 57 M2
Carrhouse N Linc 58 C5
Carrick Ag & B 87 S8
Carrick Castle Ag & B 88 E7
Carriden Falk 82 K2
Carrington Lincs 49 M2
Carrington Mdloth 83 R6
Carrington Traffd 55 R8
Carrog Conwy 43 Q4
Carrog Denbgs 44 D5
Carron Falk 82 G2
Carron Moray 103 V7
Carronbridge D & G 74 G6
Carron Bridge Stirlg 89 R9
Carronshore Falk 82 G2
Carrow Hill Mons 27 S9
Carr Shield Nthumb 68 H3
Carrutherstown D & G 75 M11
Carruth House Inver 88 J12
Carr Vale Derbys 57 Q13
Carrville Dur 70 D4
Carsaig Ag & B 86 J1
Carseriggan D & G 72 J6
Carsethorn D & G 74 J14
Carshalton Gt Lon 21 N10
Carsington Derbys 46 J3
Carskey Ag & B 79 M14
Carsluith D & G 73 M9
Carsphairn D & G 81 R14
Carstairs S Lans 82 H9
Carstairs Junction S Lans 82 J9
Carswell Marsh Oxon 29 R8
Carter's Clay Hants 9 L4
Carters Green Essex 22 D5
Carterton Oxon 29 Q6
Carterway Heads Nthumb 69 M2
Carthew Cnwll 3 Q5
Carthorpe N York 63 S3
Cartington Nthumb 77 L5
Cartland S Lans 82 G9
Cartledge Derbys 57 M11
Cartmel Cumb 61 R4
Cartmel Fell Cumb 61 S2
Carway Carmth 25 S9
Carwinley Cumb 75 T11
Cashe's Green Gloucs 28 F6
Cashmoor Dorset 8 D6
Cassington Oxon 29 U5
Cassop Colliery Dur 70 D5
Castallack Cnwll 2 D11
Castel Guern 6 d3
Castell Conwy 53 N9
Castell-y-bwch Torfn 27 P9
Casterton Cumb 62 C4
Castle Cnwll 3 R5
Castle Acre Norfk 50 D10
Castle Ashby Nhants 38 C9
Castlebay W Isls 106 b19
Castle Bolton N York 63 L1
Castle Bromwich Solhll 36 F3
Castle Bytham Lincs 48 E10
Castlebythe Pembks 24 H5
Castle Caereinion Powys 44 E12
Castle Camps Cambs 39 T12
Castle Carrock Cumb 67 R1
Castlecary Falk 89 S10
Castle Cary Somset 17 R10
Castle Combe Wilts 18 B5
Castle Donington Leics 47 M8
Castle Douglas D & G 74 E13
Castle Eaton Swindn 29 M8
Castle Eden Dur 70 F5
Castle End C Pete 48 H12
Castleford Wakefd 57 P1
Castle Frome Herefs 35 Q11
Castle Gate Cnwll 2 D10
Castle Green Cumb 61 U1
Castle Green Surrey 20 G10
Castle Gresley Derbys 46 J10
Castle Hedingham Essex 40 C13
Castlehill Border 83 P11
Castlehill Highld 112 E3
Castle Hill Kent 12 C7
Castle Hill Suffk 40 K11
Castlehill W Duns 88 J10
Castle Howard N York 64 G5
Castle Kennedy D & G 72 E8
Castle Lachlan Ag & B 87 U6
Castlemartin Pembks 24 F11
Castlemilk C Glas 89 N14
Castle Morris Pembks 24 F4
Castlemorton Worcs 35 S13
Castlemorton Common Worcs 35 S13
Castle O'er D & G 75 P7
Castle Pulverbatch Shrops 44 K13
Castle Rising Norfk 49 U9
Castleside Dur 69 N3
Castle Stuart Highld 102 K6
Castlethorpe M Keyn 30 H4
Castlethorpe N Linc 58 G5
Castleton Border 75 V8
Castleton Derbys 56 J10
Castleton N York 71 L11
Castleton Newpt 27 P11
Castleton Rochdl 56 C4
Castletown Dorset 7 S10
Castletown Highld 112 E3
Castletown IoM 60 d9
Castletown Sundld 77 T14
Castley N York 63 R10
Caston Norfk 50 G14
Castor C Pete 48 H14
Caswell Bay Swans 25 U13
Catacol N Ayrs 79 S6
Cat and Fiddle Derbys 56 F12
Catbrain S Glos 27 V11
Catbrook Mons 27 U7
Catch Flints 54 F12
Catchall Cnwll 2 C11
Catchem's Corner Solhll 36 J5
Catchgate Dur 69 Q2
Catcliffe Rothm 57 P9
Catcomb Wilts 18 F5
Catcott Somset 17 L9
Catcott Burtle Somset 17 M8
Caterham Surrey 21 P11
Catfield Norfk 51 Q9
Catfield Common Norfk 51 R9
Catford Gt Lon 21 Q8
Catforth Lancs 61 T12
Cathcart C Glas 89 N13
Cathedine Powys 27 L2
Catherine-de-Barnes Solhll 36 G4
Catherine Slack C Brad 63 M14
Catherington Hants 9 T6
Catherston Leweston Dorset 7 L6
Catherton Shrops 35 Q5
Catisfield Hants 9 R7
Catley Herefs 35 Q12
Catley Lane Head Rochdl 56 C3
Catlodge Highld 96 J5
Catlow Lancs 62 H12
Catlowdy Cumb 75 U10
Catmere End Essex 39 Q13
Catmore W Berk 19 Q4
Caton Devon 5 T6
Caton Lancs 61 U7
Caton Green Lancs 62 B6
Cator Court Devon 5 R5
Catrine E Ayrs 81 Q7
Cat's Ash Newpt 27 R9
Catsfield E Susx 12 D13
Catsfield Stream E Susx 12 D13
Catsgore Somset 17 P11
Catsham Somset 17 Q10
Catshill Worcs 36 C6
Catstree Shrops 35 R1
Cattadale Ag & B 79 M13
Cattal N York 63 U9
Cattawade Suffk 40 K14
Catterall Lancs 61 T11
Catteralslane Shrops 45 N5
Catterick N York 69 R13
Catterick Bridge N York 69 R13
Catterick Garrison N York 69 Q13
Catterlen Cumb 67 Q6
Catterline Abers 99 R8
Catterton N York 64 C10
Catteshall Surrey 10 F2
Catthorpe Leics 37 Q5
Cattishall Suffk 40 E7
Cattistock Dorset 7 Q5
Catton N York 63 T4
Catton Nthumb 76 G14
Catwick E R Yk 65 Q10
Catworth Cambs 38 G6
Caudle Green Gloucs 28 H5
Caulcott C Beds 31 M4
Caulcott Oxon 30 B8
Cauldcots Angus 91 U2
Cauldhame Stirlg 89 P7
Cauldmill Border 76 A2
Cauldon Staffs 46 E4
Cauldon Lowe Staffs 46 E4
Cauldwell Derbys 46 J10
Caulkerbush D & G 66 D1
Caulside D & G 75 T9
Caundle Marsh Dorset 7 S2
Caunsall Worcs 35 U4
Caunton Notts 47 T1
Causeway Hants 9 U4
Causeway End Cumb 61 T2
Causeway End D & G 73 L8
Causeway End Essex 22 G4
Causewayend S Lans 82 K11
Causewayhead Cumb 66 H2
Causewayhead Stirlg 89 T6
Causeyend Abers 105 Q12
Causey Park Nthumb 77 P7
Causey Park Bridge Nthumb 77 P7
Cavendish Suffk 40 D11
Cavenham Suffk 40 C6
Caversfield Oxon 30 C7
Caversham Readg 20 B8
Caverswall Staffs 46 C5
Caverton Mill Border 84 J13
Cavil E R Yk 64 H13
Cawdor Highld 103 M5
Cawkwell Lincs 59 N11
Cawood N York 64 D12
Cawsand Cnwll 5 L10
Cawston Norfk 50 K9
Cawston Warwks 37 N6
Cawthorn N York 64 H2
Cawthorne Barns 57 L5
Cawton N York 64 E4
Caxton Cambs 39 M9
Caxton End Cambs 39 M9
Caxton Gibbet Cambs 39 L8
Caynham Shrops 35 N6
Caythorpe Lincs 48 D4
Caythorpe Notts 47 S4
Cayton N York 65 P3
Ceann a Bhaigh W Isls 106 c12
Ceannacroc Lodge Highld 101 U9
Cearsiadar W Isls 106 i6
Ceciliford Mons 27 U7
Cefn Newpt 27 P10
Cefn Berain Conwy 53 S9
Cefn-brith Conwy 43 T3
Cefn-bryn-brain Carmth 26 C5
Cefn Byrle Powys 26 E5
Cefn Canel Powys 44 F7
Cefn Coch Powys 44 D8
Cefn-coed-y-cymmer Myr Td 26 J6
Cefn Cribwr Brdgnd 26 F11
Cefn Cross Brdgnd 26 F11
Cefn-ddwysarn Gwynd 43 U6
Cefn-Einion Shrops 34 G3
Cefneithin Carmth 25 U8
Cefngorwydd Powys 33 T11
Cefn-mawr Wrexhm 44 G5
Cefnpennar Rhondd 26 J7
Cefn-y-bedd Flints 44 H2
Cefn-y-pant Carmth 25 L5
Ceint IoA 52 G7
Cellan Cerdgn 33 M11
Cellardyke Fife 91 S11
Cellarhead Staffs 46 C4
Celleron Cumb 67 Q7
Celynen Caerph 27 N8
Cemaes IoA 52 E4
Cemmaes Powys 43 R12
Cemmaes Road Powys 43 R13
Cenarth Cerdgn 32 E12
Cerbyd Pembks 24 D5
Ceres Fife 91 P9
Cerne Abbas Dorset 7 S4
Cerney Wick Gloucs 29 L8
Cerrigceinwen IoA 52 F8
Cerrigydrudion Conwy 43 U4
Cess Norfk 51 R10
Ceunant Gwynd 52 H10
Chaceley Gloucs 28 G1
Chacewater Cnwll 2 K8
Chackmore Bucks 30 E5
Chacombe Nhants 37 N12
Chadbury Worcs 36 D11
Chadderton Oldham 56 D5
Chadderton Fold Oldham 56 D5
Chaddesden C Derb 47 L6
Chaddesley Corbett Worcs 35 U6
Chaddlehanger Devon 5 M5
Chaddleworth W Berk 19 P5
Chadlington Oxon 29 R3
Chadshunt Warwks 36 K10
Chadwell Leics 47 U9
Chadwell Shrops 45 S11
Chadwell End Bed 38 G7
Chadwell Heath Gt Lon 21 S5
Chadwell St Mary Thurr 22 F12
Chadwick Worcs 35 T7
Chadwick End Solhll 36 H6
Chadwick Green St Hel 55 M7
Chaffcombe Somset 7 L2
Chafford Hundred Thurr 22 F12
Chagford Devon 5 S3
Chailey E Susx 11 P7
Chainbridge Cambs 49 P13
Chainhurst Kent 12 D6
Chalbury Dorset 8 E7
Chalbury Common Dorset 8 E7
Chaldon Surrey 21 P11
Chale IoW 9 P13
Chale Green IoW 9 P13
Chalfont Common Bucks 20 H4
Chalfont St Giles Bucks 20 G4
Chalfont St Peter Bucks 20 H4
Chalford Gloucs 28 G7
Chalford Oxon 30 F12
Chalford Wilts 18 C10
Chalgrave C Beds 31 M7
Chalgrove Oxon 30 D13
Chalk Kent 22 G13
Chalk End Essex 22 F5
Chalkhouse Green Oxon 20 B7
Chalkway Somset 7 L3
Chalkwell Kent 12 G3
Challaborough Devon 5 R12
Challacombe Devon 15 Q4
Challoch D & G 72 K6
Challock Kent 12 K5
Chalmington Dorset 7 Q4
Chalton C Beds 31 M7
Chalton C Beds 38 H10
Chalton Hants 9 U5
Chalvey Slough 20 G7
Chalvington E Susx 11 S9
Chambers Green Kent 12 H7
Chandler's Cross Herts 20 J3
Chandlers Cross Worcs 35 S13
Chandler's Ford Hants 9 N5
Channel's End Bed 38 H9
Chanterlands Crematorium C KuH 65 P13
Chantry Somset 17 T7
Chantry Suffk 40 K12
Chapel Cumb 66 K6
Chapel Fife 91 L13
Chapel Allerton Leeds 63 S12
Chapel Allerton Somset 17 M6
Chapel Amble Cnwll 3 P1
Chapel Brampton Nhants 37 T7
Chapelbridge Cambs 39 L2
Chapel Chorlton Staffs 45 T6
Chapel Cross E Susx 11 U6
Chapel End Bed 38 H9
Chapel End C Beds 31 N4
Chapel End Cambs 38 H4
Chapel End Warwks 36 K2
Chapelend Way Essex 40 B13
Chapel-en-le-Frith Derbys 56 G10
Chapel Field Bury 55 S5
Chapelgate Lincs 49 P9
Chapel Green Warwks 36 J3
Chapel Green Warwks 37 N8
Chapel Haddlesey N York 57 S1
Chapelhall N Lans 82 E6
Chapel Hill Abers 105 T8
Chapel Hill Lincs 48 K3
Chapel Hill Mons 27 U8
Chapel Hill N York 63 S10
Chapelhope Border 75 P2
Chapelknowe D & G 75 R11
Chapel Lawn Shrops 34 H5
Chapel-le-Dale N York 62 E4
Chapel Leigh Somset 16 F11
Chapel Milton Derbys 56 G10
Chapel of Garioch Abers 105 L11
Chapel Rossan D & G 72 E11
Chapel Row E Susx 11 U8
Chapel Row Essex 22 J7
Chapel Row W Berk 19 S7
Chapels Cumb 61 N3
Chapel St Leonards Lincs 59 U12
Chapel Stile Cumb 67 M11
Chapelton Angus 91 T2
Chapelton Devon 15 N7
Chapelton S Lans 82 C9
Chapeltown Bl w D 55 R3
Chapel Town Cnwll 3 M5
Chapeltown Moray 104 A11
Chapeltown Sheff 57 N7
Chapmanslade Wilts 18 B11
Chapmans Well Devon 4 K2
Chapmore End Herts 31 T9
Chappel Essex 23 L2
Charaton Cnwll 4 J7
Chard Somset 6 K3
Chard Junction Somset 6 K4
Chardleigh Green Somset 6 K2
Chardstock Devon 6 K4
Charfield S Glos 28 D9
Chargrove Gloucs 28 H4
Charing Kent 12 J6
Charing Crematorium Kent 12 J6
Charing Heath Kent 12 H6
Charing Hill Kent 12 J5
Charingworth Gloucs 36 G13
Charlbury Oxon 29 S4
Charlcombe BaNES 17 T3
Charlcutt Wilts 18 E5
Charlecote Warwks 36 J9
Charlemont Sandw 36 D2
Charles Devon 15 Q6
Charleshill Surrey 10 D2
Charleston Angus 91 N2
Charlestown C Aber 99 S3
Charlestown C Brad 63 P12
Charlestown Calder 56 E1
Charlestown Cnwll 3 Q6
Charlestown Cnwll 3 Q6
Charlestown Derbys 56 F8
Charlestown Dorset 7 S9
Charlestown Fife 83 L2
Charlestown Highld 102 H6
Charlestown Highld 107 P10
Charlestown Salfd 55 T6
Charles Tye Suffk 40 H10
Charlesworth Derbys 56 F8
Charlinch Somset 16 H9
Charlottetown Fife 91 L9
Charlton Gt Lon 21 R7
Charlton Hants 19 N11
Charlton Herts 31 Q7
Charlton Nhants 30 B5
Charlton Nthumb 76 G9
Charlton Oxon 29 T10
Charlton Somset 16 J11
Charlton Somset 17 R8
Charlton Somset 17 S6
Charlton Surrey 20 J9
Charlton W Susx 10 D8
Charlton Wilts 8 C4
Charlton Wilts 28 J10
Charlton Worcs 35 T6
Charlton Worcs 36 D11
Charlton Wrekin 45 N11
Charlton Abbots Gloucs 28 K3
Charlton Adam Somset 17 P11
Charlton All Saints Wilts 8 H4
Charlton Down Dorset 7 S5
Charlton Hill Shrops 45 N12
Charlton Horethorne Somset 17 S12
Charlton Kings Gloucs 28 J3
Charlton Mackrell Somset 17 P11
Charlton Marshall Dorset 8 C8
Charlton Musgrove Somset 17 T11
Charlton-on-Otmoor Oxon 30 C9
Charlton on the Hill Dorset 8 B8
Charlton St Peter Wilts 18 H9
Charlwood Hants 9 T2
Charlwood Surrey 11 L2
Charminster Dorset 7 S6
Charmouth Dorset 7 L6
Charndon Bucks 30 E8
Charney Bassett Oxon 29 S9
Charnock Green Lancs 55 N3
Charnock Richard Lancs 55 N3
Charnock Richard Crematorium Lancs 55 N3
Charnock Richard Services Lancs 55 M3
Charsfield Suffk 41 N9
Chart Corner Kent 12 E5
Charter Alley Hants 19 S9
Charterhall Border 84 K9
Charterhouse Somset 17 N5
Chartershall Stirlg 89 S7
Charterville Allotments Oxon 29 R5
Chartham Kent 13 M5
Chartham Hatch Kent 13 M4
Chart Hill Kent 12 E6
Chartridge Bucks 30 K12
Chart Sutton Kent 12 F6
Chartway Street Kent 12 F5
Charvil Wokham 20 C7
Charwelton Nhants 37 P9
Chase Terrace Staffs 46 D12
Chasetown Staffs 46 D12
Chastleton Oxon 29 P2
Chasty Devon 14 H12
Chatburn Lancs 62 F11
Chatcull Staffs 45 S7
Chatham Caerph 27 N10
Chatham Medway 12 E2
Chatham Green Essex 22 H4
Chathill Nthumb 85 T13
Chatley Worcs 35 U8
Chatsworth House Derbys 57 L12
Chattenden Medway 22 J13
Chatter End Essex 22 C2
Chatteris Cambs 39 N3
Chatterton Lancs 55 S3
Chattisham Suffk 40 J12
Chatto Border 76 F2
Chatton Nthumb 85 R13
Chaul End C Beds 31 N8
Chawleigh Devon 15 R10
Chawley Oxon 29 U7
Chawston Bed 38 J9
Chawton Hants 19 V13
Chaxhill Gloucs 28 D5
Chazey Heath Oxon 19 U5
Cheadle Staffs 46 D5
Cheadle Stockp 56 C9
Cheadle Heath Stockp 56 C9
Cheadle Hulme Stockp 56 C9
Cheam Gt Lon 21 M10
Cheapside W & M 20 F9
Chearsley Bucks 30 F10
Chebsey Staffs 45 U8
Checkendon Oxon 19 U4
Checkley Ches E 45 R4
Checkley Herefs 35 N13
Checkley Staffs 46 D6
Checkley Green Ches E 45 R4
Chedburgh Suffk 40 C9
Cheddar Somset 17 N6
Cheddington Bucks 30 K9
Cheddleton Staffs 46 C3
Cheddleton Heath Staffs 46 C3
Cheddon Fitzpaine Somset 16 H11
Chedglow Wilts 28 H9
Chedgrave Norfk 51 Q14
Chedington Dorset 7 N3
Chediston Suffk 41 Q5
Chediston Green Suffk 41 Q5
Chedworth Gloucs 29 L5
Chedzoy Somset 16 K9
Cheeseman's Green Kent 12 K8
Cheetham Hill Manch 55 T6
Cheldon Devon 15 R10
Chelford Ches E 55 T12
Chellaston C Derb 47 L7
Chellington Bed 38 E9
Chelmarsh Shrops 35 R3
Chelmick Shrops 35 L2
Chelmondiston Suffk 41 M13
Chelmorton Derbys 56 H13
Chelmsford Essex 22 H6
Chelmsford Crematorium Essex 22 G6
Chelmsley Wood Solhll 36 G3
Chelsea Gt Lon 21 N7
Chelsfield Gt Lon 21 S10
Chelsham Surrey 21 Q11
Chelston Somset 16 G12
Chelsworth Suffk 40 G11
Cheltenham Gloucs 28 H3
Cheltenham Crematorium Gloucs 28 J3
Chelveston Nhants 38 E7
Chelvey N Som 17 N3
Chelwood BaNES 17 R4
Chelwood Common E Susx 11 Q5
Chelwood Gate E Susx 11 Q4
Chelworth Wilts 28 J9
Chelworth Lower Green Wilts 29 L9
Chelworth Upper Green Wilts 29 L9
Cheney Longville Shrops 34 K4
Chenies Bucks 20 H3
Chepstow Mons 27 U9
Chequerbent Bolton 55 Q5
Chequers Corner Norfk 49 Q12
Cherhill Wilts 18 F6
Cherington Gloucs 28 H8
Cherington Warwks 36 J13
Cheriton Devon 15 R3
Cheriton Hants 9 R3
Cheriton Kent 13 P8
Cheriton Swans 25 S12
Cheriton Bishop Devon 5 T2
Cheriton Fitzpaine Devon 15 U11
Cheriton or Stackpole Elidor Pembks 24 G11
Cherrington Wrekin 45 Q10
Cherry Burton E R Yk 65 M11
Cherry Hinton Cambs 39 Q9
Cherry Orchard Worcs 35 U10
Cherry Willingham Lincs 58 H12
Chertsey Surrey 20 H9
Cherwell Valley Services Oxon 30 B7
Cheselbourne Dorset 7 U5
Chesham Bucks 31 L12
Chesham Bury 55 T4
Chesham Bois Bucks 20 G3
Cheshire Farm Ice Cream Ches W 45 M2
Cheshunt Herts 31 U12
Chesil Beach Dorset 7 R9
Chesley Kent 12 G3
Cheslyn Hay Staffs 46 C12
Chessetts Wood Warwks 36 G6
Chessington Gt Lon 21 L10
Chessington World of Adventures Gt Lon 21 L10
Chester Ches W 54 K13
Chesterblade Somset 17 S8
Chester Crematorium Ches W 54 J13
Chesterfield Derbys 57 N12
Chesterfield Staffs 46 E12
Chesterfield Crematorium Derbys 57 N12
Chesterhill Mdloth 83 S6
Chester-le-Street Dur 69 S2
Chester Moor Dur 69 S3
Chesters Border 76 C3
Chesters Border 84 G14
Chester Services Ches W 55 L12
Chesterton Cambs 38 H1
Chesterton Cambs 39 Q8
Chesterton Gloucs 28 K7
Chesterton Oxon 30 C8
Chesterton Shrops 35 S1
Chesterton Staffs 45 T4
Chesterton Green Warwks 37 L9
Chesterwood Nthumb 76 G12
Chester Zoo Ches W 54 K12
Chestfield Kent 13 M2
Chestnut Street Kent 12 G3
Cheston Devon 5 R9
Cheswardine Shrops 45 R7
Cheswick Nthumb 85 Q9
Cheswick Green Solhll 36 F5
Chetnole Dorset 7 R3
Chettiscombe Devon 6 C2
Chettisham Cambs 39 R4
Chettle Dorset 8 D6
Chetton Shrops 35 Q2
Chetwode Bucks 30 D7
Chetwynd Wrekin 45 R9
Chetwynd Aston Wrekin 45 S10
Cheveley Cambs 39 U8
Chevening Kent 21 S11
Cheverton IoW 9 P12
Chevington Suffk 40 C9
Cheviot Hills 76 F4
Chevithorne Devon 16 C13
Chew Magna BaNES 17 Q4
Chew Moor Bolton 55 Q5
Chew Stoke BaNES 17 Q4
Chewton Keynsham BaNES 17 S3
Chewton Mendip Somset 17 Q6
Chichacott Devon 15 P13
Chicheley M Keyn 38 D11
Chichester W Susx 10 D10
Chichester Crematorium W Susx 10 D9
Chickerell Dorset 7 R8
Chickering Suffk 41 M5
Chicklade Wilts 8 C2
Chickward Herefs 34 G10
Chidden Hants 9 T5
Chiddingfold Surrey 10 F3
Chiddingly E Susx 11 S8
Chiddingstone Kent 11 S2
Chiddingstone Causeway Kent 21 T13
Chideock Dorset 7 M6
Chidham W Susx 10 B10
Chidswell Kirk 57 L2
Chieveley W Berk 19 Q6
Chieveley Services W Berk 19 Q6
Chignall St James Essex 22 G5
Chignall Smealy Essex 22 G5
Chigwell Essex 21 R4
Chigwell Row Essex 21 S4
Chilbolton Hants 19 N12
Chilcomb Hants 9 Q3
Chilcombe Dorset 7 P6
Chilcompton Somset 17 R6
Chilcote Leics 46 J11
Childer Thornton Ches W 54 J11
Child Okeford Dorset 8 A6
Childrey Oxon 29 S10
Child's Ercall Shrops 45 Q8
Childswickham Worcs 36 E13
Childwall Lpool 54 K9
Childwick Bury Herts 31 P10
Childwick Green Herts 31 P10
Chilfrome Dorset 7 Q5
Chilgrove W Susx 10 C8
Chilham Kent 13 L5
Chilla Devon 14 K12
Chillaton Devon 5 L4
Chillenden Kent 13 Q5
Chillerton IoW 9 P12
Chillesford Suffk 41 Q10
Chillingham Nthumb 85 R13
Chillington Devon 5 T12
Chillington Somset 7 L2
Chilmark Wilts 8 D2
Chilmington Green Kent 12 J7
Chilson Oxon 29 R4
Chilsworthy Cnwll 5 L6
Chilsworthy Devon 14 H11
Chiltern Green C Beds 31 P9
Chiltern Hills 20 C3
Chilterns Crematorium Bucks 20 F3
Chilthorne Domer Somset 17 P13
Chilton Bucks 30 E10
Chilton Devon 15 U12
Chilton Dur 69 S7
Chilton Kent 13 Q7
Chilton Oxon 29 U10
Chilton Suffk 40 E12
Chilton Candover Hants 19 S12
Chilton Cantelo Somset 17 Q12
Chilton Foliat Wilts 19 M6
Chilton Polden Somset 17 L8
Chilton Street Suffk 40 C11
Chilton Trinity Somset 16 J9
Chilwell Notts 47 P6
Chilworth Hants 9 N5
Chilworth Surrey 20 H13
Chimney Oxon 29 S7
Chineham Hants 19 U9
Chingford Gt Lon 21 Q4
Chinley Derbys 56 F10
Chinnor Oxon 30 G12
Chipchase Castle Nthumb 76 H10
Chipnall Shrops 45 R7
Chippenham Cambs 39 U7
Chippenham Wilts 18 D6
Chipperfield Herts 31 M12
Chipping Herts 31 U6
Chipping Lancs 62 C11
Chipping Campden Gloucs 36 G13
Chipping Hill Essex 22 K4
Chipping Norton Oxon 29 R2
Chipping Ongar Essex 22 E7
Chipping Sodbury S Glos 28 D11
Chipping Warden Nhants 37 N11
Chipshop Devon 5 L5
Chipstable Somset 16 D11
Chipstead Kent 21 T11
Chipstead Surrey 21 N11
Chirbury Shrops 44 G14
Chirk Wrexhm 44 G6
Chirnside Border 85 M7
Chirnsidebridge Border 85 M7
Chirton Wilts 18 G9
Chisbury Wilts 19 L7
Chiselborough Somset 7 N2
Chiseldon Swindn 18 J4
Chiselhampton Oxon 30 C13
Chisholme Border 75 T3
Chislehurst Gt Lon 21 R8
Chislet Kent 13 P3
Chisley Calder 63 L14
Chiswell Green Herts 31 P12
Chiswick Gt Lon 21 M7
Chiswick End Cambs 39 N11
Chisworth Derbys 56 E8
Chitcombe E Susx 12 F11
Chithurst W Susx 10 C6
Chittering Cambs 39 Q7
Chitterne Wilts 18 E12
Chittlehamholt Devon 15 Q8
Chittlehampton Devon 15 P7
Chittoe Wilts 18 E7
Chivelstone Devon 5 T13
Chivenor Devon 15 M6
Chlenry D & G 72 E7
Chobham Surrey 20 G10
Cholderton Wilts 18 K12
Cholesbury Bucks 30 K11
Chollerford Nthumb 76 J11
Chollerton Nthumb 76 J11
Cholmondeston Ches E 45 P2
Cholsey Oxon 19 S3
Cholstrey Herefs 35 L9
Chop Gate N York 70 J13
Choppington Nthumb 77 R9
Chopwell Gatesd 77 N14
Chorley Ches E 45 N3
Chorley Lancs 55 N3
Chorley Shrops 35 Q4
Chorley Staffs 46 E11
Chorleywood Herts 20 H3
Chorleywood West Herts 20 H3
Chorlton Ches E 45 R3
Chorlton-cum-Hardy Manch 55 T8
Chorlton Lane Ches W 45 L4
Choulton Shrops 34 J3
Chowley Ches W 45 L2
Chrishall Essex 39 P13
Chrisswell Inver 88 F11
Christchurch Cambs 39 Q1
Christchurch Dorset 8 H10
Christchurch Gloucs 27 V5
Christchurch Newpt 27 Q10
Christian Malford Wilts 18 E5
Christleton Ches W 54 K13
Christmas Common Oxon 20 B4
Christon N Som 17 L5
Christon Bank Nthumb 85 U14
Christow Devon 5 U3
Christ's Hospital W Susx 10 J5
Chuck Hatch E Susx 11 R4
Chudleigh Devon 5 V5
Chudleigh Knighton Devon 5 U5
Chulmleigh Devon 15 Q10
Chunal Derbys 56 F8
Church Lancs 62 E14
Churcham Gloucs 28 E4
Church Aston Wrekin 45 R10
Church Brampton Nhants 37 T7
Church Brough Cumb 68 G10
Church Broughton Derbys 46 H7
Church Cove Cnwll 2 J14
Church Crookham Hants 20 D12
Churchdown Gloucs 28 G4
Church Eaton Staffs 45 T10
Church End Bed 38 G9
Church End Bed 38 H9
Church End Bucks 30 F11
Church End C Beds 31 L6
Church End C Beds 31 L8
Church End C Beds 31 M6
Church End C Beds 31 M9
Church End C Beds 31 Q5
Church End C Beds 38 J10
Church End Cambs 38 G6
Church End Cambs 38 K4
Church End Cambs 39 M5
Church End Cambs 39 Q9
Church End Essex 22 F3
Church End Essex 22 H2
Church End Essex 22 H4
Churchend Essex 23 P9
Church End Gloucs 35 U13
Church End Gt Lon 21 M4
Church End Herts 22 B3
Church End Herts 31 P10
Church End Herts 31 S6
Church End Lincs 48 K7
Church End Lincs 59 R7
Church End Warwks 36 H2
Church End Warwks 36 J2
Church Enstone Oxon 29 S2
Church Fenton N York 64 C12
Churchfield Sandw 36 D2
Churchgate Herts 31 T12
Churchgate Street Essex 22 C5
Church Green Devon 6 G5
Church Gresley Derbys 46 J10
Church Hanborough Oxon 29 T5
Church Hill Staffs 46 D11
Church Houses N York 71 L13
Churchill Devon 6 J4
Churchill Devon 15 N4
Churchill N Som 17 M5
Churchill Oxon 29 Q3
Churchill Worcs 35 U5
Churchill Worcs 36 B10
Churchinford Somset 6 H2
Church Knowle Dorset 8 C12
Church Laneham Notts 58 D11
Church Langton Leics 37 T2
Church Lawford Warwks 37 N5
Church Lawton Ches E 45 T2
Church Leigh Staffs 46 D6
Church Lench Worcs 36 D10
Church Mayfield Staffs 46 G5
Church Minshull Ches E 45 Q1
Church Norton W Susx 10 D11
Churchover Warwks 37 P4
Church Preen Shrops 45 M14
Church Pulverbatch Shrops 44 K13
Churchstanton Somset 6 G2
Churchstoke Powys 34 G2
Churchstow Devon 5 S11
Church Stowe Nhants 37 R9
Church Street Essex 40 C12
Church Street Kent 22 H13
Church Street Suffk 41 S4
Church Stretton Shrops 35 L2
Churchthorpe Lincs 59 P7
Churchtown Bpool 61 Q11
Churchtown Cnwll 4 D5
Churchtown Derbys 57 L14
Churchtown Devon 15 Q4
Churchtown IoM 60 g4
Churchtown Lancs 61 T11
Church Town N Linc 58 C5
Churchtown Sefton 54 J3
Church Village Rhondd 26 K10
Church Warsop Notts 57 S13
Church Wilne Derbys 47 M7
Churnsike Lodge Nthumb 76 D10
Churston Ferrers Torbay 6 B13
Churt Surrey 10 D3
Churton Ches W 44 K2
Churwell Leeds 63 R14
Chwilog Gwynd 42 H6
Chyandour Cnwll 2 D10
Chyanvounder Cnwll 2 H12
Chyeowling Cnwll 2 K8
Chyvarloe Cnwll 2 H12
Cil Powys 44 E13
Cilcain Flints 54 E13
Cilcennin Cerdgn 32 K8
Cilcewydd Powys 44 F13
Cilfrew Neath 26 D7
Cilfynydd Rhondd 26 K9
Cilgerran Pembks 32 C12
Cilgwyn Carmth 26 C2
Cilgwyn Gwynd 52 G12
Ciliau-Aeron Cerdgn 32 K9
Cilmaengwyn Neath 26 C6
Cilmery Powys 34 B10
Cilrhedyn Pembks 25 N4
Cilsan Carmth 25 U6
Ciltalgarth Gwynd 43 S5
Cilycwm Carmth 33 Q13
Cimla Neath 26 D8
Cinderford Gloucs 28 C5
Cinder Hill Wolves 36 B2
Cippenham Slough 20 G6
Cirencester Gloucs 28 K7
Citadilla N York 69 R13
City Gt Lon 21 P6
City V Glam 26 H12
City Airport Gt Lon 21 R6
City Dulas IoA 52 G5
City of London Crematorium Gt Lon 21 R5
Clabhach Ag & B 92 F7
Clachaig Ag & B 88 D9
Clachan Ag & B 79 P4
Clachan Ag & B 87 P2
Clachan Ag & B 94 B10
Clachan Highld 100 e6
Clachan-a-Luib W Isls 106 d12
Clachan Mor Ag & B 92 B9
Clachan na Luib W Isls 106 d12
Clachan of Campsie E Duns 89 P10
Clachan-Seil Ag & B 87 P2
Clachnaharry Highld 102 H6
Clachtoll Highld 110 A11
Clackavoid P & K 97 U11
Clacket Lane Services Surrey 21 R12
Clackmannan Clacks 90 D13
Clackmarras Moray 104 A4
Clacton-on-Sea Essex 23 S4
Cladich Ag & B 88 C1
Cladswell Worcs 36 E9
Claggan Highld 93 S9
Claigan Highld 100 b4
Clandown BaNES 17 S5
Clanfield Hants 9 T5
Clanfield Oxon 29 Q7
Clannaborough Devon 15 R12
Clanville Hants 19 M11
Clanville Somset 17 R10
Claonaig Ag & B 79 R4
Clapgate Dorset 8 E8
Clapgate Herts 22 B3
Clapham Bed 38 F10
Clapham Devon 6 A7
Clapham Gt Lon 21 N7
Clapham N York 62 E6
Clapham W Susx 10 H9
Clapham Green Bed 38 F10
Clap Hill Kent 13 L8
Clappersgate Cumb 67 N12
Clapton Somset 7 M3
Clapton Somset 17 R6
Clapton-in-Gordano N Som 27 T13
Clapton-on-the-Hill Gloucs 29 N4
Clapworthy Devon 15 Q8
Clarach Cerdgn 33 M4
Claravale Gatesd 77 N13
Clarbeston Pembks 24 J6
Clarbeston Road Pembks 24 H6
Clarborough Notts 58 B10
Clare Suffk 40 C11
Clarebrand D & G 74 E12
Clarencefield D & G 75 L12
Clarewood Nthumb 77 L12
Clarilaw Border 76 A2
Clark's Green Surrey 10 K3
Clarkston E Rens 89 N14
Clashmore Highld 109 N7
Clashmore Highld 110 A10
Clashnessie Highld 110 B10
Clashnoir Moray 104 A11
Clathy P & K 90 E7
Clathymore P & K 90 F7
Clatt Abers 104 G10
Clatter Powys 33 U2
Clatterford End Essex 22 F5
Clatworthy Somset 16 E10
Claughton Lancs 61 U11
Claughton Lancs 62 B6
Claughton Wirral 54 H9
Clavelshay Somset 16 J10
Claverdon Warwks 36 G7
Claverham N Som 17 N3
Clavering Essex 22 C1
Claverley Shrops 35 S2
Claverton BaNES 17 U4
Claverton Down BaNES 17 U4
Clawdd-coch V Glam 26 K12
Clawdd-newydd Denbgs 44 C3
Clawthorpe Cumb 61 U4
Clawton Devon 14 J13
Claxby Lincs 58 K8
Claxby Lincs 59 S12
Claxton N York 64 F8
Claxton Norfk 51 P13
Claybrooke Magna Leics 37 N3
Clay Common Suffk 41 S4
Clay Coton Nhants 37 Q5
Clay Cross Derbys 57 N14
Claydon Oxon 37 N11
Claydon Suffk 40 K11
Clay End Herts 31 T8
Claygate D & G 75 S10
Claygate Kent 12 D7
Claygate Surrey 21 L10
Claygate Cross Kent 12 B4
Clayhall Gt Lon 21 R4
Clayhanger Devon 16 D12
Clayhanger Wsall 46 D13
Clayhidon Devon 16 G13
Clayhill E Susx 12 F11
Clayhill Hants 9 L7
Clayhithe Cambs 39 R8
Clayock Highld 112 E5
Claypit Hill Cambs 39 N10
Claypits Gloucs 28 E6
Claypole Lincs 48 B4
Claythorpe Lincs 59 R11
Clayton C Brad 63 N13
Clayton Donc 57 Q5
Clayton W Susx 11 M8
Clayton Green Lancs 55 N2
Clayton-le-Moors Lancs 62 F13
Clayton-le-Woods Lancs 55 N2
Clayton West Kirk 57 L4
Clayworth Notts 58 B9
Cleadale Highld 100 d11
Cleadon S Tyne 77 T13
Clearbrook Devon 5 N7
Clearwell Gloucs 27 V6
Clearwell Meend Gloucs 28 A6
Cleasby N York 69 S10
Cleat Ork 106 t21
Cleatlam Dur 69 P9
Cleator Cumb 66 F10
Cleator Moor Cumb 66 F9
Cleckheaton Kirk 56 J1
Cleedownton Shrops 35 N4
Cleehill Shrops 35 N5
Cleekhimin N Lans 82 E7
Clee St Margaret Shrops 35 N4
Cleestanton Shrops 35 N5
Cleethorpes NE Lin 59 P5
Cleeton St Mary Shrops 35 P5
Cleeve N Som 17 N3
Cleeve Oxon 19 T4
Cleeve Hill Gloucs 28 J2
Cleeve Prior Worcs 36 E11
Cleghornie E Loth 84 F2
Clehonger Herefs 34 K13
Cleish P & K 90 G12
Cleland N Lans 82 E7
Clement's End C Beds 31 M10
Clement Street Kent 22 D13
Clenamacrie Ag & B 94 C13
Clench Common Wilts 18 J7
Clenchwarton Norfk 49 S9

Clenerty Abers....105 M3
Clent Worcs....36 B5
Cleobury Mortimer Shrops....35 Q5
Cleobury North Shrops....35 P3
Cleongart Ag & B....79 M9
Clephanton Highld....103 M5
Clerkhill D & G....75 Q6
Clevancy Wilts....18 H5
Clevedon N Som....17 M2
Cleveley Oxon....29 S3
Cleveleys Lancs....61 Q11
Clevertton Wilts....18 F11
Clewer Somset....17 M7
Cley next the Sea Norfk....50 H5
Cliburn Cumb....67 S8
Cliddesden Hants....19 U11
Cliff Warwk....46 H14
Cliffe Lancs....62 E13
Cliffe Medway....22 H13
Cliffe N York....64 F13
Cliff End E Susx....12 G13
Clifford Leeds....63 U11
Clifford Chambers Warwks....36 G10
Clifford's Mesne Gloucs....28 D3
Cliffsend Kent....13 R3
Clifton Bristl....27 V13
Clifton C Beds....31 Q5
Clifton C Nott....47 P7
Clifton C York....64 D9
Clifton Calder....56 J2
Clifton Cumb....67 R8
Clifton Derbys....45 U4
Clifton Devon....15 P4
Clifton Donc....57 R7
Clifton Lancs....61 P13
Clifton Nthumb....77 Q9
Clifton Oxon....29 U1
Clifton Salfd....55 S6
Clifton Worcs....35 T11
Clifton Campville Staffs....46 J11
Clifton Hampden Oxon....30 B13
Clifton Reynes M Keyn....38 D10
Clifton upon Dunsmore Warwks....37 P5
Clifton upon Teme Worcs....35 R8
Cliftonville Kent....13 S1
Climping W Susx....10 F10
Clink Somset....17 U7
Clint N York....63 R8
Clint Green Norfk....50 H11
Clintmains Border....84 G12
Cliobh W Isls....106 f5
Clipiau Gwynd....43 R3
Clippesby Norfk....51 R11
Clipsham Rutlnd....48 E10
Clipston Nhants....37 T4
Clipston Notts....47 R7
Clipstone C Beds....31 L6
Clipstone Notts....57 S14
Clitheroe Lancs....62 F11
Clive Shrops....45 M9
Cliveden Bucks....20 F5
Clixby Lincs....58 J6
Cloatley Wilts....28 J9
Clocaenog Denbgs....44 C3
Clock Face St Hel....55 M8
Cloddiau Powys....44 F12
Clodock Herefs....27 T8
Cloford Somset....17 T8
Clola Abers....105 R7
Clophill C Beds....31 N5
Clopton Nhants....38 G4
Clopton Suffk....41 M10
Clopton Corner Suffk....41 M10
Clopton Green Suffk....40 C10
Clos du Valle Guern....6 e1
Closeburn D & G....74 H7
Closeburnmill D & G....74 H6
Closeclark IoM....60 d7
Closworth Somset....7 Q2
Clothall Herts....31 S6
Clotton Ches W....55 M14
Cloudesley Bush Warwks....37 N4
Clouds Herefs....35 N13
Clough Oldham....56 D5
Clough Foot Calder....56 G2
Clough Head Calder....56 G3
Cloughton N York....71 T14
Cloughton Newlands N York....71 T13
Clousta Shet....106 t8
Clova Angus....98 E9
Clovelly Devon....14 H8
Clovulin Highld....94 E6
Clow Bridge Lancs....62 G14
Clowne Derbys....57 Q11
Clows Top Worcs....35 R6
Cloy Wrexhm....44 J6
Cluanie Inn Highld....101 R9
Cluanie Lodge Highld....101 R9
Clubworthy Cnwll....4 J2
Clugston D & G....72 K8
Clun Shrops....34 H4
Clunas Highld....103 N6
Clunbury Shrops....34 J4
Clunderwen Carmth....24 K7
Clune Highld....103 N14
Clunes Highld....101 T14
Clungunford Shrops....34 K5
Clunie P & K....90 H3
Clunton Shrops....34 H4
Cluny Fife....90 K12
Clutton BaNES....17 R5
Clutton Ches W....45 L3
Clutton Hill BaNES....17 R5
Cwrt-y-bont Gwynd....52 J10
Clydach Mons....27 N5
Clydach Swans....26 B7
Clydach Vale Rhondd....26 H9
Clydebank W Duns....89 L11
Clydebank Crematorium W Duns....89 L11
Clydey Pembks....25 M3
Clyffe Pypard Wilts....18 G5
Clynder Ag & B....88 F9
Clyne Neath....26 F7
Clynnog-fawr Gwynd....52 F4
Clyro Powys....34 F12
Clyst Honiton Devon....6 C6
Clyst Hydon Devon....6 D4
Clyst St George Devon....6 C7
Clyst St Lawrence Devon....6 D4
Clyst St Mary Devon....6 C6
Cnoc W Isls....106 j5
Cnwch Coch Cerdgn....33 N6
Coad's Green Cnwll....4 H5
Coal Aston Derbys....57 N11
Coalbrookvale Blae G....27 M6
Coalburn S Lans....82 H12
Coalburns Gatesd....77 N13
Coaley Gloucs....28 E7
Coalhill Essex....22 J8
Coalmoor Wrekin....45 Q12
Coalpit Heath S Glos....28 C11
Coal Pool Wsall....46 D13
Coalport Wrekin....45 Q13
Coalsnaughton Clacks....90 D12
Coal Street Suffk....41 M6
Coaltown of Balgonie Fife....91 L12
Coaltown of Wemyss Fife....91 M12
Coalville Leics....47 M11
Coanwood Nthumb....76 D14
Coat Somset....17 N12
Coatbridge N Lans....82 D5
Coatdyke N Lans....82 D5
Coate Swindn....29 N11
Coate Wilts....18 H8
Cobairdy Abers....104 H7
Cobbaton Devon....15 P7
Coberley Gloucs....28 J4
Cobhall Common Herefs....35 L13
Cobham Kent....12 C2
Cobham Surrey....20 K11
Cobham Services Surrey....20 K11
Coblers Green Essex....22 G4
Cobley Dorset....8 E4
Cobnash Herefs....35 L8
Coburby Abers....105 R2
Cock Alley Derbys....57 P12
Cock Bank Wrexhm....44 J4
Cock Bevington Warwks....36 E10
Cock Bridge Abers....98 D2
Cock Clarks Essex....22 K7
Cock & End Suffk....40 B10
Cockenzie and Port Seton E Loth....83 U4
Cocker Bar Lancs....55 M2
Cocker Brook Lancs....62 E13
Cockerham Lancs....61 T9
Cockermouth Cumb....66 H6

Cockernhoe Herts....31 P8
Cockersdale Leeds....63 Q14
Cockett Swans....26 A9
Cockfield Dur....69 P8
Cockfield Suffk....40 F10
Cockfosters Gt Lon....21 N3
Cock Green Essex....22 G4
Cocking W Susx....10 D7
Cockington Torbay....6 A12
Cocklake Somset....17 M7
Cockley Beck Cumb....66 K12
Cockley Cley Norfk....50 C13
Cockpole Green Wokham....20 C6
Cocks Cnwll....2 J7
Cockshutt Shrops....44 K8
Cock Street Kent....12 E5
Cockthorpe Norfk....50 F5
Cockwells Cnwll....2 E10
Cockwood Devon....6 C8
Cockwood Somset....16 H8
Cockyard Derbys....56 F11
Cockyard Herefs....27 T1
Coddenham Suffk....40 K10
Coddington Herefs....35 R12
Coddington Notts....48 B3
Codford St Mary Wilts....18 E13
Codford St Peter Wilts....18 E13
Codicote Herts....31 R9
Codmore Hill W Susx....10 H6
Codnor Derbys....47 M4
Codrington S Glos....28 D12
Codsall Staffs....45 U13
Codsall Wood Staffs....45 T13
Coed Morgan Mons....27 R5
Coedely Rhondd....26 J10
Coedkernew Newpt....27 P11
Coed Talon Flints....44 G2
Coedway Powys....44 H11
Coed-y-Bryn Cerdgn....32 G11
Coed-y-caerau Newpt....27 R9
Coed-y-paen Mons....27 Q8
Coed-yr-ynys Powys....27 M3
Coed Ystumgwern Gwynd....43 L9
Coelbren Powys....26 F5
Coffinswell Devon....6 A12
Coffle End Bed....38 F9
Cofton Devon....6 C8
Cofton Hackett Worcs....36 D5
Cogan V Glam....16 G2
Cogenhoe Nhants....38 B9
Cogges Oxon....29 S6
Coggeshall Essex....23 L3
Coggin's Mill E Susx....11 T5
Coilacriech Abers....98 E4
Coilantogle Stirlg....89 N5
Coillore Highld....100 c6
Coity Brdgnd....26 H11
Col W Isls....106 j5
Colaboll Highld....108 K2
Colan Cnwll....3 M4
Colaton Raleigh Devon....6 E7
Colbost Highld....100 b5
Colburn N York....69 Q13
Colby Cumb....68 E8
Colby IoM....60 d8
Colby Norfk....51 M7
Colchester Essex....23 N3
Colchester Crematorium Essex....23 N3
Colchester Zoo Essex....23 N3
Cold Ash W Berk....19 R7
Cold Ashby Nhants....37 S5
Cold Ashton S Glos....28 E13
Cold Aston Gloucs....29 N4
Coldbackie Highld....111 N4
Coldbeck Cumb....68 F12
Cold Blow Pembks....24 K8
Cold Brayfield M Keyn....38 D10
Cold Cotes N York....62 F6
Coldeast Devon....5 U6
Colden Calder....62 K14
Colden Common Hants....9 P4
Cold Hanworth Lincs....58 H10
Coldharbour Cnwll....2 K7
Coldharbour Devon....6 E3
Coldharbour Gloucs....27 V7
Coldharbour Surrey....10 J2
Cold Harbour Wilts....18 B10
Cold Hatton Wrekin....45 P9
Cold Hatton Heath Wrekin....45 P9
Cold Hesledon Dur....70 F3
Cold Hiendley Wakefd....57 N4
Cold Higham Nhants....37 S10
Coldingham Border....85 N5
Cold Kirby N York....64 C3
Coldmeece Staffs....45 U7
Cold Newton Leics....47 T12
Cold Northcott Cnwll....4 G3
Cold Norton Essex....22 K8
Cold Overton Leics....48 B11
Coldred Kent....13 P6
Coldridge Devon....15 Q11
Coldstream Border....85 L11
Coldwaltham W Susx....10 G7
Coldwell Herefs....34 K13
Coldwells Abers....105 R6
Cold Weston Shrops....35 N4
Cole Somset....17 S10
Colebatch Shrops....34 J3
Colebrook C Plym....5 N9
Colebrook Devon....6 D3
Colebrooke Devon....15 S13
Coleby Lincs....48 F1
Coleby N Linc....58 E2
Cole End Warwks....36 H3
Coleford Devon....15 S12
Coleford Gloucs....27 V6
Coleford Somset....17 S7
Coleford Water Somset....16 F10
Cole Green Herts....31 S10
Cole Green Herts....22 B6
Cole Henley Hants....19 Q10
Colehill Dorset....8 E8
Coleman Green Herts....31 Q10
Coleman's Hatch E Susx....11 Q4
Colemere Shrops....44 K7
Colemore Hants....9 V3
Colemore Green Shrops....45 R14
Colenden P & K....90 H6
Coleorton Leics....47 M10
Colerne Wilts....18 B6
Colesbourne Gloucs....28 K5
Coles Cross Dorset....7 L3
Coles Cross Devon....6 K4
Colesden Bed....38 H9
Coles Green Suffk....40 K12
Coleshill Bucks....20 F3
Coleshill Oxon....29 P9
Coleshill Warwks....36 H3
Colestocks Devon....6 E4
Colethrop Gloucs....28 F5
Coley BaNES....17 P5
Colgate W Susx....11 L4
Colinsburgh Fife....91 R11
Colinton C Edin....83 P5
Colkirk Norfk....50 F8
Coll Ag & B....92 G7
Collace P & K....90 K5
Collafirth Shet....106 u6
Coll Airport Ag & B....92 G7
Collaton Devon....5 N12
Collaton St Mary Torbay....5 V8
College of Roseisle Moray....103 T2
Collessie Fife....91 L9
Colleton Mills Devon....15 Q9
Collier Row Gt Lon....22 D9
Collier's End Herts....31 U8
Collier's Green E Susx....12 E11
Colliers Green Kent....12 E7
Colliery Row Sundld....70 D3
Collieston Abers....105 S11
Collin D & G....74 K10
Collingbourne Ducis Wilts....18 K9
Collingbourne Kingston Wilts....18 K9
Collingham Leeds....63 S11
Collingham Notts....48 B1
Collington Herefs....35 P8
Collingtree Nhants....37 U9
Collins Green Warrtn....55 N8
Collins Green Worcs....35 S9
Colliston Angus....91 T2
Colliton Devon....6 D4
Collyweston Nhants....48 F13
Colmonell S Ayrs....72 E2
Colmworth Bed....38 G9
Colnabaichin Abers....98 E2
Colnbrook Slough....20 H7
Colne Cambs....39 N6
Colne Lancs....62 H11
Colne Bridge Kirk....56 J3
Colne Engaine Essex....22 K1
Colney Norfk....51 L12
Colney Heath Herts....31 R11

Colney Street Herts....31 Q12
Coln Rogers Gloucs....29 M6
Coln St Aldwyns Gloucs....29 M6
Coln St Dennis Gloucs....29 L5
Colonsay Ag & B....86 F6
Colonsay Airport Ag & B....104 B9
Colpy Border....83 R10
Colquhar Border....83 R10
Colquite Cnwll....3 Q2
Colscott Devon....14 J9
Colsterdale N York....63 N3
Colsterworth Lincs....48 E9
Colston Bassett Notts....47 S7
Coltfield Moray....103 U3
Colt Hill Hants....20 C12
Colton Cumb....61 Q2
Colton Leeds....63 T13
Colton N York....64 C11
Colton Norfk....50 K12
Colton Staffs....46 D9
Colt's Hill Kent....12 C7
Columbjohn Devon....6 C5
Colva Powys....34 F10
Colvend D & G....66 C2
Colwall Herefs....35 R12
Colwell Nthumb....76 K10
Colwich Staffs....46 D9
Colwick Notts....47 R5
Colwinston V Glam....26 G12
Colworth W Susx....10 E10
Colwyn Bay Conwy....53 Q7
Colyford Devon....6 J6
Colyton Devon....6 J6
Combe Herefs....34 H8
Combe Oxon....29 T5
Combe W Berk....19 N8
Combe Almer Dorset....8 B9
Combe Common Surrey....10 E3
Combe Down BaNES....17 U4
Combe Fishacre Devon....5 U7
Combe Florey Somset....16 F10
Combe Hay BaNES....17 T5
Combeinteignhead Devon....6 B10
Combe Martin Devon....15 N3
Combe Raleigh Devon....6 G4
Comberbach Ches W....55 P11
Comberford Staffs....46 G12
Comberton Cambs....39 N9
Comberton Herefs....35 L7
Combe St Nicholas Somset....6 K2
Combpyne Devon....6 J6
Combridge Staffs....46 E6
Combrook Warwks....36 K10
Combs Derbys....56 F11
Combs Suffk....40 H9
Combs Ford Suffk....40 H9
Combwich Somset....16 H8
Comers Abers....99 M2
Comhampton Worcs....35 T7
Commercial End Cambs....39 R8
Commins Coch Powys....43 R13
Commondale N York....71 L10
Common Edge Bpool....61 Q13
Common End Cumb....66 F8
Common Moor Cnwll....4 G7
Common Platt Wilts....29 N10
Commonside Ches W....55 M12
Commonside Derbys....46 H5
Common Side Derbys....57 M11
Commonwood Wrexhm....44 J3
Compass Somset....16 J10
Compstall Stockp....56 E8
Compstonend D & G....73 R9
Compton Devon....5 V8
Compton Hants....9 N3
Compton Hants....19 S10
Compton Staffs....35 T4
Compton Surrey....20 G13
Compton W Berk....19 R5
Compton Wolts....10 B9
Compton W Susx....10 B8
Compton Abbas Dorset....8 B4
Compton Abdale Gloucs....29 L4
Compton Bassett Wilts....18 F6
Compton Beauchamp Oxon....29 Q10
Compton Bishop Somset....17 L5
Compton Chamberlayne Wilts....8 E3
Compton Dando BaNES....17 R4
Compton Dundon Somset....17 N10
Compton Durville Somset....17 M13
Compton Greenfield S Glos....27 V11
Compton Martin BaNES....17 P5
Compton Pauncefoot Somset....17 R11
Compton Valence Dorset....7 P5
Compton Verney Warwks....36 K10
Comrie Fife....90 E13
Comrie P & K....89 S3
Conaglen House Highld....94 E5
Conchra Highld....101 M6
Concraigie P & K....90 G3
Conder Green Lancs....61 T9
Conderton Worcs....36 C13
Condicote Gloucs....29 N2
Condorrat N Lans....89 S11
Condover Shrops....45 L12
Coney Hill Gloucs....28 G4
Coneyhurst Common W Susx....10 J6
Coneysthorpe N York....64 G6
Coneythorpe N York....63 T8
Conford Hants....10 C4
Congdon's Shop Cnwll....4 H5
Congerstone Leics....47 L12
Congham Norfk....50 B9
Congleton Ches E....56 C14
Congl-y-wal Gwynd....43 N4
Congresbury N Som....17 M4
Congreve Staffs....45 U11
Conham Bristl....27 V13
Conicavel Moray....103 Q5
Coningsby Lincs....48 K2
Conington Cambs....38 K6
Conington Cambs....39 N7
Conisbrough Donc....57 R7
Conisholme Lincs....59 S7
Coniston Cumb....67 N13
Coniston E R Yk....65 R13
Coniston Cold N York....62 J9
Conistone N York....62 K6
Connah's Quay Flints....54 G13
Connel Ag & B....94 C12
Connel Park E Ayrs....81 S10
Connor Downs Cnwll....2 F9
Conon Bridge Highld....102 F5
Cononley N York....62 K11
Cononsyth Angus....91 T2
Consall Staffs....46 C4
Consett Dur....69 P2
Constable Burton N York....63 P1
Constable Lee Lancs....55 T2
Constantine Cnwll....2 J11
Constantine Bay Cnwll....3 M2
Contin Highld....102 E5
Conwy Conwy....53 N7
Conwy Castle Conwy....53 N7
Conyer Kent....12 J3
Conyer's Green Suffk....40 E7
Cooden E Susx....12 D14
Cooil IoM....60 d7
Cookbury Devon....14 K11
Cookbury Wick Devon....14 J11
Cookham W & M....20 E5
Cookham Dean W & M....20 E5
Cookham Rise W & M....20 E5
Cookhill Worcs....36 E9
Cookley Suffk....41 Q5
Cookley Worcs....35 T4
Cookley Green Oxon....19 U2
Cookney Abers....99 R6
Cooksbridge E Susx....11 Q8
Cooksey Green Worcs....36 B7
Cook's Green Essex....23 S4
Cooks Green Suffk....40 G10
Cooksland Cnwll....3 R3
Cooksmill Green Essex....22 F6
Cookson Green Ches W....55 N12
Coolham W Susx....10 J6
Cooling Medway....22 H13
Cooling Street Medway....22 H13
Coombe Cnwll....8 G4
Coombe Cnwll....2 F8
Coombe Cnwll....3 L5
Coombe Devon....6 E6
Coombe Devon....6 F5
Coombe Devon....15 U5
Coombe Gloucs....28 D8
Coombe Hants....9 S5
Coombe Wilts....18 H9
Coombe Bissett Wilts....8 G3
Coombe Cellars Devon....6 B10
Coombe Cross Hants....9 S5
Coombe Hill Gloucs....28 G3
Coombe Keynes Dorset....8 A12
Coombe Pafford Torbay....6 B11
Coombes W Susx....10 J9
Coombes-Moor Herefs....34 J8
Coombeswood Dudley....36 C3
Coopersale Common Essex....22 C7
Coopersale Street Essex....22 C7
Cooper's Corner Kent....21 S13

Coopers Green E Susx....11 R6
Coopers Green Herts....31 Q11
Cooper Street Kent....13 R4
Cooper Turning Bolton....55 P5
Cootham W Susx....10 H8
Copdock Suffk....40 K13
Copford Essex....23 M3
Copford Green Essex....23 M3
Copgrove N York....63 S7
Copister Shet....106 u6
Cople Bed....38 H11
Copley Calder....56 G2
Copley Dur....69 N7
Copley Tamesd....56 D7
Coplow Dale Derbys....56 J11
Copmanthorpe C York....64 D10
Copmere End Staffs....45 S8
Copp Lancs....61 S12
Coppathorne Cnwll....14 F11
Coppenhall Staffs....45 U10
Coppenhall Moss Ches E....45 R2
Copperhouse Cnwll....2 F9
Coppingford Cambs....38 J4
Copplestone Devon....15 S12
Coppull Lancs....55 N3
Coppull Moor Lancs....55 N3
Copsale W Susx....10 K6
Copster Green Lancs....62 D13
Copston Magna Warwks....37 N3
Cop Street Kent....13 Q4
Copthall Green Essex....22 C7
Copt Heath Solhll....36 G5
Copt Hewick N York....63 S5
Copthorne Cnwll....4 J4
Copthorne W Susx....11 N3
Copt Oak Leics....47 N11
Copy's Green Norfk....50 F6
Copythorne Hants....9 L6
Coram Street Suffk....40 H12
Corbets Tey Gt Lon....22 E10
Corbière Jersey....7 a3
Corbridge Nthumb....76 K13
Corby Nhants....38 C3
Corby Glen Lincs....48 F9
Corby Hill Cumb....75 T14
Cordon N Ayrs....80 E6
Cordwell Derbys....57 M11
Coreley Shrops....35 P5
Cores End Bucks....20 F5
Corfe Somset....16 H13
Corfe Castle Dorset....8 D12
Corfe Mullen Dorset....8 D9
Corfton Shrops....35 L4
Corgarff Abers....98 D2
Corhampton Hants....9 S5
Corks Pond Kent....12 C7
Corley Warwks....36 J4
Corley Ash Warwks....36 H4
Corley Moor Warwks....36 J4
Corley Services Warwks....37 L4
Cormuir Angus....98 E8
Cornard Tye Suffk....40 F12
Corndon Devon....5 R4
Cornel Conwy....53 N10
Corner Row Lancs....61 S13
Corney Cumb....66 J1
Cornforth Dur....70 D5
Cornhill Abers....104 H4
Cornhill-on-Tweed Nthumb....85 M11
Cornholme Calder....56 D1
Cornish Hall End Essex....39 U14
Cornoigmore Ag & B....92 B9
Cornriggs Dur....68 J4
Cornsay Dur....69 P4
Cornsay Colliery Dur....69 P4
Corntown Highld....102 F4
Corntown V Glam....26 G12
Cornwell Oxon....29 Q2
Cornwood Devon....5 Q8
Cornworthy Devon....5 U9
Corpach Highld....94 F3
Corpusty Norfk....50 K8
Corrachree Abers....98 H3
Corran Highld....94 F6
Corran Highld....101 L9
Corrany IoM....60 h5
Corriecravie N Ayrs....79 S11
Corriegills N Ayrs....80 E5
Corrieglen Lodge Hotel Highld....96 B5
Corriemoille Highld....102 C3
Corrimony Highld....102 C9
Corringham Lincs....58 D8
Corringham Thurr....22 H11
Corris Gwynd....43 Q12
Corris Uchaf Gwynd....43 Q12
Corry Highld....100 f7
Corrye Highld....100 f7
Corscombe Devon....5 R4
Corscombe Dorset....7 P3
Corse Gloucs....28 E3
Corse Lawn Gloucs....28 F2
Corsham Wilts....18 C6
Corsindae Abers....99 M2
Corsley Wilts....18 B11
Corsley Heath Wilts....18 B11
Corsock D & G....74 E12
Corston BaNES....17 S3
Corston Wilts....28 H11
Corstorphine C Edin....83 N4
Cortachy Angus....98 F11
Corton Suffk....41 T1
Corton Wilts....18 D12
Corton Denham Somset....17 R12
Coruanan Lodge Highld....94 F5
Corwen Denbgs....44 B4
Coryates Dorset....7 R7
Coryton Devon....5 M4
Coryton Thurr....22 J11
Cosby Leics....37 P1
Coseley Dudley....36 B2
Cosford Shrops....45 S12
Cosgrove Nhants....30 G4
Cosham C Port....9 T7
Cosheston Pembks....24 H10
Coshieville P & K....95 U9
Cossall Notts....47 N5
Cossall Marsh Notts....47 N5
Cossington Leics....47 R11
Cossington Somset....17 L8
Costessey Norfk....51 L11
Costock Notts....47 Q8
Coston Leics....48 B10
Coston Norfk....50 J12
Cote Oxon....29 R7
Cote Somset....16 K8
Cotebrook Ches W....55 N13
Cotehill Cumb....67 Q2
Cotes Cumb....61 R3
Cotes Leics....47 Q9
Cotes Staffs....45 T7
Cotes Heath Staffs....45 T7
Cotford St Luke Somset....16 F11
Cotgrave Notts....47 R6
Cotham Notts....48 B4
Cothal Abers....105 P12
Cotham Notts....48 B4
Cothelstone Somset....16 G10
Cotheridge Worcs....35 S10
Cotherstone Dur....69 L9
Cothill Oxon....29 U8
Cotleigh Devon....6 H4
Cotmanhay Derbys....47 N5
Coton Cambs....39 N9
Coton Nhants....37 S6
Coton Shrops....45 M7
Coton Staffs....45 U8
Coton Staffs....45 T9
Coton Staffs....46 G9
Coton Clanford Staffs....45 U9
Coton Hayes Staffs....45 U8
Coton Hill Staffs....45 U7
Coton in the Clay Staffs....46 F8
Coton in the Elms Derbys....46 H10
Cotswold Wildlife Park & Gardens Oxon....29 P6
Cott Devon....5 T8
Cottam Lancs....61 U13
Cottam Notts....58 C11
Cottenham Cambs....39 P7
Cotterdale N York....68 J14
Cottered Herts....31 T7
Cotteridge Birm....36 D4
Cotterstock Nhants....38 F2
Cottesbrooke Nhants....37 T6
Cottesmore Rutlnd....48 D11
Cottingham E R Yk....65 P13
Cottingham Nhants....38 C2
Cottingley C Brad....63 N13
Cottingley Hall Crematorium Leeds....63 R13
Cottisford Oxon....30 C5
Cotton Suffk....40 J7
Cotton End Bed....38 G11
Cotton Tree Lancs....62 H11
Cottown Abers....104 J10
Cottown Abers....105 N10
Cottown of Gight Abers....105 N7
Cotts Devon....5 L7
Cotwall Wrekin....45 P10
Cotwalton Staffs....45 V7
Couch's Mill Cnwll....4 E9
Coughton Herefs....27 V3
Coughton Warwks....36 E8
Coulaghailtro Ag & B....87 N10
Coulags Highld....101 Q3
Coulderton Cumb....66 E11
Coull Abers....98 K3
Coulport Ag & B....88 F8

Coulsdon Gt Lon....21 N11
Coulston Wilts....18 E10
Coulter S Lans....82 K12
Coultershaw Bridge W Susx....10 F7
Coultings Somset....16 H9
Coulton N York....64 F5
Coultra Fife....91 N7
Cound Shrops....45 N12
Coundlane Shrops....45 N12
Coundon Dur....69 R7
Coundon Grange Dur....69 R7
Countersett N York....62 J2
Countess Wilts....18 H12
Countess Cross Essex....23 L1
Countess Wear Devon....6 C7
Countesthorpe Leics....37 Q2
Countisbury Devon....15 R3
Coupar Angus P & K....90 K3
Coupland Cumb....68 F9
Coupland Nthumb....85 P12
Cour Ag & B....79 Q6
Courance D & G....75 L7
Court-at-Street Kent....13 L8
Courteachan Highld....100 f10
Courteenhall Nhants....37 U9
Court Henry Carmth....25 U7
Courtsend Essex....23 P9
Courtway Somset....16 H10
Cousland Mdloth....83 S5
Cousley Wood E Susx....12 C9
Cove Ag & B....88 F9
Cove Border....84 J4
Cove Devon....16 C13
Cove Hants....20 E11
Cove Highld....107 P6
Cove Bay C Aber....99 S3
Cove Bottom Suffk....41 S5
Covehithe Suffk....41 T4
Coven Staffs....46 B12
Coveney Cambs....39 Q4
Covenham St Bartholomew Lincs....59 P8
Covenham St Mary Lincs....59 P8
Coven Heath Staffs....45 U12
Coventry Covtry....36 K5
Coventry Airport Warwks....37 L6
Coverack Cnwll....2 K13
Coverack Bridges Cnwll....2 H10
Coverham N York....63 N2
Covington Cambs....38 G6
Covington S Lans....82 J11
Cowan Bridge Lancs....62 C5
Cowbeech E Susx....11 U8
Cowbit Lincs....49 L10
Cowbridge V Glam....26 H13
Cowdale Derbys....56 G12
Cowden Kent....11 R2
Cowdenbeath Fife....90 J13
Cowden Pound Kent....11 R2
Cowden Station Kent....11 S2
Cowers Lane Derbys....46 K4
Cowes IoW....9 P9
Cowesby N York....64 B2
Cowesfield Green Wilts....8 K3
Cowfold W Susx....11 L6
Cowgill Cumb....62 F2
Cow Green Suffk....40 H6
Cowhill S Glos....28 B9
Cowie Abers....99 R7
Cowie Stirlg....89 U8
Cowley Devon....6 B6
Cowley Gloucs....28 J5
Cowley Gt Lon....20 J6
Cowley Oxon....30 B12
Cowling Lancs....55 N3
Cowling N York....62 J11
Cowling N York....63 R2
Cowlinge Suffk....40 B10
Cowmes Kirk....56 J4
Cowpe Lancs....55 T2
Cowpen Nthumb....77 R9
Cowpen Bewley S on T....70 G7
Cowplain Hants....9 T7
Cowshill Dur....68 J4
Cowslip Green N Som....17 N4
Cowthorpe N York....63 U9
Coxall Herefs....34 J6
Coxbank Ches E....45 Q5
Coxbench Derbys....47 L5
Cox Common Suffk....41 Q4
Coxford Norfk....50 D8
Coxgreen Staffs....35 T3
Cox Green Gatesd....70 D1
Coxheath Kent....12 D5
Coxhoe Dur....70 D5
Coxley Somset....17 P8
Coxley Wick Somset....17 P8
Coxpark Cnwll....5 L7
Coxtie Green Essex....22 E8
Coxwold N York....64 C4
Coychurch Brdgnd....26 H11
Coychurch Crematorium Brdgnd....26 G11
Coylton S Ayrs....81 N9
Coylumbridge Highld....103 P13
Coytrahen Brdgnd....26 F10
Crabbs Cross Worcs....36 D7
Crab Orchard Dorset....8 F7
Crabtree W Susx....11 L6
Crackenthorpe Cumb....68 E8
Crackington Haven Cnwll....14 D13
Crackley Staffs....45 U3
Crackley Warwks....36 J6
Crackleybank Shrops....45 S11
Crackpot N York....69 L14
Cracoe N York....62 K7
Craddock Devon....6 F2
Cradle End Herts....22 B3
Cradley Dudley....36 B3
Cradley Herefs....35 R11
Cradley Heath Sandw....36 B3
Cradoc Powys....26 J2
Crafthole Cnwll....4 J10
Crafton Bucks....30 J9
Cragg Vale Calder....56 F2
Craggan Highld....103 R10
Craghead Dur....69 R2
Cragside House & Garden Nthumb....77 M5
Crai Powys....26 F2
Craibstone Moray....104 F4
Craichie Angus....91 T1
Craig Angus....99 M12
Craig D & G....73 S7
Craig Highld....101 S4
Craigbank E Ayrs....81 R10
Craigburn Border....83 P7
Craigcleuch D & G....75 R8
Craigdam Abers....105 N9
Craigdhu Ag & B....87 N3
Craigearn Abers....105 L13
Craigellachie Moray....104 B7
Craigend P & K....90 H6
Craigend Rens....88 K12
Craigendoran Ag & B....88 H9
Craigends Rens....88 K12
Craigens Ag & B....86 D13
Craighlaw D & G....72 K6
Craighat Stirlg....89 L9
Craigie P & K....90 H3
Craigie S Ayrs....81 P6
Craigiefold Abers....105 R3
Craiglockhart C Edin....83 P4
Craigmillar C Edin....83 Q4
Craignant Shrops....44 G6
Craigneston D & G....74 E9
Craigneuk N Lans....82 E6
Craigneuk N Lans....82 D5
Craigo Angus....99 M11
Craigrothie Fife....91 N10
Craigruie Stirlg....95 N14
Craig's End Essex....40 B13
Craigton Angus....91 R4
Craigton C Aber....99 R3
Craigton E Rens....89 N14
Craigton Angus....91 T2
Craig-y-Duke Neath....26 D7
Craig-y-nos Powys....26 F4
Craik Border....75 R4
Crailing Border....84 H14
Craiselound N Linc....58 C7
Crakehall N York....63 R1
Crakehill N York....63 U5
Crakemarsh Staffs....46 E6
Crambe N York....64 G7
Cramlington Nthumb....77 Q11
Cramond C Edin....83 N3
Cramond Bridge C Edin....83 N3
Crampmoor Hants....9 M4
Cranage Ches E....55 R13
Cranberry Staffs....45 T6
Cranborne Dorset....8 F6
Cranbourne Br For....20 F8
Cranbrook Devon....6 D5
Cranbrook Kent....12 E8
Cranbrook Common Kent....12 E8
Crane Moor Barns....57 M6
Crane's Corner Norfk....50 G11
Cranfield C Beds....31 L4
Cranford Gt Lon....20 K7

Cranford St Andrew Nhants....38 D5
Cranford St John Nhants....38 D5
Cranham Gloucs....28 G5
Cranham Gt Lon....22 E10
Cranhill Warwks....36 F10
Crank St Hel....55 M7
Cranleigh Surrey....10 H3
Cranmer Green Suffk....40 H6
Cranmore IoW....9 M10
Cranmore Somset....17 S8
Cranoe Leics....37 U1
Cransford Suffk....41 P8
Cranshaws Border....84 H6
Cranstal IoM....60 h2
Cranswick E R Yk....65 N9
Crantock Cnwll....2 K4
Cranwell Lincs....48 F4
Cranwich Norfk....40 C2
Cranworth Norfk....50 G13
Craobh Haven Ag & B....87 P4
Crapstone Devon....5 N7
Crarae Ag & B....87 T6
Crask Inn Highld....111 L12
Crask of Aigas Highld....102 E7
Craskins Abers....98 K3
Craster Nthumb....77 R2
Craswall Herefs....34 G13
Crateford Staffs....46 B12
Cratfield Suffk....41 P5
Crathes Abers....99 P4
Crathie Abers....98 E4
Crathie Highld....96 H5
Crathorne N York....70 H11
Craven Arms Shrops....35 K4
Crawcrook Gatesd....77 N13
Crawford Lancs....55 L6
Crawford S Lans....74 H2
Crawfordjohn S Lans....82 G14
Crawley Hants....9 N2
Crawley Oxon....29 R5
Crawley W Susx....11 M3
Crawley Down W Susx....11 N3
Crawleyside Dur....69 L3
Crawshawbooth Lancs....55 T1
Crawton Abers....99 R8
Craxe's Green Essex....23 P3
Cray N York....62 J4
Crayford Gt Lon....22 D12
Crayke N York....64 D6
Craymere Beck Norfk....50 J7
Crays Hill Essex....22 H9
Cray's Pond Oxon....19 T4
Craythorne Staffs....46 H9
Craze Lowman Devon....16 C13
Crazies Hill Wokham....20 C6
Creacombe Devon....16 B12
Creagan Inn Ag & B....94 C9
Creag Choraidh W Isls....106 c14
Creagorry W Isls....106 c14
Creaguaineach Lodge Highld....96 C10
Creamore Bank Shrops....45 M7
Creaton Nhants....37 T6
Creca D & G....75 P11
Credenhill Herefs....35 L12
Crediton Devon....15 T12
Creebank D & G....72 K4
Creebridge D & G....73 L6
Creech Heathfield Somset....16 J11
Creech St Michael Somset....16 J11
Creed Cnwll....3 N7
Creekmouth Gt Lon....21 S6
Creekmoor Poole....8 D10
Creeting St Mary Suffk....40 J9
Creeton Lincs....48 F9
Creetown D & G....73 M8
Cregneash IoM....60 b9
Cregny Baa IoM....60 f6
Cregrina Powys....34 D10
Creich Fife....91 M7
Creigiau Cardif....26 K11
Cremyll Cnwll....5 M10
Cressage Shrops....45 N13
Cressbrook Derbys....56 J12
Cresselly Pembks....24 J9
Cressex Bucks....20 D3
Cressing Essex....22 J3
Cresswell Nthumb....77 S8
Cresswell Pembks....24 J9
Cresswell Staffs....46 B6
Creswell Derbys....57 R12
Creswell Green Staffs....46 E11
Cretingham Suffk....41 M8
Cretshengan Ag & B....87 N11
Crewe Ches E....45 R2
Crewe Ches W....44 K3
Crewe Crematorium Ches E....45 R2
Crewe Green Ches E....45 R2
Crew Green Powys....44 H10
Crewkerne Somset....7 N2
Crews Hill Gt Lon....21 R3
Crewton C Derb....47 L6
Crianlarich Stirlg....95 M13
Cribbs Causeway S Glos....27 V11
Cribyn Cerdgn....32 K10
Criccieth Gwynd....42 K6
Crich Derbys....46 K2
Crich Carr Derbys....46 K2
Crichton Mdloth....83 S6
Crick Mons....27 T9
Crick Nhants....37 Q6
Crickadarn Powys....34 C12
Cricket St Thomas Somset....7 L3
Crickheath Shrops....44 G9
Crickhowell Powys....27 N4
Cricklade Wilts....29 L9
Cricklewood Gt Lon....21 M5
Cridling Stubbs N York....57 R2
Crieff P & K....90 B7
Criggan Cnwll....3 Q4
Criggion Powys....44 G11
Crigglestone Wakefd....57 M3
Crimble Rochdl....56 C4
Crimond Abers....105 T5
Crimonmogate Abers....105 T5
Crimplesham Norfk....49 T13
Crimscote Warwks....36 H11
Crinaglack Highld....102 E8
Crinan Ag & B....87 P7
Crindledyke N Lans....82 F7
Cringleford Norfk....51 L13
Crinow Pembks....24 K7
Cripplesease Cnwll....2 E9
Cripplestyle Dorset....8 F6
Cripp's Corner E Susx....12 E11
Croachy Highld....102 K10
Croanford Cnwll....3 Q2
Crockenhill Kent....21 S10
Crocker End Oxon....19 U5
Crockerhill W Susx....10 D9
Crockernwell Devon....5 S2
Crocker's Ash Herefs....27 U5
Crockerton Wilts....18 C12
Crockerton Green Wilts....18 C12
Crocketford D & G....74 F11
Crockey Hill C York....64 E10
Crockham Hill Kent....21 R12
Crockhurst Street Kent....12 B7
Crockleford Heath Essex....23 P3
Crock Street Somset....6 K2
Croeserw Neath....26 F8
Croes-goch Pembks....24 D4
Croes-lan Cerdgn....32 G12
Croesor Gwynd....43 M5
Croespenmaen Caerph....27 M7
Croes-wen Cardif....27 M11
Croesyceiliog Carmth....25 R7
Croesyceiliog Torfn....27 Q8
Croes-y-mwyalch Torfn....27 Q9
Croes-y-pant Mons....27 Q6
Croford Somset....16 F11
Croft Leics....37 P1
Croft Lincs....59 S14
Croft Warrtn....55 P8
Croftamie Stirlg....89 L9
Crofton Cumb....67 M2
Crofton Wakefd....57 N3
Crofton Wilts....19 L8
Croft-on-Tees N York....69 R11
Croftown Highld....108 A8
Crofts D & G....74 D11
Crofts Bank Traffd....55 S7
Crofts of Dipple Moray....104 C4
Crofts of Savoch Abers....105 T5
Crofty Swans....25 T12
Crogen Gwynd....44 B6
Croggan Ag & B....93 S13
Croglin Cumb....67 R3
Croick Highld....108 H7
Cromarty Highld....102 K3
Crombie Fife....90 G14
Cromdale Highld....103 R10
Cromer Herts....31 S7
Cromer Norfk....51 L5
Cromford Derbys....46 J2
Cromhall S Glos....28 C9
Cromhall Common S Glos....28 C10
Cromor W Isls....106 j6
Crompton Fold Oldham....56 D5
Cromwell Notts....47 U1
Cronberry E Ayrs....81 R8
Crondall Hants....20 B13
Cronkbourne IoM....60 f6
Cronk-y-Voddy IoM....60 e5
Cronton Knows....55 L9
Crook Cumb....67 Q13
Crook Dur....69 Q5
Crookdake Cumb....66 K4
Crooked End Gloucs....28 B4
Crookedholm E Ayrs....81 P5
Crookes Sheff....57 M9
Crookham Nthumb....85 N11

Crookham W Berk....19 S8
Crookham Village Hants....20 C12
Crook Inn Border....83 M13
Crookedack Cumb....61 U3
Crook of Devon P & K....90 F11
Crymych Pembks....25 L4
Crynant Neath....26 E7
Crystal Palace Gt Lon....21 P8
Cubbington Warwks....36 K7
Cubert Cnwll....2 K5
Cubley Barns....57 L6
Cubley Common Derbys....46 G6
Cublington Bucks....30 H8
Cublington Herefs....34 K13
Cuckfield W Susx....11 N5
Cucklington Somset....17 T11
Cuckney Notts....57 S12
Cuckoo Bridge Lincs....48 K9
Cuckoo's Corner Hants....10 A2
Cuckoo's Nest Ches W....44 J1
Cuddesdon Oxon....30 C12
Cuddington Bucks....30 F10
Cuddington Ches W....55 N12
Cuddington Heath Ches W....44 K4
Cuddy Hill Lancs....61 T12
Cudham Gt Lon....21 R11
Cudliptown Devon....5 N5
Cudnell Bmouth....8 F9
Cudworth Barns....57 N5
Cudworth Somset....7 L2
Cudworth Surrey....11 M2
Cuerdley Cross Warrtn....55 M9
Cufaud Hants....19 U9
Cuffley Herts....31 T12
Cuidhir W Isls....106 b17
Cuil Highld....94 F9
Culbokie Highld....102 H5
Culbone Somset....15 U3
Culburnie Highld....102 E7
Culcabock Highld....102 J7
Culcharry Highld....103 N5
Culcheth Warrtn....55 P8
Culdrain Highld....104 G8
Culduie Highld....100 g7
Culford Suffk....40 D6
Culgaith Cumb....68 D7
Culham Oxon....30 B13
Culkein Highld....110 A10
Culkein Drumbeg Highld....110 D10
Culkerton Gloucs....28 H8
Cullen Moray....104 G2
Cullercoats N Tyne....77 T11
Cullicudden Highld....102 J4
Cullingworth C Brad....63 M12
Cuillin Hills Highld....100 d9
Cullipool Ag & B....87 N3
Cullivoe Shet....106 v3
Culloden Highld....102 K6
Cullompton Devon....6 D3
Cullompton Services Devon....6 D3
Culm Davy Devon....16 F13
Culmington Shrops....35 L4
Culmstock Devon....16 F13
Culnacraig Highld....107 U3
Culnaightrie D & G....73 T9
Culnaknock Highld....100 f3
Culpho Suffk....41 M11
Culrain Highld....108 K6
Culross Fife....82 K1
Culroy S Ayrs....81 L10
Culsalmond Abers....104 K9
Culscadden D & G....73 M10
Culshabbin D & G....72 K9
Culswick Shet....106 s9
Cultercullen Abers....105 Q10
Cults C Aber....99 R3
Culverstone Green Kent....12 B3
Culverthorpe Lincs....48 F5
Culworth Nhants....37 P11
Culzean Castle & Country Park S Ayrs....80 J10
Cumbernauld N Lans....89 S10
Cumbernauld Village N Lans....89 S10
Cumberworth Lincs....59 T12
Cumdivock Cumb....67 M3
Cuminestown Abers....105 N5
Cummertrees D & G....75 M12
Cummingston Moray....103 T2
Cumnock E Ayrs....81 R8
Cumnor Oxon....29 U7
Cumrew Cumb....67 R3
Cumrue D & G....74 K9
Cumwhinton Cumb....67 Q2
Cumwhitton Cumb....67 R2
Cundall N York....63 U5
Cunningsburgh Shet....106 u11
Cupar Fife....91 N9
Cupar Muir Fife....91 N9
Curbar Derbys....57 L12
Curbridge Hants....9 Q6
Curbridge Oxon....29 R6
Curdridge Hants....9 Q6
Curdworth Warwks....36 G2
Curland Somset....16 H13
Curridge W Berk....19 Q6
Currie C Edin....83 N5
Curry Mallet Somset....16 K12
Curry Rivel Somset....17 L12
Curteis Corner Kent....12 F7
Curtisden Green Kent....12 D7
Curtisknowle Devon....5 S10
Cury Cnwll....2 H12
Cusgarne Cnwll....2 K8
Cushnie Abers....104 K4
Cushuish Somset....16 G10
Cusop Herefs....34 G12
Cutcloy D & G....73 L13
Cutcombe Somset....16 B9
Cuthill Highld....109 P7
Cutiau Gwynd....43 M10
Cutler's Green Essex....22 E1
Cutnall Green Worcs....35 U7
Cutsdean Gloucs....29 L1
Cutsyke Wakefd....57 P2
Cutthorpe Derbys....57 M12
Cuttivett Cnwll....4 J8
Cuxham Oxon....19 U2
Cuxton Medway....12 D2
Cuxwold Lincs....59 L6
Cwm Blae G....27 M6
Cwm Denbgs....54 C11
Cwmafan Neath....26 E9
Cwmaman Rhondd....26 J8
Cwmann Carmth....33 L11
Cwmavon Torfn....27 N6
Cwmbach Carmth....25 L6
Cwmbach Carmth....25 U11
Cwmbach Powys....34 D14
Cwmbach Rhondd....26 J7
Cwmbach Llechrhyd Powys....34 B10
Cwmbelan Powys....33 U4
Cwmbran Torfn....27 P8
Cwmbrwyno Cerdgn....33 Q4
Cwm Capel Carmth....25 S10
Cwmcarn Caerph....27 N8
Cwmcarvan Mons....27 T6
Cwm-celyn Blae G....27 N6
Cwm-Cewydd Gwynd....43 S11
Cwm-cou Cerdgn....32 E11
Cwm Crawnon Powys....27 L4
Cwmdare Rhondd....26 H7
Cwmdu Carmth....33 L13
Cwmdu Powys....27 M3
Cwmduad Carmth....25 P3
Cwm Dulais Swans....25 U10
Cwmdwr Carmth....33 N13
Cwmfelin Brdgnd....26 F10
Cwmfelin Myrd T....26 K6
Cwmfelin Boeth Carmth....25 L7
Cwmfelinfach Caerph....27 M8
Cwmfelin Mynach Carmth....25 M6
Cwmffrwd Carmth....25 R7
Cwmgiedd Powys....26 E5
Cwmgorse Carmth....26 C6
Cwmgwili Carmth....25 U8
Cwmgwrach Neath....26 F7
Cwmhiraeth Carmth....25 P3
Cwm Irfon Powys....33 S11
Cwmisfael Carmth....25 S7
Cwm-Llinau Powys....43 S12
Cwmllynfell Neath....26 D6
Cwmmawr Carmth....25 U8
Cwm Morgan Carmth....25 M4
Cwm-parc Rhondd....26 G8
Cwm Penmachno Conwy....43 P3
Cwmpengraig Carmth....25 P3
Cwmpennar Rhondd....26 J7
Cwm Plysgog Pembks....32 C12
Cwmrhos Powys....27 M3
Cwmrhydyceirw Swans....26 B8
Cwmsychpant Cerdgn....32 J11
Cwmtillery Blae G....27 N6
Cwm-twrch Isaf Powys....26 E5
Cwm-twrch Uchaf Powys....26 E5
Cwm-y-glo Carmth....25 U8
Cwm-y-glo Gwynd....52 J10
Cwmyoy Mons....27 Q3
Cwmystwyth Cerdgn....33 R6
Cwrt Gwynd....43 P13
Cwrt-newydd Cerdgn....32 J11
Cwrt-y-gollen Powys....27 N4

Cyfarthfa Castle Museum - Edenhall 129

Cyfarthfa Castle Museum Myr Td 26 J6
Cyfronydd Powys 44 D12
Cylibebyll Neath 26 C7
Cymau Flints 44 G2
Cymer Neath 26 F8
Cymmer Rhondd 26 J9
Cynghordy Carmth 33 R12
Cynheidre Carmth 25 S9
Cynonville Neath 26 E8
Cynwyd Denbgs 44 C5
Cynwyl Elfed Carmth 25 Q5

D

Daccombe Devon 6 B11
Dacre Cumb 67 Q7
Dacre N York 63 P7
Dacre Banks N York 63 P7
Daddry Shield Dur 68 J5
Dadford Bucks 30 E5
Dadlington Leics 47 M14
Dafen Carmth 25 T10
Daffy Green Norfk 50 G12
Dagenham Gt Lon 22 D11
Daglingworth Gloucs 28 J6
Dagnall Bucks 31 L9
Dagworth Suffk 40 H8
Dailly S Ayrs 80 K12
Dainton Devon 5 V7
Dairsie Fife 91 P8
Daisy Hill Bolton 55 Q6
Daisy Hill Leeds 63 R14
Dalabrog W Isls 106 c16
Dalavich Ag & B 87 T3
Dalbeattie D & G 74 F13
Dalbury Derbys 46 J7
Dalby IoM 60 c7
Dalby Lincs 59 R13
Dalby N York 64 E5
Dalcapon P & K 97 R13
Dalchalm Highld 109 S3
Dalchreichart Highld 102 A13
Dalchruin P & K 89 R2
Dalcrue P & K 90 F6
Dalderby Lincs 59 N13
Dalditch Devon 6 D8
Daldowie Crematorium C Glas 82 C6
Dale Cumb 67 R4
Dale Derbys 47 M6
Dale Pembks 24 D9
Dale Bottom Cumb 67 L8
Dale End Derbys 46 H1
Dale End N York 62 K10
Dale Hill E Susx 12 D9
Dalehouse N York 71 N9
Dalelia Highld 93 S5
Dalgarven N Ayrs 80 K3
Dalgety Bay Fife 83 N2
Dalgig E Ayrs 81 R10
Dalginross P & K 89 S1
Dalguise P & K 90 E2
Dalhalvaig Highld 111 T6
Dalham Suffk 40 B8
Daliburgh W Isls 106 c16
Dalkeith Mdloth 83 R5
Dallas Moray 103 T5
Dallinghoo Suffk 41 N9
Dallington E Susx 11 V7
Dallington Nhants 37 T8
Dallow N York 63 P5
Dalmally Ag & B 94 H13
Dalmary Stirlg 89 M6
Dalmellington E Ayrs 81 P11
Dalmeny C Edin 83 M3
Dalmore Highld 109 M11
Dalmuir W Duns 89 L11
Dalnabreck Highld 93 S5
Dalnacardoch P & K 97 L9
Dalnahaitnach Highld 103 N12
Dalnaspidal P & K 96 J9
Dalnawillan Lodge Highld 112 B8
Daloist P & K 97 M12
Dalqueich P & K 90 G11
Dalquhairn S Ayrs 81 L13
Dalreavoch Lodge Highld 109 P3
Dalry N Ayrs 80 K3
Dalrymple E Ayrs 81 M10
Dalserf S Lans 82 E8
Dalsmeran Ag & B 79 L13
Dalston Cumb 67 N2
Dalston Gt Lon 21 P6
Dalswinton D & G 74 H8
Dalton Cumb 61 U4
Dalton D & G 75 M11
Dalton Lancs 55 L5
Dalton N York 63 U4
Dalton N York 69 P11
Dalton Nthumb 77 N11
Dalton Rothm 57 Q8
Dalton-in-Furness Cumb 61 N5
Dalton-le-Dale Dur 70 F3
Dalton Magna Rothm 57 Q8
Dalton-on-Tees N York 69 S11
Dalton Parva Rothm 57 Q8
Dalton Piercy Hartpl 70 G6
Dalveich Stirlg 95 S14
Dalwhinnie Highld 96 J7
Dalwood Devon 6 H4
Damask Green Herts 31 S7
Damerham Hants 8 G5
Damgate Norfk 51 R12
Dam Green Norfk 40 H3
Damnaglaur D & G 72 E12
Danaway Kent 12 G3
Danbury Essex 22 J6
Danby N York 71 M11
Danby Bottom N York 71 L12
Danby Wiske N York 70 D13
Dandaleith Moray 104 B6
Danderhall Mdloth 83 R5
Danebridge Ches E 56 E13
Dane End Herts 31 T8
Danegate E Susx 11 T4
Danehill E Susx 11 Q5
Dane Hills C Leic 47 Q13
Danemoor Green Norfk 50 J12
Danesford Shrops 35 R2
Danesmoor Derbys 57 P14
Dane Street Kent 13 L5
Daniel's Water Kent 12 J7
Danshillock Abers 105 L4
Danskine E Loth 84 F5
Danthorpe E R Yk 65 T13
Danzey Green Warwks 36 F7
Dapple Heath Staffs 46 D8
Darby Green Hants 20 D10
Darcy Lever Bolton 55 R5
Dardy Powys 27 N4
Daren-felen Mons 27 N5
Darenth Kent 22 E13
Daresbury Halton 55 N10
Darfield Barns 57 P6
Darfoulds Notts 57 S11
Dargate Kent 13 L3
Darite Cnwll 4 H7
Darland Medway 12 E2
Darland Wrexhm 44 J2
Darlaston Wsall 36 C1
Darlaston Green Wsall 36 C1
Darley N York 63 Q8
Darley Abbey C Derb 47 L6
Darley Bridge Derbys 46 J1
Darley Dale Derbys 57 L14
Darley Green Solhll 36 G6
Darleyhall Herts 31 P8
Darley Head N York 63 P8
Darlingscott Warwks 36 H12
Darlington Darltn 69 S10
Darlington Crematorium Darltn 69 S10
Darliston Shrops 45 N7
Darlton Notts 58 C12
Darnford Staffs 46 F12
Darnick Border 84 E12
Darowen Powys 43 R13
Darra Abers 105 L6
Darracott Devon 14 F9
Darracott Devon 15 L5
Darras Hall Nthumb 77 P11
Darrington Wakefd 57 Q3
Darsham Suffk 41 R7
Darshill Somset 17 R8
Dartford Kent 22 D13
Dartington Devon 5 T8
Dartmeet Devon 5 R6
Dartmoor National Park Devon 5 R5
Dartmouth Devon 5 V10
Darton Barns 57 M4
Darvel E Ayrs 81 R5
Darwell Hole E Susx 12 C12
Darwen Bl w D 55 Q2
Datchet W & M 20 G7
Datchworth Herts 31 S9
Datchworth Green Herts 31 S9
Daubhill Bolton 55 R5
Daugh of Kinermony Moray 104 A7
Dauntsey Wilts 18 E4
Dava Highld 103 R8
Davenham Ches W 55 Q12
Davenport Stockp 56 D9
Davenport Green Ches E 55 T11
Davenport Green Traffd 55 T9
Daventry Nhants 37 Q8
Davidson's Mains C Edin 83 P3
Davidstow Cnwll 4 F3
David Street Kent 12 B3
Davington D & G 75 P5
Davington Hill Kent 12 K3
Daviot Abers 105 L10
Daviot Highld 102 K8
Daviot House Highld 102 K7
Davis's Town E Susx 11 S7
Davoch of Grange Moray 104 F5
Davyhulme Traffd 55 S7
Daw End Wsall 46 D13
Dawesgreen Surrey 21 M13
Dawley Wrekin 45 Q12
Dawlish Devon 6 C9
Dawlish Warren Devon 6 C9
Dawn Conwy 53 Q8
Daws Green Somset 16 G12
Daws Heath Essex 22 K10
Daw's House Cnwll 4 J4
Dawsmere Lincs 49 P7
Daybrook Notts 47 Q4
Day Green Ches E 45 S2
Dayhills Staffs 46 C7
Dayhouse Bank Worcs 36 C5
Daylesford Gloucs 29 P2
Ddol Flints 54 D12
Ddol-Cownwy Powys 44 B10
Deal Kent 13 S5
Dean Cumb 66 G7
Dean Devon 5 S8
Dean Devon 15 P3
Dean Devon 15 R3
Dean Dorset 8 D5
Dean Hants 9 N2
Dean Hants 9 R5
Dean Lancs 56 C1
Dean Oxon 29 R3
Dean Somset 17 S8
Dean Bottom Kent 21 U9
Deanburnhaugh Border 75 S3
Deancombe Devon 5 S8
Dean Court Oxon 29 U6
Deane Bolton 55 Q5
Deane Hants 19 R10
Dean End Dorset 8 D5
Dean Head Barns 57 L6
Deanhead Kirk 56 F3
Deanland Dorset 8 D5
Deanlane End W Susx 9 U6
Dean Prior Devon 5 S8
Deanraw Nthumb 76 G13
Dean Row Ches E 56 C10
Deans W Loth 82 K5
Deanscales Cumb 66 G7
Deanshanger Nhants 30 G5
Deanshaugh Moray 104 D5
Deanston Stirlg 89 R5
Dean Street Kent 12 D5
Dearham Cumb 66 G5
Dearnley Rochdl 56 D3
Debach Suffk 41 M10
Debden Essex 21 R3
Debden Essex 39 S14
Debden Green Essex 22 E1
Debenham Suffk 41 L8
Deblin's Green Worcs 35 T11
Dechmont W Loth 82 K4
Dechmont Road W Loth 82 K5
Deddington Oxon 29 U1
Dedham Essex 40 J14
Dedham Heath Essex 23 Q1
Dedworth W & M 20 F7
Deene Nhants 38 D2
Deenethorpe Nhants 38 E2
Deepcar Sheff 57 L7
Deepcut Surrey 20 F11
Deepdale Cumb 62 E3
Deepdale N York 62 H4
Deeping Gate C Pete 48 H12
Deeping St James Lincs 48 J12
Deeping St Nicholas Lincs 48 K10
Deerhurst Gloucs 28 G1
Deerhurst Walton Gloucs 28 G2
Deerton Street Kent 12 J3
Defford Worcs 36 B12
Defynnog Powys 26 G2
Deganwy Conwy 53 N7
Degnish Ag & B 87 P3
Deighton C York 64 E11
Deighton N York 70 E12
Deiniolen Gwynd 52 J10
Delabole Cnwll 4 D4
Delamere Ches W 55 N13
Delfrigs Abers 105 R11
Delley Devon 15 M8
Delliefure Highld 103 S9
Dell Quay W Susx 10 C10
Delly End Oxon 29 S5
Delnabo Moray 103 U12
Delnashaugh Inn Moray 103 U8
Delny Highld 109 N10
Delph Oldham 56 E5
Delves Dur 69 P3
Delvin End Essex 40 C13
Dembleby Lincs 48 F6
Demelza Cnwll 3 P4
Denaby Donc 57 Q7
Denaby Main Donc 57 Q7
Denbies Surrey 20 K12
Denbigh Denbgs 54 C13
Denbrae Fife 91 N8
Denbury Devon 5 U7
Denby Derbys 47 L4
Denby Bottles Derbys 47 L4
Denby Dale Kirk 56 K5
Denchworth Oxon 29 S9
Dendron Cumb 61 N5
Denel End C Beds 31 M5
Denfield P & K 90 E8
Denford Nhants 38 E5
Dengie Essex 23 N7
Denham Bucks 20 H5
Denham Suffk 40 C8
Denham Suffk 41 L6
Denham End Suffk 40 C8
Denham Green Bucks 20 H5
Denham Green Suffk 41 L6
Denhead Abers 105 R5
Denhead Fife 91 Q9
Denhead of Gray C Dund 91 N5
Denholm Border 76 B2
Denholme C Brad 63 M13
Denholme Clough C Brad 63 M13
Denio Gwynd 42 G6
Denmead Hants 9 T6
Denmore C Aber 105 Q13
Denne Park W Susx 10 K5
Dennington Suffk 41 N7
Denny Falk 89 T9
Dennyloanhead Falk 89 T9
Den of Lindores Fife 91 L8
Denshaw Oldham 56 E4
Denside Abers 99 Q4
Densole Kent 13 P7
Denston Suffk 40 C10
Denstone Staffs 46 E5
Denstroude Kent 13 M3
Dent Cumb 62 E2
Denton Cambs 38 J3
Denton Darltn 69 R9
Denton E Susx 11 R10
Denton Kent 13 P6
Denton Kent 22 G13
Denton Lincs 48 C7
Denton N York 63 N10
Denton Nhants 38 B9
Denton Norfk 41 N3
Denton Oxon 30 C12
Denton Tamesd 56 D7
Denver Norfk 49 T13
Denwick Nthumb 77 Q3
Deopham Norfk 50 H13
Deopham Green Norfk 50 H14
Depden Suffk 40 C9
Depden Green Suffk 40 C9
Deptford Gt Lon 21 Q7
Deptford Wilts 18 F13
Derby C Derb 47 L6
Derby Devon 15 N6
Derbyhaven IoM 60 d9
Derculich P & K 97 P13
Dereham Norfk 50 G11
Deri Caerph 27 L7
Derril Devon 14 H12
Derringstone Kent 13 P6
Derrington Staffs 45 U9
Derriton Devon 14 H12
Derry Hill Wilts 18 E6
Derrythorpe N Linc 58 D5
Dersingham Norfk 49 U7
Dervaig Ag & B 93 L8
Derwen Denbgs 44 C3
Derwen Fawr Carmth 25 U6
Derwenlas Powys 43 P14
Derwent Valley Mills Derbys 46 K2
Derwent Water Cumb 67 L8
Derwydd Carmth 25 V7
Desborough Nhants 38 B4
Desford Leics 47 N13
Deskford Moray 104 G3
Detchant Nthumb 85 R11
Detling Kent 12 E4
Deuxhill Shrops 35 Q3
Devauden Mons 27 T8
Devil's Bridge Cerdgn 33 P5
Devitts Green Warwks 36 J2
Devizes Wilts 18 F8
Devonport C Plym 5 M10
Devonside Clacks 90 D12
Devoran Cnwll 2 K9
Devoran & Perran Cnwll 2 K9
Dewarton Mdloth 83 S6
Dewlish Dorset 7 U5
Dewsbury Kirk 56 K2
Dewsbury Moor Kirk 56 K2
Dewsbury Moor Crematorium Kirk 56 K2
Deytheur Powys 44 F10
Dial N Som 17 P3
Dial Green W Susx 10 E5
Dial Post W Susx 10 K7
Dibberford Dorset 7 N4
Dibden Hants 9 N7
Dibden Purlieu Hants 9 N7
Dickens Heath Solhll 36 F5
Dickleburgh Norfk 41 L4
Didbrook Gloucs 29 L1
Didcot Oxon 19 R2
Diddington Cambs 38 J7
Diddlebury Shrops 35 M3
Didley Herefs 27 T1
Didling W Susx 10 C7
Didmarton Gloucs 28 F10
Didsbury Manch 55 T8
Didworthy Devon 5 R8
Digby Lincs 48 G3
Digg Highld 100 d3
Diggle Oldham 56 F5
Digmoor Lancs 55 L5
Digswell Herts 31 R9
Digswell Water Herts 31 S10
Dihewyd Cerdgn 32 J9
Dilham Norfk 51 P8
Dilhorne Staffs 46 C5
Dill Hall Lancs 62 F14
Dillington Cambs 38 H7
Dilston Nthumb 76 K13
Dilton Wilts 18 C11
Dilton Marsh Wilts 18 B11
Dilwyn Herefs 34 K10
Dimple Bolton 55 R3
Dimple Derbys 46 J1
Dinas Carmth 25 N4
Dinas Cnwll 3 N2
Dinas Gwynd 42 E6
Dinas Pembks 24 H3
Dinas Rhondd 26 J9
Dinas Dinlle Gwynd 52 F11
Dinas-Mawddwy Gwynd 43 S10
Dinas Powys V Glam 16 G2
Dinder Somset 17 Q8
Dinedor Herefs 35 M13
Dingestow Mons 27 T5
Dingle Lpool 54 J9
Dingleden Kent 12 F9
Dingley Nhants 37 U3
Dingwall Highld 102 F4
Dinmael Conwy 44 B5
Dinnet Abers 98 H4
Dinnington N u Ty 77 Q11
Dinnington Rothm 57 R9
Dinnington Somset 7 M2
Dinorwic Gwynd 52 J10
Dinton Bucks 30 G10
Dinton Wilts 8 E2
Dinwoodie D & G 75 M7
Dinworthy Devon 14 H9
Dipford Somset 16 H12
Dipley Hants 20 B11
Dippen Ag & B 79 Q8
Dippen N Ayrs 80 E8
Dippenhall Surrey 20 D13
Dippermill Devon 14 K11
Dippertown Devon 5 L4
Dipple Moray 104 C4
Dipple S Ayrs 80 J12
Diptford Devon 5 S9
Dipton Dur 69 Q2
Diptonmill Nthumb 76 J13
Dirleton E Loth 84 E2
Dirt Pot Nthumb 68 J3
Discoed Powys 34 G8
Diseworth Leics 47 N9
Dishforth N York 63 T5
Disley Ches E 56 E10
Diss Norfk 40 K4
Disserth Powys 34 B9
Distington Cumb 66 F8
Distington Hall Crematorium Cumb 66 F8
Ditchampton Wilts 8 F2
Ditcheat Somset 17 R9
Ditchingham Norfk 41 P2
Ditchling E Susx 11 N7
Ditherington Shrops 45 M11
Ditteridge Wilts 18 B7
Dittisham Devon 5 V9
Ditton Kent 12 D4
Ditton Green Cambs 39 U9
Ditton Priors Shrops 35 P3
Dixton Gloucs 28 J1
Dixton Mons 27 U5
Dizzard Cnwll 14 E13
Dobcross Oldham 56 E5
Dobwalls Cnwll 4 G7
Doccombe Devon 5 T3
Dochgarroch Highld 102 H7
Dockenfield Surrey 10 C2
Docker Lancs 62 B5
Docking Norfk 50 C6
Docklow Herefs 35 N9
Dockray Cumb 67 L3
Dockray Cumb 67 N8
Dodbrooke Devon 5 S12
Doddinghurst Essex 22 E8
Doddington Cambs 39 P2
Doddington Kent 12 H4
Doddington Lincs 58 E12
Doddington Nthumb 85 P12
Doddington Shrops 35 P5
Doddiscombsleigh Devon 5 V3
Dodd's Green Ches E 45 P5
Doddshill Norfk 49 U7
Doddy Cross Cnwll 4 J8
Dodford Nhants 37 R8
Dodford Worcs 36 B6
Dodington S Glos 28 E11
Dodington Somset 16 G8
Dodleston Ches W 44 J1
Dodscott Devon 15 M9
Dodside E Rens 81 Q2
Dod's Leigh Staffs 46 D7
Dodworth Barns 57 M5
Dodworth Bottom Barns 57 M6
Dodworth Green Barns 57 M6
Doe Bank Birm 46 F14
Doe Lea Derbys 57 Q13
Dogdyke Lincs 48 K2
Dogley Lane Kirk 56 J4
Dogmersfield Hants 20 C12
Dogridge Wilts 29 L10
Dogsthorpe C Pete 48 J13
Dog Village Devon 6 C5
Dolanog Powys 44 C11
Dolau Powys 34 D7
Dolaucothi Carmth 33 N12
Dolbenmaen Gwynd 42 K5
Doley Staffs 45 R8
Dolfach Powys 43 T13
Dolfor Powys 34 D3
Dol-for Powys 43 R12
Dolgarrog Conwy 53 N9
Dolgellau Gwynd 43 P10
Dolgoch Gwynd 43 N13
Dol-gran Carmth 25 R4
Doll Highld 109 R4
Dollar Clacks 90 E12
Dollarfield Clacks 90 E12
Dolley Green Powys 34 G7
Dollwen Cerdgn 33 N4
Dolphin Flints 54 E12
Dolphinholme Lancs 61 U9
Dolphinton S Lans 83 M9
Dolton Devon 15 N10
Dolwen Conwy 53 Q8
Dolwyddelan Conwy 43 P3
Dolybont Cerdgn 33 M3
Dolyhir Powys 34 F9
Domgay Powys 44 G10
Donaldson's Lodge Nthumb 85 M10
Doncaster Donc 57 S6
Doncaster Carr Donc 57 S6
Doncaster North Services Donc 57 U4
Donhead St Andrew Wilts 8 C4
Donhead St Mary Wilts 8 C4
Donibristle Fife 90 J14
Doniford Somset 16 E8
Donington Lincs 48 K6
Donington on Bain Lincs 59 M10
Donington Park Services Leics 47 N8
Donington Southing Lincs 48 K7
Donisthorpe Leics 46 K11
Donkey Street Kent 13 M9
Donkey Town Surrey 20 F10
Donnington Gloucs 29 N2
Donnington Herefs 35 R14
Donnington Shrops 45 N12
Donnington W Berk 19 Q7
Donnington W Susx 10 D10
Donnington Wrekin 45 R11
Donnington Wood Wrekin 45 R11
Donyatt Somset 6 K2
Doomsday Green W Susx 10 K5
Doonfoot S Ayrs 81 L9
Dorback Lodge Highld 103 S12
Dorchester Dorset 7 S6
Dorchester Oxon 19 S2
Dordon Warwks 46 J13
Dore Sheff 57 M10
Dores Highld 102 G9
Dorking Surrey 21 L13
Dorking Tye Suffk 40 F13
Dormans Land Surrey 11 Q2
Dormans Park Surrey 11 P2
Dormington Herefs 35 N12
Dormston Worcs 36 C9
Dorn Gloucs 36 H14
Dorney Bucks 20 F7
Dornie Highld 101 M6
Dornoch Highld 109 P7
Dornock D & G 75 P12
Dorrery Highld 112 C6
Dorridge Solhll 36 G6
Dorrington Lincs 48 G3
Dorrington Shrops 45 L13
Dorrington Shrops 45 R5
Dorsington Warwks 36 F11
Dorstone Herefs 34 H12
Dorton Bucks 30 E10
Dosthill Staffs 46 H14
Dothan IoA 52 E8
Dottery Dorset 7 N5
Doublebois Cnwll 4 F8
Doughton Gloucs 28 G9
Douglas IoM 60 f7
Douglas S Lans 82 F12
Douglas and Angus C Dund 91 P5
Douglas Borough Crematorium IoM 60 f7
Douglas Pier Ag & B 88 E6
Douglastown Angus 91 P2
Douglas Water S Lans 82 G11
Douglas West S Lans 82 F12
Doulting Somset 17 R8
Dounby Ork 106 r17
Doune Highld 108 G4
Doune Stirlg 89 R5
Dounepark S Ayrs 80 H13
Dounie Highld 108 K6
Dousland Devon 5 N7
Dovaston Shrops 44 J9
Dove Green Notts 47 N3
Dove Holes Derbys 56 G11
Dovenby Cumb 66 G6
Dover Kent 13 R7
Dover Wigan 55 P6
Dover Castle Kent 13 R7
Dovercourt Essex 23 T1
Doverdale Worcs 35 U7
Doveridge Derbys 46 F7
Doversgreen Surrey 21 N13
Dowally P & K 90 F2
Dowbridge Lancs 61 S13
Dowdeswell Gloucs 28 K4
Dowlais Myr Td 26 K6
Dowland Devon 15 N10
Dowlish Ford Somset 7 L2
Dowlish Wake Somset 7 L2
Down Ampney Gloucs 29 L8
Downderry Cnwll 4 J10
Downe Gt Lon 21 R10
Downend Gloucs 28 F8
Downend IoW 9 Q11
Downend S Glos 28 C12
Downend W Berk 19 Q5
Downfield C Dund 91 N5
Downgate Cnwll 4 H6
Downgate Cnwll 4 K6
Downham Essex 22 H8
Downham Gt Lon 21 Q8
Downham Lancs 62 F11
Downham Market Norfk 49 T13
Down Hatherley Gloucs 28 G3
Downhead Somset 17 Q11
Downhead Somset 17 S7
Downhill Cnwll 3 M3
Downhill P & K 90 G6
Downholland Cross Lancs 54 J5
Downholme N York 69 P13
Downicarey Devon 4 K2
Downies Abers 99 S5
Downing Flints 54 E11
Downley Bucks 20 D3
Down St Mary Devon 15 R12
Downs Crematorium Br & H 11 N9
Downside Somset 17 R6
Downside Somset 17 R8
Downside Surrey 20 K11
Down Thomas Devon 5 N10
Downton Hants 8 K10
Downton Wilts 8 H4
Dowsby Lincs 48 H8
Dowsdale Lincs 49 L11
Doxey Staffs 45 U9
Doxford Nthumb 85 T14
Doynton S Glos 28 D13
Draethen Caerph 27 N10
Draffan S Lans 82 E9
Dragonby N Linc 58 F4
Dragons Green W Susx 10 J6
Drakeholes Notts 58 B8
Drakelow Worcs 35 T4
Drakemyre N Ayrs 80 K2
Drakes Broughton Worcs 36 B11
Drakewalls Cnwll 5 L6
Draughton N York 63 L9
Draughton Nhants 37 U5
Drax N York 57 U1
Drax Hales N York 57 U1
Draycote Warwks 37 M6
Draycot Foliat Swindn 18 J5
Draycott Derbys 47 M7
Draycott Gloucs 36 G13
Draycott Shrops 35 T2
Draycott Somset 17 N6
Draycott Somset 17 Q12
Draycott Worcs 35 U11
Draycott in the Clay Staffs 46 G8
Draycott in the Moors Staffs 46 C5
Drayford Devon 15 S10
Drayton C Port 9 T7
Drayton Leics 38 B2
Drayton Lincs 48 K6
Drayton Norfk 51 L11
Drayton Oxon 29 U9
Drayton Oxon 37 M12
Drayton Somset 17 M12
Drayton Worcs 36 B5
Drayton Bassett Staffs 46 G13
Drayton Beauchamp Bucks 30 K10
Drayton Manor Park Staffs 46 G13
Drayton Parslow Bucks 30 H7
Drayton St Leonard Oxon 30 C13
Drebley N York 63 M8
Dreemskerry IoM 60 h4
Dreen Hill Pembks 24 F8
Drefach Carmth 25 Q3
Drefach Carmth 25 T8
Drefach Cerdgn 32 J11
Drefelin Carmth 25 Q3
Dreghorn N Ayrs 81 M5
Drellingore Kent 13 P7
Drem E Loth 84 E3
Dresden C Stke 46 B5
Drewsteignton Devon 5 S2
Driby Lincs 59 Q12
Driffield E R Yk 65 N8
Driffield Gloucs 29 L8
Driffield Cross Roads Gloucs 29 L8
Drift Cnwll 2 C11
Drigg Cumb 66 G13
Drighlington Leeds 63 Q14
Drimnin Highld 93 P8
Drimpton Dorset 7 M4
Drimsallie Highld 94 D3
Dringhouses C York 64 D10
Drinkstone Suffk 40 G8
Drinkstone Green Suffk 40 G8
Drive End Dorset 7 Q3
Driver's End Herts 31 R8
Drointon Staffs 46 D8
Droitwich Worcs 35 U8
Dron P & K 90 H8
Dronfield Derbys 57 N11
Dronfield Woodhouse Derbys 57 M11
Drongan E Ayrs 81 N9
Dronley Angus 91 M4
Droop Dorset 7 U3
Dropping Well Rothm 57 N8
Droxford Hants 9 S5
Droylsden Tamesd 56 D7
Druid Denbgs 44 B5
Druidston Pembks 24 E7
Druimarbin Highld 94 F4
Druimavuic Ag & B 94 E9
Druimdrishaig Ag & B 87 N11
Druimindarroch Highld 93 R2
Drum Ag & B 87 S10
Drum P & K 90 F11
Drumalbin S Lans 82 H11
Drumbeg Highld 110 C10
Drumblade Abers 104 H7
Drumbreddon D & G 72 D11
Drumbuie Highld 100 g6
Drumburgh Cumb 75 Q14
Drumburn D & G 66 C2
Drumchapel C Glas 89 M11
Drumchastle P & K 95 T7
Drumclog S Lans 81 S5
Drumeldrie Fife 91 P11
Drumelzier Border 83 M12
Drumfearn Highld 100 f8
Drumfrennie Abers 99 N4
Drumgley Angus 98 G13
Drumguish Highld 97 M3
Drumin Moray 103 U9
Drumjohn D & G 81 Q13
Drumlamford S Ayrs 72 H4
Drumlasie Abers 99 L2
Drumleaning Cumb 67 L2
Drumlemble Ag & B 79 M12
Drumlithie Abers 99 P7
Drummoddie D & G 72 K10
Drummore D & G 72 E12
Drummuir Moray 104 D7
Drumnadrochit Highld 102 F9
Drumnagorrach Moray 104 G5
Drumpark D & G 74 G10
Drumrunie Lodge Highld 108 B4
Drumshang S Ayrs 80 K10
Drumuie Highld 100 d5
Drumuillie Highld 103 P11
Drumvaich Stirlg 89 Q5
Drunzie P & K 90 H10
Druridge Nthumb 77 R6
Drury Flints 54 G14
Drybeck Cumb 68 E9
Drybridge Moray 104 E3
Drybridge N Ayrs 81 M5
Drybrook Gloucs 28 B4
Dryburgh Border 84 F12
Dry Doddington Lincs 48 C4
Dry Drayton Cambs 39 N8
Drymen Stirlg 89 L8
Drymuir Abers 105 Q6
Drynoch Highld 100 d6
Dry Sandford Oxon 29 U7
Dryslwyn Carmth 25 U6
Dry Street Essex 22 G10
Dryton Shrops 45 N12
Dubford Abers 105 M3
Dublin Suffk 41 L7
Duchally Highld 110 H13
Duck End Bed 31 N4
Duck End Cambs 38 K8
Duck End Essex 22 G2
Duck End Essex 39 U14
Duckend Green Essex 22 H3
Duckington Ches W 45 L3
Ducklington Oxon 29 S6
Duck's Cross Bed 38 H9
Duddenhoe End Essex 39 Q13
Duddingston C Edin 83 Q4
Duddington Nhants 48 E13
Duddlestone Somset 16 H12
Duddleswell E Susx 11 R5
Duddlewick Shrops 35 Q4
Duddo Nthumb 85 N10
Duddon Ches W 55 M14
Duddon Bridge Cumb 61 M2
Duddon Common Ches W 55 M13
Dudleston Shrops 44 H6
Dudleston Heath Shrops 44 J6
Dudley Dudley 36 B2
Dudley N Tyne 77 R11
Dudley Hill C Brad 63 P13
Dudley Port Sandw 36 C2
Dudnill Shrops 35 P6
Dudsbury Dorset 8 F9
Dudswell Herts 31 L11
Duffield Derbys 46 K5
Duffryn Neath 26 E8
Dufftown Moray 104 C7
Duffus Moray 103 U2
Dufton Cumb 68 E7
Duggleby N York 64 K6
Duirinish Highld 100 g6
Duisdalemore Highld 100 g8
Duisky Highld 94 E3
Dukestown Blae G 27 L5
Duke Street Suffk 40 J12
Dukinfield Tamesd 56 D7
Dukinfield Crematorium Tamesd 56 D7
Dulas IoA 52 G5
Dulcote Somset 17 Q8
Dulford Devon 6 E3
Dull P & K 90 B2
Dullatur N Lans 89 R10
Dullingham Cambs 39 T9
Dullingham Ley Cambs 39 T9
Dulnain Bridge Highld 103 Q11
Duloe Bed 38 J8
Duloe Cnwll 4 G9
Dulverton Somset 16 B11
Dulwich Gt Lon 21 P8
Dumbarton W Duns 88 J10
Dumbleton Gloucs 36 D13
Dumfries D & G 74 J10
Dumgoyne Stirlg 89 M9
Dummer Hants 19 S11
Dumpton Kent 13 S2
Dun Angus 99 M12
Dunalastair P & K 95 U7
Dunan Ag & B 88 E11
Dunan Highld 100 e7
Dunan P & K 95 P7
Dunaverty Ag & B 79 M14
Dunball Somset 16 K8
Dunbar E Loth 84 H3
Dunbeath Highld 112 E11
Dunbeg Ag & B 94 B12
Dunblane Stirlg 89 S5
Dunbog Fife 91 L8
Dunbridge Hants 9 L3
Duncanston Highld 102 G4
Duncanstone Abers 104 H10
Dunchideock Devon 6 A7
Dunchurch Warwks 37 N6
Duncote Nhants 37 S10
Duncow D & G 74 J9
Duncrievie P & K 90 H10
Duncton W Susx 10 F7
Dundee C Dund 91 P5
Dundee Airport C Dund 91 N6
Dundee Crematorium C Dund 91 N5
Dundon Somset 17 N10
Dundonald S Ayrs 81 M6
Dundonnell Highld 107 U7
Dundraw Cumb 66 K3
Dundreggan Highld 102 B13
Dundrennan D & G 73 S10
Dundry N Som 17 Q3
Dunecht Abers 99 P2
Dunfermline Fife 83 L1
Dunfermline Crematorium Fife 83 M1
Dunfield Gloucs 29 M8
Dunford Bridge Barns 56 J6
Dungate Kent 12 H4
Dungavel S Lans 81 T5
Dunge Wilts 18 C10
Dungeness Kent 13 L12
Dungworth Sheff 57 L9
Dunham Notts 58 D12
Dunham-on-the-Hill Ches W 55 L12
Dunhampstead Worcs 36 B8
Dunhampton Worcs 35 T7
Dunham Town Traffd 55 R9
Dunham Woodhouses Traffd 55 R9
Dunholme Lincs 58 H11
Dunino Fife 91 R9
Dunipace Falk 89 T9
Dunkeld P & K 90 F3
Dunkerton BaNES 17 T5
Dunkeswell Devon 6 F3
Dunkeswick N York 63 S10
Dunkirk Ches W 54 J12
Dunkirk Kent 13 L4
Dunkirk S Glos 28 E10
Dunkirk Wilts 18 E8
Dunk's Green Kent 12 B5
Dunlappie Angus 98 K10
Dunley Hants 19 Q10
Dunley Worcs 35 S7
Dunlop E Ayrs 81 N3
Dunmaglass Highld 102 G11
Dunmere Cnwll 3 Q3
Dunmore Falk 90 C14
Dunnet Highld 112 F2
Dunnichen Angus 91 R2
Dunning P & K 90 F9
Dunnington C York 64 F9
Dunnington E R Yk 65 R9
Dunnington Warwks 36 E10
Dunnockshaw Lancs 62 G14
Dunn Street Kent 12 E3
Dunoon Ag & B 88 E10
Dunphail Moray 103 R6
Dunragit D & G 72 F8
Duns Border 84 K8
Dunsa Derbys 56 K12
Dunsby Lincs 48 H8
Dunscar Bolton 55 R4
Dunscore D & G 74 G9
Dunscroft Donc 57 T5
Dunsdale R & Cl 70 K9
Dunsden Green Oxon 20 B7
Dunsdon Devon 14 H11
Dunsfold Surrey 10 G3
Dunsford Devon 5 U3
Dunshalt Fife 90 K9
Dunshillock Abers 105 R6
Dunsill Notts 47 N1
Dunsley N York 71 Q10
Dunsley Staffs 35 U4
Dunsmore Bucks 30 J11
Dunsop Bridge Lancs 62 D10
Dunstable C Beds 31 M8
Dunstall Staffs 46 G9
Dunstall Common Worcs 35 U12
Dunstall Green Suffk 40 B8
Dunstan Nthumb 77 Q2
Dunstan Steads Nthumb 77 Q1
Dunster Somset 16 C8
Duns Tew Oxon 29 U2
Dunston Gatesd 77 Q13
Dunston Lincs 58 J14
Dunston Norfk 51 M13
Dunston Staffs 46 B10
Dunstone Devon 5 P10
Dunstone Devon 5 S5
Dunston Heath Staffs 46 B10
Dunsville Donc 57 T5
Dunswell E R Yk 65 P12
Dunsyre S Lans 83 L9
Dunterton Devon 4 K5
Dunthrop Oxon 29 S2
Duntisbourne Abbots Gloucs 28 J6
Duntisbourne Leer Gloucs 28 J6
Duntisbourne Rouse Gloucs 28 J6
Duntish Dorset 7 S3
Duntocher W Duns 89 L11
Dunton Bucks 30 H8
Dunton C Beds 31 R4
Dunton Norfk 50 E7
Dunton Bassett Leics 37 P2
Dunton Green Kent 21 T11
Dunton Wayletts Essex 22 G9
Duntulm Highld 100 d2
Dunure S Ayrs 80 K9
Dunvant Swans 25 U12
Dunvegan Highld 100 b5
Dunwich Suffk 41 S6
Dunwood Staffs 46 B2
Durdar Cumb 67 P2
Durgan Cnwll 2 K11
Durham Dur 69 S4
Durham Cathedral Dur 69 S4
Durham Crematorium Dur 69 S4
Durham Services Dur 70 D5
Durham Tees Valley Airport S on T 70 E10
Durisdeer D & G 74 G5
Durisdeermill D & G 74 G5
Durkar Wakefd 57 M3
Durleigh Somset 16 J9
Durley Hants 9 Q5
Durley Wilts 18 K8
Durley Street Hants 9 Q5
Durlock Kent 13 Q4
Durlock Kent 13 R3
Durlow Common Herefs 35 P13
Durn Rochdl 56 D3
Durness Highld 110 J3
Durno Abers 105 L10
Duror Highld 94 D7
Durran Ag & B 87 T4
Durrington W Susx 10 J9
Durrington Wilts 18 J12
Durris Abers 99 P4
Dursley Gloucs 28 E8
Dursley Cross Gloucs 28 C3
Durston Somset 16 J11
Durweston Dorset 8 B7
Duston Nhants 37 T8
Duthil Highld 103 P11
Dutlas Powys 34 F5
Duton Hill Essex 22 F2
Dutson Cnwll 4 J3
Dutton Ches W 55 N11
Duxford Cambs 39 Q11
Duxford Oxon 29 S8
Duxford IWM Cambs 39 Q11
Dwygyfylchi Conwy 53 M7
Dwyran IoA 52 F9
Dyce C Aber 105 P13
Dyer's End Essex 40 B13
Dyfatty Carmth 25 S10
Dyffrydan Gwynd 43 N11
Dyffryn Brdgnd 26 F9
Dyffryn Myr Td 26 K7
Dyffryn V Glam 16 E2
Dyffryn Ardudwy Gwynd 43 L9
Dyffryn Castell Cerdgn 33 Q4
Dyffryn Cellwen Neath 26 F5
Dyke Lincs 48 H9
Dyke Moray 103 Q4
Dykehead Angus 98 C13
Dykehead Angus 98 F12
Dykehead N Lans 82 G7
Dykehead Stirlg 89 N6
Dykelands Abers 99 N10
Dykends Angus 98 D12
Dykeside Abers 105 L7
Dylife Powys 33 S2
Dymchurch Kent 13 M10
Dymock Gloucs 28 D1
Dyrham S Glos 28 D12
Dysart Fife 91 M13
Dyserth Denbgs 54 C11

E

Eachway Worcs 36 C5
Eachwick Nthumb 77 N11
Eagland Hill Lancs 61 S10
Eagle Lincs 58 E13
Eagle Barnsdale Lincs 58 E13
Eagle Moor Lincs 58 E13
Eaglescliffe S on T 70 F9
Eaglesfield Cumb 66 G7
Eaglesfield D & G 75 P11
Eaglesham E Rens 81 R2
Eagley Bolton 55 R4
Eairy IoM 60 d7
Eakring Notts 47 S1
Ealand N Linc 58 C4
Ealing Gt Lon 21 L6
Eals Nthumb 68 E1
Eamont Bridge Cumb 67 R7
Earby Lancs 62 J10
Earcroft Bl w D 55 Q2
Eardington Shrops 35 R2
Eardisland Herefs 34 K9
Eardisley Herefs 34 H11
Eardiston Shrops 44 J8
Eardiston Worcs 35 Q7
Earith Cambs 39 N5
Earle Nthumb 85 P13
Earlestown St Hel 55 N7
Earley Wokham 20 B8
Earlham Norfk 51 L12
Earlham Crematorium Norfk 51 M12
Earlish Highld 100 c3
Earls Barton Nhants 38 C8
Earls Colne Essex 23 L2
Earls Common Worcs 36 C9
Earl's Croome Worcs 35 U12
Earlsditton Shrops 35 P5
Earlsdon Covtry 36 K5
Earl's Down E Susx 11 U7
Earlsferry Fife 91 Q11
Earlsfield Gt Lon 21 N8
Earlsford Abers 105 N9
Earl's Green Suffk 40 H7
Earlsheaton Kirk 57 L2
Earl Shilton Leics 47 N14
Earl Soham Suffk 41 M8
Earl Sterndale Derbys 56 G13
Earlston Border 84 F11
Earlston E Ayrs 81 N5
Earl Stonham Suffk 40 K9
Earlswood Surrey 21 N13
Earlswood Warwks 36 F6
Earlswood Common Mons 27 T9
Earnley W Susx 10 C11
Earnshaw Bridge Lancs 55 M2
Earsdon N Tyne 77 S11
Earsdon Nthumb 77 P7
Earsham Norfk 41 P3
Earswick C York 64 E8
Eartham W Susx 10 E9
Earthcott S Glos 28 C10
Easby N York 70 J11
Easdale Ag & B 87 N2
Easebourne W Susx 10 E6
Easenhall Warwks 37 N5
Eashing Surrey 10 E2
Easington Bucks 30 E10
Easington Dur 70 F4
Easington E R Yk 59 Q3
Easington Nthumb 85 S12
Easington Oxon 30 E13
Easington R & Cl 71 M9
Easington Colliery Dur 70 F4
Easington Lane Sundld 70 E3
Easingwold N York 64 C6
Easole Street Kent 13 Q5
Eassie and Nevay Angus 91 M3
East Aberthaw V Glam 16 D3
East Allington Devon 5 T11
East Anstey Devon 15 U7
East Anton Hants 19 N11
East Appleton N York 69 R13
East Ashey IoW 9 R11
East Ashling W Susx 10 C9
East Aston Hants 19 P11
East Ayton N York 65 M2
East Balsdon Cnwll 14 G13
East Bank Blae G 27 N6
East Barkwith Lincs 59 L10
East Barming Kent 12 D5
East Barnby N York 71 P10
East Barnet Gt Lon 21 N3
East Barns E Loth 84 J3
East Barsham Norfk 50 F7
East Beckham Norfk 51 L6
East Bedfont Gt Lon 20 J8
East Bergholt Suffk 40 J14
East Bierley Kirk 63 P14
East Bilney Norfk 50 G10
East Blatchington E Susx 11 R10
East Bloxworth Dorset 8 B10
East Boldon S Tyne 77 T13
East Boldre Hants 9 M8
East Bolton Nthumb 77 N2
Eastbourne Darltn 70 D10
Eastbourne E Susx 11 U11
Eastbourne Crematorium E Susx 11 U10
East Bower Somset 16 K9
East Bradenham Norfk 50 F12
East Brent Somset 16 K6
Eastbridge Suffk 41 S7
East Bridgford Notts 47 S5
East Briscoe Dur 69 L9
Eastbrook V Glam 16 G2
East Buckland Devon 15 Q6
East Budleigh Devon 6 E8
Eastburn C Brad 63 L11
Eastburn E R Yk 65 M8
East Burnham Bucks 20 G6
East Burton Dorset 8 A11
Eastbury Herts 20 K4
Eastbury W Berk 19 M5
East Butsfield Dur 69 P3
East Butterwick N Linc 58 D5
Eastby N York 63 L9
East Calder W Loth 83 L5
East Carleton Norfk 51 L13
East Carlton Leeds 63 Q11
East Carlton Nhants 38 B3
East Chaldon (Chaldon Herring) Dorset 7 U8
East Challow Oxon 29 S10
East Charleton Devon 5 T12
East Chelborough Dorset 7 Q3
East Chiltington E Susx 11 P7
East Chinnock Somset 7 N2
East Chisenbury Wilts 18 H10
East Cholderton Hants 19 L11
Eastchurch Kent 23 N13
East Clandon Surrey 20 J12
East Claydon Bucks 30 F7
East Clevedon N Som 17 M2
East Coker Somset 7 P2
Eastcombe Gloucs 28 G7
Eastcombe Somset 16 G10
East Compton Somset 17 R8
East Cornworthy Devon 5 U9
East Cote Cumb 66 H1
Eastcote Gt Lon 20 K5
Eastcote Nhants 37 S10
Eastcote Solhll 36 G5
Eastcott Cnwll 14 G9
Eastcott Wilts 18 F9
East Cottingwith E R Yk 64 G11
Eastcourt Wilts 18 K8
Eastcourt Wilts 28 J9
East Cowes IoW 9 Q9
East Cowick E R Yk 57 U2
East Cowton N York 70 D12
East Cramlington Nthumb 77 R10
East Cranmore Somset 17 S8
East Creech Dorset 8 C12
East Curthwaite Cumb 67 M3
East Dean E Susx 11 T11
East Dean Gloucs 28 C3
East Dean Hants 8 K3
East Dean W Susx 10 E8
East Devon Crematorium Devon 6 E5
Eastdown Devon 5 U11
East Down Devon 15 P4
East Drayton Notts 58 C11
East Dulwich Gt Lon 21 P7
East Dundry N Som 17 Q3
East Ella C KuH 65 P14
East End Bed 38 H9
East End C Beds 31 L4
East End E R Yk 59 N1
East End E R Yk 65 R13
East End Essex 22 B5
Eastend Essex 23 M9
East End Hants 9 M9
East End Hants 19 P8
East End Herts 22 C2
East End Kent 12 F8
East End Kent 23 N13
East End M Keyn 30 K4
East End N Som 17 N2
East End Oxon 29 S4
East End Somset 17 S7
East End Suffk 40 K13
Easter Balmoral Abers 98 D5
Easter Compton S Glos 27 V11
Easter Dalziel Highld 103 L5
Eastergate W Susx 10 E9
Easterhouse C Glas 82 C5
Easter Howgate Mdloth 83 P6
Easter Kinkell Highld 102 G4
Easter Moniack Highld 102 G7
Eastern Green Covtry 36 J5
Easter Ord Abers 99 Q3
Easter Pitkierie Fife 91 S10
Easter Skeld Shet 106 t9
Easter Softlaw Border 84 K12
Easterton Wilts 18 F10
Eastertown Somset 16 K6
East Everleigh Wilts 18 K10
East Farleigh Kent 12 D5
East Farndon Nhants 37 T4
East Ferry Lincs 58 D7
Eastfield N Lans 82 G6
Eastfield N York 65 N3
East Firsby Lincs 58 H9
East Fortune E Loth 84 E3
East Garforth Leeds 63 U13
East Garston W Berk 19 N5
Eastgate Dur 69 L5
Eastgate Lincs 48 H10
Eastgate Norfk 50 K9
East Ginge Oxon 29 T10
East Goscote Leics 47 R11
East Grafton Wilts 19 L8
East Green Suffk 41 R7
East Grimstead Wilts 8 J3
East Grinstead W Susx 11 P3
East Guldeford E Susx 12 H11
East Haddon Nhants 37 S7
East Hagbourne Oxon 19 R3
East Halton N Linc 58 K3
East Ham Gt Lon 21 R6
Eastham Wirral 54 J10
Eastham Ferry Wirral 54 J10
Easthampstead Park Crematorium Br For 20 D9
Easthampton Herefs 34 K8
East Hanney Oxon 29 T9
East Hanningfield Essex 22 J7
East Hardwick Wakefd 57 Q3
East Harling Norfk 40 G3
East Harlsey N York 70 F13
East Harnham Wilts 8 G3
East Harptree BaNES 17 Q5
East Hartburn S on T 70 F9
East Hartford Nthumb 77 R10
East Harting W Susx 10 B7
East Hatch Wilts 8 C3
East Hatley Cambs 39 L10
East Hauxwell N York 69 Q14
East Haven Angus 91 S4
Eastheath Wokham 20 C9
East Heckington Lincs 48 J5
East Hedleyhope Dur 69 Q4
East Helmsdale Highld 112 B13
East Hendred Oxon 29 U10
East Heslerton N York 65 L4
East Hewish N Som 17 M4
East Hoathly E Susx 11 S7
East Holme Dorset 8 B11
Easthope Shrops 35 N1
Easthorpe Essex 23 M3
Easthorpe Notts 47 T3
East Horrington Somset 17 Q7
East Horsley Surrey 20 J12
East Horton Nthumb 85 Q12
East Howe Bmouth 8 F9
East Huntington C York 64 E8
East Huntspill Somset 16 K7
East Hyde C Beds 31 P9
East Ilkerton Devon 15 R3
East Ilsley W Berk 19 Q4
Eastington Devon 15 R11
Eastington Gloucs 28 E6
Eastington Gloucs 29 M5
East Keal Lincs 59 Q14
East Kennett Wilts 18 H7
East Keswick Leeds 63 T11
East Kilbride S Lans 81 S2
East Kimber Devon 15 L13
East Kirkby Lincs 49 M1
East Knighton Dorset 7 V7
East Knowstone Devon 15 T8
East Knoyle Wilts 8 B2
East Lambrook Somset 17 M13
East Lancashire Crematorium Bury 55 S5
Eastlands D & G 74 F11
East Langdon Kent 13 R6
East Langton Leics 37 T2
East Lavant W Susx 10 D9
East Lavington W Susx 10 E7
East Layton N York 69 Q11
Eastleach Martin Gloucs 29 P7
Eastleach Turville Gloucs 29 N6
East Leake Notts 47 Q8
East Learmouth Nthumb 85 M11
East Leigh Devon 5 R10
East Leigh Devon 5 T9
Eastleigh Devon 15 L7
East Leigh Devon 15 Q11
Eastleigh Hants 9 P5
East Lexham Norfk 50 E10
Eastling Kent 12 J4
East Linton E Loth 84 F3
East Liss Hants 10 B5
East Lockinge Oxon 29 T10
East London Crematorium Gt Lon 21 Q6
East Lound N Linc 58 C7
East Lulworth Dorset 8 B12
East Lutton N York 65 L6
East Lydeard Somset 16 G11
East Lydford Somset 17 Q10
East Malling Kent 12 D4
East Malling Heath Kent 12 C4
East Marden W Susx 10 C8
East Markham Notts 58 B12
East Martin Hants 8 F5
East Marton N York 62 J9
East Meon Hants 9 T4
East Mere Devon 16 C13
East Mersea Essex 23 P5
East Midlands Airport Leics 47 N8
East Molesey Surrey 20 K9
Eastmoor Norfk 50 B13
East Morden Dorset 8 C10
East Morton C Brad 63 M11
East Morton D & G 74 G5
East Ness N York 64 F4
East Newton E R Yk 65 T12
Eastney C Port 9 T9
Eastnor Herefs 35 R13
East Norton Leics 47 U13
Eastoft N Linc 58 D3
East Ogwell Devon 5 U6
Easton Cambs 38 H6
Easton Cumb 75 Q14
Easton Devon 5 S3
Easton Dorset 7 S10
Easton Hants 9 Q2
Easton Lincs 48 D8
Easton Norfk 50 K11
Easton Somset 17 P7
Easton Suffk 41 N9
Easton W Berk 19 P6
Easton Wilts 18 C6
Easton Grey Wilts 28 G10
Easton-in-Gordano N Som 27 U12
Easton Maudit Nhants 38 C9
Easton-on-the-Hill Nhants 48 F13
Easton Royal Wilts 18 K8
East Orchard Dorset 8 A5
East Ord Nthumb 85 P8
East Panson Devon 4 K2
East Parley Dorset 8 F9
East Peckham Kent 12 C6
East Pennar Pembks 24 G10
East Pennard Somset 17 Q9
East Perry Cambs 38 J7
East Portlemouth Devon 5 T13
East Prawle Devon 5 T13
East Preston W Susx 10 H10
East Pulham Dorset 7 T3
East Putford Devon 14 J9
East Quantoxhead Somset 16 F8
East Rainham Medway 12 F2
East Rainton Sundld 70 D3
East Ravendale NE Lin 59 M7
East Raynham Norfk 50 E8
Eastrea Cambs 39 L1
East Riding Crematorium E R Yk 65 N6
Eastriggs D & G 75 P12
East Rigton Leeds 63 T11
Eastrington E R Yk 64 H14
East Rolstone N Som 17 L4
Eastrop Swindn 29 P9
East Rounton N York 70 F12
East Rudham Norfk 50 D8
East Runton Norfk 51 L5
East Ruston Norfk 51 P8
Eastry Kent 13 R5
East Saltoun E Loth 84 D5
Eastshaw W Susx 10 D6
East Sheen Gt Lon 21 M8
East Shefford W Berk 19 N6
East Sleekburn Nthumb 77 R9
East Somerton Norfk 51 S10
East Stockwith Lincs 58 C8
East Stoke Dorset 8 B11
East Stoke Notts 47 U4
East Stour Dorset 17 V12
East Stourmouth Kent 13 Q3
East Stowford Devon 15 P7
East Stratton Hants 19 R12
East Studdal Kent 13 R6
East Sutton Kent 12 F6
East Taphouse Cnwll 4 F8
East-the-Water Devon 15 L7
East Thirston Nthumb 77 P5
East Tilbury Thurr 22 G12
East Tisted Hants 9 U2
East Torrington Lincs 58 K10
East Tuddenham Norfk 50 J11
East Tytherley Hants 8 K3
East Tytherton Wilts 18 E6
East Village Devon 15 T11
Eastville Bristl 28 B13
Eastville Lincs 49 P2
East Wall Shrops 35 M2
East Walton Norfk 50 B10
East Water Somset 17 P6
East Week Devon 5 R2
Eastwell Leics 47 U8
East Wellow Hants 9 L4
East Wemyss Fife 91 M12
East Whitburn W Loth 82 J5
Eastwick Herts 22 B5
East Wickham Gt Lon 21 S7
East Williamston Pembks 24 J10
East Winch Norfk 49 U10
East Winterslow Wilts 8 J2
East Wittering W Susx 10 B11
East Witton N York 63 N2
Eastwood Notts 47 N4
Eastwood Sthend 22 K10
East Woodburn Nthumb 76 J8
Eastwood End Cambs 39 P2
East Woodhay Hants 19 P8
East Woodlands Somset 17 U8
East Worldham Hants 10 B3
East Wretham Norfk 40 F2
East Youlstone Devon 14 G9
Eathorpe Warwks 37 L7
Eaton Ches E 56 C13
Eaton Ches W 55 N14
Eaton Leics 47 U8
Eaton Norfk 51 M12
Eaton Notts 58 B11
Eaton Oxon 29 T7
Eaton Shrops 34 J3
Eaton Shrops 35 M3
Eaton Bishop Herefs 34 K13
Eaton Bray C Beds 31 L8
Eaton Constantine Shrops 45 N12
Eaton Ford Cambs 38 J9
Eaton Green C Beds 31 L8
Eaton Hastings Oxon 29 Q8
Eaton Mascott Shrops 45 M12
Eaton Socon Cambs 38 J9
Eaton upon Tern Shrops 45 Q9
Eaves Brow Warrtn 55 P8
Eaves Green Solhll 36 J4
Ebberston N York 64 K3
Ebbesborne Wake Wilts 8 D4
Ebbw Vale Blae G 27 M6
Ebchester Dur 69 P1
Ebdon N Som 17 L4
Ebford Devon 6 C7
Ebley Gloucs 28 F6
Ebnal Ches W 45 L4
Ebnall Herefs 35 L9
Ebrington Gloucs 36 G12
Ebsworthy Devon 5 N2
Ecchinswell Hants 19 Q9
Ecclaw Border 84 K5
Ecclefechan D & G 75 N11
Eccles Border 84 K10
Eccles Kent 12 D3
Eccles Salfd 55 S7
Ecclesall Sheff 57 M10
Eccles Crematorium Salfd 55 R7
Ecclesfield Sheff 57 N8
Eccles Green Herefs 34 J11
Eccleshall Staffs 45 T8
Eccleshill C Brad 63 P12
Ecclesmachan W Loth 83 L4
Eccles on Sea Norfk 51 R8
Eccles Road Norfk 40 H3
Eccleston Ches W 44 K1
Eccleston Lancs 55 M3
Eccleston St Hel 55 L7
Eccleston Green Lancs 55 M3
Echt Abers 99 N2
Eckford Border 84 J13
Eckington Derbys 57 P11
Eckington Worcs 36 B12
Ecton Nhants 38 B8
Ecton Staffs 46 E2
Edale Derbys 56 H9
Eday Ork 106 u16
Eday Airport Ork 106 u16
Edburton W Susx 11 L8
Edderside Cumb 66 H3
Edderton Highld 109 N8
Eddington Kent 13 N2
Eddleston Border 83 P9
Eddlewood S Lans 82 D8
Edenbridge Kent 21 R13
Edenfield Lancs 55 T3
Edenhall Cumb 67 S6

Column 1

Edenham Lincs 48 G9
Edenthorpe Donc 57 T5
Edentaggart Ag & B 88 K13
Edenthorpe Donc 57 T5
Edern Gwynd 42 E6
Edgarley Somset 17 P9
Edgbaston Birm 36 F7
Edgcombe Cnwll 2 J10
Edgcott Bucks 30 E8
Edgcott Somset 15 T5
Edge Shrops 44 J12
Edgebolton Shrops 45 N9
Edge End Gloucs 28 A5
Edge Green Ches W 45 L3
Edgefield Norfk 50 J7
Edgefield Green Norfk 50 J7
Edgefold Bolton 55 R5
Edge Green Ches W 45 L3
Edgehill Warwks 37 L11
Edgeley Shrops 45 N6
Edgerton Kirk 56 H3
Edgeside Lancs 55 T2
Edgeworth Gloucs 28 H7
Edgeworthy Devon 15 T10
Edginswell Torbay 6 A11
Edgiock Worcs 36 D8
Edgmond Wrekin 45 R9
Edgmond Marsh Wrekin 34 J3
Edgton Shrops 34 J3
Edgware Gt Lon 21 L4
Edgworth Bl w D 55 R3
Edinbane Highld 100 c4
Edinburgh C Edin 83 Q4
Edinburgh Airport C Edin 83 M4
Edinburgh Castle C Edin 83 Q4
Edinburgh Old & New Town C Edin 83 Q4
Edinburgh Royal Botanic Gardens C Edin 83 P3
Edinburgh Zoo C Edin 83 N4
Edingale Staffs 46 H11
Edingham D & G 74 F13
Edingley Notts 47 S2
Edingthorpe Norfk 51 P7
Edingthorpe Green Norfk 51 P7
Edington Border 85 M7
Edington Nthumb 77 P9
Edington Somset 17 L8
Edington Wilts 18 D10
Edington Burtle Somset 17 L8
Edingworth Somset 17 L6
Edistone Devon 14 F8
Edithmead Somset 16 K7
Edith Weston Rutlnd 48 D12
Edlesborough Bucks 31 L9
Edlingham Nthumb 77 P4
Edlington Lincs 59 L12
Edmond Castle Cumb 75 U14
Edmondsham Dorset 8 F6
Edmondsley Dur 69 S4
Edmondthorpe Leics 48 C10
Edmonton Cnwll 3 N2
Edmonton Gt Lon 21 P4
Edmundbyers Dur 69 N3
Ednam Border 84 J11
Ednaston Derbys 46 H5
Edradynate P & K 97 P13
Edrom Border 85 L7
Edstaston Shrops 45 M7
Edstone Warwks 36 G8
Edvin Loach Herefs 35 Q9
Edwalton Notts 47 Q6
Edwardstone Suffk 40 F12
Edwardsville Myr Td 26 K8
Edwinsford Carmth 33 N13
Edwinstowe Notts 57 T13
Edworth C Beds 31 R4
Edwyn Ralph Herefs 35 Q9
Edzell Angus 99 L10
Edzell Woods Abers 99 L10
Efail-fach Neath 26 D8
Efail Isaf Rhondd 26 K11
Efailnewydd Gwynd 42 F6
Efail-Rhyd Powys 44 E8
Efailwen Carmth 24 K5
Efenechtyd Denbgs 44 D2
Effgill D & G 75 R7
Effingham Surrey 20 K12
Effirth Shet 106 t8
Efford Devon 15 U12
Efford Crematorium C Plym 5 N9
Egbury Hants 19 P10
Egdean W Susx 10 F6
Egerton Bolton 55 R4
Egerton Kent 12 H6
Egerton Forstal Kent 12 G6
Eggborough N York 57 S2
Eggbuckland C Plym 5 N9
Eggesford Devon 15 R10
Eggington C Beds 31 L7
Egginton Derbys 46 J8
Egglescliffe S on T 70 G10
Eggleston Dur 69 L8
Egham Surrey 20 G8
Egham Wick Surrey 20 G8
Egleton Rutlnd 48 C12
Eglingham Nthumb 77 N2
Egloshayle Cnwll 3 Q2
Egloskerry Cnwll 4 H3
Eglwysbach Conwy 53 P8
Eglwys-Brewis V Glam 16 D3
Eglwys Cross Wrexhm 45 L5
Eglwys Fach Cerdgn 33 N3
Eglwyswrw Pembks 24 K3
Egmanton Notts 58 B13
Egremont Cumb 66 F10
Egremont Wirral 54 H8
Egton N York 71 P11
Egton Bridge N York 71 P12
Egypt Buck 20 G12
Egypt Hants 19 Q12
Eigg Highld 93 M1
Eight Ash Green Essex 23 M3
Eilanreach Highld 100 h8
Eilean Donan Castle Highld 101 M6
Eisteddfa Gurig Cerdgn 33 Q4
Elan Valley Powys 33 S8
Elan Village Powys 33 S7
Elberton S Glos 28 B10
Elbridge W Susx 10 E10
Elburton C Plym 5 N10
Elcombe Swindn 18 H4
Elcot W Berk 19 P6
Eldernell Cambs 49 M14
Eldersfield Worcs 35 S14
Elderslie Rens 88 K13
Elder Street Essex 39 S14
Eldon Dur 69 S7
Eldwick C Brad 63 N11
Elfhill Abers 99 Q8
Elford Nthumb 85 S12
Elford Staffs 46 G11
Elgin Moray 103 V3
Elgol Highld 100 e8
Elham Kent 13 N7
Elie Fife 91 R11
Elilaw Nthumb 76 K4
Elim IoA 52 E6
Eling Hants 9 L6
Eling W Berk 19 S5
Elkesley Notts 57 U11
Elkstone Gloucs 28 H5
Ella Abers 104 J4
Ellacombe Torbay 6 B12
Elland Calder 56 H2
Elland Lower Edge Calder 56 H2
Ellary Ag & B 87 N10
Ellastone Staffs 46 F5
Ellel Lancs 61 T8
Ellemford Border 84 J6
Ellenabeich Ag & B 87 N3
Ellenborough Cumb 66 G6
Ellenbrook Salfd 55 R7
Ellenhall Staffs 45 T8
Ellen's Green Surrey 10 H3
Ellerbeck N York 70 F13
Ellerby N York 71 N10
Ellerdine Heath Wrekin 45 P9
Ellerhayes Devon 6 C4
Elleric Ag & B 94 E9
Ellerker E R Yk 58 H1
Ellerton E R Yk 64 G11
Ellerton N York 69 S13
Ellerton Shrops 45 R8
Ellesborough Bucks 30 H11
Ellesmere Shrops 44 J7
Ellesmere Port Ches W 54 K11
Ellingham Hants 8 H7
Ellingham Norfk 41 Q2
Ellingham Nthumb 77 T13
Ellingstring N York 63 P3
Ellington Cambs 38 J6
Ellington Nthumb 77 R7
Ellington Thorpe Cambs 38 J6
Elliots Green Somset 17 T8
Ellisfield Hants 19 U11
Ellishader Highld 100 e3
Ellistown Leics 47 M12
Ellon Abers 105 R9
Ellonby Cumb 67 P5
Elloughton E R Yk 58 G1
Ellwood Gloucs 27 V7
Elm Cambs 49 Q12
Elmbridge Worcs 36 B7
Elmdon Essex 39 Q13
Elmdon Solhll 36 G4

Column 2

Elmdon Heath Solhll 36 G4
Elmer W Susx 10 F10
Elmers End Gt Lon 21 Q9
Elmer's Green Lancs 55 M5
Elmesthorpe Leics 37 N1
Elm Green Essex 22 J6
Elmhurst Staffs 46 F11
Elmley Castle Worcs 36 C12
Elmley Lovett Worcs 35 T7
Elmore Gloucs 28 E4
Elmore Back Gloucs 28 E4
Elm Park Gt Lon 22 D10
Elmscott Devon 14 F8
Elmsett Suffk 40 J11
Elmstead Essex 23 R3
Elmstead Heath Essex 23 R3
Elmstead Market Essex 23 Q3
Elmsted Kent 13 M7
Elmstone Kent 13 Q3
Elmstone Hardwicke Gloucs 28 H3
Elmswell E R Yk 65 M8
Elmswell Suffk 40 G8
Elmton Derbys 57 R12
Elphin Highld 108 C2
Elphinstone E Loth 83 S4
Elrick Abers 99 R2
Elrig D & G 72 J10
Elrington Nthumb 76 H13
Elsecar Barns 57 N7
Elsenham Essex 22 C2
Elsfield Oxon 30 B10
Elsham N Linc 58 H4
Elsing Norfk 50 J10
Elslack N York 62 J10
Elson Hants 9 S8
Elson Shrops 44 J6
Elsrickle S Lans 83 L10
Elstead Surrey 10 E2
Elsted W Susx 10 C7
Elsthorpe Lincs 48 G9
Elston Lancs 62 B13
Elston Notts 47 U4
Elston Wilts 18 G12
Elstone Devon 15 R9
Elstow Bed 38 G11
Elstree Herts 21 L3
Elstronwick E R Yk 65 S13
Elswick Lancs 61 S12
Elswick N u Ty 77 Q13
Elsworth Cambs 39 M8
Elterwater Cumb 67 M12
Eltham Gt Lon 21 R8
Eltham Crematorium Gt Lon 21 R8
Eltisley Cambs 39 L9
Elton Bury 55 S4
Elton Cambs 38 G2
Elton Ches W 55 L11
Elton Derbys 46 H1
Elton Gloucs 28 D5
Elton Herefs 35 L6
Elton Notts 47 U6
Elton S on T 70 F9
Elton Green Ches W 55 L11
Eltringham Nthumb 77 M13
Elvanfoot S Lans 74 J2
Elvaston Derbys 47 M7
Elveden Suffk 40 C4
Elvetham Heath Hants 20 D11
Elvingston E Loth 84 D4
Elvington C York 64 G10
Elvington Kent 13 Q6
Elwell Devon 15 Q6
Elwick Hartpl 70 G6
Elwick Nthumb 85 S11
Elworth Ches E 45 R1
Elworthy Somset 16 E9
Ely Cambs 39 R4
Ely Cardif 27 L12
Emberton M Keyn 38 C11
Embleton Cumb 66 J6
Embleton Dur 70 F7
Embleton Nthumb 85 U14
Embo Highld 109 Q6
Emborough Somset 17 R6
Embo Street Highld 109 Q6
Embsay N York 63 L9
Emery Down Hants 9 L7
Emley Kirk 56 K4
Emley Moor Kirk 56 K4
Emmbrook Wokham 20 D9
Emmer Green Readg 20 B7
Emmett Carr Derbys 57 Q11
Emmington Oxon 30 F12
Emneth Norfk 49 Q12
Emneth Hungate Norfk 49 R12
Empingham Rutlnd 48 D12
Empshott Hants 10 B4
Empshott Green Hants 9 U2
Emstrey Crematorium Shrops 45 M11
Emsworth Hants 10 B9
Enborne W Berk 19 P8
Enborne Row W Berk 19 P8
Enchmarsh Shrops 35 M2
Enderby Leics 37 P1
Endmoor Cumb 61 U3
Endon Staffs 46 B3
Endon Bank Staffs 46 B3
Enfield Gt Lon 21 P3
Enfield Crematorium Gt Lon 21 Q3
Enfield Lock Gt Lon 21 Q3
Enfield Wash Gt Lon 21 Q3
Enford Wilts 18 H10
Engine Common S Glos 28 C11
England's Gate Herefs 35 N10
Englefield W Berk 19 T6
Englefield Green Surrey 20 G8
Engleseabrook Ches E 45 S3
English Bicknor Gloucs 27 V5
Englishcombe BaNES 17 T4
English Frankton Shrops 45 M8
Enham-Alamein Hants 19 N11
Enmore Somset 16 H9
Enmore Green Dorset 8 B4
Ennerdale Bridge Cumb 66 G9
Enniscaven Cnwll 3 P5
Enochdhu P & K 97 T11
Ensay Ag & B 92 K9
Ensbury Bmouth 8 F9
Ensdon Shrops 44 K10
Ensis Devon 15 N7
Enson Staffs 45 U8
Enstone Oxon 29 S3
Enterkinfoot D & G 74 G5
Enterpen N York 70 G11
Enville Staffs 35 T3
Eolaigearraidh W Isls 106 c18
Epney Gloucs 28 E6
Epperstone Notts 47 S4
Epping Essex 22 C7
Epping Green Essex 22 C7
Epping Green Herts 31 S11
Epping Upland Essex 22 C7
Eppleby N York 69 R10
Eppleworth E R Yk 65 N13
Epsom Surrey 21 M10
Epwell Oxon 37 M12
Epworth N Linc 58 C6
Epworth Turbary N Linc 58 C6
Erbistock Wrexhm 44 J5
Erbusaig Highld 100 g6
Erdington Birm 36 F2
Eridge Green E Susx 11 S4
Eridge Station E Susx 11 S4
Erines Ag & B 87 R10
Eriska Ag & B 94 C10
Eriskay W Isls 106 c18
Eriswell Suffk 40 B5
Erith Gt Lon 22 D12
Erlestoke Wilts 18 E10
Ermington Devon 5 Q10
Erpingham Norfk 51 L7
Errogie Highld 102 G11
Errol P & K 90 K6
Erskine Rens 88 K12
Ervie D & G 72 C6
Erwarton Suffk 41 M13
Erwood Powys 34 C12
Eryholme N York 70 D11
Eryrys Denbgs 44 F2
Escalls Cnwll 2 B11
Escomb Dur 69 R7
Escott Somset 16 E9
Escrick N York 64 E11
Esgair Carmth 25 M6
Esgair Cerdgn 33 M5
Esgairgeiliog Powys 43 Q12
Esgerdawe Carmth 33 M3
Esgyryn Conwy 53 P7
Esh Dur 69 Q4
Esher Surrey 21 L9
Esholt C Brad 63 P11
Eshott Nthumb 77 Q6
Eshton N York 62 J8
Esh Winning Dur 69 Q4
Eskadale Highld 102 E8
Eskbank Mdloth 83 R5
Eskdale Green Cumb 66 J12
Eskdalemuir D & G 75 Q6
Eskham Lincs 59 R6
Esperley Lane Ends Dur 69 Q8
Esprick Lancs 61 S12
Essendine Rutlnd 48 F11
Essendon Herts 31 S11
Essich Highld 102 H8
Essington Staffs 46 C13
Esslemont Abers 105 Q10

Column 3

Eston R & Cl 70 H9
Etal Nthumb 85 N11
Etchilhampton Wilts 18 F8
Etchingham E Susx 12 D10
Etchinghill Kent 13 N8
Etchinghill Staffs 46 D10
Etchingwood E Susx 11 S6
Etling Green Norfk 50 H11
Eton W & M 20 G7
Eton Wick W & M 20 F7
Etruria C Stke 45 U4
Etteridge Highld 96 J5
Ettersgill Dur 68 J7
Ettiley Heath Ches E 45 R1
Ettingshall Wolves 36 B1
Ettington Warwks 36 J11
Etton C Pete 48 J12
Etton E R Yk 65 M11
Ettrick Border 75 Q3
Ettrickbridge Border 83 S14
Ettrickhill Border 75 Q3
Etwall Derbys 46 J7
Eudon George Shrops 35 Q3
Euston Suffk 40 E5
Euximoor Drove Cambs 49 Q14
Euxton Lancs 55 N3
Evancoyd Powys 34 G8
Evanton Highld 102 J3
Evedon Lincs 48 F4
Evelix Highld 109 P6
Evenjobb Powys 34 G7
Evenley Nhants 30 C6
Evenlode Gloucs 29 P2
Evenwood Dur 69 Q8
Evenwood Gate Dur 69 Q8
Evercreech Somset 17 R9
Everingham E R Yk 64 J11
Everleigh Wilts 18 K10
Everley N York 65 M2
Eversholt C Beds 31 L6
Evershot Dorset 7 Q4
Eversley Hants 20 C10
Eversley Cross Hants 20 C10
Everthorpe E R Yk 65 L13
Everton C Beds 38 K10
Everton Hants 9 L10
Everton Lpool 54 H8
Everton Notts 57 U8
Evertown D & G 75 S11
Evesbatch Herefs 35 Q11
Evesham Worcs 36 D12
Evington C Leic 47 R13
Ewden Village Sheff 57 L7
Ewell Surrey 21 M10
Ewell Minnis Kent 13 Q7
Ewelme Oxon 19 T2
Ewen Gloucs 28 K8
Ewenny V Glam 26 G12
Ewerby Lincs 48 H4
Ewerby Thorpe Lincs 48 H4
Ewhurst Surrey 10 H2
Ewhurst Green E Susx 12 E11
Ewhurst Green Surrey 10 H3
Ewloe Flints 54 H13
Ewloe Green Flints 54 G13
Ewood Bl w D 55 Q1
Eworthy Devon 14 K13
Ewshot Hants 20 D13
Ewyas Harold Herefs 27 S1
Exbourne Devon 15 P12
Exbury Hants 9 N8
Exceat E Susx 11 S11
Exebridge Somset 16 B12
Exelby N York 63 R2
Exeter Devon 6 C6
Exeter Airport Devon 6 C6
Exeter & Devon Crematorium Devon 6 B6
Exeter Services Devon 6 C6
Exford Somset 15 U5
Exfordsgreen Shrops 45 L12
Exhall Warwks 36 F10
Exhall Warwks 37 L10
Exlade Street Oxon 19 U4
Exley Head C Brad 63 L11
Exminster Devon 6 B7
Exmoor National Park 15 U5
Exmouth Devon 6 E8
Exning Suffk 39 T7
Exton Devon 6 C7
Exton Hants 9 S4
Exton Rutlnd 48 D11
Exton Somset 16 B10
Exwick Devon 6 B6
Eyam Derbys 56 K12
Eydon Nhants 37 P10
Eye C Pete 48 K13
Eye Herefs 35 L8
Eye Suffk 40 K6
Eye Kettleby Leics 47 T10
Eyemouth Border 85 N6
Eyeworth C Beds 39 L11
Eyhorne Street Kent 12 F5
Eyke Suffk 41 P10
Eynesbury Cambs 38 J9
Eynsford Kent 21 T9
Eynsham Oxon 29 T6
Eype Dorset 7 N6
Eyre Highld 100 d4
Eythorne Kent 13 Q6
Eyton Herefs 35 L8
Eyton Shrops 34 J3
Eyton Shrops 44 J7
Eyton Wrexhm 44 K9
Eyton on Severn Shrops 45 N12
Eyton upon the Weald Moors Wrekin 45 Q11

Column 4 (F)

Faccombe Hants 19 N9
Faceby N York 70 H12
Fachwen Powys 44 B10
Facit Lancs 56 C3
Fackley Notts 47 N1
Faddiley Ches E 45 N3
Fadmoor N York 64 F2
Faerdre Swans 26 B7
Fagwyr Swans 26 B7
Faifley W Duns 89 L11
Failand N Som 17 P2
Failford S Ayrs 81 P7
Failsworth Oldham 56 C6
Fairbourne Gwynd 43 M11
Fairburn N York 64 B14
Fairfield Derbys 56 G12
Fairfield Herefs 35 T14
Fairfield Kent 12 J10
Fairfield Worcs 36 B6
Fairford Gloucs 29 N7
Fairford Park Gloucs 29 N7
Fairgirth D & G 66 C1
Fairhaven Lancs 61 Q14
Fair Isle Shet 106 r11
Fairlands Surrey 20 G12
Fairlie N Ayrs 80 J2
Fairlight E Susx 12 G13
Fairlight Cove E Susx 12 G13
Fairmile Devon 6 E5
Fairmile Surrey 20 K10
Fairmilehead C Edin 83 P4
Fair Oak Hants 9 P5
Fairoak Staffs 45 S7
Fair Oak Green Hants 19 U8
Fairseat Kent 12 B3
Fairstead Essex 22 J4
Fairstead Norfk 49 S10
Fairwarp E Susx 11 R5
Fairwater Cardif 27 L12
Fairy Cross Devon 14 K8
Fakenham Norfk 50 F8
Fakenham Magna Suffk 40 F5
Fala Mdloth 84 C6
Fala Dam Mdloth 84 C6
Faldingworth Lincs 58 H10
Faldouët Jersey 7 f2
Falfield S Glos 28 C9
Falkenham Suffk 41 N13
Falkirk Falk 82 G3
Falkirk Crematorium Falk 82 G2
Falkirk Wheel Falk 82 G2
Falkland Fife 91 L10
Fallburn S Lans 82 J11
Fallgate Derbys 57 M14
Fallin Stirlg 89 T7
Faldon Nthumb 85 R12
Fallowfield Manch 56 C8
Fallowfield Nthumb 76 J12
Falls of Blarghour Ag & B 87 R4
Falmer E Susx 11 P9
Falmouth Cnwll 3 L10
Falnash Border 75 R4
Falsgrave N York 65 P2
Falstone Nthumb 76 F9
Fanagmore Highld 110 D6
Fancott C Beds 31 N7
Fanellan Highld 102 E7
Fangdale Beck N York 70 J14
Fangfoss E R Yk 64 H9
Fanmore Ag & B 92 K10
Fannich Lodge Highld 108 J11
Fans Border 84 F10
Far Bletchley M Keyn 30 J6

Column 5

Farcet Cambs 38 K2
Far Cotton Nhants 37 U9
Farden Shrops 35 N5
Fareham Hants 9 R7
Farewell Staffs 46 E11
Far Forest Worcs 35 R5
Farforth Lincs 59 P11
Far Green Gloucs 28 D7
Farington Lancs 55 M1
Farlam Cumb 76 B14
Farleigh N Som 17 N3
Farleigh Surrey 21 Q10
Farleigh Hungerford Somset 18 B9
Farleigh Wallop Hants 19 U11
Farlesthorpe Lincs 59 S12
Farleton Cumb 61 U3
Farleton Lancs 62 B6
Farley Staffs 46 E5
Farley Wilts 8 J3
Farley Green Suffk 40 B10
Farley Green Surrey 10 J2
Farley Hill Wokham 20 B10
Farleys End Gloucs 28 E5
Farlington C Port 9 T7
Farlington N York 64 E6
Farlow Shrops 35 P4
Farmborough BaNES 17 S4
Farmbridge End Essex 22 F5
Farmcote Gloucs 29 L2
Farmcote Shrops 35 S2
Farmers Carmth 33 M12
Farmington Gloucs 29 M5
Farmoor Oxon 29 T6
Far Moor Wigan 55 M6
Farms Common Cnwll 2 H10
Farnah Green Derbys 46 K4
Farnborough Gt Lon 21 R10
Farnborough Hants 20 E12
Farnborough W Berk 19 P4
Farnborough Warwks 37 N11
Farnborough Park Hants 20 E11
Farnborough Street Hants 20 E11
Farncombe Surrey 10 F2
Farndish Bed 38 D8
Farndon Ches W 44 K3
Farndon Notts 47 U3
Farne Islands Nthumb 85 U11
Farnell Angus 99 L12
Farnham Dorset 8 D6
Farnham Essex 22 C2
Farnham N York 63 S7
Farnham Suffk 41 Q8
Farnham Surrey 20 D13
Farnham Common Bucks 20 G5
Farnham Green Essex 22 C2
Farnham Royal Bucks 20 G6
Farningham Kent 21 T9
Farnley Leeds 63 R13
Farnley N York 63 Q10
Farnley Tyas Kirk 56 J4
Farnsfield Notts 47 T2
Farnworth Bolton 55 R5
Farnworth Halton 55 M9
Far Oakridge Gloucs 28 H7
Farr Highld 102 J8
Farr Highld 111 Q4
Farraline Highld 102 G10
Farringdon Devon 6 D6
Farrington Gurney BaNES 17 R5
Farther Howegreen Essex 22 K7
Farthing Green Kent 12 F6
Farthinghoe Nhants 30 B5
Farthingloe Kent 13 Q7
Farthingstone Nhants 37 R10
Farthing Street Gt Lon 21 R10
Fartown Kirk 56 J3
Fartown Leeds 63 Q13
Farway Devon 6 F5
Fasnacloich Ag & B 94 E9
Fasnakyle Highld 102 B10
Fassfern Highld 94 E3
Fatfield Sundld 69 S2
Faugh Cumb 67 R2
Fauld Staffs 46 G8
Fauldhouse W Loth 82 H6
Faulkbourne Essex 22 J4
Faulkland Somset 17 T6
Fauls Shrops 45 N7
Faversham Kent 12 K3
Fawdington N York 63 U5
Fawdon N u Ty 77 Q12
Fawdon Nthumb 77 M2
Fawfieldhead Staffs 56 G14
Fawkham Green Kent 21 T9
Fawler Oxon 29 S4
Fawley Bucks 20 C5
Fawley Hants 9 P8
Fawley W Berk 19 N4
Fawley Chapel Herefs 28 A3
Fawnog Flints 54 F13
Fawsley Nhants 37 Q9
Faxfleet E R Yk 58 F1
Faygate W Susx 11 L4
Fazakerley Lpool 54 J7
Fazeley Staffs 46 H13
Fearby N York 63 P3
Fearn Highld 109 R9
Fearnan P & K 95 U10
Fearnbeg Highld 107 M13
Fearnhead Warrtn 55 P8
Fearnmore Highld 107 M12
Fearnoch Ag & B 87 S10
Featherstone Staffs 46 C12
Featherstone Wakefd 57 P2
Feckenham Worcs 36 D8
Feering Essex 23 L4
Feetham N York 69 L13
Feizor N York 62 F6
Felbridge Surrey 11 N3
Felbrigg Norfk 51 L6
Felcourt Surrey 11 P2
Felden Herts 31 M12
Felindre Carmth 25 R7
Felindre Carmth 26 A5
Felindre Cerdgn 32 K10
Felindre Powys 34 E3
Felindre Powys 33 S3
Felindre Swans 26 A7
Felindre Farchog Pembks 24 K3
Felin Fach Cerdgn 32 K9
Felinfach Powys 34 C14
Felinfoel Carmth 25 T10
Felingwmisaf Carmth 25 T6
Felingwm Uchaf Carmth 25 T6
Felin-newydd Powys 34 D13
Felixkirk N York 64 B3
Felixstowe Suffk 41 P14
Felixstoweferry Suffk 41 Q14
Felkirk Wakefd 57 N4
Felling Gatesd 77 R13
Fell Lane C Brad 63 L11
Fell Side Cumb 67 M5
Felmersham Bed 38 E9
Felmingham Norfk 51 N8
Felpham W Susx 10 F11
Felsham Suffk 40 F9
Felsted Essex 22 G3
Feltham Gt Lon 20 K8
Felthamhill Surrey 20 K8
Felthorpe Norfk 51 L10
Felton Herefs 35 N11
Felton N Som 17 P3
Felton Nthumb 77 P5
Felton Butler Shrops 44 J10
Feltwell Norfk 50 B14
Fenay Bridge Kirk 56 J3
Fence Lancs 62 G12
Fence Rothm 57 P9
Fence Houses Sundld 70 D2
Fencott Oxon 30 B9
Fendike Corner Lincs 59 R14
Fen Ditton Cambs 39 Q8
Fen Drayton Cambs 39 L7
Fen End Lincs 49 L8
Fen End Solhll 36 H5
Fenham Nthumb 85 R10
Feniscowles Bl w D 55 P1
Feniton Devon 6 E5
Fenn Green Shrops 35 S4
Fenn Street Medway 22 K13
Fenny Bentley Derbys 46 G3
Fenny Bridges Devon 6 F5
Fenny Compton Warwks 37 M10
Fenny Drayton Leics 37 L2
Fenny Stratford M Keyn 30 J6
Fenrother Nthumb 77 P7
Fenstanton Cambs 39 L7
Fenstead End Suffk 40 D11
Fen Street Norfk 40 H3
Fen Street Suffk 40 K6
Fenton C Stke 45 U4
Fenton Cambs 39 M5
Fenton Cumb 76 A14
Fenton Lincs 58 C13
Fenton Lincs 58 D13
Fenton Notts 58 C10
Fenton Nthumb 85 P12
Fenton Barns E Loth 84 E2
Fenwick Donc 57 S3
Fenwick E Ayrs 81 P4
Fenwick Nthumb 77 M11
Fenwick Nthumb 85 R10

Column 6

Feock Cnwll 3 L9
Feolin Ferry Ag & B 86 G12
Fergushill N Ayrs 81 L4
Feriniquarrie Highld 100 a4
Fermain Bay Guern 7 e4
Fern Angus 98 H11
Ferndale Rhondd 26 J8
Ferndown Dorset 8 F8
Ferness Highld 103 P7
Fernham Oxon 29 Q9
Fernhill Heath Worcs 35 U9
Fernhurst W Susx 10 D5
Fernie Fife 91 L9
Ferniegair S Lans 82 E8
Fernilea Highld 100 c6
Fernilee Derbys 56 F11
Fernwood Notts 48 B3
Ferrensby N York 63 T7
Ferrindonald Highld 100 f9
Ferring W Susx 10 H10
Ferrybridge Wakefd 57 Q2
Ferryden Angus 99 N12
Ferry Point Highld 109 P7
Ferryside Carmth 25 Q8
Ferrytown Highld 109 N7
Fersfield Norfk 40 J4
Fersit Highld 96 D5
Feshiebridge Highld 97 N4
Fetcham Surrey 21 K12
Fetlar Shet 106 w4
Fetterangus Abers 105 R5
Fettercairn Abers 99 M9
Fewcott Oxon 30 B7
Fewston N York 63 P9
Ffairfach Carmth 26 A3
Ffair Rhos Cerdgn 33 P7
Ffaldybrenin Carmth 33 M12
Ffawyddog Powys 27 N5
Ffestiniog Gwynd 43 P5
Ffestiniog Railway Gwynd 43 N5
Ffordd-las Denbgs 54 D14
Fforest Carmth 25 U10
Fforest Mons 27 P3
Fforest Fach Swans 26 A8
Fforest Goch Neath 26 D7
Ffostrasol Cerdgn 32 G11
Ffrith Flints 44 G2
Ffynnonddewi Cerdgn 32 G10
Ffynnongroyw Flints 54 D10
Ffynnon-oer Cerdgn 32 K10
Fiag Lodge Highld 110 K11
Fickleshole Surrey 21 Q10
Fiddington Gloucs 28 H1
Fiddington Somset 16 H8
Fiddleford Dorset 7 V2
Fiddlers Green Cnwll 3 L5
Fiddlers Hamlet Essex 22 C7
Field Staffs 46 D7
Field Broughton Cumb 61 R3
Field Dalling Norfk 50 H6
Fieldhead Cumb 67 Q5
Field Head Leics 47 M12
Fifehead Magdalen Dorset 17 U12
Fifehead Neville Dorset 7 U2
Fifehead St Quintin Dorset 7 U2
Fife Keith Moray 104 E5
Fifield Oxon 29 P4
Fifield W & M 20 F7
Fifield Wilts 18 H10
Fifield Bavant Wilts 8 E3
Figheldean Wilts 18 H12
Filands Wilts 28 J10
Filby Norfk 51 S11
Filey N York 65 R3
Filgrave M Keyn 38 C11
Filkins Oxon 29 P7
Filleigh Devon 15 Q7
Filleigh Devon 15 R10
Fillingham Lincs 58 F10
Fillongley Warwks 36 J3
Filmore Hill Hants 9 T3
Filton S Glos 28 B12
Fimber E R Yk 64 K8
Finavon Angus 98 H12
Fincham Norfk 49 U12
Finchampstead Wokham 20 C10
Fincharn Ag & B 87 S5
Finchdean Hants 9 U6
Finchingfield Essex 22 G1
Finchley Gt Lon 21 N4
Findern Derbys 46 K7
Findhorn Moray 103 R3
Findhorn Bridge Highld 103 M10
Findochty Moray 104 E2
Findo Gask P & K 90 F7
Findon Abers 99 S4
Findon W Susx 10 J9
Findon Mains Highld 102 H3
Findrack House Abers 99 L3
Finedon Nhants 38 D6
Fineshade Nhants 38 E1
Fingal Street Suffk 41 M7
Fingask P & K 90 K6
Fingerpost Worcs 35 R6
Fingest Bucks 20 C4
Finghall N York 63 P1
Fingland Cumb 67 L1
Fingland D & G 74 F3
Finglesham Kent 13 R5
Fingringhoe Essex 23 P4
Finkle Green Essex 40 B12
Finkle Street Barns 57 M7
Finlarig Stirlg 95 R11
Finmere Oxon 30 D5
Finnart P & K 95 N8
Finningham Suffk 40 J7
Finningley Donc 57 V7
Finsbay W Isls 106 f10
Finstall Worcs 36 C6
Finsthwaite Cumb 61 R2
Finstock Oxon 29 S5
Finstown Ork 106 s18
Fintry Abers 105 L5
Fintry Stirlg 89 P8
Finzean Abers 99 L4
Fionnphort Ag & B 92 J13
Fionnsbhagh W Isls 106 f10
Firbank Cumb 62 C2
Firbeck Rothm 57 S9
Firby N York 64 G6
Firby N York 63 S2
Firgrove Rochdl 56 D4
Firle E Susx 11 R9
Firsby Lincs 59 R14
Firsdown Wilts 8 J2
Fir Tree Dur 69 Q6
Fishbourne IoW 9 R10
Fishbourne W Susx 10 C9
Fishburn Dur 70 E6
Fishcross Clacks 90 C13
Fisher W Susx 10 D9
Fisherford Abers 104 K8
Fisher's Pond Hants 9 P4
Fisher's Row Lancs 61 S10
Fisherstreet W Susx 10 F4
Fisherton Highld 102 K5
Fisherton S Ayrs 80 J9
Fisherton de la Mere Wilts 18 F13
Fishery Estate W & M 20 F7
Fishguard Pembks 24 G4
Fishlake Donc 57 U3
Fishleigh Devon 15 N11
Fishmere End Lincs 49 M5
Fishnish Pier Ag & B 93 R10
Fishpond Bottom Dorset 7 L5
Fishponds Bristl 28 B13
Fishtoft Lincs 49 N4
Fishtoft Drove Lincs 49 M4
Fishwick Lancs 62 B13
Fiskavaig Highld 100 c6
Fiskerton Lincs 58 H12
Fiskerton Notts 47 U3
Fitling E R Yk 65 S13
Fittleton Wilts 18 H11
Fittleworth W Susx 10 G7
Fitton End Cambs 49 P11
Fitz Shrops 44 K10
Fitzhead Somset 16 F11
Fitzwilliam Wakefd 57 P4
Five Ash Down E Susx 11 R5
Five Ashes E Susx 11 S5
Five Bells Somset 16 E8
Five Bridges Herefs 35 Q11
Fivecrosses Ches W 55 M11
Fivehead Somset 17 L11
Fivelanes Cnwll 4 G4
Five Lanes Mons 27 S9
Five Oak Green Kent 12 B6
Five Oaks Jersey 7 f3
Five Oaks W Susx 10 H5
Five Roads Carmth 25 S9
Five Wents Kent 12 F5
Flack's Green Essex 22 J4
Flackwell Heath Bucks 20 E4
Fladbury Worcs 36 C11
Fladdabister Shet 106 u10
Flagg Derbys 56 H13
Flamborough E R Yk 65 T5
Flamborough Head E R Yk 65 U5

Column 7

Flamingo Land Theme Park N York 64 H4
Flamstead Herts 31 N10
Flamshaw Wakefd 57 M2
Flansham W Susx 10 F10
Flanshaw Wakefd 57 M2
Flasby N York 62 J8
Flash Staffs 56 F13
Flashader Highld 100 c4
Flaunden Herts 31 M12
Flawborough Notts 47 U5
Flawith N York 63 U6
Flax Bourton N Som 17 P3
Flaxby N York 63 T8
Flaxley Gloucs 28 C4
Flaxmere Ches W 55 N12
Flaxpool Somset 16 F9
Flaxton N York 64 F6
Fleckney Leics 37 R2
Flecknoe Warwks 37 P8
Fledborough Notts 58 D12
Fleet Dorset 7 R8
Fleet Hants 20 D12
Fleet Hants 9 T9
Fleet Lincs 49 N9
Fleetend Hants 9 Q7
Fleet Hargate Lincs 49 N9
Fleet Services Hants 20 C11
Fleetwood Lancs 61 Q10
Flemingston V Glam 16 D3
Flemington S Lans 81 U1
Flempton Suffk 40 D7
Fletchersbridge Cnwll 4 E7
Fletching E Susx 11 R5
Fleur-de-lis Caerph 27 M8
Flexbury Cnwll 14 F11
Flexford Surrey 20 F12
Flimby Cumb 66 F6
Flimwell E Susx 12 D9
Flint Flints 54 F12
Flintham Notts 47 U4
Flint Mountain Flints 54 F12
Flinton E R Yk 65 S12
Flishinghurst Kent 12 E8
Flitcham Norfk 50 B8
Flitton C Beds 31 N5
Flitwick C Beds 31 N5
Flixborough N Linc 58 E4
Flixborough Stather N Linc 58 E4
Flixton Gt Man 55 S8
Flixton N York 65 N4
Flixton Suffk 41 P3
Flixton Traffd 55 S8
Flockton Kirk 56 K4
Flockton Green Kirk 57 L4
Flodden Nthumb 85 N12
Flodigarry Highld 100 e3
Flookburgh Cumb 61 R4
Flordon Norfk 41 L1
Flore Nhants 37 R8
Flotterton Nthumb 77 M5
Flowers Green E Susx 11 U8
Flowton Suffk 40 J11
Flushdyke Wakefd 57 L2
Flushing Cnwll 3 L10
Fluxton Devon 6 E6
Flyford Flavell Worcs 36 C10
Fobbing Thurr 22 H11
Fochabers Moray 104 C4
Fochriw Caerph 27 L6
Fockerby N Linc 58 E3
Foddington Somset 17 Q11
Foel Powys 43 U11
Foel-gastell Carmth 25 U8
Foggathorpe E R Yk 64 H12
Fogo Border 84 J9
Fogwatt Moray 104 B4
Foindle Highld 110 D7
Folda Angus 98 C11
Fole Staffs 46 D6
Foleshill Covtry 37 L4
Folke Dorset 7 S2
Folkestone Kent 13 P8
Folkingham Lincs 48 G7
Folkington E Susx 11 T10
Folksworth Cambs 38 J3
Folkton N York 65 N3
Folla Rule Abers 105 L8
Follifoot N York 63 S9
Folly Gate Devon 15 N13
Fonmon V Glam 16 E3
Fonthill Bishop Wilts 8 C2
Fonthill Gifford Wilts 8 C2
Fontmell Magna Dorset 8 B5
Fontmell Parva Dorset 8 A6
Fontwell W Susx 10 F9
Font-y-gary V Glam 16 E3
Foolow Derbys 56 J11
Foots Cray Gt Lon 21 S8
Forbestown Abers 104 D13
Forcett N York 69 R10
Ford Ag & B 87 R5
Ford Bucks 30 F11
Ford Derbys 57 Q10
Ford Devon 15 N5
Ford Devon 5 S7
Ford Devon 5 P10
Ford Gloucs 29 L2
Ford Nthumb 85 N12
Ford Shrops 44 K11
Ford Somset 16 E11
Ford Somset 16 F9
Ford Staffs 46 D3
Ford W Susx 10 G10
Ford Wilts 28 C12
Ford Wilts 18 B5
Forda Devon 14 K13
Fordcombe Kent 11 S2
Fordell Fife 90 J14
Forden Powys 44 F12
Ford End Essex 22 G4
Forder Green Devon 5 U7
Ford Green Lancs 61 T11
Fordham Cambs 39 T6
Fordham Essex 23 N3
Fordham Norfk 49 S14
Fordham Heath Essex 23 N3
Ford Heath Shrops 44 K11
Fordingbridge Hants 8 G6
Fordon E R Yk 65 N4
Fordoun Abers 99 N8
Ford's Green Suffk 40 J7
Fordstreet Essex 23 M3
Ford Street Somset 16 G13
Fordton Devon 15 T13
Fordwells Oxon 29 R5
Fordwich Kent 13 N4
Fordyce Abers 104 H3
Forebridge Staffs 46 B9
Foreland Ag & B 86 C13
Foremark Derbys 47 L8
Forest N York 69 S11
Forest Becks Lancs 62 E9
Forestburn Gate Nthumb 77 M6
Forest Chapel Ches E 56 E12
Forest Gate Gt Lon 21 R6
Forest Green Surrey 10 J2
Forest Hall Cumb 67 R12
Forest Hall N Tyne 77 R12
Forest Head Cumb 76 B14
Forest Hill Gt Lon 21 Q8
Forest Hill Oxon 30 C11
Forest-in-Teesdale Dur 68 J7
Forest Lane Head N York 63 S8
Forest Lodge Ag & B 94 J4
Forest Mill Clacks 90 D13
Forest Row E Susx 11 Q3
Forest Side IoW 9 P11
Forestside W Susx 10 B8
Forest Town Notts 57 R13
Forfar Angus 98 H13
Forgandenny P & K 90 G7
Forge Powys 33 Q2
Forge Hammer Torfn 27 Q8
Forge Side Torfn 27 N6
Forgie Moray 104 D4
Forgue Abers 104 J6
Forhill Worcs 36 E5
Formby Sefton 54 H6
Forncett End Norfk 40 K2
Forncett St Mary Norfk 41 L2
Forncett St Peter Norfk 41 L2
Fornham All Saints Suffk 40 D7
Fornham St Martin Suffk 40 D7
Fornighty Highld 103 P5
Forres Moray 103 R4
Forsbrook Staffs 46 C5
Forse Highld 112 G10
Forshaw Heath Warwks 36 F5
Forsinard Highld 111 T7
Fort Augustus Highld 96 F4
Forteviot P & K 90 F7
Fort George Highld 102 K4
Forth S Lans 82 J8
Forthampton Gloucs 28 G1
Forth Rail Bridge C Edin 83 M2
Forth Road Bridge Fife 83 L2
Fortingall P & K 95 U10
Forton Hants 19 Q11
Forton Lancs 61 T9
Forton Shrops 44 K10
Forton Somset 7 L4
Forton Staffs 45 S9
Fortrie Abers 104 K6
Fortrose Highld 102 K4
Fortuneswell Dorset 7 R10
Fort William Highld 94 G3

Column 8

Forty Green Bucks 20 F3
Forty Hill Gt Lon 21 P3
Forward Green Suffk 40 J9
Fosbury Wilts 19 M9
Foscot Oxon 29 P3
Foscote Nhants 37 T5
Fosdyke Lincs 49 M7
Fosdyke Bridge Lincs 49 M7
Foss P & K 97 M12
Fossebridge Gloucs 29 L5
Foster Street Essex 22 C6
Foston Derbys 46 G7
Foston Leics 37 R2
Foston Lincs 48 C5
Foston N York 64 F6
Foston on the Wolds E R Yk 65 Q8
Fotherby Lincs 59 P8
Fothergill Cumb 66 F6
Fotheringhay Nhants 38 F2
Foulbridge Cumb 67 N3
Foulby Wakefd 57 N3
Foulden Border 85 N8
Foulden Norfk 50 C14
Foul End Warwks 36 H2
Foul Mile E Susx 11 U7
Foulridge Lancs 62 H11
Foulsham Norfk 50 H8
Foundry Cnwll 2 G9
Fountainhall Border 84 C9
Four Ashes Solhll 36 G5
Four Ashes Staffs 46 B12
Four Ashes Staffs 35 T4
Four Cabots Guern 7 d3
Four Crosses Powys 44 G10
Four Crosses Powys 44 C12
Four Crosses Staffs 46 C11
Four Elms Kent 21 S13
Four Forks Somset 16 H9
Four Gates Bolton 55 P5
Four Gotes Cambs 49 P11
Four Lane End Barns 57 L6
Four Lane Ends Ches W 45 N1
Four Lanes Cnwll 2 H9
Fourlanes End Ches E 45 T2
Four Marks Hants 9 U2
Four Mile Bridge IoA 52 C7
Four Oaks Birm 36 F14
Four Oaks E Susx 12 G11
Four Oaks Gloucs 28 D2
Four Oaks Solhll 36 G5
Fourpenny Highld 109 Q6
Four Points W Berk 19 S5
Four Roads Carmth 25 R9
Four Shire Stone Warwks 29 P1
Fourstones Nthumb 76 H12
Four Throws Kent 12 E10
Four Wents Kent 12 C8
Fovant Wilts 8 E3
Foveran Abers 105 R11
Fowey Cnwll 4 F10
Fowlershill Aberdn 105 Q13
Fowley Common Warrtn 55 Q7
Fowlhall Kent 12 D6
Fowlis Angus 91 M4
Fowlis Wester P & K 90 D7
Fowlmere Cambs 39 P11
Fownhope Herefs 35 N13
Foxbar Rens 89 L13
Foxcombe Devon 15 P13
Fox Corner Surrey 20 G12
Foxcote Gloucs 29 L5
Foxcote Somset 17 T5
Foxdale IoM 60 d7
Foxearth Essex 40 D12
Foxendown Kent 12 B2
Foxfield Cumb 61 N2
Foxhole Cnwll 3 P6
Foxholes N York 65 N5
Foxhunt Green E Susx 11 S7
Foxley Nhants 37 S10
Foxley Norfk 50 H9
Foxley Wilts 28 G10
Foxlydiate Worcs 36 D7
Fox Street Essex 23 P3
Foxt Staffs 46 D4
Foxton Cambs 39 P11
Foxton Dur 70 E7
Foxton Leics 37 T3
Foxton N York 70 G12
Foxup N York 62 H4
Foxwist Green Ches W 55 P13
Foxwood Shrops 35 P5
Foy Herefs 28 A3
Foyers Highld 102 F10
Foynesfield Highld 103 N5
Fraddam Cnwll 2 F10
Fraddon Cnwll 3 N5
Fradley Staffs 46 F11
Fradswell Staffs 46 C7
Fraisthorpe E R Yk 65 Q7
Framfield E Susx 11 R6
Framingham Earl Norfk 51 N13
Framingham Pigot Norfk 51 N13
Framlingham Suffk 41 N8
Frampton Dorset 7 R6
Frampton Lincs 49 M6
Frampton Cotterell S Glos 28 C11
Frampton Mansell Gloucs 28 H7
Frampton-on-Severn Gloucs 28 D6
Frampton West End Lincs 49 M5
Framsden Suffk 41 L9
Framwellgate Moor Dur 69 S4
Franche Worcs 35 T5
Frankaborough Devon 14 K13
Frankby Wirral 54 F9
Frankfort Norfk 51 P8
Franklands Gate Herefs 35 M11
Frankley Worcs 36 C4
Frankley Services Worcs 36 C4
Franksbridge Powys 34 D9
Frankton Warwks 37 N6
Frankton Green E Susx 11 T3
Frating Essex 23 Q3
Frating Green Essex 23 Q3
Fratton C Port 9 T8
Freathy Cnwll 4 K10
Freckenham Suffk 39 U6
Freckleton Lancs 61 T14
Freebirch Derbys 57 M12
Freeby Leics 48 B9
Freefolk Hants 19 R11
Freehay Staffs 46 D5
Freeland Oxon 29 T5
Freestone Pembks 24 H9
Freethorpe Norfk 51 R12
Freethorpe Common Norfk 51 R12
Freiston Lincs 49 N4
Fremington Devon 15 N6
Fremington N York 69 N13
Frenchay S Glos 28 B12
Frenchbeer Devon 5 R3
French Street Kent 21 R12
Frenich P & K 95 U6
Frensham Surrey 10 D2
Freshfield Sefton 54 H5
Freshford Wilts 17 U4
Freshwater IoW 9 L11
Freshwater Bay IoW 9 L11
Freshwater East Pembks 24 H11
Fressingfield Suffk 41 M5
Freston Suffk 41 L13
Freswick Highld 112 J3
Fretherne Gloucs 28 D6
Frettenham Norfk 51 M10
Freuchie Fife 91 L10
Freystrop Pembks 24 G8
Friar Park Sandw 36 D2
Friar's Gate E Susx 11 R4
Friars' Hel Cambs 39 M4
Friar Waddon Dorset 7 R7
Friday Bridge Cambs 49 Q13
Friday Street E Susx 11 T10
Friday Street Suffk 41 P9
Friday Street Suffk 41 Q9
Friday Street Surrey 10 K2
Fridaythorpe E R Yk 64 K9
Friden Derbys 56 H14
Friendly Calder 56 G2
Friern Barnet Gt Lon 21 N4
Friesland Ag & B 92 F8
Friesthorpe Lincs 58 H10
Frieston Lincs 48 D4
Frieth Bucks 20 C4
Friezeland Notts 47 N3
Frilford Oxon 29 T8
Frilsham W Berk 19 S6
Frimley Surrey 20 F11
Frimley Green Surrey 20 F11
Frindsbury Medway 12 D2
Fring Norfk 50 C7
Fringford Oxon 30 C7
Frinsted Kent 12 G4
Frinton-on-Sea Essex 23 T4
Friockheim Angus 91 S2
Friog Gwynd 43 M11
Frisby on the Wreake Leics 47 S11

Column 9

Fritchley Derbys 47 L3
Frith Bank Lincs 49 M4
Frith Common Worcs 35 Q7
Fritham Hants 8 K6
Frithelstock Devon 15 L9
Frithelstock Stone Devon 15 L9
Frithend Hants 10 C3
Frithsden Herts 31 M11
Frithville Lincs 49 M3
Frittenden Kent 12 F7
Frittiscombe Devon 5 U12
Fritton Norfk 41 M2
Fritton Norfk 51 S13
Fritwell Oxon 30 B7
Frizinghall C Brad 63 N12
Frizington Cumb 66 F10
Frocester Gloucs 28 E7
Frodesley Shrops 45 M13
Frodsham Ches W 55 M11
Frog End Cambs 39 Q10
Frogden Border 84 K13
Froggatt Derbys 56 K11
Froghall Staffs 46 D4
Frogham Hants 8 H6
Frogham Kent 13 Q5
Frogmore Devon 5 S12
Frognall Lincs 48 H11
Frogpool Cnwll 2 K8
Frog Pool Worcs 35 S7
Frogwell Cnwll 4 J7
Frolesworth Leics 37 P2
Frome Somset 17 U7
Frome St Quintin Dorset 7 Q4
Fromes Hill Herefs 35 Q11
Fron Denbgs 54 C13
Fron Gwynd 42 G6
Fron Gwynd 52 H12
Fron Powys 34 E14
Fron Powys 44 F13
Froncysyllte Denbgs 44 G5
Fron-goch Gwynd 43 T6
Fron Isaf Wrexhm 44 G5
Frostenden Suffk 41 S4
Frosterley Dur 69 M5
Froxfield C Beds 31 L5
Froxfield Wilts 19 L7
Froxfield Green Hants 9 U4
Fryern Hill Hants 9 P4
Fryerning Essex 22 F7
Fryton N York 64 F5
Fulbeck Lincs 48 D3
Fulbourn Cambs 39 R9
Fulbrook Oxon 29 Q5
Fulflood Hants 9 P3
Fulford C York 64 E10
Fulford Somset 16 H11
Fulford Staffs 46 C6
Fulham Gt Lon 21 N7
Fulking W Susx 11 L8
Fullaford Devon 15 Q5
Fuller's End Essex 22 C2
Fuller's Moor Ches W 45 L3
Fuller Street Essex 22 H4
Fuller Street Kent 12 B4
Fullerton Hants 19 N13
Fulletby Lincs 59 N12
Fullready Warwks 36 J11
Full Sutton E R Yk 64 G9
Fullwood E Ayrs 81 M2
Fulmer Bucks 20 G5
Fulmodeston Norfk 50 G7
Fulnetby Lincs 58 J11
Fulney Lincs 49 L9
Fulstone Kirk 56 J5
Fulstow Lincs 59 Q6
Fulwell Oxon 29 S3
Fulwell Sundld 77 T14
Fulwood Lancs 61 U13
Fulwood Notts 47 N3
Fulwood Sheff 57 M9
Fulwood Somset 16 H12
Fundenhall Norfk 41 L1
Funtington W Susx 10 C9
Funtley Hants 9 R7
Funtullich P & K 95 V13
Furley Devon 6 J4
Furnace Ag & B 87 U5
Furnace Carmth 25 T10
Furnace Cerdgn 33 N2
Furnace End Warwks 36 J2
Furner's Green E Susx 11 Q5
Furness Vale Derbys 56 F10
Further Quarter Kent 12 G8
Furtho Nhants 30 G4
Furzehill Devon 15 Q3
Furzehill Dorset 8 E8
Furzeley Corner Hants 9 S7
Furze Platt W & M 20 E6
Furzley Hants 8 K6
Fyfett Somset 6 H2
Fyfield Essex 22 E6
Fyfield Hants 19 L12
Fyfield Oxon 29 T8
Fyfield Wilts 18 H8
Fyfield Wilts 18 J7
Fyfield Bavant Wilts 8 E3
Fylingthorpe N York 71 R12
Fyning W Susx 10 C6
Fyvie Abers 105 M8

Column 10 (G)

Gabroc Hill E Ayrs 81 P2
Gaddesby Leics 47 S11
Gaddesden Row Herts 31 N10
Gadfa IoA 52 G5
Gadlas Shrops 44 J6
Gaer Powys 27 M3
Gaer-llwyd Mons 27 S8
Gaerwen IoA 52 G8
Gagingwell Oxon 29 T3
Gailes N Ayrs 81 L5
Gailey Staffs 46 B11
Gainford Dur 69 Q9
Gainsborough Lincs 58 D9
Gainsford End Essex 40 B13
Gairloch Highld 107 N9
Gairlochy Highld 96 D2
Gairneybridge P & K 90 H12
Gaisgill Cumb 68 D11
Gaitsgill Cumb 67 N3
Galashiels Border 84 D12
Galgate Lancs 61 T8
Galhampton Somset 17 R11
Gallanachbeg Ag & B 94 B13
Gallanachmore Ag & B 94 B13
Gallantry Bank Ches E 45 M3
Gallatown Fife 91 L13
Galley Common Warwks 36 K2
Galleywood Essex 22 H7
Gallovie Highld 96 H6
Galloway Forest Park 73 M4
Gallowfauld Angus 91 P3
Gallowhill P & K 90 K5
Gallows Green Worcs 36 B7
Gallows Green Staffs 46 D5
Gallowstree Common Oxon 19 U4
Galltair Highld 100 h7
Gallt-y-foel Gwynd 52 J10
Galmisdale Highld 92 J2
Galmpton Devon 5 R12
Galmpton Torbay 6 A13
Galphay N York 63 R5
Galston E Ayrs 81 Q5
Gamballs Green Staffs 56 F13
Gambles Green Essex 22 J4
Gamblesby Cumb 68 C4
Gamelsby Cumb 67 L2
Gamlingay Cambs 39 L10
Gamlingay Cinques Cambs 39 L10
Gamlingay Great Heath Cambs 38 K10
Gammersgill N York 63 L2
Gamston Notts 47 R6
Gamston Notts 58 B11
Ganarew Herefs 27 U4
Ganavan Bay Ag & B 94 B12
Gang Cnwll 4 J7
Ganllwyd Gwynd 43 P9
Gannachy Angus 98 K9
Ganstead E R Yk 65 R13
Ganthorpe N York 64 F5
Ganton N York 65 M4
Ganwick Corner Herts 21 N3
Gappah Devon 5 V4
Garbity Moray 104 C5
Garboldisham Norfk 40 H4
Garbole Highld 102 K11
Garchory Abers 104 C13
Gardeners Green Wokham 20 D9
Gardenstown Abers 105 M3
Garden City Flints 54 H13
Garden Village Sheff 57 L7
Garderhouse Shet 106 t9
Gardham E R Yk 65 M11
Gare Hill Somset 17 U8
Garelochhead Ag & B 88 F8
Garford Oxon 29 T8
Garforth Leeds 63 U13

132 Hanley Child - Hopton Castle

Hanley Child Worcs 35 Q7
Hanley Swan Worcs 35 T12
Hanley William Worcs 35 Q7
Hanlith N York 62 H7
Hanmer Wrexhm 45 L6
Hannaford Devon 15 P7
Hannah Lincs 59 S11
Hannington Hants 19 R9
Hannington Nhants 38 B6
Hannington Swindn 29 N9
Hannington Wick Swindn 29 N8
Hanscombe End C Beds 31 P6
Hanslope M Keyn 38 B11
Hanthorpe Lincs 48 G9
Hanwell Gt Lon 21 L7
Hanwell Oxon 37 M12
Hanwood Shrops 44 K12
Hanworth Gt Lon 20 K8
Hanworth Norfk 51 L6
Happendon S Lans 82 G12
Happendon Services S Lans 82 G12
Happisburgh Norfk 51 Q7
Happisburgh Common Norfk 51 Q8
Hapsford Ches W 55 L12
Hapton Lancs 62 F13
Hapton Norfk 41 L1
Harberton Devon 5 T9
Harbertonford Devon 5 T9
Harbledown Kent 13 M4
Harborne Birm 36 D4
Harborough Magna Warwks 37 N5
Harbottle Nthumb 76 J5
Harbourneford Devon 5 S8
Harbours Hill Worcs 36 C7
Harbridge Hants 8 G6
Harbridge Green Hants 8 G6
Harbury Warwks 37 L9
Harby Leics 47 T7
Harby Notts 58 E12
Harcombe Devon 6 A8
Harcombe Devon 6 G6
Harcombe Bottom Devon 6 K5
Harden C Brad 63 M12
Harden Wsall 46 D13
Hardenhuish Wilts 18 D6
Hardgate Abers 99 P3
Hardgate D & G 74 F12
Hardgate N York 63 R7
Hardgate W Duns 89 M11
Hardham W Susx 10 G7
Hardhorn Lancs 61 R12
Hardingham Norfk 50 H13
Hardingstone Nhants 37 U9
Hardington Somset 17 T6
Hardington Mandeville Somset 7 P2
Hardington Marsh Somset 7 P3
Hardington Moor Somset 7 P2
Hardisworthy Devon 14 F8
Hardley Hants 9 N7
Hardley Street Norfk 51 Q13
Hardmead M Keyn 38 D11
Hardraw N York 62 H1
Hardsough Lancs 55 S2
Hardstoft Derbys 57 P14
Hardway Hants 9 S8
Hardway Somset 17 T10
Hardwick Bucks 30 H9
Hardwick Cambs 39 N9
Hardwick Nhants 38 B7
Hardwick Norfk 41 M3
Hardwick Oxon 29 S6
Hardwick Oxon 30 C7
Hardwick Rothm 57 Q9
Hardwick Wsall 46 E14
Hardwicke Gloucs 28 E5
Hardwicke Gloucs 28 H2
Hardwick Hall Dur 70 D7
Hardy's Green Essex 23 M3
Harebeating E Susx 11 T8
Hareby Lincs 59 P13
Hare Croft C Brad 63 M12
Harefield Gt Lon 20 J4
Hare Green Essex 23 R2
Hare Hatch Wokham 20 D7
Harehill Derbys 46 G6
Harehills Leeds 63 S13
Harehope Nthumb 77 M1
Harelaw Border 84 E14
Harelaw D & G 75 T10
Harelaw Dur 69 Q2
Hareplain Kent 12 F8
Haresceugh Cumb 68 D4
Harescombe Gloucs 28 F5
Haresfield Gloucs 28 F5
Harestock Hants 9 P2
Hare Street Essex 22 B6
Hare Street Essex 22 D7
Hare Street Herts 31 U7
Harewood Leeds 63 S10
Harewood End Herefs 27 U2
Harford Devon 5 Q9
Hargate Norfk 40 K2
Hargatewall Derbys 56 H11
Hargrave Ches W 45 L1
Hargrave Nhants 38 F6
Hargrave Suffk 40 C9
Harker Cumb 75 S13
Harkstead Suffk 41 L14
Harlaston Staffs 46 H11
Harlaxton Lincs 48 C7
Harlech Gwynd 43 L7
Harlech Castle Gwynd 43 L7
Harlescott Shrops 45 L10
Harlesden Gt Lon 21 M6
Harlesthorpe Derbys 57 Q11
Harleston Devon 5 T11
Harleston Norfk 41 M4
Harleston Suffk 40 H8
Harlestone Nhants 37 T8
Harle Syke Lancs 62 H12
Harley Rothm 57 N7
Harley Shrops 45 N13
Harlington C Beds 31 M6
Harlington Donc 57 Q6
Harlington Gt Lon 20 J7
Harlosh Highld 100 b5
Harlow Essex 22 B5
Harlow Carr RHS N York 63 R9
Harlow Hill Nthumb 77 M12
Harlthorpe E R Yk 64 G12
Harlton Cambs 39 N10
Harlyn Cnwll 3 M1
Harman's Cross Dorset 8 D12
Harmby N York 63 N2
Harmer Green Herts 31 S9
Harmer Hill Shrops 45 L9
Harmondsworth Gt Lon 20 J7
Harmston Lincs 48 E1
Harnage Shrops 45 N13
Harnham Nthumb 77 M9
Harnhill Gloucs 29 L7
Harold Hill Gt Lon 22 D9
Haroldston West Pembks 24 E7
Haroldswick Shet 106 w2
Harold Wood Gt Lon 22 E9
Harome N York 64 E3
Harpenden Herts 31 P10
Harpford Devon 6 E6
Harpham E R Yk 65 P7
Harpley Norfk 50 C8
Harpley Worcs 35 Q8
Harpole Nhants 37 S8
Harpsdale Highld 112 D5
Harpsden Oxon 20 C6
Harpswell Lincs 58 F9
Harpurhey Manch 56 C6
Harpur Hill Derbys 56 G12
Harraby Cumb 67 P2
Harracott Devon 15 N7
Harrapool Highld 100 f7
Harrietfield P & K 90 E6
Harrietsham Kent 12 G5
Harringay Gt Lon 21 P5
Harrington Cumb 66 E7
Harrington Lincs 59 Q12
Harrington Nhants 37 U4
Harringworth Nhants 38 D1
Harris W Isls 106 f9
Harriseahead Staffs 45 U2
Harriston Cumb 66 J4
Harrogate N York 63 S9
Harrogate Crematorium N York 63 S9
Harrold Bed 38 D9
Harrop Dale Oldham 56 F5
Harrow Gt Lon 21 L5
Harrowbarrow Cnwll 5 L6
Harrowden Bed 38 G11
Harrowgate Village Darltn 69 S9
Harrow Green Suffk 40 E10
Harrow on the Hill Gt Lon 21 L5
Harrow Weald Gt Lon 21 L4
Harston Cambs 39 P10
Harston Leics 48 B7
Harswell E R Yk 64 J11
Hart Hartpl 70 G6
Hartburn Nthumb 77 M8
Hartest Suffk 40 D10
Hartfield E Susx 11 R3
Hartford Cambs 39 L6
Hartford Ches W 55 P12
Hartford Somset 16 C11
Hartfordbridge Hants 20 C11
Hartford End Essex 22 G4
Hartforth N York 69 Q11
Hartgrove Dorset 8 A5
Harthill Ches W 45 L2
Harthill N Lans 82 H6
Harthill Rothm 57 Q10
Hartington Derbys 46 F1
Hartington Nthumb 77 L8
Hartland Devon 14 G8
Hartland Quay Devon 14 F8
Hartlebury Worcs 35 T6
Hartlepool Hartpl 70 H6
Hartlepool Crematorium Hartpl 70 H6
Hartley Cumb 68 G11
Hartley Kent 12 B2
Hartley Kent 12 E9
Hartley Nthumb 77 S10
Hartley Green Kent 12 B2
Hartley Green Staffs 46 C8
Hartley Wespall Hants 19 U9
Hartley Wintney Hants 20 C11
Hartlip Kent 12 F3
Hartoft End N York 71 M14
Harton N York 64 G7
Harton S Tyne 77 T12
Harton Shrops 35 L3
Hartpury Gloucs 28 E3
Hartshead Kirk 56 J2
Hartshead Moor Services Calder 56 J2
Hartshill C Stke 45 U4
Hartshill Warwks 36 K2
Hartshorne Derbys 46 K9
Hartside Nthumb 76 K2
Hartsop Cumb 67 P10
Hart Station Hartpl 70 G5
Hartswell Somset 16 E11
Hartwell Nhants 37 U10
Hartwith N York 63 Q7
Hartwood N Lans 82 F7
Hartwoodmyres Border 84 C14
Harvel Kent 12 C3
Harvington Worcs 35 U6
Harvington Worcs 36 E11
Harwell Notts 57 U8
Harwell Oxon 29 U10
Harwich Essex 23 U1
Harwood Bolton 55 R4
Harwood Dur 68 H6
Harwood Dale N York 71 S13
Harwood Lee Bolton 55 R4
Harwood Park Crematorium Herts 31 S8
Harworth Notts 57 T8
Hasbury Dudley 36 C4
Hascombe Surrey 10 G3
Haselbech Nhants 37 T5
Haselbury Plucknett Somset 7 N2
Haseley Warwks 36 H7
Haseley Green Warwks 36 H7
Haseley Knob Warwks 36 H6
Haselor Warwks 36 F9
Hasfield Gloucs 28 F2
Hasguard Pembks 24 E9
Hasholme E R Yk 64 J13
Haskayne Lancs 54 J5
Hasketon Suffk 41 M10
Hasland Derbys 57 N13
Haslemere Surrey 10 E4
Haslingden Lancs 55 S2
Haslingfield Cambs 39 P10
Haslington Ches E 45 R2
Hassall Ches E 45 S2
Hassall Green Ches E 45 S2
Hassell Street Kent 13 L6
Hassingham Norfk 51 Q12
Hassness Cumb 66 J9
Hassocks W Susx 11 N7
Hassop Derbys 56 K12
Haste Hill Surrey 10 E4
Haster Highld 112 H6
Hasthorpe Lincs 59 S13
Hastingleigh Kent 13 L6
Hastings E Susx 12 F14
Hastings Somset 16 K13
Hastings Borough Crematorium E Susx 12 F13
Hastingwood Essex 22 C6
Hastoe Herts 30 K11
Haswell Dur 70 E4
Haswell Plough Dur 70 E4
Hatch C Beds 38 J11
Hatch Beauchamp Somset 16 K12
Hatch End Bed 38 G8
Hatch End Gt Lon 20 K4
Hatchet Gate Hants 9 M8
Hatching Green Herts 31 P10
Hatchmere Ches W 55 N12
Hatcliffe NE Lin 59 M6
Hatfield Donc 57 U5
Hatfield Herefs 35 N9
Hatfield Herts 31 R11
Hatfield Worcs 35 U10
Hatfield Broad Oak Essex 22 D4
Hatfield Heath Essex 22 D4
Hatfield Peverel Essex 22 J5
Hatfield Woodhouse Donc 57 U5
Hatford Oxon 29 R9
Hatherden Hants 19 M10
Hatherleigh Devon 15 M12
Hathern Leics 47 P9
Hatherop Gloucs 29 N6
Hathersage Derbys 56 K10
Hathersage Booths Derbys 56 K10
Hatherton Ches E 45 Q4
Hatherton Staffs 46 C11
Hatley St George Cambs 39 L10
Hatt Cnwll 5 L8
Hattersley Tamesd 56 E8
Hattingley Hants 19 T13
Hatton Abers 105 T8
Hatton Angus 91 Q3
Hatton Derbys 46 H7
Hatton Gt Lon 20 J7
Hatton Lincs 59 L11
Hatton Shrops 35 L2
Hatton Warrtn 55 N10
Hatton Warwks 36 H7
Hatton Heath Ches W 45 L1
Hatton of Fintray Abers 105 N12
Haugh E Ayrs 81 P7
Haugh Lincs 59 R11
Haugh Rochdl 56 D4
Haugham Lincs 59 P10
Haughhead E Duns 89 P10
Haugh Head Nthumb 85 Q13
Haughley Suffk 40 H8
Haughley Green Suffk 40 H8
Haugh of Glass Moray 104 E8
Haugh of Urr D & G 74 F12
Haughs of Kinnaird Angus 99 L12
Haughton Notts 57 U12
Haughton Powys 44 H10
Haughton Shrops 35 Q1
Haughton Shrops 44 J8
Haughton Shrops 45 N10
Haughton Shrops 45 R12
Haughton Staffs 45 U9
Haughton Green Tamesd 56 D8
Haughton le Skerne Darltn 70 D9
Haughton Moss Ches E 45 N2
Haultwick Herts 31 T8
Haunton Staffs 46 H11
Hautes Croix Jersey 7 d1
Hauxton Cambs 39 P10
Havannah Ches E 56 C14
Havant Hants 9 U7
Havant Crematorium Hants 9 U7
Haven Herefs 34 K10
Haven Bank Lincs 48 K3
Haven Side E R Yk 65 R14
Havenstreet IoW 9 R10
Havercroft Wakefd 57 N4
Haverfordwest Pembks 24 G7
Haverhill Suffk 39 U11
Haverigg Cumb 61 M4
Havering-atte-Bower Gt Lon 22 D9
Haversham M Keyn 30 H4
Haverthwaite Cumb 61 Q3
Haverton Hill S on T 70 G8
Havyat N Som 17 N4
Havyatt Somset 17 P9
Hawarden Flints 54 H13
Hawbridge Worcs 36 B11
Hawbush Green Essex 22 J3
Hawcoat Cumb 61 N5
Hawen Cerdgn 32 F11
Hawes N York 62 H2
Hawe's Green Norfk 51 M14
Hawford Worcs 35 T8
Hawick Border 75 V3
Hawkchurch Devon 6 K4
Hawkedon Suffk 40 C10
Hawkenbury Kent 12 F6
Hawkeridge Wilts 18 C10
Hawkerland Devon 6 E7
Hawker's Cove Cnwll 3 N1
Hawkesbury S Glos 28 E10
Hawkesbury Warwks 37 L4
Hawkesbury Upton S Glos 28 E10
Hawkes End Covtry 36 J4
Hawk Green Stockp 56 E9
Hawkhill Nthumb 77 Q3
Hawkhurst Kent 12 E9
Hawkhurst Common E Susx 11 S7
Hawkinge Kent 13 P8
Hawkinge Crematorium Kent 13 P7
Hawkley Hants 9 U3
Hawkley Wigan 55 N6
Hawkridge Somset 15 U6
Hawksdale Cumb 67 N3
Hawkshaw Bury 55 S3
Hawkshead Cumb 67 N13
Hawkshead Hill Cumb 67 M13
Hawksland S Lans 82 F11
Hawkspur Green Essex 22 G1
Hawkstone Shrops 45 N7
Hawkswick N York 62 K5
Hawksworth Leeds 63 P11
Hawksworth Notts 47 U5
Hawkwell Essex 23 L9
Hawkwell Nthumb 77 M11
Hawley Hants 20 E11
Hawley Kent 22 D13
Hawling Gloucs 29 L3
Hawnby N York 64 C2
Haworth C Brad 63 L12
Hawridge Bucks 30 K11
Hawstead Suffk 40 E9
Hawstead Green Suffk 40 E9
Hawthorn Dur 70 F3
Hawthorn Hants 9 T2
Hawthorn Rhondd 26 K10
Hawthorn Hill Br For 20 E8
Hawthorn Hill Lincs 48 K2
Hawthorpe Lincs 48 F8
Hawton Notts 47 U3
Haxby C York 64 E8
Haxby Gates C York 64 E8
Haxey N Linc 58 C7
Haxey Carr N Linc 58 C6
Haxted Surrey 21 R13
Haxton Wilts 18 H11
Hay Cnwll 3 P2
Hay Cnwll 3 P6
Haycombe Crematorium BaNES 17 T4
Haydock St Hel 55 N7
Haydon BaNES 17 S6
Haydon Dorset 17 S13
Haydon Somset 16 J12
Haydon Bridge Nthumb 76 G13
Haydon Wick Swindn 29 M10
Haye Cnwll 4 K6
Hayes Gt Lon 20 J6
Hayes Gt Lon 21 R9
Hayes End Gt Lon 20 J6
Hayfield Ag & B 94 F14
Hayfield Derbys 56 F9
Haygate Wrekin 45 P11
Hay Green Norfk 49 R10
Hayhillock Angus 91 R3
Hayle Cnwll 2 F9
Hayle Port Cnwll 2 F9
Hayley Green Dudley 36 C4
Hayling Island Hants 9 U8
Haymoor Green Ches E 45 Q3
Hayne Devon 5 T3
Hayne Devon 16 C13
Haynes (Church End) C Beds 31 N4
Haynes (Northwood End) C Beds 31 N4
Haynes (Silver End) C Beds 31 P4
Haynes (West End) C Beds 31 N4
Hay-on-Wye Powys 34 F12
Hayscastle Pembks 24 E5
Hayscastle Cross Pembks 24 F5
Haysden Kent 21 U13
Hay Street Herts 31 U7
Hayton Cumb 66 H4
Hayton Cumb 75 V14
Hayton E R Yk 64 J10
Hayton Notts 58 B10
Hayton's Bent Shrops 35 M4
Haytor Vale Devon 5 T5
Haytown Devon 14 J10
Haywards Heath W Susx 11 N6
Haywood Donc 57 S4
Haywood Herefs 35 L14
Haywood Oaks Notts 47 R2
Hazards Green E Susx 12 C13
Hazelbank S Lans 82 F9
Hazelbury Bryan Dorset 7 T3
Hazeleigh Essex 22 K7
Hazeley Hants 20 B11
Hazelford Notts 47 T4
Hazel Grove Stockp 56 D9
Hazelhurst Tamesd 56 E6
Hazelslade Staffs 46 D11
Hazel Street Kent 12 C8
Hazel Stub Suffk 39 U12
Hazelton Walls Fife 91 M7
Hazelwood Derbys 46 K4
Hazlemere Bucks 20 E3
Hazlerigg N u Ty 77 Q11
Hazles Staffs 46 D4
Hazleton Gloucs 29 L4
Heacham Norfk 49 U6
Headbourne Worthy Hants 9 P2
Headbrook Herefs 34 G9
Headcorn Kent 12 F7
Headingley Leeds 63 R12
Headington Oxon 30 B11
Headlam Dur 69 Q9
Headlesscross N Lans 82 H7
Headless Cross Worcs 36 D7
Headley Hants 10 C3
Headley Hants 19 R8
Headley Surrey 21 M12
Headley Down Hants 10 C3
Headley Heath Worcs 36 E5
Headon Devon 14 J12
Headon Notts 58 B11
Heads Nook Cumb 67 R2
Heage Derbys 47 L3
Healaugh N York 64 C10
Healaugh N York 69 M13
Heald Green Stockp 55 T9
Heale Devon 15 P3
Heale Somset 16 H12
Heale Somset 17 L11
Healey N York 63 P3
Healey Nthumb 77 L14
Healey Rochdl 56 C3
Healey Wakefd 57 L3
Healeyfield Dur 69 N3
Healing NE Lin 59 M4
Heamoor Cnwll 2 D10
Heanor Derbys 47 M4
Heanton Punchardon Devon 15 M5
Heapham Lincs 58 E9
Hearn Hants 10 C3
Heart of England Crematorium Warwks 37 L2
Heart of Scotland Services N Lans 82 H6
Hearts Delight Kent 12 G3
Heasley Mill Devon 15 R6
Heast Highld 100 f8
Heath Derbys 57 Q13
Heath Wakefd 57 N2
Heath and Reach C Beds 30 K7
Heath Common W Susx 10 H7
Heathcote Derbys 46 F1
Heathcote Shrops 45 Q8
Heath End Bucks 20 E3
Heath End Hants 19 P8
Heath End Leics 47 L9
Heath End Warwks 36 H8
Heather Leics 47 L11
Heathfield Devon 5 U5
Heathfield E Susx 11 T6
Heathfield N York 63 N6
Heathfield Somset 16 G11
Heathfield Village Oxon 30 B9
Heath Green Worcs 36 E6
Heath Hall D & G 74 J10
Heath Hayes & Wimblebury Staffs 46 D11
Heath Hill Shrops 45 S11
Heath House Somset 17 M7
Heathrow Airport Gt Lon 20 J7
Heathstock Devon 6 H4
Heathton Shrops 35 T2
Heath Town Wolves 46 B14
Heathwaite N York 70 G12
Heatley Staffs 46 E8
Heatley Warrtn 55 R9
Heaton Bolton 55 Q5
Heaton C Brad 63 N12
Heaton Lancs 61 S7
Heaton N u Ty 77 R12
Heaton Staffs 56 E14
Heaton Chapel Stockp 56 C8
Heaton Mersey Stockp 56 C8
Heaton Norris Stockp 56 C8
Heaton's Bridge Lancs 54 K4
Heaverham Kent 21 U11
Heaviley Stockp 56 D9
Heavitree Devon 6 B6
Hebburn S Tyne 77 S13
Hebden N York 63 L7
Hebden Bridge Calder 56 E1
Hebden Green Ches W 55 P13
Hebing End Herts 31 T8
Hebron Carmth 25 L5
Hebron IoA 52 G6
Hebron Nthumb 77 P8
Heckfield Hants 20 B10
Heckfield Green Suffk 41 L5
Heckfordbridge Essex 23 M3
Heckington Lincs 48 H5
Heckmondwike Kirk 56 K2
Heddington Wilts 18 E7
Heddon-on-the-Wall Nthumb 77 N12
Hedenham Norfk 41 P2
Hedge End Hants 9 P6
Hedgerley Bucks 20 G5
Hedgerley Green Bucks 20 G5
Hedging Somset 16 K11
Hedley on the Hill Nthumb 77 M14
Hednesford Staffs 46 C11
Hedon E R Yk 65 R14
Hedsor Bucks 20 F5
Hegdon Hill Herefs 35 N10
Heglibister Shet 106 t8
Heighington Darltn 69 R8
Heighington Lincs 58 H13
Heightington Worcs 35 S6
Heiton Border 84 J12
Hele Devon 5 S6
Hele Devon 6 C4
Hele Devon 15 M3
Hele Somset 16 G12
Helebridge Cnwll 14 F12
Hele Lane Devon 15 S10
Helensburgh Ag & B 88 G9
Helenton S Ayrs 81 M6
Helford Cnwll 2 K11
Helford Passage Cnwll 2 K11
Helhoughton Norfk 50 E8
Helions Bumpstead Essex 39 U12
Hellaby Rothm 57 R8
Helland Cnwll 3 R2
Hellandbridge Cnwll 3 R2
Hell Corner W Berk 19 N8
Hellescott Cnwll 4 H3
Hellesdon Norfk 51 M11
Hellesveor Cnwll 2 E8
Hellidon Nhants 37 P9
Hellifield N York 62 H8
Hellingly E Susx 11 T8
Hellington Norfk 51 P13
Helm Nthumb 77 P6
Helmdon Nhants 30 C4
Helme Kirk 56 G4
Helmingham Suffk 41 L9
Helmington Row Dur 69 Q5
Helmsdale Highld 112 B13
Helmshore Lancs 55 S2
Helmsley N York 64 E3
Helperby N York 63 U6
Helperthorpe N York 65 M5
Helpringham Lincs 48 H5
Helpston C Pete 48 H12
Helsby Ches W 55 L11
Helsey Lincs 59 T12
Helston Cnwll 2 H11
Helstone Cnwll 4 D4
Helton Cumb 67 R8
Helwith N York 69 N12
Helwith Bridge N York 62 G6
Hemblington Norfk 51 P11
Hembridge Somset 17 Q9
Hemel Hempstead Herts 31 N11
Hemerdon Devon 5 P9
Hemingbrough N York 64 F13
Hemingby Lincs 59 M12
Hemingfield Barns 57 N6
Hemingford Abbots Cambs 39 L6
Hemingford Grey Cambs 39 L6
Hemingstone Suffk 40 K10
Hemington Leics 47 N8
Hemington Nhants 38 G3
Hemington Somset 17 T6
Hemley Suffk 41 N12
Hemlington Middsb 70 H10
Hempholme E R Yk 65 P9
Hempnall Norfk 41 M2
Hempnall Green Norfk 41 M2
Hempriggs Moray 103 T3
Hempstead Essex 39 T13
Hempstead Medway 12 E3
Hempstead Norfk 50 K6
Hempstead Norfk 51 R8
Hempsted Gloucs 28 F4
Hempton Norfk 50 F8
Hempton Oxon 29 T1
Hemsby Norfk 51 S10
Hemswell Lincs 58 F8
Hemswell Cliff Lincs 58 F9
Hemsworth Wakefd 57 P4
Hemyock Devon 6 F2
Henbury Bristl 27 V12
Henbury Ches E 56 C12
Hendham Devon 5 S10
Hendomen Powys 44 F14
Hendon Gt Lon 21 M5
Hendon Sundld 70 F1
Hendon Crematorium Gt Lon 21 M4
Hendra Cnwll 2 J9
Hendra Cnwll 3 Q1
Hendre Brdgnd 26 G11
Hendre Flints 54 E13
Hendre Mons 27 T5
Hendy Carmth 25 U10
Heneglwys IoA 52 F7
Henfield W Susx 11 L7
Henford Devon 4 K2
Henghurst Kent 12 J8
Hengoed Caerph 27 M9
Hengoed Powys 34 F10
Hengoed Shrops 44 G7
Hengrave Suffk 40 D7
Henham Essex 22 D2
Heniarth Powys 44 D12
Henlade Somset 16 J12
Henley Dorset 7 S4
Henley Gloucs 28 H4
Henley Shrops 35 L3
Henley Shrops 35 M5
Henley Somset 17 M10
Henley Suffk 41 L10
Henley W Susx 10 D5
Henley Green Covtry 37 L4
Henley-in-Arden Warwks 36 G7
Henley-on-Thames Oxon 20 C6
Henley Park Surrey 20 F12
Henley's Down E Susx 12 D13
Henley Street Kent 12 C2
Henllan Cerdgn 32 G12
Henllan Denbgs 53 T9
Henllan Amgoed Carmth 25 L7
Henllys Torfn 27 P9
Henlow C Beds 31 Q5
Hennock Devon 5 U4
Henny Street Essex 40 E13
Henryd Conwy 53 N8
Henry's Moat (Castell Hendre) Pembks 24 H5
Hensall N York 57 S2
Henshaw Nthumb 76 F13
Hensingham Cumb 66 E9
Henstead Suffk 41 S3
Hensting Hants 9 P4
Henstridge Somset 17 T13
Henstridge Ash Somset 17 T12
Henstridge Marsh Somset 17 T12
Henton Oxon 30 G12
Henton Somset 17 N7
Henwick Worcs 35 T9
Henwood Cnwll 4 H6
Henwood Oxon 29 U7
Heol-las Swans 26 B8
Heol Senni Powys 26 G3
Heol-y-Cyw Brdgnd 26 G11
Hepburn Nthumb 85 R14
Hepple Nthumb 76 K5
Hepscott Nthumb 77 Q9
Heptonstall Calder 62 K14
Hepworth Kirk 56 J5
Hepworth Suffk 40 G6
Herbrandston Pembks 24 E9
Hereford Herefs 35 M13
Hereford Crematorium Herefs 35 L12
Hereson Kent 13 S2
Heribusta Highld 100 c2
Heriot Border 83 T8
Hermiston C Edin 83 N4
Hermitage Border 75 V6
Hermitage Dorset 7 S3
Hermitage W Berk 19 R6
Hermitage W Susx 10 B9
Hermit Hill Barns 57 M6
Hermon Carmth 25 Q4
Hermon IoA 52 E9
Hermon Pembks 25 M4
Herne Kent 13 N2
Herne Bay Kent 13 N2
Herne Common Kent 13 N2
Herne Hill Gt Lon 21 P8
Herne Pound Kent 12 C5
Herner Devon 15 N7
Hernhill Kent 13 L3
Herodsfoot Cnwll 4 G8
Heronden Kent 13 Q5
Herongate Essex 22 F9
Heronsford S Ayrs 72 E3
Heronsgate Herts 20 H4
Herriard Hants 19 U11
Herringfleet Suffk 51 S14
Herring's Green Bed 31 N4
Herringswell Suffk 40 B6
Herringthorpe Rothm 57 P8
Herrington Sundld 70 E2
Hersden Kent 13 P3
Hersham Cnwll 14 G11
Hersham Surrey 20 K10
Herstmonceux E Susx 11 U8
Herston Dorset 8 E13
Herston Ork 106 t20
Hertford Herts 31 T10
Hertford Heath Herts 31 U10
Hertingfordbury Herts 31 T10
Hesketh Bank Lancs 54 K2
Hesketh Lane Lancs 62 C11
Hesket Newmarket Cumb 67 M5
Heskin Green Lancs 55 M3
Hesleden Dur 70 F5
Hesleden N York 62 H5
Hesley Donc 57 T8
Hesleyside Nthumb 76 G9
Heslington C York 64 E9
Hessay C York 64 C9
Hessenford Cnwll 4 J9
Hessett Suffk 40 F8
Hessle E R Yk 58 H1
Hessle Wakefd 57 P3
Hest Bank Lancs 61 T6
Hestley Green Suffk 41 L7
Heston Gt Lon 20 K7
Heston Services Gt Lon 20 K7
Hestwall Ork 106 r18
Heswall Wirral 54 G10
Hethe Oxon 30 C7
Hethersett Norfk 50 K13
Hethersgill Cumb 75 U12
Hetherside Cumb 75 T12
Hetherson Green Ches W 45 M3
Hethpool Nthumb 85 M13
Hett Dur 69 S5
Hetton N York 62 K8
Hetton-le-Hole Sundld 70 E3
Hetton Steads Nthumb 85 Q11
Heugh Nthumb 77 M11
Heughhead Abers 104 D13
Heugh Head Border 85 M6
Heveningham Suffk 41 P6
Hever Kent 21 S13
Heversham Cumb 61 T3
Hevingham Norfk 51 L9
Hewas Water Cnwll 3 P7
Hewelsfield Gloucs 27 V7
Hewenden C Brad 63 M12
Hewish N Som 17 M4
Hewish Somset 7 M3
Hewood Dorset 7 L4
Hexham Nthumb 76 J13
Hextable Kent 22 D13
Hexthorpe Donc 57 S6
Hexton Herts 31 P6
Hexworthy Cnwll 4 K4
Hexworthy Devon 5 R6
Hey Lancs 62 H11
Heybridge Essex 22 F8
Heybridge Essex 23 L6
Heybridge Basin Essex 23 L6
Heybrook Bay Devon 5 M11
Heydon Cambs 39 P13
Heydon Norfk 50 K8
Heydour Lincs 48 F6
Heyhead Manch 55 T9
Hey Houses Lancs 61 Q14
Heylipoll Ag & B 92 B10
Heylor Shet 106 s5
Heyrod Tamesd 56 E7
Heysham Lancs 61 S7
Heyshaw N York 63 P7
Heyshott W Susx 10 D7
Heyside Oldham 56 D5
Heytesbury Wilts 18 D12
Heythrop Oxon 29 S2
Heywood Rochdl 56 C4
Heywood Wilts 18 C10
Hibaldstow N Linc 58 G6
Hickleton Donc 57 Q5
Hickling Norfk 51 R9
Hickling Notts 47 S8
Hickling Green Norfk 51 R9
Hickling Heath Norfk 51 R9
Hickmans Green Kent 13 L4
Hicks Forstal Kent 13 N3
Hickstead W Susx 11 M6
Hidcote Bartrim Gloucs 36 G12
Hidcote Boyce Gloucs 36 G12
High Ackworth Wakefd 57 P3
Higham Barns 57 M5
Higham Derbys 47 L2
Higham Kent 12 B6
Higham Kent 22 H13
Higham Lancs 62 G12
Higham Suffk 40 B7
Higham Suffk 40 H13
Higham Dykes Nthumb 77 N10
Higham Ferrers Nhants 38 E7
Higham Gobion C Beds 31 P6
Higham Hill Gt Lon 21 Q4
Higham on the Hill Leics 37 L1
Highampton Devon 15 L12
Highams Park Gt Lon 21 Q4
High Angerton Nthumb 77 M8
High Ardwell D & G 72 D10
High Auldgirth D & G 74 H8
High Bankhill Cumb 67 S4
High Beach Essex 21 R3
High Bentham N York 62 D6
High Bewaldeth Cumb 66 K6
High Bickington Devon 15 P8
High Biggins Cumb 62 C4
High Birkwith N York 62 G4
High Blantyre S Lans 82 C7
High Bonnybridge Falk 89 T10
High Borrans Cumb 67 P12
High Bradley N York 63 L10
High Bray Devon 15 Q6
Highbridge Hants 9 P4
Highbridge Somset 16 K7
Highbrook W Susx 11 P4
High Brooms Kent 11 T2
High Bullen Devon 15 M8
Highburton Kirk 56 J4
Highbury Gt Lon 21 P5
Highbury Somset 17 S7
High Buston Nthumb 77 Q4
High Callerton Nthumb 77 P11
High Casterton Cumb 62 C4
High Catton E R Yk 64 G9
Highclere Hants 19 P9
Highcliffe Dorset 8 J10
High Close Dur 69 Q9
High Cogges Oxon 29 S6
High Common Norfk 50 G12
High Coniscliffe Darltn 69 R9
High Crosby Cumb 75 U14
High Cross Cnwll 2 J11
High Cross E Ayrs 81 N3
High Cross Hants 9 U3
High Cross Herts 31 U9
Highcross Lancs 61 Q12
High Cross W Susx 11 L7
High Cross Warwks 36 H7
High Drummore D & G 72 E12
High Dubmire Sundld 70 D3
High Easter Essex 22 F5
High Eggborough N York 57 S2
High Ellington N York 63 P3
Higher Alham Somset 17 S8
Higher Ansty Dorset 7 U4
Higher Ballam Lancs 61 R13
Higher Bartle Lancs 61 U13
Higher Berry End C Beds 31 L6
Higher Bockhampton Dorset 7 T6
Higher Brixham Torbay 6 B14
Higher Burrowton Devon 6 D5
Higher Burwardsley Ches W 45 M2
High Ercall Wrekin 45 N10
Higher Chillington Somset 7 L2
Higher Clovelly Devon 14 H8
Highercombe Somset 16 B10
Higher Coombe Dorset 7 P6
Higher Disley Ches E 56 E10
Higher Folds Wigan 55 Q6
Higherford Lancs 62 H11
Higher Gabwell Devon 6 B11
Higher Halstock Leigh Dorset 7 P3
Higher Harpers Lancs 62 G12
Higher Heysham Lancs 61 S7
Higher Hurdsfield Ches E 56 D12
Higher Irlam Salfd 55 R7
Higher Kingcombe Dorset 7 P5
Higher Kinnerton Flints 44 H1
Higher Marston Ches W 55 Q11
Higher Muddiford Devon 15 N5
Higher Nyland Dorset 17 T12
Higher Ogden Rochdl 56 E4
Higher Pentire Cnwll 2 H11
Higher Penwortham Lancs 61 U14
Higher Prestacott Devon 14 J13
Higher Studfold N York 62 G5
Higher Town Cnwll 3 L8
Higher Town Cnwll 3 Q4
Higher Town IoS 2 c1
Higher Tregantle Cnwll 5 L10
Higher Walton Lancs 55 N1
Higher Walton Warrtn 55 N9
Higher Wambrook Somset 6 J3
Higher Waterston Dorset 7 T5
Higher Whatcombe Dorset 8 A8
Higher Wheelton Lancs 55 P2
Higher Whitley Ches W 55 P10
Higher Wincham Ches W 55 Q11
Higher Wraxhall Dorset 7 Q4
Higher Wych Ches W 45 L5
High Etherley Dur 69 Q7
High Ferry Lincs 49 N4
Highfield E R Yk 64 G12
Highfield Gatesd 77 N14
Highfield N Ayrs 81 L2
Highfields Donc 57 R5
High Flats Kirk 56 K5
High Garrett Essex 22 J2
Highgate E Susx 11 Q4
Highgate Gt Lon 21 N5
Highgate Kent 12 E9
High Grange Dur 69 Q6
High Grantley N York 63 Q6
High Green Cumb 67 P12
High Green Kirk 56 K4
High Green Norfk 41 L3
High Green Norfk 50 K12
High Green Sheff 57 M7
High Green Shrops 35 R4
High Green Suffk 40 E8
High Green Worcs 35 U11
Highgreen Manor Nthumb 76 G7
High Halden Kent 12 G8
High Halstow Medway 22 J12
High Ham Somset 17 M10
High Harrington Cumb 66 F7
High Harrogate N York 63 S8
High Haswell Dur 70 E4
High Hatton Shrops 45 P9
High Hauxley Nthumb 77 R5
High Hawsker N York 71 R11
High Hesket Cumb 67 Q4
High Hoyland Barns 57 L5
High Hunsley E R Yk 65 M12
High Hurstwood E Susx 11 R5
High Hutton N York 64 H6
High Ireby Cumb 66 K5
High Kelling Norfk 50 K5
High Kilburn N York 64 C4
High Killerby N York 65 P3
High Knipe Cumb 67 R9
High Lands Dur 69 P7
Highlane Ches E 56 C13
Highlane Derbys 57 P10
High Lane Stockp 56 E9
High Lanes Cnwll 2 F9
High Laver Essex 22 D6
Highlaws Cumb 66 H3
Highleadon Gloucs 28 E3
High Legh Ches E 55 R10
Highleigh W Susx 10 C11
High Leven S on T 70 G10
Highley Shrops 35 R4
High Littleton BaNES 17 R5
High Lorton Cumb 66 J7
High Marishes N York 64 J4
High Marnham Notts 58 D12
High Melton Donc 57 R6
High Mickley Nthumb 77 M13
Highmoor Cumb 67 L3
Highmoor Oxon 20 B6
Highmoor Cross Oxon 20 B6
Highmoor Hill Mons 27 T10
High Moorsley Sundld 70 D3
Highnam Gloucs 28 E4
Highnam Green Gloucs 28 E3
High Newport Sundld 70 E2
High Newton Cumb 61 S3
High Nibthwaite Cumb 61 P2
High Offley Staffs 45 S8
High Ongar Essex 22 E7
High Onn Staffs 45 T10
High Park Corner Essex 23 P3
High Pennyvenie E Ayrs 81 P11
High Post Wilts 18 J13
Highridge N Som 17 Q3
High Roding Essex 22 F4
High Row Cumb 67 N5
High Row Cumb 67 N8
High Salter Lancs 62 C7
High Salvington W Susx 10 J9
High Scales Cumb 66 J3
High Seaton Cumb 66 F6
High Shaw N York 62 H1
High Side Cumb 66 K6
High Spen Gatesd 77 N14
Highstead Kent 13 P2
Highsted Kent 12 H3
High Stoop Dur 69 P4
High Street Cnwll 3 P6
High Street Kent 12 D9
Highstreet Kent 13 L3
High Street Suffk 41 R6
High Street Suffk 41 R9
Highstreet Green Essex 40 C14
Highstreet Green Surrey 10 F3
Hightae D & G 75 L10
Highter's Heath Birm 36 E5
High Throston Hartpl 70 G6
Hightown Ches E 45 U1
Hightown Hants 8 H8
Hightown Sefton 54 H6
High Town Staffs 46 C11
Hightown Green Suffk 40 G9
High Toynton Lincs 59 N13
High Trewhitt Nthumb 77 L4
High Urpeth Dur 69 R2
High Valleyfield Fife 82 K1
High Warden Nthumb 76 J12
Highway Herefs 35 L11
Highway Wilts 18 F6
Highweek Devon 5 U6
High Westwood Dur 69 P1
Highwood Staffs 46 E7
Highwood Hill Gt Lon 21 M4
High Woolaston Gloucs 28 A8
High Worsall N York 70 E11
Highworth Swindn 29 P9
High Wray Cumb 67 N13
High Wych Herts 22 C5
High Wycombe Bucks 20 E4
Hilborough Norfk 50 D13
Hilcote Derbys 47 N2
Hilcott Wilts 18 H9
Hildenborough Kent 21 U13
Hilden Park Kent 21 U13
Hildersham Cambs 39 R11
Hilderstone Staffs 46 C7
Hilderthorpe E R Yk 65 R6
Hilfield Dorset 7 R3
Hilgay Norfk 49 T14
Hill S Glos 28 B8
Hill Warwks 37 N7
Hillam N York 64 C14
Hillbeck Cumb 68 G9
Hillborough Kent 13 P2
Hill Brow Hants 10 B5
Hillbutts Dorset 8 D8
Hill Chorlton Staffs 45 S6
Hillclifflane Derbys 46 J4
Hill Common Norfk 51 R9
Hill Common Somset 16 F11
Hill Deverill Wilts 18 C12
Hilldyke Lincs 49 M4
Hill End Dur 69 M5
Hillend Fife 83 M2
Hill End Fife 90 F12
Hill End Gloucs 36 B13
Hillend Mdloth 83 Q5
Hillend N Lans 82 F5
Hillend Swans 25 R12
Hillersland Gloucs 27 V5
Hillerton Devon 15 R13
Hillesden Bucks 30 E7
Hillesley Gloucs 28 E10
Hillfarrance Somset 16 G12
Hill Green Kent 12 F3
Hillgrove W Susx 10 E5
Hillhampton Herefs 35 N11
Hillhead Abers 104 H8
Hillhead Devon 6 B14
Hill Head Hants 9 Q8
Hillhead S Lans 82 J10
Hillhead of Cocklaw Abers 105 T7
Hilliard's Cross Staffs 46 G11
Hilliclay Highld 112 E4
Hillingdon Gt Lon 20 J6
Hillington C Glas 89 M13
Hillington Norfk 50 B8
Hillis Corner IoW 9 P10
Hillmorton Warwks 37 P6
Hillock Vale Lancs 62 F14
Hill of Beath Fife 90 J13
Hill of Fearn Highld 109 Q9
Hillowton D & G 74 E13
Hillpool Worcs 35 U5
Hillpound Hants 9 R5
Hill Ridware Staffs 46 E10
Hillside Abers 99 S4
Hillside Angus 99 N11
Hillside Devon 5 S8
Hill Side Kirk 56 J3
Hill Side Worcs 35 S8
Hills Town Derbys 57 Q13
Hillstreet Hants 9 L5
Hillswick Shet 106 s6
Hill Top Dur 69 L8
Hill Top Hants 9 N8
Hill Top Kirk 56 G4
Hill Top Rothm 57 N8
Hill Top Sandw 36 C2
Hill Top Wakefd 57 M3
Hillwell Shet 106 t12
Hilmarton Wilts 18 F5
Hilperton Wilts 18 C9
Hilperton Marsh Wilts 18 C9
Hilsea C Port 9 T8
Hilston E R Yk 65 T13
Hiltingbury Hants 9 N4
Hilton Border 85 M8
Hilton Cambs 39 L7
Hilton Cumb 68 F8
Hilton Derbys 46 H7
Hilton Dorset 7 U4
Hilton Dur 69 Q8
Hilton Highld 109 R9
Hilton S on T 70 G10
Hilton Shrops 35 S1
Hilton Park Services Staffs 46 C13
Himbleton Worcs 36 B9
Himley Staffs 35 U2
Hincaster Cumb 61 U3
Hinchley Wood Surrey 21 L9
Hinckley Leics 37 M2
Hinderclay Suffk 40 H5
Hinderwell N York 71 N9
Hindford Shrops 44 H7
Hindhead Surrey 10 D3
Hindle Fold Lancs 62 E13
Hindley Nthumb 77 L14
Hindley Wigan 55 P6
Hindley Green Wigan 55 P6
Hindlip Worcs 35 U9
Hindolveston Norfk 50 H8
Hindon Wilts 8 C2
Hindringham Norfk 50 G6
Hingham Norfk 50 H13
Hinksford Staffs 35 U3
Hinstock Shrops 45 Q8
Hintlesham Suffk 40 J12
Hinton Gloucs 28 C7
Hinton Hants 8 J9
Hinton Herefs 34 H13
Hinton S Glos 28 D12
Hinton Shrops 35 Q4
Hinton Shrops 44 K12
Hinton Admiral Hants 8 J9
Hinton Ampner Hants 9 S3
Hinton Blewett BaNES 17 Q5
Hinton Charterhouse BaNES 17 U5
Hinton Green Worcs 36 D12
Hinton-in-the-Hedges Nhants 30 C5
Hinton Marsh Hants 9 R3
Hinton Martell Dorset 8 E7
Hinton on the Green Worcs 36 D12
Hinton Parva Swindn 29 P11
Hinton St George Somset 7 M2
Hinton St Mary Dorset 17 U13
Hinton Waldrist Oxon 29 S8
Hints Shrops 35 P6
Hints Staffs 46 G13
Hinwick Bed 38 D8
Hinxhill Kent 12 K7
Hinxton Cambs 39 Q11
Hinxworth Herts 31 R4
Hipperholme Calder 56 H1
Hipsburn Nthumb 77 Q3
Hipswell N York 69 Q13
Hirn Abers 99 N3
Hirnant Powys 44 B9
Hirst Nthumb 77 R8
Hirst Courtney N York 57 T2
Hirwaen Denbgs 44 D1
Hirwaun Rhondd 26 H6
Hiscott Devon 15 M7
Histon Cambs 39 P8
Hitcham Suffk 40 G10
Hitcham Causeway Suffk 40 G10
Hitcham Street Suffk 40 G10
Hitchin Herts 31 Q7
Hither Green Gt Lon 21 Q8
Hittisleigh Devon 15 R13
Hive E R Yk 64 J13
Hixon Staffs 46 D8
Hoaden Kent 13 Q4
Hoar Cross Staffs 46 F9
Hoarwithy Herefs 27 U2
Hoath Kent 13 P3
Hoathly Kent 12 C8
Hobarris Shrops 34 H5
Hobbles Green Suffk 40 B10
Hobbs Cross Essex 21 S3
Hobbs Cross Essex 22 C5
Hobkirk Border 76 B3
Hobland Hall Norfk 51 T13
Hobsick Notts 47 N4
Hobson Dur 69 Q1
Hoby Leics 47 S10
Hoccombe Somset 16 F11
Hockering Norfk 50 J11
Hockerton Notts 47 T2
Hockley Ches E 56 D10
Hockley Covtry 36 J5
Hockley Essex 22 K9
Hockley Staffs 46 H13
Hockley Heath Solhll 36 G6
Hockliffe C Beds 31 L7
Hockwold cum Wilton Norfk 40 B3
Hockworthy Devon 16 D13
Hoddesdon Herts 31 U11
Hoddlesden Bl w D 55 R2
Hoddom Cross D & G 75 N11
Hoddom Mains D & G 75 N11
Hodgehill Ches E 55 T13
Hodgeston Pembks 24 H11
Hodnet Shrops 45 P8
Hodsock Notts 57 T9
Hodsoll Street Kent 12 B3
Hodson Swindn 18 J4
Hodthorpe Derbys 57 R11
Hoe Hants 9 R5
Hoe Norfk 50 G10
Hoe Gate Hants 9 S6
Hoff Cumb 68 E9
Hogben's Hill Kent 12 K4
Hoggards Green Suffk 40 E9
Hoggeston Bucks 30 H8
Hoggrill's End Warwks 36 H2
Hog Hill E Susx 12 G12
Hoghton Lancs 55 P1
Hoghton Bottoms Lancs 55 P1
Hognaston Derbys 46 H3
Hogsthorpe Lincs 59 T12
Holbeach Lincs 49 N9
Holbeach Bank Lincs 49 N8
Holbeach Clough Lincs 49 N8
Holbeach Drove Lincs 49 M11
Holbeach Hurn Lincs 49 N8
Holbeach St Johns Lincs 49 N10
Holbeach St Mark's Lincs 49 N7
Holbeach St Matthew Lincs 49 P7
Holbeck Notts 57 R12
Holbeck Woodhouse Notts 57 R12
Holberrow Green Worcs 36 D9
Holbeton Devon 5 Q10
Holborn Gt Lon 21 P6
Holborough Kent 12 D3
Holbrook Derbys 47 L5
Holbrook Sheff 57 P10
Holbrook Suffk 41 L13
Holbrook Moor Derbys 47 L4
Holbrooks Covtry 36 K4
Holburn Nthumb 85 Q11
Holbury Hants 9 N8
Holcombe Devon 6 C10
Holcombe Somset 17 S7
Holcombe Rogus Devon 16 E13
Holcot Nhants 37 U7
Holden Lancs 62 F10
Holdenby Nhants 37 S7
Holden Gate Calder 56 C2
Holder's Green Essex 22 F2
Holdgate Shrops 35 N3
Holdingham Lincs 48 G4
Holditch Dorset 6 K4
Holdsworth Calder 63 M14
Holehouse Derbys 56 F8
Hole-in-the-Wall Herefs 28 B2
Holemoor Devon 14 K11
Hole Street W Susx 10 J8
Holford Somset 16 G8
Holgate C York 64 D9
Holker Cumb 61 R4
Holkham Norfk 50 E5
Hollacombe Devon 14 J12
Holland Fen Lincs 48 K4
Holland Lees Lancs 55 M5
Holland-on-Sea Essex 23 S4
Hollandstoun Ork 106 w14
Hollee D & G 75 Q12
Hollesley Suffk 41 Q12
Hollicombe Torbay 6 A12
Hollingbourne Kent 12 F4
Hollingbury Br & H 11 N9
Hollingdon Bucks 30 J7
Hollingthorpe Leeds 63 T13
Hollington Derbys 46 H6
Hollington Staffs 46 E6
Hollingworth Tamesd 56 F7
Hollinlane Ches E 55 T10
Hollins Bury 55 T5
Hollins Derbys 57 M12
Hollins Staffs 46 C4
Hollinsclough Staffs 56 G13
Hollins End Sheff 57 N10
Hollins Green Warrtn 55 Q8
Hollins Lane Lancs 61 T9
Hollinswood Wrekin 45 R12
Hollinwood Shrops 45 M6
Hollinwood Crematorium Oldham 56 D6
Holllingrove E Susx 12 C11
Hollocombe Devon 15 P10
Holloway Derbys 46 K2
Holloway Gt Lon 21 P5
Holloway Wilts 8 B2
Hollowell Nhants 37 S6
Hollowmoor Heath Ches W 55 L13
Hollows D & G 75 S10
Hollybush Caerph 27 M7
Hollybush E Ayrs 81 M9
Hollybush Herefs 35 S13
Holly End Norfk 49 Q12
Holly Green Worcs 35 U12
Hollyhurst Ches E 45 N5
Hollym E R Yk 59 P1
Hollywood Worcs 36 E5
Holmbridge Kirk 56 H5
Holmbury St Mary Surrey 10 J2
Holmbush Cnwll 3 Q6
Holmcroft Staffs 46 B9
Holme Cambs 38 J3
Holme Cumb 61 U4
Holme Kirk 56 H5
Holme N Linc 58 F5
Holme N York 63 T3
Holme Notts 48 B2
Holme Chapel Lancs 62 H14
Holme Green N York 64 D11
Holme Hale Norfk 50 E12
Holme Lacy Herefs 35 N13
Holme Marsh Herefs 34 H10
Holme next the Sea Norfk 50 B5
Holme on the Wolds E R Yk 65 M10
Holme Pierrepont Notts 47 R6
Holmer Herefs 35 M12
Holmer Green Bucks 20 F3
Holme St Cuthbert Cumb 66 H3
Holmes Chapel Ches E 55 S13
Holmesfield Derbys 57 M11
Holmes Hill E Susx 11 S8
Holmeswood Lancs 54 K3
Holmethorpe Surrey 21 N12
Holme upon Spalding Moor E R Yk 64 J12
Holmewood Derbys 57 P13
Holmfield Calder 63 M14
Holmfirth Kirk 56 H5
Holmhead E Ayrs 81 R8
Holmpton E R Yk 59 Q2
Holmrook Cumb 66 G13
Holmsford Bridge Crematorium N Ayrs 81 M5
Holmshurst E Susx 12 B10
Holmside Dur 69 R3
Holmwrangle Cumb 67 R3
Holne Devon 5 S7
Holnest Dorset 7 S3
Holnicote Somset 16 B7
Holsworthy Devon 14 H12
Holsworthy Beacon Devon 14 J11
Holt Dorset 8 E8
Holt Norfk 50 J6
Holt Wilts 18 C8
Holt Worcs 35 T8
Holt Wrexhm 44 K3
Holtby C York 64 F9
Holt End Worcs 36 E7
Holt Fleet Worcs 35 T8
Holt Green Lancs 54 J5
Holt Heath Dorset 8 F8
Holt Heath Worcs 35 T8
Holton Oxon 30 D11
Holton Somset 17 S11
Holton Suffk 41 R5
Holton cum Beckering Lincs 58 K10
Holton Heath Dorset 8 C10
Holton Hill E Susx 12 C10
Holton le Clay Lincs 59 N6
Holton le Moor Lincs 58 J7
Holton St Mary Suffk 40 J13
Holt Street Kent 13 Q5
Holtye E Susx 11 R3
Holway Flints 54 E11
Holwell Dorset 7 S2
Holwell Herts 31 Q6
Holwell Leics 47 T9
Holwell Oxon 29 P6
Holwick Dur 68 K7
Holworth Dorset 7 U8
Holybourne Hants 10 A2
Holy Cross Worcs 36 B5
Holyfield Essex 31 U12
Holyhead IoA 52 B6
Holy Island IoA 52 C6
Holy Island Nthumb 85 S10
Holy Island Nthumb 85 S10
Holymoorside Derbys 57 M13
Holyport W & M 20 E7
Holystone Nthumb 76 K5
Holytown N Lans 82 E6
Holytown Crematorium N Lans 82 E6
Holywell C Beds 31 M9
Holywell Cambs 39 M6
Holywell Cnwll 2 K5
Holywell Dorset 7 Q4
Holywell Flints 54 E11
Holywell Nthumb 77 S11
Holywell Warwks 36 H7
Holywell Green Calder 56 G3
Holywell Lake Somset 16 F12
Holywell Row Suffk 40 B5
Holywood D & G 74 H9
Holywood Village D & G 74 J10
Homer Shrops 45 P13
Homer Green Sefton 54 H6
Homersfield Suffk 41 N3
Homescales Cumb 62 B2
Hom Green Herefs 28 A3
Homington Wilts 8 G3
Honeyborough Pembks 24 F9
Honeybourne Worcs 36 F12
Honeychurch Devon 15 P12
Honey Hill Kent 13 M3
Honeystreet Wilts 18 H8
Honey Tye Suffk 40 G13
Honiley Warwks 36 H6
Honing Norfk 51 P8
Honingham Norfk 50 K11
Honington Lincs 48 D5
Honington Suffk 40 F6
Honington Warwks 36 J12
Honiton Devon 6 G4
Honley Kirk 56 H4
Honnington Wrekin 45 R10
Honor Oak Crematorium Gt Lon 21 Q8
Hoo Kent 13 Q3
Hoobrook Worcs 35 T6
Hood Green Barns 57 M6
Hood Hill Rothm 57 N7
Hooe C Plym 5 N10
Hooe E Susx 12 C13
Hoo End Herts 31 Q8
Hoo Green Ches E 55 R10
Hoohill Bpool 61 Q12
Hook Cambs 39 P2
Hook Devon 6 K3
Hook E R Yk 58 C1
Hook Gt Lon 21 L10
Hook Hants 9 Q7
Hook Hants 20 B12
Hook Pembks 24 G8
Hook Wilts 29 L11
Hookagate Shrops 45 L12
Hook Bank Worcs 35 T12
Hooke Dorset 7 P4
Hook End Essex 22 E7
Hookgate Staffs 45 R6
Hook Green Kent 12 C8
Hook Green Kent 22 F13
Hook Norton Oxon 37 L14
Hook Street Gloucs 28 C8
Hook Street Wilts 29 L11
Hookway Devon 15 U13
Hookwood Surrey 11 M2
Hooley Surrey 21 N11
Hooley Bridge Rochdl 56 C4
Hoo Meavy Devon 5 N7
Hoo St Werburgh Medway 22 J13
Hooton Ches W 54 J11
Hooton Levitt Rothm 57 R8
Hooton Pagnell Donc 57 Q5
Hooton Roberts Rothm 57 Q7
Hopcrofts Holt Oxon 29 U2
Hope Derbys 56 J10
Hope Devon 5 R12
Hope Flints 44 H2
Hope Powys 44 G12
Hope Shrops 44 H13
Hope Staffs 46 F3
Hope Bagot Shrops 35 N6
Hope Bowdler Shrops 35 L2
Hope End Green Essex 22 E3
Hopehouse Border 75 Q2
Hopeman Moray 103 T2
Hope Mansell Herefs 28 B4
Hopesay Shrops 34 J4
Hopetown Wakefd 57 N2
Hope under Dinmore Herefs 35 M10
Hopgrove C York 64 E9
Hopperton N York 63 U8
Hop Pole Lincs 48 J11
Hopsford Warwks 37 M4
Hopstone Shrops 35 S2
Hopton Derbys 46 J3
Hopton Shrops 44 J9
Hopton Staffs 46 B8
Hopton Suffk 40 G5
Hopton Cangeford Shrops 35 M4
Hopton Castle Shrops 34 J5

Hoptonheath - Kirkoswald 133

Hoptonheath Shrops 34 J5
Hopton on Sea Norfk 51 T14
Hopton Wafers Shrops 35 P5
Hopwas Staffs 46 G13
Hopwood Rochdl 56 C5
Hopwood Worcs 36 D5
Hopwood Park Services Worcs 36 D6
Horam E Susx 11 T7
Horbling Lincs 48 H6
Horbury Wakefd 57 L3
Horcott Gloucs 29 N7
Horden Dur 70 F4
Horderley Shrops 34 K3
Hordle Hants 8 K9
Hordley Shrops 44 J7
Horeb Carmth 25 S9
Horeb Cerdgn 32 G12
Horfield Bristl 28 A12
Horham Suffk 41 M6
Horkesley Heath Essex 23 N2
Horkstow N Linc 58 G3
Horley Oxon 37 M12
Horley Surrey 11 M2
Hornblotton Green Somset 17 Q10
Hornby Lancs 62 B6
Hornby N York 69 R14
Hornby N York 70 E11
Horncastle Lincs 59 N13
Hornchurch Gt Lon 22 D10
Horncliffe Nthumb 85 N9
Horndean Border 85 N9
Horndean Hants 9 U6
Horndon Devon 5 N4
Horndon on the Hill Thurr 22 G11
Horne Surrey 11 N2
Horner Somset 16 B7
Horne Row Essex 22 J7
Horners Green Suffk 40 G12
Horney Common E Susx 11 R5
Horn Hill Bucks 20 H4
Horning Norfk 51 P10
Horninghold Leics 38 B1
Horninglow Staffs 46 H8
Horningsea Cambs 39 Q8
Horningsham Wilts 18 B12
Horningtoft Norfk 50 F9
Horningtops Cnwll 4 H8
Hornsbury Somset 6 K2
Hornsby Cumb 67 R2
Hornsbygate Cumb 67 R2
Horns Cross Devon 14 J8
Horns Cross E Susx 12 F11
Hornsea E R Yk 65 R10
Hornsey Gt Lon 21 P5
Horn's Green Gt Lon 21 S11
Horn Street Kent 13 N8
Hornton Oxon 37 L11
Horpit Swindn 29 P11
Horra Shet 106 u4
Horrabridge Devon 5 N7
Horringer Suffk 40 D8
Horringford IoW 9 Q11
Horrocks Fold Bolton 55 R4
Horrocksford Lancs 62 F11
Horsacott Devon 15 M6
Horsebridge Devon 5 L5
Horsebridge E Susx 11 T9
Horsebridge Hants 9 L2
Horsebridge Shrops 44 J12
Horsebridge Staffs 46 C3
Horsebrook Staffs 45 U11
Horsecastle N Som 17 M3
Horsedown Cnwll 2 G10
Horsegate Lincs 48 J11
Horsehay Wrekin 45 Q12
Horseheath Cambs 39 T11
Horsehouse N York 63 L3
Horsell Surrey 20 G11
Horseman's Green Wrexhm 44 K5
Horsenden Bucks 30 G12
Horsey Norfk 51 S9
Horsey Somset 16 K9
Horsey Corner Norfk 51 S9
Horsford Norfk 51 L10
Horsforth Leeds 63 Q12
Horsham W Susx 10 K4
Horsham Worcs 35 R9
Horsham St Faith Norfk 51 M10
Horsington Lincs 59 L13
Horsington Somset 17 T12
Horsley Derbys 47 L5
Horsley Gloucs 28 F8
Horsley Nthumb 76 G6
Horsley Nthumb 77 M12
Horsley Cross Essex 23 R2
Horsleycross Street Essex 23 R2
Horsley-Gate Derbys 57 M11
Horsleyhill Border 76 A2
Horsley's Green Bucks 20 C4
Horsley Woodhouse Derbys 47 L5
Horsmonden Kent 12 D7
Horspath Oxon 30 C11
Horstead Norfk 51 N10
Horsted Keynes W Susx 11 P5
Horton Bucks 30 K9
Horton Dorset 8 E7
Horton Lancs 62 H9
Horton Nhants 38 B10
Horton S Glos 28 E11
Horton Shrops 45 L8
Horton Somset 6 K2
Horton Staffs 46 B2
Horton Surrey 21 L10
Horton Swans 25 S13
Horton W & M 20 H7
Horton Wilts 18 F8
Horton Wrekin 45 Q11
Horton Cross Somset 16 K13
Horton-cum-Studley Oxon 30 C10
Horton Green Ches W 45 L4
Horton Heath Hants 9 P5
Horton-in-Ribblesdale N York 62 G5
Horton Kirby Kent 21 U9
Horwich Bolton 55 P4
Horwich End Derbys 56 F10
Horwood Devon 15 M7
Hoscar Lancs 55 L4
Hoscote Border 75 S3
Hose Leics 47 T8
Hosey Hill Kent 21 S12
Hosh P & K 90 C7
Hoswick Shet 106 u11
Hotham E R Yk 64 K13
Hothfield Kent 12 J7
Hoton Leics 47 Q9
Hott Nthumb 76 F8
Hough Ches E 45 S3
Hough Ches E 56 C11
Hougham Lincs 48 C5
Hough End Leeds 63 R13
Hough Green Halton 55 L9
Hough-on-the-Hill Lincs 48 D4
Houghton Cambs 39 L6
Houghton Cumb 75 T14
Houghton Hants 19 M13
Houghton Nthumb 77 N12
Houghton Pembks 24 G9
Houghton W Susx 10 G8
Houghton Conquest C Beds 31 M4
Houghton Gate Dur 70 D2
Houghton Green E Susx 12 H11
Houghton Green Warrtn 55 P8
Houghton le Side Darltn 69 R8
Houghton-le-Spring Sundld 70 D3
Houghton on the Hill Leics 47 S13
Houghton Regis C Beds 31 M8
Houghton St Giles Norfk 50 F6
Hound Green Hants 20 B11
Houndslow Border 84 G9
Houndsmoor Somset 16 F11
Houndwood Border 85 L6
Hounslow Gt Lon 20 K7
Househill Highld 103 N4
Houses Hill Kirk 56 J3
Housieside Abers 105 P10
Houston Rens 88 K12
Houstry Highld 112 E10
Houton Ork 106 s19
Hove Br & H 11 M10
Hove Edge Calder 56 H2
Hoveringham Notts 47 S4
Hoveton Norfk 51 P10
Hovingham N York 64 F4
Howbrook Barns 57 M7
How Caple Herefs 28 B1
Howden E R Yk 64 G14
Howden-le-Wear Dur 69 Q6
Howe Highld 112 H4
Howe IoM 60 b9
Howe N York 63 T3
Howe Norfk 51 N14
Howe Bridge Wigan 55 Q6
Howe Bridge Crematorium Wigan 55 Q6
Howe Green Essex 22 H7
Howegreen Essex 22 K7
Howell Lincs 48 H4
How End C Beds 31 M4
Howe of Teuchar Abers 105 M6
Howes D & G 75 N12
Howe Street Essex 22 G5
Howe Street Essex 39 U14
Howey Powys 34 B9
Howgate Cumb 66 E8
Howgate Mdloth 83 P7
Howgill Lancs 62 G10
Howick Nthumb 77 R2
Howle Wrekin 45 Q9
Howle Hill Herefs 28 B3
Howlett End Essex 39 S14
Howley Somset 6 J3
How Mill Cumb 67 R1
Howmore W Isls 106 c15
Hownam Border 76 F2
Howrigg Cumb 67 M3
Howsham N Linc 58 H6
Howsham N York 64 G7
Howtel Nthumb 85 M12
Howt Green Kent 12 G2
Howton Herefs 27 S2
Howtown Cumb 67 P9
Howwood Rens 88 J13
Hoxne Suffk 41 L5
Hoy Ork 106 r20
Hoylake Wirral 54 F9
Hoyland Common Barns 57 N6
Hoyland Nether Barns 57 N6
Hoyland Swaine Barns 57 L6
Hoyle W Susx 10 E7
Hoyle Mill Barns 57 N5
Hubberholme N York 62 J4
Hubberston Pembks 24 E9
Hubbert's Bridge Lincs 49 L5
Huby N York 63 R10
Huby N York 64 D6
Huccaby Devon 5 R6
Hucclecote Gloucs 28 G4
Hucking Kent 12 F4
Hucknall Notts 47 P4
Huddersfield Kirk 56 H3
Huddersfield Crematorium Kirk 56 H2
Huddington Worcs 36 B9
Hudnall Herts 31 M10
Hudswell N York 69 P12
Huggate E R Yk 64 K8
Hugglescote Leics 47 M11
Hughenden Valley Bucks 20 E3
Hughley Shrops 45 N14
Hugh Town IoS 2 c2
Huish Devon 15 M10
Huish Wilts 18 H8
Huish Champflower Somset 16 E11
Huish Episcopi Somset 17 M11
Hulcote C Beds 30 K5
Hulcott Bucks 30 J9
Hulham Devon 6 D8
Hulland Derbys 46 H4
Hulland Ward Derbys 46 J4
Hullavington Wilts 18 C4
Hullbridge Essex 22 K8
Hull, Kingston upon C KuH 65 P14
Hulme Manch 55 T7
Hulme Staffs 46 B4
Hulme Warrtn 55 P8
Hulme End Staffs 46 F2
Hulme Walfield Ches E 55 T13
Hulse Heath Ches E 55 R10
Hulton Lane Ends Bolton 55 Q5
Hulverstone IoW 9 M12
Hulver Street Norfk 50 F11
Hulver Street Suffk 41 S3
Humber Devon 6 A9
Humber Herefs 35 M9
Humberside Airport N Linc 58 J4
Humberston NE Lin 59 P5
Humberstone C Leic 47 R12
Humbie E Loth 84 D6
Humbleton E R Yk 65 S13
Humbleton Nthumb 85 P13
Humby Lincs 48 F7
Hume Border 84 J10
Humshaugh Nthumb 76 J11
Huna Highld 112 J2
Huncoat Lancs 62 F13
Huncote Leics 47 P14
Hundalee Border 76 C2
Hundall Derbys 57 N11
Hunderthwaite Dur 69 L8
Hundleby Lincs 59 Q13
Hundle Houses Lincs 48 K3
Hundleton Pembks 24 G10
Hundon Suffk 40 B11
Hundred End Lancs 54 K2
Hundred House Powys 34 D10
Hungarton Leics 47 S12
Hungerford Hants 8 H6
Hungerford Somset 16 D8
Hungerford W Berk 19 M7
Hungerford Newtown W Berk 19 N6
Hunger Hill Bolton 55 Q5
Hunger Hill Lancs 55 M4
Hungerstone Herefs 34 K13
Hungerton Lincs 48 C8
Hungryhatton Shrops 45 Q8
Hunmanby N York 65 P4
Hunningham Warwks 37 L7
Hunnington Worcs 36 C4
Hunsbury Hill Nhants 37 U9
Hunsdon Herts 22 B5
Hunsingore N York 63 U9
Hunslet Leeds 63 S13
Hunsonby Cumb 67 S5
Hunstanton Norfk 49 U5
Hunstanworth Dur 68 K3
Hunsterson Ches E 45 Q4
Hunston Suffk 40 G7
Hunston W Susx 10 D10
Hunston Green Suffk 40 G7
Hunstrete BaNES 17 R4
Hunsworth Kirk 56 J1
Hunt End Worcs 36 D8
Hunter's Inn Devon 15 Q3
Hunter's Quay Ag & B 88 E10
Huntham Somset 16 K11
Hunthill Lodge Angus 98 H9
Huntingdon Cambs 38 K6
Huntingfield Suffk 41 P6
Huntingford Dorset 17 V11
Huntington C York 64 E8
Huntington Ches W 54 K14
Huntington E Loth 84 D4
Huntington Herefs 34 G10
Huntington Herefs 35 L12
Huntington Staffs 46 C11
Huntley Gloucs 28 D4
Huntly Abers 104 G8
Hunton Hants 19 Q12
Hunton Kent 12 D6
Hunton N York 63 P1
Hunton Bridge Herts 31 N12
Hunt's Corner Norfk 40 J3
Huntscott Somset 16 B8
Hunt's Cross Lpool 54 K9
Hunts Green Bucks 30 J12
Hunts Green Warwks 36 G1
Huntsham Devon 16 D12
Huntshaw Devon 15 M8
Huntshaw Cross Devon 15 M8
Huntspill Somset 16 K7
Huntstile Somset 16 J10
Huntworth Somset 16 K10
Hunwick Dur 69 Q6
Hunworth Norfk 50 J6
Hurcott Somset 17 L13
Hurdcott Wilts 8 H2
Hurdsfield Ches E 56 D12
Hurley W & M 20 D6
Hurley Warwks 36 H1
Hurley Bottom W & M 20 D6
Hurley Common Warwks 36 H1
Hurlford E Ayrs 81 P5
Hurlston Green Lancs 54 J4
Hurn Dorset 8 G9
Hurn's End Lincs 49 P4
Hursley Hants 9 N3
Hurst Dorset 7 U6
Hurst N York 69 M12
Hurst Somset 17 N13
Hurst Wokham 20 C8
Hurstbourne Priors Hants 19 P11
Hurstbourne Tarrant Hants 19 N10
Hurst Green E Susx 12 D10
Hurst Green Essex 23 Q5
Hurst Green Lancs 62 D12
Hurst Green Surrey 21 Q12
Hurst Hill Dudley 36 B2
Hurstley Herefs 34 J11
Hurstpierpoint W Susx 11 M7
Hurst Wickham W Susx 11 M7
Hurstwood Lancs 62 H13
Hurtiso Ork 106 u19
Hurtmore Surrey 20 F13
Hurworth Burn Dur 70 F6
Hurworth-on-Tees Darltn 70 D11
Hurworth Place Darltn 69 S11
Hury Dur 69 L9
Husbands Bosworth Leics 37 R4
Husborne Crawley C Beds 31 L5
Husthwaite N York 64 C4
Hutcherleigh Devon 5 T10
Hutcliffe Wood Crematorium Sheff 57 M10
Hut Green N York 57 S2
Huthwaite Notts 47 N2
Huttoft Lincs 59 T11
Hutton Border 85 N8
Hutton Cumb 67 P7
Hutton E R Yk 65 N9
Hutton Essex 22 F8
Hutton Lancs 55 L1
Hutton N Som 17 L5
Hutton Bonville N York 70 D12
Hutton Buscel N York 65 M3
Hutton Conyers N York 63 S5
Hutton Cranswick E R Yk 65 N9
Hutton End Cumb 67 Q5
Hutton Hang N York 63 P2
Hutton Henry Dur 70 F5
Hutton-le-Hole N York 64 G1
Hutton Lowcross R & Cl 70 J10
Hutton Magna Dur 69 P10
Hutton Mulgrave N York 71 P11
Hutton Roof Cumb 62 B4
Hutton Roof Cumb 67 N6
Hutton Rudby N York 70 G11
Hutton Sessay N York 64 B4
Hutton Wandesley N York 64 C9
Huxham Devon 6 B5
Huxham Green Somset 17 Q9
Huxley Ches W 45 M1
Huyton Knows 54 K8
Hycemoor Cumb 60 K2
Hyde Gloucs 28 G7
Hyde Hants 8 H6
Hyde Tamesd 56 D8
Hyde End Wokham 20 B9
Hyde Heath Bucks 30 K12
Hyde Lea Staffs 46 B10
Hydestile Surrey 10 F2
Hykeham Moor Lincs 58 F13
Hylands House & Park Essex 22 G7
Hyndford Bridge S Lans 82 H10
Hynish Ag & B 92 B11
Hyssington Powys 34 H2
Hystfield Gloucs 28 C8
Hythe Essex 23 P2
Hythe Hants 9 N7
Hythe Kent 13 N9
Hythe Somset 17 M6
Hythe End W & M 20 H8
Hyton Cumb 60 K2

I

Ibberton Dorset 7 U3
Ible Derbys 46 H2
Ibsley Hants 8 H7
Ibstock Leics 47 M12
Ibstone Bucks 20 C4
Ibthorpe Hants 19 N10
Iburndale N York 71 Q11
Ibworth Hants 19 S10
Icelton N Som 17 L3
Ichrachan Ag & B 94 E12
Ickburgh Norfk 40 D1
Ickenham Gt Lon 20 J5
Ickford Bucks 30 D11
Ickham Kent 13 P4
Ickleford Herts 31 Q6
Icklesham E Susx 12 G12
Ickleton Cambs 39 Q12
Icklingham Suffk 40 C6
Ickornshaw N York 62 K11
Ickwell Green C Beds 38 J11
Icomb Gloucs 29 P3
Idbury Oxon 29 P4
Iddesleigh Devon 15 N11
Ide Devon 6 A6
Ideford Devon 6 A9
Ide Hill Kent 21 S12
Iden E Susx 12 H11
Iden Green Kent 12 D9
Iden Green Kent 12 F9
Idle C Brad 63 P12
Idless Cnwll 3 L7
Idlicote Warwks 36 J12
Idmiston Wilts 18 J13
Idole Carmth 25 R7
Idridgehay Derbys 46 J4
Idrigill Highld 100 c3
Idstone Oxon 29 Q11
Iffley Oxon 30 B12
Ifield W Susx 11 M3
Ifold W Susx 10 H4
Iford Bmouth 8 G10
Iford E Susx 11 Q9
Ifton Mons 27 T10
Ifton Heath Shrops 44 H6
Ightfield Shrops 45 N6
Ightham Kent 21 U11
Iken Suffk 41 R9
Ilam Staffs 46 F3
Ilchester Somset 17 P12
Ilderton Nthumb 77 L1
Ilford Gt Lon 21 R5
Ilford Somset 17 L13
Ilfracombe Devon 15 M3
Ilkeston Derbys 47 N5
Ilketshall St Andrew Suffk 41 Q3
Ilketshall St John Suffk 41 Q3
Ilketshall St Lawrence Suffk 41 Q4
Ilketshall St Margaret Suffk 41 P3
Ilkley C Brad 63 N10
Illand Cnwll 4 H5
Illey Dudley 36 C4
Illidge Green Ches E 55 S14
Illingworth Calder 63 M14
Illogan Cnwll 2 H8
Illston on the Hill Leics 47 T14
Ilmer Bucks 30 G11
Ilmington Warwks 36 H12
Ilminster Somset 7 L2
Ilsington Devon 5 T5
Ilsington Dorset 7 U6
Ilston Swans 25 U12
Ilton N York 63 N4
Ilton Somset 17 L13
Imachar N Ayrs 79 R8
Immingham NE Lin 59 L3
Immingham Dock NE Lin 59 L3
Impington Cambs 39 P8
Ince Ches W 55 L11
Ince Blundell Sefton 54 H6
Ince-in-Makerfield Wigan 55 N6
Inchbae Lodge Hotel Highld 108 G11
Inchbare Angus 99 L10
Inchberry Moray 104 C4
Incheril Highld 108 B11
Inchinnan Rens 89 L12
Inchlaggan Highld 101 T11
Inchmichael P & K 91 K6
Inchnacardoch Hotel Highld 102 C13
Inchnadamph Highld 110 E12
Inchture P & K 91 L6
Inchvuilt Highld 101 U3
Inchyra P & K 90 J7
Indian Queens Cnwll 3 N5
Ingatestone Essex 22 F8
Ingbirchworth Barns 56 K5
Ingerthorpe N York 63 R6
Ingestre Staffs 46 C9
Ingham Lincs 58 F10
Ingham Norfk 51 Q8
Ingham Suffk 40 E6
Ingham Corner Norfk 51 Q8
Ingleborough Norfk 49 Q10
Ingleby Derbys 46 K8
Ingleby Arncliffe N York 70 F12
Ingleby Barwick S on T 70 G10
Ingleby Cross N York 70 G12
Ingleby Greenhow N York 70 J11
Ingleigh Green Devon 15 P11
Inglesbatch BaNES 17 T4
Inglesham Swindn 29 P8
Ingleston D & G 74 J12
Ingleton Dur 69 Q8
Ingleton N York 62 D5
Inglewhite Lancs 61 U12
Ingoe Nthumb 77 L11
Ingol Lancs 61 U13
Ingoldisthorpe Norfk 49 U7
Ingoldmells Lincs 59 U13
Ingoldsby Lincs 48 F8
Ingram Nthumb 77 L2
Ingrave Essex 22 F9
Ingrow C Brad 63 M12
Ings Cumb 67 P13
Ingst S Glos 28 A10
Ingthorpe Rutlnd 48 E12
Ingworth Norfk 51 L8
Inkberrow Worcs 36 D9
Inkerman Dur 69 P5
Inkhorn Abers 105 Q8
Inkpen W Berk 19 N8
Inkstack Highld 112 G2
Inmarsh Wilts 18 D8
Innellan Ag & B 88 E11
Innerleithen Border 83 R11
Innerleven Fife 91 N11
Innermessan D & G 72 D7
Innerwick E Loth 84 J4
Innesmill Moray 104 B3
Innsworth Gloucs 28 G3
Insch Abers 104 J10
Insh Highld 97 N3
Inskip Lancs 61 T12
Inskip Moss Side Lancs 61 T12
Instow Devon 15 L6
Insworke Cnwll 5 L10
Intake Sheff 57 S5
Inver Abers 98 C5
Inver Highld 109 R8
Inver P & K 90 F3
Inverailort Highld 93 T2
Inveralligin Highld 107 P13
Inverallochy Abers 105 S2
Inveran Highld 108 K5
Inveraray Ag & B 88 C4
Inverarish Highld 100 e6
Inverarity Angus 91 Q3
Inverarnan Stirlg 88 H2
Inverasdale Highld 107 P8
Inverbeg Ag & B 88 H6
Inverbervie Abers 99 Q9
Inver-boyndie Abers 104 K3
Invercreran House Hotel Ag & B 94 E9
Inverdruie Highld 103 N13
Inveresk E Loth 83 R4
Inveresragan Ag & B 94 D11
Inverey Abers 97 T6
Inverfarigaig Highld 102 F11
Inverfolla Ag & B 94 D10
Invergarry Highld 96 C3
Invergeldie P & K 95 U13
Invergloy Highld 101 U14
Invergordon Highld 109 N11
Invergowrie P & K 91 M5
Inverguseran Highld 100 g9
Inverhadden P & K 95 S7
Inverherive Hotel Stirlg 95 M13
Inverie Highld 100 g9
Inverinan Ag & B 87 T2
Inverinate Highld 101 N7
Inverkeilor Angus 91 U2
Inverkeithing Fife 83 M2
Inverkeithny Abers 104 J6
Inverkip Inver 88 F11
Inverkirkaig Highld 110 B13
Inverlael Highld 108 B7
Inverlair Highld 96 C7
Inverliever Lodge Ag & B 87 R4
Inverlochy Ag & B 94 H13
Invermark Angus 98 H7
Invermoriston Highld 102 D12
Invernaver Highld 111 Q4
Inverness Highld 102 J6
Inverness Airport Highld 103 L5
Inverness Crematorium Highld 102 H7
Invernoaden Ag & B 88 D6
Inveroran Hotel Ag & B 94 K10
Inverquharity Angus 98 G12
Inverquhomery Abers 105 S6
Inverroy Highld 96 B7
Inversanda Highld 94 C7
Invershiel Highld 101 N8
Invershin Highld 108 K5
Invershore Highld 112 F9
Inversnaid Hotel Stirlg 88 H4
Inverugie Abers 105 U6
Inveruglas Ag & B 88 H4
Inveruglass Highld 97 N3
Inverurie Abers 105 M11
Inwardleigh Devon 15 N13
Inworth Essex 23 L4
Iochdar W Isls 106 c14
Iona Ag & B 92 H13
Iping W Susx 10 D6
Ipplepen Devon 5 U7
Ipsden Oxon 19 T3
Ipstones Staffs 46 D4
Ipswich Suffk 41 L12
Ipswich Crematorium Suffk 41 L11
Irby Wirral 54 G10
Irby in the Marsh Lincs 59 S14
Irby upon Humber NE Lin 59 L6
Irchester Nhants 38 D7
Ireby Cumb 66 K5
Ireby Lancs 62 D4
Ireland C Beds 31 P4
Ireleth Cumb 61 N4
Ireshopeburn Dur 68 J5
Ireton Wood Derbys 46 J4
Irlam Salfd 55 R8
Irnham Lincs 48 F8
Iron Acton S Glos 28 C11
Iron Bridge Cambs 49 Q14
Ironbridge Wrekin 45 Q13
Ironbridge Gorge Wrekin 45 Q13
Iron Cross Warwks 36 E10
Ironmacannie D & G 73 R4
Irons Bottom Surrey 21 M13
Ironville Derbys 47 M3
Irstead Norfk 51 Q9
Irthington Cumb 75 U13
Irthlingborough Nhants 38 E6
Irton N York 65 N3
Irvine N Ayrs 81 L5
Isauld Highld 112 A3
Isbister Shet 106 t4
Isbister Shet 106 v7
Isfield E Susx 11 Q7
Isham Nhants 38 C6
Isington Hants 10 B2
Islandpool Worcs 35 U4
Islay Ag & B 86 F10
Islay Airport Ag & B 78 E5
Isle Abbotts Somset 17 L12
Isle Brewers Somset 17 L12
Isleham Cambs 39 T6
Isle of Dogs Gt Lon 21 Q7
Isle of Grain Medway 23 L12
Isle of Lewis W Isls 106 f5
Isle of Man IoM 60 f5
Isle of Man Ronaldsway Airport IoM 60 d9
Isle of Mull Ag & B 93 Q11
Isle of Purbeck Dorset 8 E12
Isle of Sheppey Kent 23 N13
Isle of Skye Highld 100 d6
Isle of Thanet Kent 13 R2
Isle of Walney Cumb 61 M6
Isle of Whithorn D & G 73 M12
Isle of Wight IoW 9 Q11
Isle of Wight Crematorium IoW 9 Q10
Isleornsay Highld 100 g8
Isles of Scilly IoS 2 c2
Isles of Scilly St Mary's Airport IoS 2 c2
Islesteps D & G 74 J11
Islet Village Guern 6 e2
Isleworth Gt Lon 21 L7
Isley Walton Leics 47 M9
Islibhig W Isls 106 f6
Islington Gt Lon 21 P6
Islip Nhants 38 E5
Islip Oxon 30 B10
Islivig W Isls 106 f6
Isombridge Wrekin 45 P11
Istead Rise Kent 22 F13
Itchen Abbas Hants 9 R2
Itchen Stoke Hants 9 R2
Itchingfield W Susx 10 J5
Itchington S Glos 28 C10
Itteringham Norfk 50 K7
Itton Devon 15 R13
Itton Mons 27 T8
Itton Common Mons 27 T8
Ivegill Cumb 67 P4
Ivelet N York 68 K13
Iver Bucks 20 H6
Iver Heath Bucks 20 H6
Iveston Dur 69 P2
Ivinghoe Bucks 30 K9
Ivinghoe Aston Bucks 31 L9
Ivington Herefs 35 L9
Ivington Green Herefs 35 L9
Ivybridge Devon 5 Q9
Ivychurch Kent 12 K10
Ivy Cross Dorset 8 B4
Ivy Hatch Kent 21 U12
Ivy Todd Norfk 50 E12
Iwade Kent 12 H2
Iwerne Courtney or Shroton Dorset 8 B6
Iwerne Minster Dorset 8 B6
Ixworth Suffk 40 F6
Ixworth Thorpe Suffk 40 F6

J

Jack Green Lancs 55 N1
Jack Hill N York 63 P9
Jack-in-the-Green Devon 6 D5
Jack's Bush Hants 19 L13
Jacksdale Notts 47 M3
Jackson Bridge Kirk 56 J5
Jackton S Lans 81 R1
Jacobstow Cnwll 14 E13
Jacobstowe Devon 15 N12
Jacobs Well Surrey 20 G12
Jameston Pembks 24 J11
Jamestown Highld 102 E4
Jamestown W Duns 88 J9
Janetstown Highld 112 D4
Janetstown Highld 112 J6
Jardine Hall D & G 75 M8
Jarrow S Tyne 77 S13
Jarvis Brook E Susx 11 S5
Jasper's Green Essex 22 H2
Jawcraig Falk 89 T10
Jaywick Essex 23 S5
Jealott's Hill Br For 20 E8
Jeater Houses N York 70 F14
Jedburgh Border 76 C1
Jeffreyston Pembks 24 J9
Jemimaville Highld 102 K2
Jerbourg Guern 6 e4
Jersey Jersey 7 d2
Jersey Airport Jersey 7 b2
Jersey Crematorium Jersey 7 d3
Jersey Marine Neath 26 C9
Jerusalem Lincs 58 F12
Jesmond N u Ty 77 R12
Jevington E Susx 11 T10
Jingle Street Mons 27 T5
Jockey End Herts 31 M10
Jodrell Bank Ches E 55 S12
Johnby Cumb 67 P6
John Lennon Airport Lpool 54 K10
John o' Groats Highld 112 J2
John's Cross E Susx 12 D11
Johnshaven Abers 99 P10
Johnson's Street Norfk 51 Q10
Johnston Pembks 24 F8
Johnstone D & G 75 P5
Johnstone Rens 88 K13
Johnstonebridge D & G 75 M7
Johnstown Carmth 25 R7
Johnstown Wrexhm 44 H4
Joppa C Edin 83 R4
Joppa Cerdgn 33 L7
Joppa S Ayrs 81 N9
Jordans Bucks 20 G4
Jordanston Pembks 24 F4
Jordanthorpe Sheff 57 N10
Joyden's Wood Kent 22 D13
Jubilee Corner Kent 12 F6
Jump Barns 57 N6
Jumper's Town E Susx 11 R4
Juniper Nthumb 76 J14
Juniper Green C Edin 83 N5
Jura Ag & B 86 J9
Jurassic Coast Devon 6 F7
Jurby IoM 60 f3
Jurston Devon 5 R4

K

Kaber Cumb 68 G10
Kaimend S Lans 82 J9
Kames Ag & B 87 T11
Kames E Ayrs 82 C13
Kea Cnwll 3 L8
Keadby N Linc 58 D4
Keal Cotes Lincs 49 N1
Kearby Town End N York 63 S10
Kearsley Bolton 55 S6
Kearsley Nthumb 77 L11
Kearsney Kent 13 Q7
Kearstwick Cumb 62 C4
Kearton N York 69 L13
Keasden N York 62 E6
Keaton Devon 5 Q10
Keckwick Halton 55 N10
Keddington Lincs 59 Q9
Keddington Corner Lincs 59 Q9
Kedington Suffk 40 B12
Kedleston Derbys 46 K5
Keelby Lincs 59 L4
Keele Staffs 45 T4
Keele Services Staffs 45 T5
Keele University Staffs 45 T4
Keeley Green Bed 38 F11
Keelham C Brad 63 M13
Keeston Pembks 24 F7
Keevil Wilts 18 D9
Kegworth Leics 47 N8
Kehelland Cnwll 2 G8
Keig Abers 104 J12
Keighley C Brad 63 M11
Keighley Crematorium C Brad 63 L12
Keilarsbrae Clacks 90 C13
Keillour P & K 90 E6
Keiloch Abers 98 B5
Keils Ag & B 86 J12
Keinton Mandeville Somset 17 P10
Keir Mill D & G 74 G7
Keirsleywell Row Nthumb 68 G2
Keisby Lincs 48 F8
Keisley Cumb 68 F8
Keiss Highld 112 H4
Keith Moray 104 E5
Keithick P & K 90 K4
Keithock Angus 99 L11
Keithtown Highld 102 F4
Kelbrook Lancs 62 J11
Kelby Lincs 48 F5
Keld Cumb 67 S10
Keld N York 68 J12
Keld Head N York 64 H3
Keldholme N York 64 G2
Kelfield N Linc 58 D6
Kelfield N York 64 D12
Kelham Notts 47 U2
Kelhead D & G 75 M12
Kellacott Devon 5 L3
Kellamergh Lancs 61 S14
Kellas Angus 91 Q4
Kellas Moray 103 U5
Kellaton Devon 5 U13
Kelleth Cumb 68 E11
Kelling Norfk 50 J5
Kellington N York 57 S2
Kelloe Dur 70 D5
Kelloholm D & G 74 D3
Kells Cumb 66 E9
Kelly Devon 4 K4
Kelly Bray Cnwll 4 K6
Kelmarsh Nhants 37 T5
Kelmscott Oxon 29 P8
Kelsale Suffk 41 Q7
Kelsall Ches W 55 M13
Kelshall Herts 31 T5
Kelsick Cumb 66 J2
Kelso Border 84 J12
Kelstedge Derbys 57 M14
Kelstern Lincs 59 M9
Kelsterton Flints 54 G12
Kelston BaNES 17 T3
Keltneyburn P & K 95 V9
Kelton D & G 74 J11
Kelty Fife 90 H13
Kelvedon Essex 23 L4
Kelvedon Hatch Essex 22 E8
Kelynack Cnwll 2 B11
Kemacott Devon 15 Q3
Kemback Fife 91 P9
Kemberton Shrops 45 R13
Kemble Gloucs 28 J8
Kemble Wick Gloucs 28 J8
Kemerton Worcs 36 C13
Kemeys Commander Mons 27 Q7
Kemnay Abers 105 L12
Kempe's Corner Kent 12 K6
Kempley Gloucs 28 C2
Kempley Green Gloucs 28 C2
Kempsey Worcs 35 T11
Kempsford Gloucs 29 N8
Kemps Green Warwks 36 F6
Kempshott Hants 19 T10
Kempston Bed 38 F11
Kempston Hardwick Bed 31 M4
Kempton Shrops 34 J4
Kemp Town Br & H 11 N10
Kemsing Kent 21 U11
Kemsley Kent 12 H2
Kemsley Street Kent 12 F3
Kenardington Kent 12 J9
Kenchester Herefs 34 K12
Kencot Oxon 29 Q7
Kendal Cumb 67 R14
Kenderchurch Herefs 27 S2
Kendleshire S Glos 28 C12
Kenfig Brdgnd 26 E11
Kenfig Hill Brdgnd 26 E11
Kenilworth Warwks 36 J6
Kenley Gt Lon 21 P10
Kenley Shrops 45 N13
Kenmore Highld 107 N13
Kenmore P & K 95 V9
Kenn Devon 6 B7
Kenn N Som 17 M3
Kennacraig Ag & B 79 Q3
Kennall Vale Cnwll 2 J9
Kennards House Cnwll 4 H4
Kenneggy Cnwll 2 F11
Kennerleigh Devon 15 T11
Kennessee Green Sefton 54 J6
Kennet Clacks 90 D13
Kennethmont Abers 104 G10
Kennett Cambs 39 U7
Kennford Devon 6 B7
Kenninghall Norfk 40 H3
Kennington Kent 12 K7
Kennington Oxon 30 B12
Kennoway Fife 91 N11
Kenny Somset 16 K13
Kenny Hill Suffk 39 T5
Kennythorpe N York 64 H6
Kenovay Ag & B 92 B9
Kensaleyre Highld 100 d4
Kensington Gt Lon 21 N7
Kensington Palace Gt Lon 21 N6
Kensworth Common C Beds 31 M9
Kentallen Highld 94 E7
Kent and Sussex Crematorium Kent 11 T3
Kentchurch Herefs 27 S2
Kentford Suffk 40 B7
Kent Green Ches E 45 T2
Kent International Airport Kent 13 R2
Kentisbeare Devon 6 E3
Kentisbury Devon 15 P4
Kentisbury Ford Devon 15 P4
Kentish Town Gt Lon 21 N6
Kentmere Cumb 67 Q12
Kenton Devon 6 C8
Kenton Gt Lon 21 L5
Kenton N u Ty 77 Q12
Kenton Suffk 41 L7
Kenton Bankfoot N u Ty 77 Q12
Kentra Highld 93 R5
Kents Bank Cumb 61 R4
Kent's Green Gloucs 28 D3
Kent's Oak Hants 9 L4
Kent Street E Susx 12 E12
Kent Street Kent 12 C5
Kenwick Shrops 44 K7
Kenwyn Cnwll 3 L7
Kenyon Warrtn 55 P7
Keoldale Highld 110 H3
Keppoch Highld 101 M7
Kepwick N York 64 B1
Keresley Covtry 36 K4
Kermincham Ches E 55 T13
Kernborough Devon 5 T12
Kerne Bridge Herefs 28 A4
Kerrera Ag & B 93 U13
Kerridge Ches E 56 D11
Kerridge-end Ches E 56 D12
Kerris Cnwll 2 C11
Kerry Powys 34 D2
Kerrycroy Ag & B 88 D13
Kersall Notts 47 T1
Kersbrook Devon 6 E8
Kerscott Devon 15 P7
Kersey Suffk 40 H12
Kersey Tye Suffk 40 G12
Kersey Upland Suffk 40 G12
Kershader W Isls 106 i6
Kershopefoot Cumb 75 U9
Kersoe Worcs 36 C12
Kerswell Devon 6 E3
Kerswell Green Worcs 35 U11
Kerthen Wood Cnwll 2 F10
Kesgrave Suffk 41 M11
Kessingland Suffk 41 T3
Kessingland Beach Suffk 41 T3
Kestle Cnwll 3 P7
Kestle Mill Cnwll 3 L5
Keston Gt Lon 21 R10
Keswick Cumb 67 L8
Keswick Norfk 51 M13
Ketsby Lincs 59 Q11
Kettering Nhants 38 C5
Kettering Crematorium Nhants 38 C5
Ketteringham Norfk 51 L13
Kettins P & K 90 K4
Kettlebaston Suffk 40 G10
Kettlebridge Fife 91 M10
Kettlebrook Staffs 46 H13
Kettleburgh Suffk 41 N8
Kettle Green Herts 22 B4
Kettleholm D & G 75 M10
Kettleness N York 71 P9
Kettleshulme Ches E 56 E11
Kettlesing N York 63 Q8
Kettlesing Bottom N York 63 Q8
Kettlestone Norfk 50 G7
Kettlethorpe Lincs 58 D11
Kettletoft Ork 106 v16
Kettlewell N York 62 K5
Ketton Rutlnd 48 E13
Kew Gt Lon 21 L7
Kew Royal Botanic Gardens Gt Lon 21 L7
Kewstoke N Som 16 K4
Kexbrough Barns 57 M5
Kexby C York 64 G9
Kexby Lincs 58 E9
Key Green Ches E 56 C14
Key Green N York 71 P12
Keyham Leics 47 S12
Keyhaven Hants 9 L10
Keyingham E R Yk 59 M1
Keymer W Susx 11 N8
Keynsham BaNES 17 S3
Keysoe Bed 38 G8
Keysoe Row Bed 38 G8
Keyston Cambs 38 F5
Key Street Kent 12 G3
Keyworth Notts 47 R7
Kibbear Somset 16 H12
Kibblesworth Gatesd 69 R1
Kibworth Beauchamp Leics 37 S2
Kibworth Harcourt Leics 37 S2
Kidbrooke Gt Lon 21 R7
Kidburngill Cumb 66 G8
Kiddemore Green Staffs 45 U12
Kidderminster Worcs 35 T5
Kiddington Oxon 29 T3
Kidd's Moor Norfk 50 K13
Kidlington Oxon 29 U5
Kidmore End Oxon 19 U5
Kidsdale D & G 73 L12
Kidsgrove Staffs 45 T3
Kidstones N York 62 K3
Kidwelly Carmth 25 R9
Kiel Crofts Ag & B 94 C11
Kielder Nthumb 76 C7
Kielder Forest 76 D8
Kiells Ag & B 86 G12
Kilbarchan Rens 88 K13
Kilbeg Highld 100 f9
Kilberry Ag & B 79 N3
Kilbirnie N Ayrs 88 J14
Kilbride Ag & B 87 N10
Kilbride Ag & B 88 C12
Kilbuiack Moray 103 S3
Kilburn Derbys 47 L4
Kilburn Gt Lon 21 M6
Kilburn N York 64 C4
Kilby Leics 37 R1
Kilchamaig Ag & B 79 Q3
Kilchattan Ag & B 80 F2
Kilchattan Ag & B 86 F6
Kilcheran Ag & B 93 U11
Kilchoan Highld 93 M6
Kilchoman Ag & B 78 C3
Kilchrenan Ag & B 94 E14
Kilconquhar Fife 91 Q11
Kilcot Gloucs 28 C2
Kilcoy Highld 102 F5
Kilcreggan Ag & B 88 F9
Kildale N York 70 K11
Kildalloig Ag & B 79 P12
Kildary Highld 109 P10
Kildavaig Ag & B 87 T12
Kildavanan Ag & B 88 B12
Kildonan Highld 111 U12
Kildonan N Ayrs 80 E8
Kildonan Lodge Highld 111 U12
Kildonnan Highld 93 M1
Kildrochet House D & G 72 D8
Kildrummy Abers 104 F12
Kildwick N York 63 L10
Kilfinan Ag & B 87 S10
Kilfinnan Highld 96 B4
Kilford Denbgs 54 C13
Kilgetty Pembks 24 K9
Kilgrammie S Ayrs 80 K12
Kilgwrrwg Common Mons 27 T8
Kilham E R Yk 65 P7
Kilham Nthumb 85 M12
Kilkenneth Ag & B 92 A10
Kilkenzie Ag & B 79 M11
Kilkerran Ag & B 79 N12
Kilkhampton Cnwll 14 G10
Killamarsh Derbys 57 Q10
Killay Swans 25 V12
Killearn Stirlg 89 M8
Killen Highld 102 J4
Killerby Darltn 69 Q9
Killerton Devon 6 C4
Killichonan P & K 95 Q7
Killiechonate Highld 94 J2
Killiechronan Ag & B 93 N10
Killiecrankie P & K 97 Q11
Killilan Highld 101 N5
Killimster Highld 112 H5
Killin Stirlg 95 R12
Killinghall N York 63 R8
Killington Cumb 62 C2
Killington Devon 15 Q3
Killington Lake Services Cumb 62 B1
Killingworth N Tyne 77 R11
Killiow Cnwll 3 L8
Killochyett Border 84 D10
Kilmacolm Inver 88 J11
Kilmahog Stirlg 89 P4
Kilmahumaig Ag & B 87 P7
Kilmaluag Highld 100 d2
Kilmany Fife 91 N7
Kilmarnock E Ayrs 81 N5
Kilmartin Ag & B 87 Q6
Kilmaurs E Ayrs 81 N4
Kilmelford Ag & B 87 R2
Kilmersdon Somset 17 S6
Kilmeston Hants 9 R3
Kilmichael Ag & B 79 M11
Kilmichael Glassary Ag & B 87 R7
Kilmichael of Inverlussa Ag & B 87 P8
Kilmington Devon 6 J5
Kilmington Wilts 17 U9
Kilmington Common Wilts 17 U9
Kilmington Street Wilts 17 U9
Kilmorack Highld 102 E7
Kilmore Ag & B 94 B13
Kilmore Highld 100 f9
Kilmory Ag & B 87 N11
Kilmory Highld 93 N4
Kilmory N Ayrs 80 D8
Kilmuir Highld 100 b5
Kilmuir Highld 100 c2
Kilmuir Highld 102 J6
Kilmuir Highld 109 P10
Kilmun Ag & B 88 E9
Kilnave Ag & B 86 D11
Kilncadzow S Lans 82 G9
Kilndown Kent 12 D8
Kiln Green Wokham 20 D7
Kilnhill Cumb 66 K6
Kilnhouses Ches W 55 P13
Kilnhurst Rothm 57 Q7
Kilninver Ag & B 87 Q1
Kiln Pit Hill Nthumb 69 M1
Kilnsea E R Yk 59 R3
Kilnsey N York 62 K6
Kilnwick E R Yk 65 M10
Kilnwick Percy E R Yk 64 J10
Kiloran Ag & B 86 F6
Kilpatrick N Ayrs 79 S10
Kilpeck Herefs 27 S1
Kilpin E R Yk 58 C1
Kilpin Pike E R Yk 58 C1
Kilrenny Fife 91 S11
Kilsby Nhants 37 Q6
Kilspindie P & K 90 K6
Kilstay D & G 72 E12
Kilsyth N Lans 89 R10
Kiltarlity Highld 102 F7
Kilton R & Cl 71 M9
Kilton Thorpe R & Cl 71 L9
Kilvaxter Highld 100 c3
Kilve Somset 16 F8
Kilvington Notts 48 B5
Kilwinning N Ayrs 81 L4
Kimberley Norfk 50 J13
Kimberley Notts 47 N5
Kimberworth Rothm 57 P8
Kimblesworth Dur 69 S3
Kimble Wick Bucks 30 H11
Kimbolton Cambs 38 H7
Kimbolton Herefs 35 M8
Kimcote Leics 37 Q3
Kimmeridge Dorset 8 C13
Kimmerston Nthumb 85 P11
Kimpton Hants 19 L11
Kimpton Herts 31 Q9
Kimworthy Devon 14 H10
Kinbrace Highld 111 T10
Kinbuck Stirlg 89 S4
Kincaple Fife 91 Q8
Kincardine Fife 90 D14
Kincardine Highld 109 L7
Kincardine O'Neil Abers 98 K4
Kinclaven P & K 90 J4
Kincorth C Aber 99 S3
Kincorth House Moray 103 R3
Kincraig Highld 97 N2
Kincraigie P & K 90 E2
Kindallachan P & K 90 E2
Kinerarach Ag & B 79 M5
Kineton Gloucs 29 L2
Kineton Warwks 36 K10
Kinfauns P & K 90 J7
Kingarth Ag & B 80 F1
Kingcausie Abers 99 R4
Kingcoed Mons 27 S6
Kingerby Lincs 58 J8
Kingford Devon 14 G11
Kingham Oxon 29 P3
Kingholm Quay D & G 74 J11
Kinghorn Fife 83 Q1
Kinglassie Fife 90 K12
Kingoldrum Angus 98 E12
Kingoodie P & K 91 M6
King's Acre Herefs 35 L12
Kingsand Cnwll 5 L10
Kingsash Bucks 30 J11
Kingsbarns Fife 91 S9
Kingsbridge Devon 5 S12
Kingsbridge Somset 16 C9
Kings Bridge Swans 25 U11
King's Bromley Staffs 46 F10
Kingsburgh Highld 100 c4
Kingsbury Gt Lon 21 L5
Kingsbury Warwks 36 H1
Kingsbury Episcopi Somset 17 M12
King's Caple Herefs 27 V2
Kingsclere Hants 19 R9
King's Cliffe Nhants 38 F1
Kings Clipstone Notts 57 T14
Kingscote Gloucs 28 F8
Kingscott Devon 15 M9
King's Coughton Warwks 36 E9
Kingscross N Ayrs 80 E7
Kingsdon Somset 17 P11
Kingsdown Kent 13 S6
Kingsdown Swindn 29 N10
Kingsdown Wilts 18 B7
Kingsdown Crematorium Swindn 29 N10
Kingseat Fife 90 H13
Kingsey Bucks 30 F11
Kingsfold W Susx 10 K3
Kingsford C Aber 99 R2
Kingsford E Ayrs 81 N3
Kingsford Worcs 35 T4
Kingsgate Kent 13 S1
Kings Green Gloucs 35 S14
Kingshall Street Suffk 40 F8
Kingsheanton Devon 15 N5
King's Heath Birm 36 E4
Kings Hill Kent 12 C4
King's Hill Wsall 36 C1
Kings House Hotel Highld 94 K8
Kingshouse Hotel Stirlg 89 N1
Kingshurst Solhll 36 G3
Kingside Hill Cumb 66 J2
Kingskerswell Devon 6 A11
Kingskettle Fife 91 M10
Kingsland Dorset 7 N5
Kingsland Herefs 34 K8
Kingsland IoA 52 C6
Kings Langley Herts 31 N12
Kingsley Ches W 55 N12
Kingsley Hants 10 B3
Kingsley Staffs 46 D4
Kingsley Green W Susx 10 D4
Kingsley Holt Staffs 46 D4
Kingsley Park Nhants 37 U8
Kingslow Shrops 45 S14
King's Lynn Norfk 49 T9
Kings Meaburn Cumb 68 D8
Kingsmead Hants 9 R6
King's Mills Guern 6 c3
King's Moss St Hel 55 M6
Kingsmuir Angus 91 Q2
Kings Muir Border 83 Q11
Kingsmuir Fife 91 R10
Kings Newnham Warwks 37 N5
King's Newton Derbys 47 L8
Kingsnorth Kent 12 K8
King's Norton Birm 36 E5
King's Norton Leics 47 S13
Kings Nympton Devon 15 Q9
King's Pyon Herefs 34 K10
Kings Ripton Cambs 39 L5
King's Somborne Hants 9 M2
King's Stag Dorset 7 T2
King's Stanley Gloucs 28 F7
King's Sutton Nhants 37 N13
Kingstanding Birm 36 E2
Kingsteignton Devon 5 V6
Kingsteps Highld 103 Q4
King Sterndale Derbys 56 G12
Kingsthorne Herefs 27 U1
Kingsthorpe Nhants 37 U8
Kingston Cambs 39 M9
Kingston Cnwll 4 K5
Kingston Devon 5 Q11
Kingston Devon 6 E7
Kingston Dorset 7 U3
Kingston Dorset 8 D13
Kingston E Loth 84 E2
Kingston Hants 8 H8
Kingston IoW 9 P12
Kingston Kent 13 N5
Kingston W Susx 10 H10
Kingston Bagpuize Oxon 29 T8
Kingston Blount Oxon 20 B3
Kingston Deverill Wilts 18 B13
Kingstone Herefs 34 K13
Kingstone Somset 7 L2
Kingstone Staffs 46 E8
Kingstone Winslow Oxon 29 Q10
Kingston Lacy House & Gardens Dorset 8 D8
Kingston Lisle Oxon 29 R10
Kingston near Lewes E Susx 11 P9
Kingston on Soar Notts 47 P8
Kingston on Spey Moray 104 C2
Kingston Russell Dorset 7 Q6
Kingston St Mary Somset 16 H11
Kingston Seymour N Som 17 M3
Kingston Stert Oxon 30 F12
Kingston upon Hull C KuH 65 P14
Kingston upon Thames Gt Lon 21 L9
Kingston upon Thames Crematorium Gt Lon 21 L9
Kingstown Cumb 75 S14
King's Walden Herts 31 Q8
Kingswear Devon 5 V10
Kingswells C Aber 99 R2
Kings Weston Bristl 27 U12
Kingswinford Dudley 35 U3
Kingswood Bucks 30 E9
Kingswood Gloucs 28 D9
Kingswood Kent 12 F5
Kingswood Powys 44 F13
Kingswood S Glos 28 B13
Kingswood Somset 16 F9
Kingswood Surrey 21 M11
Kingswood Warwks 36 G6
Kingswood Brook Warwks 36 G6
Kingswood Common Herefs 34 G10
Kingswood Common Staffs 45 T13
Kings Worthy Hants 9 P2
Kingthorpe Lincs 58 K11
Kington Herefs 34 G9
Kington S Glos 28 B9
Kington Worcs 36 C9
Kington Langley Wilts 18 D5
Kington Magna Dorset 17 U12
Kington St Michael Wilts 18 D5
Kingussie Highld 97 M3
Kingweston Somset 17 P10
Kinharrachie Abers 105 Q9
Kinharvie D & G 74 H12
Kinkell Bridge P & K 90 D8
Kinknockie Abers 105 S7
Kinleith C Edin 83 N5
Kinlet Shrops 35 R4
Kinloch Highld 100 d10
Kinloch Highld 110 F10
Kinloch Highld 111 M6
Kinloch P & K 90 H3
Kinlochard Stirlg 89 L5
Kinlochbervie Highld 110 E5
Kinlocheil Highld 94 D3
Kinlochewe Highld 107 T12
Kinloch Hourn Highld 101 P10
Kinlochlaggan Highld 96 G6
Kinlochleven Highld 94 H6
Kinlochmoidart Highld 93 S4
Kinlochnanuagh Highld 93 S2
Kinloch Rannoch P & K 95 T7
Kinloss Moray 103 S3
Kinmel Bay Conwy 53 S6
Kinmuck Abers 105 N12
Kinmundy Abers 105 P12
Kinnabus Ag & B 78 D7
Kinnadie Abers 105 R7
Kinnaird P & K 97 R12
Kinneff Abers 99 Q8
Kinnelhead D & G 75 L4
Kinnell Angus 99 L13
Kinnerley Shrops 44 H9
Kinnersley Herefs 34 H11
Kinnersley Worcs 35 U12
Kinnerton Powys 34 F8
Kinnerton Shrops 34 J1
Kinnerton Green Flints 44 H1
Kinnesswood P & K 90 J11
Kinninvie Dur 69 N8
Kinnordy Angus 98 F12
Kinoulton Notts 47 S7
Kinross P & K 90 H11
Kinrossie P & K 90 J5
Kinross Services P & K 90 H11
Kinsbourne Green Herts 31 P9
Kinsey Heath Ches E 45 Q5
Kinsham Herefs 34 J7
Kinsham Worcs 36 B13
Kinsley Wakefd 57 P4
Kinson Bmouth 8 F9
Kintail Highld 101 P8
Kintbury W Berk 19 N7
Kintessack Moray 103 R3
Kintillo P & K 90 H8
Kinton Herefs 34 K6
Kinton Shrops 44 J10
Kintore Abers 105 M12
Kintour Ag & B 78 H5
Kintra Ag & B 78 E6
Kintra Ag & B 92 J13
Kintraw Ag & B 87 Q5
Kintyre Ag & B 79 N8
Kinveachy Highld 103 P12
Kinver Staffs 35 T4
Kiplin N York 69 S13
Kippax Leeds 63 U13
Kippen Stirlg 89 P7
Kippford or Scaur D & G 66 B2
Kipping's Cross Kent 12 B7
Kirbister Ork 106 s19
Kirby Bedon Norfk 51 N12
Kirby Bellars Leics 47 T10
Kirby Cane Norfk 41 Q2
Kirby Corner Covtry 36 J5
Kirby Cross Essex 23 T3
Kirby Fields Leics 47 P13
Kirby Grindalythe N York 65 L6
Kirby Hill N York 63 T6
Kirby Hill N York 69 P11
Kirby Knowle N York 64 B2
Kirby-le-Soken Essex 23 T3
Kirby Misperton N York 64 H4
Kirby Muxloe Leics 47 P13
Kirby Sigston N York 70 F14
Kirby Underdale E R Yk 64 J8
Kirby Wiske N York 63 T3
Kirdford W Susx 10 G5
Kirk Highld 112 G5
Kirkabister Shet 106 u10
Kirkandrews D & G 73 Q10
Kirkandrews upon Eden Cumb 75 S14
Kirkbampton Cumb 67 M1
Kirkbean D & G 66 C1
Kirk Bramwith Donc 57 T4
Kirkbride Cumb 66 K1
Kirkbridge N York 63 R1
Kirkbuddo Angus 91 R3
Kirkburn Border 83 Q11
Kirkburn E R Yk 65 M8
Kirkburton Kirk 56 J4
Kirkby Knows 54 K7
Kirkby Lincs 58 J8
Kirkby N York 70 H11
Kirkby Fleetham N York 69 S14
Kirkby Green Lincs 48 G2
Kirkby in Ashfield Notts 47 N2
Kirkby-in-Furness Cumb 61 N3
Kirkby la Thorpe Lincs 48 G4
Kirkby Lonsdale Cumb 62 C4
Kirkby Malham N York 62 H7
Kirkby Mallory Leics 47 N13
Kirkby Malzeard N York 63 Q5
Kirkby Mills N York 64 G2
Kirkbymoorside N York 64 F2
Kirkby on Bain Lincs 48 K1
Kirkby Overblow N York 63 S10
Kirkby Stephen Cumb 68 G11
Kirkby Thore Cumb 68 D7
Kirkby Underwood Lincs 48 G8
Kirkby Wharf N York 64 C11
Kirkby Woodhouse Notts 47 N3
Kirkcaldy Fife 91 L13
Kirkcaldy Crematorium Fife 91 L13
Kirkcambeck Cumb 76 A12
Kirkchrist D & G 73 R9
Kirkcolm D & G 72 C6
Kirkconnel D & G 74 E3
Kirkconnell D & G 74 J12
Kirkcowan D & G 72 J7
Kirkcudbright D & G 73 R9
Kirkdale Lpool 54 H8
Kirk Deighton N York 63 T9
Kirk Ella E R Yk 65 N14
Kirkfieldbank S Lans 82 G10
Kirkgunzeon D & G 74 G12
Kirk Hallam Derbys 47 N5
Kirkham Lancs 61 S13
Kirkham N York 64 G6
Kirkhamgate Wakefd 57 L2
Kirk Hammerton N York 64 B8
Kirkharle Nthumb 77 L9
Kirkhaugh Nthumb 68 E3
Kirkheaton Kirk 56 J3
Kirkheaton Nthumb 77 L10
Kirkhill Highld 102 G6
Kirkhope S Lans 74 J4
Kirkhouse Cumb 76 B14
Kirkhouse Green Donc 57 T4
Kirkibost Highld 100 e8
Kirkinch P & K 91 M3
Kirkinner D & G 73 L9
Kirkintilloch E Duns 89 Q11
Kirk Ireton Derbys 46 J3
Kirkland Cumb 66 G9
Kirkland Cumb 68 D6
Kirkland D & G 74 E3
Kirkland D & G 74 G7
Kirkland D & G 75 L8
Kirkland Guards Cumb 66 J4
Kirk Langley Derbys 46 J6
Kirkleatham R & Cl 70 J8
Kirklevington S on T 70 F11
Kirkley Suffk 41 T2
Kirklington N York 63 S3
Kirklington Notts 47 S3
Kirklinton Cumb 75 T12
Kirkliston C Edin 83 M4
Kirkmabreck D & G 73 N8
Kirkmaiden D & G 72 E12
Kirk Merrington Dur 69 S6
Kirk Michael IoM 60 e4
Kirkmichael P & K 97 T12
Kirkmichael S Ayrs 81 L11
Kirkmuirhill S Lans 82 E10
Kirknewton Nthumb 85 N12
Kirknewton W Loth 83 M5
Kirkney Abers 104 G9
Kirk of Shotts N Lans 82 F5
Kirkoswald Cumb 67 S4

Kirkoswald S Ayrs....80 J11
Kirkpatrick D & G....74 H7
Kirkpatrick Durham D & G....8 E11
Kirkpatrick-Fleming D & G....75 Q11
Kirk Sandall Donc....57 T5
Kirksanton Cumb....61 L13
Kirk Smeaton N York....57 R3
Kirkstall Leeds....63 R12
Kirkstead Lincs....48 J1
Kirkstile Abers....104 G8
Kirkstile D & G....75 Q7
Kirkstone Pass Inn Cumb....67 P11
Kirkstyle Highld....112 H2
Kirkthorpe Wakefd....57 N2
Kirkton Abers....104 J10
Kirkton D & G....75 N6
Kirkton Fife....91 N6
Kirkton Highld....101 L6
Kirkton Highld....90 E8
Kirkton Highld....101 P3
Kirkton Manor Border....83 P11
Kirkton of Airlie Angus....98 E13
Kirkton of Auchterhouse Highld....91 M4
Kirkton of Barevan Highld....103 N4
Kirkton of Collace P & K....90 J5
Kirkton of Glenbuchat Abers....104 D12
Kirkton of Logie Buchan Abers....105 R10
Kirkton of Menmuir Angus....98 J11
Kirkton of Monikie Angus....91 M4
Kirkton of Rayne Abers....104 K9
Kirkton of Skene Abers....99 Q2
Kirkton of Strathmartine Angus....91 N4
Kirkton of Tealing Angus....91 N4
Kirkton of Tough Abers....104 J13
Kirktown Abers....105 T5
Kirktown Abers....105 T5
Kirktown of Alvah Abers....104 K4
Kirktown of Bourtie Abers....105 N10
Kirktown of Fetteresso Abers....99 R6
Kirktown of Mortlach Moray....104 C8
Kirktown of Slains Abers....105 S10
Kirkurd Border....83 M10
Kirkwall Ork....106 t18
Kirkwall Airport Ork....106 t19
Kirkwhelpington Nthumb....76 K9
Kirk Yetholm Border....85 L13
Kirmington N Linc....58 K4
Kirmond le Mire Lincs....59 L8
Kirn Ag & B....88 E10
Kirriemuir Angus....98 F13
Kirstead Green Norfk....51 N1
Kirtlebridge D & G....75 P11
Kirtling Cambs....39 U9
Kirtling Green Cambs....39 U9
Kirtlington Oxon....29 U4
Kirtomy Highld....111 Q4
Kirton Lincs....49 M6
Kirton Notts....57 U13
Kirton Suffk....41 N12
Kirton End Lincs....49 L5
Kirtonhill W Duns....88 J10
Kirton Holme N Linc....58 F7
Kirwaugh D & G....73 L9
Kishorn Highld....101 L4
Kislingbury Nhants....37 S9
Kitebrook Warwks....29 P1
Kites Green Warwks....36 G7
Kites Hardwick Warwks....37 N7
Kittisford Somset....16 E12
Kittle Swans....25 U13
Kitt's Green Birm....36 G3
Kittybrewster C Aber....99 S2
Kitwood Hants....9 T2
Kivernoll Herefs....27 T1
Kiveton Park Rothm....57 Q10
Knaith Lincs....58 D9
Knaith Park Lincs....58 D9
Knap Corner Dorset....17 V12
Knaphill Surrey....20 G11
Knapp Somset....16 K11
Knapp Hill Hants....9 N4
Knapthorpe Notts....47 T2
Knapton N York....64 D9
Knapton Norfk....51 P7
Knapton Green Herefs....34 K10
Knapwell Cambs....39 M8
Knaresborough N York....63 T8
Knarsdale Nthumb....68 E2
Knaven Abers....105 P7
Knayton N York....63 U2
Knebworth Herts....31 R8
Knedlington E R Yk....64 G14
Kneesall Notts....47 U14
Kneesworth Cambs....31 T4
Kneeton Notts....47 T4
Knelston Swans....25 S13
Knenhall Staffs....46 B6
Knettishall Suffk....40 G4
Knightacott Devon....15 Q5
Knightcote Warwks....37 M10
Knightley Staffs....45 T9
Knightley Dale Staffs....45 T9
Knighton C Leic....47 R13
Knighton Devon....5 N11
Knighton Dorset....7 R2
Knighton Poole....8 E9
Knighton Somset....16 G8
Knighton Staffs....45 R5
Knighton Staffs....45 S8
Knighton Wilts....19 L6
Knighton on Teme Worcs....35 P7
Knightsbridge Gloucs....28 G2
Knightsmill Cnwll....4 A6
Knightwick Worcs....35 R9
Knill Herefs....34 G8
Knipton Leics....48 B7
Knitsley Dur....69 P3
Kniveton Derbys....46 H3
Knock Cumb....68 E7
Knock Highld....100 f9
Knock Moray....104 G5
Knock W Isls....106 j5
Knockally Highld....112 D11
Knockan Highld....108 C2
Knockando Moray....103 U7
Knockbain Highld....102 H4
Knockbain Highld....102 H3
Knock Castle N Ayrs....88 E13
Knockdee Highld....112 E4
Knockdow Ag & B....88 D10
Knockdown Wilts....28 F10
Knockeen S Ayrs....81 L4
Knockenkelly N Ayrs....80 E7
Knockentiber E Ayrs....81 N5
Knockhall Kent....22 E13
Knockholt Kent....21 S11
Knockholt Pound Kent....21 S11
Knockin Shrops....44 H9
Knockinlaw E Ayrs....81 N5
Knocknain D & G....72 B7
Knocksharry IoM....60 d5
Knocksheen D & G....73 P5
Knockvennie Smithy D & G....74 E11
Knodishall Suffk....41 R8
Knodishall Common Suffk....41 R8
Knole Somset....17 M11
Knole Park S Glos....28 A11
Knolls Green Ches E....55 T11
Knook Wilts....18 D12
Knossington Leics....48 B12
Knott End-on-Sea Lancs....61 R10
Knotting Bed....38 F8
Knotting Green Bed....38 F8
Knottingley Wakefd....57 S2
Knotty Ash Lpool....54 K8
Knotty Green Bucks....20 F3
Knowbury Shrops....35 N5
Knowe D & G....72 K6
Knowehead D & G....73 R3
Knowes of Elrick Abers....104 K5
Knoweside S Ayrs....80 K9
Knowle Bristl....27 V13
Knowle Devon....6 D3
Knowle Devon....15 M4
Knowle Devon....15 S12
Knowle Shrops....35 N6
Knowle Solhll....36 G5
Knowle Green Lancs....62 C12
Knowle Hill Surrey....20 G9
Knowle St Giles Somset....16 K13
Knowle Village Hants....9 R7
Knowle Wood Calder....56 D2
Knowl Green Essex....40 C12
Knowl Hill W & M....20 D7
Knowlton Dorset....8 E7
Knowlton Kent....13 P4
Knowsley Knows....54 K7

Knowsley Safari Park Knows....55 L8
Knowstone Devon....15 T8
Knox N York....63 R8
Knox Bridge Kent....12 E7
Knucklas Powys....34 G6
Knuston Nhants....38 D7
Knutsford Ches E....55 T11
Knutsford Services Ches E....55 R11
Knutton Staffs....45 T4
Krumlin Calder....56 G3
Kuggar Cnwll....2 J13
Kyleakin Highld....100 g7
Kyle of Lochalsh Highld....100 g7
Kylerhea Highld....100 g7
Kylesku Highld....110 E10
Kylesmorar Highld....100 h10
Kyles Scalpay W Isls....106 h9
Kylestrome Highld....110 E10
Kynaston Herefs....35 P13
Kynaston Shrops....44 J9
Kynnersley Wrekin....45 Q10
Kyre Green Worcs....35 N7
Kyre Park Worcs....35 P8
Kyrewood Worcs....35 N7
Kyrle Somset....16 E12

L

La Bellieuse Guern....6 d3
Lacasaigh W Isls....106 i6
Lacasdal W Isls....106 j5
Laceby NE Lin....59 M5
Lacey Green Bucks....30 H12
Lach Dennis Ches E....55 R12
Lackenby R & Cl....70 J9
Lackford Suffk....40 C6
Lackford Green Suffk....40 C6
Lacock Wilts....18 D7
Ladbroke Warwks....37 M9
Ladderedge Staffs....46 B2
Laddingford Kent....12 C6
Lade Bank Lincs....49 N3
Ladock Cnwll....3 M6
Lady Ork....106 v15
Ladybank Fife....91 M10
Ladycross Cnwll....4 J3
Lady Hall Cumb....61 M2
Ladykirk Border....85 M9
Ladyridge Herefs....28 A1
Lady's Green Suffk....40 C9
Ladywood Birm....36 E3
Ladywood Worcs....35 U8
La Fontenelle Guern....6 e1
La Fosse Guern....6 d4
Lagavulin Ag & B....79 R5
Lagg N Ayrs....80 D8
Laggan Highld....96 G4
Laggan Highld....97 P5
Lagganlia Highld....97 P3
La Greve Guern....6 e2
La Greve de Lecq Jersey....7 b1
La Houguette Guern....6 d3
Laid Highld....110 K4
Laide Highld....107 Q6
Laigh Clunch E Ayrs....81 P3
Laigh Fenwick E Ayrs....81 P3
Laigh Glenmuir E Ayrs....81 S8
Laighstonehall S Lans....82 D8
Laindon Essex....22 G10
Lair Highld....101 P3
Lairg Highld....109 L4
Laisterdyke C Brad....63 P13
Laithes Cumb....67 Q6
Lake Devon....15 N9
Lake IoW....9 R12
Lake Wilts....18 H13
Lakenheath Suffk....40 B4
Laker's Green Surrey....10 G3
Lakesend Norfk....39 R1
Lakeside Cumb....61 R2
Laleham Surrey....20 J9
Laleston Brdgnd....26 F12
Lamanva Cnwll....2 K10
Lamarsh Essex....40 E13
Lamas Norfk....51 M9
Lamb Corner Essex....23 Q1
Lambden Border....84 J10
Lamberhurst Kent....12 C8
Lamberhurst Down Kent....12 C8
Lamberton Border....85 P7
Lambeth Gt Lon....21 P7
Lambeth Crematorium Gt Lon....21 N8
Lambfair Green Suffk....40 B10
Lambley Notts....47 R4
Lambley Nthumb....76 D14
Lambourn W Berk....19 M5
Lambourne End Essex....21 S3
Lambourn Woodlands W Berk....19 L6
Lamb Roe Lancs....62 E12
Lambs Green W Susx....11 L4
Lambston Pembks....24 F7
Lamellion Cnwll....4 G8
Lamerton Devon....5 L6
Lamesley Gatesd....77 R14
Lamington S Lans....82 H11
Lamlash N Ayrs....80 E6
Lamonby Cumb....67 P5
Lamorick Cnwll....3 Q4
Lamorna Cnwll....2 C12
Lamorran Cnwll....3 M8
Lampen Cnwll....4 G6
Lampeter Cerdgn....33 L11
Lampeter Velfrey Pembks....25 L8
Lamphey Pembks....24 H10
Lamplugh Cumb....66 G8
Lamport Nhants....37 U6
Lamyatt Somset....17 S9
Lana Devon....14 H12
Lana Devon....14 H13
Lanark S Lans....82 G11
Lancaster Lancs....61 T7
Lancaster & Morecambe Crematorium Lancs....61 T7
Lancaster Services Lancs....61 U10
Lancaut Gloucs....27 V8
Lanchester Dur....69 Q3
Lancing W Susx....10 K10
L'Ancresse Guern....6 e1
Landbeach Cambs....39 Q7
Landcross Devon....14 K8
Landerberry Abers....99 N2
Landford Wilts....8 K5
Land-hallow Highld....112 D10
Landican Crematorium Wirral....54 G9
Landimore Swans....25 S12
Landkey Devon....15 N6
Landore Swans....26 B8
Landrake Cnwll....4 K8
Landscove Devon....5 U7
Land's End Cnwll....2 A11
Land's End Airport Cnwll....2 B11
Landshipping Pembks....24 H8
Landulph Cnwll....5 L8
Landwade Suffk....39 U7
Landywood Staffs....46 C13
Lane Cnwll....3 L4
Lane Bottom Lancs....62 H12
Lane End Bucks....20 D4
Lane End Cnwll....3 Q3
Lane End Hants....9 R3
Lane End Lancs....62 H10
Lane End Wilts....18 B11
Lane Ends Derbys....46 H7
Lane Ends Lancs....62 F6
Lane Ends N York....62 K6
Lane Green Staffs....45 U13
Lane Head Dur....69 P9
Lane Head Wigan....55 P7
Lane Heads Lancs....61 S12
Laneshaw Bridge Lancs....62 K6
Lane Side Lancs....55 S1
Langaford Devon....14 K3
Langaller Somset....16 J11
Langar Notts....47 U6
Langbank Rens....88 J11
Langbar N York....63 L9
Langcliffe N York....62 H7
Langdale End N York....65 L1
Langdon Cnwll....4 J3
Langdon Beck Dur....68 J6
Langdon Hills Essex....22 G10
Langdyke Fife....91 M11
Langenhoe Essex....23 Q4
Langford C Beds....31 Q4
Langford Devon....6 D4
Langford Essex....23 L6
Langford Notts....48 B2
Langford Oxon....29 P7
Langford Somset....16 F11
Langford Budville Somset....16 F12
Langham Dorset....17 U11
Langham Essex....23 P1
Langham Norfk....50 H5
Langham Rutlnd....48 B11
Langham Suffk....40 G7
Langho Lancs....62 E13
Langholm D & G....75 S9
Langland Swans....25 V13
Langley Ches E....56 D12
Langley Derbys....47 N4
Langley Essex....39 Q13
Langley Gloucs....28 K2
Langley Hants....9 N8
Langley Herts....31 R8
Langley Kent....12 F5
Langley Nthumb....76 G13
Langley Oxon....29 Q4
Langley Rochdl....56 C5
Langley Slough....20 H7
Langley Somset....16 E11
Langley W Susx....10 C5
Langley Warwks....36 G8
Langley Burrell Wilts....18 D5
Langley Common Derbys....46 J6
Langley Green Derbys....46 J6
Langley Green Essex....23 L3
Langley Green W Susx....11 M3
Langley Lower Green Essex....39 P14
Langley Marsh Somset....16 E11
Langley Mill Derbys....47 M4
Langley Moor Dur....69 S4
Langley Park Dur....69 R3
Langley Street Norfk....51 P1
Langley Upper Green Essex....39 P14
Langney E Susx....11 U10
Langold Notts....57 S9
Langore Cnwll....4 H3
Langport Somset....17 M11
Langrick Lincs....49 L4
Langridge BaNES....17 T3
Langridgeford Devon....15 N8
Langrigg Cumb....66 J3
Langrish Hants....9 U3
Langsett Barns....56 K6
Langside P & K....89 S3
Langstone Hants....9 U8
Langthorne N York....63 R1
Langthorpe N York....63 U6
Langthwaite N York....69 M12
Langtoft E R Yk....65 M7
Langtoft Lincs....48 H11
Langton Dur....69 Q9
Langton Lincs....48 K1
Langton Lincs....59 M13
Langton N York....64 H6
Langton by Wragby Lincs....58 K11
Langton Green Kent....11 S3
Langton Green Suffk....40 K6
Langton Herring Dorset....7 R8
Langton Long Blandford Dorset....8 C7
Langton Matravers Dorset....8 E13
Langtree Devon....15 L9
Langtree Week Devon....15 L9
Langwathby Cumb....67 S6
Langwell House Highld....112 D12
Langwith Derbys....57 R13
Langwith Junction Derbys....57 R13
Langworth Lincs....58 J11
Lanhydrock House & Gardens Cnwll....3 R4
Lanivet Cnwll....3 Q4
Lanjeth Cnwll....3 P6
Lank Cnwll....4 R1
Lanlivery Cnwll....3 R5
Lanner Cnwll....2 J9
Lanoy Cnwll....4 H5
Lanreath Cnwll....4 F9
Lansallos Cnwll....4 F10
Lanteglos Cnwll....3 U1
Lanteglos Highway Cnwll....4 E10
Lanton Border....76 C1
Lanton Nthumb....85 N12
La Passee Guern....6 d3
Lapford Devon....15 R11
Laphroaig Ag & B....78 F6
Lapley Staffs....45 U11
La Pulente Jersey....7 a3
Lapworth Warwks....36 G6
Larachbeg Highld....93 R9
Larbert Falk....82 G2
Larbreck Lancs....61 S11
Larches Lancs....61 T13
Larden Green Ches E....45 N2
Largie Abers....104 J8
Largiemore Ag & B....87 S8
Largoward Fife....91 Q10
Largs N Ayrs....88 E14
Largymore N Ayrs....80 E8
Larkbeare Devon....6 E5
Larkfield Inver....88 F10
Larkfield Kent....12 D4
Larkhall S Lans....82 E8
Larkhill Wilts....18 H12
Larling Norfk....40 G3
La Rocque Jersey....7 d4
La Rousaillerie Guern....6 d2
Lartington Dur....69 M9
Lasborough Gloucs....28 F9
Lasham Hants....19 U12
Lashbrook Devon....14 K11
Lashbrook Devon....14 K12
Lashenden Kent....12 F7
Lask Edge Staffs....46 B2
Lasswade Mdloth....83 R5
Lastingham N York....64 H1
Latcham Somset....17 M7
Latchford Herts....31 U8
Latchford Oxon....30 E12
Latchingdon Essex....23 L7
Latchley Cnwll....5 L6
Lately Common Warrtn....55 Q7
Lathbury M Keyn....30 J4
Latheron Highld....112 F10
Latheronwheel Highld....112 F10
Lathones Fife....91 Q10
Latimer Bucks....20 H3
Latteridge S Glos....28 C10
Lattiford Somset....17 R11
Latton Wilts....29 L8
Lauder Border....84 E9
Laugharne Carmth....25 Q8
Laughterton Lincs....58 D11
Laughton E Susx....11 R8
Laughton Leics....37 S3
Laughton Lincs....48 D7
Laughton Lincs....58 E7
Laughton-en-le-Morthen Rothm....57 R9
Launcells Cnwll....14 F11
Launcells Cross Cnwll....14 G11
Launceston Cnwll....4 J4
Launton Oxon....30 C8
Laurencekirk Abers....99 M9
Laurieston D & G....73 R7
Laurieston Falk....82 H3
Lavendon M Keyn....38 D10
Lavenham Suffk....40 F11
Laverhay D & G....75 N5
Lavernock V Glam....16 G3
Laversdale Cumb....75 U13
Laverstock Wilts....8 H2
Laverstoke Hants....19 R11
Laverton Gloucs....36 E14
Laverton N York....63 R5
Laverton Somset....17 U5
La Villette Guern....6 d4
Lavister Wrexhm....44 J2
Law S Lans....82 F8
Lawers P & K....95 T11
Lawford Essex....23 R1
Lawford Somset....16 F9
Law Hill S Lans....82 F8
Lawhitton Cnwll....4 J4
Lawkland N York....62 F6
Lawkland Green N York....62 F6
Lawley Wrekin....45 Q12
Lawnhead Staffs....45 T9
Lawns Wood Crematorium Leeds....63 R12
Lawrenny Pembks....24 H9
Lawshall Suffk....40 E10
Lawshall Green Suffk....40 E10
Lawton Herefs....34 K9
Laxay W Isls....106 i6
Laxdale W Isls....106 j5
Laxey IoM....60 g6
Laxfield Suffk....41 N6
Laxford Bridge Highld....110 E7
Laxo Shet....106 u7
Laxton E R Yk....58 B1
Laxton Nhants....38 E1
Laxton Notts....58 B13
Laycock C Brad....63 L11
Layer Breton Essex....23 M4
Layer-de-la-Haye Essex....23 N4
Layer Marney Essex....23 M4
Laymore Dorset....7 L3
Layter's Green Bucks....20 G4
Laytham E R Yk....64 F12
Lazenby R & Cl....70 J9
Lazonby Cumb....67 S5
Lea Derbys....47 L2
Lea Herefs....28 B3
Lea Lincs....58 D9
Lea Shrops....34 K2
Lea Shrops....44 K13
Lea Wilts....28 J10
Leachkin Highld....102 H7
Leadburn Border....83 P6
Leadenham Lincs....48 D3
Leaden Roding Essex....22 E5
Leadgate Cumb....68 F4
Leadgate Dur....69 P2
Leadgate Nthumb....77 P14
Leadhills S Lans....74 G2
Leadingcross Green Kent....12 G5
Leadmill Derbys....56 K10
Leafield Oxon....29 R4
Leagrave Luton....31 N8
Leahead Ches W....55 Q14
Lea Heath Staffs....46 D8
Leake N York....63 U1
Leake Common Side Lincs....49 N3
Lealholm N York....71 M11
Lealholm Side N York....71 N11
Lealt Highld....100 e3
Lea Marston Warwks....36 H2
Leamington Hastings Warwks....37 M7
Leamington Spa Warwks....36 K7
Leamside Dur....70 D3
Leap Cross E Susx....11 T8
Leasgill Cumb....61 T3
Leasingham Lincs....48 G4
Leasingthorne Dur....69 S6
Leatherhead Surrey....21 L11
Leathley N York....63 Q10
Leaton Shrops....45 L10
Leaton Wrekin....45 P11
Leaveland Kent....13 L5
Leavenheath Suffk....40 F13
Leavening N York....64 H7
Leaves Green Gt Lon....21 R10
Lea Town Lancs....61 T13
Lebberston N York....65 P3
Le Bigard Guern....6 d4
Le Bourg Guern....6 d4
Le Bourg Jersey....7 e4
Lechlade on Thames Gloucs....29 P8
Lecht Gruinart Ag & B....78 D3
Leck Lancs....62 C4
Leckbuie P & K....95 U10
Leckford Hants....19 N13
Leckhampstead Bucks....30 F5
Leckhampstead W Berk....19 P5
Leckhampstead Thicket W Berk....19 P5
Leckhampton Gloucs....28 H4
Leckmelm Highld....108 B7
Leckwith V Glam....27 M13
Leconfield E R Yk....65 N11
Ledaig Ag & B....94 C11
Ledburn Bucks....30 K8
Ledbury Herefs....35 R13
Ledgemoor Herefs....34 K10
Ledicot Herefs....34 K8
Ledmore Junction Highld....108 C2
Ledsham Ches W....54 J12
Ledsham Leeds....57 S1
Ledston Leeds....57 R1
Ledstone Devon....5 S11
Ledston Luck Leeds....57 S1
Ledwell Oxon....29 U3
Lee Devon....15 L3
Lee Gt Lon....21 Q8
Lee Hants....9 M5
Lee Shrops....44 K7
Lee Brockhurst Shrops....45 M8
Leebotwood Shrops....45 L14
Lee Chapel Essex....22 G10
Lee Clump Bucks....30 K12
Lee Common Bucks....30 K12
Leeds Kent....12 F5
Leeds Leeds....63 R13
Leeds Bradford Airport Leeds....63 Q11
Leeds Castle Kent....12 F5
Leedstown Cnwll....2 G9
Lee Green Ches E....45 Q1
Leek Staffs....46 C2
Leek Wootton Warwks....36 J7
Lee Mill Devon....5 P9
Leeming C Brad....63 M13
Leeming N York....63 R2
Leeming Bar N York....63 R2
Lee Moor Devon....5 P8
Lee-on-the-Solent Hants....9 R8
Lees C Brad....63 L13
Lees Derbys....46 H6
Lees Oldham....56 E6
Lees Green Derbys....46 H6
Leesthorpe Leics....47 U11
Lee Street Surrey....11 M2
Leeswood Flints....44 F1
Leetown P & K....90 K7
Leftwich Ches W....55 Q12
Legar Powys....27 N4
Legbourne Lincs....59 Q10
Legburthwaite Cumb....67 N8
Legerwood Border....84 F10
Legoland W & M....20 F8
Le Gron Guern....6 d3
Legsby Lincs....58 K9
Le Haguais Jersey....7 e4
Le Hocq Jersey....7 e4
Leicester C Leic....47 Q13
Leicester Forest East Services Leics....47 P13
Leigh Devon....15 R10
Leigh Dorset....7 R3
Leigh Gloucs....28 G3
Leigh Kent....21 T13
Leigh Shrops....44 J12
Leigh Surrey....11 M2
Leigh Wigan....55 Q6
Leigh Wilts....29 L9
Leigh Worcs....35 S10
Leigh Beck Essex....23 L11
Leigh Delamere Wilts....18 C5
Leigh Delamere Services Wilts....18 C5
Leigh Green Kent....12 J9
Leigh Knoweglass S Lans....81 S2
Leighland Chapel Somset....16 E9
Leigh-on-Sea Sthend....22 K10
Leigh Park Dorset....8 E9
Leigh Sinton Worcs....35 S10
Leighswood Wsall....46 D14
Leighterton Gloucs....28 F9
Leighton Powys....44 F13
Leighton Shrops....45 P12
Leighton Somset....17 T7
Leighton Bromswold Cambs....38 H5
Leighton Buzzard C Beds....30 K7
Leigh upon Mendip Somset....17 S7
Leigh Woods N Som....27 V13
Leinthall Earls Herefs....34 K7
Leinthall Starkes Herefs....34 K6
Leintwardine Herefs....34 J6
Leire Leics....37 P3
Leiston Suffk....41 R8
Leith C Edin....83 Q3
Leitholm Border....84 J10
Lelant Cnwll....2 E9
Lelley E R Yk....65 S13
Lem Hill Worcs....35 R6
Lempitlaw Border....84 K12
Lemreway W Isls....106 j7
Lemsford Herts....31 Q10
Lenchwick Worcs....36 D11
Lendalfoot S Ayrs....80 G13
Lendrick Stirlg....89 M4
Lendrum Terrace Abers....105 U7
Lenham Kent....12 G5
Lenham Heath Kent....12 H6
Lenie Highld....102 F10
Lennel Border....85 L10
Lennox Plunton D & G....73 Q9
Lennoxtown E Duns....89 N11
Lenton C Nott....47 Q6
Lenton Lincs....48 F7
Lenwade Norfk....50 J10
Leny W Isls....106 j5
Lenzie E Duns....89 P12
Leochel-Cushnie Abers....104 H13
Leomansley Staffs....46 F12
Leominster Herefs....34 K9
Leonard Stanley Gloucs....28 F7
Leoville Jersey....7 a2
Lepe Hants....9 N9
Lephin Highld....100 a5
Leppington N York....64 G7
Lepton Kirk....56 K4
Lerags Ag & B....94 B13
Le Rondin Guern....6 d4
Lerryn Cnwll....4 E9
Lerwick Shet....106 u9
Les Arquets Guern....6 d3
Lesbury Nthumb....77 Q3
Les Hubits Guern....6 e4
Leslie Abers....104 H10
Leslie Fife....91 L11
Lesmahagow S Lans....82 F11
Les Murchez Guern....6 d4
Les Nicolles Guern....6 d4
Lesnewth Cnwll....4 E2
Les Quartiers Guern....6 d2
Les Quennevais Jersey....7 b3
Les Sages Guern....6 d4
Lessingham Norfk....51 Q8
Lessonhall Cumb....66 K2
Lestowder Cnwll....2 K11
Les Villets Guern....6 d4
Leswalt D & G....72 C7
L'Etacq Jersey....7 a2
Letchmore Heath Herts....21 L3
Letchworth Garden City Herts....31 R6
Letcombe Bassett Oxon....29 R10
Letcombe Regis Oxon....29 R10
Letham Angus....91 R2
Letham Border....76 C3
Letham Falk....82 H2
Letham Fife....91 M9
Letham Grange Angus....91 U3
Lethendy P & K....90 H3
Lethenty Abers....104 H11
Lethenty Abers....105 N7
Letheringham Suffk....41 N9
Letheringsett Norfk....50 J6
Lettaford Devon....5 S3
Letterewe Highld....107 S10
Letterfinlay Lodge Highld....96 B5
Lettermorar Highld....100 J11
Letters Highld....108 B7
Lettershaw S Lans....74 G1
Letterston Pembks....24 G5
Lettoch Highld....103 R12
Lettoch Highld....103 R9
Letton Herefs....34 H11
Letton Herefs....34 H6
Lett's Green Kent....21 S11
Letty Green Herts....31 S10
Letwell Rothm....57 S9
Leuchars Fife....91 Q7
Leumrabagh W Isls....106 j7
Leurbost W Isls....106 i6
Levalsa Meor Cnwll....3 Q7
Levedale Staffs....45 U10
Leven E R Yk....65 R10
Leven Fife....91 M11
Levens Cumb....61 T2
Levens Green Herts....31 U8
Levenshulme Manch....56 C8
Levenwick Shet....106 u11
Leverburgh W Isls....106 f10
Leverington Cambs....49 P11
Leverstock Green Herts....31 M11
Leverton Lincs....49 P4
Le Villocq Guern....6 d3
Levington Suffk....41 M13
Levisham N York....64 J1
Lew Oxon....29 R6
Lewannick Cnwll....4 H5
Lewdown Devon....4 K3
Lewes E Susx....11 Q8
Leweston Pembks....24 F6
Lewisham Gt Lon....21 Q8
Lewisham Crematorium Gt Lon....21 Q8
Lewiston Highld....102 F10
Lewistown Brdgnd....26 G10
Lewis Wych Herefs....34 H11
Lewknor Oxon....20 B3
Leworthy Devon....15 Q6
Leworthy Devon....14 J12
Lewson Street Kent....12 K3
Lewth Lancs....61 T13
Lewtrenchard Devon....5 M3
Lexden Essex....23 N2
Lexworthy Somset....16 H9
Ley Cnwll....4 F7
Leybourne Kent....12 C4
Leyburn N York....63 N1
Leycett Staffs....45 S4
Leygreen Herts....31 Q8
Ley Hill Bucks....20 K2
Leyland Lancs....55 M2
Leylodge Abers....105 N13
Leys Abers....105 S5
Leys P & K....90 K5
Leysdown-on-Sea Kent....23 P13
Leysmill Angus....91 U2
Leys of Cossans Angus....91 N2
Leysters Herefs....35 N8
Leyton Gt Lon....21 Q5
Leytonstone Gt Lon....21 Q5
Lezant Cnwll....4 J5
Lezerea Cnwll....2 H10
Lhanbryde Moray....104 B3
Libanus Powys....26 G2
Libberton S Lans....82 H10
Liberton C Edin....83 Q5
Lichfield Staffs....46 F12
Lickey Worcs....36 C6
Lickey End Worcs....36 C6
Lickey Rock Worcs....36 C6
Lickfold W Susx....10 E5
Liddaton Devon....5 L4
Liddesdale Highld....93 R6
Liddington Swindn....18 K4
Lidgate Suffk....40 B9
Lidget Donc....57 T6
Lidgett Notts....57 S13
Lidham Hill E Susx....12 F12
Lidlington C Beds....31 L5
Lidsing Kent....12 E3
Liff Angus....91 M5
Lifford Birm....36 E5
Lifton Devon....4 K3
Liftondown Devon....4 K3
Lighthorne Warwks....36 K9
Lighthorne Heath Warwks....37 L9
Lightwater Surrey....20 G10
Lightwater Valley Theme Park N York....63 R4
Lightwood C Stke....46 B5
Lightwood Green Ches E....45 P5
Lightwood Green Wrexhm....44 J5
Lilbourne Nhants....37 Q5
Lilburn Tower Nthumb....85 Q14
Lilleshall Wrekin....45 R10
Lilley Herts....31 P7
Lilley W Berk....19 R5
Lilliesleaf Border....84 E13
Lillingstone Dayrell Bucks....30 F5
Lillingstone Lovell Bucks....30 F5
Lillington Dorset....7 R2
Lilliput Poole....8 E11
Lilstock Somset....16 G7
Lilyhurst Shrops....45 R11
Limbrick Lancs....55 N3
Limbury Luton....31 N8
Limebrook Herefs....34 H7
Limefield Bury....55 T4
Limekilnburn S Lans....82 D8
Limekilns Fife....82 K2
Limerigg Falk....82 G4
Limerstone IoW....9 N12
Limestone Brae Nthumb....68 G3
Limington Somset....17 P12
Limmerhaugh E Ayrs....81 S7
Limpenhoe Norfk....51 R13
Limpley Stoke Wilts....17 U4
Limpsfield Surrey....21 R12
Limpsfield Chart Surrey....21 R12
Linby Notts....47 P3
Linchmere W Susx....10 D4
Lincluden D & G....74 J11
Lincoln Lincs....58 G12
Lincoln Crematorium Lincs....58 G12
Lincomb Worcs....35 T7
Lincombe Devon....15 S12
Lincombe Devon....5 S11
Lindal in Furness Cumb....61 N4
Lindfield W Susx....11 N5
Lindford Hants....10 C3
Lindley Kirk....56 H3
Lindley N York....63 Q10
Lindores Fife....91 L8
Lindow End Ches E....55 T11
Lindridge Worcs....35 Q7
Lindsell Essex....22 F2
Lindsey Suffk....40 G12
Lindsey Tye Suffk....40 G11
Liney Somset....17 L9
Linford Hants....8 H7
Linford Thurr....22 F12
Lingbob C Brad....63 M12
Lingdale R & Cl....70 K9
Lingen Herefs....34 H7
Lingfield Surrey....11 P2
Lingwood Norfk....51 Q12
Linhope Border....75 U3
Linicro Highld....100 c3
Linkend Worcs....35 U14
Linkenholt Hants....19 N9
Linkhill Kent....12 F10
Linkinhorne Cnwll....4 J6
Linktown Fife....91 L13
Linley Shrops....34 J1
Linley Green Herefs....35 R10
Linleygreen Shrops....35 Q1
Linlithgow W Loth....82 K3
Linshiels Nthumb....76 H4
Linsidemore Highld....108 K6
Linslade C Beds....30 K7
Linstead Parva Suffk....41 N5
Linstock Cumb....75 U14
Linthurst Worcs....36 C6
Linthwaite Kirk....56 H4
Lintlaw Border....85 L7
Lintmill Moray....104 G2
Linton Border....84 K13
Linton Cambs....39 S11
Linton Derbys....46 J10
Linton Herefs....28 C2
Linton Kent....12 D6
Linton Leeds....63 T10
Linton N York....62 K6
Linton-on-Ouse N York....64 B7
Linwood Hants....8 H7
Linwood Lincs....58 J9
Linwood Rens....88 K13
Lional W Isls....106 k2
Lions Green E Susx....11 T7
Liphook Hants....10 C3
Lipley Shrops....45 R7
Liscard Wirral....54 G8
Liscombe Somset....15 U6
Liskeard Cnwll....4 G8
Lismore Ag & B....94 B11
Liss Hants....10 B5
Lissett E R Yk....65 Q9
Liss Forest Hants....10 B5
Lissington Lincs....58 K10
Liston Essex....40 E12
Lisvane Cardif....27 M11
Liswerry Newpt....27 R10
Litcham Norfk....50 E10
Litchard Brdgnd....26 G11
Litchborough Nhants....37 R10
Litchfield Hants....19 R10
Litherland Sefton....54 H7
Litlington Cambs....31 T4
Litlington E Susx....11 S10
Little Abington Cambs....39 R11
Little Addington Nhants....38 E6
Little Airies D & G....73 L9
Little Almshoe Herts....31 R7
Little Alne Warwks....36 F8
Little Altcar Sefton....54 H5
Little Amwell Herts....31 U10
Little Asby Cumb....68 E10
Little Aston Staffs....46 E14
Little Atherfield IoW....9 P13
Little Ayton N York....70 H10
Little Baddow Essex....22 H6
Little Badminton S Glos....28 F11
Little Bampton Cumb....67 L1
Little Bardfield Essex....22 G1
Little Barford Bed....38 J9
Little Barningham Norfk....50 K7
Little Barrington Gloucs....29 P5
Little Barrow Ches W....54 K13
Little Barugh N York....64 G4
Little Bavington Nthumb....76 K10
Little Bealings Suffk....41 M11
Littlebeck N York....71 Q12
Little Bedwyn Wilts....19 L7
Little Bentley Essex....23 R2
Little Berkhamsted Herts....31 S11
Little Billing Nhants....38 B8
Little Billington C Beds....30 K8
Little Birch Herefs....35 M14
Little Bispham Bpool....61 Q11
Little Blakenham Suffk....40 K11
Little Blencow Cumb....67 Q6
Little Bloxwich Wsall....46 D13
Little Bognor W Susx....10 G6
Little Bollington Ches E....55 R9
Little Bookham Surrey....20 K12
Littleborough Notts....58 D10
Littleborough Rochdl....56 E4
Littlebourne Kent....13 P4
Little Bourton Oxon....37 M12
Little Bowden Leics....37 U3
Little Bradley Suffk....40 B10
Little Brampton Herefs....34 H7
Little Brampton Shrops....34 J3
Little Braxted Essex....23 L5
Little Brechin Angus....98 K11
Littlebredy Dorset....7 P6
Little Brickhill M Keyn....30 K6
Little Bridgeford Staffs....45 T8
Little Brington Nhants....37 R8
Little Bromley Essex....23 Q2
Little Broughton Cumb....66 G6
Little Budworth Ches W....55 N13
Little Burstead Essex....22 F9
Little Bytham Lincs....48 F10
Little Canfield Essex....22 E3
Little Carlton Lincs....59 R9
Little Carlton Notts....47 U2
Little Casterton Rutlnd....48 F12
Little Catwick E R Yk....65 Q10
Little Catworth Cambs....38 H6
Little Cawthorpe Lincs....59 Q10
Little Chalfont Bucks....20 H3
Little Chart Kent....12 J6
Little Chesterford Essex....39 R12
Little Cheveney Kent....12 D7
Little Cheverell Wilts....18 E10
Little Chishill Cambs....39 Q13
Little Clacton Essex....23 S4
Little Clanfield Oxon....29 Q7
Little Clifton Cumb....66 G8
Little Coates NE Lin....59 M5
Little Comberton Worcs....36 C12
Little Common E Susx....12 D14
Little Comp Kent....12 B4
Little Compton Warwks....29 P1
Little Corby Cumb....75 U14
Little Cornard Suffk....40 E13
Littlecott Wilts....18 H9
Little Cowarne Herefs....35 N10
Little Coxwell Oxon....29 Q9
Little Crakehall N York....63 R1
Little Cransley Nhants....38 B5
Little Crosby Sefton....54 H6
Little Crosthwaite Cumb....67 L7
Little Cubley Derbys....46 G6
Little Dalby Leics....47 U11
Little Dewchurch Herefs....35 M13
Little Ditton Cambs....39 U9
Little Doward Herefs....27 U4
Littledown Hants....19 N9
Little Downham Cambs....39 R4
Little Driffield E R Yk....65 N9
Little Dunham Norfk....50 E11
Little Dunkeld P & K....90 G3
Little Dunmow Essex....22 G3
Little Durnford Wilts....8 G2
Little Easton Essex....22 F3
Little Eaton Derbys....47 L5
Little Ellingham Norfk....50 H14
Little Elm Somset....17 T7
Little Everdon Nhants....37 Q9
Little Eversden Cambs....39 N10
Little Faringdon Oxon....29 P7
Little Fencote N York....63 R1
Little Fenton N York....64 C13
Littleferry Highld....109 Q5
Little Fransham Norfk....50 F11
Little Gaddesden Herts....31 L10
Little Garway Herefs....27 S3
Little Gidding Cambs....38 H4
Little Glemham Suffk....41 P9
Little Gorsley Herefs....28 C2
Little Gransden Cambs....39 L9
Little Green Somset....17 T7
Little Grimsby Lincs....59 P8
Little Gringley Notts....58 B10
Little Habton N York....64 G5
Little Hadham Herts....22 C3
Little Hale Lincs....48 J5
Little Hallam Derbys....47 N5
Little Hallingbury Essex....22 D4
Littleham Devon....15 L8
Littleham Devon....6 E8
Little Hampden Bucks....30 J12
Littlehampton W Susx....10 G10
Little Hanford Dorset....8 B6
Little Harrowden Nhants....38 B6
Little Haseley Oxon....30 D12
Little Hatfield E R Yk....65 R11
Little Haven Pembks....24 E8
Little Hay Staffs....46 F13
Little Hayfield Derbys....56 F8
Little Haywood Staffs....46 D9
Little Heath Ches W....54 K12
Little Heath Warwks....37 L4
Little Hereford Herefs....35 N7
Little Horkesley Essex....23 N1
Little Hormead Herts....22 B2
Little Horsted E Susx....11 R6
Little Horton C Brad....63 N13
Little Horwood Bucks....30 G5
Little Houghton Barns....57 P5
Little Houghton Nhants....38 B9
Littlehoughton Nthumb....77 Q2
Little Hucklow Derbys....56 J11
Little Hulton Salfd....55 R6
Little Hungerford W Berk....19 S5
Little Hutton N York....64 B4
Little Irchester Nhants....38 D8
Little Keyford Somset....17 T8
Little Kimble Bucks....30 H11
Little Kineton Warwks....36 K10
Little Kingshill Bucks....20 E3
Little Knox D & G....74 F13
Little Langdale Cumb....67 L12
Little Langford Wilts....8 F2
Little Laver Essex....22 D6
Little Leigh Ches W....55 P11
Little Leighs Essex....22 H5
Little Lever Bolton....55 S5
Little Load Somset....17 M12
Little London E Susx....11 T7
Little London Essex....39 R14
Little London Gloucs....28 D4
Little London Hants....19 N10
Little London Hants....19 T10
Little London Leeds....63 R13
Little London Lincs....49 N9
Little London Lincs....49 P10
Little London Norfk....49 R10
Little London Powys....34 C5
Little Longstone Derbys....56 J12
Little Malvern Worcs....35 S12
Little Mancot Flints....54 H13
Little Maplestead Essex....40 D14
Little Marcle Herefs....35 P13
Little Marland Devon....15 M9
Little Marlow Bucks....20 E5
Little Massingham Norfk....50 C9
Little Melton Norfk....51 L12
Littlemill Abers....98 D4
Littlemill Highld....103 P5
Little Mill Mons....27 R6
Little Milton Oxon....30 D12
Little Missenden Bucks....20 G3
Littlemoor Derbys....57 N14
Littlemoor Dorset....7 S7
Little Mongeham Kent....13 R5
Littlemore Oxon....30 B12
Little Moor Somset....16 K10
Little Musgrave Cumb....68 G10
Little Ness Shrops....44 K10
Little Neston Ches W....54 G12
Little Newcastle Pembks....24 G5
Little Newsham Dur....69 P9
Little Norton Somset....17 N13
Little Oakley Essex....23 T2
Little Oakley Nhants....38 C3
Little Odell Bed....38 E9
Little Offley Herts....31 P7
Little Onn Staffs....45 T10
Little Ormside Cumb....68 F9
Little Orton Cumb....67 M1
Little Ouse Cambs....39 T4
Little Ouseburn N York....63 U8
Little Packington Warwks....36 H4
Little Pattenden Kent....36 H4
Little Paxton Cambs....38 J8
Little Petherick Cnwll....3 N2
Little Plumpton Lancs....61 R13
Little Plumstead Norfk....51 P11
Little Ponton Lincs....48 E7
Littleport Cambs....39 S3
Littleport Bridge Cambs....39 S3
Little Posbrook Hants....9 Q8
Little Potheridge Devon....15 M10
Little Preston Leeds....57 M13
Little Preston Nhants....37 Q9
Littler Ches W....55 P13
Little Raveley Cambs....39 L5
Little Reedness E R Yk....58 D2
Little Ribston N York....63 U9
Little Rissington Gloucs....29 N4
Little Rollright Oxon....29 Q1
Little Rowsley Derbys....57 L13
Little Ryburgh Norfk....50 G8
Little Ryle Nthumb....77 M3
Little Ryton Shrops....45 L13
Little Salkeld Cumb....67 S5
Little Sampford Essex....22 G1
Little Sandhurst Br For....20 E10
Little Saredon Staffs....46 B12
Little Saughall Ches W....54 J13
Little Saxham Suffk....40 D8
Little Scatwell Highld....102 C5
Little Shelford Cambs....39 P10
Little Shrewbsury Warwks....36 H7
Little Silver Devon....15 V11
Little Singleton Lancs....61 R13
Little Skipwith N York....64 E12
Little Smeaton N York....57 S3
Little Snoring Norfk....50 G7
Little Sodbury S Glos....28 E11
Little Sodbury End S Glos....28 E11
Little Somborne Hants....9 M2
Little Somerford Wilts....28 J10
Little Soudley Shrops....45 R8
Little Stainforth N York....62 H7
Little Stainton Darltn....70 D8
Little Stanney Ches W....54 K12
Little Staughton Bed....38 H8
Little Steeping Lincs....59 R14
Little Stoke Staffs....46 B7
Littlestone-on-Sea Kent....13 L11
Little Stonham Suffk....40 K8
Little Stretton Leics....47 S13
Little Stretton Shrops....34 K2
Little Strickland Cumb....67 R9
Little Stukeley Cambs....38 K6
Little Sugnall Staffs....45 T7
Little Sutton Ches W....54 J11
Little Sutton Shrops....35 M4
Little Swinburne Nthumb....76 J10
Little Sypland D & G....73 S9
Little Tarrington Herefs....35 N12
Little Tey Essex....23 M3
Little Thetford Cambs....39 R5
Little Thirkleby N York....64 B4
Little Thornage Norfk....50 J6
Little Thornton Lancs....61 R11
Little Thorpe Dur....70 F3
Littlethorpe Leics....37 Q1
Littlethorpe N York....63 S6
Little Thurlow Suffk....39 U10
Little Thurrock Thurr....22 F12
Littleton BaNES....17 Q4
Littleton Ches W....54 K13
Littleton D & G....73 M9
Littleton Dorset....8 D8
Littleton Hants....9 N2
Littleton Somset....17 M10
Littleton Surrey....20 H9
Littleton Surrey....20 K11
Littleton Drew Wilts....28 F11
Littleton-on-Severn S Glos....28 A10
Littleton Pannell Wilts....18 E9
Little Torrington Devon....15 L10
Little Totham Essex....23 L5
Little Town Cumb....67 L8
Little Town Lancs....62 D13
Little Town Warrtn....55 P8
Little Twycross Leics....46 K12
Little Urswick Cumb....61 N5
Little Wakering Essex....23 M10
Little Walden Essex....39 R12
Little Waldingfield Suffk....40 F12
Little Walsingham Norfk....50 F6
Little Waltham Essex....22 H5
Little Warley Essex....22 F9
Little Washbourne Gloucs....36 C14
Little Weighton E R Yk....65 M13
Little Weldon Nhants....38 D3
Little Welnetham Suffk....40 E8
Little Welton Lincs....59 P9
Little Wenham Suffk....40 J13
Little Wenlock Wrekin....45 Q12
Little Weston Somset....17 R11
Little Whitefield IoW....9 R11
Little Whittington Nthumb....76 K12
Littlewick Green W & M....20 D7
Little Wilbraham Cambs....39 R9
Littlewindsor Dorset....7 M3
Little Witcombe Gloucs....28 H4
Little Witley Worcs....35 S8
Little Wittenham Oxon....19 S2
Little Wolford Warwks....36 K14
Littleworth Oxon....29 R8
Littleworth Staffs....46 D10
Littleworth Staffs....46 C11
Littleworth Worcs....35 U9
Little Wratting Suffk....40 B11
Little Wymington Bed....38 E8
Little Wymondley Herts....31 R7
Little Wyrley Staffs....46 D13
Little Wytheford Shrops....45 M10
Little Yeldham Essex....40 C13
Litton Derbys....56 J12
Litton N York....62 J5
Litton Somset....17 P6
Litton Cheney Dorset....7 P6
Liurbost W Isls....106 i6
Liverpool Lpool....54 H8
Liverpool Maritime Mercantile City Lpool....54 H9
Liversedge Kirk....56 K2
Liverton Devon....5 U5
Liverton R & Cl....71 M9
Liverton Mines R & Cl....71 M9
Liverton Street Kent....12 G5
Livingston W Loth....83 L5
Livingston Village W Loth....82 K5
Lixwm Flints....54 E12
Lizard Cnwll....2 J14
Llaingoch IoA....52 C6
Llaithddu Powys....34 B3
Llan Powys....43 S13
Llanaber Gwynd....43 M10
Llanaelhaearn Gwynd....42 F4
Llanafan Cerdgn....33 N6
Llanafan-fawr Powys....33 U9
Llanafan-fechan Powys....33 U10
Llanallgo IoA....52 G5
Llanarmon Gwynd....42 H6
Llanarmon Dyffryn Ceiriog Wrexhm....44 E7
Llanarmon-yn-Ial Denbgs....44 E2
Llanarth Cerdgn....32 H9
Llanarth Mons....27 R4
Llanarthne Carmth....25 U6
Llanasa Flints....54 D10
Llanbabo IoA....52 E4
Llanbadarn Fawr Cerdgn....33 M4
Llanbadarn-y-garreg Powys....34 C11
Llanbadarn Fynydd Powys....34 C5
Llanbadoc Mons....27 R7
Llanbadrig IoA....52 E2
Llanbeder Newpt....27 R9
Llanbedr Gwynd....43 L8
Llanbedr Powys....27 N3
Llanbedr Powys....34 D12
Llanbedr-Dyffryn-Clwyd Denbgs....44 D2
Llanbedrgoch IoA....52 G5
Llanbedrog Gwynd....42 F7
Llanbedr-y-Cennin Conwy....53 N9
Llanberis Gwynd....52 J10
Llanbethery V Glam....16 D3
Llanbister Powys....34 D6
Llanblethian V Glam....26 H13
Llanboidy Carmth....25 M6
Llanbradach Caerph....27 L8
Llanbrynmair Powys....43 S13
Llancadle V Glam....16 D3
Llancarfan V Glam....26 J13
Llancayo Mons....27 R7
Llancloudy Herefs....27 T3
Llandanwg Gwynd....43 L8
Llandarcy Neath....26 C8
Llandawke Carmth....25 M8
Llanddaniel Fab IoA....52 G8
Llanddarog Carmth....25 T7
Llanddeiniol Cerdgn....33 L6
Llanddeiniolen Gwynd....52 H9
Llandderfel Gwynd....43 U6
Llanddeusant Carmth....26 E2
Llanddeusant IoA....52 D4
Llanddew Powys....26 H1
Llanddewi Swans....25 S13
Llanddewi Brefi Cerdgn....33 N9
Llanddewi'r Cwm Powys....34 B11
Llanddewi Rhydderch Mons....27 R5
Llanddewi Velfrey Pembks....24 K7
Llanddewi Ystradenni Powys....34 D7
Llanddoged Conwy....53 P10
Llanddona IoA....52 H6
Llanddowror Carmth....25 M8
Llanddulas Conwy....53 R7
Llanddwywe Gwynd....43 L9
Llanddyfnan IoA....52 H7
Llandecwyn Gwynd....43 M6
Llandefaelog-Tre'r-Graig Powys....27 L2
Llandefalle Powys....34 C13
Llandegfan IoA....52 J8
Llandegla Denbgs....44 E3
Llandegley Powys....34 D8
Llandegveth Mons....27 Q8
Llandegwning Gwynd....42 E7
Llandeilo Carmth....26 A3
Llandeilo Graban Powys....34 C12
Llandeilo'r Fan Powys....33 S14
Llandeloy Pembks....24 E5
Llandenny Mons....27 S7
Llandevaud Newpt....27 S9
Llandevenny Mons....27 S10
Llandinabo Herefs....27 U2
Llandinam Powys....34 B3
Llandissilio Pembks....24 K6
Llandogo Mons....27 U7
Llandough V Glam....26 H13
Llandough V Glam....27 M13
Llandovery Carmth....33 R14
Llandow V Glam....26 G13
Llandre Carmth....33 N12
Llandre Cerdgn....33 M4
Llandre Isaf Pembks....24 K5
Llandrillo Denbgs....44 C6
Llandrillo-yn-Rhos Conwy....53 P6
Llandrindod Wells Powys....34 C8
Llandrinio Powys....44 G10
Llandudno Conwy....53 N6
Llandudno Junction Conwy....53 N7
Llandulas Powys....33 S10
Llandwrog Gwynd....52 G11
Llandybie Carmth....25 V7
Llandyfaelog Carmth....25 R8
Llandyfan Carmth....26 A5
Llandyfriog Cerdgn....32 G12
Llandyfrydog IoA....52 F5
Llandygai Gwynd....52 K8
Llandygwydd Cerdgn....32 D12
Llandynan Denbgs....44 E4
Llandyrnog Denbgs....53 U12
Llandysilio Powys....44 G10
Llandyssil Powys....34 D1
Llandysul Cerdgn....32 H11
Llanedeyrn Cardif....27 N11
Llanedi Carmth....25 U9
Llaneglwys Powys....34 C13
Llanegryn Gwynd....43 M11
Llanegwad Carmth....25 U5
Llaneilian IoA....52 G3
Llanelian-yn-Rhôs Conwy....53 Q7
Llanelidan Denbgs....44 D3
Llanelieu Powys....34 E14
Llanellen Mons....27 Q5
Llanelli Carmth....25 T10
Llanelli Crematorium Carmth....25 T10
Llanelltyd Gwynd....43 P10
Llanelly Mons....27 N5
Llanelwedd Powys....34 B10
Llanenddwyn Gwynd....43 L9
Llanengan Gwynd....42 E8
Llanerch Powys....34 J2
Llanerchymedd IoA....52 F5
Llanerfyl Powys....44 B12
Llanfachraeth IoA....52 D5
Llanfachreth Gwynd....43 Q9
Llanfaelog IoA....52 D7
Llanfaelrhys Gwynd....42 D8
Llanfaenor Mons....27 S4
Llanfaes IoA....53 L7
Llanfaes Powys....26 J2
Llanfaethlu IoA....52 D4
Llanfaglan Gwynd....52 G10
Llanfair Gwynd....43 L8
Llanfair Caereinion Powys....44 D12
Llanfair Clydogau Cerdgn....33 M10
Llanfair Dyffryn Clwyd Denbgs....44 D2
Llanfairfechan Conwy....53 L7
Llanfair Kilgeddin Mons....27 R5
Llanfair-Nant-Gwyn Pembks....24 K4
Llanfair P G IoA....52 H8
Llanfair Talhaiarn Conwy....53 R8
Llanfair Waterdine Shrops....34 F5
Llanfairynghornwy IoA....52 D3
Llanfair-yn-Neubwll IoA....52 D6
Llanfallteg Carmth....24 K7
Llanfallteg West Carmth....24 K7
Llanfarian Cerdgn....33 L5
Llanfechain Powys....44 E9
Llanfechell IoA....52 E3
Llanferres Denbgs....44 E1
Llan Ffestiniog Gwynd....43 P4
Llanfflewyn IoA....52 E4
Llanfigael IoA....52 D5
Llanfihangel-ar-arth Carmth....32 H12
Llanfihangel Glyn Myfyr Conwy....43 U4
Llanfihangel Nant Bran Powys....33 T14
Llanfihangel-nant-Melan Powys....34 E9

Medway Services
Medway 12 F3
Meerbrook Staffs 46 C1
Meer Common Herefs 34 J10
Meesden Herts 22 B1
Meeson Wrekin 45 P9
Meeth Devon 15 M11
Meeting Green Suffk 40 B9
Meeting House Hill Norfk 51 P8
Meidrim Carmth 25 N6
Meifod Powys 44 E11
Meigle P & K 91 J6
Meikle Carco D & G 74 E3
Meikle Earnock S Lans 82 D8
Meikle Kilmory Ag & B 88 C13
Meikle Obney P & K 90 F4
Meiklour P & K 90 J4
Meikle Wartle Abers 105 L9
Meinciau Carmth 25 S8
Melbourn Cambs 31 U4
Melbourne Derbys 47 L8
Melbourne E R Yk 64 H11
Melbur Cnwll 3 N6
Melbury Devon 14 J9
Melbury Abbas Dorset 8 B4
Melbury Bubb Dorset 7 Q3
Melbury Osmond Dorset 7 Q3
Melbury Sampford Dorset 7 Q3
Melchbourne Bed 38 F7
Melcombe Bingham Dorset 7 U4
Meldon Devon 5 P2
Meldon Nthumb 77 N8
Meldreth Cambs 39 N11
Meldrum Stirlg 89 S6
Melfort Ag & B 87 Q3
Meliden Denbgs 54 C10
Melinau Pembks 25 L8
Melin-byrheolydd Powys 43 R14
Melin-y-coed Conwy 53 P10
Melin-y-ddol Powys 44 C12
Melin-y-wig Denbgs 44 B2
Melkinthorpe Cumb 67 S7
Melkridge Nthumb 76 E13
Melksham Wilts 18 D8
Mellangoose Cnwll 2 H11
Mell Green W Berk 19 Q5
Mellguards Cumb 67 P3
Melling Lancs 62 B5
Melling Sefton 54 J6
Melling Mount Sefton 54 K6
Mellis Suffk 40 J6
Mellon Charles Highld 107 P6
Mellon Udrigle Highld 107 Q5
Mellor Lancs 62 D13
Mellor Stockp 56 E9
Mellor Brook Lancs 62 C13
Mells Somset 17 T7
Mells Suffk 41 R5
Melmerby Cumb 68 D5
Melmerby N York 63 M3
Melmerby N York 63 S4
Melness Highld 111 M4
Melon Green Suffk 40 D9
Melplash Dorset 7 N5
Melrose Border 84 E12
Melsetter Ork 106 r21
Melsonby N York 69 Q11
Meltham Kirk 56 H4
Meltham Mills Kirk 56 H4
Melton E R Yk 58 C1
Melton Suffk 41 N10
Meltonby E R Yk 64 H9
Melton Constable Norfk 50 H7
Melton Mowbray Leics 47 U10
Melton Ross N Linc 58 J4
Melvaig Highld 107 M7
Melverley Shrops 44 H10
Melverley Green Shrops 44 H10
Melvich Highld 111 U4
Membury Devon 6 J4
Membury Services W Berk 19 M5
Memsie Abers 105 R3
Memus Angus 98 G12
Menabilly Cnwll 3 R6
Menagissey Cnwll 2 J7
Menai Bridge IoA 52 J8
Mendham Suffk 41 N4
Mendip Crematorium Somset 17 Q8
Mendip Hills 17 P6
Mendlesham Suffk 40 K7
Mendlesham Green Suffk 40 J8
Menethorpe N York 64 G7
Menheniot Cnwll 4 H8
Menithwood Worcs 35 R7
Mennock D & G 74 F4
Menston C Brad 63 P11
Menstrie Clacks 90 C12
Mentmore Bucks 30 K9
Meoble Highld 100 g11
Meole Brace Shrops 45 L11
Meonstoke Hants 9 S5
Meopham Kent 12 B2
Meopham Green Kent 12 B2
Meopham Station Kent 12 B2
Mepal Cambs 39 P4
Meppershall C Beds 31 P5
Merbach Herefs 34 H11
Mere Ches E 55 R10
Mere Wilts 17 V10
Mere Brow Lancs 54 K3
Mereclough Lancs 62 H13
Mere Green Birm 46 F14
Mere Green Worcs 36 B8
Mere Heath Ches W 55 Q12
Meresborough Medway 12 F2
Mereworth Kent 12 C4
Meriden Solhll 36 H4
Merkadale Highld 100 c6
Merley Poole 8 E9
Merlin's Bridge Pembks 24 F8
Merrington Shrops 45 L9
Merrion Pembks 24 F11
Merriott Somset 7 M2
Merrivale Devon 5 N6
Merrow Surrey 20 H12
Merry Field Hill Dorset 8 E8
Merry Hill Herts 20 K4
Merryhill Wolves 35 U2
Merry Lees Leics 47 N12
Merrymeet Cnwll 4 H7
Mersea Island Essex 23 P4
Mersham Kent 13 L7
Merstham Surrey 21 N11
Merston W Susx 10 D10
Merstone IoW 9 Q12
Merther Cnwll 3 M8
Merthyr Carmth 25 Q5
Merthyr Cynog Powys 33 T15
Merthyr Dyfan V Glam 16 F3
Merthyr Mawr Brdgnd 26 F12
Merthyr Tydfil Myr Td 26 K8
Merthyr Vale Myr Td 26 K9
Merton Devon 15 M9
Merton Gt Lon 21 M8
Merton Norfk 50 F14
Merton Oxon 30 C9
Meshaw Devon 15 S9
Messing Essex 23 L4
Messingham N Linc 58 E6
Metfield Suffk 41 N4
Metherell Cnwll 5 L7
Metheringham Lincs 48 G1
Methil Fife 91 N12
Methilhill Fife 91 N12
Methley Leeds 57 N1
Methley Junction Leeds 57 N1
Methlick Abers 105 P8
Methven P & K 90 F6
Methwold Norfk 50 B14
Methwold Hythe Norfk 49 U14
Mettingham Suffk 41 Q3
Metton Norfk 51 L6
Mevagissey Cnwll 3 Q7
Mexborough Donc 57 Q6
Mey Highld 112 G2
Meysey Hampton Gloucs 29 M7
Miabhig W Isls 106 f5
Miavaig W Isls 106 f5
Michaelchurch Herefs 27 U3
Michaelchurch Escley Herefs 34 H14
Michaelchurch-on-Arrow Powys 34 F10
Michaelston-y-Fedw Newpt 27 N11
Michaelston-le-Pit V Glam 16 F2
Michaelstow Cnwll 4 D5
Michaelwood Services Gloucs 28 D8
Michelcombe Devon 5 R7
Micheldever Hants 19 R12
Micheldever Station Hants 19 R12
Michelmersh Hants 9 L3
Mickfield Suffk 40 K8
Micklebring Donc 57 R8
Mickleby N York 71 P10
Micklefield Leeds 64 B13
Micklefield Green Herts 20 H3
Mickleham Surrey 21 L12
Mickleover C Derb 46 K7
Micklethwaite C Brad 63 M11
Micklethwaite Cumb 67 L2

Mickleton Dur 69 L8
Mickleton Gloucs 36 G12
Mickletown Leeds 57 P1
Mickle Trafford Ches W 54 K13
Mickley Derbys 57 L11
Mickley N York 63 R4
Mickley Green Suffk 40 D9
Mickley Square Nthumb 77 M13
Mid Ardlaw Abers 105 Q3
Midbea Ork 106 t15
Mid Beltie Abers 99 L3
Mid Bockhampton Dorset 8 H9
Mid Calder W Loth 83 L5
Mid Clyth Highld 112 G11
Mid Culbeuchly Abers 104 K3
Middle Aston Oxon 29 U2
Middle Barton Oxon 29 T2
Middlebie D & G 75 P10
Middlebridge P & K 97 P10
Middle Chinnock Somset 7 P2
Middle Claydon Bucks 30 F7
Middlecliffe Barns 57 P5
Middlecott Devon 5 S3
Middle Duntisbourne Gloucs 28 J6
Middleham N York 63 N2
Middle Handley Derbys 57 P11
Middle Harling Norfk 40 G3
Middlehill Cnwll 4 H7
Middlehill Wilts 18 B7
Middlehope Shrops 35 L3
Middle Kames Ag & B 87 S8
Middle Littleton Worcs 36 E11
Middle Madeley Staffs 45 S4
Middlemarsh Dorset 7 S3
Middle Mayfield Staffs 46 F5
Middle Mill Pembks 24 D5
Middlemore Devon 5 M6
Middle Quarter Kent 12 G8
Middle Rasen Lincs 58 J9
Middle Rocombe Devon 6 B11
Middle Salter Lancs 62 C7
Middlesbrough Middsb 70 G9
Middlesceugh Cumb 67 N4
Middleshaw Cumb 62 B2
Middlesmoor N York 63 M5
Middlestone Dur 69 S5
Middlestone Moor Dur 69 R5
Middle Stoford Somset 16 G12
Middle Stoke Medway 12 F13
Middlestown Wakefd 57 M3
Middlethird Border 84 F10
Middleton Ag & B 92 B10
Middleton Cumb 62 C2
Middleton Derbys 46 J2
Middleton Derbys 46 H1
Middleton Essex 40 E13
Middleton Hants 19 Q11
Middleton Herefs 35 M7
Middleton Lancs 61 S8
Middleton Leeds 63 S14
Middleton N York 63 N10
Middleton N York 64 H3
Middleton Nthumb 77 M9
Middleton Nthumb 85 R12
Middleton Norfk 49 U10
Middleton P & K 90 H7
Middleton Rochdl 56 C5
Middleton Shrops 35 M6
Middleton Shrops 45 L7
Middleton Suffk 41 R7
Middleton Swans 25 R13
Middleton Warwks 46 G14
Middleton Cheney Nhants 37 N12
Middleton Crematorium Rochdl 56 C5
Middleton Green Staffs 46 C6
Middleton Hall Nthumb 85 P13
Middleton-in-Teesdale Dur 68 K7
Middleton Moor Suffk 41 R7
Middleton One Row Darltn 70 D10
Middleton-on-Leven N York 70 G11
Middleton-on-Sea W Susx 10 F10
Middleton on the Hill Herefs 35 M8
Middleton on the Wolds E R Yk 65 L10
Middleton Park C Aber 105 Q13
Middleton Priors Shrops 35 P2
Middleton Quernhow N York 63 S4
Middleton St George Darltn 70 D10
Middleton Scriven Shrops 35 Q3
Middleton Stoney Oxon 30 B8
Middleton Tyas N York 69 R11
Middletown C Aber 105 Q3
Middle Town IoS 2 b3
Middletown N Som 17 L2
Middle Tysoe Warwks 36 K12
Middle Wallop Hants 19 L13
Middlewich Ches E 55 R14
Middle Winterslow Wilts 18 H13
Middlewood Cnwll 4 H5
Middle Woodford Wilts 18 G13
Middlewood Green Suffk 40 J8
Middleyard E Ayrs 81 Q6
Middle Yard Gloucs 28 F7
Middlezoy Somset 17 L10
Middridge Dur 69 R7
Midford BaNES 17 U4
Midge Hall Lancs 55 M1
Midgeholme Cumb 76 B14
Midgham W Berk 19 S7
Midgley Calder 56 F1
Midgley Wakefd 57 L4
Mid Holmwood Surrey 21 L13
Midhopestones Sheff 56 K6
Midhurst W Susx 10 D6
Mid Lavant W Susx 10 D9
Midlem Border 84 E13
Mid Mains Highld 102 D8
Midney Somset 17 P11
Midpark Ag & B 87 U14
Midsomer Norton BaNES 17 S6
Midtown Highld 111 N5
Midville Lincs 49 N2
Mid Warwickshire Crematorium Warwks 36 K9
Midway Ches E 56 D10
Mid Yell Shet 106 v4
Migvie Abers 98 G3
Milborne Port Somset 17 S13
Milborne St Andrew Dorset 7 V5
Milborne Wick Somset 17 S12
Milbourne Nthumb 77 N10
Milbourne Wilts 28 J10
Milburn Cumb 68 E7
Milbury Heath S Glos 28 C9
Milby N York 63 U6
Milcombe Oxon 37 M14
Milden Suffk 40 G11
Mildenhall Suffk 40 B6
Mildenhall Wilts 18 K7
Milebrook Powys 34 H6
Milebush Kent 12 E6
Mile Elm Wilts 18 E7
Mile End Essex 23 N3
Mile End Gloucs 28 A5
Mile Oak Br & H 11 L9
Mile Oak Kent 12 C5
Mile Oak Staffs 46 G13
Miles Hope Herefs 35 N8
Milesmark Fife 90 G14
Mile Town Kent 23 M13
Milfield Nthumb 85 N12
Milford Derbys 47 L4
Milford Powys 44 C14
Milford Staffs 46 C9
Milford Surrey 10 F2
Milford Haven Pembks 24 F9
Milford on Sea Hants 8 K10
Milkwall Gloucs 28 A6
Millais Jersey 7 a1
Milland W Susx 10 C5
Mill Bank Calder 56 F2
Millbeck Cumb 67 L8
Millbreck Abers 105 R7
Millbridge Surrey 10 D2
Millbrook C Beds 31 N5
Millbrook Cnwll 5 L10
Millbrook C Sotn 9 M6
Millbrook Jersey 7 b2
Millbrook Tamesd 56 E7
Mill Brow Stockp 56 E9
Millcorner E Susx 12 F11

Millcraig Highld 109 M10
Mill Cross Devon 5 S8
Milldale Staffs 46 F3
Mill End Bucks 20 C5
Mill End Cambs 39 S8
Mill End Herts 31 T6
Mill End Herts 31 M9
Millerhill Mdloth 83 R5
Miller's Dale Derbys 56 H12
Miller's Green Derbys 46 H3
Millers Green Essex 22 E6
Miller's Green C Glas 89 P12
Millgate Lancs 56 C3
Mill Green Cambs 39 T11
Mill Green Essex 22 F7
Mill Green Herts 31 R10
Mill Green Lincs 48 K9
Mill Green Norfk 40 K4
Mill Green Shrops 45 Q8
Mill Green Staffs 46 E13
Mill Green Staffs 46 E10
Mill Green Suffk 40 E12
Mill Green Suffk 40 G7
Mill Green Suffk 40 H12
Mill Green Suffk 41 P8
Millhalf Herefs 34 G11
Millhayes Devon 6 H4
Millheugh S Lans 82 D8
Mill Hill Gt Lon 21 M4
Millhouse Ag & B 87 T11
Millhouse Cumb 67 N5
Millhousebridge D & G 75 M9
Millhouse Green Barns 56 K6
Millhouses Sheff 57 M10
Millhouses Barns 57 N5
Millikenpark Rens 88 K13
Millin Cross Pembks 24 G8
Millington E R Yk 64 J9
Mill Lane Hants 20 C12
Millmeece Staffs 45 T7
Mill of Drummond P & K 89 T2
Mill of Haldane W Duns 88 J9
Millom Cumb 61 M3
Millook Cnwll 14 E13
Millpool Cnwll 4 F6
Millpool Cnwll 2 H11
Millport Ag & B 80 K2
Mill Side Cumb 61 S3
Mill Street Kent 12 C4
Mill Street Norfk 50 J10
Mill Street Suffk 40 K6
Millthorp Cumb 62 D1
Millthorpe Nhants 37 Q11
Milltimber C Aber 99 R2
Milltown Abers 104 D12
Milltown Abers 104 F11
Milltown Cnwll 4 F9
Milltown D & G 75 T9
Milltown Derbys 47 L1
Milltown Devon 15 N5
Milltown of Campfield Abers 99 M3
Milltown of Edinville Moray 104 B7
Milltown of Learney Abers 99 L3
Milnacraig Angus 98 D12
Milnathort P & K 90 H11
Milngavie E Duns 89 N11
Milnrow Rochdl 56 D4
Milnthorpe Cumb 61 T3
Milnthorpe Wakefd 57 M3
Milovaig Highld 100 a4
Milson Shrops 35 P6
Milstead Kent 12 H4
Milston Wilts 18 J11
Milthorpe Nhants 37 Q11
Milton C Stke 46 B3
Milton Cambs 39 Q8
Milton Cumb 76 B13
Milton D & G 72 G7
Milton D & G 74 H11
Milton Derbys 47 L8
Milton Highld 102 G5
Milton Highld 102 E7
Milton Highld 102 H11
Milton Highld 109 M10
Milton Inver 88 G11
Milton Kent 22 H13
Milton Moray 104 H2
Milton Moray 103 V12
Milton N Som 17 L4
Milton Newpt 27 R10
Milton Notts 58 B12
Milton Oxon 29 U9
Milton Oxon 37 M13
Milton P & K 97 R13
Milton Pembks 24 H10
Milton Somset 17 N11
Milton Stirlg 88 K5
Milton Stirlg 89 K11
Milton Abbas Dorset 7 U4
Milton Abbot Devon 5 L5
Milton Bridge Mdloth 83 P6
Milton Bryan C Beds 31 L6
Milton Clevedon Somset 17 S9
Milton Combe Devon 5 M7
Milton Common Oxon 30 E12
Milton Damerel Devon 14 J10
Milton End Gloucs 28 M7
Milton Ernest Bed 38 F9
Milton Green Ches W 45 L2
Milton Hill Oxon 29 U8
Milton Keynes M Keyn 30 J5
Milton Lilbourne Wilts 18 J8
Milton Malsor Nhants 37 T9
Milton Morenish P & K 95 S11
Milton-under-Wychwood Oxon 29 Q4

Milverton Somset 16 F11
Milverton Warwks 36 K7
Milwich Staffs 46 C7
Milwr Flints 54 F12
Minard Ag & B 87 T6
Minchington Dorset 8 D6
Minchinhampton Gloucs 28 G7
Mindrum Nthumb 85 L12
Minehead Somset 16 B7
Minera Wrexhm 44 G2
Minety Wilts 28 K9
Minffordd Gwynd 43 L6
Miningsby Lincs 49 M1
Minions Cnwll 4 H6
Minishant S Ayrs 81 L10
Minllyn Gwynd 43 S11
Minnis Bay Kent 13 Q2
Minnonie Abers 105 M3
Minshull Vernon Ches E 45 R1
Minskip N York 63 T7
Minstead Hants 9 L6
Minsted W Susx 10 D6
Minster Kent 13 R2
Minster Kent 23 R13
Minsterley Shrops 44 J12
Minster Lovell Oxon 29 R5
Minsterworth Gloucs 28 E4
Minterne Magna Dorset 7 S4
Minterne Parva Dorset 7 S4
Minting Lincs 59 L12
Mintlyn Crematorium Norfk 49 U10
Minto Border 84 E14
Minwear Pembks 24 H8
Minworth Birm 36 G2
Mirehouse Cumb 66 E9
Mireland Highld 112 H4
Mirfield Kirk 56 K3
Miserden Gloucs 28 H6
Miskin Rhondd 26 K11
Miskin Rhondd 26 J8
Misson Notts 57 U7
Misterton Leics 37 Q4
Misterton Notts 58 C8
Misterton Somset 7 N3
Mistley Essex 23 R1
Mistley Heath Essex 23 R1
Mitcham Gt Lon 21 N9
Mitchel Troy Mons 27 T5
Mitcheldean Gloucs 28 C4
Mitchell Cnwll 3 L5
Mitchellslacks D & G 74 J7
Mitford Nthumb 77 P8
Mithian Cnwll 2 J6
Mitton Staffs 45 U10
Mixbury Oxon 30 D6
Mixenden Calder 63 M14
Moats Tye Suffk 40 H9
Mobberley Ches E 55 S11
Mobberley Staffs 46 D4
Moccas Herefs 34 J12
Mochdre Conwy 53 P7
Mochdre Powys 34 C3
Mochrum D & G 72 K10
Mockbeggar Hants 8 H7

Mockbeggar Kent 12 D6
Mockerkin Cumb 66 G8
Modbury Devon 5 R10
Moddershall Staffs 46 B6
Modsarie Highld 111 P4
Moelfre IoA 52 H5
Moelfre Powys 44 D8
Moel Tryfan Gwynd 52 H11
Moffat D & G 75 L5
Mogerhanger C Beds 38 H11
Moira Leics 46 K10
Molash Kent 12 K5
Mol-chlach Highld 100 d8
Mold Flints 54 F14
Moldgreen Kirk 56 J3
Molehill Green Essex 22 E3
Molehill Green Essex 22 H2
Molescroft E R Yk 65 N11
Molesden Nthumb 77 N9
Molesworth Cambs 38 G5
Moll Highld 100 e6
Molland Devon 15 U7
Mollington Ches W 54 J12
Mollington Oxon 37 M11
Mollinsburn N Lans 82 B4
Monachty Cerdgn 32 K8
Mondynes Abers 99 N9
Monevechadan Ag & B 88 E5
Monewden Suffk 41 M9
Moneydie P & K 90 G5
Moneyrow Green W & M 20 E7
Monifieth Angus 91 Q5
Monikie Angus 91 Q4
Monimail Fife 91 L9
Monington Pembks 32 B12
Monk Bretton Barns 57 N5
Monken Hadley Gt Lon 21 M3
Monk Fryston N York 57 T1
Monkhide Herefs 35 P12
Monkhill Cumb 75 R14
Monkhopton Shrops 35 P2
Monkland Herefs 35 L9
Monkleigh Devon 15 L8
Monknash V Glam 26 G12
Monkokehampton Devon 15 N11
Monkseaton N Tyne 77 S11
Monks Eleigh Suffk 40 G11
Monk's Gate W Susx 11 L5
Monks Heath Ches E 55 T12
Monk Sherborne Hants 19 T9
Monkshill Abers 105 L6
Monksilver Somset 16 E9
Monks Kirby Warwks 37 N4
Monk Soham Suffk 41 M7
Monkspath Solhll 36 F5
Monks Risborough Bucks 30 H12
Monksthorpe Lincs 59 R13
Monk Street Essex 22 F2
Monkswood Mons 27 Q7
Monkton Devon 6 H4
Monkton Kent 13 Q3
Monkton S Ayrs 81 M7
Monkton S Tyne 77 S13
Monkton V Glam 16 E3
Monkton Combe BaNES 17 U4
Monkton Deverill Wilts 18 C13
Monkton Farleigh Wilts 18 B7
Monkton Heathfield Somset 16 J11
Monkton Up Wimborne Dorset 8 E6
Monkton Wyld Dorset 6 K5
Monkwearmouth Sundld 77 T14
Monkwood Hants 19 U13
Monmore Green Wolves 36 B1
Monmouth Mons 27 U5
Monnington on Wye Herefs 34 J12
Monreith D & G 72 K11
Montacute Somset 17 N13
Montcliffe Bolton 55 Q4
Montford Shrops 44 K10
Montford Bridge Shrops 44 K10
Montgarrie Abers 104 H12
Montgarswood E Ayrs 81 R6
Montgomery Powys 44 F1
Montrave Fife 91 M10
Montrose Angus 99 N11
Mont Saint Guern 6 c3
Monxton Hants 19 M11
Monyash Derbys 56 H13
Monymusk Abers 104 K12
Monzie P & K 90 C6
Moodiesburn N Lans 82 C4
Moonzie Fife 91 M8
Moorbath Dorset 7 M5
Moorby Lincs 59 L14
Moorcot Herefs 34 J9
Moor Crichel Dorset 8 D7
Moordown BCP 8 F10
Moore Halton 55 N10
Moor End C Beds 31 L8
Moor End Calder 56 F1
Moor End Devon 15 Q11
Moorend Gloucs 28 D7
Moor End Lancs 61 R11
Moor End N York 64 E10
Moorends Donc 57 U3
Moorgreen Hants 9 P5
Moor Green Herts 31 T7
Moorgreen Notts 47 N4
Moorhall Derbys 57 M12
Moorhampton Herefs 34 J12
Moorhead C Brad 63 P12
Moorhouse Cumb 75 R14
Moorhouse Cumb 67 M2
Moorhouse Donc 57 U4
Moorhouse Notts 58 B13
Moorhouse Bank Surrey 21 R12
Moorland Somset 16 K10
Moorlinch Somset 17 L9
Moor Monkton N York 64 C8
Moor Row Cumb 66 F10
Moor Row Cumb 67 M3
Moorsholm R & C 71 L9
Moorside Dorset 17 U13
Moor Side Lancs 61 S12
Moor Side Lancs 61 T12
Moorside Leeds 63 Q13
Moorside Oldham 56 D5
Moor Side Lincs 49 L2
Moorstock Kent 13 L7
Moor Street Kent 12 F2
Moor Street Medway 12 F2
Moorswater Cnwll 4 G8
Moorthorpe Wakefd 57 Q4
Moortown Devon 5 N5
Moortown Hants 8 H7
Moortown IoW 9 N12
Moortown Leeds 63 S12
Moortown Lincs 58 J7
Moortown Wrekin 45 P10
Morangie Highld 109 P8
Morar Highld 100 f10
Moray Crematorium Moray 104 D3
Morborne Cambs 38 H2
Morchard Bishop Devon 15 S11
Morcombelake Dorset 7 M6
Morcott Rutlnd 48 D13
Morda Shrops 44 G8
Morden Dorset 8 C9
Morden Gt Lon 21 M9
Mordiford Herefs 35 N13
Mordon Dur 70 D7
More Shrops 34 J2
Morebath Devon 16 C11
Morebattle Border 84 K14
Morecambe Lancs 61 S7
Moredon Swindn 29 M10
Morefield Highld 107 V5
Morehall Kent 13 P8
Moreleigh Devon 5 S10
Morenish P & K 95 S11
Moresby Parks Cumb 66 E9
Morestead Hants 9 Q3
Moreton Dorset 7 V7
Moreton Essex 22 E6
Moreton Herefs 35 M8
Moreton Oxon 30 E12
Moreton Staffs 46 E11
Moreton Wirral 54 G9
Moreton Corbet Shrops 45 N9
Moretonhampstead Devon 5 S3
Moreton-in-Marsh Gloucs 29 P1
Moreton Jeffries Herefs 35 P11
Moreton Morrell Warwks 36 K9
Moreton on Lugg Herefs 35 M12
Moreton Paddox Warwks 36 K10
Moreton Pinkney Nhants 37 P11
Moreton Say Shrops 45 P7
Moreton Valence Gloucs 28 E6
Morfa Cerdgn 32 F10
Morfa Bychan Gwynd 42 K6
Morfa Dinlle Gwynd 52 F11
Morfa Glas Neath 26 F6
Morfa Nefyn Gwynd 42 E4
Morganstown Cardif 27 L11
Morgan's Vale Wilts 8 G4
Moriah Cerdgn 33 M5
Morland Cumb 68 D8
Morley Ches E 55 S11
Morley Derbys 47 L5
Morley Dur 69 Q7
Morley Leeds 57 L1

Morley Green Ches E 55 T10
Morley St Botolph Norfk 50 J14
Mornick Cnwll 4 J6
Morningside C Edin 83 P4
Morningside N Lans 82 G7
Morningthorpe Norfk 41 M2
Morpeth Nthumb 77 P9
Morphie Abers 99 N11
Morrey Staffs 46 F10
Morridge Side Staffs 46 E2
Morriston Swans 26 A8
Morston Norfk 50 H5
Mortehoe Devon 15 L3
Morthen Rothm 57 Q9
Mortimer W Berk 19 U7
Mortimer Common W Berk 19 U7
Mortimer's Cross Herefs 34 K8
Mortimer West End Hants 19 T8
Mortlake Gt Lon 21 M7
Mortlake Crematorium Gt Lon 21 L7
Morton Cumb 67 N1
Morton Cumb 75 R14
Morton Derbys 47 M1
Morton Lincs 48 G9
Morton Lincs 58 D8
Morton Lincs 58 D6
Morton Notts 47 U3
Morton Shrops 44 G9
Morton Hall Lincs 58 E14
Mortonhall Crematorium C Edin 83 Q5
Morton-on-Swale N York 63 S1
Morton on the Hill Norfk 50 K10
Morton Tinmouth Dur 69 Q8
Morvah Cnwll 2 C9
Morval Cnwll 4 H9
Morvich Highld 101 P7
Morville Shrops 35 Q2
Morville Heath Shrops 35 Q2
Morwenstow Cnwll 14 E9
Mosborough Sheff 57 P10
Moscow E Ayrs 81 P4
Mose Shrops 35 S2
Mosedale Cumb 67 N6
Moseley Birm 36 E4
Moseley Wolves 36 B1
Moseley Worcs 35 T9
Moses Gate Bolton 55 R5
Moss Ag & B 92 B10
Moss Donc 57 S4
Moss Wrexhm 44 H3
Moss Bank St Hel 55 M7
Mossbay Cumb 66 F7
Mossblown S Ayrs 81 N8
Mossbrow Traffd 55 R9
Mossburnford Border 76 D2
Mossdale D & G 73 R5
Mossdale E Ayrs 81 P12
Moss Edge Lancs 61 S11
Moss End Ches E 55 R10
Mossend N Lans 82 C6
Mossgiel E Ayrs 81 P7
Mosshead Abers 104 H9
Mossley Ches E 45 U1
Mossley Tamesd 56 E6
Mossley Hill Lpool 54 J9
Moss-side Highld 103 N4
Moss Side Cumb 75 L14
Moss Side Lancs 61 R13
Moss Side Lancs 54 J1
Moss Side Sefton 54 J6
Mosspaul Hotel Border 75 S6
Mosstodloch Moray 104 C4
Mossyard D & G 73 N9
Mossy Lea Lancs 55 M4
Mosterton Dorset 7 N4
Moston Manch 56 C6
Moston Shrops 45 N9
Moston Green Ches E 45 S1
Mostyn Flints 54 E10
Motcombe Dorset 17 V12
Mothecombe Devon 5 Q11
Motherby Cumb 67 P7
Motherwell N Lans 82 D7
Motspur Park Gt Lon 21 M9
Mottingham Gt Lon 21 R8
Mottisfont Hants 9 L3
Mottistone IoW 9 N12
Mottram in Longdendale Tamesd 56 E7
Mottram St Andrew Ches E 56 C11
Mouilpied Guern 6 d3
Mouldsworth Ches W 55 M12
Moulin P & K 97 Q12
Moulsecoomb Br & H 11 N9
Moulsford Oxon 19 S4
Moulsoe M Keyn 30 K4
Moultavie Highld 109 L10
Moulton Ches W 55 Q13
Moulton Lincs 49 M9
Moulton Nhants 37 U7
Moulton N York 69 R11
Moulton Suffk 39 U8
Moulton V Glam 16 E3
Moulton Chapel Lincs 49 L10
Moulton St Mary Norfk 51 Q12
Moulton Seas End Lincs 49 M8
Mount Cnwll 3 N3
Mount Cnwll 4 E7
Mount Kent 13 M7
Mount Hawke Cnwll 2 J7
Mount Hermon Cnwll 2 H11
Mountjoy Cnwll 3 M4
Mount Lothian Mdloth 83 P7
Mountnessing Essex 22 F8
Mounton Mons 27 U8
Mount Pleasant Ches E 45 U2
Mount Pleasant Derbys 46 K10
Mount Pleasant Derbys 47 L3
Mount Pleasant Dur 70 E4
Mount Pleasant E R Yk 65 T12
Mount Pleasant E Susx 11 R7
Mount Pleasant Norfk 40 G3
Mount Pleasant Suffk 40 B11
Mount Sorrel Wilts 8 E4
Mount Tabor Calder 56 F1
Mousehole Cnwll 2 C11
Mouswald D & G 75 L11
Mow Cop Ches E 45 U2
Mowhaugh Border 85 L13
Mowmacre Hill C Leic 47 R12
Mowsley Leics 37 R3
Moy Highld 103 L8
Moy Highld 96 E1
Moylegrove Pembks 32 C11
Muasdale Ag & B 79 M7
Muchalls Abers 99 S4
Much Birch Herefs 27 U1
Much Cowarne Herefs 35 P11
Much Dewchurch Herefs 27 T1
Muchelney Somset 17 M12
Muchelney Ham Somset 17 M12
Much Hadham Herts 22 B4
Much Hoole Lancs 55 L2
Much Hoole Town Lancs 55 L2
Muchlarnick Cnwll 4 G9
Much Marcle Herefs 35 Q14
Much Wenlock Shrops 45 P13
Muck Highld 93 L3
Mucking Thurr 22 G11
Muckingford Thurr 22 G12
Muckleburgh Collection Norfk 50 K5
Muckleford Dorset 7 R6
Mucklestone Staffs 45 R7
Muckton Lincs 59 Q11
Muddiford Devon 15 N5
Muddles Green E Susx 11 S8
Mudeford BCP 8 H10
Mudford Somset 17 Q13
Mudford Sock Somset 17 Q13
Mudgley Somset 17 N8
Mugdock Stirlg 89 M11
Mugeary Highld 100 d6
Mugginton Derbys 46 J5
Muggintonlane End Derbys 46 J5
Muggleswick Dur 69 M2
Muirden Abers 105 L5
Muirdrum Angus 91 R4
Muiresk Abers 105 L6
Muirhead Angus 91 N5
Muirhead Fife 91 L10
Muirhead N Lans 82 B5
Muirhouses Falk 83 L1

Muirkirk E Ayrs 81 T9
Muir of Fowlis Abers 104 H12
Muir of Miltonduff Moray 103 V4
Muir of Ord Highld 102 F6
Muir of Ardblair Abers 90 J3
Muirshearlich Highld 94 F2
Muirtack Abers 105 R8
Muirton P & K 90 H6
Muirton Mains Highld 102 E5
Muirton of Ardblair Abers 90 J3
Muker N York 68 K13
Mulbarton Norfk 51 L13
Mulben Moray 104 D5
Mulfra Cnwll 2 C10
Mulindry Ag & B 78 E4
Mullacott Cross Devon 15 M4
Mullion Cnwll 2 H13
Mullion Cove Cnwll 2 H13
Mumby Lincs 59 S11
Munderfield Row Herefs 35 P10
Munderfield Stocks Herefs 35 P10
Mundesley Norfk 51 P6
Mundford Norfk 50 D14
Mundham Norfk 51 P14
Mundon Essex 23 L7
Mundurno C Aber 105 R12
Munerigie Highld 101 V9
Mungrisdale Cumb 67 N6
Munlochy Highld 102 H5
Munnoch N Ayrs 80 K3
Munsley Herefs 35 Q12
Munslow Shrops 35 M3
Murchington Devon 5 R3
Murcot Worcs 36 D12
Murcott Oxon 30 C9
Murcott Wilts 28 J9
Murkle Highld 112 E3
Murlaggan Highld 101 S14
Murrell Green Hants 20 C11
Murroes Angus 91 Q4
Murrow Cambs 49 N12
Mursley Bucks 30 H7
Murston Kent 12 K3
Murthill Angus 98 H12
Murthly P & K 90 G4
Murton C York 64 E9
Murton Cumb 68 F8
Murton Dur 70 E3
Murton Nthumb 85 P9
Murton N Nthumb 85 R11
Murton N York 63 U6
Musbury Devon 6 J5
Muscoates N York 64 F3
Musselburgh E Loth 83 R4
Muston Leics 48 B6
Muston N York 65 P4
Mustow Green Worcs 35 T6
Muswell Hill Gt Lon 21 N5
Mutehill D & G 73 R10
Mutford Suffk 41 S3
Muthill P & K 90 C8
Mutterton Devon 6 D3
Muxton Wrekin 45 R11
Mybster Highld 112 E6
Myddfai Carmth 26 E1
Myddle Shrops 45 L9
Mydroilyn Cerdgn 32 J9
Myerscough Lancs 61 T12
Mylor Cnwll 3 L9
Mylor Bridge Cnwll 3 L9
Mynachlog ddu Pembks 24 K4
Myndd-llan Flints 54 E12
Mynydd-bach Swans 26 B8
Mynydd-Bach Swans 26 B8
Mynyddgarreg Carmth 25 R9
Mynydd Isa Flints 54 F14
Mynydd Llandygai Gwynd 52 K9
Myntho Gwynd 42 E7
Myrebird Abers 99 N4
Myredykes Border 76 B7
Mytchett Surrey 20 F11
Mytholm Calder 56 E1
Mytholmroyd Calder 56 F1
Mythop Lancs 61 R13
Myton-on-Swale N York 63 U6

N

Naast Highld 107 P8
Nab's Head Lancs 62 C14
Na Buirgh W Isls 106 f9
Naburn C York 64 D10
Nab Wood Crematorium C Brad 63 N12
Naccolt Kent 13 L7
Nackington Kent 13 N5
Nacton Suffk 41 M12
Nafferton E R Yk 65 P8
Nag's Head Gloucs 28 G8
Nailbridge Gloucs 28 C4
Nailsbourne Somset 16 H11
Nailsea N Som 17 M3
Nailstone Leics 47 M12
Nailsworth Gloucs 28 F8
Nairn Highld 103 N4
Nalderswood Surrey 21 M13
Nancegollan Cnwll 2 H10
Nancledra Cnwll 2 D10
Nangreaves Bury 55 T4
Nanhoron Gwynd 42 E7
Nannerch Flints 54 E13
Nanpantan Leics 47 P10
Nanpean Cnwll 3 P5
Nanquidno Cnwll 2 B11
Nanstallon Cnwll 3 Q3
Nant-ddu Powys 26 K6
Nanternis Cerdgn 32 G9
Nantgaredig Carmth 25 S6
Nantgarw Rhondd 27 L10
Nant-glas Powys 33 U7
Nantglyn Denbgs 53 U13
Nantgwyn Powys 33 U5
Nantlle Gwynd 52 H11
Nantmawr Shrops 44 G9
Nantmel Powys 33 U8
Nantmor Gwynd 43 L4
Nant Peris Gwynd 52 K11
Nantwich Ches E 45 Q3
Nant-y-Bwch Blae G 27 M5
Nant-y-caws Carmth 25 S7
Nant-y-derry Mons 27 Q6
Nantyffyllon Brdgnd 26 F9
Nantyglo Blae G 27 M6
Nant-y-gollen Shrops 44 F8
Nant-y-moel Brdgnd 26 G9
Nant-y-pandy Conwy 53 L8
Naphill Bucks 20 D3
Napleton Worcs 35 U11
Nappa N York 62 H9
Napton on the Hill Warwks 37 N8
Narberth Pembks 24 K7
Narborough Leics 37 P1
Narborough Norfk 50 B11
Narkurs Cnwll 4 J9
Nasareth Gwynd 42 H3
Naseby Nhants 37 S5
Nash Bucks 30 G5
Nash Gt Lon 21 R10
Nash Herefs 34 H8
Nash Newpt 27 R11
Nash Shrops 35 P6
Nash End Worcs 35 S5
Nash Lee Bucks 30 H11
Nash's Green Hants 19 V11
Nash Street Suffk 40 B7
Nassington Nhants 38 G1
Nasty Herts 31 U8
Nateby Cumb 68 G11
Nateby Lancs 61 T11
National Memorial Arboretum Staffs 46 F10
National Motor Museum (Beaulieu) Hants 9 M8
National Space Science Centre C Leic 47 Q12
Natland Cumb 61 U2
Naughton Suffk 40 H11
Naunton Gloucs 29 M3
Naunton Worcs 35 U13
Naunton Beauchamp Worcs 36 C10

Navenby Lincs 48 E2
Navestock Essex 22 D8
Navestock Side Essex 22 D8
Navidale House Hotel Highld 112 B13
Navity Highld 109 Q10
Nawton N York 64 E3
Nayland Suffk 40 G13
Nazeing Essex 31 U12
Nazeing Gate Essex 22 B7
Neal's Green Warwks 37 L4
Neap Shet 106 v8
Near Cotton Staffs 46 E4
Near Sawrey Cumb 67 N13
Neasden Gt Lon 21 M5
Neasham Darltn 70 D10
Neath Neath 26 D8
Neatham Hants 10 B2
Neatishead Norfk 51 P9
Nebo Cerdgn 32 K7
Nebo Conwy 53 P11
Nebo Gwynd 42 H3
Nebo IoA 52 G4
Necton Norfk 50 E12
Nedd Highld 110 D10
Nedderton Nthumb 77 Q9
Nedging Suffk 40 G11
Nedging Tye Suffk 40 H11
Needham Norfk 41 M3
Needham Market Suffk 40 J9
Needham Street Suffk 40 B7
Needingworth Cambs 39 M6

Neen Savage Shrops 35 Q5
Neen Sollars Shrops 35 Q6
Neenton Shrops 35 P3
Nefyn Gwynd 42 F5
Neilston E Rens 81 M1
Nelson Caerph 27 L9
Nelson Lancs 62 H12
Nelson Village Nthumb 77 R10
Nemphlar S Lans 82 G10
Nempnett Thrubwell BaNES 17 P4
Nenthall Cumb 68 F3
Nenthead Cumb 68 G4
Nenthorn Border 84 H11
Neopardy Devon 15 S12
Nerabus Ag & B 78 D4
Nercwys Flints 44 F1
Nereabolls Ag & B 78 C4
Nesbit Nthumb 85 P12
Nesfield N York 63 M10
Ness Ches W 54 H11
Nesscliffe Shrops 44 J10
Neston Ches W 54 G11
Neston Wilts 18 C7
Netchwood Shrops 35 P2
Nether Alderley Ches E 55 T11
Netheravon Wilts 18 H11
Nether Blainslie Border 84 E10
Netherbrae Abers 105 L4
Netherbury Dorset 7 N5
Netherby Cumb 75 S10
Nether Cerne Dorset 7 S5
Nethercleuch D & G 75 M8
Nether Compton Dorset 17 Q13
Nethercote Warwks 37 P7
Nethercott Devon 14 J13
Nether Crimond Abers 105 N11
Nether Dallachy Moray 104 D3
Nether Exe Devon 6 B4
Netherfield E Susx 12 D12
Netherfield Leics 47 Q10
Netherfield Notts 47 R5
Nether Fingland S Lans 74 G2
Nethergate N Linc 58 C7
Nethergate Norfk 50 J8
Netherhampton Wilts 8 G3
Nether Handley Derbys 57 P11
Nether Haugh Rothm 57 P7
Netherhay Dorset 7 M3
Nether Headon Notts 58 B11
Nether Heage Derbys 47 L3
Nether Heyford Nhants 37 R9
Nether Howcleugh S Lans 74 K3
Nether Kellet Lancs 61 U6
Nether Kinmundy Abers 105 S7
Netherland Green Staffs 46 F7
Nether Langwith Notts 57 R12
Netherley Abers 99 R4
Nethermill D & G 74 K9
Nethermuir Abers 105 Q7
Netherne-on-the-Hill Surrey 21 N11
Netheroyd Hill Kirk 56 H3
Nether Padley Derbys 56 K11
Nether Poppleton C York 64 D9
Nether Silton N York 64 B1
Nether Skyborry Shrops 34 G6
Nether Stowey Somset 16 G9
Netherstreet Wilts 18 E8
Netherthong Kirk 56 H5
Netherthorpe Derbys 57 Q12
Netherton Angus 98 J12
Netherton Devon 6 B8
Netherton Dudley 36 B3
Netherton Hants 19 M9
Netherton Herefs 28 A2
Netherton Kirk 56 J3
Netherton N Lans 82 E8
Netherton Nthumb 76 K5
Netherton Oxon 29 U8
Netherton P & K 90 G2
Netherton Sefton 54 J6
Netherton Shrops 35 R4
Netherton Stirlg 89 M10
Netherton Wakefd 57 L4
Netherton Worcs 36 C11
Nethertown Cumb 66 E11
Nethertown Highld 112 J1
Nethertown Lancs 62 D10
Nethertown Staffs 46 F10
Netherurd Border 83 N10
Nether Wallop Hants 19 L13
Nether Wasdale Cumb 66 J11
Nether Welton Cumb 67 N3
Nether Westcote Gloucs 29 P3
Nether Whitacre Warwks 36 H2
Nether Whitecleuch S Lans 74 F2
Nether Winchendon Bucks 30 F10
Netherwitton Nthumb 77 M7
Nethy Bridge Highld 103 R11
Netley Hants 9 P7
Netley Marsh Hants 9 L6
Nettlebed Oxon 19 U4
Nettlebridge Somset 17 R7
Nettlecombe Dorset 7 P5
Nettlecombe IoW 9 Q13
Nettleden Herts 31 M10
Nettleham Lincs 58 H12
Nettlestead Kent 12 C5
Nettlestead Green Kent 12 C5
Nettlestone IoW 9 S10
Nettlesworth Dur 69 S3
Nettleton Lincs 58 K6
Nettleton Wilts 18 B5
Nettleton Shrub Wilts 18 B5
Netton Devon 5 P11
Netton Wilts 18 H13
Neuadd Carmth 26 B3
Neuadd-ddu Powys 33 T6
Nevendon Essex 22 H9
Nevern Pembks 32 D12
Nevill Holt Leics 38 B2
New Abbey D & G 74 J12
New Addington Gt Lon 21 Q10
Newall Leeds 63 P10
New Alresford Hants 9 R2
New Alyth P & K 90 K2
Newark C Pete 48 K13
Newark Ork 106 w15
Newark-on-Trent Notts 48 B3
Newarthill N Lans 82 E7
New Ash Green Kent 12 B3
New Balderton Notts 48 B3
New Barn Kent 12 B2
Newbarn Kent 13 M7
New Barnet Gt Lon 21 M3
New Barton Nhants 38 B7
Newbattle Mdloth 83 R5
New Bewick Nthumb 85 R13
Newbie D & G 75 N12
Newbiggin Cumb 68 D6
Newbiggin Cumb 67 R6
Newbiggin Cumb 66 K7
Newbiggin Cumb 67 S3
Newbiggin Dur 68 K4
Newbiggin N York 63 L2
Newbiggin N York 63 L1
Newbiggin-by-the-Sea Nthumb 77 S8
Newbigging Angus 91 Q5
Newbigging Angus 91 N4
Newbigging Angus 91 P4
Newbigging S Lans 82 K9
Newbiggin-on-Lune Cumb 68 F12

Newbridge-on-Usk Mons 27 R9
Newbridge-on-Wye Powys 34 B9
New Brighton Flints 54 G13
New Brighton Wirral 54 G8
New Brinsley Notts 47 N3
New Brotton R & C 71 L8
Newbrough Nthumb 76 H12
New Buckenham Norfk 40 J2
New Byth Abers 105 N5
Newbury Somset 17 T7
Newbury W Berk 19 Q7
Newbury Park Gt Lon 21 R5
Newby Cumb 67 R6
Newby Lancs 62 G11
Newby N York 62 E6
Newby N York 70 H10
Newby N York 63 U3
Newby Bridge Cumb 61 R3
Newby East Cumb 67 P1
Newby Head Cumb 67 R7
Newby West Cumb 67 N1
Newby Wiske N York 63 S2
Newcastle Mons 27 S4
Newcastle Shrops 34 G4
Newcastle Airport Nthumb 77 P11
Newcastle Emlyn Carmth 32 F12
Newcastleton Border 75 U8
Newcastle-under-Lyme Staffs 45 T4
Newcastle upon Tyne N u Ty 77 Q13
Newchapel Pembks 25 L3
Newchapel Staffs 45 U3
Newchapel Surrey 11 N2
Newchurch Blae G 27 M7
Newchurch Herefs 34 G10
Newchurch IoW 9 R12
Newchurch Kent 13 L8
Newchurch Mons 27 T9
Newchurch Powys 34 F10
Newchurch Staffs 46 F9
Newchurch in Pendle Lancs 62 G12
New Costessey Norfk 51 L11
New Cowper Cumb 66 H3
Newcraighall C Edin 83 R4
New Crofton Wakefd 57 N3
New Cross Cerdgn 33 M5
New Cross Gt Lon 21 Q7
New Cross Somset 17 M11
New Cumnock E Ayrs 81 S11
New Deer Abers 105 N6
New Delaval Nthumb 77 S10
New Denham Bucks 20 H6
New Duston Nhants 37 T8
New Earswick C York 64 E8
New Eastwood Notts 47 N4
New Edlington Donc 57 R7
New Elgin Moray 104 B3
New Ellerby E R Yk 65 R12
Newell Green Br For 20 E8
New Eltham Gt Lon 21 R8
New End Worcs 36 E8
Newenden Kent 12 F10
New England Essex 40 B12
New England C Pete 48 J13
Newent Gloucs 28 D3
New Farnley Leeds 63 R13
New Ferry Wirral 54 H9
Newfield Dur 69 R5
Newfield Dur 69 S2
Newfield Highld 109 P9
New Fletton C Pete 48 J14
New Forest National Park 8 K7
Newfound Hants 19 S10
New Fryston Wakefd 57 Q1
Newgale Pembks 24 E6
New Galloway D & G 73 R4
Newgate Norfk 50 J5
Newgate Street Herts 31 S12
New Gilston Fife 91 P10
New Grimsby IoS 2 b1
Newhall Ches E 45 Q4
Newhall Derbys 46 J9
Newham Nthumb 85 T13
New Hartley Nthumb 77 S10
Newhaven C Edin 83 Q3
Newhaven E Susx 11 Q10
New Haw Surrey 20 J10
New Hedges Pembks 24 K10
New Herrington Sundld 70 D2
Newhey Rochdl 56 D4
New Holkham Norfk 50 E6
New Holland N Linc 58 J2
Newholm N York 71 Q10
New Houghton Derbys 57 Q13
New Houghton Norfk 50 C8
Newhouse N Lans 82 E6
New Houses N York 62 G5
New Houses Wigan 55 N6
New Hutton Cumb 61 U1
New Hythe Kent 12 D4
Newick E Susx 11 Q6
Newingreen Kent 13 M8
Newington Kent 12 G3
Newington Kent 13 N8
Newington Oxon 19 U2
Newington Shrops 34 K4
Newington Bagpath Gloucs 28 F8
New Inn Carmth 32 H12
New Inn Torfn 27 Q8
New Invention Shrops 34 G5
New Lakenham Norfk 51 M12
New Lanark S Lans 82 G10
New Lanark Village S Lans 82 G10
Newland C KuH 65 P13
Newland Gloucs 28 A6
Newland N York 57 S1
Newland Oxon 29 S5
Newland Worcs 35 S11
Newland Somset 15 U6
Newlandrig Mdloth 83 R6
Newlands Border 75 T7
Newlands Cumb 67 M2
Newlands Nthumb 77 L14
Newlands of Dundurcas Moray 104 C5
New Lane Lancs 54 K4
New Lane End Warrtn 55 P8
New Langholm D & G 75 R9
New Leake Lincs 49 P2
New Leeds Abers 105 R5
New Longton Lancs 55 L1
New Luce D & G 72 F7
Newlyn Cnwll 2 C11
Newmachar Abers 105 P12
Newmains N Lans 82 G7
New Malden Gt Lon 21 M9
Newman's End Essex 22 D5
Newman's Green Suffk 40 E12
Newmarket Suffk 39 T8
Newmarket W Isls 106 j5
New Marske R & C 71 L8
New Marston Oxon 30 B11
New Marton Shrops 44 H7
New Mill Abers 99 N2
New Mill Cnwll 2 C10
New Mill Herts 30 K10
New Mill Kirk 56 J5
Newmill Border 75 U3
Newmill Moray 104 F5
New Mills Cnwll 3 M4
New Mills Derbys 56 E9
New Mills Mons 27 U6
New Mills Powys 44 C13
Newmills C Edin 82 K4
Newmills Fife 82 K2
Newmiln P & K 90 H5
Newmilns E Ayrs 81 R5
New Milton Hants 8 J10
New Mistley Essex 23 R1
New Moat Pembks 24 H5
Newney Green Essex 22 F6
Newnham Gloucs 28 C5
Newnham Hants 20 B11
Newnham Herts 31 R5
Newnham Kent 12 J4
Newnham Nhants 37 Q9
Newnham Worcs 35 Q7
Newnham Bridge Worcs 35 Q7
New Ollerton Notts 57 U13
New Oscott Birm 36 F2
New Pitsligo Abers 105 P4
New Polzeath Cnwll 4 B4
Newport Cnwll 4 J4
Newport Dorset 8 D10
Newport E R Yk 64 K13
Newport Essex 22 D1
Newport Gloucs 28 C9

Newport Essex 39 R14
Newport Gloucs 28 D8
Newport Highld 112 D12
Newport IoW 9 Q11
Newport Newpt 27 Q10
Newport Norfk 51 T10
Newport Pembks 24 J3
Newport Wrekin 45 R10
Newport-on-Tay Fife 91 P6
Newport Pagnell M Keyn 30 J4
Newport Pagnell Services M Keyn 30 J4
Newpound Common W Susx 10 H5
New Prestwick S Ayrs 81 L8
New Quay Cerdgn 32 G9
Newquay Cnwll 3 L4
New Quay Essex 23 P3
Newquay Airport Cnwll 3 M4
New Rackheath Norfk 51 N11
New Radnor Powys 34 F8
New Rent Cumb 67 Q5
New Ridley Nthumb 77 M14
New Road Side N York 62 K11
New Romney Kent 13 L11
New Rossington Donc 57 T7
New Row Cerdgn 33 P6
New Row Lancs 62 C12
New Sauchie Clacks 90 C13
Newsbank Ches E 55 T13
Newseat Abers 105 L9
Newsham Lancs 61 U12
Newsham N York 63 T3
Newsham N York 69 P10
Newsham Nthumb 77 S10
New Sharlston Wakefd 57 N3
Newsholme E R Yk 64 G14
Newsholme Lancs 62 G9
New Shoreston Nthumb 85 T12
New Silksworth Sundld 70 E2
New Skelton R & Cl 71 L9
Newsome Kirk 56 J4
New Somerby Lincs 48 D6
New Southgate Crematorium Gt Lon 21 N4
New Springs Wigan 55 N5
Newstead Border 84 F12
Newstead Notts 47 P3
Newstead Nthumb 85 T13
New Stevenston N Lans 82 E7
New Street Herefs 34 H9
New Swanington Leics 47 M10
Newthorpe N York 64 B13
Newthorpe Notts 47 N4
New Thundersley Essex 22 J10
Newtimber W Susx 11 M8
Newtoft Lincs 58 H9
Newton Ag & B 88 B6
Newton Border 76 C1
Newton Brdgnd 26 E12
Newton C Beds 31 R4
Newton Cambs 39 P11
Newton Cambs 49 P11
Newton Cardif 27 N12
Newton Ches W 45 M2
Newton Ches W 54 K13
Newton Ches W 55 M11
Newton Cumb 61 N5
Newton Derbys 47 M2
Newton Herefs 34 H14
Newton Herefs 35 L7
Newton Herefs 35 M10
Newton Highld 102 G5
Newton Highld 102 K6
Newton Highld 103 L2
Newton Highld 112 H7
Newton Lancs 61 Q12
Newton Lancs 62 B5
Newton Lancs 62 C7
Newton Lincs 48 G6
Newton Mdloth 83 R5
Newton Moray 103 U3
Newton Moray 104 C3
Newton N York 64 K5
Newton Nhants 38 C4
Newton Norfk 50 D10
Newton Notts 47 S5
Newton Nthumb 76 K4
Newton Nthumb 77 L13
Newton S Lans 82 H12
Newton S Lans 89 Q13
Newton Sandw 36 D2
Newton Shrops 44 K7
Newton Somset 16 F9
Newton Staffs 46 D8
Newton Suffk 40 F12
Newton W Loth 83 L3
Newton Warwks 37 P5
Newton Wilts 8 J4
Newton Abbot Devon 5 V6
Newton Arlosh Cumb 66 K1
Newton Aycliffe Dur 69 S8
Newton Bewley Hartpl 70 G7
Newton Blossomville M Keyn 38 D10
Newton Bromswold Nhants 38 E7
Newton Burgoland Leics 47 L12
Newton-by-the-Sea Nthumb 85 U13
Newton by Toft Lincs 58 H9
Newton Ferrers Devon 5 P11
Newton Ferry W Isls 106 d11
Newton Flotman Norfk 51 M14
Newtongrange Mdloth 83 R6
Newton Green Mons 27 U9
Newton Harcourt Leics 37 R1
Newton Heath Manch 56 C6
Newtonhill Abers 99 S5
Newton Hill Wakefd 57 M2
Newton-in-Bowland Lancs 62 D9
Newton Kyme N York 64 B11
Newton-le-Willows N York 63 Q2
Newton-le-Willows St Hel 55 N7
Newtonloan Mdloth 83 R6
Newton Longville Bucks 30 H6
Newton Mearns E Rens 81 Q1
Newtonmill Angus 99 L11
Newtonmore Highld 97 L4
Newton Morrell N York 69 R11
Newton Mountain Pembks 24 G9
Newton Mulgrave N York 71 N9
Newton of Balcanquhal P & K 90 J9
Newton of Balcormo Fife 91 R11
Newton on Ouse N York 64 C8
Newton-on-Rawcliffe N York 64 J1
Newton on the Hill Shrops 45 L9
Newton-on-the-Moor Nthumb 77 P4
Newton on Trent Lincs 58 D12
Newton Poppleford Devon 6 E7
Newton Purcell Oxon 30 D6
Newton Regis Warwks 46 J12
Newton Reigny Cumb 67 Q6
Newton St Cyres Devon 15 U13
Newton St Faith Norfk 51 M10
Newton St Loe BaNES 17 T4
Newton St Petrock Devon 14 K10
Newton Solney Derbys 46 J8
Newton Stacey Hants 19 P12
Newton Stewart D & G 73 L6
Newton Tony Wilts 18 K12
Newton Tracey Devon 15 M7
Newton under Roseberry R & Cl 70 J10
Newton Underwood Nthumb 77 N8
Newton upon Derwent E R Yk 64 G10
Newton Valence Hants 9 U2
Newton Wamphray D & G 75 M7
Newton with Scales Lancs 61 T13
Newtown Blae G 27 M6
Newtown Ches W 55 M11
Newtown Cnwll 2 F11
Newtown Cnwll 4 H5
Newtown Cumb 66 G3
Newtown Cumb 67 R8
Newtown Cumb 75 S13
Newtown Cumb 75 V13
Newtown D & G 74 E4
Newtown Derbys 56 E10
Newtown Devon 6 E5
Newtown Devon 15 S7
Newtown Dorset 7 N4
New Town Dorset 8 D5
New Town Dorset 8 D6
New Town Dorset 8 D7
New Town E Susx 11 R6
Newtown Gloucs 28 C7
Newtown Hants 8 K6
Newtown Hants 9 S6
Newtown Hants 19 Q8
Newtown Herefs 35 L9
Newtown Herefs 35 M14
Newtown Herefs 35 P12
Newtown Herefs 35 R12
Newtown Highld 96 D3
Newtown IoW 9 N10
Newtown Lancs 55 M2
New Town Nhants 38 E5
Newtown Nthumb 77 L5
Newtown Nthumb 85 P12
Newtown Nthumb 85 Q13
Newtown Poole 8 E10
Newtown Powys 34 D2
Newtown Rhondd 26 K8
Newtown Shrops 44 K9
Newtown Shrops 45 L7
Newtown Somset 6 J2
Newtown Staffs 46 B1
Newtown Staffs 46 C13
Newtown Wigan 55 N6
Newtown Wilts 8 C3
New Town Wilts 19 L6
Newtown Wilts 19 N8
Newtown Worcs 35 U9
Newtown Worcs 36 B5
Newtown-in-St Martin Cnwll 2 J12
Newtown Linford Leics 47 P12
Newtown of Beltrees Rens 88 J14
Newtown St Boswells Border 84 F12
Newtown Unthank Leics 47 N13
New Tredegar Caerph 27 L7
New Trows S Lans 82 F11
New Tupton Derbys 57 N13
Newtyle Angus 91 L3
New Walsoken Cambs 49 Q12
New Waltham NE Lin 59 N6
New Whittington Derbys 57 N11
New Winton E Loth 84 C4
New Yatt Oxon 29 S5
Newyears Green Gt Lon 20 J5
Newyork Ag & B 87 T3
New York Lincs 48 K2
New York N Tyne 77 S11
New York N York 63 P7
Nextend Herefs 34 H9
Neyland Pembks 24 G9
Niarbyl IoM 60 c7
Nibley Gloucs 28 C6
Nibley S Glos 28 C11
Nibley Green Gloucs 28 D8
Nicholashayne Devon 16 F13
Nicholaston Swans 25 T13
Nickies Hill Cumb 76 A12
Nidd N York 63 S7
Nigg C Aber 99 S3
Nigg Highld 109 Q10
Nigg Ferry Highld 109 P11
Nimlet BaNES 17 T2
Ninebanks Nthumb 68 G2
Nine Elms Swindn 29 M10
Nine Wells Pembks 24 C6
Ninfield E Susx 12 D13
Ningwood IoW 9 M11
Nisbet Border 84 H13
Nisbet Hill Border 84 K8
Niton IoW 9 Q13
Nitshill C Glas 89 M13
Noah's Ark Kent 21 U11
Noak Bridge Essex 22 G9
Noak Hill Gt Lon 22 D9
Noblethorpe Barns 57 L5
Nobold Shrops 45 L11
Nobottle Nhants 37 S8
Nocton Lincs 58 J14
Nogdam End Norfk 51 Q13
Noke Oxon 30 B10
Nolton Pembks 24 E7
Nolton Haven Pembks 24 E7
No Man's Heath Ches W 45 M4
No Man's Heath Warwks 46 J12
No Man's Land Cnwll 4 H9
Nomansland Devon 15 T10
Nomansland Wilts 8 K5
Noneley Shrops 45 L8
Nonington Kent 13 Q5
Nook Cumb 61 U3
Nook Cumb 75 U10
Norbiton Gt Lon 21 L9
Norbreck Bpool 61 Q11
Norbridge Herefs 35 R12
Norbury Ches E 45 N4
Norbury Derbys 46 F5
Norbury Gt Lon 21 P9
Norbury Shrops 34 J2
Norbury Staffs 45 S9
Norbury Common Ches E 45 N4
Norbury Junction Staffs 45 S9
Norchard Worcs 35 T7
Norcott Brook Ches W 55 P10
Norcross Lancs 61 Q11
Nordelph Norfk 49 S13
Norden Rochdl 56 C4
Nordley Shrops 35 Q1
Norfolk Broads Norfk 51 S12
Norham Nthumb 85 N9
Norland Town Calder 56 G2
Norley Ches W 55 N12
Norleywood Hants 9 M9
Norlington E Susx 11 Q8
Normanby Lincs 58 G9
Normanby N Linc 58 E3
Normanby N York 64 G3
Normanby R & Cl 70 H9
Normanby le Wold Lincs 58 K7
Norman Cross Cambs 38 J2
Normandy Surrey 20 F12
Norman's Bay E Susx 12 C14
Norman's Green Devon 6 E4
Normanton C Derb 46 K7
Normanton Leics 48 B5
Normanton Lincs 48 D4
Normanton Notts 47 T3
Normanton RutInd 48 D12
Normanton Wakefd 57 N2
Normanton Wilts 18 H12
Normanton le Heath Leics 47 L11
Normanton on Soar Notts 47 P9
Normanton on the Wolds Notts 47 R7
Normanton on Trent Notts 58 C13
Normoss Lancs 61 Q12
Norney Surrey 10 E2
Norrington Common Wilts 18 C8
Norris Green Cnwll 5 L7
Norris Green Lpool 54 J8
Norris Hill Leics 46 K10
Norristhorpe Kirk 56 K2
Northacre Norfk 50 G14
Northall Bucks 31 L8
Northallerton N York 70 E14
Northall Green Norfk 50 G11
Northam C Soth 9 N6
Northam Devon 15 L7
Northampton Nhants 37 U8
Northampton Worcs 35 T7
Northampton Services Nhants 37 T9
North Anston Rothm 57 R10
North Ascot Br For 20 F9
North Aston Oxon 29 U2
Northaw Herts 31 S12
Northay Somset 6 J2
North Baddesley Hants 9 M4
North Ballachulish Highld 94 F6
North Barrow Somset 17 R11
North Barsham Norfk 50 F6
North Benfleet Essex 22 J10
North Bersted W Susx 10 E10
North Berwick E Loth 84 E1
North Bitchburn Dur 69 Q6
North Blyth Nthumb 77 S9
North Boarhunt Hants 9 S6
North Bockhampton Dorset 8 H9
Northborough C Pete 48 J12
Northbourne Kent 13 R5
North Bovey Devon 5 S4
North Bradley Wilts 18 C9
North Brentor Devon 5 M4
North Brewham Somset 17 T9
North Bridge Surrey 10 F3
Northbridge Street E Susx 12 D11
Northbrook Hants 19 R13
Northbrook Oxon 29 U3
North Brook End Cambs 31 S4
North Buckland Devon 15 L4
North Burlingham Norfk 51 Q12
North Cadbury Somset 17 R11
North Carlton Lincs 58 F11
North Carlton Notts 57 S10
North Cave E R Yk 64 K13
North Cerney Gloucs 28 K6
North Chailey E Susx 11 P6
Northchapel W Susx 10 F5
North Charford Hants 8 H5
North Charlton Nthumb 85 T14
North Cheam Gt Lon 21 M9
North Cheriton Somset 17 S11
North Chideock Dorset 7 M6
Northchurch Herts 31 L11
North Cliffe E R Yk 64 K12
North Clifton Notts 58 D12
North Close Dur 69 S6
North Cockerington Lincs 59 Q9
North Connel Ag & B 94 C12
North Cornelly Brdgnd 26 E11
North Corner Cnwll 2 K13
North Cotes Lincs 59 P6
Northcott Devon 4 J2
Northcott Devon 6 E2
Northcott Devon 6 F3
North Country Cnwll 2 H8
Northcourt Oxon 29 U8
North Cove Suffk 41 S3
North Cowton N York 69 S12
North Crawley M Keyn 30 K4
North Cray Gt Lon 21 S8
North Creake Norfk 50 E6
North Curry Somset 16 K11
North Dalton E R Yk 65 L9
North Deighton N York 63 T9
North Devon Crematorium Devon 15 M6
Northdown Kent 13 S1
North Downs 12 H4
North Duffield N York 64 F12
North Duntulm Highld 100 d2
North East Surrey Crematorium Gt Lon 21 M9
Northedge Derbys 57 N13
North Elham Kent 13 N7
North Elkington Lincs 59 N8
North Elmham Norfk 50 G9
North Elmsall Wakefd 57 Q4
Northend Bucks 20 B4
North End C Port 9 T8
North End Cumb 75 R14
North End Dorset 8 A3
North End E R Yk 65 R11
North End E R Yk 65 T13
North End Essex 22 G4
North End Hants 8 G5
North End Hants 9 R3
North End Leics 47 Q10
North End Lincs 48 K5
North End Lincs 58 H7
North End Lincs 59 P6
North End Lincs 59 R9
North End N Linc 58 K2
North End N Som 17 M4
North End Nhants 38 E7
North End Norfk 40 G2
North End Nthumb 77 N5
North End Sefton 54 H6
North End W Susx 10 F10
North End W Susx 10 J9
Northend Warwks 37 L10
Northenden Manch 55 T9
Northend Woods Bucks 20 F5
North Erradale Highld 107 M8
North Evington C Leic 47 R13
North Fambridge Essex 23 L8
North Ferriby E R Yk 58 G1
Northfield Birm 36 D5
Northfield C Aber 99 S2
Northfield E R Yk 58 H1
Northfields Lincs 48 F12
Northfleet Kent 22 F13
North Frodingham E R Yk 65 Q9
North Gorley Hants 8 H6
North Green Norfk 41 M3
North Green Suffk 41 P8
North Green Suffk 41 Q7
North Greetwell Lincs 58 H12
North Grimston N York 64 J6
North Halling Medway 12 D2
North Haven Shet 106 r11
North Hayling Hants 9 U8
North Hazelrigg Nthumb 85 R12
North Heasley Devon 15 R6
North Heath W Susx 10 H6
North Hele Devon 16 D12
North Hill Cnwll 4 H5
North Hillingdon Gt Lon 20 J6
North Hinksey Village Oxon 29 U6
North Holmwood Surrey 21 L13
North Huish Devon 5 S9
North Hykeham Lincs 58 F13
Northiam E Susx 12 F11
Northill C Beds 38 H11
Northington Gloucs 28 D6
Northington Hants 19 S13
North Kelsey Lincs 58 H6
North Kessock Highld 102 J6
North Killingholme N Linc 58 K3
North Kilvington N York 63 U2
North Kilworth Leics 37 R4
North Kingston Hants 8 H8
North Kyme Lincs 48 J3
North Landing E R Yk 65 S5
Northlands Lincs 49 M3
Northleach Gloucs 29 M5
North Lee Bucks 30 H11
North Lees N York 63 R5
Northleigh Devon 6 G5
Northleigh Devon 15 P6
North Leigh Kent 13 M7
North Leigh Oxon 29 S5
North Leverton with Habblesthorpe Notts 58 C10
Northlew Devon 15 M13
North Littleton Worcs 36 E11
Northload Bridge Somset 17 N9
North Lopham Norfk 40 H3
North Luffenham RutInd 48 D13
North Marden W Susx 10 C7
North Marston Bucks 30 G8
North Middleton Mdloth 83 S7
North Middleton Nthumb 85 P14
North Millbrex Abers 105 N7
North Milmain D & G 72 D9
North Molton Devon 15 R7
Northmoor Oxon 29 T7
North Moreton Oxon 19 S3
Northmuir Angus 98 F13
North Mundham W Susx 10 D10
North Muskham Notts 47 U2
North Newbald E R Yk 65 L12
North Newington Oxon 37 M12
North Newnton Wilts 18 H9
North Newton Somset 16 K10
Northney Hants 9 U8
North Nibley Gloucs 28 D8
North Oakley Hants 19 R10
North Ockendon Gt Lon 22 E10
Northolt Gt Lon 20 K6
Northop Flints 54 F13
Northop Hall Flints 54 G13
North Ormesby Middsb 70 H9
North Ormsby Lincs 59 N8
Northorpe Kirk 56 K2
Northorpe Lincs 48 G10
Northorpe Lincs 48 K6
Northorpe Lincs 58 E7
North Otterington N York 63 T2
Northover Somset 17 N9
Northover Somset 17 P12
North Owersby Lincs 58 J8
Northowram Calder 56 H1
North Perrott Somset 7 N3
North Petherton Somset 16 J10
North Petherwin Cnwll 4 H3
North Pickenham Norfk 50 E12
North Piddle Worcs 36 C10
North Poorton Dorset 7 P5
Northport Dorset 8 C11
North Poulner Hants 8 H7
North Queensferry Fife 83 M2
North Radworthy Devon 15 S6
North Rauceby Lincs 48 F4
Northrepps Norfk 51 M6
North Reston Lincs 59 Q10
North Rigton N York 63 R10
North Ripley Hants 8 H9
North Rode Ches E 56 C13
North Ronaldsay Ork 106 w14
North Ronaldsay Airport Ork 106 w14
North Row Cumb 66 K6
North Runcton Norfk 49 T10
North Scale Cumb 61 M6
North Scarle Lincs 58 D13
North Seaton Nthumb 77 R8
North Seaton Colliery Nthumb 77 R8
North Shian Ag & B 94 C10
North Shields N Tyne 77 T12
North Shoebury Sthend 23 M10
North Shore Bpool 61 Q12
North Side C Pete 49 L14
North Side Cumb 66 E7
North Skelton R & Cl 71 L9
North Somercotes Lincs 59 R7
North Stainley N York 63 R4
North Stainmore Cumb 68 H10
North Stifford Thurr 22 F11
North Stoke BaNES 17 T3
North Stoke Oxon 19 T3
North Stoke W Susx 10 G8
North Street Cambs 39 R7
North Street Hants 8 J5
North Street Hants 9 S2
North Street Kent 12 K4
North Street Medway 22 K13
North Street W Berk 19 T6
North Sunderland Nthumb 85 U12
North Tamerton Cnwll 14 H13
North Tawton Devon 15 Q12
North Third Stirlg 89 S8
North Thoresby Lincs 59 N7
North Togston Nthumb 77 Q5
North Town Devon 15 M11
North Town Somset 17 Q8
North Town W & M 20 E6
North Tuddenham Norfk 50 J11
North Uist W Isls 106 c12
Northumberland National Park Nthumb 76 H5
North Walbottle N u Ty 77 P12
North Walsham Norfk 51 N7
North Waltham Hants 19 S11
North Warnborough Hants 20 B12
Northway Somset 16 F11
Northway Swans 25 U13
North Weald Bassett Essex 22 C7
North Wheatley Notts 58 C9
North Whilborough Devon 5 V7
Northwich Ches W 55 Q12
North Wick BaNES 17 Q3
Northwick S Glos 27 V10
Northwick Somset 17 L7
Northwick Worcs 35 T9
North Widcombe BaNES 17 Q5
North Willingham Lincs 59 L9
North Wingfield Derbys 57 P13
North Witham Lincs 48 D9
Northwold Norfk 40 C1
Northwood C Stke 45 U4
Northwood Derbys 57 L14
Northwood Gt Lon 20 J4
Northwood IoW 9 P10
Northwood Shrops 45 L7
Northwood Green Gloucs 28 D4
North Wootton Dorset 7 S2
North Wootton Norfk 49 T9
North Wootton Somset 17 Q8
North Wraxall Wilts 18 B5
North Wroughton Swindn 18 H4
North York Moors National Park 71 M12
Norton Donc 57 R3
Norton E Susx 11 R10
Norton Gloucs 28 G3
Norton Halton 55 N10
Norton Herts 31 R6
Norton IoW 9 L11
Norton Mons 27 S3
Norton N Som 16 K4
Norton Nhants 37 R8
Norton Notts 57 S12
Norton Powys 34 H7
Norton S on T 70 F8
Norton Sheff 57 N10
Norton Shrops 35 L4
Norton Shrops 35 P4
Norton Shrops 45 N12
Norton Shrops 45 R13
Norton Suffk 40 G7
Norton Swans 25 V13
Norton W Susx 10 E9
Norton Wilts 28 G11
Norton Worcs 35 U10
Norton Worcs 36 D11
Norton Bavant Wilts 18 D12
Norton Bridge Staffs 45 U7
Norton Canes Staffs 46 D12
Norton Canes Services Staffs 46 D12
Norton Canon Herefs 34 J11
Norton Corner Norfk 50 J8
Norton Disney Lincs 48 C2
Norton Ferris Wilts 17 U9
Norton Fitzwarren Somset 16 G11
Norton Green IoW 9 L11
Norton Hawkfield BaNES 17 Q4
Norton Heath Essex 22 F7
Norton in Hales Shrops 45 R6
Norton in the Moors C Stke 45 U3
Norton-Juxta-Twycross Leics 46 K12
Norton-le-Clay N York 63 U5
Norton Lindsey Warwks 36 H8
Norton Little Green Suffk 40 G7
Norton Malreward BaNES 17 R4
Norton Mandeville Essex 22 E7
Norton-on-Derwent N York 64 H5
Norton St Philip Somset 17 U5
Norton Subcourse Norfk 51 R14
Norton sub Hamdon Somset 17 N13
Norton Wood Herefs 34 J11
Norwell Notts 47 U1
Norwell Woodhouse Notts 58 B14
Norwich Norfk 51 M12
Norwich Airport Norfk 51 M11
Norwich (St Faith) Crematorium Norfk 51 M10
Norwick Shet 106 w2
Norwood Clacks 90 C13
Norwood Derbys 57 Q10
Norwood Kent 12 K10
Norwood End Essex 22 E6
Norwood Green Calder 56 H1
Norwood Green Gt Lon 20 K7
Norwood Hill Surrey 11 L2
Norwoodside Cambs 49 P14
Noseley Leics 47 T14
Noss Mayo Devon 5 P11
Nosterfield N York 63 R3
Nosterfield End Cambs 39 T12
Nostie Highld 101 M6
Notgrove Gloucs 29 M3
Nottage Brdgnd 26 E12
Notter Cnwll 4 K8
Nottingham C Nott 47 Q6
Nottington Dorset 7 S8
Notton Wakefd 57 M4
Notton Wilts 18 D7
Nounsley Essex 22 J5
Noutard's Green Worcs 35 S7
Nowton Suffk 40 E8
Nox Shrops 44 K11
Nuffield Oxon 19 U3
Nunburnholme E R Yk 64 J10
Nuncargate Notts 47 P3
Nunclose Cumb 67 Q3
Nuneaton Warwks 37 L2
Nuneham Courtenay Oxon 30 C13
Nunhead Gt Lon 21 P7
Nunkeeling E R Yk 65 Q10
Nun Monkton N York 64 C8
Nunney Somset 17 T8
Nunney Catch Somset 17 T8
Nunnington Herefs 35 M12
Nunnington N York 64 F4
Nunsthorpe NE Lin 59 N5
Nunthorpe C York 64 E9
Nunthorpe Middsb 70 H10
Nunthorpe Village Middsb 70 H10
Nunton Wilts 8 H3
Nunwick N York 63 S5
Nunwick Nthumb 76 H11
Nupdown S Glos 28 B8
Nup End Bucks 30 J9
Nupend Gloucs 28 E6
Nuptown Br For 20 E8
Nursling Hants 9 M5
Nursted Hants 10 B6
Nursteed Wilts 18 F8
Nurton Staffs 45 U14
Nutbourne W Susx 10 B9
Nutbourne W Susx 10 H7
Nutfield Surrey 21 P12
Nuthall Notts 47 P5
Nuthampstead Herts 39 P14
Nuthurst W Susx 10 K5
Nutley E Susx 11 Q5
Nutley Hants 19 T12
Nuttall Bury 55 S3
Nutwell Donc 57 T6
Nybster Highld 112 J4
Nyetimber W Susx 10 D11
Nyewood W Susx 10 C6
Nymans W Susx 11 M5
Nymet Rowland Devon 15 R11
Nymet Tracey Devon 15 R12
Nympsfield Gloucs 28 F7
Nynehead Somset 16 F12
Nythe Somset 17 M10
Nyton W Susx 10 E9

O

Oadby Leics 47 R13
Oad Street Kent 12 G3
Oakall Green Worcs 35 T8
Oakamoor Staffs 46 D5
Oakbank W Loth 83 L5
Oak Cross Devon 15 M13
Oakdale Caerph 27 M8
Oake Somset 16 G11
Oaken Staffs 45 U13
Oakenclough Lancs 61 U10
Oakengates Wrekin 45 R11
Oakenholt Flints 54 G12
Oakenshaw Dur 69 R5
Oakenshaw Kirk 63 P14
Oakerthorpe Derbys 47 L3
Oakford Cerdgn 32 J9
Oakford Devon 16 B12
Oakfordbridge Devon 16 B12
Oakgrove Ches E 56 D13
Oakham RutInd 48 C12
Oakhanger Ches E 45 S3
Oakhanger Hants 10 B3
Oakhill Somset 17 R7
Oakhurst Kent 21 U12
Oakington Cambs 39 P8
Oaklands Powys 34 B10
Oakle Street Gloucs 28 E4
Oakley Bed 38 F10
Oakley Bucks 30 D10
Oakley Fife 90 F14
Oakley Hants 19 S10
Oakley Oxon 30 G12
Oakley Poole 8 E9
Oakley Suffk 41 L5
Oakley Green W & M 20 F7
Oakley Park Powys 33 U3
Oakridge Lynch Gloucs 28 H7
Oaks Lancs 62 D13
Oaks Shrops 44 K13
Oaksey Wilts 28 J9
Oaks Green Derbys 46 G7
Oakshaw Ford Cumb 75 V10
Oakshott Hants 9 U3
Oakthorpe Leics 46 K11
Oak Tree Darltn 70 E10
Oakwood C Derb 47 L6
Oakwood Nthumb 76 J12
Oakworth C Brad 63 L12
Oare Kent 12 K3
Oare Somset 15 S3
Oare Wilts 18 J8
Oasby Lincs 48 F6
Oath Somset 17 L11
Oathlaw Angus 98 H12
Oatlands Park Surrey 20 J9
Oban Ag & B 94 B13
Oban Airport Ag & B 94 C11
Obley Shrops 34 H5
Obney P & K 90 F4
Oborne Dorset 17 S13
Obthorpe Lincs 48 G11
Occold Suffk 41 L6
Occumster Highld 112 G9
Ochiltree E Ayrs 81 Q8
Ockbrook Derbys 47 M6
Ocker Hill Sandw 36 C2
Ockeridge Worcs 35 S8
Ockham Surrey 20 J11
Ockle Highld 93 N4
Ockley Surrey 10 J3
Ocle Pychard Herefs 35 N11
Octon E R Yk 65 N6
Odcombe Somset 17 P13
Odd Down BaNES 17 T4
Oddingley Worcs 36 B9
Oddington Gloucs 29 P2
Oddington Oxon 30 B9
Odell Bed 38 E9
Odham Devon 15 L12
Odiham Hants 20 B12
Odsal C Brad 63 P14
Odsey Cambs 31 S5
Odstock Wilts 8 G3
Odstone Leics 47 L12
Offchurch Warwks 37 L7
Offenham Worcs 36 E11
Offerton Stockp 56 D9
Offerton Sundld 70 D1
Offham E Susx 11 Q8
Offham Kent 12 C4
Offham W Susx 10 G9
Offleymarsh Staffs 45 S8
Offord Cluny Cambs 38 K7
Offord D'Arcy Cambs 38 K7
Offton Suffk 40 J11
Offwell Devon 6 G5
Ogbourne Maizey Wilts 18 J6
Ogbourne St Andrew Wilts 18 J6
Ogbourne St George Wilts 18 K6
Ogden Calder 63 M13
Ogle Nthumb 77 N10
Oglet Lpool 54 K10
Ogmore V Glam 26 F12
Ogmore-by-Sea V Glam 26 F12
Ogmore Vale Brdgnd 26 G9
Ogwen Bank Gwynd 52 K9
Okeford Fitzpaine Dorset 7 V2
Okehampton Devon 15 N13
Oker Side Derbys 46 J1
Okewood Hill Surrey 10 J4
Olchard Devon 6 A9
Old Nhants 37 U6
Old Aberdeen C Aber 99 S2
Old Alresford Hants 9 R2
Oldany Highld 110 B10
Old Auchenbrack D & G 74 E6
Old Basford C Nott 47 P5
Old Basing Hants 19 U10
Old Beetley Norfk 50 G10
Oldberrow Warwks 36 F7
Old Bewick Nthumb 77 M1
Old Bolingbroke Lincs 59 Q13
Old Bramhope Leeds 63 Q11
Old Brampton Derbys 57 M12
Old Bridge of Urr D & G 74 E12
Old Buckenham Norfk 40 J2
Old Burghclere Hants 19 Q9
Oldbury Kent 21 U11
Oldbury Sandw 36 C3
Oldbury Shrops 35 R2
Oldbury Warwks 36 K2
Oldbury Naite S Glos 28 B9
Oldbury-on-Severn S Glos 28 B9
Oldbury on the Hill Gloucs 28 F10
Old Byland N York 64 D2
Old Cantley Donc 57 T6
Old Cassop Dur 70 D5
Oldcastle Mons 27 Q3
Oldcastle Heath Ches W 45 L4
Old Catton Norfk 51 M11
Old Churchstoke Powys 34 G2
Old Clee NE Lin 59 N5
Old Cleeve Somset 16 D8
Old Clipstone Notts 57 T14
Old Colwyn Conwy 53 Q7
Oldcotes Notts 57 S9
Old Dailly S Ayrs 80 J13
Old Dalby Leics 47 S9
Old Dam Derbys 56 H11
Old Deer Abers 105 R6
Old Ditch Somset 17 P7
Old Edlington Donc 57 R7
Old Eldon Dur 69 R7
Old Ellerby E R Yk 65 R12
Old Felixstowe Suffk 41 P13
Oldfield C Brad 63 L12
Oldfield Worcs 35 T8
Old Fletton C Pete 38 J1
Oldford Somset 17 U6
Old Forge Herefs 27 V4
Old Furnace Herefs 27 T3
Old Glossop Derbys 56 F8
Old Goole E R Yk 58 B2
Old Grimsby IoS 2 b1
Old Hall Green Herts 31 U8
Oldhall Green Suffk 40 E9
Old Hall Street Norfk 51 P7
Oldham Oldham 56 D6
Oldhamstocks E Loth 84 J4
Old Harlow Essex 22 C5
Old Heath Essex 23 P3
Old Hunstanton Norfk 49 U5
Old Hurst Cambs 39 L5
Old Hutton Cumb 62 B2
Old Inns Services N Lans 89 S10
Old Kea Cnwll 3 L8
Old Kilpatrick W Duns 89 L11
Old Knebworth Herts 31 R8
Old Lakenham Norfk 51 M12
Oldland S Glos 17 S2
Old Langho Lancs 62 E12
Old Laxey IoM 60 g6
Old Leake Lincs 49 P3
Old Malton N York 64 H5
Oldmeldrum Abers 105 N10
Oldmill Cnwll 4 K6
Old Milverton Warwks 36 J7
Oldmixon N Som 16 K5
Old Newton Suffk 40 J8
Old Quarrington Dur 70 D5
Old Radford C Nott 47 P5
Old Radnor Powys 34 G9
Old Rayne Abers 104 K10
Old Romney Kent 12 K11
Old Shoreham W Susx 11 L9
Oldshoremore Highld 110 E5
Old Soar Kent 12 B5
Old Sodbury S Glos 28 E11
Old Somerby Lincs 48 E7
Oldstead N York 64 C4
Old Stratford Nhants 30 G4
Old Struan P & K 97 N10
Old Swarland Nthumb 77 P5
Old Swinford Dudley 36 B4
Old Tebay Cumb 68 D11
Old Thirsk N York 63 U3
Old Town Calder 62 K14
Old Town Cumb 62 B3
Old Town Cumb 67 Q4
Old Town E Susx 11 T11
Old Town IoS 2 c2
Old Trafford Traffd 55 T7
Old Tupton Derbys 57 N13
Oldwall Cumb 75 U13
Oldwalls Swans 25 S12
Old Warden C Beds 31 P4
Oldways End Somset 15 U8
Old Weston Cambs 38 G5
Old Wick Highld 112 J7
Old Windsor W & M 20 G8
Old Wives Lees Kent 13 L5
Old Woking Surrey 20 H11
Old Wolverton M Keyn 30 H4
Old Woodhall Lincs 59 M13
Old Woods Shrops 45 L9
Olgrinmore Highld 112 C6
Olive Green Staffs 46 F10
Oliver's Battery Hants 9 P3
Ollaberry Shet 106 t5
Ollach Highld 100 e6
Ollerton Ches E 55 S11
Ollerton Notts 57 U13
Ollerton Shrops 45 P8
Olmarch Cerdgn 33 M9
Olmstead Green Cambs 39 T12
Olney M Keyn 38 C10
Olrig House Highld 112 E3
Olton Solhll 36 F4
Olveston S Glos 28 B10
Ombersley Worcs 35 T8
Ompton Notts 57 U13
Once Brewed Nthumb 76 E12
Onchan IoM 60 f7
Onecote Staffs 46 D2
Onehouse Suffk 40 H9
Onen Mons 27 S5
Ongar Street Herefs 34 J7
Onibury Shrops 35 L5
Onich Highld 94 E6
Onllwyn Neath 26 E5
Onneley Staffs 45 S5
Onslow Green Essex 22 G4
Onslow Village Surrey 20 G13
Onston Ches W 55 N12
Openwoodgate Derbys 47 L4
Opinan Highld 107 M10
Orbliston Moray 104 C4
Orbost Highld 100 b5
Orby Lincs 59 S13
Orchard Portman Somset 16 H12
Orcheston Wilts 18 G11
Orcop Herefs 27 T2
Orcop Hill Herefs 27 T2
Ord Abers 104 J4
Ordhead Abers 104 K13
Ordie Abers 98 H3
Ordiequish Moray 104 C4
Ordley Nthumb 76 J14
Ordsall Notts 58 B11
Ore E Susx 12 F13
Oreleton Common Herefs 35 L7
Oreton Shrops 35 Q4
Orford Suffk 41 R10
Orford Warrtn 55 P8
Organford Dorset 8 C10
Orgreave Staffs 46 G10
Orkney Islands Ork 106 t19
Orkney Neolithic Ork 106 r18
Orlestone Kent 12 K9
Orleton Herefs 35 L7
Orleton Worcs 35 R7
Orlingbury Nhants 38 C6
Ormathwaite Cumb 67 L7
Ormesby R & Cl 70 H9
Ormesby St Margaret Norfk 51 S11
Ormesby St Michael Norfk 51 S11
Ormiscaig Highld 107 Q6
Ormiston E Loth 84 C5
Ormsaigmore Highld 93 M6
Ormsary Ag & B 87 N11
Ormskirk Lancs 54 K5
Ornsby Hill Dur 69 Q3
Oronsay Ag & B 86 F8
Orphir Ork 106 s19
Orpington Gt Lon 21 S9
Orrell Sefton 54 H7
Orrell Wigan 55 M6
Orrell Post Wigan 55 M6
Orrisdale IoM 60 e4
Orroland D & G 73 T10
Orsett Thurr 22 F11
Orslow Staffs 45 T10
Orston Notts 47 U5
Orthwaite Cumb 67 L6
Ortner Lancs 61 U9
Orton Cumb 68 D11
Orton Nhants 38 B5
Orton Staffs 35 U1
Orton Longueville C Pete 38 J1
Orton-on-the-Hill Leics 46 K13
Orton Rigg Cumb 67 M2
Orton Waterville C Pete 38 J1
Orwell Cambs 39 N10
Osbaldeston Lancs 62 C13
Osbaldeston Green Lancs 62 C13
Osbaldwick C York 64 E9
Osbaston Leics 47 M13
Osbaston Shrops 44 H9
Osborne IoW 9 Q10
Osborne House IoW 9 Q10
Osbournby Lincs 48 G6
Oscroft Ches W 55 M13
Ose Highld 100 c5
Osgathorpe Leics 47 M10
Osgodby Lincs 58 J8
Osgodby N York 64 E13
Osgodby N York 65 P3
Oskaig Highld 100 e6
Oskamull Ag & B 93 M10
Osmaston Derbys 46 H5
Osmington Dorset 7 T8
Osmington Mills Dorset 7 T8
Osmondthorpe Leeds 63 S13
Osmotherley N York 70 G13
Osney Oxon 29 U6
Ospringe Kent 12 K3
Ossett Wakefd 57 L2
Ossington Notts 58 C14
Ostend Essex 23 M8
Osterley Gt Lon 20 K7
Oswaldkirk N York 64 E4
Oswaldtwistle Lancs 62 E14
Oswestry Shrops 44 G8
Otford Kent 21 T11
Otham Kent 12 E5
Otham Hole Kent 12 F5
Othery Somset 17 L10
Otley Leeds 63 Q10
Otley Suffk 41 M9
Otley Green Suffk 41 M9
Otterbourne Hants 9 P4
Otterburn N York 62 H8
Otterburn Nthumb 76 H7
Otter Ferry Ag & B 87 S8
Otterham Cnwll 4 F2
Otterhampton Somset 16 H8
Otterham Quay Kent 12 F2
Otterham Station Cnwll 4 F3
Otternish W Isls 106 e11
Ottershaw Surrey 20 H10
Otterswick Shet 106 v5
Otterton Devon 6 E7
Otterwood Hants 9 N8
Ottery St Mary Devon 6 F5
Ottinge Kent 13 N7
Ottringham E R Yk 59 N2
Oughterby Cumb 67 L1
Oughtershaw N York 62 H3
Oughterside Cumb 66 H4
Oughtibridge Sheff 57 M8
Oughtrington Warrtn 55 Q9
Oulston N York 64 C5
Oulton Cumb 66 K2
Oulton Leeds 63 T14
Oulton Norfk 50 K8
Oulton Staffs 45 S9
Oulton Staffs 46 B6
Oulton Suffk 41 T2
Oulton Broad Suffk 41 T2
Oulton Street Norfk 51 L8
Oundle Nhants 38 F3
Ounsdale Staffs 35 U2
Our Dynamic Earth C Edin 83 Q4
Ousby Cumb 68 D6
Ousden Suffk 40 B9
Ousefleet E R Yk 58 D2
Ouston Dur 69 S2
Outchester Nthumb 85 S12
Out Elmstead Kent 13 P5
Outgate Cumb 67 N13
Outhgill Cumb 68 G12
Outhill Warwks 36 F7
Outlands Staffs 45 S8
Outlane Kirk 56 G3
Out Newton E R Yk 59 Q2
Out Rawcliffe Lancs 61 S11
Outwell Norfk 49 R13
Outwick Hants 8 G5
Outwood Surrey 21 P13
Outwood Wakefd 57 M2
Outwood Gate Bury 55 S5
Outwoods Leics 47 M10
Outwoods Staffs 45 S10
Ouzlewell Green Leeds 57 M1
Ovenden Calder 63 M14
Over Cambs 39 N6
Over Ches W 55 P13
Over Gloucs 28 F4
Over S Glos 28 A11
Over Burrows Derbys 46 J6
Overbury Worcs 36 C13
Overcombe Dorset 7 S8
Over Compton Dorset 17 Q13
Overdale Crematorium Bolton 55 Q5
Over End Cambs 38 G2
Overgreen Derbys 57 M12
Over Green Warwks 36 G2
Over Haddon Derbys 56 K13
Over Kellet Lancs 61 U6
Over Kiddington Oxon 29 T3
Overleigh Somset 17 N9
Overley Staffs 46 G10
Over Monnow Mons 27 U5
Over Norton Oxon 29 R2
Over Peover Ches E 55 S12
Overpool Ches W 54 J11
Overscaig Hotel Highld 110 C12
Overseal Derbys 46 J10
Over Silton N York 70 F14
Oversland Kent 13 L4
Oversley Green Warwks 36 E9
Overstone Nhants 37 U7
Over Stowey Somset 16 G9
Overstrand Norfk 51 M5
Over Stratton Somset 17 M13
Overstreet Wilts 18 G13
Over Tabley Ches E 55 R11
Overthorpe Nhants 37 N12
Overton C Aber 105 P13
Overton Ches W 55 M11
Overton Hants 19 R11
Overton Lancs 61 S8
Overton N York 64 D8
Overton Shrops 35 M6
Overton Swans 25 S13
Overton Wakefd 57 L3
Overton Wrexhm 44 J5
Overton Bridge Wrexhm 44 J5
Overton Green Ches E 45 T1
Overtown Lancs 62 C4
Overtown N Lans 82 F8
Overtown Swindn 18 J5
Overtown Wakefd 57 N3
Over Wallop Hants 19 L13
Over Whitacre Warwks 36 J2
Over Woodhouse Derbys 57 Q12
Over Worton Oxon 29 T2
Overy Oxon 19 S2
Oving Bucks 30 G8
Oving W Susx 10 E10
Ovingdean Br & H 11 P10
Ovingham Nthumb 77 M13
Ovington Dur 69 P10
Ovington Essex 40 C12
Ovington Hants 9 R2
Ovington Norfk 50 F13
Ovington Nthumb 77 M13
Ower Hants 9 L5
Ower Hants 9 P8
Owermoigne Dorset 7 U7
Owlbury Shrops 34 H2
Owlerton Sheff 57 M9
Owlpen Gloucs 28 E8
Owl's Green Suffk 41 N7
Owlsmoor Br For 20 D10
Owlswick Bucks 30 G11
Owmby Lincs 58 H9
Owmby Lincs 58 J6
Owslebury Hants 9 Q4
Owston Donc 57 S4
Owston Leics 47 U12
Owston Ferry N Linc 58 D6
Owstwick E R Yk 65 T13
Owthorne E R Yk 65 U14
Owthorpe Notts 47 S7
Owton Manor Hartpl 70 G7
Oxborough Norfk 50 B13
Oxbridge Dorset 7 N5
Oxcombe Lincs 59 P11
Oxcroft Derbys 57 Q12
Oxen End Essex 22 G2
Oxenholme Cumb 61 U2
Oxenhope C Brad 63 L13
Oxen Park Cumb 61 Q2
Oxenpill Somset 17 M8
Oxenton Gloucs 28 J1
Oxenwood Wilts 19 M9
Oxford Oxon 30 B11
Oxford Airport Oxon 29 U4
Oxford Crematorium Oxon 30 C11
Oxford Services Oxon 30 D11
Oxhey Herts 20 K3
Oxhill Dur 69 Q2
Oxhill Warwks 36 K11
Oxley Wolves 46 B13
Oxley Green Essex 23 M5
Oxley's Green E Susx 12 C11
Oxlode Cambs 39 Q3
Oxnam Border 76 D2
Oxnead Norfk 51 M9
Oxshott Surrey 20 K10
Oxshott Heath Surrey 20 K10
Oxspring Barns 57 L6
Oxted Surrey 21 Q12
Oxton Border 84 D8
Oxton N York 64 C11
Oxton Notts 47 R3
Oxton Wirral 54 H9
Oxwich Swans 25 S13
Oxwich Green Swans 25 S13
Oxwick Norfk 50 F8
Oykel Bridge Hotel Highld 108 F4
Oyne Abers 104 K10
Oystermouth Swans 25 V13
Ozleworth Gloucs 28 E9

P

Pabail W Isls 106 k5
Packers Hill Dorset 7 T2
Packington Leics 47 L11
Packmoor C Stke 45 U3
Packmores Warwks 36 J7
Padanaram Angus 98 G13
Padbury Bucks 30 F6
Paddington Gt Lon 21 N6
Paddington Warrtn 55 P9
Paddlesworth Kent 12 C3
Paddlesworth Kent 13 N8
Paddock Wood Kent 12 C7
Paddolgreen Shrops 45 M7
Padfield Derbys 56 F7
Padgate Warrtn 55 P9
Padhams Green Essex 22 F8
Padiham Lancs 62 F13
Padside N York 63 P8
Padstow Cnwll 3 N1
Padworth W Berk 19 T7
Page Bank Dur 69 R5
Pagham W Susx 10 D11
Paglesham Essex 23 M9
Paignton Torbay 6 A12
Pailton Warwks 37 N4
Paine's Cross E Susx 12 B11
Painleyhill Staffs 46 D7
Painscastle Powys 34 E11
Painshawfield Nthumb 77 M13
Painsthorpe E R Yk 64 J8
Painswick Gloucs 28 G6
Painter's Forstal Kent 12 J4
Paisley Rens 89 L13
Paisley Woodside Crematorium Rens 89 L13
Pakefield Suffk 41 T2
Pakenham Suffk 40 F7
Pale Gwynd 43 U6
Pale Green Essex 39 U12
Palestine Hants 19 L12
Paley Street W & M 20 E7
Palfrey Wsall 36 D1
Palgrave Suffk 40 K5
Pallington Dorset 7 U6
Palmarsh Kent 13 M9
Palmersbridge Cnwll 4 F5
Palmers Green Gt Lon 21 P4
Palmerston E Ayrs 81 P9
Palmerstown V Glam 16 F3
Palnackie D & G 74 G14
Palnure D & G 73 M7
Palterton Derbys 57 Q13
Pamber End Hants 19 T9
Pamber Green Hants 19 T9
Pamber Heath Hants 19 T8
Pamington Gloucs 36 B14
Pamphill Dorset 8 D8
Pampisford Cambs 39 Q11
Panbride Angus 91 S4
Pancrasweek Devon 14 G11
Pancross V Glam 16 D3
Pandy Caerph 27 M10
Pandy Gwynd 43 M13
Pandy Gwynd 43 T7
Pandy Mons 27 Q3
Pandy Powys 43 U13
Pandy Wrexhm 44 E6
Pandy'r Capel Denbgs 44 C3
Pandy Tudur Conwy 53 Q10
Panfield Essex 22 H2
Pangbourne W Berk 19 T5
Pangdean W Susx 11 M8
Panks Bridge Herefs 35 P11
Pannal N York 63 S9
Pannal Ash N York 63 R9
Pannanich Wells Hotel Abers 98 G4
Pant Shrops 44 G9
Pantasaph Flints 54 E11
Panteg Pembks 24 F4
Pantersbridge Cnwll 4 F7
Pant-ffrwyth Brdgnd 26 G11
Pant Glas Gwynd 42 J4
Pantglas Powys 43 Q14
Pant-Gwyn Carmth 25 U5
Pant-lasau Swans 26 B8
Pant Mawr Powys 33 R4
Panton Lincs 59 L11
Pant-pastynog Denbgs 53 T10
Pantperthog Gwynd 43 P13
Pant-y-caws Carmth 24 K5
Pant-y-dwr Powys 33 U6
Pant-y-ffridd Powys 44 E13
Pantyffynnon Carmth 25 V8
Pantygasseg Torfn 27 P8
Pant-y-gog Brdgnd 26 G9
Pantymenyn Carmth 24 K5
Pant-y-mwyn Flints 54 E14
Panxworth Norfk 51 Q11
Papa Westray Airport Ork 106 t14
Papcastle Cumb 66 H6
Papigoe Highld 112 J6
Papple E Loth 84 F4
Papplewick Notts 47 P3
Papworth Everard Cambs 39 L8
Papworth St Agnes Cambs 39 L8
Par Cnwll 3 R6
Paramour Street Kent 13 Q3
Parbold Lancs 55 L4
Parbrook Somset 17 Q9
Parbrook W Susx 10 H5
Parc Gwynd 43 S7
Parc Gwyn Crematorium Pembks 24 K8
Parc Seymour Newpt 27 S9
Pardshaw Cumb 66 G8
Parham Suffk 41 P8
Park D & G 74 H7
Park Nthumb 76 D13
Park Bottom Cnwll 2 H8
Park Bridge Tamesd 56 D6
Park Corner E Susx 11 S3
Park Corner Oxon 19 U3
Park Corner W & M 20 E6
Park Crematorium Lancs 61 R14
Park End Bed 38 E10
Parkend Gloucs 28 B6
Park End Nthumb 76 H10
Parkers Green Kent 12 B6
Parkeston Essex 23 T1
Parkeston Quay Essex 41 M14
Park Farm Kent 12 K8
Parkgate Ches W 54 G11
Parkgate Cumb 66 K3
Parkgate D & G 74 J8
Parkgate E Susx 12 D13
Parkgate Essex 22 G2
Park Gate Hants 9 Q7
Parkgate Kent 12 G9
Parkgate Kent 21 T10
Park Gate Leeds 63 P11
Parkgate Surrey 11 L2
Park Gate Worcs 36 B6
Park Green Essex 22 C2
Park Green Suffk 40 K8
Parkgrove Crematorium Angus 91 T2
Parkhall W Duns 89 L11
Parkham Devon 14 J8
Parkham Ash Devon 14 J8
Park Head Derbys 47 L3
Park Hill Gloucs 27 V8
Parkhouse Mons 27 T7
Parkmill Swans 25 T13
Park Royal Gt Lon 21 L6
Parkside Dur 70 F3
Parkside N Lans 82 F7
Parkside Wrexhm 44 J2
Parkstone Poole 8 E10
Park Street Herts 31 P12
Park Street W Susx 10 J4
Park Wood Crematorium Calder 56 H2
Parley Green Dorset 8 G9
Parmoor Bucks 20 C5
Parndon Essex 22 B6
Parndon Wood Crematorium Essex 22 B6
Parracombe Devon 15 Q3
Parrog Pembks 24 J3
Parsonby Cumb 66 H5
Parson Cross Sheff 57 M8
Parson Drove Cambs 49 N12
Parson's Heath Essex 23 P2
Parson's Hill Derbys 46 J8
Partick C Glas 89 M12
Partington Traffd 55 R8
Partney Lincs 59 R13
Parton Cumb 66 E8
Partridge Green W Susx 10 K7
Partrishow Powys 27 P3
Parwich Derbys 46 G3
Paslow Wood Common Essex 22 E7
Passenham Nhants 30 G5
Passfield Hants 10 C4
Passingford Bridge Essex 22 D8
Paston C Pete 48 J13
Paston Norfk 51 P7
Pasturefields Staffs 46 C9
Patchacott Devon 15 L13
Patcham Br & H 11 N9
Patchetts Green Herts 20 K3
Patching W Susx 10 H9
Patchole Devon 15 P4
Patchway S Glos 28 B11
Pateley Bridge N York 63 P6
Paternoster Heath Essex 23 M4
Pathe Somset 17 L10
Pathhead Fife 91 L13
Pathhead Mdloth 83 S6
Pathlow Warwks 36 G9
Path of Condie P & K 90 G9
Patmore Heath Herts 22 B2
Patna E Ayrs 81 N10
Patney Wilts 18 G9
Patrick IoM 60 c6
Patrick Brompton N York 63 Q1
Patricroft Salfd 55 S7
Patrington E R Yk 59 P2
Patrington Haven E R Yk 59 P2
Patrixbourne Kent 13 N4
Patterdale Cumb 67 N9
Pattingham Staffs 45 T14
Pattishall Nhants 37 S10
Pattiswick Green Essex 22 K3
Patton Shrops 35 N1
Paul Cnwll 2 D11
Paulerspury Nhants 37 T11
Paull E R Yk 59 L1
Paul's Dene Wilts 8 G2
Paulton BaNES 17 S5
Paunton Herefs 35 Q10
Pauperhaugh Nthumb 77 N6
Pave Lane Wrekin 45 S10
Pavenham Bed 38 E9
Pawlett Somset 16 J8
Pawston Nthumb 85 M12
Paxford Gloucs 36 G13
Paxton Border 85 N8
Payden Street Kent 12 H5
Payhembury Devon 6 E4
Paynter's Lane End Cnwll 2 H8
Paythorne Lancs 62 G9
Paytoe Herefs 34 K6
Peacehaven E Susx 11 Q10
Peak Dale Derbys 56 G11
Peak District National Park 56 J8
Peak Forest Derbys 56 H11
Peak Hill Lincs 49 L10
Peakirk C Pete 48 J12
Pearson's Green Kent 12 C7
Peartree Green Herefs 35 N14
Peasedown St John BaNES 17 T5
Peasehill Derbys 47 M4
Peaseland Green Norfk 50 J10
Peasemore W Berk 19 Q5
Peasenhall Suffk 41 Q7
Pease Pottage W Susx 11 M4
Peaslake Surrey 10 H2
Peasley Cross St Hel 55 M8
Peasmarsh E Susx 12 G11
Peasmarsh Somset 6 K2
Peasmarsh Surrey 20 G13
Peathill Abers 105 Q2
Peat Inn Fife 91 Q10
Peatling Magna Leics 37 Q2
Peatling Parva Leics 37 Q3
Peaton Shrops 35 M3
Pebmarsh Essex 40 E14
Pebworth Worcs 36 F11
Pecket Well Calder 62 K14
Peckforton Ches E 45 M2
Peckham Gt Lon 21 P7
Peckleton Leics 47 N13
Pedairffordd Powys 44 D9
Pedlinge Kent 13 M8
Pedmore Dudley 36 B4
Pedwell Somset 17 M9
Peebles Border 83 Q10
Peel IoM 60 c6
Peel Lancs 61 R13
Peel Common Hants 9 R8
Peene Kent 13 N8
Peening Quarter Kent 12 G10
Peggs Green Leics 47 M10
Pegsdon C Beds 31 P6
Pegswood Nthumb 77 Q8
Pegwell Kent 13 S3
Peinchorran Highld 100 e6
Peinlich Highld 100 d4
Pelcomb Pembks 24 F7
Pelcomb Bridge Pembks 24 F7
Pelcomb Cross Pembks 24 F7
Peldon Essex 23 N4
Pell Green E Susx 12 B9
Pelsall Wsall 46 D13
Pelsall Wood Wsall 46 D13
Pelton Dur 69 S2
Pelton Fell Dur 69 S2
Pelutho Cumb 66 H3
Pelynt Cnwll 4 G9

Place	County	Page	Grid
Pemberton	Carmth	25	T10
Pemberton	Wigan	55	N6
Pembles Cross	Kent	12	G6
Pembrey	Carmth	25	R10
Pembridge	Herefs	34	J9
Pembroke	Pembks	24	G10
Pembroke Dock	Pembks	24	G10
Pembrokeshire Coast National Park		24	D6
Pembury	Kent	12	F7
Pen-allt	Herefs	27	V2
Penallt	Mons	27	U5
Penally	Pembks	24	K11
Penare	Cnwll	3	P8
Penarth V Glam		16	G2
Penblewin	Pembks	24	K7
Pen-bont Rhydybeddau Cerdgn		33	N4
Penbryn	Cerdgn	32	E10
Pencader	Carmth	25	S12
Pencaenewydd	Gwynd	42	H5
Pencaitland	E Loth	84	G5
Pencarnisiog	IoA	52	E8
Pencarreg	Carmth	32	K11
Pencarrow	Cnwll	4	E4
Pencelli	Powys	26	E3
Penclawdd	Swans	25	T11
Pencoed	Brdgnd	26	H11
Pencombe	Herefs	35	N10
Pencoyd	Herefs	27	V2
Pencraig	Herefs	27	V3
Pencraig	Powys	44	B10
Pendeen	Cnwll	2	B7
Penderyn	Rhondd	26	E4
Pendine	Carmth	25	M9
Pendlebury	Salfd	55	S6
Pendleton	Lancs	62	G10
Pendock	Worcs	35	S14
Pendoggett	Cnwll	4	E5
Pendomer	Somset	7	N2
Pendre	V Glam	26	K12
Pendre	Brdgnd	26	G4
Penegoes	Powys	43	Q13
Penelewey	Cnwll	3	L5
Pen-ffordd	Pembks	24	J5
Pengam	Caerph	27	M8
Pengam	Cardif	27	N12
Penge	Gt Lon	21	Q8
Pengelly	Cnwll	4	F3
Pengorffwysfa	IoA	52	G4
Pen-groes-oped	Mons	27	Q6
Pengwern	Denbgs	53	T7
Penhale	Cnwll	2	H13
Penhale	Cnwll	3	N5
Penhale	Cnwll	4	K8
Penhale	Cnwll	5	L10
Penhallow	Cnwll	2	K6
Penhalurick	Cnwll	2	H9
Penhalvean	Cnwll	2	H9
Penhill	Swindn	29	N10
Penhow	Newpt	27	S9
Penhurst	E Susx	12	D13
Peniarth	Gwynd	43	P7
Penicuik	Mdloth	83	P6
Peniel	Carmth	25	S8
Peniel	Denbgs	53	T10
Penifiler	Highld	100	d5
Peninver	Ag & B	79	P11
Penisarwaun	Gwynd	52	J8
Penistone	Barns	56	L6
Penkerrick	Cnwll	3	N9
Penketh	Warrtn	55	M9
Penkill	S Ayrs	80	J13
Penkridge	Staffs	46	B11
Penlean	Cnwll	4	H4
Penleigh	Wilts	18	C10
Penley	Wrexhm	44	K5
Penllergaer	Swans	25	V11
Pen-llyn	IoA	52	E6
Penllyn	V Glam	26	H12
Pen-lon	IoA	52	F9
Penmachno	Conwy	43	P3
Penmaen	Caerph	27	M8
Penmaen	Swans	25	T13
Penmaenan	Conwy	53	M7
Penmaenmawr	Conwy	53	M7
Penmaenpool	Gwynd	43	N10
Penmark	V Glam	16	E3
Penmon	IoA	53	K6
Penmorfa	Gwynd	42	K5
Penmount Crematorium	Cnwll	3	L7
Penmynydd	IoA	52	H8
Penn	Bucks	20	F3
Penn	Wolves	35	U1
Pennal	Gwynd	43	N13
Pennan	Abers	105	N2
Pennant	Cerdgn	32	K7
Pennant	Denbgs	44	B2
Pennant	Powys	43	S14
Pennant-Melangell Powys		44	B8
Pennard	Swans	25	U13
Pennerley	Shrops	44	J14
Pennicott	Devon	15	U12
Pennines		62	K12
Pennington	Cumb	61	P4
Pennington	Hants	9	L9
Pennington Green Wigan		55	P5
Penn Street	Bucks	20	F3
Pennsylvania	S Glos	17	Q13
Penny Bridge	Cumb	61	Q3
Pennycross	Ag & B	93	P9
Pennygate	Norfk	51	P9
Pennyghael	Ag & B	93	P9
Pennyglen	S Ayrs	80	K10
Penny Green	Derbys	57	R11
Penny Hill	Lincs	49	N8
Pennymoor	Devon	15	U10
Pennywell	Sundld	70	E1
Penparc	Cerdgn	32	D10
Penparcau	Cerdgn	33	L4
Penpedairheol	Caerph	27	L7
Penpedairheol	Mons	27	Q7
Penperlleni	Mons	27	Q7
Penpethy	Cnwll	4	D4
Penpillick	Cnwll	3	R5
Penpol	Cnwll	3	L9
Penpoll	Cnwll	4	F9
Penponds	Cnwll	2	G9
Penpont	D & G	74	F7
Penpont	Powys	26	H2
Penquit	Devon	5	Q10
Penrest	Cnwll	4	J5
Penrherber	Carmth	25	N3
Pen-rhiw	Pembks	32	D12
Penrhiwceiber	Rhondd	26	K8
Pen-Rhiw-fawr	Neath	26	C6
Penrhiw-Ilan	Cerdgn	32	G12
Penrhiw-pal	Cerdgn	32	F11
Penrhos	Gwynd	52	E8
Penrhos	Herefs	34	K9
Penrhos	IoA	52	C6
Penrhos	Mons	27	S5
Penrhos	Powys	26	C4
Penrhos garnedd Gwynd		52	J8
Penrhyn Bay	Conwy	53	P6
Penrhyncoch	Cerdgn	33	N4
Penrhyndeudraeth Gwynd		43	M6
Penrhyn-side	Conwy	53	P6
Penrice	Swans	25	S13
Penrioch	N Ayrs	79	R7
Penrith	Cumb	67	Q7
Penrose	Cnwll	4	M2
Penruddock	Cumb	67	P7
Penryn	Cnwll	2	K10
Pensarn	Conwy	53	S7
Pensax	Worcs	35	S7
Pensby	Wirral	54	H10
Penselwood	Somset	17	U10
Pensford	BaNES	17	R4
Pensham	Worcs	36	B12
Penshaw	Sundld	70	D2
Penshurst	Kent	11	S2
Penshurst Station Kent		21	T14
Pensilva	Cnwll	4	H7
Pensnett	Dudley	36	B3
Penstone	Devon	15	S12
Penstrowed	Powys	34	C2
Pentewan	Cnwll	3	Q7
Pentir	Gwynd	52	J8
Pentireglaze	Cnwll	4	B4
Pentlepoir	Pembks	24	K9
Pentlow	Essex	40	D11
Pentlow Street Essex		40	D11
Pentney	Norfk	50	B11
Pentonbridge Cumb		75	T10
Penton Grafton Hants		19	M11
Penton Mewsey Hants		19	M11
Pentraeth	IoA	52	H7
Pentre	Denbgs	44	C1
Pentre	Mons	27	S8
Pentre	Powys	34	C5
Pentre	Powys	34	E1
Pentre	Rhondd	26	H8
Pentre	Shrops	44	H11
Pentre	Wrexhm	44	G4
Pentre-bach Cerdgn		33	N11
Pentre Bach Flints		54	F12
Pentrebach Myr Td		26	K6
Pentre-bach Powys		33	U13
Pentrebeirdd Powys		44	E11
Pentre Berw IoA		52	G8
Pentre-bont Conwy		43	P3
Pentre-cagel Carmth		32	F12
Pentre-celyn Denbgs		44	D3
Pentre-celyn Powys		43	S12
Pentre-chwyth Swans		26	B9
Pentre-clawdd Shrops		44	G7
Pentre-cwrt Carmth		25	Q3
Pentredwr Denbgs		44	E4
Pentrefelin Carmth		25	V7
Pentrefelin Conwy		53	N8
Pentrefelin IoA		52	F7
Pentre Ffwrndan Flints		54	G12
Pentrefoelas Conwy		43	S3
Pentregalar Pembks		25	L4
Pentregat Cerdgn		32	F10
Pentre-Gwenlais Carmth		25	V7
Pentre Gwynfryn Gwynd		43	L8
Pentre Halkyn Flints		54	F12
Pentre Hodrey Shrops		34	H5
Pentre Isaf Conwy		53	Q8
Pentre Llanrhaeadr Denbgs		54	C14
Pentre Llifior Powys		34	E1
Pentre-Ilwyn-Ilwyd Powys		33	U10
Pentre-Ilyn Cerdgn		33	N5
Pentre-Ilyn-cymmer Conwy		43	U3
Pentre Maelor Wrexhm		44	J4
Pentre-Maw Powys		43	S13
Pentre Meyrick V Glam		26	H12
Pentre-piod Torfn		27	P8
Pentre-poeth Newpt		27	P10
Pentre'r-felin Cerdgn		33	M11
Pentre'r Felin Conwy		53	P9
Pentre'r-felin Powys		33	U13
Pentre Saron Denbgs		53	T10
Pentre-tafarn-y-fedw Conwy		53	P10
Pentrich Derbys		47	L3
Pentridge Dorset		8	E5
Pen-twyn Caerph		27	N7
Pen-twyn Mons		27	U5
Pen-twyn Torfn		27	P7
Pentwynmaur Caerph		27	M8
Pentwyn Cardif		27	L11
Pentyrch Cardif		27	L11
Penwithick Cnwll		3	Q5
Penwood Hants		19	P8
Penwyllt Powys		26	E3
Penybanc Carmth		25	V6
Penybont Powys		34	D8
Pen-y-bont Powys		44	G9
Pen-y-bont-fawr Powys		44	C9
Pen-y-bryn Pembks		32	C12
Pen-y-cae Powys		26	E4
Penycae Wrexhm		44	G4
Pen-y-cae-mawr Mons		27	S8
Penycaerau Gwynd		42	C8
Pen-y-cefn Flints		54	D11
Pen-y-clawdd Mons		27	T6
Pen-y-coedcae Rhondd		26	K10
Pen-y-cwm Pembks		24	E6
Pen-y-fai Brdgnd		26	F11
Pen-y-felin Flints		54	E13
Penyffordd Flints		44	H1
Penyffordd Flints		54	H14
Penyffridd Gwynd		52	H11
Pen-y-garn Cerdgn		33	M3
Pen-y-genffordd Powys		27	M2
Pen-y-graig Gwynd		42	D7
Penygraig Rhondd		26	J8
Penygroes Carmth		25	U8
Penygroes Gwynd		52	G11
Pen-y-Gwryd Gwynd		53	L12
Pen-y-lan V Glam		26	H12
Pen-y-Mynydd Carmth		25	S10
Penymynydd Flints		44	H1
Pen-y-pass Gwynd		52	K11
Pen-yr-Heol Mons		27	S5
Pen-yr-Heolgerrig Myr Td		26	J6
Penysarn IoA		52	G4
Pen-y-stryt Denbgs		44	F3
Penywaun Rhondd		26	H7
Penzance Cnwll		2	D10
Peopleton Worcs		36	B10
Peover Heath Ches E		55	S12
Peper Harow Surrey		10	E2
Peplow Shrops		45	P9
Pepper's Green Essex		22	F6
Pepperstock C Beds		31	N9
Perceton N Ayrs		81	M4
Percyhorner Abers		105	R2
Perelle Guern		6	d3
Perham Down Wilts		19	L11
Periton Somset		16	C7
Perivale Gt Lon		21	L6
Perkins Village Devon		6	D6
Perkinsville Dur		69	S2
Perlethorpe Notts		57	T12
Perranarworthal Cnwll		2	K9
Perranporth Cnwll		2	K5
Perranuthnoe Cnwll		2	E11
Perranwell Cnwll		2	K6
Perranwell Cnwll		2	K9
Perran Wharf Cnwll		2	K9
Perranzabuloe Cnwll		2	K6
Perrott's Brook Gloucs		28	K6
Perry Barr Birm		36	E2
Perry Barr Crematorium Birm		36	E2
Perry Green Essex		22	H4
Perry Green Herts		22	B4
Perry Green Wilts		28	J10
Perrystone Hill Herefs		35	N14
Perry Street Somset		6	K3
Pershall Staffs		45	T8
Pershore Worcs		36	B11
Pertenhall Bed		38	G7
Perth P & K		90	G6
Perth Crematorium P & K		90	G6
Perthy Shrops		44	J7
Perton Herefs		35	N12
Perton Staffs		45	U14
Pertwood Wilts		8	B2
Peterborough C Pete		48	J14
Peterborough Crematorium C Pete		38	J13
Peterborough Services P & K		27	P12
Peterburn Highld		107	N6
Peterchurch Herefs		34	H13
Peterculter C Aber		99	Q3
Peterhead Abers		105	U6
Peterlee Dur		70	F4
Petersfield Hants		9	U4
Peter's Green Herts		31	P9
Petersham Gt Lon		21	L8
Peters Marland Devon		14	J10
Peterstone Wentlooge Newpt		27	P12
Peterston-super-Ely V Glam		26	K12
Peterstow Herefs		27	V3
Peter Tavy Devon		5	N5
Petham Kent		13	M5
Petherwin Gate Cnwll		4	J4
Petrockstowe Devon		15	M11
Petsoe End M Keyn		38	C11
Pett E Susx		12	F13
Pettaugh Suffk		41	L9
Pett Bottom Kent		13	M5
Petterden Angus		91	P3
Pettinain S Lans		82	H10
Pettistree Suffk		41	N10
Petton Devon		16	D12
Petton Shrops		45	L8
Petts Wood Gt Lon		21	R9
Pettycur Fife		83	Q1
Petty France S Glos		28	E10
Pettymuk Abers		105	Q11
Petworth W Susx		10	F6
Pevensey E Susx		11	U10
Pevensey Bay E Susx		11	V10
Peverell C Plym		5	N9
Pewsey Wilts		18	H8
Pheasant's Hill Bucks		20	C5
Phepson Worcs		36	B9
Philadelphia Sundld		70	D2
Philham Devon		14	F8
Philiphaugh Border		84	C13
Phillack Cnwll		2	F9
Philleigh Cnwll		3	M9
Phocle Green Herefs		35	R14
Phoenix Green Hants		20	B11
Phones Highld		97	L5
Pica Cumb		66	F8
Piccadilly Warwks		46	H14
Piccotts End Herts		31	M11
Pickburn Donc		57	R5
Pickering N York		64	H3
Picket Piece Hants		19	M11
Picket Post Hants		8	H7
Pickford Covtry		36	J4
Pickford Green Covtry		36	J4
Pickhill N York		63	S3
Picklescott Shrops		44	K14
Pickmere Ches E		55	Q11
Pickney Somset		16	G11
Pickstock Wrekin		45	R9
Pickup Bank Bl w D		55	R2
Pickwell Devon		14	K3
Pickwell Leics		47	U11
Pickwick Wilts		18	B6
Pickworth Lincs		48	F6
Pickworth Rutlnd		48	E11
Picton Ches W		54	K12
Picton Flints		54	D10
Picton N York		70	F11
Piddington Oxon		30	D9
Piddinghoe E Susx		7	T5
Piddlehinton Dorset		7	T5
Piddletrenthide Dorset		7	T4
Pidley Cambs		39	M5
Piercebridge Darltn		69	R9
Pierowall Ork		106	t15
Piff's Elm Gloucs		28	H2
Pigdon Nthumb		77	P8
Pigeon Green Warwks		36	H8
Pig Oak Dorset		8	E8
Pig Street Herefs		34	J11
Pikehall Derbys		46	G2
Pilford Dorset		8	E8
Pilgrims Hatch Essex		22	E8
Pilham Lincs		58	E8
Pill N Som		27	U12
Pillaton Cnwll		4	K8
Pillatonmill Cnwll		4	K8
Pillerton Hersey Warwks		36	K11
Pillerton Priors Warwks		36	J11
Pilleth Powys		34	G7
Pilley Barns		57	N5
Pilley Hants		9	L9
Pilley Bailey Hants		9	L9
Pilligwenlly Newpt		27	R11
Pillhead Devon		15	L7
Pilling Lancs		61	S10
Pilling Lane Lancs		61	R9
Pilning S Glos		27	T10
Pilot Inn Kent		13	L12
Pilsbury Derbys		56	H14
Pilsdon Dorset		7	M5
Pilsgate C Pete		48	G12
Pilsley Derbys		47	M1
Pilsley Derbys		56	K12
Pilson Green Norfk		51	Q11
Piltdown E Susx		11	Q6
Pilton Devon		15	N5
Pilton Nhants		38	F4
Pilton Rutlnd		48	C13
Pilton Somset		17	Q8
Pilton Green Swans		25	R13
Pimlico Lancs		62	E11
Pimlico Nhants		30	D6
Pimperne Dorset		8	C7
Pinchbeck Lincs		48	K9
Pinchbeck Bars Lincs		48	J9
Pinchbeck West Lincs		48	K9
Pincheon Green Donc		57	U3
Pinchinthorpe R & Cl		70	J10
Pincock Lancs		55	N3
Pinfold Lancs		54	K4
Pinford End Suffk		40	D9
Pinged Carmth		25	R10
Pingewood W Berk		19	U7
Pin Green Herts		31	S7
Pinhoe Devon		6	C6
Pinkett's Booth Covtry		36	J4
Pinkney Wilts		28	G10
Pinkneys Green W & M		20	E6
Pinley Covtry		37	L5
Pinley Green Warwks		36	H7
Pin Mill Suffk		41	M13
Pinminnoch S Ayrs		80	J10
Pinmore S Ayrs		80	K11
Pinn Devon		6	F7
Pinner Gt Lon		20	K5
Pinner Green Gt Lon		20	K5
Pinsley Green Ches E		45	N4
Pinvin Worcs		36	C11
Pinwherry S Ayrs		72	G1
Pinxton Derbys		47	M2
Pipe and Lyde Herefs		35	L12
Pipe Aston Herefs		35	L6
Pipe Gate Shrops		45	R5
Pipehill Staffs		46	E12
Piperhill Highld		103	N5
Pipers Pool Cnwll		4	H4
Pipewell Nhants		38	B3
Pippacott Devon		15	M5
Pippin Street Lancs		55	N2
Pipton Powys		34	E13
Pirbright Surrey		20	G12
Pirbright Camp Surrey		20	G12
Pirnie Border		84	H13
Pirnmill N Ayrs		79	R7
Pirton Herts		31	Q6
Pirton Worcs		35	U11
Pisgah Cerdgn		33	N5
Pishill Oxon		20	B5
Pistyll Gwynd		42	F5
Pitagowan P & K		97	N10
Pitblae Abers		105	R3
Pitcairngreen P & K		90	F6
Pitcalnie Highld		109	Q10
Pitcaple Abers		105	L10
Pitcarity Angus		98	E10
Pitchcombe Gloucs		28	G6
Pitchcott Bucks		30	G8
Pitcher Row Lincs		49	L6
Pitchford Shrops		45	M13
Pitch Green Bucks		30	G12
Pitch Place Surrey		10	D3
Pitch Place Surrey		20	G12
Pitchroy Moray		104	A8
Pitcombe Somset		17	S10
Pitcot V Glam		26	F12
Pitcox E Loth		84	H3
Pitfichie Abers		104	K12
Pitglassie Abers		105	L5
Pitgrudy Highld		109	P6
Pitlessie Fife		91	M10
Pitlochry P & K		97	Q12
Pitmachie Abers		104	K10
Pitmain Highld		97	M3
Pitmedden Abers		105	P10
Pitmedden Garden Abers		105	P10
Pitminster Somset		16	H13
Pitmuies Angus		91	M2
Pitmunie Abers		104	K12
Pitney Somset		17	M11
Pitroddie P & K		90	K6
Pitscottie Fife		91	P9
Pitsea Essex		22	H10
Pitses Oldham		56	D6
Pitsford Nhants		37	U7
Pitstone Bucks		30	K9
Pitt Devon		16	D13
Pitt Hants		9	P3
Pittarrow Abers		99	N8
Pitteuchar Fife		91	L11
Pittington Dur		70	D4
Pittodrie House Hotel Abers		104	K11
Pitton Wilts		8	J2
Pitt's Wood Kent		12	B6
Pittulie Abers		105	R2
Pityme Cnwll		3	P1
Pity Me Dur		69	S4
Pivington Kent		12	H6
Pixey Green Suffk		41	M6
Pixham Surrey		21	L12
Pixley Herefs		35	Q13
Plaidy Abers		105	L4
Plain Street Cnwll		4	B5
Plaish Shrops		45	L14
Plaistow Derbys		47	L1
Plaistow Gt Lon		21	R6
Plaistow W Susx		10	G4
Plaitford Hants		8	K5
Plank Lane Wigan		55	Q7
Plas Cymyran IoA		52	C7
Plastow Green Hants		19	S8
Platt Kent		12	B5
Platt Bridge Wigan		55	P6
Platt Lane Shrops		45	M6
Platts Heath Kent		12	G5
Plawsworth Dur		69	S3
Plaxtol Kent		12	B5
Playden E Susx		12	H11
Playford Suffk		41	M11
Play Hatch Oxon		20	B7
Playing Place Cnwll		3	L8
Playley Green Gloucs		28	E1
Plealey Shrops		44	K12
Plean Stirlg		89	T8
Pleasance Fife		90	K9
Pleasington Bl w D		55	P1
Pleasley Derbys		57	R14
Pleasleyhill Notts		57	R14
Pleck Dorset		7	T2
Pledgdon Green Essex		22	E3
Pledwick Wakefd		57	M3
Pleinheaume Guern		6	d2
Plemstall Ches W		55	L12
Plenmeller Nthumb		76	E13
Pleshey Essex		22	F5
Plockton Highld		100	h6
Plocrapol W Isls		106	g9
Plordiwick Staffs		45	T10
Plowden Shrops		34	J3
Ploxgreen Shrops		44	J13
Pluckley Kent		12	H6
Pluckley Station Kent		12	H7
Pluckley Thorne Kent		12	H7
Plucks Gutter Kent		13	Q3
Plumbland Cumb		66	K5
Plumgarths Cumb		67	Q14
Plumley Ches E		55	R12
Plumpton Cumb		67	Q5
Plumpton E Susx		11	P7
Plumpton Nhants		37	Q11
Plumpton Green E Susx		11	P7
Plumpton Head Cumb		67	R5
Plumstead Gt Lon		21	S7
Plumstead Norfk		50	K6
Plumtree Notts		47	R6
Plumtree Green Kent		12	F6
Plungar Leics		47	U7
Plurenden Kent		12	H8
Plush Dorset		7	T4
Plusha Cnwll		4	H4
Plushabridge Cnwll		4	J6
Plwmp Cerdgn		32	G10
Plymouth C Plym		5	M10
Plymouth Airport C Plym		5	N8
Plympton C Plym		5	N9
Plymstock C Plym		5	N10
Plymtree Devon		6	E4
Pockley N York		64	E2
Pocklington E R Yk		64	J10
Pode Hole Lincs		48	K9
Podimore Somset		17	P12
Podington Bed		38	E8
Podmore Staffs		45	S6
Point Clear Essex		23	Q5
Pointon Lincs		48	H7
Pokesdown Bmouth		8	G10
Polbain Highld		107	J2
Polbathic Cnwll		4	J9
Polbeth W Loth		82	K6
Polbrock Cnwll		3	R3
Poldark Mine Cnwll		2	H10
Polebrook Nhants		38	G3
Pole Elm Worcs		35	T10
Polegate E Susx		11	T10
Pole Moor Kirk		56	G3
Polesden Lacey Surrey		20	K12
Polesworth Warwks		46	J13
Polgigga Cnwll		2	B12
Polglass Highld		107	T3
Polgooth Cnwll		3	P6
Poling W Susx		10	G9
Poling Corner W Susx		10	G9
Polkerris Cnwll		3	R6
Pollard Street Norfk		51	P7
Pollington E R Yk		57	T3
Polloch Highld		93	T5
Pollokshaws C Glas		89	N13
Pollokshields C Glas		89	N13
Polmassick Cnwll		3	P7
Polmear Cnwll		3	R6
Polmont Falk		82	H3
Polnish Highld		93	R2
Polperro Cnwll		4	G10
Polruan Cnwll		4	E10
Polsham Somset		17	P8
Polstead Suffk		40	H13
Polstead Heath Suffk		40	G12
Poltalloch Ag & B		87	Q6
Poltescoe Cnwll		2	J13
Poltimore Devon		6	C5
Polton Mdloth		83	Q5
Polwarth Border		84	K9
Polyphant Cnwll		4	H4
Polzeath Cnwll		4	B5
Pomathorn Mdloth		83	P7
Pomeroy Derbys		56	H13
Ponde Powys		34	D13
Ponders End Gt Lon		21	Q3
Pondersbridge Cambs		39	L2
Ponsanooth Cnwll		2	K9
Ponsonby Cumb		66	F11
Ponsongath Cnwll		2	K13
Ponsworthy Devon		5	S6
Pont Abraham Services Carmth		25	U9
Pontac Jersey		7	e4
Pontamman Carmth		26	A5
Pontantwn Carmth		25	R8
Pontardawe Neath		26	C7
Pontarddulais Swans		25	U10
Pont-ar-gothi Carmth		25	T6
Pont-ar-Hydfer Powys		26	E2
Pont-ar-Ilechau Carmth		26	C3
Pontarsais Carmth		25	R5
Pontblyddyn Flints		44	G1
Pont Cyfyng Conwy		53	M11
Pontcysyllte Aqueduct Wrexhm		44	G5
Pont Dolgarrog Conwy		53	N9
Pontdolgoch Powys		34	B2
Pont-Ebbw Newpt		27	P11
Pontefract Wakefd		57	Q2
Pontefract Crematorium Wakefd		57	P2
Ponteland Nthumb		77	P11
Ponterwyd Cerdgn		33	P4
Pontesbury Shrops		44	J12
Pontesbury Hill Shrops		44	J12
Pontesford Shrops		44	K12
Pontfadog Wrexhm		44	F6
Pontfaen Pembks		24	H4
Pont-faen Powys		33	U14
Pontgarreg Cerdgn		32	F10
Pontgarreg Pembks		32	B12
Ponthenry Carmth		25	S9
Ponthir Torfn		27	Q9
Ponthirwaun Cerdgn		32	E11
Pontlanfraith Caerph		27	M8
Pontliw Swans		25	V11
Pontllyfni Gwynd		52	F11
Pont Morlais Carmth		25	T9
Pontnewydd Torfn		27	P8
Pontneddfechan Powys		26	F6
Pontnewydd Torfn		27	P7
Pont Pen-y-benglog Gwynd		53	L10
Pontrhydfendigaid Cerdgn		33	P7
Pont Rhyd-sarn Gwynd		43	S8
Pont Rhyd-y-cyff Brdgnd		26	F10
Pont-rhyd-y-fen Neath		26	D9
Pontrhydygroes Cerdgn		33	P6
Pontrhydyrun Torfn		27	P8
Pontrilas Herefs		27	R2
Pont-rug Gwynd		52	H10
Ponts Green E Susx		12	C12
Pontshaen Cerdgn		32	H11
Pontshill Herefs		35	B3
Pontsticill Myr Td		26	K5
Pont Walby Neath		26	F6
Pontwelly Carmth		32	H12
Pontyates Carmth		25	S9
Pontyberem Carmth		25	T8
Pont-y-blew Wrexhm		44	H6
Pontybodkin Flints		44	G2
Pontyclun Rhondd		26	J11
Pontycymer Brdgnd		26	G9
Pontyglasier Pembks		24	K3
Pontygwaith Rhondd		26	J9
Pont-y-pant Conwy		53	N12
Pontypool Torfn		27	P7
Pontypool Road Torfn		27	Q7
Pontypridd Rhondd		26	K10
Pont-yr-hafod Pembks		24	F5
Pont-y-Rhyl Brdgnd		26	H10
Pontywaun Caerph		27	N9
Pool Cnwll		2	H8
Pool IoS		2	b2
Pool Leeds		63	Q10
Poole Poole		8	E10
Poole Keynes Gloucs		28	J8
Poolewe Highld		107	Q8
Pooley Bridge Cumb		67	P7
Pooley Street Norfk		40	H4
Poolfold Staffs		45	U2
Pool Head Herefs		35	N10
Poolhill Gloucs		28	D2
Pool of Muckhart Clacks		90	F11
Pool Quay Powys		44	F11
Pool Street Essex		40	C13
Pooting's Kent		21	S12
Popham Hants		19	S12
Poplar Gt Lon		21	Q6
Poplar Street Pembks		24	K7
Porchfield IoW		9	N10
Poringland Norfk		51	N13
Porkellis Cnwll		2	H9
Porlock Somset		15	U3
Porlock Weir Somset		15	U3
Port-an-Eorna Highld		100	g6
Portachoillan Ag & B		79	N5
Port Appin Ag & B		94	C9
Port Askaig Ag & B		86	G12
Portavadie Ag & B		88	B12
Port Bannatyne Ag & B		88	C12
Portbury N Som		27	U12
Port Carlisle Cumb		75	N13
Port Charlotte Ag & B		86	C13
Portchester Hants		9	S7
Portchester Crematorium Hants		9	S7
Port Clarence S on T		70	H7
Port Driseach Ag & B		87	T11
Port Ellen Ag & B		86	E14
Port-Eynon Swans		25	S13
Porter's Fen Corner Norfk		49	R12
Portesham Dorset		7	R7
Portessie Moray		104	E2
Port e Vullen IoM		60	h4
Port Eynon Swans		25	S13
Portfield Gate Pembks		24	F7
Portgate Devon		5	L3
Port Gaverne Cnwll		4	D3
Port Glasgow Inver		88	H11
Portgordon Moray		104	D3
Portgower Highld		110	A8
Porth Cnwll		3	M3
Porth Rhondd		26	J9
Porthallow Cnwll		2	K12
Porthallow Cnwll		4	G10
Porthcawl Brdgnd		26	E12
Porthcothan Cnwll		3	M2
Porthcurno Cnwll		2	B12
Port Henderson Highld		107	N10
Porthgain Pembks		24	D4
Porthgwarra Cnwll		2	B12
Porthill Staffs		45	T4
Porthkea Cnwll		3	L8
Porthkerry V Glam		16	E3
Porthleven Cnwll		2	G11
Porthmadog Gwynd		43	L6
Porthmeor Cnwll		2	C9
Porth Navas Cnwll		2	K11
Portholland Cnwll		3	P7
Porthoustock Cnwll		3	L12
Porthpean Cnwll		3	Q6
Porthtowan Cnwll		2	J6
Porthwgan Wrexhm		44	J4
Porthyrhyd Carmth		25	T8
Porth-y-Waen Shrops		44	G9
Portincaple Ag & B		88	F7
Portinfer Jersey		7	a1
Portington E R Yk		64	H13
Portinnisherrich Ag & B		87	T3
Portinscale Cumb		67	L8
Port Isaac Cnwll		4	C3
Portishead N Som		27	T12
Portknockie Moray		104	F2
Portland Dorset		7	S10
Portlethen Abers		99	S4
Portling D & G		66	C2
Portloe Cnwll		3	N9
Port Logan D & G		72	D11
Portlooe Cnwll		4	H10
Portmahomack Highld		109	S8
Portmeirion Gwynd		43	L6
Portmellon Cnwll		3	Q7
Port Mor Highld		93	L3
Portmore Hants		9	L9
Port Mulgrave N York		71	M9
Portnacroish Ag & B		94	C9
Portnaguran W Isls		106	k5
Portnahaven Ag & B		78	B5
Portnalong Highld		100	c6
Port nan Giuran W Isls		106	k5
Port nan Long W Isls		106	d11
Port Nis W Isls		106	k2
Portobello C Edin		83	R4
Portobello Gatesd		69	S1
Portobello Wolves		46	C14
Port of Menteith Stirlg		89	N5
Port of Ness W Isls		106	k2
Porton Wilts		8	H2
Portontown Devon		5	L5
Portpatrick D & G		72	B9
Port Quin Cnwll		4	B4
Port Ramsay Ag & B		94	B9
Portreath Cnwll		2	H7
Portreath Harbour Cnwll		2	H7
Portree Highld		100	d5
Port St Mary IoM		60	c9
Portscatho Cnwll		3	N9
Portsea C Port		9	S8
Portskerra Highld		111	T3
Portskewett Mons		27	U10
Portslade Br & H		11	M9
Portslade-by-Sea Br & H		11	M10
Portslogan D & G		72	B8
Portsmouth Calder		56	D1
Portsmouth C Port		9	S9
Portsmouth Dockyard C Port		9	S8
Port Soderick IoM		60	e8
Port Solent C Port		9	S7
Portsonachan Hotel Ag & B		88	B1
Portsoy Abers		104	H2
Port Sunlight Wirral		54	H10
Portswood C Sotn		9	N6
Port Talbot Neath		26	D10
Port Tennant Swans		26	B9
Portuairk Highld		93	L5
Portway Herefs		35	L13
Portway Herefs		35	L12
Portway Worcs		36	E6
Port Wemyss Ag & B		78	B5
Port William D & G		72	J11
Portwrinkle Cnwll		4	K10
Portyerrock D & G		73	M11
Posbury Devon		15	S13
Posenhall Shrops		45	Q13
Poslingford Suffk		40	C11
Posso Border		83	P12
Postbridge Devon		5	R5
Postcombe Oxon		30	F12
Post Green Dorset		8	D10
Postling Kent		13	M8
Postwick Norfk		51	N12
Potarch Abers		99	L4
Potten End Herts		31	M11
Potten Street Kent		13	Q2
Potterhanworth Lincs		58	H13
Potterhanworth Booths Lincs		58	H13
Potter Heigham Norfk		51	R10
Potterne Wilts		18	E9
Potterne Wick Wilts		18	E9
Potter Row Bucks		31	L12
Potters Bar Herts		31	R12
Potters Brook Lancs		61	T9
Potter's Cross Staffs		35	T3
Potters Crouch Herts		31	P11
Potter's Forstal Kent		12	G6
Potter's Green E Susx		11	S6
Potters Green Covtry		37	L4
Pottersheath Herts		31	R10
Potters Marston Leics		37	N2
Potterspury Nhants		30	F4
Potter Street Essex		22	C6
Potterton Abers		105	Q12
Potthorpe Norfk		50	F9
Pottle Street Wilts		18	B12
Potto N York		70	G11
Potton C Beds		39	L11
Pott Row Norfk		49	U9
Pott Shrigley Ches E		56	D11
Poughill Cnwll		14	F11
Poughill Devon		15	U11
Poulner Hants		8	H7
Poulshot Wilts		18	E8
Poulton Gloucs		29	L6
Poulton Wirral		54	H9
Poulton-le-Fylde Lancs		61	Q12
Poulton Priory Gloucs		29	L7
Pound Bank Worcs		35	S5
Poundbury Dorset		7	S6
Poundffald Swans		25	U12
Poundgate E Susx		11	R5
Pound Green E Susx		11	S5
Pound Green Suffk		40	B10
Pound Green Worcs		35	S5
Pound Hill W Susx		11	M3
Poundon Bucks		30	E7
Poundsbridge Kent		11	S2
Poundsgate Devon		5	S6
Pound Street Hants		19	P8
Poundstock Cnwll		14	F13
Pound Street Hants		19	P8
Pouton D & G		73	L9
Pouy Street Suffk		41	P6
Povey Cross Surrey		11	M2
Powburn Nthumb		77	M3
Powderham Devon		6	C8
Powerstock Dorset		7	P5
Powfoot D & G		75	N12
Powhill Cumb		66	K1
Powick Worcs		35	T10
Powmill P & K		90	F12
Poxwell Dorset		7	T7
Poyle Slough		20	H7
Poynings W Susx		11	M8
Poyntington Dorset		17	S12
Poynton Ches E		56	D10
Poynton Wrekin		45	N10
Poynton Green Wrekin		45	N10
Poystreet Green Suffk		40	G9
Praa Sands Cnwll		2	F11
Pratt's Bottom Gt Lon		21	S10
Praze-an-Beeble Cnwll		2	G9
Predannack Wollas Cnwll		2	H13
Prees Shrops		45	N7
Preesall Lancs		61	R10
Prees Green Shrops		45	N7
Prees Heath Shrops		45	N6
Prees Higher Heath Shrops		45	N6
Prees Lower Heath Shrops		45	N7
Prendwick Nthumb		77	L2
Pren-gwyn Cerdgn		32	H12
Prenteg Gwynd		42	K4
Prenton Wirral		54	H9
Prescot Knows		54	K8
Prescott Devon		16	E13
Prescott Shrops		35	N2
Prescott Shrops		45	L9
Presnerb Angus		98	C11
Pressen Nthumb		85	M12
Prestatyn Denbgs		54	C10
Prestbury Ches E		56	C11
Prestbury Gloucs		28	H3
Presteigne Powys		34	H8
Prestleigh Somset		17	R8
Preston Border		84	K8
Preston Br & H		11	N9
Preston Devon		5	V6
Preston Dorset		7	T8
Preston E R Yk		65	R13
Preston Gloucs		28	K7
Preston Gloucs		35	N13
Preston Herts		31	Q8
Preston Kent		12	K3
Preston Kent		13	P3
Preston Lancs		61	U14
Preston Nthumb		85	T13
Preston Rutlnd		48	C13
Preston Shrops		45	M11
Preston Somset		16	E9
Preston Suffk		40	F10
Preston Torbay		6	A12
Preston Wilts		18	H6
Preston Bagot Warwks		36	G7
Preston Bissett Bucks		30	E7
Preston Bowyer Somset		16	F11
Preston Brockhurst Shrops		45	M9
Preston Brook Halton		55	M10
Preston Candover Hants		19	T12
Preston Capes Nhants		37	Q10
Preston Crematorium Lancs		62	B13
Preston Crowmarsh Oxon		19	T2
Preston Deanery Nhants		37	U9
Preston Green Warwks		36	G7
Preston Gubbals Shrops		45	L10
Preston Montford Shrops		44	K11
Preston on Stour Warwks		36	H11
Preston on Tees S on T		70	F9
Preston on the Hill Halton		55	M10
Preston on Wye Herefs		34	J12
Prestonpans E Loth		83	S4
Preston Patrick Cumb		61	U3
Preston Plucknett Somset		17	P13
Preston-under-Scar N York		69	N14
Preston upon the Weald Moors Wrekin		45	Q10
Preston Wynne Herefs		35	N11
Prestwich Bury		55	T6
Prestwick Nthumb		77	P11
Prestwick S Ayrs		81	M7
Prestwick Airport S Ayrs		81	M7
Prestwood Bucks		30	H12
Prestwood Staffs		35	U3
Price Town Brdgnd		26	H9
Prickwillow Cambs		39	S4
Priddy Somset		17	P6
Priest Hutton Lancs		61	U5
Priestcliffe Derbys		56	H12
Priestcliffe Ditch Derbys		56	H12
Priest Weston Shrops		34	G2
Priestland E Ayrs		81	R5
Priestley Green Calder		56	H1
Priestwood Green Kent		12	C3
Primethorpe Leics		37	P2
Primrose Green Norfk		50	H10
Primrosehill Border		84	K7
Primrose Hill Cambs		39	N3
Primrose Hill Derbys		47	M2
Primrose Hill Dudley		36	B3
Primrose Hill Lancs		54	K6
Primsidemill Border		85	L13
Princes Gate Pembks		24	K7
Princes Risborough Bucks		30	H12
Princethorpe Warwks		37	M6
Princetown Devon		5	P6
Prinsted W Susx		9	U8
Prion Denbgs		44	C1
Prior Rigg Cumb		75	U12
Priors Halton Shrops		35	L6
Priors Hardwick Warwks		37	N9
Priorslee Wrekin		45	R11
Priors Marston Warwks		37	N9
Priors Norton Gloucs		28	G3
Priory Vale Swindn		29	M10
Priory Wood Herefs		34	G12
Prisk V Glam		16	D2
Pristow Green Norfk		41	L3
Prittlewell Sthend		23	L10
Privett Hants		9	T4
Prixford Devon		15	M5
Probus Cnwll		3	M7
Prora E Loth		84	E3
Prospect Cumb		66	H4
Prospidnick Cnwll		2	G10
Prostonhill Abers		105	M3
Prudhoe Nthumb		77	M13
Prussia Cove Cnwll		2	F11
Publow BaNES		17	R4
Puckeridge Herts		31	U8
Puckington Somset		17	L13
Pucklechurch S Glos		28	C12
Puckrup Gloucs		35	U13
Puddinglake Ches W		55	R13
Puddington Ches W		54	H12
Puddington Devon		15	T10
Puddledock Norfk		40	J2
Puddletown Dorset		7	U6
Pudleston Herefs		35	M9
Pudsey Leeds		63	Q13
Pulborough W Susx		10	H7
Puleston Wrekin		45	R9
Pulford Ches W		44	J2
Pulham Dorset		7	T3
Pulham Market Norfk		41	L3
Pulham St Mary Norfk		41	M3
Pullens Green S Glos		28	B9
Puloxhill C Beds		31	N5
Pumpherston W Loth		82	K5
Pumsaint Carmth		33	M13
Puncheston Pembks		24	H5
Puncknowle Dorset		7	P6
Punnett's Town E Susx		11	V6
Purbrook Hants		9	T7
Purfleet Thurr		22	E12
Puriton Somset		16	K8
Purleigh Essex		23	L7
Purley Gt Lon		21	P10
Purley W Berk		19	U5
Purlogue Shrops		34	G5
Purlpit Wilts		18	C7
Purls Bridge Cambs		39	Q3
Purse Caundle Dorset		17	S13
Purshull Green Worcs		35	U6
Purslow Shrops		34	J4
Purston Jaglin Wakefd		57	P3
Purtington Somset		7	L3
Purton Gloucs		28	C6
Purton Gloucs		28	C6
Purton Wilts		29	L10
Purton Stoke Wilts		29	L9
Pury End Nhants		37	U11
Pusey Oxon		29	S7
Putley Herefs		35	P13
Putley Green Herefs		35	P13
Putloe Gloucs		28	E6
Putney Gt Lon		21	N8
Putney Vale Crematorium Gt Lon		21	M8
Putsborough Devon		14	K3
Puttenham Herts		30	K9
Puttenham Surrey		20	F13
Puttock End Essex		40	D12
Puxley Nhants		30	F4
Puxton N Som		17	M4
Pwll Carmth		25	S10
Pwll-du Mons		27	N5
Pwll-glâs Denbgs		44	D3
Pwllgloyw Powys		34	C14
Pwllheli Gwynd		42	G6
Pwllmeyric Mons		27	U8
Pwll Trap Carmth		25	N7
Pwll-y-glaw Neath		26	D9
Pye Bridge Derbys		47	M3
Pyecombe W Susx		11	M8
Pye Corner Newpt		27	Q11
Pye Green Staffs		46	B11
Pyle Brdgnd		26	E11
Pyleigh Somset		16	F10
Pylle Somset		17	R9
Pymoor Cambs		39	Q3
Pymore Dorset		7	N5
Pyrford Surrey		20	H11
Pyrton Oxon		30	E13
Pytchley Nhants		38	B6
Pyworthy Devon		14	H12

Q

Place	County	Page	Grid
Quabbs Shrops		34	F4
Quadring Lincs		48	K7
Quadring Eaudike Lincs		48	K6
Quainton Bucks		30	F8
Quaking Houses Dur		69	Q2
Quantock Hills Somset		16	F9
Quarff Shet		106	u10
Quarley Hants		19	L12
Quarndon Derbys		46	K5
Quarr Hill IoW		9	R10
Quarrier's Village Inver		88	J12
Quarrington Lincs		48	G5
Quarrington Hill Dur		70	D5
Quarry Bank Dudley		36	B3

Quarrywood Moray		103	U3
Quarter N Ayrs		88	D13
Quarter S Lans		82	D8
Quatford Shrops		35	R2
Quatt Shrops		35	S3
Quebec Dur		69	Q4
Quedgeley Gloucs		28	F5
Queen Adelaide Cambs		39	S4
Queenborough Kent		23	M13
Queen Camel Somset		17	Q12
Queen Charlton BaNES		17	R3
Queen Dart Devon		15	T9
Queen Elizabeth Forest Park Stirlg		89	M5
Queenhill Worcs		35	U13
Queen Oak Dorset		17	U10
Queen's Bower IoW		9	R12
Queensbury C Brad		63	N13
Queensferry Flints		54	H13
Queenslie C Glas		89	Q12
Queen's Park Bed		38	G10
Queen's Park Nhants		37	U8
Queen Street Kent		12	C7
Queen Street Wilts		28	K10
Queenzieburn N Lans		89	P10
Quendon Essex		22	D1
Queniborough Leics		47	R11
Quenington Gloucs		29	M7
Quernmore Lancs		61	U8
Quethiock Cnwll		4	J8
Quick's Green W Berk		19	S5
Quidenham Norfk		40	H3
Quidhampton Hants		19	R10
Quidhampton Wilts		8	G2
Quina Brook Shrops		45	M7
Quinbury End Nhants		37	R10
Quinton Birm		36	C4
Quinton Nhants		37	U9
Quinton Green Nhants		37	U10
Quintrell Downs Cnwll		3	L4
Quixhall Staffs		46	F4
Quixwood Border		84	K6
Quoditch Devon		14	K13
Quoig P & K		90	C7
Quoisley Ches E		45	M4
Quoyburray Ork		106	u19
Quoyloo Ork		106	r17

R

Place	County	Page	Grid
Raasay Highld		100	e5
Rabbit's Cross Kent		12	E6
Rableyheath Herts		31	R9
Raby Wirral		54	H11
Rachan Mill Border		83	M12
Rachub Gwynd		52	K9
Rackenford Devon		15	U9
Rackham W Susx		10	H7
Rackheath Norfk		51	N11
Racks D & G		75	L11
Rackwick Ork		106	r20
Radbourne Derbys		46	J6
Radcliffe Bury		55	S5
Radcliffe Nthumb		77	R5
Radcliffe on Trent Notts		47	R6
Radclive Bucks		30	E6
Radcot Oxon		29	Q8
Raddery Highld		102	K4
Raddington Somset		16	D11
Radernie Fife		91	Q10
Radford Covtry		37	K4
Radford Semele Warwks		36	K8
Radlet Somset		16	H9
Radlett Herts		31	Q12
Radley Devon		15	U7
Radley Oxon		30	B13
Radley W Susx		10	G5
Radley Green Essex		22	F6
Radmore Green Ches E		45	N3
Radnage Bucks		20	C3
Radstock BaNES		17	S5
Radstone Nhants		30	C4
Radway Warwks		37	L11
Radwell Bed		38	F9
Radwell Herts		31	R5
Radwinter Essex		39	T13
Radwinter End Essex		39	T13
Radyr Cardif		27	L11
RAF College (Cranwell) Lincs		48	E4
RAF Museum Cosford Shrops		45	S12
RAF Museum Hendon Gt Lon		21	M4
Ragdale Leics		47	S10
Raginnis Cnwll		2	D11
Raglan Mons		27	S6
Ragnall Notts		58	D12
Raigbeg Highld		103	M10
Rainbow Hill Worcs		35	U9
Rainford St Hel		54	K6
Rainham Gt Lon		22	D11
Rainham Medway		12	F2
Rainhill St Hel		54	K8
Rainhill Stoops St Hel		55	L8
Rainow Ches E		56	D12
Rainsbrook Warwks		37	P6
Rainsough Bury		55	T6
Rainton N York		63	T4
Rainworth Notts		47	Q2
Raisbeck Cumb		68	D11
Raise Cumb		68	B3
Rait P & K		90	K6
Raithby Lincs		59	P11
Raithby Lincs		59	Q13
Raithwaite N York		71	Q10
Rake Hants		10	B5
Rakewood Rochdl		56	D4
Ralia Highld		97	M4
Ram Carmth		33	L11
Ramasaig Highld		100	a5
Rame Cnwll		2	K9
Rame Cnwll		5	L11
Ram Hill S Glos		28	C12
Ram Lane Kent		12	H6
Rampisham Dorset		7	Q4
Rampside Cumb		61	N6
Rampton Cambs		39	P8
Rampton Notts		58	C11
Ramsbottom Bury		55	S3
Ramsbury Wilts		19	L6
Ramscraigs Highld		112	D11
Ramsdean Hants		9	U4
Ramsdell Hants		19	S9
Ramsden Oxon		29	S4
Ramsden Worcs		36	C12
Ramsden Bellhouse Essex		22	H9
Ramsden Heath Essex		22	H8
Ramsey Cambs		39	L3
Ramsey Essex		23	T1
Ramsey IoM		60	h3
Ramsey Forty Foot Cambs		39	M3
Ramsey Heights Cambs		39	K4
Ramsey Island Essex		23	M7
Ramsey Island Pembks		24	B6
Ramsey Mereside Cambs		39	L3
Ramsey St Mary's Cambs		39	L3
Ramsgate Kent		13	S2
Ramsgill N York		63	N6
Ramshaw Dur		68	K3
Ramshaw Dur		69	P4
Ramsholt Suffk		41	P12
Ramshope Nthumb		76	H5
Ramshorn Staffs		46	E4
Ramsley Devon		15	Q13
Ramsnest Common Surrey		10	E4
Ranby Lincs		59	M11
Ranby Notts		57	U10
Rand Lincs		58	J11
Randalls Park Crematorium Surrey		21	L11
Randwick Gloucs		28	F6
Ranfurly Rens		88	J12
Rangemore Staffs		46	G9
Rangeworthy S Glos		28	C10
Rankinston E Ayrs		81	P10
Ranksborough Rutlnd		48	B11
Rank's Green Essex		22	H5
Rannoch Station P & K		95	L8
Ranochan Highld		100	h11
Ranscombe Somset		16	B8
Ranskill Notts		57	U9
Ranton Staffs		45	U9
Ranton Green Staffs		45	T9
Ranworth Norfk		51	Q11
Raploch Stirlg		89	S7
Rapness Ork		106	u15
Rapps Somset		17	L13
Rascarrel D & G		73	T10
Rashfield Ag & B		88	E9
Rashwood Worcs		35	U7
Raskelf N York		64	B6
Rassau Blae G		27	M5
Rastrick Calder		56	H2
Ratagan Highld		101	M7
Ratby Leics		47	P12

Rathen Abers		105	R3
Rathillet Fife		91	N7
Rathmell N York		62	H8
Ratho C Edin		83	M4
Ratho Station C Edin		83	M4
Rathven Moray		104	F2
Ratlake Hants		9	N4
Ratley Warwks		37	L11
Ratling Kent		13	P5
Ratlinghope Shrops		34	K1
Rattan Row N York		64	H3
Rattar Highld		112	G2
Ratten Row Cumb		67	M4
Ratten Row Cumb		67	N3
Ratten Row Lancs		61	S11
Rattery Devon		5	S8
Rattlesden Suffk		40	G9
Ratton Village E Susx		11	T10
Rattray P & K		90	K2
Raughton Cumb		67	N3
Raughton Head Cumb		67	N3
Raunds Nhants		38	E6
Ravenfield Rothm		57	Q7
Ravenglass Cumb		66	G13
Ravenhills Green Worcs		35	R10
Raveningham Norfk		41	Q1
Ravenscar N York		71	S12
Ravenscraig N Lans		82	E7
Ravensdale IoM		60	f3
Ravensden Bed		38	G10
Ravenseat N York		68	K12
Ravenshead Notts		47	Q2
Ravensmoor Ches E		45	P3
Ravensthorpe Kirk		56	K2
Ravensthorpe Nhants		37	S6
Ravenstone Leics		47	M11
Ravenstone M Keyn		38	B10
Ravenstonedale Cumb		68	E12
Ravenstruther S Lans		82	H9
Ravensworth N York		69	P11
Raw N York		71	R11
Rawcliffe C York		64	D9
Rawcliffe E R Yk		57	U2
Rawcliffe Bridge E R Yk		57	U2
Rawdon Leeds		63	Q12
Rawdon Crematorium Leeds		63	Q12
Rawling Street Kent		12	H4
Rawmarsh Rothm		57	P7
Rawnsley Staffs		46	D11
Rawreth Essex		22	J9
Rawridge Devon		6	H3
Rawtenstall Lancs		55	T2
Raydon Suffk		40	H13
Raylees Nthumb		76	K7
Rayleigh Essex		22	K9
Raymond's Hill Devon		6	K5
Rayne Essex		22	H3
Raynes Park Gt Lon		21	M9
Reach Cambs		39	S7
Read Lancs		62	F13
Reading Readg		20	B8
Reading Services W Berk		19	U7
Reading Street Kent		12	J9
Reading Street Kent		13	S2
Reagill Cumb		68	D9
Realwa Cnwll		2	G9
Rearquhar Highld		109	N6
Rearsby Leics		47	S11
Rease Heath Ches E		45	P3
Reay Highld		111	V4
Reculver Kent		13	P2
Red Ball Devon		16	E13
Redberth Pembks		24	J10
Redbourn Herts		31	P10
Redbourne N Linc		58	G7
Redbrook Gloucs		27	U6
Redbrook Wrexhm		45	M5
Redbrook Street Kent		12	H8
Redburn Highld		103	P6
Redcar R & Cl		71	L8
Redcastle D & G		74	J12
Redcastle Highld		102	G6
Red Dial Cumb		67	L3
Redding Falk		82	H3
Reddingmuirhead Falk		82	H3
Reddish Stockp		56	C8
Redditch Worcs		36	D7
Redditch Crematorium Worcs		36	D7
Rede Suffk		40	D9
Redenhall Norfk		41	N4
Redenham Hants		19	M11
Redesmouth Nthumb		76	H9
Redford Abers		99	P8
Redford Angus		91	S3
Redford W Susx		10	D5
Redfordgreen Border		75	R2
Redgate Rhondd		26	J10
Redgorton P & K		90	F5
Redgrave Suffk		40	H5
Redhill Abers		99	P3
Redhill Herts		31	T6
Red Hill Bmouth		8	F9
Redhill N Som		17	N4
Redhill Surrey		21	N12
Red Hill Warwks		36	F9
Redisham Suffk		41	R4
Redland Bristl		27	V12
Redland Ork		106	s18
Redlingfield Suffk		41	L6
Redlingfield Green Suffk		41	L6
Red Lodge Suffk		39	T6
Red Lumb Rochdl		55	T4
Redlynch Somset		17	T10
Redlynch Wilts		8	J4
Redmain Cumb		66	J6
Redmarley D'Abitot Gloucs		28	E1
Redmarshall S on T		70	E7
Redmile Leics		47	U6
Redmire N York		69	N13
Redmyre Abers		99	N7
Rednal Birm		36	D5
Rednal Shrops		44	J8
Redpath Border		84	F12
Redpoint Highld		107	M11
Red Rock Wigan		55	N5
Red Roses Carmth		25	L8
Red Row Nthumb		77	R7
Redruth Cnwll		2	J8
Redstocks Wilts		18	D8
Redstone Cross Pembks		24	J7
Red Street Staffs		45	T3
Redvales Bury		55	T5
Red Wharf Bay IoA		52	H6
Redwick Newpt		27	R11
Redwick S Glos		27	T10
Redworth Darltn		69	S7
Reed Herts		31	T5
Reedham Norfk		51	R13
Reedness E R Yk		58	C2
Reeds Beck Lincs		59	L13
Reeds Holme Lancs		55	S2
Reepham Lincs		58	H12
Reepham Norfk		50	H9
Reeth N York		69	N13
Reeves Green Solhll		36	J5
Regaby IoM		60	g3
Regil N Som		17	P4
Reiff Highld		107	S2
Reigate Surrey		21	N12
Reighton N York		65	Q4
Reisque Abers		105	P11
Reiss Highld		112	H5
Rejerrah Cnwll		2	K5
Releath Cnwll		2	H10
Relubbus Cnwll		2	F10
Remenham Wokhm		20	C6
Remenham Hill Wokhm		20	C6
Rempstone Notts		47	Q9
Rendcomb Gloucs		28	K5
Rendham Suffk		41	P8
Rendlesham Suffk		41	P10
Renfrew Rens		88	M12
Renhold Bed		38	G10
Renishaw Derbys		57	Q11
Rennington Nthumb		77	Q2
Renton W Duns		88	J10
Renwick Cumb		67	S3
Repps Norfk		51	R10
Repton Derbys		46	K8
Resaurie Highld		102	K6
Rescassa Cnwll		3	P7
Rescorla Cnwll		3	Q6
Resipole Highld		93	S5
Reskadinnick Cnwll		2	G8
Resolis Highld		109	M11
Resolven Neath		26	E7
Rest and be thankful Ag & B		88	G5
Reston Border		85	L7
Restronguet Cnwll		2	K9
Reswallie Angus		91	Q2
Reterth Cnwll		3	N4
Retew Cnwll		3	N5
Retford Notts		58	B10
Retire Cnwll		3	Q3
Rettendon Essex		22	J8
Retyn Cnwll		3	L5
Revesby Lincs		59	L14
Rew Devon		5	S10
Rewe Devon		6	B5
Rew Street IoW		9	P10
Rexon Devon		5	L3
Reymerston Norfk		50	H12
Reynalton Pembks		24	J9

Reynoldston - Shangton 139

Reynoldston Swans 25 S13
Rezare Cnwll 4 K5
Rhadyr Mons 27 R7
Rhandirmwyn Carmth 33 Q12
Rhayader Powys 33 U7
Rheindown Highld 102 F6
Rhes-y-cae Flints 54 E12
Rhewl Denbgs 44 D1
Rhewl Denbgs 44 E5
Rhewl-fawr Flints 54 D10
Rhewl Mostyn Flints 54 E10
Rhicarn Highld 110 B11
Rhiconich Highld 110 F6
Rhicullen Highld 109 M10
Rhigos Rhondd 26 G6
Rhireavach Highld 107 T5
Rhives Highld 109 Q4
Rhiwbina Cardif 27 M11
Rhiwbryfdir Gwynd 43 N4
Rhiwderyn Newpt 27 P10
Rhiwen Gwynd 52 J10
Rhiwinder Rhondd 26 J10
Rhiwlas Gwynd 43 T6
Rhiwlas Gwynd 52 J9
Rhiwlas Powys 44 E7
Rhiwsaeson Rhondd 26 K11
Rhode Somset 16 J10
Rhoden Green Kent 12 C6
Rhodesia Notts 57 S11
Rhodes Minnis Kent 13 N7
Rhodiad-y-brenin Pembks 24 C5
Rhonehouse D & G 74 D14
Rhoose V Glam 16 E3
Rhos Carmth 25 Q3
Rhos Denbgs 44 D1
Rhos Neath 26 C7
Rhosbeirio IoA 52 E4
Rhoscefnhir IoA 52 H7
Rhoscolyn IoA 52 C7
Rhoscrowther Pembks 24 F10
Rhosesmor Flints 54 F13
Rhos-fawr Gwynd 42 G6
Rhosgadfan Gwynd 52 H11
Rhosgoch IoA 52 F5
Rhosgoch Powys 34 E11
Rhos Haminiog Cerdgn 32 K8
Rhoshill Pembks 32 C12
Rhoshirwaun Gwynd 42 D8
Rhoslan Gwynd 42 J5
Rhoslefain Gwynd 43 L12
Rhosllanerchrugog Wrexhm 44 G4
Rhôs Lligwy IoA 52 G5
Rhosmaen Carmth 26 A3
Rhosmeirch IoA 52 G7
Rhosneigr IoA 52 D8
Rhosnesni Wrexhm 44 J3
Rhôs-on-Sea Conwy 53 P6
Rhosrobin Wrexhm 44 H3
Rhossili Swans 25 R13
Rhostryfan Gwynd 52 G11
Rhostyllen Wrexhm 44 H4
Rhosybol IoA 52 F5
Rhos y-brithdir Powys 44 D9
Rhosygadfa Shrops 44 H7
Rhos-y-garth Cerdgn 33 M6
Rhos-y-gwaliau Gwynd 43 T7
Rhos-y-llan Gwynd 42 D6
Rhosymedre Wrexhm 44 G5
Rhos-y-meirch Powys 34 G7
Rhu Ag & B 88 G9
Rhuallt Denbgs 54 C11
Rhubodach Ag & B 88 B11
Rhuddall Heath Ches W 45 N1
Rhuddlan Cerdgn 32 J12
Rhuddlan Denbgs 53 T7
Rhulen Powys 34 D11
Rhunahaorine Ag & B 79 N6
Rhyd Gwynd 43 M5
Rhydargaeau Carmth 25 R5
Rhydcymerau Carmth 25 U3
Rhydd Worcs 35 T11
Rhyd-Ddu Gwynd 52 J12
Rhydding Neath 26 C8
Rhydgaled Conwy 53 S10
Rhydlanfair Conwy 53 P12
Rhydlewis Cerdgn 32 F11
Rhydlios Gwynd 42 C8
Rhyd-lydan Conwy 43 S3
Rhydowen Cerdgn 32 H11
Rhydrosser Cerdgn 33 L7
Rhydspence Herefs 34 F11
Rhydtalog Flints 44 F3
Rhyd-uchaf Gwynd 43 T6
Rhyd-y-clafdy Gwynd 42 F7
Rhydycroesau Shrops 44 F7
Rhydyfelin Cerdgn 33 L5
Rhydyfelin Rhondd 26 K10
Rhyd-y-foel Conwy 53 R7
Rhydyfro Neath 26 C6
Rhyd-y-groes Gwynd 52 J9
Rhydymain Gwynd 43 R9
Rhyd-y-meirch Mons 27 Q6
Rhydymwyn Flints 54 F13
Rhyd-y pennau Cerdgn 33 M3
Rhyd-yr-onnen Gwynd 43 M13
Rhyd-y-sarn Gwynd 43 N5
Rhyl Denbgs 53 T6
Rhymney Caerph 27 L6
Rhynd P & K 90 J7
Rhynie Abers 104 F10
Rhynie Highld 109 Q9
Ribbesford Worcs 35 S6
Ribbleton Lancs 62 B13
Ribby Lancs 61 S13
Ribchester Lancs 62 D12
Riber Derbys 46 K2
Riby Lincs 59 L5
Riccall N York 64 E12
Riccarton Border 76 A7
Riccarton E Ayrs 81 N5
Richards Castle Herefs 35 L7
Richings Park Bucks 20 H7
Richmond Gt Lon 21 L8
Richmond N York 69 Q12
Richmond Sheff 57 P9
Richmond Fort Guern 6 C2
Rich's Holford Somset 16 F10
Rickerscote Staffs 46 B9
Rickford N Som 17 N5
Rickham Devon 5 T13
Rickinghall Suffk 40 H5
Rickling Essex 22 C1
Rickling Green Essex 22 D2
Rickmansworth Herts 20 J4
Riddell Border 84 E14
Riddings Derbys 47 M3
Riddlecombe Devon 15 P10
Riddlesden C Brad 63 M11
Ridge BaNES 17 Q5
Ridge Dorset 8 C11
Ridge Herts 31 R12
Ridge Wilts 8 D2
Ridgebourne Powys 34 C8
Ridge Green Surrey 21 P13
Ridge Lane Warwks 36 J2
Ridge Row Kent 13 P7
Ridgeway Derbys 57 P10
Ridgeway Worcs 36 D8
Ridgeway Cross Herefs 35 R11
Ridgewell Essex 40 B12
Ridgewood E Susx 11 R7
Ridgmont C Beds 31 L5
Riding Mill Nthumb 77 L13
Ridley Kent 12 B3
Ridley Nthumb 76 F13
Ridley Green Ches E 45 N3
Ridlington Norfk 51 P7
Ridlington Rutlnd 48 B13
Ridlington Street Norfk 51 P7
Ridsdale Nthumb 76 J9
Rievaulx N York 64 D2
Rigg D & G 75 Q12
Riggend N Lans 82 E4
Righoul Highld 103 N5
Rigmadon Park Cumb 62 C3
Rigsby Lincs 59 R11
Rigside S Lans 82 G11
Riley Green Lancs 55 P1
Rileyhill Staffs 46 F11
Rilla Mill Cnwll 4 H6
Rillaton Cnwll 4 H6
Rillington N York 64 K5
Rimington Lancs 62 G10
Rimpton Somset 17 R12
Rimswell E R Yk 65 U14
Rinaston Pembks 24 G5
Rindleford Shrops 35 R1
Ringford D & G 73 R8
Ringinglow Sheff 57 L10
Ringland Norfk 50 K11
Ringles Cross E Susx 11 R6
Ringlestone Kent 12 G4
Ringley Bolton 55 S5
Ringmer E Susx 11 Q8
Ringmore Devon 5 R11
Ringmore Devon 6 B10
Ring o'Bells Lancs 55 L4
Ringorm Moray 104 B7
Ring's End Cambs 49 N13
Ringsfield Suffk 41 R3
Ringsfield Corner Suffk 41 R3
Ringshall Herts 31 L10
Ringshall Suffk 40 H10
Ringshall Stocks Suffk 40 J10
Ringstead Nhants 38 E5
Ringstead Norfk 50 B5
Ringwood Hants 8 H7
Ringwould Kent 13 S6
Rinsey Cnwll 2 F11
Rinsey Croft Cnwll 2 G11
Ripe E Susx 11 S8
Ripley Derbys 47 L3
Ripley Hants 8 H9
Ripley N York 63 R7
Ripley Surrey 20 J11
Riplingham E R Yk 65 M13
Riplington Hants 9 T4
Ripon N York 63 S5
Rippingale Lincs 48 G8
Ripple Kent 13 S5
Ripple Worcs 35 U13
Ripponden Calder 56 F3
Risabus Ag & B 78 E7
Risbury Herefs 35 M10
Risby N Linc 58 F4
Risby Suffk 40 D7
Risca Caerph 27 N9
Rise E R Yk 65 R11
Riseden E Susx 11 U4
Riseden Kent 12 D8
Risegate Lincs 48 K8
Riseholme Lincs 58 G11
Risehow Cumb 66 F6
Riseley Bed 38 F8
Riseley Wokham 20 B10
Rishangles Suffk 41 L7
Rishton Lancs 62 E13
Rishworth Calder 56 F3
Rising Bridge Lancs 55 S1
Risley Derbys 47 N6
Risley Warrtn 55 Q8
Risplith N York 63 Q6
Rivar Wilts 19 M8
Rivenhall End Essex 22 K4
River Kent 13 Q7
River W Susx 10 E6
River Bank Cambs 39 R7
Riverford Highld 102 F5
Riverhead Kent 21 T11
Rivers Corner Dorset 7 U2
Rivington Lancs 55 P4
Rivington Services Lancs 55 P4
Roachill Devon 15 U8
Roade Nhants 37 U10
Road Green Norfk 41 N2
Roadhead Cumb 75 V11
Roadmeetings S Lans 82 G9
Roadside E Ayrs 81 R9
Roadside Highld 112 E4
Roadwater Somset 16 D9
Roag Highld 100 b5
Roa Island Cumb 61 N6
Roan of Craigoch S Ayrs 80 K12
Roast Green Essex 39 Q14
Roath Cardif 27 M12
Roberton Border 75 T3
Roberton S Lans 82 H13
Robertsbridge E Susx 12 D11
Roberttown Kirk 56 J2
Robeston Wathen Pembks 24 J7
Robgill Tower D & G 75 P11
Robin Hill Staffs 46 B2
Robin Hood Lancs 55 M4
Robin Hood Leeds 57 M1
Robin Hood Crematorium Solihll 36 F4
Robin Hood Doncaster Sheffield Airport Donc 57 U7
Robinhood End Essex 40 B13
Robin Hood's Bay N York 71 S11
Roborough Devon 5 N8
Roborough Devon 15 N9
Roby Knows 54 K8
Roby Mill Lancs 55 M5
Rocester Staffs 46 F6
Roch Pembks 24 E6
Rochdale Rochdl 56 C4
Rochdale Crematorium Rochdl 56 C4
Roche Cnwll 3 P4
Rochester Medway 12 D2
Rochester Nthumb 76 G6
Rochford Essex 23 L9
Rochford Worcs 35 P7
Roch Gate Pembks 24 E6
Rock Cnwll 3 N1
Rock Neath 26 D9
Rock Nthumb 77 Q1
Rock W Susx 10 J8
Rock Worcs 35 R6
Rockbeare Devon 6 D6
Rockbourne Hants 8 G5
Rockcliffe Cumb 75 S13
Rockcliffe D & G 66 B2
Rockcliffe Cross Cumb 75 R13
Rock End Staffs 45 U2
Rockend Torbay 6 B12
Rock Ferry Wirral 54 H9
Rockfield Highld 109 S8
Rockfield Mons 27 T5
Rockford Devon 15 S3
Rockford Hants 8 H7
Rockgreen Shrops 35 M5
Rockhampton S Glos 28 C9
Rockhead Cnwll 4 D4
Rockhill Shrops 34 G5
Rock Hill Worcs 36 C7
Rockingham Nhants 38 C2
Rockland All Saints Norfk 40 G1
Rockland St Mary Norfk 51 P13
Rockland St Peter Norfk 40 G1
Rockley Notts 58 B12
Rockley Wilts 18 J6
Rockliffe Lancs 56 C2
Rockville Ag & B 88 F7
Rockwell End Bucks 20 C5
Rockwell Green Somset 16 F12
Rodborough Gloucs 28 F7
Rodbourne Swindn 29 M10
Rodbourne Wilts 28 H11
Rodd Herefs 34 H8
Roddam Nthumb 77 L1
Rodden Dorset 7 R8
Roddymoor Dur 69 Q5
Rode Somset 18 B10
Rode Heath Ches E 45 T2
Rode Heath Ches E 56 C13
Rodel W Isls 106 f10
Roden Wrekin 45 N10
Rodhuish Somset 16 D9
Rodington Wrekin 45 N11
Rodington Heath Wrekin 45 N11
Rodley Gloucs 28 D5
Rodley Leeds 63 Q12
Rodmarton Gloucs 28 H8
Rodmell E Susx 11 Q9
Rodmersham Kent 12 H3
Rodmersham Green Kent 12 H3
Rodney Stoke Somset 17 N7
Rodsley Derbys 46 H5
Rodway Somset 16 J8
Roecliffe N York 63 T6
Roe Cross Tamesd 56 E7
Roe Green Herts 31 R11
Roe Green Herts 31 T6
Roe Green Salfd 55 S6
Roehampton Gt Lon 21 M8
Roffey W Susx 10 K4
Rogart Highld 109 N4
Rogate W Susx 10 C6
Roger Ground Cumb 67 N13
Rogerstone Newpt 27 P10
Roghadal W Isls 106 f10
Rogiet Mons 27 T10
Roke Oxon 19 T2
Roker Sundld 77 U14
Rollesby Norfk 51 R10
Rolleston Leics 47 T13
Rolleston Notts 47 T3
Rolleston on Dove Staffs 46 H8
Rolston E R Yk 65 S11
Rolstone N Som 17 L4
Rolvenden Kent 12 F9
Rolvenden Layne Kent 12 G9
Romaldkirk Dur 69 L8
Romanby N York 70 E14
Romanno Bridge Border 83 N9
Romansleigh Devon 15 R8
Romden Castle Kent 12 G7
Romesdal Highld 100 d4
Romford Dorset 8 F7
Romford Gt Lon 22 D10
Romiley Stockp 56 D8
Romney Street Kent 21 U10
Romsey Hants 9 M4
Romsley Shrops 35 S4
Romsley Worcs 36 C4
Rona Highld 100 f4
Ronachan Ag & B 79 N5
Rood Ashton Wilts 18 C9
Rookhope Dur 68 K4
Rookley IoW 9 Q12
Rookley Green IoW 9 Q12
Rooks Bridge Somset 17 L6
Rooks Nest Somset 16 E10
Rookwith N York 63 Q2
Roos E R Yk 65 T13
Roose Cumb 61 N6
Roosebeck Cumb 61 P6
Roothams Green Bed 38 G9
Ropley Hants 9 S2
Ropley Dean Hants 9 S2
Ropley Soke Hants 9 T2
Ropsley Lincs 48 E7
Rora Abers 105 T5
Rorrington Shrops 44 H13
Rosarie Moray 104 D5
Rose Cnwll 2 K6
Roseacre Lancs 61 S12
Rose Ash Devon 15 S8
Rosebank S Lans 82 F9
Rosebush Pembks 24 J5
Rosecare Cnwll 14 E13
Rosecliston Cnwll 3 L5
Rosedale Abbey N York 71 M13
Rose Green Essex 23 M2
Rose Green Suffk 40 F13
Rose Green Suffk 40 G12
Rose Green W Susx 10 E11
Rosehall Highld 108 H4
Rosehearty Abers 105 Q2
Rose Hill E Susx 11 R7
Rose Hill Lancs 62 G13
Roseisle Moray 103 T2
Roselands E Susx 11 U10
Rosemarket Pembks 24 G9
Rosemarkie Highld 102 K4
Rosemary Lane Devon 6 G2
Rosemount P & K 90 J3
Rosenannon Cnwll 3 P3
Rosenithon Cnwll 3 L12
Roser's Cross E Susx 11 S6
Rosevean Cnwll 3 Q5
Rosevine Cnwll 3 M9
Rosewarne Cnwll 2 G9
Rosewell Mdloth 83 Q6
Roseworth S on T 70 F8
Roseworthy Cnwll 2 G9
Rosgill Cumb 67 R9
Roskestal Cnwll 2 B12
Roskhill Highld 100 b5
Roskorwell Cnwll 2 K12
Rosley Cumb 67 M3
Roslin Mdloth 83 Q6
Rosliston Derbys 46 H10
Rosneath Ag & B 88 G9
Ross D & G 73 Q11
Ross Nthumb 85 S11
Rossett Wrexhm 44 J2
Rossett Green N York 63 R9
Rossington Donc 57 T7
Rossland Rens 88 K11
Ross-on-Wye Herefs 28 A3
Roster Highld 112 G9
Rostherne Ches E 55 R10
Rosthwaite Cumb 67 L10
Roston Derbys 46 F5
Rosudgeon Cnwll 2 F11
Rosyth Fife 83 M2
Rothbury Nthumb 77 M5
Rotherby Leics 47 S10
Rotherfield E Susx 11 T5
Rotherfield Greys Oxon 20 B6
Rotherfield Peppard Oxon 20 B6
Rotherham Rothm 57 P8
Rotherham Crematorium Rothm 57 Q8
Rothersthorpe Nhants 37 T9
Rotherwick Hants 20 B11
Rothes Moray 104 B6
Rothesay Ag & B 88 C13
Rothiebrisbane Abers 105 L8
Rothiemay Moray 104 H6
Rothiemurchus Lodge Highld 97 R2
Rothiemurchus Visitor Centre Highld 103 P13
Rothienorman Abers 105 L8
Rothley Leics 47 Q11
Rothley Nthumb 77 L8
Rothmaise Abers 104 K9
Rothwell Leeds 63 S14
Rothwell Lincs 58 K7
Rothwell Nhants 38 B4
Rotsea E R Yk 65 P9
Rottal Lodge Angus 98 F10
Rottingdean Br & H 11 P10
Rottington Cumb 66 E10
Roucan D & G 74 K10
Roucan Loch Crematorium D & G 74 K10
Roud IoW 9 Q12
Rougham Norfk 50 D9
Rougham Suffk 40 F8
Rough Close Staffs 46 B6
Rough Common Kent 13 M4
Roughlee Lancs 62 G11
Roughpark Abers 104 C13
Roughton Lincs 59 M14
Roughton Norfk 51 M6
Roughton Shrops 35 S2
Roughway Kent 12 B5
Roundbush Essex 23 L7
Round Bush Herts 20 K3
Roundbush Green Essex 22 E5
Round Green Luton 31 P8
Roundham Somset 7 M3
Roundhay Leeds 63 S12
Rounds Green Sandw 36 C3
Round Street Kent 12 C2
Roundstreet Common W Susx 10 H5
Roundway Wilts 18 F8
Roundyhill Angus 98 F13
Rousay Ork 106 s16
Rousdon Devon 6 J6
Rousham Oxon 29 U3
Rous Lench Worcs 36 D10
Routenburn N Ayrs 88 E13
Routh E R Yk 65 P11
Rout's Green Bucks 20 C3
Row Cnwll 3 R1
Row Cumb 61 T2
Row Cumb 68 D6
Rowanburn D & G 75 T10
Rowardennan Stirlg 88 J6
Rowarth Derbys 56 F9
Row Ash Hants 9 Q6
Rowberrow Somset 17 N5
Rowborough IoW 9 P12
Rowde Wilts 18 E8
Rowden Devon 15 P13
Rowen Conwy 53 N8
Rowfield Derbys 46 G4
Rowfoot Nthumb 76 D13
Rowford Somset 16 H11
Row Green Essex 22 H3
Rowhedge Essex 23 P3
Rowhook W Susx 10 J4
Rowington Warwks 36 H7
Rowland Derbys 56 K12
Rowland's Castle Hants 9 U6
Rowland's Gill Gatesd 77 P14
Rowledge Surrey 10 C2
Rowley Dur 69 N3
Rowley E R Yk 65 M13
Rowley Shrops 44 H12
Rowley Hill Kirk 56 J4
Rowley Regis Sandw 36 C3
Rowley Regis Crematorium Sandw 36 C3
Rowlstone Herefs 27 R2
Rowly Surrey 10 G2
Rowner Hants 9 R8
Rowney Green Worcs 36 D6
Rownhams Hants 9 M5
Rownhams Services Hants 9 M5
Rowrah Cumb 66 G9
Rowsham Bucks 30 H9
Rowsley Derbys 57 L13
Rows of Trees Ches E 55 T11
Rowstock Oxon 29 U10
Rowston Lincs 48 G2
Rowthorne Derbys 57 Q14
Rowton Ches W 54 K14
Rowton Shrops 34 K4
Rowton Shrops 44 J11
Rowton Wrekin 45 P10
Row Town Surrey 20 H10
Roxburgh Border 84 H12
Roxby N Linc 58 F3
Roxby N York 71 N9
Roxton Bed 38 J10
Roxwell Essex 22 F6
Royal Leamington Spa Warwks 36 K7
Royal Oak Darltn 69 R8
Royal Oak Lancs 54 K6
Royal's Green Ches E 45 P5
Royal Sutton Coldfield Birm 36 F1
Royal Tunbridge Wells Kent 11 T3
Royal Wootton Bassett Wilts 29 L11
Royal Yacht Britannia C Edin 83 Q3
Roy Bridge Highld 96 B7
Roydhouse Kirk 56 K4
Roydon Essex 22 B5
Roydon Norfk 40 K4
Roydon Norfk 50 B9
Roydon Hamlet Essex 22 B6
Royston Barns 57 N4
Royston Herts 31 U4
Royton Oldham 56 D5
Rozel Jersey 7 e2
Ruabon Wrexhm 44 H5
Ruaig Ag & B 92 D9
Ruan High Lanes Cnwll 3 N9
Ruan Lanihorne Cnwll 3 M8
Ruan Major Cnwll 2 J13
Ruan Minor Cnwll 2 J13
Ruardean Gloucs 28 B4
Ruardean Hill Gloucs 28 B4
Ruardean Woodside Gloucs 28 B4
Rubery Birm 36 C5
Rubha Ban W Isls 106 c17
Ruckcroft Cumb 67 R4
Ruckhall Herefs 35 L13
Ruckinge Kent 12 K9
Ruckland Lincs 59 P11
Ruckley Shrops 45 M13
Rudby N York 70 G11
Rudchester Nthumb 77 N12
Ruddington Notts 47 Q7
Ruddle Gloucs 28 C5
Ruddlemoor Cnwll 3 Q6
Rudford Gloucs 28 E3
Rudge Somset 18 B10
Rudgeway S Glos 28 B10
Rudgwick W Susx 10 H4
Rudhall Herefs 28 B2
Rudheath Ches W 55 Q12
Rudheath Woods Ches E 55 R12
Rudley Green Essex 22 K7
Rudloe Wilts 18 B6
Rudry Caerph 27 N10
Rudston E R Yk 65 P6
Rudyard Staffs 46 C2
Ruecastle Border 76 C1
Rufford Lancs 55 L3
Rufford Abbey Notts 57 T14
Rufforth C York 64 C9
Rug Denbgs 44 C5
Rugby Warwks 37 P5
Rugeley Staffs 46 D10
Ruishton Somset 16 J11
Ruislip Gt Lon 20 J5
Rùm Highld 100 c10
Rumbach Moray 104 D5
Rumbling Bridge P & K 90 F12
Rumburgh Suffk 41 P4
Rumby Hill Dur 69 Q6
Rumford Cnwll 3 M2
Rumford Falk 82 H3
Rumney Cardif 27 N12
Rumwell Somset 16 G12
Runcorn Halton 55 M10
Runcton W Susx 10 D10
Runcton Holme Norfk 49 T12
Runfold Surrey 20 E13
Runhall Norfk 50 J12
Runham Norfk 51 S11
Runham Norfk 51 T12
Runnington Somset 16 F12
Runsell Green Essex 22 J6
Runshaw Moor Lancs 55 M3
Runswick N York 71 P9
Runtaleave Angus 98 D10
Runway Visitor Park Manch 55 T10
Runwell Essex 22 J9
Ruscombe Wokham 20 C7
Rushall Herefs 35 P13
Rushall Norfk 41 L4
Rushall Wilts 18 H9
Rushall Wsall 46 D13
Rushbrooke Suffk 40 E8
Rushbury Shrops 35 M2
Rushden Herts 31 T6
Rushden Nhants 38 E7
Rushenden Kent 23 M13
Rusher's Cross E Susx 11 U5
Rushford Devon 5 M5
Rushford Norfk 40 F4
Rush Green Essex 23 S4
Rush Green Gt Lon 22 D10
Rush Green Herts 31 R8
Rush Green Warrtn 55 Q9
Rushlake Green E Susx 11 U7
Rushmere Suffk 41 S3
Rushmere St Andrew Suffk 41 L11
Rushmoor Surrey 10 D2
Rushock Herefs 34 H9
Rushock Worcs 35 U6
Rusholme Manch 56 C8
Rushton Ches W 55 N14
Rushton Nhants 38 B4
Rushton Shrops 45 P12
Rushton Spencer Staffs 46 B1
Rushwick Worcs 35 T10
Rushyford Dur 69 S7
Ruskie Stirlg 89 P5
Ruskington Lincs 48 G3
Rusland Cross Cumb 61 Q2
Rusper W Susx 11 L3
Ruspidge Gloucs 28 C5
Russell Green Essex 22 H5
Russell's Water Oxon 20 B5
Russel's Green Suffk 41 N6
Russ Hill Surrey 11 L2
Rusthall Kent 11 T3
Rustington W Susx 10 G10
Ruston N York 65 M3
Ruston Parva E R Yk 65 P7
Ruswarp N York 71 Q11
Ruthall Shrops 35 N2
Rutherford Border 84 G12
Rutherglen S Lans 89 P13
Ruthernbridge Cnwll 3 Q3
Ruthin Denbgs 44 D2
Ruthrieston C Aber 99 S3
Ruthven Abers 104 G6
Ruthven Angus 91 L2
Ruthven Highld 97 M4
Ruthven Highld 103 L10
Ruthvoes Cnwll 3 N4
Ruthwaite Cumb 66 K5
Ruthwell D & G 75 L12
Ruxley Corner Gt Lon 21 S8
Ruxton Green Herefs 27 U4
Ruyton-XI-Towns Shrops 44 J9
Ryal Nthumb 77 L11
Ryall Dorset 7 M5
Ryall Worcs 35 U12
Ryarsh Kent 12 C4
Rycote Oxon 30 E11
Rydal Cumb 67 N11
Ryde IoW 9 R10
Rye E Susx 12 H11
Ryebank Shrops 45 M7
Ryeford Herefs 28 B3
Rye Foreign E Susx 12 G11
Rye Harbour E Susx 12 H12
Ryehill E R Yk 59 M1
Ryeish Green Wokham 20 B9
Rye Street Worcs 35 S13
Ryhall Rutlnd 48 F11
Ryhill Wakefd 57 N4
Ryhope Sundld 70 F2
Rylah Derbys 57 Q13
Ryland Lincs 58 H11
Rylands Notts 47 P6
Rylstone N York 62 K8
Ryme Intrinseca Dorset 7 Q2
Ryther N York 64 D12
Ryton Gatesd 77 N13
Ryton N York 64 H4
Ryton Shrops 45 S13
Ryton Warwks 37 M3
Ryton-on-Dunsmore Warwks 37 L6
Ryton Woodside Gatesd 77 N13

S

Sabden Lancs 62 F12
Sabine's Green Essex 22 D8
Sacombe Herts 31 T9
Sacombe Green Herts 31 T9
Sacriston Dur 69 R3
Sadberge Darltn 70 D9
Saddell Ag & B 79 P9
Saddington Leics 37 S2
Saddle Bow Norfk 49 T10
Saddlescombe W Susx 11 M8
Sadgill Cumb 67 Q11
Saffron Walden Essex 39 R13
Sageston Pembks 24 J10
Saham Hills Norfk 50 E13
Saham Toney Norfk 50 E13
Saighton Ches W 44 K1
St Abbs Border 85 N5
St Agnes Border 84 H6
St Agnes Cnwll 2 J6
St Agnes IoS 2 b3
St Agnes Mining District Cnwll 2 J7
St Albans Herts 31 P11
St Allen Cnwll 3 L6
St Andrew Guern 6 d3
St Andrews Fife 91 R8
St Andrews Botanic Garden Fife 91 R8
St Andrew's Major V Glam 16 F2
St Andrews Well Dorset 7 N6
St Anne's Lancs 61 Q14
St Ann's D & G 75 L7
St Ann's Chapel Cnwll 5 L6
St Ann's Chapel Devon 5 R11
St Anthony Cnwll 2 K11
St Anthony's Hill E Susx 11 U10
St Arvans Mons 27 U8
St Asaph Denbgs 53 T8
St Athan V Glam 16 D3
St Aubin Jersey 7 c3
St Austell Cnwll 3 Q6
St Bees Cumb 66 E10
St Blazey Cnwll 3 R6
St Blazey Gate Cnwll 3 R6
St Boswells Border 84 F12
St Brelade Jersey 7 b3
St Brelade's Bay Jersey 7 b3
St Breock Cnwll 3 P2
St Breward Cnwll 3 R1
St Briavels Gloucs 27 V7
St Brides Pembks 24 D8
St Bride's Major V Glam 26 F13
St Brides Netherwent Mons 27 S10
St Brides-super-Ely V Glam 26 K12
St Brides Wentlooge Newpt 27 P11
St Budeaux C Plym 5 M9
Saintbury Gloucs 36 F13
St Buryan Cnwll 2 C11
St Catherine BaNES 17 U3
St Catherines Ag & B 88 D4
St Chloe Gloucs 28 F7
St Clears Carmth 25 N7
St Cleer Cnwll 4 G7
St Clement Cnwll 3 M8
St Clement Jersey 7 e4
St Clether Cnwll 4 G4
St Colmac Ag & B 88 B12
St Columb Major Cnwll 3 N4
St Columb Minor Cnwll 3 L4
St Columb Road Cnwll 3 N5
St Combs Abers 105 T3
St Cross South Elmham Suffk 41 N4
St Cyrus Abers 99 N11
St David's P & K 90 D7
St Davids Pembks 24 C5
St David's Cathedral Pembks 24 C5
St Day Cnwll 2 J8
St Decumans Somset 16 E8
St Dennis Cnwll 3 P5
St Devereux Herefs 27 S1
St Dogmaels Pembks 32 C11
St Dogwells Pembks 24 G5
St Dominick Cnwll 5 L7
St Donats V Glam 16 B3
St Edith's Marsh Wilts 18 E8
St Endellion Cnwll 4 B5
St Enoder Cnwll 3 M5
St Erme Cnwll 3 L7
St Erney Cnwll 4 K9
St Erth Cnwll 2 F9
St Erth Praze Cnwll 2 F9
St Ervan Cnwll 3 M2
St Eval Cnwll 3 M3
St Ewe Cnwll 3 P7
St Fagans Cardif 27 L12
St Fagans: National History Museum Cardif 27 L12
St Fergus Abers 105 T5
St Fillans P & K 95 T14
St Florence Pembks 24 J10
St Gennys Cnwll 14 D13
St George Conwy 53 S7
St Georges N Som 17 L4
St George's V Glam 27 L12
St George's Hill Surrey 20 J10
St Germans Cnwll 4 K9
St Giles in the Wood Devon 15 M9
St Giles-on-the-Heath Devon 4 K2
St Gluvia's Cnwll 2 K10
St Harmon Powys 33 U6
St Helen Auckland Dur 69 Q7
St Helens Cumb 66 F6
St Helen's E Susx 12 F13
St Helens IoW 9 S11
St Helens St Hel 55 M7
St Helens Crematorium St Hel 55 L7
St Helier Gt Lon 21 N9
St Helier Jersey 7 d3
St Hilary Cnwll 2 E10
St Hilary V Glam 26 J13
Saint Hill Devon 6 E3
Saint Hill W Susx 11 P3
St Illtyd Blae G 27 N7
St Ippollitts Herts 31 Q7
St Ishmael's Pembks 24 D9
St Issey Cnwll 3 N2
St Ive Cnwll 4 J7
St Ive Cross Cnwll 4 J7
St Ives Cambs 39 M6
St Ives Cnwll 2 E8
St Ives Dorset 8 G8
St James Norfk 51 N9
St James's End Nhants 37 T8
St James South Elmham Suffk 41 P4
St Jidgey Cnwll 3 N3
St John Cnwll 5 L10
St John Jersey 7 c1
St Johns Dur 69 N6
St John's E Susx 11 S4
St John's IoM 60 d6
St Johns Kent 21 T11
St Johns Surrey 20 G11
St Johns Worcs 35 T10
St John's Chapel Devon 15 M7
St John's Chapel Dur 68 J5
St John's Fen End Norfk 49 R11
St John's Highway Norfk 49 R11
St John's Kirk S Lans 82 J11
St John's Town of Dalry D & G 73 Q3
St John's Wood Gt Lon 21 N6
St Jude's IoM 60 f3
St Just Cnwll 2 B10
St Just-in-Roseland Cnwll 3 L9
St Just Mining District Cnwll 2 B10
St Katherines Abers 105 M9
St Keverne Cnwll 2 K12
St Kew Cnwll 3 Q1
St Kew Highway Cnwll 3 Q1
St Keyne Cnwll 4 G8
St Lawrence Cnwll 3 Q3
St Lawrence Essex 23 N7
St Lawrence IoW 9 Q13
St Lawrence Jersey 7 c2
St Lawrence Kent 13 S2
St Leonards Bucks 30 K11
St Leonards Dorset 8 G8
St Leonards E Susx 12 F14
St Leonard's Street Kent 12 C4
St Levan Cnwll 2 B12
St Lythans V Glam 27 L13
St Mabyn Cnwll 3 Q2
St Madoes P & K 90 J7
St Margarets Herefs 34 J14
St Margarets Herts 31 U10
St Margaret's at Cliffe Kent 13 S7
St Margaret's Hope Ork 106 t20
St Margaret South Elmham Suffk 41 P4
St Marks IoM 60 d8
St Martin Cnwll 2 J12
St Martin Cnwll 4 H9
St Martin Guern 6 d3
St Martin Jersey 7 e2
St Martin's IoS 2 c1
St Martin's P & K 90 J5
St Martins Shrops 44 H6
St Martin's Moor Shrops 44 H6
St Mary Jersey 7 c2
St Mary Bourne Hants 19 P10
St Marychurch Torbay 6 B11
St Mary Church V Glam 16 D2
St Mary Cray Gt Lon 21 S9
St Mary Hill V Glam 26 H12
St Mary in the Marsh Kent 13 L10
St Marylebone Crematorium Gt Lon 21 N5
St Mary's IoS 2 c2
St Mary's Ork 106 t19
St Mary's Bay Kent 13 L10
St Mary's Grove N Som 17 N3
St Mary's Hoo Medway 22 K12
St Maughans Mons 27 T4
St Maughans Green Mons 27 T4
St Mawes Cnwll 3 L10
St Mawgan Cnwll 3 M3
St Mellion Cnwll 4 K7
St Mellons Cardif 27 N11
St Merryn Cnwll 3 M2
St Mewan Cnwll 3 P6
St Michael Caerhays Cnwll 3 P8
St Michael Church Somset 16 K10
St Michael Penkevil Cnwll 3 M8
St Michaels Kent 12 G8
St Michaels Worcs 35 N7
St Michael's Mount Cnwll 2 E11
St Michael's on Wyre Lancs 61 T11
St Michael South Elmham Suffk 41 P4
St Minver Cnwll 4 B5
St Monans Fife 91 R11
St Neot Cnwll 4 F7
St Neots Cambs 38 J8
St Newlyn East Cnwll 3 L5
St Nicholas Pembks 24 F3
St Nicholas V Glam 26 K13
St Nicholas at Wade Kent 13 Q2
St Ninians Stirlg 89 S7
St Olaves Norfk 51 S14
St Osyth Essex 23 R4
St Ouen Jersey 7 b2
St Owens Cross Herefs 27 U3
St Paul's Cray Gt Lon 21 S9
St Paul's Walden Herts 31 Q8
St Peter Jersey 7 b2
St Peter Port Guern 6 e3
St Peter's Guern 6 c3
St Peter's Kent 13 S2
St Peter's Hill Cambs 38 K6
St Petrox Pembks 24 G11
St Pinnock Cnwll 4 G8
St Quivox S Ayrs 81 M8
St Ruan Cnwll 2 J13
St Sampson Guern 6 e2
St Saviour Guern 6 c3
St Saviour Jersey 7 d3
St Stephen Cnwll 3 N6
St Stephens Cnwll 4 J3
St Stephens Cnwll 5 L9
St Teath Cnwll 4 D4
St Margaret's Bay Kent 13 S7
St Tudy Cnwll 3 R1
St Twynnells Pembks 24 G11
St Veep Cnwll 4 E9
St Vigeans Angus 91 T3
St Wenn Cnwll 3 P4
St Weonards Herefs 27 T3
St y-Nyll V Glam 26 K12
Salcey Forest Nhants 38 B10
Salcombe Devon 5 S13
Salcombe Regis Devon 6 G7
Salcott-cum-Virley Essex 23 M5
Sale Traffd 55 S8
Saleby Lincs 59 S11
Sale Green Worcs 36 B9
Salehurst E Susx 12 E11
Salem Carmth 25 V5
Salem Cerdgn 33 N4
Salen Ag & B 93 P10
Salen Highld 93 R6
Salesbury Lancs 62 D13
Salford C Beds 30 K5
Salford Oxon 29 Q2
Salford Salfd 55 T7
Salford Priors Warwks 36 E10
Salfords Surrey 21 N13
Salhouse Norfk 51 P11
Saline Fife 90 F13
Salisbury Wilts 8 G3
Salisbury Crematorium Wilts 8 H2
Salisbury Plain Wilts 18 G12
Salkeld Dykes Cumb 67 R5
Salle Norfk 50 K9
Salmonby Lincs 59 P12
Salperton Gloucs 29 L3
Salph End Bed 38 G10
Salsburgh N Lans 82 F6
Salt Staffs 46 C8
Salta Cumb 66 G3
Saltaire C Brad 63 N12
Saltaire C Brad 63 N12
Saltash Cnwll 5 L9
Saltburn Highld 109 N10
Saltburn-by-the-Sea R & Cl 71 L8
Saltby Leics 48 C8
Salt Coates Cumb 66 J2
Saltcoats Cumb 66 G13
Saltcoats N Ayrs 80 J4
Saltcotes Lancs 61 R14
Saltdean Br & H 11 P10
Salterbeck Cumb 66 E7
Salterforth Lancs 62 H10
Salterswall Ches W 55 P13
Salterton Wilts 18 H13
Saltfleet Lincs 59 S8
Saltfleetby All Saints Lincs 59 S8
Saltfleetby St Clement Lincs 59 S8
Saltfleetby St Peter Lincs 59 R9
Saltford BaNES 17 S3
Salthouse Norfk 50 J5
Saltley Birm 36 F3
Saltmarsh Newpt 27 Q11
Saltmarshe E R Yk 58 C2
Saltney Flints 54 J14
Salton N York 64 G4
Saltrens Devon 15 L8
Saltwell Crematorium Gatesd 77 R13
Saltwick Nthumb 77 P9
Saltwood Kent 13 N8
Salvington W Susx 10 J9
Salwarpe Worcs 35 U8
Salway Ash Dorset 7 N5
Sambourne Warwks 36 E8
Sambrook Wrekin 45 R9
Samlesbury Lancs 62 B13
Samlesbury Bottoms Lancs 62 C14
Sampford Arundel Somset 16 F13
Sampford Brett Somset 16 E8
Sampford Courtenay Devon 15 P12
Sampford Moor Somset 16 F13
Sampford Peverell Devon 6 D2
Sampford Spiney Devon 5 N6
Samsonlane Ork 106 v17
Samson's Corner Essex 23 Q4
Samuelston E Loth 84 D4
Sanaigmore Ag & B 86 C11
Sancreed Cnwll 2 C11
Sancton E R Yk 64 K12
Sand Somset 17 M7
Sandaig Highld 100 g9
Sandale Cumb 66 K4
Sandal Magna Wakefd 57 M3
Sandavore Highld 93 M2
Sanday Ork 106 v15
Sanday Airport Ork 106 v15
Sandbach Ches E 45 S1
Sandbach Services Ches E 45 S1
Sandbank Ag & B 88 E9
Sandbanks Poole 8 E11
Sandend Abers 104 H2
Sanderstead Gt Lon 21 P10
Sandford Cumb 68 F9
Sandford Devon 15 T12
Sandford Dorset 8 C11
Sandford Hants 8 H8
Sandford IoW 9 Q12
Sandford N Som 17 M5
Sandford S Lans 82 D10
Sandford Shrops 44 H9
Sandford Shrops 45 N7
Sandford-on-Thames Oxon 30 B12
Sandford Orcas Dorset 17 R12
Sandford St Martin Oxon 29 T2
Sandgate Kent 13 P8
Sandhaven Abers 105 R2
Sandhead D & G 72 D10
Sandhill Rothm 57 P7
Sandhills Dorset 7 Q4
Sandhills Dorset 7 S2
Sand Hills Leeds 63 T12
Sandhills Oxon 30 C11
Sandhills Surrey 10 E3
Sandhoe Nthumb 76 K12
Sandhole Ag & B 87 U6
Sand Hole E R Yk 64 J12
Sandholme E R Yk 64 J13
Sandholme Lincs 49 M6
Sandhurst Br For 20 D10
Sandhurst Gloucs 28 F3
Sandhurst Kent 12 E10
Sandhurst Cross Kent 12 E10
Sandhutton N York 63 T3
Sand Hutton N York 64 F8
Sandiacre Derbys 47 N6
Sandilands Lincs 59 T10
Sandiway Ches W 55 P12
Sandleheath Hants 8 G5
Sandleigh Oxon 29 U7
Sandley Dorset 17 U12
Sandling Kent 12 E4
Sandlow Green Ches E 55 S13
Sandness Shet 106 r8
Sandon Essex 22 H7
Sandon Herts 31 T6
Sandon Staffs 46 B8
Sandon Bank Staffs 46 B8
Sandown IoW 9 R12
Sandplace Cnwll 4 H9
Sandridge Herts 31 Q10
Sandridge Wilts 18 D7
Sandringham Norfk 49 U8
Sands Bucks 20 D4
Sandsend N York 71 Q10
Sand Side Cumb 61 N3
Sandside Cumb 61 T3
Sandtoft N Linc 58 B5
Sandway Kent 12 G5
Sandwich Kent 13 R4
Sandwick Cumb 67 P9
Sandwick Shet 106 u11
Sandwick W Isls 106 j5
Sandwith Cumb 66 E10
Sandwith Newtown Cumb 66 E10
Sandy C Beds 38 J11
Sandy Bank Lincs 49 L2
Sandycroft Flints 54 H13
Sandy Cross E Susx 11 T6
Sandy Cross Herefs 35 Q9
Sandyford D & G 75 P7
Sandygate Devon 5 V6
Sandygate IoM 60 f3
Sandy Haven Pembks 24 E9
Sandyhills D & G 66 C1
Sandylands Lancs 61 S7
Sandy Lane C Brad 63 N12
Sandylane Staffs 45 R6
Sandylane Swans 25 U13
Sandy Lane Wilts 18 E7
Sandy Lane Wrexhm 44 K5
Sandy Park Devon 5 S3
Sandysike Cumb 75 S12
Sandyway Herefs 27 T2
Sangobeg Highld 110 J3
Sangomore Highld 110 J3
Sankey Bridges Warrtn 55 N9
Sankyn's Green Worcs 35 S7
Sanna Bay Highld 93 L5
Sanndabhaig W Isls 106 j5
Sannox N Ayrs 80 E3
Sanquhar D & G 74 E4
Santon Cumb 66 H12
Santon IoM 60 e8
Santon Bridge Cumb 66 H12
Santon Downham Suffk 40 D3
Sapcote Leics 37 N2
Sapey Common Herefs 35 R8
Sapiston Suffk 40 F5
Sapley Cambs 38 K6
Sapperton Derbys 46 G7
Sapperton Gloucs 28 H7
Sapperton Lincs 48 F7
Saracen's Head Lincs 49 M8
Sarclet Highld 112 H8
Sarisbury Hants 9 Q7
Sarn Brdgnd 26 G11
Sarn Gwynd 42 D7
Sarn Powys 34 F2
Sarn Powys 43 U14
Sarnau Carmth 25 P7
Sarnau Cerdgn 32 F10
Sarnau Gwynd 43 U6
Sarnau Powys 34 B14
Sarnau Powys 44 F10
Sarn Bach Gwynd 42 F8
Sarnesfield Herefs 34 J10
Sarn Park Services Brdgnd 26 G11
Sarn-wen Powys 44 G10
Saron Carmth 25 Q3
Saron Carmth 25 V8
Saron Gwynd 52 G11
Saron Gwynd 52 H9
Sarratt Herts 20 H3
Sarre Kent 13 Q3
Sarsden Oxon 29 Q3
Sarson Hants 19 M12
Satley Dur 69 P4
Satmar Kent 13 Q8
Satron N York 68 K13
Satterleigh Devon 15 Q8
Satterthwaite Cumb 61 Q1
Satwell Oxon 20 B6
Sauchen Abers 105 L13
Saucher P & K 90 J5
Sauchieburn Abers 99 M10
Saul Gloucs 28 D6
Saundby Notts 58 C9
Saundersfoot Pembks 24 K10
Saunderton Bucks 30 G12
Saunton Devon 15 L5
Sausthorpe Lincs 59 Q13
Saveock Cnwll 2 K7
Saverley Green Staffs 46 C6
Savile Town Kirk 56 K2
Sawbridge Warwks 37 P7
Sawbridgeworth Herts 22 C5
Sawdon N York 65 L3
Sawley Derbys 47 N7
Sawley Lancs 62 F10
Sawley N York 63 Q6
Sawston Cambs 39 Q11
Sawtry Cambs 38 J4
Saxby Leics 48 B10
Saxby Lincs 58 H9
Saxby All Saints N Linc 58 G3
Saxelbye Leics 47 S9
Saxham Street Suffk 40 J8
Saxilby Lincs 58 E11
Saxlingham Norfk 50 H6
Saxlingham Green Norfk 41 M1
Saxlingham Nethergate Norfk 41 M1
Saxlingham Thorpe Norfk 41 M1
Saxmundham Suffk 41 Q8
Saxondale Notts 47 S6
Saxon Street Cambs 39 U9
Saxtead Suffk 41 N7
Saxtead Green Suffk 41 N8
Saxtead Little Green Suffk 41 M7
Saxthorpe Norfk 50 K7
Saxton N York 64 B12
Sayers Common W Susx 11 M7
Scackleton N York 64 E5
Scafell Pike Cumb 66 K11
Scaftworth Notts 57 U8
Scagglethorpe N York 64 J5
Scalasaig Ag & B 86 F7
Scalby E R Yk 64 J14
Scalby N York 65 N1
Scald End Bed 38 F9
Scaldwell Nhants 37 U6
Scaleby Cumb 75 T13
Scalebyhill Cumb 75 T13
Scale Houses Cumb 67 S3
Scales Cumb 61 P5
Scales Cumb 67 M7
Scalesceugh Cumb 67 P3
Scalford Leics 47 U9
Scaling N York 71 M10
Scaling Dam R & Cl 71 M10
Scalloway Shet 106 u10
Scalpay Highld 100 f6
Scamblesby Lincs 59 N11
Scammonden Kirk 56 G3
Scamodale Highld 93 U4
Scampston N York 64 K4
Scampton Lincs 58 G11
Scaniport Highld 102 H8
Scapegoat Hill Kirk 56 G3
Scarba Ag & B 87 M5
Scarborough N York 65 N2
Scarcewater Cnwll 3 N6
Scarcliffe Derbys 57 Q13
Scarcroft Leeds 63 T11
Scarfskerry Highld 112 G2
Scargill Dur 69 N10
Scarinish Ag & B 92 C10
Scarisbrick Lancs 54 J4
Scarness Cumb 66 K6
Scarning Norfk 50 G11
Scarrington Notts 47 T5
Scarth Hill Lancs 54 K5
Scarthingwell N York 64 B12
Scartho NE Lin 59 N5
Scatsta Airport Shet 106 t6
Scawby N Linc 58 G5
Scawsby Donc 57 R6
Scawthorpe Donc 57 S6
Scawton N York 64 C3
Scayne's Hill W Susx 11 P6
Scethrog Powys 27 L2
Scholar Green Ches E 45 T2
Scholemoor Crematorium C Brad 63 N13
Scholes Kirk 56 J1
Scholes Kirk 56 J5
Scholes Leeds 63 T12
Scholes Rothm 57 N7
Scholes Wigan 55 N5
School Aycliffe Dur 69 S8
School Green C Brad 63 N13
School Green Ches W 55 P14
Schoolgreen Wokham 20 B9
School House Dorset 7 L4
Scissett Kirk 56 K4
Scleddau Pembks 24 F4
Scofton Notts 57 T10
Scole Norfk 41 L5
Scone P & K 90 H6
Sconser Highld 100 e6
Scoonie Fife 91 N11
Scopwick Lincs 48 G2
Scoraig Highld 107 T5
Scorborough E R Yk 65 N10
Scorrier Cnwll 2 J8
Scorriton Devon 5 S7
Scorton Lancs 61 U10
Scorton N York 69 S12
Sco Ruston Norfk 51 N9
Scotby Cumb 67 P1
Scotch Corner N York 69 R11
Scotforth Lancs 61 T8
Scot Hay Staffs 45 S4
Scothern Lincs 58 H11
Scotland Lincs 48 F7
Scotland Gate Nthumb 77 R9
Scotlandwell P & K 90 J11
Scot Lane End Bolton 55 P5
Scotscalder Station Highld 112 C5
Scotsdike Cumb 75 S11
Scot's Gap Nthumb 77 L8
Scotsmill Abers 104 H12
Scotstoun C Glas 89 M12
Scotswood N u Ty 77 Q13
Scotter Lincs 58 E6
Scotterthorpe Lincs 58 E6
Scottish Seabird Centre E Loth 84 F1
Scottish Wool Centre Stirlg 89 M5
Scottlethorpe Lincs 48 G9
Scotton Lincs 58 E7
Scotton N York 63 S8
Scotton N York 69 Q13
Scottow Norfk 51 N9
Scott Willoughby Lincs 48 G6
Scoulton Norfk 50 G13
Scounslow Green Staffs 46 E8
Scourie Highld 110 D8
Scourie More Highld 110 C8
Scousburgh Shet 106 t12
Scouthead Oldham 56 E5
Scrabster Highld 112 D2
Scraesburgh Border 76 D2
Scrafield Lincs 59 P13
Scrainwood Nthumb 76 K4
Scrane End Lincs 49 N5
Scraptoft Leics 47 R12
Scratby Norfk 51 T10
Scrayingham N York 64 G8
Scrays E Susx 12 E12
Scredington Lincs 48 G5
Scremby Lincs 59 R13
Scremerston Nthumb 85 Q9
Screveton Notts 47 T5
Scrivelsby Lincs 59 N13
Scriven N York 63 S8
Scrooby Notts 57 U8
Scropton Derbys 46 G7
Scrub Hill Lincs 48 K2
Scruton N York 63 R1
Scuggate Cumb 75 T11
Scullomie Highld 111 N4
Sculthorpe Norfk 50 E7
Scunthorpe N Linc 58 E4
Scurlage Swans 25 S13
Sea Somset 6 K2
Seaborough Dorset 7 M3
Seabridge Staffs 45 T5
Seabrook Kent 13 N8
Seaburn Sundld 77 U14
Seacombe Wirral 54 H8
Seacroft Leeds 63 T12
Seacroft Lincs 49 S1
Seadyke Lincs 49 M6
Seafield Highld 100 d5
Seafield W Loth 82 K5
Seafield Crematorium C Edin 83 Q3
Seaford E Susx 11 R11
Seaforth Sefton 54 H7
Seagrave Leics 47 R10
Seagry Heath Wilts 18 E4
Seaham Dur 70 F3
Seahouses Nthumb 85 U12
Seal Kent 21 U11
Sealand Flints 54 J13
Seale Surrey 20 E13
Seamer N York 65 N3
Seamer N York 70 G10
Seamill N Ayrs 80 J3
Sea Palling Norfk 51 R8
Searby Lincs 58 J5
Seasalter Kent 13 L3
Seascale Cumb 66 F12
Seathwaite Cumb 66 K10
Seathwaite Cumb 66 K13
Seatle Cumb 61 R3
Seatoller Cumb 66 K10
Seaton Cnwll 4 J10
Seaton Cumb 66 F6
Seaton Devon 6 H6
Seaton Dur 70 E3
Seaton E R Yk 65 R10
Seaton Kent 13 P4
Seaton Nthumb 77 S10
Seaton Rutlnd 48 D14
Seaton Burn N Tyne 77 Q11
Seaton Carew Hartpl 70 H7
Seaton Delaval Nthumb 77 S10
Seaton Ross E R Yk 64 H11
Seaton Sluice Nthumb 77 S10
Seatown Dorset 7 M6
Seave Green N York 70 J12
Seaview IoW 9 S10
Seaville Cumb 66 J2
Seavington St Mary Somset 7 M2
Seavington St Michael Somset 17 M13
Sebastopol Torfn 27 P8
Sebergham Cumb 67 N4
Seckington Warwks 46 J12
Sedbergh Cumb 62 D1
Sedbury Gloucs 27 U9
Sedbusk N York 62 H1
Sedgeberrow Worcs 36 D13
Sedgebrook Lincs 48 C6
Sedge Fen Suffk 39 U4
Sedgefield Dur 70 E7
Sedgeford Norfk 50 B6
Sedgehill Wilts 8 B3
Sedgemoor Services Somset 17 L6
Sedgley Dudley 36 B2
Sedgley Park Bury 55 T6
Sedgwick Cumb 61 U2
Sedlescombe E Susx 12 E12
Sedrup Bucks 30 H10
Seed Kent 12 H4
Seend Wilts 18 D8
Seend Cleeve Wilts 18 D8
Seer Green Bucks 20 G4
Seething Norfk 41 P1
Sefton Sefton 54 J6
Sefton Town Sefton 54 H6
Seghill Nthumb 77 R11
Seighford Staffs 45 U8
Seion Gwynd 52 H9
Seisdon Staffs 35 T1
Selattyn Shrops 44 G7
Selborne Hants 9 U2
Selby N York 64 E13
Selham W Susx 10 E6
Selhurst Gt Lon 21 P9
Selkirk Border 84 D13
Sellack Herefs 27 V2
Sellafirth Shet 106 v4
Sellan Cnwll 2 C10
Sellick's Green Somset 16 H13
Sellindge Kent 13 L8
Selling Kent 12 K4
Sells Green Wilts 18 D8
Selly Oak Birm 36 D4
Selmeston E Susx 11 S9
Selsdon Gt Lon 21 Q10
Selsey Gloucs 28 F7
Selsey W Susx 10 D12
Selsfield Common W Susx 11 N4
Selside Cumb 67 R13
Selside N York 62 F4
Selsted Kent 13 P7
Selston Notts 47 N3
Selworthy Somset 16 B7
Semer Suffk 40 G11
Semington Wilts 18 C8
Semley Wilts 8 B3
Sempringham Lincs 48 H7
Send Surrey 20 H11
Send Marsh Surrey 20 H11
Senghenydd Caerph 27 L9
Sennen Cnwll 2 B11
Sennen Cove Cnwll 2 B11
Sennybridge Powys 26 G2
Serlby Notts 57 T9
Sessay N York 64 B4
Setchey Norfk 49 T11
Setley Hants 9 L8
Seton Mains E Loth 84 C3
Settle N York 62 G7
Settrington N York 64 J5
Seven Ash Somset 16 G10
Sevenhampton Gloucs 28 K3
Sevenhampton Swindn 29 P9
Seven Hills Crematorium Suffk 41 M12
Seven Kings Gt Lon 21 S5
Sevenoaks Kent 21 T11
Sevenoaks Weald Kent 21 T12
Seven Sisters Neath 26 E6
Seven Springs Gloucs 28 J4
Seven Star Green Essex 23 M2
Severn Beach S Glos 27 U11
Severn Stoke Worcs 35 U12
Severn View Services S Glos 27 V10
Sevick End Bed 38 G10
Sevington Kent 12 K7
Sewards End Essex 39 S13
Sewardstonebury Essex 21 Q3
Sewell C Beds 31 L8
Sewerby E R Yk 65 R6
Seworgan Cnwll 2 J10
Sewstern Leics 48 C9
Sexhow N York 70 G11
Sezincote Gloucs 29 N1
Sgiogarstaigh W Isls 106 k2
Shabbington Bucks 30 E11
Shackerley Shrops 45 T12
Shackerstone Leics 47 L12
Shacklecross Derbys 47 M7
Shackleford Surrey 20 F13
Shade Calder 56 D2
Shader W Isls 106 i3
Shadforth Dur 70 D4
Shadingfield Suffk 41 R4
Shadoxhurst Kent 12 J8
Shadwell Leeds 63 S12
Shadwell Norfk 40 F4
Shaftenhoe End Herts 39 P13
Shaftesbury Dorset 8 B4
Shaftholme Donc 57 S5
Shafton Barns 57 N4
Shafton Two Gates Barns 57 N4
Shakerley Wigan 55 Q6
Shalbourne Wilts 19 M8
Shalcombe IoW 9 M11
Shalden Hants 19 U12
Shalden Green Hants 19 U12
Shaldon Devon 6 B10
Shalfleet IoW 9 N11
Shalford Essex 22 H2
Shalford Surrey 20 H13
Shalford Green Essex 22 H2
Shallowford Staffs 45 U8
Shalmsford Street Kent 13 L5
Shalstone Bucks 30 D5
Shamley Green Surrey 10 G2
Shandford Angus 98 H11
Shandon Ag & B 88 G8
Shandwick Highld 109 R9
Shangton Leics 37 T1

Shankhouse Nthumb 77 R10
Shanklin IoW 9 R12
Shap Cumb 67 S9
Shapinsay Ork 106 u18
Shapwick Dorset 8 C8
Shapwick Somset 17 M9
Shard End Birm 36 G3
Shardlow Derbys 47 M7
Shareshill Staffs 46 B12
Sharlston Wakefd 57 N3
Sharlston Common Wakefd 57 N3
Sharman's Cross Solhll 36 F5
Sharnal Street Medway 22 J13
Sharnbrook Bed 38 E9
Sharneyford Lancs 56 C2
Sharnford Leics 37 N2
Sharnhill Green Dorset 7 T3
Sharoe Green Lancs 61 U13
Sharow N York 63 S5
Sharpenhoe C Beds 31 N6
Sharperton Nthumb 76 K5
Sharp Green Norfk 51 Q9
Sharpness Gloucs 28 C7
Sharpthorne W Susx 11 P4
Sharptor Cnwll 4 H6
Sharpway Gate Worcs 36 C7
Sharrington Norfk 50 H6
Shatterford Worcs 35 S4
Shatterling Kent 13 Q4
Shatton Derbys 56 K10
Shaugh Prior Devon 5 N8
Shave Cross Dorset 7 M5
Shavington Ches E 45 Q3
Shaw C Brad 63 L12
Shaw Oldham 56 D5
Shaw Swindn 29 M10
Shaw W Berk 19 Q7
Shaw Wilts 18 C7
Shawbirch Wrekin 45 P11
Shawbost W Isls 106 h4
Shawbury Shrops 45 N9
Shawclough Rochdl 56 C4
Shaw Common Gloucs 28 C2
Shawdon Hill Nthumb 77 M3
Shawell Leics 37 P4
Shawford Hants 9 P3
Shawforth Lancs 56 C2
Shaw Green Herts 31 T6
Shaw Green Lancs 55 M3
Shaw Green N York 63 R9
Shawhead D & G 74 G10
Shaw Mills N York 63 R7
Shawsburn S Lans 82 E8
Shear Cross Wilts 18 C12
Shearington D & G 74 K12
Shearsby Leics 37 R2
Shearston Somset 16 J10
Shebbear Devon 14 K11
Shebdon Staffs 45 S8
Shebster Highld 112 B4
Sheddens E Rens 81 R1
Shedfield Hants 9 R6
Sheen Staffs 46 F1
Sheepbridge Derbys 57 N12
Sheep Hill Dur 69 Q1
Sheepridge Kirk 56 J3
Sheepscar Leeds 63 S13
Sheepscombe Gloucs 28 G5
Sheepstor Devon 5 P7
Sheepwash Devon 15 L11
Sheepwash Nthumb 77 R8
Sheepway N Som 27 T12
Sheepy Magna Leics 46 K13
Sheepy Parva Leics 46 K13
Sheering Essex 22 D5
Sheerness Kent 23 M13
Sheerwater Surrey 20 H10
Sheet Hants 10 B6
Sheffield Cnwll 2 D11
Sheffield Sheff 57 N9
Sheffield Bottom W Berk 19 T7
Sheffield City Road Crematorium Sheff 57 N9
Sheffield Green E Susx 11 Q5
Sheffield Park E Susx 11 Q6
Shefford C Beds 31 P5
Sheigra Highld 110 D4
Sheinton Shrops 45 P13
Shelderton Shrops 34 K5
Sheldon Birm 36 G4
Sheldon Derbys 56 J13
Sheldon Devon 6 F3
Sheldwich Kent 12 K4
Sheldwich Lees Kent 12 K4
Shelf Calder 63 N14
Shelfanger Norfk 40 K4
Shelfield Warwks 36 F8
Shelfield Wsall 46 D13
Shelfield Green Warwks 36 F8
Shelford Notts 47 S5
Shelford Warwks 37 M3
Shellacres Nthumb 85 M10
Shelley Essex 22 E6
Shelley Kirk 56 K4
Shelley Suffk 40 H13
Shelley Far Bank Kirk 56 K4
Shellingford Oxon 29 R9
Shellow Bowells Essex 22 F6
Shelsley Beauchamp Worcs 35 R8
Shelsley Walsh Worcs 35 R8
Shelton Bed 38 F7
Shelton Norfk 41 M2
Shelton Notts 47 U5
Shelton Shrops 45 L11
Shelton Green Norfk 41 M2
Shelton Lock C Derb 47 L7
Shelton Under Harley Staffs 45 T6
Shelve Shrops 44 H14
Shelwick Herefs 35 M12
Shenfield Essex 22 F8
Shenington Oxon 37 L12
Shenley Herts 31 Q12
Shenley Brook End M Keyn 30 H5
Shenleybury Herts 31 Q12
Shenley Church End M Keyn 30 H5
Shenmore Herefs 34 J13
Shennanton D & G 72 J7
Shenstone Staffs 46 F13
Shenstone Worcs 35 U6
Shenstone Woodend Staffs 46 F13
Shenton Leics 47 L14
Shenval Moray 103 V10
Shepeau Stow Lincs 49 M11
Shephall Herts 31 S8
Shepherd's Bush Gt Lon 21 M6
Shepherd's Green Oxon 20 B6
Shepherds Patch Gloucs 28 D7
Shepherdswell Kent 13 Q6
Shepley Kirk 56 J5
Shepperdine S Glos 28 B8
Shepperton Surrey 20 J9
Shepperton Green Surrey 20 J9
Shepreth Cambs 39 N11
Shepshed Leics 47 N10
Shepton Beauchamp Somset 17 M13
Shepton Mallet Somset 17 R8
Shepton Montague Somset 17 S10
Shepway Kent 12 E5
Sheraton Dur 70 F5
Sherborne Dorset 17 R13
Sherborne Gloucs 29 N5
Sherborne Somset 17 Q5
Sherborne St John Hants 19 T9
Sherbourne Warwks 36 J8
Sherburn Dur 70 D4
Sherburn N York 65 M4
Sherburn Hill Dur 70 D4
Sherburn in Elmet N York 64 B13
Shere Surrey 20 J13
Shereford Norfk 50 E8
Sherfield English Hants 8 K4
Sherfield on Loddon Hants 19 U9
Sherfin Lancs 55 S1
Sherford Devon 5 T12
Sherford Dorset 8 C10
Sheriffhales Shrops 45 S11
Sheriff Hutton N York 64 F6
Sheringham Norfk 51 L5
Sherington M Keyn 38 C11
Shermanbury W Susx 11 L7
Shernborne Norfk 50 B7
Sherrington Wilts 18 E13
Sherston Wilts 28 G10
Sherwood C Nott 47 Q5
Sherwood Forest Notts 47 R1
Sherwood Forest Crematorium Notts 57 U13
Shetland Islands Shet 106 u8
Shettleston C Glas 89 P13
Shevington Wigan 55 M5
Shevington Moor Wigan 55 M4
Shevington Vale Wigan 55 M5
Sheviock Cnwll 4 K9
Shibden Head C Brad 63 M14
Shide IoW 9 Q11
Shidlaw Nthumb 85 L11
Shiel Bridge Highld 101 N8
Shieldaig Highld 107 P14
Shieldhill D & G 74 K8
Shieldhill Falk 82 G3
Shieldhill House Hotel S Lans 82 K10
Shields N Lans 82 E7
Shielfoot Highld 93 R4
Shielhill Angus 98 G12
Shielhill Inver 88 F11
Shifford Oxon 29 S7
Shifnal Shrops 45 R12
Shilbottle Nthumb 77 P4
Shildon Dur 69 R7
Shillford E Rens 81 P1
Shillingford Devon 16 C12
Shillingford Oxon 19 S2
Shillingford Abbot Devon 6 B7
Shillingford St George Devon 6 B7
Shillingstone Dorset 8 A6
Shillington C Beds 31 P6
Shillmoor Nthumb 76 H4
Shilton Oxon 29 Q6
Shilton Warwks 37 M4
Shimpling Norfk 41 L4
Shimpling Suffk 40 E10
Shimpling Street Suffk 40 E10
Shincliffe Dur 69 S4
Shiney Row Sundld 70 D2
Shinfield Wokham 20 B9
Shingay Cambs 39 M11
Shingle Street Suffk 41 Q12
Shinnersbridge Devon 5 T8
Shinness Highld 108 J2
Shipbourne Kent 21 U12
Shipdham Norfk 50 G12
Shipham Somset 17 M5
Shiphay Torbay 6 A11
Shiplake Oxon 20 C7
Shiplake Row Oxon 20 B7
Shiplate N Som 17 L5
Shipley C Brad 63 P12
Shipley Derbys 47 M5
Shipley Shrops 35 T1
Shipley W Susx 10 J6
Shipley Bridge Surrey 11 N2
Shipley Hatch Kent 12 K8
Shipmeadow Suffk 41 Q2
Shippea Hill Station Cambs 39 T4
Shippon Oxon 29 U8
Shipston-on-Stour Warwks 36 J12
Shipton Bucks 30 G7
Shipton Gloucs 28 K4
Shipton N York 64 D8
Shipton Shrops 35 N2
Shipton Bellinger Hants 18 K11
Shipton Gorge Dorset 7 N6
Shipton Green W Susx 10 C11
Shipton Moyne Gloucs 28 G10
Shipton-on-Cherwell Oxon 29 U4
Shiptonthorpe E R Yk 64 K11
Shipton-under-Wychwood Oxon 29 Q4
Shirburn Oxon 30 E13
Shirdley Hill Lancs 54 J4
Shire Cumb 68 D5
Shirebrook Derbys 57 R13
Shiregreen Sheff 57 N8
Shirehampton Bristl 27 U12
Shiremoor N Tyne 77 S11
Shirenewton Mons 27 T9
Shire Oak Wsall 46 E13
Shireoaks Notts 57 S10
Shirkoak Kent 12 H8
Shirland Derbys 47 M2
Shirlett Shrops 45 P14
Shirley C Sotn 9 N6
Shirley Derbys 46 H5
Shirley Gt Lon 21 Q9
Shirley Solhll 36 F5
Shirl Heath Herefs 34 K9
Shirrell Heath Hants 9 R6
Shirvan Ag & B 87 R9
Shirwell Devon 15 P5
Shiskine N Ayrs 79 S10
Shittlehope Dur 69 M5
Shobdon Herefs 34 K8
Shobley Hants 8 H7
Shobrooke Devon 15 U12
Shoby Leics 47 S9
Shocklach Ches W 44 K4
Shocklach Green Ches W 44 K4
Shoeburyness Sthend 23 M10
Sholden Kent 13 S5
Sholing C Sotn 9 P6
Shoot Hill Shrops 44 K11
Shop Cnwll 3 M2
Shop Cnwll 14 F10
Shopwyke W Susx 10 D9
Shore Rochdl 56 D3
Shoreditch Gt Lon 21 P6
Shoreditch Somset 16 H12
Shoreham Kent 21 T10
Shoreham Airport W Susx 11 L9
Shoreham-by-Sea W Susx 11 L9
Shoreswood Nthumb 85 N9
Shorley Hants 9 R3
Shorncote Gloucs 28 K8
Shorne Kent 22 G13
Shorta Cross Cnwll 4 H9
Shortbridge E Susx 11 R6
Shortfield Common Surrey 10 C2
Shortgate E Susx 11 R7
Short Heath Birm 36 E2
Shortheath Hants 10 B3
Short Heath Wsall 46 C13
Shortlanesend Cnwll 3 L7
Shortlees E Ayrs 81 N5
Shortstown Bed 38 G11
Shorwell IoW 9 P12
Shoscombe BaNES 17 T5
Shotesham Norfk 51 M14
Shotgate Essex 22 J9
Shotley Suffk 41 M13
Shotley Bridge Dur 69 N2
Shotleyfield Nthumb 69 N2
Shotley Gate Suffk 41 M14
Shotley Street Suffk 41 M13
Shottenden Kent 12 K5
Shottermill Surrey 10 D4
Shottery Warwks 36 G10
Shotteswell Warwks 37 M11
Shottisham Suffk 41 P12
Shottle Derbys 46 K4
Shottlegate Derbys 46 K4
Shotton Dur 70 E7
Shotton Dur 70 F5
Shotton Flints 54 H13
Shotton Nthumb 77 Q10
Shotton Nthumb 85 L12
Shotton Colliery Dur 70 E4
Shotts N Lans 82 G7
Shotwick Ches W 54 H12
Shougle Moray 103 V4
Shouldham Norfk 49 U12
Shouldham Thorpe Norfk 49 U12
Shoulton Worcs 35 T9
Shover's Green E Susx 12 C9
Shraleybrook Staffs 45 S4
Shrawardine Shrops 44 J10
Shrawley Worcs 35 T7
Shreding Green Bucks 20 H6
Shrewley Warwks 36 H7
Shrewsbury Shrops 45 L11
Shrewton Wilts 18 G12
Shripney W Susx 10 E10
Shrivenham Oxon 29 P10
Shropham Norfk 40 G2
Shrub End Essex 23 N3
Shucknall Herefs 35 N12
Shudy Camps Cambs 39 T12
Shuna Ag & B 87 P4
Shurdington Gloucs 28 H4
Shurlock Row W & M 20 D8
Shurnock Worcs 36 D8
Shurrery Highld 112 B5
Shurrery Lodge Highld 112 B5
Shurton Somset 16 H8
Shustoke Warwks 36 H2
Shute Devon 6 J5
Shute Devon 15 U12
Shutford Oxon 37 L12
Shut Heath Staffs 45 U9
Shuthonger Gloucs 35 U13
Shutlanger Nhants 37 T11
Shutterton Devon 6 C9
Shutt Green Staffs 45 U12
Shuttington Warwks 46 J12
Shuttlewood Derbys 57 Q12
Shuttleworth Bury 55 T3
Siabost W Isls 106 h4
Siadar W Isls 106 i3
Sibbertoft Nhants 37 S4
Sibdon Carwood Shrops 34 K4
Sibford Ferris Oxon 37 L13
Sibford Gower Oxon 37 L13
Sible Hedingham Essex 40 C14
Sibley's Green Essex 22 F2
Siblyback Cnwll 4 G6
Sibsey Lincs 49 N3
Sibsey Fenside Lincs 49 M3
Sibson Cambs 38 G1
Sibson Leics 47 L13
Sibster Highld 112 H6
Sibthorpe Notts 47 U4
Sibthorpe Notts 58 B12
Sibton Suffk 41 Q7
Sicklesmere Suffk 40 E8
Sicklinghall N York 63 T10
Sidbrook Somset 16 J11
Sidbury Devon 6 F6
Sidbury Shrops 35 Q3
Sid Cop Barns 57 N5
Sidcot N Som 17 M5
Sidcup Gt Lon 21 S8
Siddick Cumb 66 F6
Siddington Ches E 55 T12
Siddington Gloucs 28 K8
Sidemoor Worcs 36 C6
Sidestrand Norfk 51 N6
Sidford Devon 6 F6
Sidlesham W Susx 10 D11
Sidlesham Common W Susx 10 D11
Sidley E Susx 12 D14
Sidmouth Devon 6 F7
Siefton Shrops 35 L4
Sigford Devon 5 T6
Sigglesthorne E R Yk 65 R10
Sigingstone V Glam 16 C2
Signet Oxon 29 P5
Silchester Hants 19 T8
Sileby Leics 47 R10
Silecroft Cumb 61 L3
Silfield Norfk 50 K14
Silian Cerdgn 33 L10
Silkstead Hants 9 N4
Silkstone Barns 57 L5
Silkstone Common Barns 57 L6
Silk Willoughby Lincs 48 G5
Silloth Cumb 66 H2
Silpho N York 65 M1
Silsden C Brad 63 L10
Silsoe C Beds 31 N5
Silton Dorset 17 U11
Silverburn Mdloth 83 P6
Silverdale Lancs 61 T5
Silverdale Staffs 45 T4
Silver End Essex 22 K4
Silverford Abers 105 M3
Silvergate Norfk 51 L8
Silverlace Green Suffk 41 P8
Silverley's Green Suffk 41 N5
Silverstone Nhants 30 E4
Silver Street Kent 12 G3
Silver Street Somset 17 P10
Silverton Devon 6 C4
Silverwell Cnwll 2 J7
Silvington Shrops 35 P5
Simister Bury 55 T5
Simmondley Derbys 56 F8
Simonburn Nthumb 76 H11
Simonsbath Somset 15 S5
Simonsburrow Devon 16 F13
Simonstone Lancs 62 F13
Simonstone N York 62 H1
Simprim Border 85 L9
Simpson M Keyn 30 J5
Simpson Cross Pembks 24 E7
Sinclair's Hill Border 85 L8
Sinclairston E Ayrs 81 P9
Sinderby N York 63 S3
Sinderhope Nthumb 68 H2
Sinderland Green Traffd 55 R9
Sindlesham Wokham 20 C9
Sinfin C Derb 46 K7
Singleborough Bucks 30 G6
Single Street Gt Lon 21 R11
Singleton Kent 12 K7
Singleton Lancs 61 R12
Singleton W Susx 10 D8
Singlewell Kent 22 G13
Sinkhurst Green Kent 12 F7
Sinnarhard Abers 104 F13
Sinnington N York 64 G2
Sinton Worcs 35 T8
Sinton Worcs 35 T8
Sinton Green Worcs 35 T8
Sipson Gt Lon 20 J7
Sirhowy Blae G 27 L5
Sissinghurst Kent 12 E8
Siston S Glos 28 C12
Sitcott Devon 4 K2
Sithney Cnwll 2 G11
Sithney Common Cnwll 2 G11
Sithney Green Cnwll 2 G11
Sittingbourne Kent 12 H3
Six Ashes Shrops 35 S3
Six Bells Blae G 27 N7
Sixhills Lincs 59 L9
Six Mile Bottom Cambs 39 S9
Sixmile Cottages Kent 13 M7
Sixpenny Handley Dorset 8 D5
Six Rues Jersey 7 C2
Sizewell Suffk 41 S8
Skaill Ork 106 u19
Skara Brae Ork 106 r18
Skares E Ayrs 81 Q9
Skateraw Abers 99 S5
Skateraw E Loth 84 J3
Skeabost Highld 100 d5
Skeeby N York 69 Q12
Skeffington Leics 47 T13
Skeffling E R Yk 59 Q3
Skegby Notts 47 N1
Skegby Notts 58 C13
Skegness Lincs 59 U14
Skelbo Highld 109 P5
Skelbo Street Highld 109 P6
Skelbrooke Donc 57 R4
Skeldyke Lincs 49 M6
Skellingthorpe Lincs 58 F12
Skellorn Green Ches E 56 D10
Skellow Donc 57 R4
Skelmanthorpe Kirk 56 K4
Skelmersdale Lancs 55 L5
Skelmorlie N Ayrs 88 E12
Skelpick Highld 111 Q5
Skelston D & G 74 F8
Skelton C York 64 D8
Skelton Cumb 67 P5
Skelton E R Yk 58 C1
Skelton N York 63 T6
Skelton N York 69 N12
Skelton R & Cl 71 L9
Skelwith Bridge Cumb 67 M12
Skendleby Lincs 59 R13
Skene House Abers 105 M13
Skenfrith Mons 27 T3
Skerne E R Yk 65 N8
Skerray Highld 111 P4
Skerricha Highld 110 E6
Skerton Lancs 61 T7
Sketchley Leics 37 M2
Sketty Swans 25 V12
Skewen Neath 26 C8
Skewsby N York 64 E5
Skeyton Norfk 51 M8
Skeyton Corner Norfk 51 N8
Skiall Highld 112 B3
Skidbrooke Lincs 59 R8
Skidbrooke North End Lincs 59 R7
Skidby E R Yk 65 N13
Skigersta W Isls 106 k2
Skilgate Somset 16 C11
Skillington Lincs 48 C8
Skinburness Cumb 66 H1
Skinflats Falk 82 H2
Skinidin Highld 100 b5
Skinners Green W Berk 19 P7
Skinningrove R & Cl 71 M9
Skipness Ag & B 79 S4
Skipper's Bridge D & G 75 S9
Skiprigg Cumb 67 N3
Skipsea E R Yk 65 R9
Skipsea Brough E R Yk 65 R9
Skipton N York 62 K9
Skipton-on-Swale N York 63 T4
Skipwith N York 64 F12
Skirlaugh E R Yk 65 Q12
Skirling Border 83 L11
Skirmett Bucks 20 C4
Skirpenbeck E R Yk 64 G8
Skirwith Cumb 68 D6
Skirwith N York 62 E5
Skirza Highld 112 J3
Skitby Cumb 75 T12
Skittle Green Bucks 30 G12
Skokholm Island Pembks 24 B10
Skomer Island Pembks 24 B9
Skulamus Highld 100 f7
Skyborry Green Shrops 34 G6
Skye Green Essex 23 L3
Skye of Curr Highld 103 Q11
Skyreholme N York 63 M7
Slack Calder 62 K14
Slackcote Oldham 56 E5
Slack Head Cumb 61 T4
Slackholme End Lincs 59 T12
Slacks of Cairnbanno Abers 105 N6
Slad Gloucs 28 G6
Slade Devon 6 F3
Slade Devon 15 M3
Slade Devon 15 T7
Slade End Oxon 19 S2
Slade Green Gt Lon 22 D12
Slade Heath Staffs 46 B12
Slade Hooton Rothm 57 R9
Sladesbridge Cnwll 3 Q2
Slades Green Worcs 35 T14
Slaggyford Nthumb 68 E2
Slaidburn Lancs 62 E9
Slaithwaite Kirk 56 G4
Slaley Derbys 46 J2
Slaley Nthumb 76 K14
Slamannan Falk 82 G4
Slapton Bucks 30 K8
Slapton Devon 5 U11
Slapton Nhants 37 R11
Slattocks Rochdl 56 C5
Slaugham W Susx 11 M5
Slaughterford Wilts 18 B6
Slawston Leics 37 U2
Sleaford Hants 10 C3
Sleaford Lincs 48 G4
Sleagill Cumb 67 S9
Sleap Shrops 45 L8
Sleapford Wrekin 45 P10
Sleapshyde Herts 31 Q11
Sleasdairidh Highld 109 L5
Slebech Pembks 24 H7
Sledge Green Worcs 35 T14
Sledmere E R Yk 65 L7
Sleetbeck Cumb 75 V10
Sleight Dorset 8 D9
Sleightholme Dur 69 L10
Sleights N York 71 Q11
Slepe Dorset 8 C10
Slickly Highld 112 G3
Sliddery N Ayrs 79 S11
Sligachan Highld 100 d7
Sligrachan Ag & B 88 E7
Slimbridge Gloucs 28 D7
Slimbridge Wetland Centre Gloucs 28 D6
Slindon Staffs 45 T7
Slindon W Susx 10 F9
Slinfold W Susx 10 J4
Sling Gwynd 52 K9
Slingsby N York 64 F5
Slip End C Beds 31 N9
Slip End Herts 31 S5
Slipton Nhants 38 E5
Slitting Mill Staffs 46 D10
Slockavullin Ag & B 87 Q6
Sloley Norfk 51 N9
Sloncombe Devon 5 S3
Sloothby Lincs 59 S12
Slough Slough 20 G7
Slough Crematorium Bucks 20 G6
Slough Green Somset 16 J13
Slough Green W Susx 11 M5
Slumbay Highld 101 M4
Slyfield Green Surrey 20 G12
Slyne Lancs 61 T6
Smailholm Border 84 G11
Smallbridge Rochdl 56 D3
Smallbrook Devon 15 U13
Smallbrook Gloucs 28 A7
Smallburgh Norfk 51 P9
Smalldale Derbys 56 G11
Smalldale Derbys 56 J10
Small Dole W Susx 11 L8
Smalley Derbys 47 M5
Smalley Common Derbys 47 M5
Smalley Green Derbys 47 M5
Smallfield Surrey 11 N2
Small Heath Birm 36 F3
Small Hythe Kent 12 G9
Smallridge Devon 6 K4
Smallthorne C Stke 45 U3
Smallways N York 69 P10
Smallwood Ches E 45 T1
Small Wood Hey Lancs 61 R10
Smallworth Norfk 40 H4
Smannell Hants 19 N11
Smardale Cumb 68 F11
Smarden Kent 12 G7
Smarden Bell Kent 12 G7
Smart's Hill Kent 11 S2
Smeafield Nthumb 85 R11
Smearisary Highld 93 Q3
Smeatharpe Devon 6 G2
Smeeth Kent 13 L8
Smeeton Westerby Leics 37 S2
Smelthouses N York 63 P7
Smerral Highld 112 E10
Smestow Staffs 35 U2
Smethwick Sandw 36 D3
Smethwick Green Ches E 55 T14
Smisby Derbys 46 K10
Smitheclose IoW 9 Q10
Smith End Green Worcs 35 S10
Smithfield Cumb 75 T12
Smith Green Lancs 61 T8
Smithies Barns 57 N5
Smithincott Devon 6 E2
Smith's End Herts 39 P13
Smith's Green Essex 22 E3
Smith's Green Essex 39 U12
Smithstown Highld 107 N9
Smithton Highld 102 K6
Smithy Bridge Rochdl 56 D3
Smithy Green Ches E 55 R12
Smithy Green Stockp 56 C9
Smithy Houses Derbys 47 L4
Smockington Leics 37 N3
Smoo Highld 110 J3
Smythe's Green Essex 23 M4
Snade D & G 74 F8
Snailbeach Shrops 44 J13
Snailwell Cambs 39 T7
Snainton N York 65 L3
Snaith E R Yk 57 T2
Snake Pass Inn Derbys 56 H8
Snape N York 63 R3
Snape Suffk 41 Q9
Snape Green Lancs 54 J4
Snape Street Suffk 41 Q9
Snaresbrook Gt Lon 21 R5
Snarestone Leics 46 K12
Snarford Lincs 58 H10
Snargate Kent 12 J10
Snave Kent 12 K10
Sneachill Worcs 36 B10
Snead Powys 34 H2
Sneath Common Norfk 41 L3
Sneaton N York 71 Q11
Sneatonthorpe N York 71 R11
Snelland Lincs 58 J10
Snelson Ches E 55 T12
Snelston Derbys 46 G5
Snetterton Norfk 40 G2
Snettisham Norfk 49 U7
Snibston Leics 47 M11
Snig's End Gloucs 28 E2
Snitter Nthumb 77 L5
Snitterby Lincs 58 G8
Snitterfield Warwks 36 H9
Snitterton Derbys 46 J1
Snitton Shrops 35 N5
Snoadhill Kent 12 H7
Snodhill Herefs 34 H12
Snodland Kent 12 D3
Snoll Hatch Kent 12 C6
Snowden Hill Barns 57 L6
Snowdon Gwynd 52 K12
Snowdon Kent 13 P5
Snowdonia National Park 43 R8
Snow End Herts 22 B1
Snowshill Gloucs 36 E14
Snow Street Norfk 40 J4
Soake Hants 9 T6
Soar Cardif 26 K11
Soar Devon 5 S13
Soar Powys 26 H1
Soay Highld 100 d8
Soberton Hants 9 S5
Soberton Heath Hants 9 S6
Sockbridge Cumb 67 Q7
Sockburn Darltn 70 D11
Sodom Denbgs 54 C12
Sodylt Bank Shrops 44 H6
Soham Cambs 39 S6
Soham Cotes Cambs 39 S5
Solas W Isls 106 d11
Solbury Pembks 24 E8
Soldon Devon 14 H10
Soldon Cross Devon 14 H10
Soldridge Hants 19 U13
Sole Street Kent 12 C2
Sole Street Kent 13 L6
Solihull Solhll 36 G5
Sollers Dilwyn Herefs 34 K9
Sollers Hope Herefs 35 P14
Sollom Lancs 55 L3
Solva Pembks 24 D6
Solwaybank D & G 75 R10
Somerby Leics 47 U11
Somerby Lincs 58 J5
Somercotes Derbys 47 M3
Somerford Dorset 8 H10
Somerford Keynes Gloucs 28 K8
Somerley W Susx 10 C11
Somerleyton Suffk 41 S1
Somersal Herbert Derbys 46 F6
Somersby Lincs 59 P12
Somersham Cambs 39 N5
Somersham Suffk 40 J11
Somerton Oxon 29 U2
Somerton Somset 17 N11
Somerton Suffk 40 D10
Somerwood Shrops 45 N11
Sompting W Susx 10 K9
Sonning Wokham 20 C7
Sonning Common Oxon 20 B6
Sonning Eye Oxon 20 B7
Sontley Wrexhm 44 H4
Sopley Hants 8 H9
Sopworth Wilts 28 F10
Sorbie D & G 73 L10
Sordale Highld 112 D4
Sorisdale Ag & B 92 H6
Sorn E Ayrs 81 R7
Sortat Highld 112 G4
Sotby Lincs 59 M11
Sots Hole Lincs 58 K14
Sotterley Suffk 41 R4
Soughton Flints 54 F13
Soulbury Bucks 30 J7
Soulby Cumb 67 Q7
Soulby Cumb 68 F10
Souldern Oxon 30 B6
Souldrop Bed 38 E8
Sound Ches E 45 P4
Sound Muir Moray 104 D5
Soundwell S Glos 28 C12
Sourton Devon 5 N2
Soutergate Cumb 61 N3
South Acre Norfk 50 D11
South Alkham Kent 13 P7
Southall Gt Lon 20 K7
South Allington Devon 5 T13
South Alloa Falk 90 C13
Southam Gloucs 28 J2
Southam Warwks 37 M8
South Ambersham W Susx 10 E6
Southampton C Sotn 9 N6
Southampton Airport Hants 9 P5
Southampton Crematorium Hants 9 N5
South Anston Rothm 57 R10
South Ascot W & M 20 F9
South Ashford Kent 12 K7
South Baddesley Hants 9 M9
South Ballachulish Highld 94 F7
South Bank C York 64 D9
South Bank R & Cl 70 H8
South Barrow Somset 17 R11
South Beddington Gt Lon 21 N10
South Beer Cnwll 4 J2
South Benfleet Essex 22 J10
South Bersted W Susx 10 E10
South Bockhampton Dorset 8 H9
Southborough Gt Lon 21 R9
Southborough Kent 11 T2
Southbourne Bmouth 8 G10
Southbourne W Susx 10 B9
South Bowood Dorset 7 M5
South Bramwith Donc 57 T4
South Brent Devon 5 R8
South Brewham Somset 17 T9
South Bristol Crematorium Bristl 17 Q3
South Broomhill Nthumb 77 Q6
Southburgh Norfk 50 H12
South Burlingham Norfk 51 Q12
Southburn E R Yk 65 M9
South Cadbury Somset 17 R11
South Carlton Lincs 58 F11
South Carlton Notts 57 S10
South Cave E R Yk 65 L13
South Cerney Gloucs 28 K8
South Chailey E Susx 11 P7
South Chard Somset 6 K3
South Charlton Nthumb 77 P1
South Cheriton Somset 17 S12
South Church Dur 69 R7
Southchurch Sthend 23 M10
South Cleatlam Dur 69 P9
South Cliffe E R Yk 64 K12
South Clifton Notts 58 D12
South Cockerington Lincs 59 Q9
South Cornelly Brdgnd 26 E11
Southcott Cnwll 14 E13
Southcott Devon 5 T4
Southcott Devon 14 K9
Southcott Devon 15 M13
Southcott Wilts 18 J9
Southcourt Bucks 30 H10
South Cove Suffk 41 S4
South Creake Norfk 50 E6
South Crosland Kirk 56 H4
South Croxton Leics 47 S11
South Dalton E R Yk 65 M10
South Darenth Kent 21 U9
South Downs National Park 11 P9
South Duffield N York 64 F13
Southease E Susx 11 Q9
South Elkington Lincs 59 N9
South Elmsall Wakefd 57 Q4
Southend Ag & B 79 M14
South End E R Yk 59 Q3
South End Hants 8 G5
South End Herefs 35 R12
South End N Linc 58 K2
South End Norfk 40 G2
Southend Wilts 18 J6
Southend Airport Essex 23 L10
Southend Crematorium Sthend 23 L10
Southend-on-Sea Sthend 23 L10
Southernby Cumb 67 N5
Southernden Kent 12 G6
Southerndown V Glam 26 F13
Southerness D & G 66 E2
South Erradale Highld 107 M10
Southerton Devon 6 E6
Southery Norfk 39 T2
South Essex Crematorium Gt Lon 22 E10
South Fambridge Essex 23 L9
South Fawley W Berk 19 N4
South Ferriby N Linc 58 G2
South Field E R Yk 58 H1
Southfield Falk 82 F4
Southfleet Kent 22 F13
Southford IoW 9 Q13
Southgate Gt Lon 21 N4
Southgate Norfk 49 U7
Southgate Norfk 50 E6
Southgate Norfk 50 K9
Southgate Swans 25 U13
South Godstone Surrey 21 Q13
South Gorley Hants 8 H6
South Gosforth N u Ty 77 Q12
South Green Essex 22 G9
South Green Essex 23 P4
South Green Kent 12 G3
South Green Norfk 50 J11
South Green Suffk 41 L5
South Gyle C Edin 83 N4
South Hanningfield Essex 22 H8
South Harting W Susx 10 B7
South Hayling Hants 9 U9
South Hazelrigg Nthumb 85 R12
South Heath Bucks 30 K12
South Heighton E Susx 11 Q10
South Hetton Dur 70 E3
South Hiendley Wakefd 57 N4
South Hill Cnwll 4 J6
South Hill Somset 17 N11
South Hinksey Oxon 30 B12
South Hole Devon 14 F8
South Holmwood Surrey 10 K2
South Hornchurch Gt Lon 22 D11
South Horrington Somset 17 Q7
South Huish Devon 5 R12
South Hykeham Lincs 58 F14
South Hylton Sundld 70 E1
Southill C Beds 31 Q4
Southington Hants 19 R11
South Kelsey Lincs 58 H7
South Kessock Highld 102 J6
South Killingholme N Linc 58 K3
South Kilvington N York 63 U3
South Kilworth Leics 37 R4
South Kirkby Wakefd 57 P4
South Knighton Devon 5 U6
South Kyme Lincs 48 J4
South Lanarkshire Crematorium S Lans 82 C7
Southleigh Devon 6 H6
South Leigh Oxon 29 S6
South Leverton Notts 58 C10
South Littleton Worcs 36 E11
South London Crematorium Gt Lon 21 N9
South Lopham Norfk 40 H4
South Luffenham Rutlnd 48 D13
South Malling E Susx 11 Q8
South Marston Swindn 29 N10
South Merstham Surrey 21 N12
South Middleton Nthumb 85 P14
South Milford N York 64 B13
South Milton Devon 5 S12
South Mimms Herts 31 R12
South Mimms Services Herts 31 R12
Southminster Essex 23 N8
South Molton Devon 15 R7
South Moor Dur 69 Q2
Southmoor Oxon 29 S8
South Moreton Oxon 19 S3
Southmuir Angus 98 F13
South Mundham W Susx 10 D10
South Muskham Notts 47 U2
South Newbald E R Yk 65 L12
South Newington Oxon 37 M14
South Newton Wilts 8 F2
South Normanton Derbys 47 M2
South Norwood Gt Lon 21 P9
South Nutfield Surrey 21 P13
South Ockendon Thurr 22 E11
Southoe Cambs 38 J8
Southolt Suffk 41 L7
South Ormsby Lincs 59 Q11
Southorpe C Pete 48 G13
South Ossett Wakefd 57 L3
South Otterington N York 63 T2
Southover Dorset 7 R6
Southover E Susx 12 C10
South Owersby Lincs 58 J8
Southowram Calder 56 H2
South Park Surrey 21 M13
South Perrott Dorset 7 N3
South Petherton Somset 17 M13
South Petherwin Cnwll 4 J4
South Pickenham Norfk 50 E13
South Pill Cnwll 5 L9
South Pool Devon 5 T12
South Poorton Dorset 7 P5
Southport Sefton 54 H3
Southport Crematorium Lancs 54 J4
South Queensferry C Edin 83 M3
South Radworthy Devon 15 R6
South Rauceby Lincs 48 F4
South Raynham Norfk 50 E9
South Reddish Stockp 56 C8
Southrepps Norfk 51 N6
South Reston Lincs 59 R10
Southrey Lincs 58 K13
South Ronaldsay Ork 106 t21
Southrop Gloucs 29 N7
Southrope Hants 19 U12
South Runcton Norfk 49 T12
South Scarle Notts 58 D14
Southsea C Port 9 T9
Southsea Wrexhm 44 H3
South Shian Ag & B 94 C10
South Shields S Tyne 77 T12
South Shields Crematorium S Tyne 77 S13
South Shore Bpool 61 Q13
Southside Dur 69 P7
South Somercotes Lincs 59 R8
South Stainley N York 63 S7
South Stifford Thurr 22 E12
South Stoke BaNES 17 T4
South Stoke Oxon 19 S4
South Stoke W Susx 10 G9
South Stour Kent 12 K8
South Street Kent 12 B3
South Street Kent 13 L4
South Street Kent 13 M2
South Tarbrax S Lans 82 K8
South Tawton Devon 5 R2
South Tehidy Cnwll 2 H8
South Thoresby Lincs 59 R11
South Thorpe Dur 69 P10
South Town Hants 19 U13
Southtown Norfk 51 T12
Southtown Somset 16 K13
South Uist W Isls 106 d15
Southwaite Cumb 67 P3
Southwaite Services Cumb 67 P3
South Walsham Norfk 51 Q11
Southwark Gt Lon 21 P7
South Warnborough Hants 20 B13
Southwater W Susx 10 K5
Southwater Street W Susx 10 J5
Southway Somset 17 P8
South Weald Essex 22 E9
Southwell Dorset 7 S10
Southwell Notts 47 S3
South West Middlesex Crematorium Gt Lon 20 K8
South Weston Oxon 20 B3
South Wheatley Cnwll 4 G2
Southwick Hants 9 S7
Southwick Nhants 38 F2
Southwick Somset 17 L7
Southwick Sundld 77 T14
Southwick W Susx 11 L9
Southwick Wilts 18 B9
South Widcombe BaNES 17 Q5
South Wigston Leics 47 Q14
South Willesborough Kent 12 K7
South Willingham Lincs 59 L10
South Wingate Dur 70 F6
South Wingfield Derbys 47 L2
South Witham Lincs 48 D10
Southwold Suffk 41 T5
South Wonston Hants 19 Q13
Southwood Norfk 51 Q12
Southwood Somset 17 Q10
South Woodham Ferrers Essex 22 K8
South Wootton Norfk 49 T9
South Wraxall Wilts 18 B8
South Zeal Devon 5 R2
Sowerby Calder 56 F2
Sowerby N York 63 U3
Sowerby Bridge Calder 56 G2
Sowerby Row Cumb 67 N4
Sower Carr Lancs 61 R11
Sowerhill Somset 15 U8
Sowhill Torfn 27 P7
Sowley Green Suffk 40 B10
Sowood Calder 56 G3
Sowton Devon 5 N7
Sowton Devon 6 C6
Soyland Town Calder 56 F2
Spa Common Norfk 51 N7
Spain's End Essex 39 U13
Spalding Lincs 48 K9
Spaldington E R Yk 64 H13
Spaldwick Cambs 38 H6
Spalford Notts 58 D13
Spanby Lincs 48 G6
Spanish Green Hants 19 U9
Sparham Norfk 50 J10
Sparhamill Norfk 50 J10
Spark Bridge Cumb 61 Q3
Sparket Cumb 67 P7
Sparkford Somset 17 R11
Sparkhill Birm 36 F4
Sparkwell Devon 5 P9
Sparrow Green Norfk 50 F11
Sparrowpit Derbys 56 G10
Sparrows Green E Susx 12 B9
Sparsholt Hants 9 N2
Sparsholt Oxon 29 R10
Spartylea Nthumb 68 J3
Spath Staffs 46 E6
Spaunton N York 64 G2
Spaxton Somset 16 H9
Spean Bridge Highld 94 J2
Spear Hill W Susx 10 J7
Spearywell Hants 9 L3
Speen Bucks 20 D3
Speen W Berk 19 Q7
Speeton N York 65 R5
Speke Lpool 54 K10
Speldhurst Kent 11 T2
Spellbrook Herts 22 C4
Spelmonden Kent 12 D8
Spelsbury Oxon 29 R3
Spen Kirk 56 J1
Spencers Wood Wokham 20 B9
Spen Green Ches E 45 T1
Spennithorne N York 63 N2
Spennymoor Dur 69 S6
Spernall Warwks 36 E8
Spetchley Worcs 35 U10
Spetisbury Dorset 8 C8
Spexhall Suffk 41 Q4
Spey Bay Moray 104 D2
Speybridge Highld 103 R10
Speyview Moray 104 B7
Spilsby Lincs 59 R13
Spindlestone Nthumb 85 T12
Spinkhill Derbys 57 Q11
Spinningdale Highld 109 M7
Spion Kop Notts 57 S13
Spirthill Wilts 18 E5
Spital Wirral 54 H10
Spital Hill Donc 57 T8
Spital in the Street Lincs 58 G8
Spithurst E Susx 11 Q7
Spittal E Loth 84 D3
Spittal E R Yk 64 H9
Spittal Highld 112 E6
Spittal Nthumb 85 Q8
Spittal Pembks 24 G6
Spittalfield P & K 90 H3
Spittal of Glenmuick Abers 98 E6
Spittal of Glenshee P & K 97 U10
Spittal-on-Rule Border 76 B2
Spixworth Norfk 51 M10
Splatt Cnwll 3 N1
Splatt Cnwll 4 G3
Splatt Devon 15 P11
Splayne's Green E Susx 11 Q6
Splottlands Cardif 27 N12
Spofforth N York 63 T9
Spondon C Derb 47 M6
Spon Green Flints 54 G14
Spooner Row Norfk 40 J1
Sporle Norfk 50 D11
Spott E Loth 84 H3
Spottiswoode Border 84 G9
Spratton Nhants 37 T7
Spreakley Surrey 10 C2
Spreyton Devon 15 Q13
Spriddlestone Devon 5 N10
Spridlington Lincs 58 H10
Springburn C Glas 89 P12
Springfield D & G 75 R12
Springfield Essex 22 H6
Springfield Fife 91 M9
Springhill Staffs 46 C13
Springhill Staffs 46 E12
Springholm D & G 74 F11
Springside N Ayrs 81 M5
Springthorpe Lincs 58 E9
Spring Vale Barns 57 L6
Springwell Sundld 77 R14
Springwood Crematorium Lpool 54 K9
Sproatley E R Yk 65 R13
Sproston Green Ches W 55 R13
Sprotbrough Donc 57 R6
Sproughton Suffk 40 K12
Sprouston Border 84 K11
Sprowston Norfk 51 N11
Sproxton Leics 48 C9
Sproxton N York 64 E3
Spunhill Shrops 44 K7
Spurstow Ches E 45 N2
Spyway Dorset 7 P6
Square & Compass Pembks 24 D4
Stableford Shrops 45 S14
Stableford Staffs 45 T6
Stacey Bank Sheff 57 L8
Stackhouse N York 62 G6
Stackpole Pembks 24 G11
Stacksford Norfk 40 J2
Stacksteads Lancs 56 C2
Staddiscombe C Plym 5 N10
Staddlethorpe E R Yk 64 J14
Staden Derbys 56 G12
Stadhampton Oxon 30 D13
Stadhlaigearraidh W Isls 106 c15
Staffield Cumb 67 R4
Staffin Highld 100 d3
Stafford Staffs 46 B9
Stafford Crematorium Staffs 46 C9
Stafford Services (Northbound) Staffs 45 U7
Stafford Services (Southbound) Staffs 45 U7
Stagsden Bed 38 E11
Stainborough Barns 57 M6
Stainburn Cumb 66 F7
Stainburn N York 63 R10
Stainby Lincs 48 D9
Staincross Barns 57 M4
Staindrop Dur 69 P8
Staines-upon-Thames Surrey 20 H8
Stainfield Lincs 48 G9
Stainfield Lincs 58 K12
Stainforth Donc 57 T4
Stainforth N York 62 G6
Staining Lancs 61 Q12
Stainland Calder 56 G3
Stainsacre N York 71 R11
Stainsby Derbys 57 Q13
Stainton Cumb 61 U2
Stainton Cumb 67 N1
Stainton Cumb 67 Q7
Stainton Donc 57 S8
Stainton Dur 69 N9
Stainton Middsb 70 G10
Stainton N York 69 P13
Stainton by Langworth Lincs 58 J11
Staintondale N York 71 S13
Stainton le Vale Lincs 59 L8
Stainton with Adgarley Cumb 61 N5
Stair Cumb 66 K8
Stair E Ayrs 81 N8
Stairfoot Barns 57 N5
Stairhaven D & G 72 G9
Staithes N York 71 N9
Stakeford Nthumb 77 R8
Stake Pool Lancs 61 S10
Stakes Hants 9 T7
Stalbridge Dorset 17 T13
Stalbridge Weston Dorset 17 T13
Stalham Norfk 51 Q8
Stalham Green Norfk 51 Q9
Stalisfield Green Kent 12 J5
Stalland Common Norfk 50 H14
Stallen Dorset 17 R13
Stallingborough NE Lin 59 L4
Stalling Busk N York 62 J2
Stallington Staffs 46 B6
Stalmine Lancs 61 R10
Stalmine Moss Side Lancs 61 R10
Stalybridge Tamesd 56 E7
Stambourne Essex 40 B13
Stambourne Green Essex 39 U13
Stamford Lincs 48 F12
Stamford Nthumb 77 Q2
Stamford Bridge Ches W 55 L13
Stamford Bridge E R Yk 64 G8
Stamfordham Nthumb 77 M11
Stamford Hill Gt Lon 21 P5
Stanah Lancs 61 R11
Stanborough Herts 31 R10
Stanbridge C Beds 31 L8
Stanbridge Dorset 8 E8
Stanbury C Brad 63 L12
Stand Bury 55 S5
Stand N Lans 82 E5
Standburn Falk 82 H4
Standeford Staffs 46 B12
Standen Kent 12 G7
Standen Street Kent 12 F9
Standerwick Somset 18 B10
Standford Hants 10 C4
Standingstone Cumb 66 G6
Standish Gloucs 28 E6
Standish Wigan 55 N4
Standish Lower Ground Wigan 55 N5
Standlake Oxon 29 S7
Standon Hants 9 N3
Standon Herts 31 U8
Standon Staffs 45 T6
Standon Green End Herts 31 U9
Standwell Green Suffk 40 K7
Stane N Lans 82 G7
Stanfield Norfk 50 F9
Stanford C Beds 31 Q4
Stanford Kent 13 M8
Stanford Shrops 44 H11
Stanford Bishop Herefs 35 Q10
Stanford Bridge Worcs 35 R7
Stanford Bridge Wrekin 45 R9
Stanford Dingley W Berk 19 S6
Stanford in the Vale Oxon 29 R9
Stanford le Hope Thurr 22 G11
Stanford on Avon Nhants 37 Q5
Stanford on Soar Notts 47 P9
Stanford on Teme Worcs 35 R7
Stanford Rivers Essex 22 D7
Stanfree Derbys 57 Q12
Stanghow R & Cl 71 L9
Stanground C Pete 38 K1
Stanhill Lancs 62 E14
Stanhoe Norfk 50 D6
Stanhope Border 83 M13
Stanhope Dur 69 L5
Stanhope Kent 12 K7
Stanhope Bretby Derbys 46 J9
Stanion Nhants 38 D3
Stanklin Worcs 35 U6
Stanley Derbys 47 M5
Stanley Dur 69 Q2
Stanley Notts 47 N1
Stanley P & K 90 H5
Stanley Shrops 35 R4
Stanley Staffs 46 B3
Stanley Wakefd 57 M2
Stanley Common Derbys 47 M5
Stanley Crook Dur 69 Q5
Stanley Ferry Wakefd 57 N2
Stanley Gate Lancs 54 K5
Stanley Moor Staffs 46 B3
Stanley Pontlarge Gloucs 28 K1
Stanmer Br & H 11 N9
Stanmore Gt Lon 21 L4
Stanmore Hants 9 P3
Stanmore W Berk 19 Q5
Stannersburn Nthumb 76 E8
Stanningfield Suffk 40 E9
Stanningley Leeds 63 Q13
Stannington Nthumb 77 Q10
Stannington Sheff 57 L9
Stannington Station Nthumb 77 Q9
Stansbatch Herefs 34 H8
Stansfield Suffk 40 C10
Stanshope Staffs 46 F3
Stanstead Suffk 40 D11
Stanstead Abbotts Herts 31 U10
Stansted Kent 12 B3
Stansted Airport Essex 22 D3
Stansted Mountfitchet Essex 22 D2
Stanton Derbys 46 J10
Stanton Gloucs 36 E14
Stanton Mons 27 Q3
Stanton Nthumb 77 N7
Stanton Staffs 46 F4
Stanton Suffk 40 G6
Stanton by Bridge Derbys 47 L8
Stanton by Dale Derbys 47 N6
Stanton Drew BaNES 17 Q4
Stanton Fitzwarren Swindn 29 N9
Stanton Harcourt Oxon 29 T6
Stanton Hill Notts 47 N1
Stanton in Peak Derbys 56 K14
Stanton Lacy Shrops 35 L5
Stanton Lees Derbys 57 L14
Stanton Long Shrops 35 N2
Stanton on the Wolds Notts 47 R7
Stanton Prior BaNES 17 S4
Stanton St Bernard Wilts 18 G8
Stanton St John Oxon 30 C11
Stanton St Quintin Wilts 18 D5
Stanton Street Suffk 40 G7
Stanton under Bardon Leics 47 N11
Stanton upon Hine Heath Shrops 45 N9
Stanton Wick BaNES 17 R4
Stantway Gloucs 28 D5
Stanwardine in the Field Shrops 44 K9
Stanwardine in the Wood Shrops 44 K8
Stanway Essex 23 M3
Stanway Gloucs 29 L1
Stanway Green Essex 23 N3
Stanway Green Suffk 41 M6
Stanwell Surrey 20 J8
Stanwell Moor Surrey 20 H8
Stanwick Nhants 38 E6
Stanwix Cumb 67 P1
Staoinebrig W Isls 106 c15
Stape N York 71 N14
Stapehill Dorset 8 F8
Stapeley Ches E 45 Q4
Stapenhill Staffs 46 J9
Staple Kent 13 Q4
Staple Cross Devon 16 D12
Staplecross E Susx 12 E11
Staplefield W Susx 11 M5
Staple Fitzpaine Somset 16 J13
Stapleford Cambs 39 Q10
Stapleford Herts 31 T9
Stapleford Leics 48 B10
Stapleford Lincs 48 C2
Stapleford Notts 47 N6
Stapleford Wilts 18 G13
Stapleford Abbotts Essex 22 D9
Stapleford Tawney Essex 22 D8
Staplegrove Somset 16 H11
Staplehay Somset 16 H12
Staple Hill Worcs 36 C6
Staplehurst Kent 12 E7
Staplers IoW 9 Q11
Staplestreet Kent 13 L3
Stapleton Cumb 75 V11
Stapleton Herefs 34 H7
Stapleton Leics 47 M14
Stapleton N York 69 S10
Stapleton Shrops 45 L13
Stapleton Somset 17 N12
Stapley Somset 6 G2
Staploe Bed 38 J8
Staplow Herefs 35 Q12
Star Fife 91 M11
Star Pembks 25 M4
Star Somset 17 M5
Starbeck N York 63 S8
Starbotton N York 62 K5
Starcross Devon 6 C8
Stareton Warwks 36 K6
Starkholmes Derbys 46 K2
Starlings Green Essex 22 C1
Starr's Green E Susx 12 E12
Starston Norfk 41 M4
Start Devon 5 U12
Startforth Dur 69 M9
Startley Wilts 18 D4
Statenborough Kent 13 R4
Statham Warrtn 55 Q9
Stathe Somset 17 L11
Stathern Leics 47 U7
Station Town Dur 70 F5
Staughton Green Cambs 38 H7
Staughton Highway Cambs 38 H8
Staunton Gloucs 27 V5
Staunton Gloucs 28 E2
Staunton in the Vale Notts 48 B5
Staunton on Arrow Herefs 34 J8
Staunton on Wye Herefs 34 J12
Staveley Cumb 61 R2
Staveley Cumb 67 Q13
Staveley Derbys 57 P12
Staveley N York 63 T7
Staverton Devon 5 T8
Staverton Gloucs 28 G3
Staverton Nhants 37 P8
Staverton Wilts 18 C8
Staverton Bridge Gloucs 28 G3
Stawell Somset 17 L9
Stawley Somset 16 E12
Staxigoe Highld 112 J6
Staxton N York 65 N4
Staylittle Cerdgn 33 M3
Staylittle Powys 33 S2
Staynall Lancs 61 R11
Staythorpe Notts 47 U3
Stead C Brad 63 N10
Stean N York 63 M5
Stearsby N York 64 E5
Steart Somset 16 J7
Stebbing Essex 22 G3
Stebbing Green Essex 22 G3
Stechford Birm 36 F3
Stede Quarter Kent 12 G8
Stedham W Susx 10 D6
Steel Nthumb 76 J14
Steel Cross E Susx 11 S4
Steelend Fife 90 F13
Steele Road Border 76 A7
Steel Green Cumb 61 M4
Steel Heath Shrops 45 M6
Steen's Bridge Herefs 35 M9
Steep Hants 9 U3
Steephill IoW 9 Q13
Steep Lane Calder 56 F2
Steeple Dorset 8 C12
Steeple Essex 23 M7
Steeple Ashton Wilts 18 D9
Steeple Aston Oxon 29 U2
Steeple Barton Oxon 29 T3
Steeple Bumpstead Essex 39 U12
Steeple Claydon Bucks 30 F7
Steeple Gidding Cambs 38 H4
Steeple Langford Wilts 18 F13
Steeple Morden Cambs 31 S4
Steeton C Brad 63 L11
Stein Highld 100 b4
Stella Gatesd 77 P13
Stelling Minnis Kent 13 M6
Stembridge Somset 17 M12
Stenalees Cnwll 3 Q5
Stenhouse D & G 74 F7
Stenhousemuir Falk 82 G2
Stenigot Lincs 59 M10
Stenscholl Highld 100 d3
Stenson Fields Derbys 46 K7
Stenton E Loth 84 G4
Steornabhagh W Isls 106 j5
Stepaside Pembks 24 K9
Stepford D & G 74 G9
Stepney Gt Lon 21 Q6
Stepping Hill Stockp 56 D9
Steppingley C Beds 31 M5
Stepps N Lans 89 Q12
Sternfield Suffk 41 Q8
Stert Wilts 18 F9
Stetchworth Cambs 39 T9
Stevenage Herts 31 R7
Steven's Crouch E Susx 12 D12
Stevenston N Ayrs 80 K4
Steventon Hants 19 R11
Steventon Oxon 29 U9
Steventon End Essex 39 S12
Stevington Bed 38 E10
Stewartby Bed 31 M4
Stewartfield S Lans 81 S1
Stewarton E Ayrs 81 N3
Stewkley Bucks 30 J7
Stewley Somset 16 K13
Stewton Lincs 59 Q9
Steyne Cross IoW 9 S11
Steyning W Susx 10 K8
Steynton Pembks 24 F9
Stibb Cnwll 14 F10
Stibbard Norfk 50 G8
Stibb Cross Devon 14 K10
Stibb Green Wilts 18 K8
Stibbington Cambs 48 G14
Stichill Border 84 J11
Sticker Cnwll 3 P6
Stickford Lincs 49 N1
Sticklepath Devon 5 Q2
Sticklepath Somset 16 D9
Stickling Green Essex 39 Q14
Stickney Lincs 49 M2
Stiffkey Norfk 50 G5
Stifford's Bridge Herefs 35 R11
Stiff Street Kent 12 G3
Stile Bridge Kent 12 E6
Stileway Somset 17 N8
Stilligarry W Isls 106 c15
Stillingfleet N York 64 D11
Stillington N York 64 D6
Stillington S on T 70 E8
Stilton Cambs 38 J3
Stinchcombe Gloucs 28 D8
Stinsford Dorset 7 T6
Stiperstones Shrops 44 J13
Stirchley Birm 36 E4
Stirchley Wrekin 45 Q12
Stirling Abers 105 U7
Stirling Stirlg 89 S7
Stirling Castle Stirlg 89 S7
Stirling Services Stirlg 89 T8
Stirtloe Cambs 38 J7
Stirton N York 62 K9
Stisted Essex 22 K3
Stitchcombe Wilts 18 K7
Stithians Cnwll 2 J9
Stivichall Covtry 36 K5
Stixwould Lincs 59 L13

Stoak - Timsbury 141

Stoak Ches W 54 K12
Stobo Border 83 N11
Stoborough Dorset 8 C11
Stoborough Green Dorset 8 C11
Stobs Castle Border 75 V4
Stobswood Nthumb 77 Q6
Stock Essex 22 G8
Stock N Som 17 N4
Stockbridge Hants 19 N13
Stockbriggs S Lans 82 E11
Stockbury Kent 12 F3
Stockcross W Berk 19 P7
Stockdalewath Cumb 67 N3
Stocker's Hill Kent 12 J5
Stockerston Leics 48 B14
Stock Green Worcs 36 C9
Stocking Herefs 28 B1
Stockingford Warwks 36 K2
Stocking Pelham Herts 22 C2
Stockland Devon 6 H4
Stockland Bristol Somset 16 H8
Stockland Green Kent 11 T2
Stockleigh English Devon 15 U11
Stockleigh Pomeroy Devon 15 U12
Stockley Wilts 18 E7
Stockley Hill Herefs 34 J13
Stocklinch Somset 17 L13
Stockmoor Herefs 34 J10
Stockport Stockp 56 C8
Stockport Crematorium Stockp 56 D9
Stocksbridge Sheff 57 L7
Stocksfield Nthumb 77 M13
Stockton Herefs 35 M8
Stockton Norfk 41 Q2
Stockton Shrops 44 G13
Stockton Shrops 45 R14
Stockton Warwks 37 M8
Stockton Wilts 18 E13
Stockton Wrekin 45 S10
Stockton Brook Staffs 46 B3
Stockton Heath Warrtn 55 P9
Stockton-on-Tees S on T 70 F9
Stockton on Teme Worcs 35 R7
Stockton on the Forest C York 64 F8
Stockwell Gloucs 28 H5
Stockwell End Wolves 45 U13
Stockwell Heath Staffs 46 E9
Stockwood Bristl 17 R3
Stockwood Dorset 7 Q3
Stock Wood Worcs 36 D9
Stodday Lancs 61 T8
Stodmarsh Kent 13 P3
Stody Norfk 50 J6
Stoer Highld 110 A11
Stoford Somset 7 Q2
Stoford Wilts 18 G13
Stogumber Somset 16 E9
Stogursey Somset 16 H8
Stoke Covtry 37 L5
Stoke Devon 14 F8
Stoke Hants 9 U8
Stoke Hants 19 P10
Stoke Medway 22 K13
Stoke Abbott Dorset 7 N4
Stoke Albany Nhants 38 B3
Stoke Ash Suffk 40 K6
Stoke Bardolph Notts 47 R5
Stoke Bliss Worcs 35 Q8
Stoke Bruerne Nhants 37 T11
Stoke by Clare Suffk 40 B12
Stoke-by-Nayland Suffk 40 G13
Stoke Canon Devon 6 B5
Stoke Charity Hants 19 Q13
Stoke Climsland Cnwll 4 K6
Stoke Cross Herefs 35 P10
Stoke D'Abernon Surrey 20 K11
Stoke Doyle Nhants 38 F3
Stoke Dry Rutlnd 38 C1
Stoke Edith Herefs 35 P12
Stoke End Warwks 36 G1
Stoke Farthing Wilts 8 F3
Stoke Ferry Norfk 50 B13
Stoke Fleming Devon 5 V11
Stokeford Dorset 8 B11
Stoke Gabriel Devon 5 V9
Stoke Gifford S Glos 28 B12
Stoke Golding Leics 37 L1
Stoke Goldington M Keyn 38 B11
Stoke Green Bucks 20 G6
Stokeham Notts 58 C11
Stoke Hammond Bucks 30 J7
Stoke Heath Shrops 45 Q8
Stoke Heath Worcs 36 B7
Stoke Holy Cross Norfk 51 M13
Stokeinteignhead Devon 6 B10
Stoke Lacy Herefs 35 P11
Stoke Lyne Oxon 30 C7
Stoke Mandeville Bucks 30 H10
Stokenchurch Bucks 20 C3
Stoke Newington Gt Lon 21 P5
Stokenham Devon 5 U12
Stoke-on-Trent C Stke 45 U4
Stoke Orchard Gloucs 28 H2
Stoke Poges Bucks 20 G6
Stoke Pound Worcs 36 C7
Stoke Prior Herefs 35 M9
Stoke Prior Worcs 36 B7
Stoke Rivers Devon 15 P5
Stoke Rochford Lincs 48 D8
Stoke Row Oxon 19 U4
Stoke St Gregory Somset 16 K11
Stoke St Mary Somset 16 J12
Stoke St Michael Somset 17 S7
Stoke St Milborough Shrops 35 N4
Stokesay Shrops 34 K4
Stokesby Norfk 51 R11
Stokesley N York 70 H11
Stoke sub Hamdon Somset 17 N13
Stoke Talmage Oxon 30 E13
Stoke Trister Somset 17 T11
Stoke upon Tern Shrops 45 P8
Stoke-upon-Trent C Stke 45 U4
Stoke Wake Dorset 7 U3
Stoke Wharf Worcs 36 C7
Stolford Somset 16 H7
Stondon Massey Essex 22 E7
Stone Bucks 30 G10
Stone Gloucs 28 C8
Stone Kent 22 E13
Stone Rothm 57 S9
Stone Somset 17 Q10
Stone Staffs 46 B7
Stone Worcs 35 U5
Stonea Cambs 39 Q2
Stone Allerton Somset 17 L6
Ston Easton Somset 17 R6
Stonebridge N Som 17 L5
Stonebridge Norfk 40 F2
Stonebridge Warwks 36 H4
Stone Bridge Corner C Pete 49 L13
Stonebroom Derbys 47 M2
Stone Chair Calder 63 N14
Stone Cross E Susx 11 S5
Stone Cross E Susx 11 U10
Stone Cross E Susx 12 B9
Stone Cross Kent 11 S3
Stone Cross Kent 12 K8
Stone Cross Kent 13 R4
Stonecross Green Suffk 40 D9
Stonecrouch Kent 12 D9
Stone-edge-Batch N Som 17 N2
Stoneferry C KuH 65 Q13
Stonefield Castle Hotel Ag & B 87 R11
Stonegate E Susx 12 C10
Stonegate N York 71 N11
Stonegrave N York 64 F4
Stonehall Worcs 35 U11
Stonehaugh Nthumb 76 F10
Stonehaven Abers 99 R6
Stonehenge Wilts 18 H12
Stone Hill Donc 57 U5
Stonehouse C Plym 5 M10
Stone House Cumb 62 F2
Stonehouse Gloucs 28 F6
Stonehouse Nthumb 76 D14
Stonehouse S Lans 82 E9
Stone in Oxney Kent 12 H10
Stoneleigh Warwks 36 K6
Stoneley Green Ches E 45 P3
Stonely Cambs 38 H7
Stoner Hill Hants 9 U3
Stonesby Leics 48 B9
Stonesfield Oxon 29 S4
Stones Green Essex 23 S2
Stone Street Kent 21 U12
Stone Street Suffk 40 G13
Stone Street Suffk 40 H12
Stone Street Suffk 41 Q4
Stonestreet Green Kent 13 L8
Stonethwaite Cumb 67 L10
Stonewells Moray 104 B2
Stonewood Kent 22 E13
Stoneybridge W Isls 106 c15
Stoneybridge Worcs 36 B5
Stoneyburn W Loth 82 J6
Stoney Cross Hants 8 K6
Stoneygate C Leic 47 R13
Stoneyhills Essex 23 N8
Stoneykirk D & G 72 D9
Stoney Middleton Derbys 56 K11
Stoney Stanton Leics 37 N2
Stoney Stoke Somset 17 T10
Stoney Stratton Somset 17 S9
Stoney Stretton Shrops 44 J12
Stoneywood C Aber 105 P13
Stoneywood Falk 89 S9
Stonham Aspal Suffk 40 K9
Stonnall Staffs 46 E13
Stonor Oxon 20 B5
Stonton Wyville Leics 37 T1
Stony Cross Herefs 35 M7
Stony Cross Herefs 35 R11
Stonyford Hants 9 L5
Stony Houghton Derbys 57 Q13
Stony Stratford M Keyn 30 G4
Stonywell Staffs 46 E11
Stoodleigh Devon 15 Q6
Stoodleigh Devon 16 B13
Stop 24 Services Kent 13 M8
Stopham W Susx 10 G7
Stopsley Luton 31 P8
Stoptide Cnwll 3 N1
Storeton Wirral 54 H10
Storeyard Green Herefs 35 R12
Stornoway W Isls 106 j5
Stornoway Airport W Isls 106 j5
Storridge Herefs 35 S11
Storrington W Susx 10 H8
Storth Cumb 61 T4
Storwood E R Yk 64 G11
Stotfield Moray 104 A1
Stotfold C Beds 31 R5
Stottesdon Shrops 35 Q4
Stoughton Leics 47 R13
Stoughton Surrey 20 G12
Stoughton W Susx 10 C8
Stoulton Worcs 36 B11
Stourbridge Dudley 35 U4
Stourbridge Crematorium Dudley 35 U4
Stourhead Wilts 17 U10
Stourpaine Dorset 8 B7
Stourport-on-Severn Worcs 35 T6
Stour Provost Dorset 17 U12
Stour Row Dorset 17 V12
Stourton Leeds 63 S13
Stourton Staffs 35 U4
Stourton Warwks 36 J13
Stourton Wilts 17 U10
Stourton Caundle Dorset 17 T13
Stout Somset 17 M10
Stove Shet 106 u11
Stoven Suffk 41 R4
Stow Border 84 D10
Stow Lincs 58 E10
Stow Bardolph Norfk 49 T12
Stow Bedon Norfk 40 G1
Stowbridge Norfk 49 T12
Stow-cum-Quy Cambs 39 R8
Stowe Gloucs 27 V6
Stowe Shrops 34 H6
Stowe by Chartley Staffs 46 D8
Stowehill Nhants 37 R9
Stowell Somset 17 S12
Stowey BaNES 17 Q5
Stowford Devon 5 L3
Stowford Devon 6 F7
Stowford Devon 14 K13
Stowford Devon 15 Q4
Stowlangtoft Suffk 40 G7
Stow Longa Cambs 38 H6
Stow Maries Essex 22 K8
Stowmarket Suffk 40 H9
Stow-on-the-Wold Gloucs 29 N2
Stowting Kent 13 M7
Stowting Common Kent 13 M7
Stowupland Suffk 40 J8
Straanruie Highld 103 Q12
Strachan Abers 99 M5
Strachur Ag & B 88 C5
Stradbroke Suffk 41 M6
Stradbrook Wilts 18 D10
Stradishall Suffk 40 C10
Stradsett Norfk 49 U12
Stragglethorpe Lincs 48 D3
Stragglethorpe Notts 47 S6
Straight Soley Wilts 19 M6
Straiton Mdloth 83 Q5
Straiton S Ayrs 81 M12
Straloch Abers 105 P11
Straloch P & K 97 S11
Stramshall Staffs 46 E6
Strang IoM 60 f7
Strangeways Salfd 55 T7
Strangford Herefs 28 A2
Stranraer D & G 72 D7
Strata Florida Cerdgn 33 P7
Stratfield Mortimer W Berk 19 U8
Stratfield Saye Hants 19 U8
Stratfield Turgis Hants 19 U9
Stratford C Beds 38 J11
Stratford Gt Lon 21 Q6
Stratford St Andrew Suffk 41 Q8
Stratford St Mary Suffk 40 H14
Stratford sub Castle Wilts 8 G2
Stratford Tony Wilts 8 F3
Stratford-upon-Avon Warwks 36 H9
Strath Highld 107 N9
Strathan Highld 110 B12
Strathan Highld 111 M4
Strathaven S Lans 82 D10
Strathblane Stirlg 89 N10
Strathcanaird Highld 108 B4
Strathcarron Highld 101 N3
Strathcoil Ag & B 93 R12
Strathdon Abers 104 D13
Strathkinness Fife 91 Q8
Strathloanhead W Loth 82 H4
Strathmashie House Highld 96 H5
Strathmiglo Fife 90 K10
Strathpeffer Highld 102 E4
Strathtay P & K 97 Q13
Strathwhillan N Ayrs 80 E5
Strathy Highld 111 S4
Strathy Inn Highld 111 S3
Strathyre Stirlg 89 N2
Stratton Cnwll 14 F11
Stratton Dorset 7 S6
Stratton Gloucs 28 K7
Stratton Audley Oxon 30 D7
Stratton-on-the-Fosse Somset 17 S6
Stratton St Margaret Swindn 29 N10
Stratton St Michael Norfk 41 M2
Stratton Strawless Norfk 51 M9
Stream Somset 16 E9
Streat E Susx 11 P7
Streatham Gt Lon 21 P8
Streatley C Beds 31 N7
Streatley W Berk 19 S4
Street Devon 6 G7
Street Lancs 61 U9
Street N York 71 M12
Street Somset 17 N9
Street Ashton Warwks 37 N4
Street Dinas Shrops 44 H6
Street End E Susx 11 U6
Street End Kent 13 M5
Street End W Susx 10 D11
Street Gate Gatesd 77 Q14
Streethay Staffs 46 F11
Street Houses N York 64 C10
Streetlam N York 70 D13
Street Lane Derbys 47 L4
Streetly Wsall 46 E14
Streetly Crematorium Wsall 46 E14
Streetly End Cambs 39 T11
Street on the Fosse Somset 17 R9
Strefford Shrops 34 K3
Strelitz P & K 90 J4
Strelley Notts 47 P5
Strensall C York 64 E7
Strensham Worcs 36 B12
Strensham Services (northbound) Worcs 35 U12
Strensham Services (southbound) Worcs 36 B12
Stretcholt Somset 16 J8
Strete Devon 5 U11
Stretford Herefs 34 K9
Stretford Herefs 35 M9
Stretford Traffd 55 S8
Strethall Essex 39 Q13
Stretham Cambs 39 R6
Strettington W Susx 10 D9
Stretton Ches W 44 K3
Stretton Derbys 47 L1
Stretton Rutlnd 48 D10
Stretton Staffs 45 U11
Stretton Staffs 46 J8
Stretton Warrtn 55 P10
Stretton en le Field Leics 46 K11
Stretton Grandison Herefs 35 P12
Stretton-on-Dunsmore Warwks 37 M6
Stretton on Fosse Warwks 36 H13
Stretton Sugwas Herefs 35 L12
Stretton under Fosse Warwks 37 N4
Stretton Westwood Shrops 45 N14
Strichen Abers 105 Q4
Strines Stockp 56 E9
Stringston Somset 16 G8
Strixton Nhants 38 D8
Stroat Gloucs 27 V8
Stroma Highld 112 J1
Stromeferry Highld 101 M5
Stromness Ork 106 r19
Stronachlachar Stirlg 88 K3
Stronafian Ag & B 87 U9
Stronchrubie Highld 110 E13
Strone Ag & B 88 E9
Strone Highld 94 G2
Strone Highld 102 F10
Stronenaba Highld 94 J2
Stronmilchan Ag & B 94 H13
Stronsay Ork 106 v17
Stronsay Airport Ork 106 v17
Strontian Highld 93 U6
Strood Kent 12 G9
Strood Medway 12 D2
Strood Green Surrey 21 M13
Strood Green W Susx 10 G6
Stroud Gloucs 28 G6
Stroud Hants 9 U4
Stroude Surrey 20 H9
Stroud Green Essex 23 L9
Stroud Green Gloucs 28 F6
Stroxton Lincs 48 D7
Struan Highld 100 c6
Struan P & K 97 N10
Strubby Lincs 59 S10
Strumpshaw Norfk 51 P12
Strutherhill S Lans 82 E9
Struthers Fife 91 N10
Struy Highld 102 D7
Stryd-y-Facsen IoA 52 D6
Stryt-issa Wrexhm 44 G4
Stuartfield Abers 105 R6
Stubbers Green Wsall 46 D13
Stubbington Hants 9 R8
Stubbins Lancs 55 S3
Stubbs Green Norfk 51 N14
Stubhampton Dorset 8 C6
Stubley Derbys 57 M11
Stubshaw Cross Wigan 55 N7
Stubton Lincs 48 C4
Stuckton Hants 8 H6
Studfold N York 62 G6
Stud Green W & M 20 E7
Studham C Beds 31 M9
Studholme Cumb 67 L1
Studland Dorset 8 E12
Studley Warwks 36 E8
Studley Wilts 18 E6
Studley Common Warwks 36 E8
Studley Roger N York 63 R6
Studley Royal N York 63 R5
Studley Royal Park & Fountains Abbey N York 63 R6
Stuntney Cambs 39 S5
Stunts Green E Susx 11 U8
Sturbridge Staffs 45 T7
Sturgate Lincs 58 E9
Sturmer Essex 39 U12
Sturminster Common Dorset 7 U2
Sturminster Marshall Dorset 8 D8
Sturminster Newton Dorset 7 U2
Sturry Kent 13 N3
Sturton N Linc 58 G6
Sturton by Stow Lincs 58 E10
Sturton le Steeple Notts 58 C10
Stuston Suffk 40 K5
Stutton N York 64 B11
Stutton Suffk 41 L14
Styal Ches E 55 T10
Stydd Lancs 62 D12
Stynie Moray 104 C3
Styrrup Notts 57 T8
Succoth Ag & B 88 G4
Suckley Worcs 35 R10
Suckley Green Worcs 35 R10
Sudborough Nhants 38 E4
Sudbourne Suffk 41 R10
Sudbrook Lincs 48 E5
Sudbrook Mons 27 U10
Sudbrooke Lincs 58 H11
Sudbury Derbys 46 G7
Sudbury Gt Lon 21 L5
Sudbury Suffk 40 E12
Sudden Rochdl 56 C4
Sudgrove Gloucs 28 H6
Suffield N York 65 M1
Suffield Norfk 51 M7
Sugdon Wrekin 45 P10
Sugnall Staffs 45 S7
Sugwas Pool Herefs 35 L12
Suisnish Highld 100 e8
Sulby IoM 60 f4
Sulgrave Nhants 30 C4
Sulham W Berk 19 T6
Sulhamstead W Berk 19 T7
Sulhamstead Abbots W Berk 19 T7
Sulhamstead Bannister W Berk 19 T7
Sullington W Susx 10 H8
Sullom Shet 106 t6
Sullom Voe Shet 106 u6
Sully V Glam 16 G3
Sumburgh Airport Shet 106 t12
Summerbridge N York 63 Q7
Summercourt Cnwll 3 M5
Summerfield Norfk 50 C6
Summerfield Worcs 35 T6
Summer Heath Bucks 20 B4
Summerhill Pembks 25 L9
Summerhill Staffs 46 E12
Summer Hill Wrexhm 44 H3
Summerhouse Darltn 69 R9
Summerlands Cumb 61 U2
Summerley Derbys 57 N11
Summersdale W Susx 10 D9
Summerseat Bury 55 S4
Summertown Oxon 30 B11
Summit Oldham 56 D5
Summit Rochdl 56 D3
Sunbiggin Cumb 68 E11
Sunbury-on-Thames Surrey 20 K9
Sundaywell D & G 74 F9
Sunderland Ag & B 78 C3
Sunderland Cumb 66 J5
Sunderland Lancs 61 S8
Sunderland Sundld 70 E1
Sunderland Bridge Dur 69 S5
Sunderland Crematorium Sundld 70 E1
Sundhope Border 83 R13
Sundon Park Luton 31 N7
Sundridge Kent 21 S11
Sunk Island E R Yk 59 N3
Sunningdale W & M 20 G9
Sunninghill W & M 20 F9
Sunningwell Oxon 29 U7
Sunniside Dur 69 P5
Sunniside Gatesd 77 Q14
Sunny Brow Dur 69 Q6
Sunnyhill C Derb 46 K7
Sunnyhurst Bl w D 55 Q2
Sunnylaw Stirlg 89 S6
Sunnymead Oxon 30 B11
Sunton Wilts 18 K10
Surbiton Gt Lon 21 L9
Surfleet Lincs 49 L8
Surfleet Seas End Lincs 49 L8
Surlingham Norfk 51 P12
Surrex Essex 23 L3
Surrey & Sussex Crematorium W Susx 11 M3
Sustead Norfk 51 L6
Susworth Lincs 58 D6
Sutcombe Devon 14 H10
Sutcombemill Devon 14 H10
Suton Norfk 50 J14
Sutterby Lincs 59 Q12
Sutterton Lincs 49 L6
Sutton C Beds 38 K11
Sutton C Pete 48 G14
Sutton Cambs 39 P5
Sutton Devon 5 S12
Sutton Devon 15 R12
Sutton Donc 57 S4
Sutton E Susx 11 R11
Sutton Gt Lon 21 N10
Sutton Kent 13 R6
Sutton N York 57 Q1
Sutton Norfk 51 Q9
Sutton Notts 47 U6
Sutton Oxon 29 T6
Sutton Pembks 24 F7
Sutton Shrops 35 R3
Sutton Shrops 44 J8
Sutton Shrops 45 M11
Sutton Shrops 45 Q7
Sutton St Hel 55 M8
Sutton Staffs 45 S9
Sutton Suffk 41 P11
Sutton W Susx 10 F7
Sutton Abinger Surrey 20 K13
Sutton at Hone Kent 21 U9
Sutton Bassett Nhants 37 U2
Sutton Benger Wilts 18 D5
Sutton Bingham Somset 7 P2
Sutton Bonington Notts 47 P9
Sutton Bridge Lincs 49 Q9
Sutton Cheney Leics 47 M13
Sutton Coldfield Birm 36 F1
Sutton Coldfield Crematorium Birm 46 F14
Sutton Courtenay Oxon 19 R2
Sutton Crosses Lincs 49 P9
Sutton cum Lound Notts 57 U10
Sutton Fields Notts 47 N8
Sutton Green Surrey 20 H12
Sutton Green Wrexhm 44 K4
Sutton Howgrave N York 63 S4
Sutton in Ashfield Notts 47 N2
Sutton-in-Craven N York 63 L11
Sutton in the Elms Leics 37 P2
Sutton Lane Ends Ches E 56 D12
Sutton Maddock Shrops 45 R13
Sutton Mallet Somset 17 L9
Sutton Mandeville Wilts 8 D3
Sutton Manor St Hel 55 M8
Sutton Marsh Herefs 35 N12
Sutton Montis Somset 17 R12
Sutton-on-Hull C KuH 65 Q13
Sutton on Sea Lincs 59 T10
Sutton-on-the-Forest N York 64 D7
Sutton on the Hill Derbys 46 H7
Sutton on Trent Notts 58 C13
Sutton Poyntz Dorset 7 T8
Sutton St Edmund Lincs 49 N11
Sutton St James Lincs 49 N10
Sutton St Nicholas Herefs 35 M11
Sutton Scotney Hants 19 Q13
Sutton Street Kent 12 F4
Sutton-under-Brailes Warwks 36 K13
Sutton-under-Whitestonecliffe N York 64 B3
Sutton upon Derwent E R Yk 64 G10
Sutton Valence Kent 12 F6
Sutton Veny Wilts 18 D12
Sutton Waldron Dorset 8 B5
Sutton Weaver Ches W 55 M11
Sutton Wick BaNES 17 Q5
Sutton Wick Oxon 29 U9
Swaby Lincs 59 Q11
Swadlincote Derbys 46 J10
Swaffham Norfk 50 D12
Swaffham Bulbeck Cambs 39 S8
Swaffham Prior Cambs 39 S8
Swafield Norfk 51 N7
Swainby N York 70 G12
Swainshill Herefs 35 L12
Swainsthorpe Norfk 51 M13
Swainswick BaNES 17 U3
Swalcliffe Oxon 37 L13
Swalecliffe Kent 13 M2
Swallow Lincs 59 L6
Swallow Beck Lincs 58 F13
Swallowcliffe Wilts 8 D3
Swallowfield Wokham 20 B10
Swallow Nest Rothm 57 Q9
Swallows Cross Essex 22 F8
Swampton Hants 19 P10
Swanage Dorset 8 E13
Swanbourne Bucks 30 H7
Swanbridge V Glam 16 G3
Swancote Shrops 35 R2
Swan Green Ches W 55 R12
Swanland E R Yk 65 M14
Swanley Kent 21 T9
Swanley Village Kent 21 T9
Swanmore Hants 9 R5
Swannington Leics 47 M10
Swannington Norfk 50 K10
Swanpool Garden Suburb Lincs 58 G13
Swanscombe Kent 22 F13
Swansea Swans 26 B9
Swansea Airport Swans 25 U12
Swansea Crematorium Swans 26 B8
Swansea West Services Swans 25 V11
Swan Street Essex 23 L2
Swanton Abbot Norfk 51 N8
Swanton Morley Norfk 50 H10
Swanton Novers Norfk 50 H7
Swanton Street Kent 12 G4
Swan Village Sandw 36 C2
Swanwick Derbys 47 M3
Swanwick Hants 9 Q7
Swanwick Crematorium Derbys 47 M3
Swarby Lincs 48 F5
Swardeston Norfk 51 M13
Swarkestone Derbys 47 L8
Swarland Nthumb 77 P5
Swarraton Hants 19 S13
Swartha C Brad 63 M10
Swarthmoor Cumb 61 P4
Swaton Lincs 48 H6
Swavesey Cambs 39 N7
Sway Hants 8 K9
Swayfield Lincs 48 E9
Swaythling C Sotn 9 N5
Sweet Green Worcs 35 P8
Sweetham Devon 15 U13
Sweethaws E Susx 11 S5
Sweetlands Corner Kent 12 E6
Sweets Cnwll 14 E13
Sweetshouse Cnwll 3 R4
Swefling Suffk 41 P8
Swepstone Leics 47 L11
Swerford Oxon 29 S1
Swettenham Ches E 55 T13
Swffryd Blae G 27 N8
Swift's Green Kent 12 G7
Swilland Suffk 41 L10
Swillbrook Lancs 61 T13
Swillington Leeds 63 T13
Swimbridge Devon 15 P6
Swimbridge Newland Devon 15 P6
Swinbrook Oxon 29 Q5
Swincliffe Kirk 63 Q14
Swincliffe N York 63 Q8
Swincombe Devon 15 Q4
Swinden N York 62 H9
Swinderby Lincs 58 E14
Swindon Gloucs 28 H2
Swindon Nthumb 76 K6
Swindon Staffs 35 U2
Swindon Swindn 29 M11
Swine E R Yk 65 Q12
Swinefleet E R Yk 58 C2
Swineford S Glos 17 S3
Swineshead Bed 38 G7
Swineshead Lincs 48 K5
Swineshead Bridge Lincs 48 K5
Swiney Highld 112 F9
Swinford Leics 37 Q5
Swinford Oxon 29 T6
Swingfield Minnis Kent 13 P7
Swingfield Street Kent 13 P7
Swingleton Green Suffk 40 G11
Swinhoe Nthumb 85 U13
Swinhope Lincs 59 M7
Swinithwaite N York 63 L2
Swinmore Common Herefs 35 Q12
Swinscoe Staffs 46 F4
Swinside Cumb 66 K8
Swinstead Lincs 48 F9
Swinthorpe Lincs 58 J10
Swinton Border 85 L9
Swinton N York 63 Q4
Swinton N York 64 H5
Swinton Rothm 57 Q7
Swinton Salfd 55 S6
Swithland Leics 47 Q11
Swordale Highld 102 G2
Swordland Highld 100 g10
Swordly Highld 111 Q4
Sworton Heath Ches E 55 Q10
Swyddffynnon Cerdgn 33 N7
Swyncombe Oxon 19 U2
Swynnerton Staffs 45 U6
Swyre Dorset 7 P7
Sycharth Powys 44 F8
Sychnant Powys 33 U5
Sychtyn Powys 43 U12
Sydallt Wrexhm 44 H2
Syde Gloucs 28 J5
Sydenham Gt Lon 21 Q8
Sydenham Oxon 30 F12
Sydenham Damerel Devon 5 L5
Sydenhurst Surrey 10 F4
Syderstone Norfk 50 D7
Sydling St Nicholas Dorset 7 R5
Sydmonton Hants 19 Q9
Sydnal Lane Shrops 45 T12
Syerston Notts 47 T4
Syke Rochdl 56 C3
Sykehouse Donc 57 T3
Syleham Suffk 41 M5
Sylen Carmth 25 T9
Symbister Shet 106 v7
Symington S Ayrs 81 M6
Symington S Lans 82 J11
Symondsbury Dorset 7 M6
Symonds Yat Herefs 27 V4
Sympson Green C Brad 63 P12
Synderford Dorset 7 L4
Synod Inn Cerdgn 32 H10
Syre Highld 111 P8
Syreford Gloucs 28 K3
Syresham Nhants 30 D4
Syston Leics 47 R11
Syston Lincs 48 D5
Sytchampton Worcs 35 T7
Sywell Nhants 38 B7

T

Tabley Hill Ches E 55 R11
Tackley Oxon 29 U4
Tacolneston Norfk 40 K1
Tadcaster N York 64 B11
Taddington Derbys 56 H12
Taddington Gloucs 29 L1
Taddiport Devon 15 L9
Tadley Hants 19 T8
Tadlow Cambs 39 L11
Tadmarton Oxon 37 L13
Tadwick BaNES 17 T2
Tadworth Surrey 21 M11
Tafarnaubach Blae G 27 L5
Tafarn-y-bwlch Pembks 24 J4
Tafarn-y-Gelyn Denbgs 44 E1
Taff's Well Rhondd 27 L11
Tafolwern Powys 43 S13
Taibach Neath 26 D10
Tain Highld 109 P8
Tain Highld 112 F3
Tai'n Lôn Gwynd 42 H3
Tairbeart W Isls 106 g8
Tai'r Bull Powys 26 H2
Takeley Essex 22 E3
Takeley Street Essex 22 D3
Talachddu Powys 34 C14
Talacre Flints 54 D10
Talaton Devon 6 E5
Talbenny Pembks 24 D8
Talbot Green Rhondd 26 J11
Talbot Village Bmouth 8 F10
Taleford Devon 6 E5
Talerddig Powys 43 T13
Talgarreg Cerdgn 32 H10
Talgarth Powys 34 E14
Talisker Highld 100 c6
Talke Staffs 45 T3
Talke Pits Staffs 45 T3
Talkin Cumb 67 S1
Talladale Highld 107 R10
Talla Linnfoots Border 75 M1
Tallaminnock S Ayrs 81 N13
Tallarn Green Wrexhm 44 K5
Tallentire Cumb 66 H5
Talley Carmth 33 M14
Tallington Lincs 48 G12
Tallwrn Wrexhm 44 G4
Talmine Highld 111 M4
Talog Carmth 25 P5
Talsarn Cerdgn 32 K9
Talsarnau Gwynd 43 M6
Talskiddy Cnwll 3 N3
Talwrn IoA 52 G7
Talwrn Wrexhm 44 J4
Tal-y-bont Cerdgn 33 N3
Tal-y-Bont Conwy 53 N9
Tal-y-bont Gwynd 43 L9
Tal-y-bont Gwynd 52 K8
Talybont-on-Usk Powys 27 L3
Tal-y-Cafn Conwy 53 N8
Tal-y-coed Mons 27 S4
Tal-y-garn Rhondd 26 J12
Tal-y-llyn Gwynd 43 P12
Talysarn Gwynd 52 G12
Tal-y-Waun Torfn 27 P7
Talywern Powys 43 R13
Tamar Valley Mining District Devon 5 L7
Tamer Lane End Wigan 55 P6
Tamerton Foliot C Plym 5 M8
Tamworth Staffs 46 H13
Tamworth Green Lincs 49 N5
Tamworth Services Warwks 46 H13
Tancred N York 64 B8
Tancredston Pembks 24 E5
Tandridge Surrey 21 Q12
Tanfield Dur 69 Q1
Tanfield Lea Dur 69 Q2
Tangiers Pembks 24 G7
Tangley Hants 19 M10
Tangmere W Susx 10 E9
Tangusdale W Isls 106 b18
Tan Hill N York 68 J11
Tankerness Ork 106 u19
Tankersley Barns 57 M7
Tankerton Kent 13 M2
Tannach Highld 112 H7
Tannachie Abers 99 P7
Tannadice Angus 98 H12
Tanner's Green Worcs 36 E6
Tannington Suffk 41 M7
Tannochside N Lans 82 D6
Tansley Derbys 46 K2
Tansor Nhants 38 G2
Tantobie Dur 69 Q2
Tanton N York 70 H10
Tanwood Worcs 36 B6
Tanworth in Arden Warwks 36 F6
Tan-y-Bwlch Gwynd 43 N5
Tan-y-fron Conwy 53 S10
Tan-y-fron Wrexhm 44 G3
Tan-y-grisiau Gwynd 43 N4
Tan-y-groes Cerdgn 32 E11
Taobh Tuath W Isls 106 e10
Taplow Bucks 20 F6
Tarbert Ag & B 79 M5
Tarbert Ag & B 87 R12
Tarbert W Isls 106 g8
Tarbet Ag & B 88 H5
Tarbet Highld 100 g10
Tarbet Highld 110 D7
Tarbock Green Knows 55 L9
Tarbolton S Ayrs 81 N7
Tarbrax S Lans 82 K7
Tardebigge Worcs 36 C7
Tarfside Angus 98 H8
Tarland Abers 98 H3
Tarleton Lancs 55 L2
Tarlscough Lancs 54 K4
Tarlton Gloucs 28 J8
Tarnock Somset 17 L6
Tarns Cumb 66 H3
Tarnside Cumb 61 S1
Tarporley Ches W 55 N14
Tarr Somset 15 U6
Tarrant Crawford Dorset 8 C8
Tarrant Gunville Dorset 8 C6
Tarrant Hinton Dorset 8 C6
Tarrant Keyneston Dorset 8 C8
Tarrant Launceston Dorset 8 C7
Tarrant Monkton Dorset 8 C7
Tarrant Rawston Dorset 8 C7
Tarrant Rushton Dorset 8 C7
Tarring Neville E Susx 11 Q10
Tarrington Herefs 35 P12
Tarskavaig Highld 100 e8
Tarves Abers 105 P9
Tarvin Ches W 55 L13
Tarvin Sands Ches W 55 L13
Tasburgh Norfk 41 L1
Tasley Shrops 35 Q2
Taston Oxon 29 S3
Tatenhill Staffs 46 H9
Tathall End M Keyn 38 B11
Tatham Lancs 62 C6
Tathwell Lincs 59 P10
Tatsfield Surrey 21 R11
Tattenhall Ches W 45 L2
Tatterford Norfk 50 E8
Tattersett Norfk 50 D8
Tattershall Lincs 48 K2
Tattershall Bridge Lincs 48 J2
Tattershall Thorpe Lincs 48 K2
Tattingstone Suffk 40 K13
Tattingstone White Horse Suffk 40 K13
Tatton Park Ches E 55 R10
Tatworth Somset 6 K3
Tauchers Moray 104 D6
Taunton Somset 16 H12
Taunton Deane Crematorium Somset 16 H12
Taunton Deane Services Somset 16 G12
Taverham Norfk 51 L11
Taverners Green Essex 22 E4
Tavernspite Pembks 25 L8
Tavistock Devon 5 M6
Tavistock Devon 5 M6
Taw Green Devon 15 Q13
Tawstock Devon 15 N7
Taxal Derbys 56 F11
Taychreggan Hotel Ag & B 88 B1
Tay Forest Park P & K 97 M11
Tayinloan Ag & B 79 M6
Taynton Gloucs 28 D3
Taynton Oxon 29 P5
Taynuilt Ag & B 94 E12
Tayport Fife 91 Q6
Tayvallich Ag & B 87 N8
Tealby Lincs 59 L8
Tealing Angus 91 P4
Team Valley Gatesd 77 Q14
Teangue Highld 100 f9
Teanord Highld 102 G3
Tebay Cumb 68 D12
Tebay Services Cumb 68 D11
Tebworth C Beds 31 L7
Tedburn St Mary Devon 5 U2
Teddington Gloucs 36 C14
Teddington Gt Lon 21 L8
Tedstone Delamere Herefs 35 Q9
Tedstone Wafer Herefs 35 Q9
Teesport R & Cl 70 H8
Teesside Crematorium Middsb 70 G9
Teesside Park S on T 70 G9
Teeton Nhants 37 S6
Teffont Evias Wilts 8 D2
Teffont Magna Wilts 8 D2
Tegryn Pembks 25 M4
Teigh Rutlnd 48 C10
Teigncombe Devon 5 R3
Teigngrace Devon 5 V6
Teignmouth Devon 6 B10
Teindside Border 75 T4
Telford Wrekin 45 Q12
Telford Crematorium Wrekin 45 R11
Telford Services Shrops 45 R12
Tellisford Somset 18 B9
Telscombe E Susx 11 Q10
Telscombe Cliffs E Susx 11 Q10
Tempar P & K 95 T7
Templand D & G 75 L8
Temple Cnwll 4 E6
Temple Mdloth 83 R7
Temple Balsall Solhll 36 H5
Temple Bar Cerdgn 32 K10
Temple Cloud BaNES 17 R5
Templecombe Somset 17 T12
Temple End Suffk 39 U10
Temple Ewell Kent 13 Q7
Temple Grafton Warwks 36 F9
Temple Guiting Gloucs 29 L2
Temple Herdewyke Warwks 37 L10
Temple Hirst N York 57 T2
Temple Normanton Derbys 57 P13
Temple of Fiddes Abers 99 Q7
Temple Sowerby Cumb 68 D7
Templeton Devon 15 U10
Templeton Pembks 24 K8
Templetown Dur 69 P2
Tempsford C Beds 38 J10
Tenbury Wells Worcs 35 N7
Tenby Pembks 24 K10
Tendring Essex 23 R3
Tendring Green Essex 23 R2
Tendring Heath Essex 23 R2
Ten Mile Bank Norfk 39 S1
Tenpenny Heath Essex 23 Q3
Tenterden Kent 12 G9
Terling Essex 22 J4
Tern Wrekin 45 P10
Ternhill Shrops 45 P7
Terregles D & G 74 H10
Terrington N York 64 F5
Terrington St Clement Norfk 49 S9
Terrington St John Norfk 49 R11
Terry's Green Warwks 36 F6
Teston Kent 12 D5
Testwood Hants 9 M6
Tetbury Gloucs 28 G9
Tetbury Upton Gloucs 28 G8
Tetchill Shrops 44 J7
Tetcott Devon 14 H13
Tetford Lincs 59 P12
Tetney Lincs 59 P6
Tetney Lock Lincs 59 P6
Tetsworth Oxon 30 E12
Tettenhall Wolves 45 U13
Tettenhall Wood Wolves 45 U14
Teversal Notts 47 N1
Teversham Cambs 39 Q9
Teviothead Border 75 T4
Tewin Herts 31 S10
Tewin Wood Herts 31 S9
Tewkesbury Gloucs 35 U14
Teynham Kent 12 J3
Thackley C Brad 63 P12
Thackthwaite Cumb 66 H8
Thackthwaite Cumb 67 P7
Thainstone Abers 105 M12
Thakeham W Susx 10 J7
Thame Oxon 30 F11
Thames Ditton Surrey 21 L9
Thamesmead Gt Lon 21 S6
Thamesport Medway 23 L13
Thanet Crematorium Kent 13 S2
Thanington Kent 13 M4
Thankerton S Lans 82 J11
Tharston Norfk 41 L2
Thatcham W Berk 19 R7
Thatto Heath St Hel 55 M8
Thaxted Essex 22 F1
Theakston N York 63 S2
Thealby N Linc 58 E3
Theale Somset 17 N7
Theale W Berk 19 T6
Thearne E R Yk 65 P12
The Bank Ches E 45 T2
The Bank Shrops 45 P14
The Beeches Gloucs 28 K7
Theberton Suffk 41 R7
The Blythe Staffs 46 D8
The Bog Shrops 44 J14
The Bourne Worcs 36 C9
The Braes Highld 100 e6
The Bratch Staffs 35 U2
The Broad Herefs 35 L8
The Brunt E Loth 84 H4
The Bungalow IoM 60 f5
The Burf Worcs 35 T7
The Butts Gloucs 28 G4
The Camp Gloucs 28 H6
The Chequer Wrexhm 45 L5
The City Bed 38 H9
The City Bucks 20 C3
The Common Oxon 29 Q2
The Common Wilts 8 J2
The Common Wilts 28 K10
The Corner Kent 12 D7
The Counties Crematorium Nhants 37 T9
The Cronk IoM 60 e3
Theddingworth Leics 37 S3
Theddlethorpe All Saints Lincs 59 S9
Theddlethorpe St Helen Lincs 59 S9
The Den N Ayrs 81 L2
The Forest of Dean Crematorium Gloucs 28 B5
The Forge Herefs 34 H9
The Forstal Kent 12 K8
The Fouralls Shrops 45 Q7
The Garden of England Crematorium Kent 12 G2
The Green Cumb 61 M3
The Green Essex 22 J4
The Green N York 71 N11
The Green Wilts 8 B2
The Grove Worcs 35 U12
The Haven W Susx 10 H4
The Haw Gloucs 28 F2
The Headland Hartpl 70 H6
The Hill Cumb 61 M3
The Holt Wokham 20 D7
The Hundred Herefs 35 M8
Thelbridge Cross Devon 15 S10
The Leacon Kent 12 J9
The Lee Bucks 30 K12
The Lhen IoM 60 f2
The Linn Crematorium E Rens 89 N14
Thelnetham Suffk 40 H5
The Lochs Moray 104 C3
Thelveton Norfk 41 L4
Thelwall Warrtn 55 Q9
The Manchester Crematorium Manch 55 T8
The Marsh Powys 44 H14
Themelthorpe Norfk 50 J9
The Middles Dur 69 R2
The Moor Kent 12 E10
The Mumbles Swans 25 V13
The Murray S Lans 81 S2
The Mythe Gloucs 35 U14
The Narth Mons 27 U6
The Neuk Abers 99 N4
Thenford Nhants 30 B4
Theobald's Green Wilts 18 F7
The Park Crematorium Hants 20 E13
The Quarry Gloucs 28 D8
The Quarter Kent 12 G7
The Reddings Gloucs 28 H3
Therfield Herts 31 T5
The Rhôs Powys 27 M1
The Rose Hill Crematorium Donc 57 T6
The Ross P & K 89 S1
The Sands Surrey 20 E13
The Shoe Wilts 18 B6
The Smithies Shrops 45 Q14
The Spring Warwks 36 J6
The Square Torfn 27 P8
The Stair Kent 12 B6
The Stocks Kent 12 H10
The Straits Hants 10 B3
The Strand Wilts 18 D9
Thetford Norfk 40 E4
Thetford Forest Park 40 D3
Thethwaite Cumb 67 N4
The Towans Cnwll 2 F9
The Vale Crematorium Luton 31 P8
The Vauld Herefs 35 M11
The Wyke Shrops 45 R12
Theydon Bois Essex 21 R3
Thicket Priory N York 64 F11
Thickwood Wilts 18 B6
Thimbleby Lincs 59 M12
Thimbleby N York 70 F13
Thingwall Wirral 54 G10
Thirkleby N York 64 B4
Thirlby N York 64 B3
Thirlestane Border 84 F9
Thirn N York 63 Q2
Thirsk N York 63 U3
Thirtleby E R Yk 65 R13
Thistleton Lancs 61 S12
Thistleton Rutlnd 48 D10
Thistley Green Suffk 39 U5
Thixendale N York 64 J7
Thockrington Nthumb 76 K10
Tholomas Drove Cambs 49 P12
Tholthorpe N York 64 B6
Thomas Chapel Pembks 24 K9
Thomas Close Cumb 67 P4
Thomastown Abers 104 H8
Thomas Town Warwks 36 E8
Thompson Norfk 40 F1
Thong Kent 22 G13
Thoralby N York 63 L2
Thoresby Notts 57 T12
Thoresthorpe Lincs 59 S11
Thoresway Lincs 59 L7
Thorganby Lincs 59 M7
Thorganby N York 64 F11
Thorgill N York 71 M13
Thorington Suffk 41 R6
Thorington Street Suffk 40 H13
Thorlby N York 62 K9
Thorley Herts 22 C4
Thorley IoW 9 M11
Thorley Houses Herts 22 C3
Thorley Street IoW 9 M11
Thormanby N York 64 B5
Thornaby-on-Tees S on T 70 G9
Thornage Norfk 50 J6
Thornborough Bucks 30 F6
Thornborough N York 63 R4
Thornbury C Brad 63 P13
Thornbury Devon 14 K11
Thornbury Herefs 35 P9
Thornbury S Glos 28 B9
Thornby Cumb 67 L2
Thornby Nhants 37 S5
Thorncliff Staffs 46 D2
Thorncliffe Crematorium Cumb 61 M5
Thorncombe Dorset 7 L4
Thorncombe Street Surrey 10 F2
Thorncott Green C Beds 38 J11
Thorncross IoW 9 N12
Thorndon Suffk 40 K7
Thorndon Cross Devon 5 N2
Thorne Donc 57 U4
Thorne Coffin Somset 17 P13
Thornecroft Devon 5 T7
Thornehillhead Devon 14 K9
Thorner Leeds 63 T11
Thornes Staffs 46 E13
Thornes Wakefd 57 M3
Thorne St Margaret Somset 16 F12
Thorney Bucks 20 H7
Thorney C Pete 49 L13
Thorney Notts 58 E12
Thorney Somset 17 M12
Thorney Hill Hants 8 J9
Thorney Island W Susx 10 B10
Thorney Toll Cambs 49 M13
Thornfalcon Somset 16 J12
Thornford Dorset 7 R2
Thorngrafton Nthumb 76 F12
Thorngrove Somset 17 L10
Thorngumbald E R Yk 59 M1
Thornham Norfk 50 B5
Thornham Magna Suffk 40 K6
Thornham Parva Suffk 40 K6
Thornhaugh C Pete 48 G13
Thornhill C Sotn 9 P6
Thornhill Caerph 27 M11
Thornhill Cumb 66 F11
Thornhill D & G 74 G6
Thornhill Derbys 56 J10
Thornhill Kirk 57 L3
Thornhill Stirlg 89 Q5
Thornhill Crematorium Cardif 27 M11
Thornhill Lees Kirk 56 K3
Thornhills Calder 56 J2
Thornholme E R Yk 65 Q7
Thornicombe Dorset 8 B8
Thornington Nthumb 85 M12
Thornley Dur 69 P5
Thornley Dur 70 E5
Thornley Gate Nthumb 68 H1
Thornliebank E Rens 89 N14
Thorns Suffk 40 B9
Thornsett Derbys 56 F9
Thorns Green Ches E 55 S10
Thornthwaite Cumb 66 K7
Thornthwaite N York 63 P8
Thornton Angus 91 N2
Thornton Bucks 30 F5
Thornton C Brad 63 M13
Thornton E R Yk 64 H10
Thornton Fife 91 L12
Thornton Lancs 61 Q11
Thornton Leics 47 N12
Thornton Lincs 59 M13
Thornton Middsb 70 G10
Thornton Nthumb 85 P9
Thornton Pembks 24 F9
Thornton Sefton 54 H6
Thornton Curtis N Linc 58 J3
Thornton Garden of Rest Crematorium Sefton 54 H6
Thorntonhall S Lans 81 R1
Thornton Heath Gt Lon 21 P9
Thornton Hough Wirral 54 H10
Thornton-in-Craven N York 62 J10
Thornton in Lonsdale N York 62 D5
Thornton-le-Beans N York 63 T1
Thornton-le-Clay N York 64 F6
Thornton-le-Dale N York 64 J3
Thornton le Moor Lincs 58 H7
Thornton-le-Moor N York 63 T2
Thornton-le-Moors Ches W 54 K12
Thornton-le-Street N York 63 U2
Thorntonloch E Loth 84 K4
Thornton Rust N York 62 K2
Thornton Steward N York 63 P2
Thornton Watlass N York 63 Q2
Thornwood Common Essex 22 C7
Thornydykes Border 84 G9
Thornythwaite Cumb 67 N8
Thoroton Notts 47 U5
Thorp Arch Leeds 63 U10
Thorpe Derbys 46 G3
Thorpe E R Yk 65 M10
Thorpe Lincs 59 S10
Thorpe N York 63 L7
Thorpe Norfk 51 R14
Thorpe Notts 47 U4
Thorpe Surrey 20 H9
Thorpe Abbotts Norfk 41 L5
Thorpe Acre Leics 47 P10
Thorpe Arnold Leics 47 U9
Thorpe Audlin Wakefd 57 Q3
Thorpe Bassett N York 64 K5
Thorpe Bay Sthend 23 M10
Thorpe by Water Rutlnd 38 C1
Thorpe Common Rothm 57 N7
Thorpe Constantine Staffs 46 J12
Thorpe End Norfk 51 N11
Thorpe Green Essex 23 S3
Thorpe Green Lancs 55 N2
Thorpe Green Suffk 40 F10
Thorpe Hesley Rothm 57 N7
Thorpe in Balne Donc 57 S4
Thorpe Langton Leics 37 T2
Thorpe Larches Dur 70 E7
Thorpe Lea Surrey 20 H8
Thorpe le Fallows Lincs 58 F10
Thorpe-le-Soken Essex 23 S3
Thorpe le Street E R Yk 64 J11
Thorpe Malsor Nhants 38 B5
Thorpe Mandeville Nhants 30 B4
Thorpe Market Norfk 51 M6
Thorpe Marriot Norfk 51 L10
Thorpe Morieux Suffk 40 F10
Thorpeness Suffk 41 S9
Thorpe on the Hill Leeds 57 M1
Thorpe on the Hill Lincs 58 F13
Thorpe Park Surrey 20 H9
Thorpe St Andrew Norfk 51 N12
Thorpe St Peter Lincs 49 Q1
Thorpe Salvin Rothm 57 R10
Thorpe Satchville Leics 47 T11
Thorpe Thewles S on T 70 E8
Thorpe Tilney Lincs 48 H2
Thorpe Underwood N York 64 B8
Thorpe Underwood Nhants 37 U4
Thorpe Waterville Nhants 38 F4
Thorpe Willoughby N York 64 D13
Thorpland Norfk 49 T12
Thorrington Essex 23 Q4
Thorverton Devon 6 B4
Thrales End C Beds 31 P9
Thrandeston Suffk 40 K5
Thrapston Nhants 38 E5
Threapland Cumb 66 J5
Threapland N York 62 K7
Threapwood Ches W 44 K5
Threapwood Staffs 46 D5
Threapwood Head Staffs 46 D5
Threave S Ayrs 81 L11
Three Ashes Herefs 27 U3
Three Bridges W Susx 11 M3
Three Burrows Cnwll 2 J7
Three Chimneys Kent 12 F8
Three Cocks Powys 34 E13
Three Counties Crematorium Essex 22 J2
Three Crosses Swans 25 U12
Three Cups Corner E Susx 11 U6
Three Gates Worcs 35 Q8
Threehammer Common Norfk 51 P10
Three Hammers Cnwll 4 G3
Three Holes Norfk 49 R13
Threekingham Lincs 48 G6
Three Leg Cross E Susx 12 C9
Three Legged Cross Dorset 8 F7
Three Mile Cross Wokham 20 B9
Threemilestone Cnwll 2 K7
Three Miletown W Loth 83 L3
Three Oaks E Susx 12 F13
Threlkeld Cumb 67 M7
Threshers Bush Essex 22 C6
Threshfield N York 62 K7
Thrigby Norfk 51 S11
Thringarth Dur 68 K8
Thringstone Leics 47 M10
Thrintoft N York 70 D14
Thriplow Cambs 39 P11
Throapham Rothm 57 R9
Throckenhalt Lincs 49 N12
Throcking Herts 31 T6
Throckley N u Ty 77 P12
Throckmorton Worcs 36 C10
Throop Bmouth 8 G9
Throop Dorset 8 A10
Throphill Nthumb 77 N8
Thropton Nthumb 77 L5
Throsk Stirlg 90 C13
Througham Gloucs 28 H6
Throughgate D & G 74 G9
Throwleigh Devon 5 R2
Throwley Kent 12 J4
Throwley Forstal Kent 12 J5
Thrumpton Notts 47 P7
Thrumpton Notts 58 B10
Thrumster Highld 112 H7
Thrunscoe NE Lin 59 P5
Thrunton Nthumb 77 M3
Thrup Oxon 29 Q8
Thrupp Gloucs 28 G7
Thrupp Oxon 29 U4
Thrushelton Devon 5 L3
Thrussington Leics 47 S10
Thruxton Hants 19 L11
Thruxton Herefs 34 K14
Thrybergh Rothm 57 Q7
Thulston Derbys 47 M7
Thundersley Essex 22 J10
Thurcaston Leics 47 Q11
Thurcroft Rothm 57 Q9
Thurdon Cnwll 14 G10
Thurgarton Norfk 51 L7
Thurgarton Notts 47 S4
Thurgoland Barns 57 L6
Thurlaston Leics 47 P14
Thurlaston Warwks 37 N6
Thurlbear Somset 16 J12
Thurlby Lincs 48 D1
Thurlby Lincs 48 G10
Thurlby Lincs 59 S11
Thurleigh Bed 38 G9
Thurlestone Devon 5 R12
Thurloxton Somset 16 J10
Thurlstone Barns 56 K6
Thurlton Norfk 51 R14
Thurlwood Ches E 45 T2
Thurmaston Leics 47 R12
Thurnby Leics 47 R13
Thurne Norfk 51 R10
Thurnham Kent 12 F4
Thurning Nhants 38 G4
Thurning Norfk 50 J8
Thurnscoe Barns 57 Q5
Thurrock Services Thurr 22 E12
Thursby Cumb 67 M2
Thursden Lancs 62 J13
Thursford Norfk 50 G7
Thursley Surrey 10 E3
Thurso Highld 112 D3
Thurstaston Wirral 54 F10
Thurston Suffk 40 F7
Thurston Clough Oldham 56 E5
Thurstonfield Cumb 67 M1
Thurstonland Kirk 56 J4
Thurston Planch Suffk 40 F8
Thurton Norfk 51 P13
Thurvaston Derbys 46 H6
Thuxton Norfk 50 H12
Thwaite N York 68 J13
Thwaite Suffk 40 K7
Thwaite Head Cumb 61 Q1
Thwaites C Brad 63 M11
Thwaite St Mary Norfk 41 P1
Thwaites Brow C Brad 63 M11
Thwing E R Yk 65 N5
Tibbermore P & K 90 F7
Tibbers D & G 74 G6
Tibberton Gloucs 28 E3
Tibberton Worcs 36 B9
Tibberton Wrekin 45 Q9
Tibbie Shiels Inn Border 75 P1
Tibenham Norfk 40 K3
Tibshelf Derbys 47 M1
Tibshelf Services Derbys 47 M1
Tibthorpe E R Yk 65 M8
Ticehurst E Susx 12 C9
Tichborne Hants 9 R2
Tickencote Rutlnd 48 E12
Tickenham N Som 17 N2
Tickford End M Keyn 30 J4
Tickhill Donc 57 S8
Ticklerton Shrops 35 L2
Ticknall Derbys 47 L9
Tickton E R Yk 65 P11
Tidbury Green Solhll 36 F5
Tidcombe Wilts 19 L9
Tiddington Oxon 30 D12
Tiddington Warwks 36 H9
Tiddleywink Wilts 18 C5
Tidebrook E Susx 11 U4
Tideford Cnwll 4 K9
Tideford Cross Cnwll 4 J8
Tidenham Gloucs 27 V8
Tideswell Derbys 56 J11
Tidmarsh W Berk 19 T6
Tidmington Warwks 36 J13
Tidpit Hants 8 F5
Tidworth Wilts 18 K11
Tiers Cross Pembks 24 F8
Tiffield Nhants 37 T10
Tigerton Angus 98 J11
Tigh a Ghearraidh W Isls 106 c11
Tigharry W Isls 106 c11
Tighnabruaich Ag & B 87 T11
Tigley Devon 5 T8
Tilbrook Cambs 38 G7
Tilbury Thurr 22 F12
Tilbury Dock Thurr 22 F12
Tilbury Green Essex 40 B12
Tilbury Juxta Clare Essex 40 C12
Tile Cross Birm 36 G3
Tile Hill Covtry 36 J5
Tilehouse Green Solhll 36 G5
Tilehurst Readg 19 U6
Tilford Surrey 10 D2
Tilgate W Susx 11 M4
Tilgate Forest Row W Susx 11 M4
Tilham Street Somset 17 Q9
Tillers Green Gloucs 35 Q14
Tillicoultry Clacks 90 D12
Tillietudlem S Lans 82 F9
Tillingham Essex 23 N7
Tillington Herefs 35 L12
Tillington W Susx 10 F6
Tillington Common Herefs 35 L11
Tillybirloch Abers 99 M2
Tillyfourie Abers 104 J13
Tillygreig Abers 105 P11
Tillyrie P & K 90 H10
Tilmanstone Kent 13 R5
Tilney All Saints Norfk 49 S10
Tilney High End Norfk 49 S10
Tilney St Lawrence Norfk 49 R11
Tilshead Wilts 18 F11
Tilstock Shrops 45 M6
Tilston Ches W 45 L3
Tilstone Bank Ches W 45 N2
Tilstone Fearnall Ches W 45 N1
Tilsworth C Beds 31 L8
Tilton on the Hill Leics 47 T12
Tiltups End Gloucs 28 F8
Tilty Essex 22 E2
Timberland Lincs 48 H2
Timbersbrook Ches E 56 C14
Timberscombe Somset 16 C8
Timble N York 63 P9
Timewell Devon 16 C11
Timpanheck D & G 75 R11
Timperley Traffd 55 S9
Timsbury BaNES 17 S5
Timsbury Hants 9 L4

Timsgarry W Isls 106 f5
Timsgearraidh W Isls 106 f5
Timworth Suffk 40 E7
Timworth Green Suffk 40 E7
Tincleton Dorset 7 U6
Tindale Cumb 76 C14
Tindale Crescent Dur 69 Q7
Tingewick Bucks 30 E6
Tingley Leeds 57 L1
Tingrith C Beds 31 M6
Tingwall Ork 106 t17
Tingwall Airport Shet 106 t17
Tinhay Devon 4 K3
Tinker's Hill Hants 19 P11
Tinkersley Derbys 57 L14
Tinsley Sheff 57 P8
Tinsley Green W Susx 11 M3
Tintagel Cnwll 4 D3
Tintern Parva Mons 27 U7
Tintinhull Somset 17 N13
Tintwistle Derbys 56 F7
Tinwald D & G 74 K9
Tinwell Rutlnd 48 F12
Tipacott Devon 15 S5
Tipp's End Norfk 39 Q1
Tiptoe Hants 8 K9
Tipton Sandw 36 C2
Tipton Green Sandw 36 C2
Tipton St John Devon 6 F6
Tiptree Essex 23 L4
Tiptree Heath Essex 23 L4
Tirabad Powys 33 S12
Tiree Ag & B 92 C10
Tiree Airport Ag & B 92 C10
Tirley Gloucs 28 F2
Tiroran Ag & B 93 M13
Tirphil Caerph 27 L7
Tirril Cumb 67 R7
Tir-y-fron Flints 44 H2
Tisbury Wilts 8 C3
Tisman's Common W Susx 10 H4
Tissington Derbys 46 G3
Titchberry Devon 14 F7
Titchfield Hants 9 Q7
Titchfield Common Hants 9 Q7
Titchmarsh Nhants 38 F5
Titchwell Norfk 50 C5
Tithby Notts 47 S6
Titley Herefs 34 H8
Titmore Green Herts 31 R7
Titsey Surrey 21 R12
Titson Cnwll 14 G12
Tittensor Staffs 45 U6
Tittleshall Norfk 50 E9
Titton Worcs 35 T7
Tiverton Ches W 45 N1
Tiverton Devon 6 C2
Tivetshall St Margaret Norfk 41 L3
Tivetshall St Mary Norfk 41 L3
Tivington Somset 16 B7
Tivy Dale Barns 57 L5
Tixall Staffs 46 C9
Tixover Rutlnd 48 E13
Toab Shet 106 t12
Toadhole Derbys 47 L2
Toadmoor Derbys 46 K3
Tobermory Ag & B 93 N7
Toberonochy Ag & B 87 N4
Tobha Mor W Isls 106 c15
Tocher Abers 104 K8
Tochieneal Moray 104 G4
Tockenham Wilts 18 F5
Tockenham Wick Wilts 18 F4
Tocketts R & Cl 70 K9
Tockholes Bl w D 55 Q2
Tockington S Glos 28 B10
Tockwith N York 64 B9
Todber Dorset 17 U13
Todburn Nthumb 77 N6
Toddington C Beds 31 M7
Toddington Gloucs 36 D14
Toddington Services C Beds 31 M7
Todds Green Herts 31 R7
Todenham Gloucs 36 H13
Todhills Angus 91 P4
Todhills Cumb 75 S13
Todhills Dur 69 R6
Todhills Services Cumb 75 S13
Todmorden Calder 56 D2
Todwick Rothm 57 Q10
Toft Cambs 39 N9
Toft Ches E 55 S11
Toft Lincs 48 G11
Toft Shet 106 u6
Toft Warwks 37 N6
Toft Hill Dur 69 Q7
Toft Hill Lincs 48 K1
Toft Monks Norfk 41 R2
Toft next Newton Lincs 58 H9
Toftrees Norfk 50 E8
Tofts Norfk 50 B1
Togston Nthumb 77 Q5
Tokavaig Highld 100 f8
Tokers Green Oxon 20 B7
Tolastadh W Isls 106 k4
Toldish Cnwll 3 N4
Tolland Somset 16 F10
Tollard Farnham Dorset 8 C5
Tollard Royal Wilts 8 C5
Toll Bar Donc 57 S5
Tollbar End Covtry 37 L5
Toller Fratrum Dorset 7 Q5
Toller Porcorum Dorset 7 Q5
Tollerton N York 64 C7
Tollerton Notts 47 R6
Toller Whelme Dorset 7 P4
Tollesbury Essex 23 M5
Tolleshunt D'Arcy Essex 23 M5
Tolleshunt Knights Essex 23 M5
Tolleshunt Major Essex 23 M5
Tollingham E R Yk 64 J13
Tolpuddle Dorset 7 U6
Tolsta W Isls 106 k4
Tolworth Gt Lon 21 L9
Tomatin Highld 103 M10
Tomchrasky Highld 101 V9
Tomdoun Highld 101 T10
Tomich Highld 102 B10
Tomich Highld 102 F6
Tomich Highld 109 M10
Tomintoul Moray 103 U12
Tomlow Warwks 37 N8
Tomnacross Highld 102 F7
Tomnavoulin Moray 103 V10
Tompkin Staffs 46 B2
Ton Mons 27 R8
Tonbridge Kent 21 U12
Tondu Brdgnd 26 G11
Tonedale Somset 16 F12
Ton fanau Gwynd 43 L13
Tong C Brad 63 Q13
Tong Kent 12 G4
Tong Shrops 45 S12
Tong Green Kent 12 K4
Tongham Surrey 20 F13
Tongland D & G 73 R9
Tong Norton Shrops 45 S12
Tongue Highld 111 M6
Tongue End Lincs 48 J11
Tongwynlais Cardif 27 L11
Tonmawr Neath 26 E8
Tonna Neath 26 D8
Ton-teg Rhondd 26 K10
Tonwell Herts 31 T9
Tonypandy Rhondd 26 H9
Tonyrefail Rhondd 26 J10
Toot Baldon Oxon 30 C12
Toot Hill Essex 22 D7
Toothill Hants 9 M5
Toothill Swindn 29 N11
Tooting Gt Lon 21 N8
Tooting Bec Gt Lon 21 N8
Topcliffe N York 63 T4
Topcroft Norfk 41 N2
Topcroft Street Norfk 41 N2
Topham Donc 57 T4
Top of Hebers Rochdl 56 C5
Toppesfield Essex 22 H1
Toprow Norfk 51 L14
Topsham Devon 6 C7
Top-y-rhos Flints 44 G2
Torbeg N Ayrs 79 R10
Torboll Highld 109 Q5
Torbreck Highld 102 H7
Torbryan Devon 5 U7
Torcastle Highld 94 G3
Torcross Devon 5 U12
Tore Highld 102 H5
Torfrey Cnwll 4 E10
Torinturk Ag & B 79 Q3
Torksey Lincs 58 D11
Tormarton S Glos 28 E12
Tormore N Ayrs 79 R9
Tornagrain Highld 103 L5
Tornaveen Abers 99 L3
Torpenhow Cumb 66 K5
Torphichen W Loth 82 H4
Torphins Abers 99 L3
Torpoint Cnwll 5 L9
Torquay Torbay 6 B12
Torquay Crematorium Torbay 6 B12
Torquhan Border 84 D10

Torran Highld 100 e5
Torrance E Duns 89 P11
Torranyard N Ayrs 81 M4
Torre Somset 16 C9
Torridon Highld 107 R13
Torridon House Highld 107 Q13
Torrin Highld 100 e7
Torrisdale Ag & B 79 P8
Torrisdale Highld 111 P4
Torrisholme Lancs 61 T7
Torroble Highld 108 K4
Torry C Aber 99 S2
Torryburn Fife 82 K1
Torteval Guern 6 b3
Torthorwald D & G 74 K10
Tortington W Susx 10 G10
Torton Worcs 35 T6
Tortworth S Glos 28 D9
Torvaig Highld 100 d5
Torver Cumb 67 L14
Torwood Falk 89 T8
Torwoodlee Border 84 D11
Torworth Notts 57 U10
Toscaig Highld 100 g6
Tosberry Devon 14 G8
Toseland Cambs 38 K8
Tosside Lancs 62 F8
Tostock Suffk 40 G8
Totaig Highld 100 a4
Tote Highld 100 d5
Tote Hill W Susx 10 D6
Totford Hants 19 S13
Tothill Lincs 59 R10
Totland IoW 9 L11
Totley Sheff 57 M11
Totley Brook Sheff 57 M10
Totnes Devon 5 U8
Toton Notts 47 P7
Totronald Ag & B 92 F7
Totscore Highld 100 c3
Tottenham Gt Lon 21 P4
Tottenhill Norfk 49 T11
Tottenhill Row Norfk 49 T11
Totteridge Gt Lon 21 N3
Totternhoe C Beds 31 M8
Tottington Bury 55 S4
Tottleworth Lancs 62 E13
Totton Hants 9 M6
Touchen End W & M 20 E7
Toulston N York 64 B12
Toulton Somset 16 G10
Toulvaddie Highld 109 R8
Tovil Kent 12 E5
Towan Cnwll 3 L4
Toward Ag & B 88 D12
Toward Quay Ag & B 88 D12
Towcester Nhants 37 S11
Towednack Cnwll 2 D9
Tower of London Gt Lon 21 P6
Towersey Oxon 30 F11
Towie Abers 104 E13
Tow Law Dur 69 P5
Town End Cambs 39 P1
Town End Cumb 61 S3
Town End Cumb 67 M11
Townend W Duns 88 J10
Town End Cumb 67 R3
Town Green Lancs 54 K5
Town Green Norfk 51 Q11
Town Head Barns 56 J6
Townhead Cumb 66 G5
Town Head Cumb 67 P12
Townhead Cumb 68 D6
Townhead D & G 73 R11
Town Head N York 62 H8
Townhead of Greenlaw D & G 74 D13
Townhill Fife 90 H14
Town Kelloe Dur 70 E5
Townlake Devon 5 L6
Town Lane Wigan 55 Q7
Town Littleworth E Susx 11 Q7
Town of Lowton Wigan 55 P7
Town Row E Susx 11 T4
Towns End Hants 19 S9
Townsend Somset 17 L12
Townshend Cnwll 2 F10
Town Street Suffk 40 C3
Townwell S Glos 28 D9
Town Yetholm Border 85 L13
Towthorpe C York 64 E8
Towthorpe E R Yk 64 K7
Towton N York 64 B12
Towyn Conwy 53 Q7
Toxteth Lpool 54 J9
Toynton All Saints Lincs 59 Q14
Toynton Fen Side Lincs 48 K1
Toynton St Peter Lincs 59 R14
Toy's Hill Kent 21 S12
Trabboch E Ayrs 81 N8
Trabbochburn E Ayrs 81 P8
Traboe Cnwll 2 J12
Tracebridge Somset 16 E12
Tradespark Highld 103 N5
Trallong Powys 26 H2
Tranent E Loth 84 C4
Tranmere Wirral 54 H9
Trantelbeg Highld 111 T6
Trantlemore Highld 111 T6
Tranwell Nthumb 77 P9
Trapp Carmth 26 A4
Traprain E Loth 84 F4
Trap's Green Warwks 36 F7
Trapshill W Berk 19 N8
Traquair Border 83 R12
Trash Green W Berk 19 U7
Trawden Lancs 62 J12
Trawscoed Cerdgn 33 N6
Trawsfynydd Gwynd 43 P6
Trealaw Rhondd 26 J9
Treales Lancs 61 S13
Trearddur Bay IoA 52 C7
Treaslane Highld 100 c4
Treator Cnwll 3 N1
Tre Aubrey V Glam 16 D2
Trebanog Rhondd 26 J9
Trebanos Neath 26 C7
Trebartha Cnwll 4 H5
Trebarwith Cnwll 4 D3
Trebeath Cnwll 4 H3
Trebetherick Cnwll 4 C2
Treborough Somset 16 C9
Trebudannon Cnwll 3 M3
Trebullett Cnwll 4 J5
Treburgett Cnwll 4 E4
Treburley Cnwll 4 J5
Treburrick Cnwll 3 M2
Trebyan Cnwll 3 R4
Trecastle Powys 26 F2
Trecogo Cnwll 4 J7
Treccott Devon 15 N12
Trecwn Pembks 24 G4
Trecynon Rhondd 26 H7
Tredaule Cnwll 4 H4
Tredavoe Cnwll 2 D11
Tredegar Blae G 27 L6
Tredethy Cnwll 3 R2
Tredington Gloucs 28 H3
Tredington Warwks 36 J12
Tredinnick Cnwll 3 M3
Tredinnick Cnwll 3 Q5
Tredinnick Cnwll 3 R3
Tredinnick Cnwll 4 H7
Tredinnick Cnwll 4 J7
Tredomen Powys 34 D14
Tredrissi Pembks 24 J2
Tredrizzick Cnwll 4 C4
Tredunnock Mons 27 R9
Tredustan Powys 34 D14
Treen Cnwll 2 B12
Treen Cnwll 2 C9
Treesmill Cnwll 3 R5
Treeton Rothm 57 P9
Trefasser Pembks 24 E4
Trefdraeth IoA 52 F8
Trefecca Powys 34 D14
Trefeglwys Powys 33 T3
Trefenter Cerdgn 33 M7
Treffgarne Pembks 24 G5
Treffgarne Owen Pembks 24 E5

Tre-Gibbon Rhondd 26 H6
Tregidden Cnwll 2 J12
Tregiskey Cnwll 3 Q7
Treglemais Pembks 24 D5
Tregole Cnwll 14 F13
Tregonce Cnwll 3 N2
Tregonetha Cnwll 3 P4
Tregonning & Gwinear Mining District Cnwll 2 F10
Tregony Cnwll 3 N8
Tregoodwell Cnwll 4 E4
Tregorrick Cnwll 3 Q6
Tregoss Cnwll 3 P4
Tregoyd Powys 34 E13
Tregregan Cnwll 3 N4
Tre-groes Cerdgn 32 H12
Tregullon Cnwll 3 R4
Tregunna Cnwll 3 P2
Tregunnon Cnwll 4 G4
Tregurrian Cnwll 3 M3
Tregynon Powys 44 C14
Tre-gynwr Carmth 25 R7
Trehafod Rhondd 26 J9
Trehan Cnwll 5 L9
Treharris Myr Td 26 K8
Treharrock Cnwll 4 D4
Trehemborne Cnwll 3 M2
Treherbert Carmth 33 L11
Treherbert Rhondd 26 G8
Trehunist Cnwll 4 J8
Trekenner Cnwll 4 J5
Treknow Cnwll 4 D3
Trelan Cnwll 2 J13
Trelash Cnwll 4 G2
Trelassick Cnwll 3 M6
Trelawne Cnwll 4 G9
Trelawnyd Flints 54 C11
Treleague Cnwll 2 K12
Treleaver Cnwll 2 K13
Trelech Carmth 25 N4
Trelech a'r Betws Carmth 25 P5
Treleddyd-fawr Pembks 24 C5
Trelew Cnwll 3 L9
Trelewis Myr Td 27 L7
Treligga Cnwll 4 C4
Trelights Cnwll 4 B5
Trelill Cnwll 4 C5
Trelinnoe Cnwll 4 J4
Trelion Cnwll 3 N6
Trelissick Cnwll 3 L8
Trelleck Mons 27 U6
Trelleck Grange Mons 27 T7
Trelogan Flints 54 D10
Trelow Cnwll 3 N3
Trelowarren Cnwll 2 H12
Trelowia Cnwll 4 H9
Treluggan Cnwll 4 J9
Trelystan Powys 44 G13
Tremadog Gwynd 43 L5
Tremail Cnwll 4 F3
Tremaine Cnwll 4 G3
Tremar Cnwll 4 G7
Trematon Cnwll 4 K9
Tremeirchion Denbgs 54 C12
Tremethick Cross Cnwll 2 C10
Tre-Mostyn Flints 54 D11
Trenance Cnwll 3 L3
Trenance Cnwll 3 L12
Trenance Cnwll 3 M2
Trenance Cnwll 3 Q7
Trenarren Cnwll 3 Q7
Trench Wrekin 45 Q11
Trench Green Oxon 19 U5
Trendeal Cnwll 3 M6
Trendrine Cnwll 2 D9
Treneague Cnwll 3 P2
Trenear Cnwll 2 H10
Treneglos Cnwll 4 G3
Trenewan Cnwll 4 F10
Trenewth Cnwll 4 E5
Trengune Cnwll 4 F2
Treninnick Cnwll 3 L4
Trenoweth Cnwll 2 K10
Trent Dorset 17 Q13
Trentham C Stke 45 U5
Trentishoe Devon 15 P3
Trentlock Derbys 47 N7
Trent Port Lincs 58 D10
Trent Vale C Stke 45 U5
Trenwheal Cnwll 2 G10
Treoes V Glam 26 H11
Treorchy Rhondd 26 H8
Treowen Mons 27 P6
Trequite Cnwll 4 C5
Tre'r-ddol Cerdgn 33 N2
Trerhyngyll V Glam 26 J12
Trerulefoot Cnwll 4 J9
Tresaith Cerdgn 32 E10
Tresawle Cnwll 3 M7
Trescott Staffs 35 U1
Trescowe Cnwll 2 F10
Tresean Cnwll 3 L5
Tresham Gloucs 28 E9
Treshnish Isles Ag & B 92 G10
Tresillian Cnwll 3 M7
Tresinney Cnwll 4 F4
Treskinnick Cross Cnwll 14 F13
Tresmeer Cnwll 4 H3
Tresparrett Cnwll 4 E2
Tressait P & K 97 N11
Tresta Shet 106 t8
Tresta Shet 106 v4
Treswell Notts 58 C11
Treswithian Downs Crematorium Cnwll 2 G8
Tre Taliesin Cerdgn 33 N2
Trethevey Cnwll 4 E3
Trethewey Cnwll 2 B12
Trethomas Caerph 27 M10
Trethosa Cnwll 3 N6
Trethurgy Cnwll 3 Q5
Tretio Pembks 24 C5
Tretire Herefs 27 U3
Tretower Powys 27 M4
Treuddyn Flints 44 G2
Trevadlock Cnwll 4 H5
Trevalga Cnwll 4 D3
Trevalyn Wrexhm 44 J3
Trevanger Cnwll 4 B5
Trevanson Cnwll 3 P2
Trevarrack Cnwll 2 D10
Trevarren Cnwll 3 N4
Trevarrian Cnwll 3 M3
Trevarrick Cnwll 3 P7
Tre-vaughan Carmth 25 R6
Trevaughan Carmth 25 Q8
Treveal Cnwll 3 L5
Treveighan Cnwll 4 D5
Trevellas Downs Cnwll 2 J5
Trevelmond Cnwll 4 G8
Trevemper Cnwll 3 L5
Treveor Cnwll 3 P7
Treverbyn Cnwll 3 M7
Treverva Cnwll 2 K10
Trevescan Cnwll 2 B12
Trevethin Torfn 27 Q6
Trevia Cnwll 4 E4
Trevigro Cnwll 4 J7
Trevilla Cnwll 3 L8
Treviscoe Cnwll 3 N5
Treviskey Cnwll 3 M8
Trevithick Cnwll 3 N2
Trevithick Cnwll 3 P5
Trevone Cnwll 3 M1
Trevor Wrexhm 44 F5
Trevorgans Cnwll 2 C11
Trevorrick Cnwll 3 N2
Trevowah Cnwll 3 L5
Trewalder Cnwll 4 D4
Trewalkin Powys 27 M1
Trewarmett Cnwll 4 D3
Trewarthenick Cnwll 3 N7
Trewassa Cnwll 4 F3
Trewavas Mining District Cnwll 2 F11
Treween Cnwll 4 H4
Trewellard Cnwll 2 B10
Trewen Cnwll 4 H4
Trewennack Cnwll 2 H11
Trewent Pembks 24 H11
Trewern Powys 44 F11
Trewetha Cnwll 4 C4
Trewethern Cnwll 4 C5
Trewidland Cnwll 4 H8
Trewillis Cnwll 2 K13
Trewint Cnwll 4 F2
Trewint Cnwll 4 H4
Trewithian Cnwll 3 M9
Trewoodloe Cnwll 4 J6
Trewoofe Cnwll 2 C11
Trewoon Cnwll 3 N5
Treworga Cnwll 3 M8
Treworlas Cnwll 3 M9
Treworld Cnwll 4 F2
Tre-wyn Mons 27 Q3
Treyarnon Cnwll 3 M2
Treyford W Susx 10 C7
Trezaise Cnwll 3 N5
Triangle Calder 56 G2

Trillacott Cnwll 4 H3
Trimdon Dur 70 E6
Trimdon Colliery Dur 70 E5
Trimdon Grange Dur 70 E5
Trimingham Norfk 51 N6
Trimley Lower Street Suffk 41 N13
Trimley St Martin Suffk 41 N13
Trimley St Mary Suffk 41 N13
Trimpley Worcs 35 S5
Trimsaran Carmth 25 S9
Trims Green Herts 22 C4
Trimstone Devon 15 M4
Trinafour P & K 97 N11
Trinant Caerph 27 N8
Tring Herts 30 K10
Tringford Herts 30 K10
Tring Wharf Herts 30 K10
Trinity Angus 99 L11
Trinity Jersey 7 d2
Trinity Gask P & K 90 E8
Triscombe Somset 16 G9
Trislaig Highld 94 F4
Trispen Cnwll 3 L6
Tritlington Nthumb 77 Q7
Troan Cnwll 3 M5
Trochry P & K 90 D3
Troedrhiwfuwch Caerph 27 L7
Troedyraur Cerdgn 32 G11
Troedyrhiw Myr Td 26 K7
Trofarth Conwy 53 Q8
Trois Bois Jersey 7 c1
Troon Cnwll 2 H9
Troon S Ayrs 81 L6
Tropical World Roundhay Park Leeds 63 S12
Trossachs Stirlg 89 M4
Trossachs Pier Stirlg 89 M4
Troston Suffk 40 E6
Troswell Cnwll 4 H2
Trotshill Worcs 35 U9
Trottiscliffe Kent 12 C3
Trotton W Susx 10 C6
Troughend Nthumb 76 J6
Trough Gate Lancs 56 C2
Troutbeck Cumb 67 N7
Troutbeck Cumb 67 P2
Troutbeck Bridge Cumb 57 N11
Troway Derbys 57 N11
Trowbridge Wilts 18 C9
Trowell Notts 47 N6
Trowell Services Notts 47 N6
Trowle Common Wilts 18 B9
Trowley Bottom Herts 31 N10
Trowse Newton Norfk 51 N12
Troy Leeds 63 Q12
Trudoxhill Somset 17 T8
Trull Somset 16 H12
Trumfleet Donc 57 T4
Trumpan Highld 100 b3
Trumpet Herefs 35 Q13
Trumpington Cambs 39 P10
Trumpsgreen Surrey 20 G9
Trunch Norfk 51 N6
Trunnah Lancs 61 Q11
Truro Cnwll 3 L8
Truscott Cnwll 4 J4
Trusham Devon 6 A4
Trusley Derbys 46 J6
Trusthorpe Lincs 59 T10
Trysull Staffs 35 U2
Tubney Oxon 29 T8
Tuckenhay Devon 5 U9
Tuckhill Shrops 35 S3
Tuckingmill Cnwll 2 H8
Tuckingmill Wilts 8 C3
Tuckton Bmouth 8 G10
Tucoyse Cnwll 3 P7
Tuddenham Suffk 40 B6
Tuddenham Suffk 41 L11
Tudeley Kent 12 B6
Tudhoe Dur 69 S5
Tudorville Herefs 28 A3
Tudweiliog Gwynd 42 D6
Tuesley Surrey 10 F2
Tuffley Gloucs 28 F5
Tufton Hants 19 Q11
Tufton Pembks 24 H5
Tugby Leics 47 U13
Tugford Shrops 35 M3
Tughall Nthumb 85 U13
Tullibody Clacks 90 C12
Tullich Abers 102 H10
Tullich Highld 109 N13
Tulliemet P & K 97 R13
Tulloch Abers 105 N9
Tullochgorm Ag & B 87 T6
Tulloch Station Highld 96 B3
Tullymurdoch P & K 97 U12
Tullynessle Abers 104 H12
Tulse Hill Gt Lon 21 P8
Tumble Carmth 25 T8
Tumbler's Green Essex 22 K3
Tumby Lincs 48 K2
Tumby Woodside Lincs 49 L2
Tummel Bridge P & K 97 N12
Tunbridge Wells Kent 11 T3
Tunga W Isls 106 j5
Tungate Norfk 51 N8
Tunley BaNES 17 S5
Tunstall C Stke 45 U3
Tunstall E R Yk 65 U13
Tunstall Kent 12 G3
Tunstall Lancs 62 C5
Tunstall N York 69 R13
Tunstall Norfk 51 R12
Tunstall Staffs 45 S9
Tunstall Staffs 45 T11
Tunstall Suffk 41 Q9
Tunstall Sundld 70 E1
Tunstead Derbys 56 H12
Tunstead Norfk 51 N9
Tunstead Milton Derbys 56 F10
Tunworth Hants 19 U11
Tupsley Herefs 35 M12
Tupton Derbys 57 N14
Turgis Green Hants 19 U9
Turkdean Gloucs 29 L5
Tur Langton Leics 37 T2
Turleigh Wilts 18 B8
Turleygreen Shrops 35 S3
Turn Lancs 55 S3
Turnastone Herefs 34 J13
Turnberry S Ayrs 80 K11
Turnchapel C Plym 5 M10
Turnditch Derbys 46 J4
Turner Green Lancs 62 D13
Turner's Green E Susx 11 U6
Turner's Green Warwks 36 G7
Turner's Hill W Susx 11 N3
Turners Puddle Dorset 8 A9
Turnford Herts 31 U12
Turnhouse C Edin 83 N4
Turnworth Dorset 8 A7
Turriff Abers 105 L5
Turton Bottoms Bl w D 55 R3
Turves Cambs 39 M1
Turville Bucks 20 C4
Turville Heath Bucks 20 C4
Turweston Bucks 30 D5
Tushielaw Inn Border 75 R3
Tutbury Staffs 46 H8
Tutnall Worcs 36 C6
Tutshill Gloucs 27 U8
Tuttington Norfk 51 M8
Tutts Clump W Berk 19 S6
Tutwell Cnwll 4 K5
Tuxford Notts 58 B12
Twatt Ork 106 r17
Twatt Shet 106 t8
Twechar E Duns 89 Q10
Tweedmouth Border 85 P8
Tweedsmuir Border 83 M14
Twelve Heads Cnwll 3 L7
Twelve Oaks E Susx 12 C12
Twelvewoods Cnwll 4 G7
Twemlow Green Ches E 55 S13
Twenty Lincs 48 J9
Twerton BaNES 17 T4
Twickenham Gt Lon 21 L8
Twigworth Gloucs 28 F3
Twineham W Susx 11 L6
Twineham Green W Susx 11 L6
Twinhoe BaNES 17 U5
Twinstead Essex 40 E13
Twitchen Devon 15 S7
Twitchen Shrops 34 J5
Twitham Kent 13 Q4
Two Bridges Devon 5 Q6
Two Dales Derbys 57 L14
Two Gates Staffs 46 H13
Two Mile Oak Cross Devon 5 U7
Two Pots Devon 15 M4
Two Waters Herts 31 N11
Twycross Leics 46 K12
Twycross Zoo Leics 46 K12
Twyford Bucks 30 E7
Twyford Hants 9 P4
Twyford Leics 47 T11
Twyford Lincs 48 D9
Twyford Norfk 50 H8
Twyford Wokham 20 C7
Twyford Common Herefs 35 M13
Twyn-carno Caerph 27 L6
Twynholm D & G 73 Q9
Twyning Gloucs 36 H13
Twyning Green Gloucs 36 H13
Twynllanan Carmth 26 E2
Twyn-yr-Odyn V Glam 27 L12
Twyn-y-Sheriff Mons 27 S6
Twywell Nhants 38 E5
Tyberton Herefs 34 J13
Tyburn Birm 36 G2
Tycroes Carmth 25 U9
Tycroes IoA 52 G7

Tycrwyn Powys 44 D10
Tydd Gote Lincs 49 Q10
Tydd St Giles Cambs 49 P10
Tydd St Mary Lincs 49 P10
Tye Hants 9 U7
Tye Green Essex 22 J3
Tye Green Essex 22 J3
Tye Green Essex 39 S13
Tyersal C Brad 63 P13
Tyldesley Wigan 55 Q6
Tyler Hill Kent 13 M3
Tylers Green Bucks 20 F4
Tyler's Green Essex 22 D7
Tyler's Green Surrey 21 Q12
Tylorstown Rhondd 26 J8
Tylwch Powys 33 U4
Ty-nant Conwy 43 T5
Ty-nant Gwynd 43 T8
Tyndrum Stirlg 95 Q14
Tynemouth N Tyne 77 T12
Tynemouth Crematorium N Tyne 77 S12
Tynewydd Rhondd 26 G8
Tyninghame E Loth 84 G3
Tynron D & G 74 F7
Ty'n-y-bryn Rhondd 26 J10
Ty'n-y-coedcae Caerph 27 M10
Tynygongl IoA 52 H6
Tynygraig Cerdgn 33 N7
Ty'n-y-Groes Conwy 53 N8
Tyn-y-nant Rhondd 26 J10
Tyrie Abers 105 Q3
Tyringham M Keyn 38 C11
Tyseley Birm 36 F4
Tythegston Brdgnd 26 F12
Tytherington Ches E 56 C11
Tytherington S Glos 28 C10
Tytherington Somset 18 B12
Tytherington Wilts 18 D12
Tytherleigh Devon 6 K4
Tytherton Lucas Wilts 18 D6
Tyttenhanger Herts 31 Q11
Tywardreath Cnwll 3 R5
Tywardreath Highway Cnwll 3 R5
Tywyn Conwy 53 N7
Tywyn Gwynd 43 L13

U

Ubbeston Green Suffk 41 P6
Ubley BaNES 17 P5
Uckerby N York 69 R12
Uckfield E Susx 11 Q6
Uckinghall Worcs 35 U13
Uckington Gloucs 28 H3
Uckington Shrops 45 N11
Uddingston S Lans 82 C6
Uddington S Lans 82 G11
Udimore E Susx 12 G12
Udny Green Abers 105 P10
Udny Station Abers 105 Q11
Uffcott Wilts 18 H5
Uffculme Devon 6 E2
Uffington Lincs 48 G12
Uffington Oxon 29 R10
Uffington Shrops 45 M11
Ufford C Pete 48 G13
Ufford Suffk 41 N9
Ufton Warwks 37 L8
Ufton Nervet W Berk 19 T7
Ugadale Ag & B 79 P10
Ugborough Devon 5 Q9
Uggeshall Suffk 41 R4
Ugglebarnby N York 71 Q11
Ughill Sheff 57 L8
Ugley Essex 22 D2
Ugley Green Essex 22 D2
Ugthorpe N York 71 N10
Uibhist A Deas W Isls 106 d15
Uibhist A Tuath W Isls 106 d12
Uig Ag & B 88 B7
Uig Highld 100 c3
Uig Highld 100 a4
Uig W Isls 106 f6
Uigshader Highld 100 d5
Uisken Ag & B 86 J2
Ulbster Highld 112 H8
Ulcat Row Cumb 67 P8
Ulceby Lincs 59 R11
Ulceby N Linc 58 K3
Ulceby Skitter N Linc 58 K3
Ulcombe Kent 12 F6
Uldale Cumb 66 K5
Uley Gloucs 28 E7
Ulgham Nthumb 77 Q7
Ullapool Highld 108 B6
Ullenhall Warwks 36 F7
Ullenwood Gloucs 28 H4
Ulleskelf N York 64 C12
Ullesthorpe Leics 37 P3
Ulley Rothm 57 P9
Ullingswick Herefs 35 N11
Ullinish Lodge Hotel Highld 100 c6
Ullock Cumb 66 G8
Ullswater Cumb 67 N8
Ullswater Steamers Cumb 67 N9
Ulpha Cumb 61 L1
Ulpha Cumb 61 J14
Ulrome E R Yk 65 R8
Ulsta Shet 106 u5
Ulting Wick Essex 22 K6
Ulva Ag & B 93 L11
Ulverley Green Solhll 36 F4
Ulverston Cumb 61 P4
Ulwell Dorset 8 E12
Ulzieside D & G 74 E4
Umberleigh Devon 15 P8
Unapool Highld 110 E10
Underbarrow Cumb 67 P14
Under Burnmouth Border 75 U9
Undercliffe C Brad 63 P13
Underdale Shrops 45 M11
Underling Green Kent 12 E6
Under River Kent 21 T12
Underwood Notts 47 N3
Undley Suffk 39 T4
Undy Mons 27 S10
Union Mills IoM 60 e7
Union Street E Susx 12 D9
Unst Shet 106 v3
Unstone Derbys 57 N11
Unstone Green Derbys 57 N11
Unthank Cumb 67 N3
Unthank Cumb 67 R5
Unthank Cumb 68 C4
Unthank Derbys 57 M11
Unthank Nthumb 85 M11
Upavon Wilts 18 H10
Up Cerne Dorset 7 S4
Upchurch Kent 12 F2
Upcott Devon 15 S7
Upcott Herefs 34 H10
Upend Cambs 39 U9
Up Exe Devon 6 C4
Upgate Norfk 50 K10
Upgate Street Norfk 40 K2
Upgate Street Norfk 41 N2
Uphall Dorset 7 Q4
Uphall W Loth 82 K4
Uphall Station W Loth 82 K4
Upham Devon 15 U11
Upham Hants 9 Q4
Uphampton Herefs 34 J8
Uphampton Worcs 35 T8
Uphill N Som 16 K5
Up Holland Lancs 55 M5
Uplawmoor E Rens 81 M2
Upleadon Gloucs 28 D2
Upleatham R & Cl 70 K9
Uplees Kent 12 K3
Uploders Dorset 7 P6
Uplowman Devon 16 D13
Uplyme Devon 6 K6
Up Marden W Susx 10 B8
Up Mudford Somset 17 Q13
Up Nately Hants 19 U10
Upottery Devon 6 H3
Upper Affcot Shrops 34 K3
Upper Ardchronie Highld 109 M7
Upper Arley Worcs 35 S4
Upper Arncott Oxon 30 C9
Upper Astrop Nhants 30 B5
Upper Badcall Highld 110 D9
Upper Basildon W Berk 19 T5
Upper Batley Kirk 63 Q14
Upper Beeding W Susx 11 L8
Upper Benefield Nhants 38 F3
Upper Bentley Worcs 36 C7
Upper Bighouse Highld 111 T5
Upper Birchwood Derbys 47 M3
Upper Boat Rhondd 27 L10
Upper Boddington Nhants 37 N10
Upper Borth Cerdgn 33 M2
Upper Brailes Warwks 36 K13
Upper Breakish Highld 100 f7
Upper Breinton Herefs 35 L12
Upper Broadheath Worcs 35 T9
Upper Broughton Notts 47 S8
Upper Buckenhill Herefs 35 N13
Upper Bucklebury W Berk 19 S7
Upper Burgate Hants 8 H5
Upper Bush Medway 12 C2
Upperby Cumb 67 P2
Upper Caldecote C Beds 38 J11
Upper Canada N Som 17 L5
Upper Canterton Hants 9 L7

Upper Catesby Nhants 37 P9
Upper Catshill Worcs 36 C6
Upper Chapel Powys 34 B12
Upper Cheddon Somset 16 H11
Upper Chicksgrove Wilts 8 D3
Upper Chute Wilts 19 L10
Upper Clapton Gt Lon 21 P5
Upper Clatford Hants 19 N11
Upper Coberley Gloucs 28 J4
Upper Cokeham W Susx 11 K10
Upper Cotton Staffs 46 E4
Upper Cound Shrops 45 N12
Upper Cudworth Barns 57 N4
Upper Cumberworth Kirk 56 K5
Upper Dallachy Moray 104 D3
Upper Dean Bed 38 F7
Upper Denby Kirk 56 K5
Upper Denton Cumb 76 B12
Upper Dicker E Susx 11 T9
Upper Dinchope Shrops 35 L4
Upper Dounreay Highld 112 B3
Upper Dovercourt Essex 23 T1
Upper Drumbane Stirlg 89 Q4
Upper Dunsforth N York 63 U7
Upper Eashing Surrey 10 F2
Upper Eathie Highld 103 L3
Upper Egleton Herefs 35 P12
Upper Elkstone Staffs 46 E2
Upper Ellastone Staffs 46 F5
Upper Enham Hants 19 N10
Upper Farmcote Shrops 35 S2
Upper Farringdon Hants 19 V13
Upper Framilode Gloucs 28 D5
Upper Froyle Hants 19 U12
Upper Godney Somset 17 N8
Upper Gravenhurst C Beds 31 Q4
Upper Green Mons 27 R4
Upper Green Suffk 39 U9
Upper Green W Berk 19 M8
Upper Grove Common Herefs 28 A3
Upper Hackney Derbys 46 J1
Upper Hale Surrey 20 E13
Upper Halliford Surrey 20 J9
Upper Halling Medway 12 C3
Upper Hambleton Rutlnd 48 D12
Upper Harbledown Kent 13 M4
Upper Hardres Court Kent 13 N5
Upper Hardwick Herefs 34 K9
Upper Hartfield E Susx 11 R4
Upper Hartshay Derbys 47 L3
Upper Hatherley Gloucs 28 H4
Upper Haugh Rothm 57 P7
Upper Hayton Shrops 35 M4
Upper Heaton Kirk 56 J3
Upper Helmsley N York 64 F8
Upper Hergest Herefs 34 G10
Upper Heyford Nhants 37 S9
Upper Heyford Oxon 29 U3
Upper Hill Herefs 35 L10
Upper Hockenden Kent 21 S9
Upper Hopton Kirk 56 J3
Upper Howsell Worcs 35 S11
Upper Hulme Staffs 46 D1
Upper Ifold Surrey 10 G3
Upper Inglesham Swindn 29 P8
Upper Kilcott Gloucs 28 E9
Upper Killay Swans 25 U12
Upper Kinchrackine Ag & B 94 H13
Upper Lambourn W Berk 19 M4
Upper Landywood Staffs 46 C12
Upper Langford N Som 17 N5
Upper Langwith Derbys 57 R13
Upper Largo Fife 91 P11
Upper Leigh Staffs 46 D6
Upper Littleton N Som 17 P4
Upper Lochton Abers 99 M4
Upper Longdon Staffs 46 E11
Upper Ludstone Shrops 35 T1
Upper Lybster Highld 112 G9
Upper Lydbrook Gloucs 28 A4
Upper Lye Herefs 34 J7
Upper Maes-coed Herefs 34 J13
Upper Midhope Sheff 56 K6
Uppermill Oldham 56 E5
Upper Milton Worcs 35 T6
Upper Minety Wilts 28 J9
Upper Moor Worcs 36 C11
Upper Moor Side Leeds 63 Q13
Upper Mulben Moray 104 D5
Upper Netchwood Shrops 35 P2
Upper Nobut Staffs 46 D6
Upper Norwood W Susx 10 D6
Upper Padley Derbys 56 K11
Upper Pennington Hants 9 L9
Upper Pollicott Bucks 30 E9
Upper Poppleton C York 64 D9
Upper Quinton Warwks 36 G11
Upper Ratley Hants 9 L4
Upper Rissington Gloucs 29 P4
Upper Rochford Worcs 35 P7
Upper Ruscoe D & G 73 P7
Upper Sapey Herefs 35 Q8
Upper Seagry Wilts 18 E5
Upper Shelton C Beds 38 C11
Upper Sheringham Norfk 50 K5
Upper Skelmorlie N Ayrs 88 F12
Upper Slaughter Gloucs 29 M3
Upper Soudley Gloucs 28 C5
Upper Spond Herefs 34 H10
Upper Standen Kent 13 N7
Upper Staploe Bed 38 J9
Upper Stoke Norfk 51 N13
Upper Stowe Nhants 37 S9
Upper Street Hants 8 H5
Upper Street Norfk 51 P10
Upper Street Norfk 51 P11
Upper Street Suffk 40 C10
Upper Street Suffk 40 J11
Upper Strensham Worcs 36 B12
Upper Sundon C Beds 31 N7
Upper Swell Gloucs 29 M3
Upper Tankersley Barns 57 M6
Upper Tasburgh Norfk 41 M2
Upper Tean Staffs 46 D6
Upperthong Kirk 56 J5
Upperthorpe N Linc 58 C5
Upper Threapwood Ches W 44 K4
Upperton W Susx 10 F6
Uppertown Derbys 57 M14
Upper Town Dur 69 M4
Upper Town Herefs 35 M11
Upper Town N Som 17 P3
Uppertown Highld 112 H1
Upper Town Suffk 40 E7
Upper Tumble Carmth 25 T8
Upper Tysoe Warwks 36 K12
Upper Ufford Suffk 41 N9
Upper Upham Wilts 19 K6
Upper Upnor Medway 12 E2
Upper Victoria Angus 91 T4
Upper Vobster Somset 17 T7
Upper Wardington Oxon 37 N11
Upper Weald M Keyn 30 H5
Upper Weedon Nhants 37 R9
Upper Welland Worcs 35 S12
Upper Wellingham E Susx 11 Q8
Upper Weston BaNES 17 T3
Upper Weybread Suffk 41 N5
Upper Wick Worcs 35 T10
Upper Wield Hants 19 U13
Upper Winchendon Bucks 30 F9
Upper Woodford Wilts 18 H13
Upper Wootton Hants 19 S9
Upper Wraxall Wilts 18 B6
Upperwood Derbys 46 H2

Upper Wyche Worcs 35 S12
Uppincott Devon 15 U12
Uppingham Rutlnd 48 C14
Uppington Dorset 8 F8
Uppington Shrops 45 N12
Upsall N York 64 B2
Upsettlington Border 85 M9
Upshire Essex 31 U12
Up Somborne Hants 9 M2
Upstreet Kent 13 P3
Up Sydling Dorset 7 R4
Upthorpe Suffk 40 G6
Upton Bucks 30 F10
Upton C Pete 48 H13
Upton Cambs 38 J6
Upton Ches W 54 K13
Upton Cnwll 4 H11
Upton Cnwll 15 L13
Upton Cumb 67 M6
Upton Devon 6 E5
Upton Devon 5 S11
Upton Dorset 8 D10
Upton Dorset 8 B9
Upton E R Yk 65 Q8
Upton Halton 55 L9
Upton Hants 9 M5
Upton Hants 19 N9
Upton Leics 47 L14
Upton Lincs 58 E9
Upton Nhants 37 T9
Upton Norfk 51 Q11
Upton Notts 47 T3
Upton Notts 58 B11
Upton Oxon 19 R3
Upton Oxon 29 P5
Upton Pembks 24 H9
Upton R & Cl 71 M9
Upton Slough 20 G7
Upton Somset 16 C11
Upton Somset 17 N11
Upton Wakefd 57 Q3
Upton Warwks 36 G9
Upton Wilts 8 B2
Upton Wirral 54 G8
Upton Bishop Herefs 35 P14
Upton Cheyney S Glos 17 S3
Upton Cressett Shrops 35 Q2
Upton Crews Herefs 35 P14
Upton Cross Cnwll 4 H6
Upton End C Beds 31 P6
Upton Grey Hants 19 U11
Upton Heath Ches W 54 K13
Upton Hellions Devon 15 T12
Upton Lovell Wilts 18 D12
Upton Magna Shrops 45 N11
Upton Noble Somset 17 T9
Upton Pyne Devon 6 B5
Upton St Leonards Gloucs 28 G4
Upton Scudamore Wilts 18 C11
Upton Snodsbury Worcs 36 B10
Upton Towans Cnwll 2 F8
Upton-upon-Severn Worcs 35 U12
Upton Warren Worcs 36 B7
Upwaltham W Susx 10 F8
Upware Cambs 39 R6
Upwell Norfk 49 Q13
Upwey Dorset 7 S7
Upwick Green Herts 22 C3
Upwood Cambs 39 L4
Urchfont Wilts 18 F9
Urdimarsh Herefs 35 M11
Ure Bank N York 63 S5
Urlay Nook S on T 70 E10
Urmston Traffd 55 S8
Urquhart Moray 104 B3
Urquhart Castle Highld 102 F9
Urra N York 70 J12
Urray Highld 102 F5
Usan Angus 99 N13
Ushaw Moor Dur 69 R4
Usk Mons 27 R7
Usselby Lincs 58 J8
Usworth Sundld 77 S14
Utkinton Ches W 55 M13
Utley C Brad 63 L11
Uton Devon 15 T13
Utterby Lincs 59 P8
Uttoxeter Staffs 46 E7
Uwchmynydd Gwynd 42 B8
Uxbridge Gt Lon 20 J6
Uyeasound Shet 106 v3
Uzmaston Pembks 24 G8

V

Vale Guern 6 e2
Vale of Glamorgan Crematorium V Glam 16 C2
Valley IoA 52 C7
Valley End Surrey 20 G10
Valley Truckle Cnwll 4 E4
Valtos Highld 100 e3
Valtos W Isls 106 f5
Vange Essex 22 H10
Varteg Torfn 27 P6
Vatsetter Shet 106 v5
Vatten Highld 100 b5
Vaynor Myr Td 27 K6
Vazon Bay Guern 6 c2
Veensgarth Shet 106 u9
Velindre Powys 34 E13
Vellow Somset 16 E9
Velly Devon 14 F8
Venngreen Devon 14 K10
Vennington Shrops 44 H12
Venn Ottery Devon 6 E6
Venny Tedburn Devon 15 T13
Venterdon Cnwll 4 J6
Ventnor IoW 9 R13
Venton Devon 5 P9
Vernham Dean Hants 19 M9
Vernham Street Hants 19 M9
Vernolds Common Shrops 35 L4
Verwood Dorset 8 F7
Veryan Cnwll 3 N8
Veryan Green Cnwll 3 N7
Vicarage Devon 6 J7
Vickerstown Cumb 61 M6
Victoria Barns 56 K4
Victoria Blae G 27 M6
Victoria Cnwll 3 P4
Vidlin Shet 106 u7
Viewfield Moray 104 B3
Viewpark N Lans 82 C6
Vigo Kent 12 B3
Village de Putron Guern 6 e3
Ville la Bas Jersey 7 a1
Villiaze Guern 6 c3
Vinehall Street E Susx 12 D11
Vines Cross E Susx 11 T7
Vinters Park Crematorium Kent 12 E4
Virginia Water Surrey 20 G9
Virginstow Devon 14 K2
Vobster Somset 17 T7
Voe Shet 106 u7
Vowchurch Herefs 34 J13
Vulcan Village St Hel 55 N8

W

Waberthwaite Cumb 66 H14
Wackerfield Dur 69 Q8
Wacton Norfk 41 L2
Wadborough Worcs 36 B11
Waddesdon Bucks 30 F9
Waddesdon Manor Bucks 30 F9
Waddeton Devon 6 A13
Waddicar Sefton 54 J7
Waddingham Lincs 58 G7
Waddington Lincs 58 F14
Waddon Devon 6 C7
Wadebridge Cnwll 3 P2
Wadeford Somset 6 K2
Wadenhoe Nhants 38 F4
Wadesmill Herts 31 U9
Wadhurst E Susx 12 B9
Wadshelf Derbys 57 M12
Wadswick Wilts 18 B7
Wadworth Donc 57 R7
Waen Denbgs 53 T9
Waen Denbgs 54 C13
Waen Flints 54 D12
Waen Powys 44 E10
Waen-pentir Gwynd 52 J9
Waen-wen Gwynd 52 J9
Wagbeach Shrops 44 J13
Wainfelin Torfn 27 P6
Wainfleet All Saints Lincs 49 R2
Wainfleet Bank Lincs 49 R2
Wainfleet St Mary Lincs 59 S14
Wainford Norfk 41 Q3
Wainhouse Corner Cnwll 14 E13
Wainscott Medway 22 H13
Wain's Hill N Som 17 L2
Wainstalls Calder 56 F1
Waitby Cumb 68 F11
Waithe Lincs 59 N6
Wakefield Wakefd 57 M3
Wakefield Crematorium Wakefd 57 M3
Wake Green Birm 36 E3
Wakerley Nhants 48 E14
Wakes Colne Essex 23 L2
Walberswick Suffk 41 S5
Walberton W Susx 10 F9
Walbottle N u Ty 77 P12
Walby Cumb 75 U13
Walcombe Somset 17 P7
Walcot Lincs 48 G7
Walcot Lincs 48 J4
Walcot N Linc 58 E2
Walcot Shrops 34 J4
Walcot Shrops 45 N11
Walcot Swindn 29 M10
Walcot Warwks 36 G10
Walcote Leics 37 Q4
Walcot Green Norfk 40 K4
Walcott Lincs 48 J2
Walcott Norfk 51 P6
Walden N York 63 L2
Walden Head N York 62 K2
Walden Stubbs N York 57 S3
Walderslade Medway 12 D3
Walderton W Susx 10 B8
Walditch Dorset 7 N6
Waldley Derbys 46 F6
Waldridge Dur 69 R2
Waldringfield Suffk 41 N11
Waldron E Susx 11 S7
Wales Rothm 57 Q10
Wales Somset 17 Q12
Walesby Lincs 58 K8
Walesby Notts 57 U12
Wales Millennium Centre Cardif 27 M13
Walford Herefs 28 A3
Walford Herefs 34 K6
Walford Shrops 44 K9
Walford Heath Shrops 44 K10
Walgherton Ches E 45 Q4
Walgrave Nhants 38 B6
Walhampton Hants 9 L9
Walkden Salfd 55 R6
Walker N u Ty 77 R12
Walkerburn Border 83 S11
Walkeringham Notts 58 C7
Walkerith Lincs 58 C8
Walkern Herts 31 S7
Walker's Green Herefs 35 M11
Walker's Heath Birm 36 E5
Walkerton Fife 90 K11
Walkford Dorset 8 J10
Walkhampton Devon 5 N7
Walkington E R Yk 65 M12
Walkley Sheff 57 M9
Walk Mill Lancs 62 H14
Walkwood Worcs 36 D8
Wall Nthumb 76 J12
Wall Staffs 46 E12
Wallacetown S Ayrs 80 K10
Wallacetown S Ayrs 81 M8
Wallands Park E Susx 11 Q8
Wallasey Wirral 54 G8
Wall End Cumb 61 N3
Wall End Herefs 35 L9
Wallend Medway 23 L13
Waller's Green Herefs 35 Q13
Wallhead Cumb 75 U13
Wall Heath Dudley 35 U3
Wall Houses Nthumb 77 L12
Wallingford Oxon 19 T3
Wallington Gt Lon 21 N10
Wallington Hants 9 R7
Wallington Herts 31 S5
Wallington Heath Wsall 46 C13
Wallis Pembks 24 H5
Walliswood Surrey 10 J3
Wall Nook Dur 69 S2
Walls Shet 106 s9
Wallsend N Tyne 77 S12
Wallthwaite Cumb 67 N7
Wall under Haywood Shrops 35 M2
Wallyford E Loth 83 S4
Walmer Kent 13 S5
Walmer Bridge Lancs 55 L1
Walmersley Bury 55 T4
Walmestone Kent 13 P4
Walmley Birm 36 F2
Walmley Ash Birm 36 F2
Walmsgate Lincs 59 Q11
Walpole Somset 16 K8
Walpole Suffk 41 Q6
Walpole Cross Keys Norfk 49 R10
Walpole Highway Norfk 49 R10
Walpole St Andrew Norfk 49 R10
Walpole St Peter Norfk 49 R10
Walrow Somset 16 K7
Walsall Wsall 46 D14
Walsall Wood Wsall 46 D13
Walsden Calder 56 D2
Walsgrave on Sowe Covtry 37 L4
Walsham le Willows Suffk 40 H6
Walshaw Bury 55 S4
Walshford N York 63 U9
Walsoken Norfk 49 Q11
Walston S Lans 83 L9
Walsworth Herts 31 Q6
Walter's Ash Bucks 20 D3
Walters Green Kent 11 S2
Walterston V Glam 16 D2
Walterstone Herefs 27 Q1
Waltham Kent 13 M6
Waltham NE Lin 59 N6
Waltham Abbey Essex 31 U12
Waltham Chase Hants 9 R5
Waltham Cross Herts 31 U11
Waltham on the Wolds Leics 48 B9
Waltham St Lawrence W & M 20 D7
Waltham's Cross Essex 22 G1
Walthamstow Gt Lon 21 Q5
Walton C Pete 48 J13
Walton Cumb 75 U13
Walton Derbys 57 M14
Walton Leeds 63 U10
Walton Leics 37 Q3
Walton M Keyn 30 J5
Walton Powys 34 G10
Walton Shrops 34 K3
Walton Somset 17 M9
Walton Staffs 45 U7
Walton Staffs 45 U8
Walton Suffk 41 N13
Walton W Susx 10 C9
Walton Wakefd 57 M3
Walton Wrekin 45 N10
Walton Cardiff Gloucs 36 B13
Walton East Pembks 24 H6
Walton Elm Dorset 17 U13
Walton Grounds Nhants 30 B6
Walton-in-Gordano N Som 27 S13
Walton Lea Crematorium Warrtn 55 P9
Walton-le-Dale Lancs 62 B14
Walton-on-Thames Surrey 20 K9
Walton-on-the-Hill Staffs 46 C9
Walton on the Hill Surrey 21 M11
Walton on the Naze Essex 23 T3
Walton on the Wolds Leics 47 Q10
Walton-on-Trent Derbys 46 H10
Walton Park N Som 17 M2
Walton West Pembks 24 E8
Walwen Flints 54 E12
Walwen Flints 54 D11
Walwen Flints 54 E11
Walwick Nthumb 76 J11
Walworth Darltn 69 R9
Walworth Gt Lon 21 P7
Walworth Gate Darltn 69 R8
Walwyn's Castle Pembks 24 E8
Wambrook Somset 6 K3
Wampool Cumb 66 K2
Wanborough Surrey 20 F13
Wanborough Swindn 29 P10
Wandon End Herts 31 P8
Wandsworth Gt Lon 21 N8
Wangford Suffk 41 S5
Wangford Suffk 40 B4
Wanlip Leics 47 Q11
Wanlockhead D & G 74 G4
Wannock E Susx 11 T10
Wansford C Pete 48 F14
Wansford E R Yk 65 N9
Wanshurst Green Kent 12 E6
Wanstead Gt Lon 21 R5
Wanswell Gloucs 28 C6
Wantage Oxon 29 S9
Wants Green Worcs 35 S9
Wappenbury Warwks 37 L7
Wappenham Nhants 37 R11
Warbleton E Susx 11 U7
Warborough Oxon 19 T2
Warboys Cambs 39 M4
Warbreck Bpool 61 Q12
Warbstow Cnwll 4 G2
Warburton Traffd 55 R9
Warcop Cumb 68 E9
Warden Kent 23 N13
Warden Nthumb 76 K12
Warden Street C Beds 31 P4
Ward End Birm 36 F3
Ward Green Suffk 40 J7
Ward Green Cross Lancs 62 C12
Wardhedges C Beds 31 N5
Wardington Oxon 37 N11
Wardle Ches E 45 Q2
Wardle Rochdl 56 D4
Wardley Gatesd 77 S13
Wardley Rutlnd 48 C13
Wardley Salfd 55 R6
Wardlow Derbys 56 J12
Wardsend Ches E 56 D10
Wardy Hill Cambs 39 Q4
Ware Herts 31 U10
Ware Kent 13 Q3
Wareham Dorset 8 C11
Warehorne Kent 12 J9
Warenford Nthumb 85 T13
Waren Mill Nthumb 85 T12
Warenton Nthumb 85 S12
Wareside Herts 31 U9
Waresley Cambs 38 K10
Waresley Worcs 35 U6
Ware Street Kent 12 E4
Warfield Br For 20 E8
Warfleet Devon 5 V11
Wargate Lincs 48 K6
Wargrave Wokham 20 C7

Warham Herefs...35 L13
Warham All Saints Norfk...50 G5
Warham St Mary Norfk...50 G5
Wark Nthumb...76 H10
Warkleigh Devon...15 P8
Warkton Nhants...38 C5
Warkworth Nhants...37 N12
Warkworth Nthumb...77 Q4
Warlaby N York...63 S1
Warland Calder...56 D2
Warleggan Cnwll...4 F7
Warlingham Surrey...21 Q11
Warmbrook Derbys...46 J3
Warmfield Wakefd...57 N3
Warmingham Ches E...45 R1
Warmington Nhants...38 G2
Warmington Warwks...37 M11
Warminster Wilts...18 C11
Warmley S Glos...17 N2
Warmsworth Donc...57 R6
Warmwell Dorset...7 U7
Warndon Worcs...35 U9
Warner Bros Studio Tour Herts...31 N12
Warnford Hants...9 S4
Warnham W Susx...10 K4
Warningcamp W Susx...10 G9
Warninglid W Susx...11 L5
Warren Pembks...24 F11
Warren Row W & M...20 D6
Warren's Green Herts...31 S7
Warren Street Kent...12 H5
Warrington M Keyn...38 C10
Warrington Warrtn...55 P9
Warriston C Edin...83 Q3
Warsash Hants...9 P7
Warslow Staffs...46 F2
Warsop Vale Notts...57 R13
Warter E R Yk...64 K9
Warthermaske N York...63 Q3
Warthill N York...64 F8
Wartling E Susx...11 V9
Wartnaby Leics...47 U9
Warton Lancs...61 S14
Warton Lancs...61 T5
Warton Nthumb...77 N5
Warton Warwks...36 J7
Warwick Warwks...36 J8
Warwick Bridge Cumb...67 Q1
Warwick Castle Warwks...36 J8
Warwick-on-Eden Cumb...67 Q1
Warwicksland Cumb...75 U10
Wasbister Ork...106 s16
Wasdale Head Cumb...66 K12
Washall Hants...22 B1
Washaway Cnwll...3 Q3
Washbourne Devon...5 S9
Washbrook Somset...17 M6
Washbrook Suffk...40 K12
Washfield Devon...16 B13
Washfold N York...69 N12
Washford Somset...16 E8
Washford Pyne Devon...15 T10
Washingborough Lincs...58 H12
Washington Sundld...70 D1
Washington W Susx...10 J8
Washington Services Gatesd...69 S1
Washwood Heath Birm...36 F3
Wasing W Berk...19 S8
Waskerley Dur...69 N3
Wasperton Warwks...36 J9
Wasps Nest Lincs...58 J14
Wass N York...64 D4
Watchet Somset...16 E8
Watchfield Oxon...29 P9
Watchfield Somset...16 K7
Watchgate Cumb...67 R13
Watchhill Cumb...66 J4
Watcombe Torbay...6 B11
Watendlath Cumb...67 L9
Water Devon...5 T4
Water Lancs...55 T1
Waterbeach Cambs...39 Q7
Waterbeck D & G...75 P10
Waterden Norfk...50 E6
Water Eaton Oxon...30 B10
Water Eaton Staffs...45 U12
Water End Bed...38 H11
Water End C Beds...31 N5
Water End E R Yk...64 H11
Water End Herts...31 M10
Water End Herts...31 N10
Waterfall Staffs...46 E3
Waterfoot E Rens...81 R1
Waterford Herts...31 T10
Water Fryston Wakefd...57 Q2
Watergate Cnwll...4 F5
Waterhead Cumb...67 N12
Waterheads Border...83 P8
Waterhouses Dur...69 Q4
Waterhouses Staffs...46 E3
Wateringbury Kent...12 C5
Waterlane Gloucs...28 H7
Waterloo Derbys...57 P14
Waterloo Herefs...34 H11
Waterloo Highld...100 f7
Waterloo N Lans...82 F7
Waterloo P & K...90 G4
Waterloo Pembks...24 G10
Waterloo Poole...8 D10
Waterloo Sefton...54 J7
Waterloo Cross Devon...6 F2
Waterloo Port Gwynd...52 G10
Waterlooville Hants...9 T7
Water Newton Cambs...38 H1
Water Orton Warwks...36 G2
Waterperry Oxon...30 D11
Waterrow Somset...16 E11
Watersfield W Susx...10 G7
Waterside Bl w D...55 R2
Waterside Bucks...30 K11
Waterside Cumb...66 K3
Waterside Donc...57 U4
Waterside E Ayrs...81 N11
Waterside E Ayrs...81 P3
Waterside E Duns...89 P10
Water's Nook Bolton...55 Q5
Waterstein Highld...100 a5
Waterstock Oxon...30 D11
Waterston Pembks...24 F10
Water Stratford Bucks...30 F6
Water Street Neath...26 E11
Waters Upton Wrekin...45 P10
Water Yeat Cumb...61 P2
Watford Herts...20 K3
Watford Nhants...37 R7
Watford Gap Services Nhants...37 R7
Wath N York...63 N6
Wath N York...63 S3
Wath upon Dearne Rothm...57 P6
Watlington Norfk...49 T11
Watlington Oxon...19 U2
Watnall Notts...47 N4
Watten Highld...112 F6
Wattisfield Suffk...40 H6
Wattisham Suffk...40 H10
Watton Dorset...7 N6
Watton E R Yk...65 N9
Watton Norfk...50 F13
Watton-at-Stone Herts...31 T9
Wattons Green Essex...22 D8
Wattston N Lans...82 E4
Wattstown Rhondd...26 J9
Wattsville Caerph...27 N7
Waulkmill Abers...98 K4
Waunarlwydd Swans...25 V11
Waunfawr Cerdgn...33 M4
Waunfawr Gwynd...52 H11
Waungron Swans...25 U10
Waunlwyd Blae G...27 N6
Wavendon M Keyn...30 K5
Waverbridge Cumb...66 K3
Waverton Ches W...45 L1
Waverton Cumb...66 K3
Wawne E R Yk...65 P13
Waxham Norfk...51 R9
Waxholme E R Yk...65 U14
Way Kent...13 Q3
Waye Devon...5 S7
Way Village Devon...15 U10
Wayford Somset...7 M3
Waytown Dorset...7 N5
Way Wick N Som...17 L4
Weacombe Somset...16 F8
Weald Oxon...29 R7
Wealdstone Gt Lon...21 L5
Weardley Leeds...63 R10
Wearhead Dur...68 J5
Wearne Somset...17 M11

Wear Valley Crematorium Dur...69 S6
Weasdale Cumb...68 E12
Weasenham All Saints Norfk...50 D9
Weasenham St Peter Norfk...50 E9
Weaste Salfd...55 T7
Weatheroak Hill Worcs...36 E6
Weaverham Ches W...55 P12
Weaverslake Staffs...46 F10
Weaverthorpe N York...65 M5
Webbington Somset...17 L5
Webb's Heath S Glos...28 C13
Webheath Worcs...36 D7
Webton Herefs...34 K13
Wedderlairs Abers...105 P8
Wedding Hall Fold...62 J10
Weddington Kent...13 Q4
Weddington Warwks...37 L2
Wedhampton Wilts...18 G9
Wedmore Somset...17 M7
Wednesbury Sandw...36 C1
Wednesfield Wolves...46 B13
Weecar Notts...58 D13
Weedon Bucks...30 H9
Weedon Nhants...37 R9
Weedon Lois Nhants...37 R11
Weeford Staffs...46 F12
Week Devon...15 N7
Week Devon...15 P8
Week Somset...16 B11
Weeke Devon...15 S11
Weeke Hants...9 P2
Weekley Nhants...38 C4
Weel E R Yk...65 P13
Weeley Essex...23 R3
Weeley Heath Essex...23 R3
Weem P & K...90 B2
Weeping Cross Staffs...46 B9
Weethley Warwks...36 E9
Weeting Norfk...40 C3
Weeton E R Yk...59 Q2
Weeton Lancs...61 R13
Weeton N York...63 R10
Weetwood Leeds...63 R12
Weir Cumb...54 C1
Weir Quay Devon...5 L7
Weirbrook Shrops...44 H9
Weirside Shet...106 u8
Welbeck Norfk...50 J11
Welborne Norfk...50 J11
Welbourn Lincs...48 E3
Welburn N York...64 E6
Welburn N York...64 F4
Welbury N York...70 E12
Welby Lincs...48 E6
Welches Dam Cambs...39 Q3
Welcombe Devon...14 F9
Weldon Nthumb...77 N6
Weld Bank Lancs...55 N3
Welford Nhants...37 S4
Welford W Berk...19 P6
Welford-on-Avon Warwks...36 F10
Welham Leics...37 U2
Welham Notts...58 B10
Welham Green Herts...31 R11
Well Hants...20 C13
Well Lincs...59 R12
Well N York...63 R3
Welland Worcs...35 S12
Wellbank Angus...91 N4
Well End Bucks...20 E5
Well End Herts...21 M3
Wellesbourne Warwks...36 J9
Wellesbourne Mountford Warwks...36 J9
Well Head Herts...31 Q7
Well Hill Kent...21 S10
Wellingborough Nhants...38 C7
Wellingham Norfk...50 E9
Wellingore Lincs...48 E2
Wellington Cumb...66 G12
Wellington Herefs...35 L11
Wellington Somset...16 F12
Wellington Wrekin...45 P11
Wellington Heath Herefs...35 R12
Wellington Marsh Herefs...35 L11
Wellow BaNES...17 T5
Wellow IoW...9 M11
Wellow Notts...57 U13
Wellpond Green Herts...22 B3
Wells Somset...17 Q7
Wellsborough Leics...47 L13
Wells Green Ches E...45 Q3
Wells Head C Brad...63 M13
Wells-next-the-sea Norfk...50 F5
Wellstye Green Essex...22 F4
Well Town Devon...15 U11
Welltree P & K...90 E7
Wellwood Fife...90 G14
Welney Norfk...39 R1
Welsh Bicknor Herefs...28 A4
Welsh Frankton Shrops...44 J6
Welsh Hook Pembks...24 F5
Welsh Newton Herefs...27 U3
Welsh Newton Common Herefs...27 V3
Welshpool Powys...44 F12
Welsh St Donats V Glam...26 J12
Welton Cumb...67 N3
Welton E R Yk...58 H1
Welton Lincs...58 G11
Welton Nhants...37 Q8
Welton le Marsh Lincs...59 S13
Welton le Wold Lincs...59 N9
Welwick E R Yk...59 P1
Welwyn Herts...31 R9
Welwyn Garden City Herts...31 R10
Wembdon Somset...16 J9
Wembley Gt Lon...21 L5
Wembury Devon...5 N11
Wembworthy Devon...15 Q10
Wemyss Bay Inver...88 E12
Wenallt Cerdgn...33 N6
Wenallt Gwynd...43 R4
Wendens Ambo Essex...39 R13
Wendlebury Oxon...30 C9
Wendling Norfk...50 F11
Wendover Bucks...30 J11
Wendron Cnwll...2 H10
Wendron Mining District Cnwll...2 H10
Wendy Cambs...39 M11
Wenfordbridge Cnwll...3 Q3
Wenhaston Suffk...41 R5
Wennington Cambs...39 K5
Wennington Gt Lon...22 D11
Wennington Lancs...62 C6
Wensley Derbys...46 J1
Wensley N York...63 L1
Wentbridge Wakefd...57 Q3
Wentnor Shrops...34 J2
Wentworth Cambs...39 Q5
Wentworth Rothm...57 N7
Wentworth Castle Barns...57 M6
Wenvoe V Glam...16 F2
Weobley Herefs...34 K10
Weobley Marsh Herefs...35 L10
Wepham W Susx...10 G9
Wereham Norfk...49 U13
Wergs Wolves...45 U13
Wern Gwynd...42 K6
Wern Powys...27 L4
Wern Powys...44 F9
Wernffrwd Swans...25 T12
Wern-y-gaer Flints...54 F12
Werrington Cnwll...4 J3
Werrington C Pete...48 J13
Werrington Staffs...46 B4
Wervin Ches W...54 K12
Wesham Lancs...61 S13
Wessex Vale Crematorium...9 P5
Wessington Derbys...47 L2
West Aberthaw V Glam...16 D3
West Acre Norfk...50 B10
West Allerdean Nthumb...85 P9
West Alvington Devon...5 S12
West Amesbury Wilts...18 H12
West Anstey Devon...15 U7
West Appleton N York...69 R14
West Ashby Lincs...59 M12
West Ashling W Susx...10 C9
West Ashton Wilts...18 C9
West Auckland Dur...69 Q7
West Ayton N York...65 M3
West Bagborough Somset...16 G10
West Bank Blae G...27 N6
West Barkwith Lincs...59 L10
West Barnby N York...71 P10
West Barns E Loth...84 H3
West Barsham Norfk...50 F7
West Bay Dorset...7 N6
West Beckham Norfk...51 L6
West Bedfont Surrey...20 J8
Westbere Kent...13 N3
West Bergholt Essex...23 N2
West Berkshire Crematorium W Berk...19 Q7
West Bexington Dorset...7 P7
West Bilney Norfk...50 B11
West Blackdene Dur...68 J5
West Blatchington Br & H...11 M9

West Boldon S Tyne...77 T13
Westborough Lincs...48 C5
Westbourne Bmouth...8 F10
Westbourne W Susx...10 B9
West Bourton Dorset...17 T11
West Bowling C Brad...63 P13
West Brabourne Kent...13 L7
West Bradenham Norfk...50 F12
West Bradford Lancs...62 E11
West Bradley Somset...17 Q9
West Bretton Wakefd...57 L4
West Bridgford Notts...47 Q6
West Briscoe Dur...68 K8
West Bromwich Sandw...36 D2
West Bromwich Crematorium Sandw...36 D2
Westbrook Kent...13 R1
Westbrook W Berk...19 P6
Westbrook Wilts...18 D7
West Buckland Devon...15 Q6
West Buckland Devon...16 E3
West Buckland Somset...16 G12
West Burrafirth Shet...106 s8
West Burton N York...63 L2
West Burton W Susx...10 F7
Westbury Bucks...30 E5
Westbury Shrops...44 J12
Westbury Wilts...18 C10
Westbury Leigh Wilts...18 C11
Westbury on Severn Gloucs...28 D4
Westbury-on-Trym Bristl...27 V12
Westbury-sub-Mendip Somset...17 P7
West Butsfield Dur...69 P4
West Butterwick N Linc...58 D5
West Byfleet Surrey...20 H10
West Cairngaan D & G...72 D13
West Caister Norfk...51 T11
West Calder W Loth...82 K6
West Camel Somset...17 Q12
West Chaldon Dorset...7 U8
West Challow Oxon...29 S10
West Charleton Devon...5 T12
West Chelborough Dorset...7 P3
West Chevington Nthumb...77 Q6
West Chiltington W Susx...10 H7
West Chinnock Somset...7 N2
West Chisenbury Wilts...18 H10
West Clandon Surrey...20 H12
West Cliffe Kent...13 R7
Westcliff-on-sea Sthend...23 L10
West Coker Somset...7 P2
West Combe Devon...5 T8
Westcombe Somset...17 Q8
West Compton Abbas Dorset...7 Q5
Westcote Gloucs...29 P3
Westcote Barton Oxon...29 T2
Westcott Bucks...30 F9
Westcott Devon...6 D4
Westcott Surrey...20 K13
West Cottingwith N York...64 F11
Westcourt Wilts...18 K8
West Cowick E R Yk...57 T2
West Cross Swans...25 V13
West Curry Cnwll...14 H2
West Curthwaite Cumb...67 M3
Westdean E Susx...11 S11
West Dean Wilts...8 K3
West Deeping Lincs...48 H12
West Derby Lpool...54 J8
West Dereham Norfk...49 U13
West Ditchburn Nthumb...77 N1
West Down Devon...15 M4
West Drayton Gt Lon...20 J7
West Drayton Notts...58 B12
West Dunnet Highld...112 F2
Wested Kent...22 T9
West Ella E R Yk...65 N14
West End Bed...38 E10
West End Br For...20 E8
West End Caerph...27 N8
West End Cambs...39 N1
West End E R Yk...65 L14
West End E R Yk...65 P13
West End E R Yk...65 R13
West End Gloucs...28 D9
West End Hants...9 P6
West End Hants...19 S5
West End Herts...31 T11
West End Lancs...61 S6
West End Leeds...63 Q12
West End Lincs...59 N6
West End N Som...17 L3
West End N York...63 M8
West End N York...63 Q8
West End N York...64 C11
West End Norfk...50 J12
West End Norfk...51 T11
West End Oxon...19 R3
West End S Lans...82 H9
West End Somset...17 S10
West End Surrey...20 G10
West End Surrey...21 P9
West End W & M...20 D7
West End W Susx...11 L8
West End Wilts...8 C4
West End Wilts...18 D4
West End Green Hants...19 U8
Westend Town Nthumb...76 E13
Westenhanger Kent...13 M8
Wester Aberchalder Highld...102 G11
Westerdale Highld...112 D6
Westerdale N York...71 L11
Westerfield Suffk...41 L11
Westergate W Susx...10 E9
Wester Ochiltree W Loth...82 K4
Wester Pitkierie Fife...91 S10
Wester Ross Highld...107 S9
Westerton of Rossie Angus...91 M13
West Ewell Surrey...21 M10
West Farleigh Kent...12 D5
West Farndon Nhants...37 P10
West Felton Shrops...44 H8
Westfield BaNES...17 S6
Westfield Cumb...66 E7
Westfield E Susx...12 F13
Westfield Highld...112 C4
Westfield N Lans...89 S11
Westfield Norfk...50 G12
Westfield Surrey...20 H11
Westfields Dorset...7 S2
Westfields Herefs...35 L12
Westfields of Rattray P & K...90 J2
Westfield Sole Kent...12 D3
West Flotmanby N York...65 P4
Westford Somset...16 F12
Westgate Dur...68 K4
Westgate N Linc...58 C5
Westgate Norfk...50 F5
Westgate Hill C Brad...63 P14
Westgate-on-sea Kent...13 Q1
Westgate Street Norfk...51 L9
West Ginge Oxon...29 T10
West Grafton Wilts...18 K8
West Green Hants...20 B10
West Grimstead Wilts...8 J3
West Grinstead W Susx...10 K6
West Haddlesey N York...57 T1
West Haddon Nhants...37 S6
West Hagbourne Oxon...19 R2
West Hagley Worcs...35 U4
Westhall Suffk...41 R4
West Hallam Derbys...47 M5
West Hallam Common Derbys...47 M5
West Halton N Linc...58 F2
Westham Dorset...7 S9
Westham E Susx...11 U10
West Ham Gt Lon...21 Q6
Westham Somset...17 L7
Westhampnett W Susx...10 D9
West Handley Derbys...57 N11
West Hanney Oxon...29 T10
West Hanningfield Essex...22 H8
West Harnham Wilts...8 G3
West Harptree BaNES...17 Q5
West Harting W Susx...10 B6
West Hatch Somset...16 J12
West Hatch Wilts...8 C3
West Haven Angus...91 S5
Westhay Somset...17 M8
Westhead Lancs...54 K5
West Head Norfk...49 U12
West Heath Birm...36 D5
West Heath Hants...19 S9
West Helmsdale Highld...112 C2
West Hendred Oxon...29 T10
West Heslerton N York...65 L4
West Hewish N Som...17 L4
West Hill Devon...6 E5
Westhide Herefs...35 N12
West Hill N Som...17 M2
Westhope Herefs...35 L10

West Holme Dorset...8 B11
Westholme Somset...17 Q8
West Hope Shrops...35 L3
West Horndon Essex...22 F10
Westhorp Nhants...37 Q10
Westhorpe Lincs...48 K7
Westhorpe Suffk...40 H8
West Horrington Somset...17 Q7
West Horsley Surrey...20 J12
West Horton Nthumb...85 Q12
West Hougham Kent...13 Q7
Westhoughton Bolton...55 Q5
West Hourn N York...62 F2
West Howe Bmouth...8 F9
West Howetown Somset...16 B10
Westhouse N York...62 C5
Westhouses Derbys...47 M2
West Huntingtower P & K...90 G7
West Huntspill Somset...16 K8
West Hyde C Beds...31 N9
West Hyde Herts...20 H4
West Hythe Kent...13 M8
West Ilkerton Devon...15 R3
West Ilsley W Berk...19 R4
West Itchenor W Susx...10 B9
West Keal Lincs...59 Q14
West Kennett Wilts...18 H7
West Kilbride N Ayrs...80 J3
West Kingsdown Kent...21 U10
West Kington Wilts...18 B5
West Kirby Wirral...54 F9
West Knapton N York...64 K4
West Knighton Dorset...7 T7
West Knoyle Wilts...8 B2
West Kyloe Nthumb...85 R10
West Lambrook Somset...17 M13
Westland Green Herts...22 B3
West Langdon Kent...13 R6
West Langwell Highld...108 K3
West Lavington W Susx...10 D6
West Lavington Wilts...18 F10
West Layton N York...69 P10
West Leake Notts...47 P8
West Learmouth Nthumb...85 L11
West Lees N York...70 H11
Westleigh Devon...15 L8
West Leigh Devon...15 Q11
Westleigh Devon...16 D13
West Leigh Somset...16 F10
Westleton Suffk...41 R7
West Lexham Norfk...50 D10
Westley Shrops...44 J12
Westley Suffk...40 D8
Westley Waterless Cambs...39 T9
West Lilling N York...64 E7
Westlington Bucks...30 G10
West Linton Border...83 M8
Westlinton Cumb...75 S13
West Littleton S Glos...28 E12
West Lockinge Oxon...29 T10
West London Crematorium Gt Lon...21 M6
West Lulworth Dorset...8 A12
West Lutton N York...65 L6
West Lydford Somset...17 Q10
West Lyn Devon...15 R3
West Lyng Somset...16 K11
West Lynn Norfk...49 U10
West Malling Kent...12 C4
West Malvern Worcs...35 S11
West Marden W Susx...10 B7
West Markham Notts...58 B12
West Marsh NE Lin...59 N5
West Marton N York...62 H9
West Melbury Dorset...8 B4
West Melton Rothm...57 P6
West Meon Hants...9 T4
West Meon Woodlands Hants...9 S3
West Mersea Essex...23 N5
Westmeston E Susx...11 N8
Westmill Herts...31 U7
Westmill Herts...31 U7
West Milton Dorset...7 P5
Westminster Gt Lon...21 N7
Westminster Kent...23 M13
Westminster Abbey & Palace Gt Lon...21 N7
West Molesey Surrey...20 K9
West Monkton Somset...16 J11
West Moors Dorset...8 F8
West Morden Dorset...8 C9
West Morriston Border...84 G10
West Morton C Brad...63 M11
West Mudford Somset...17 Q12
West Ness N York...64 F4
West Newbiggin Darltn...70 D9
West Newton E R Yk...65 S12
West Newton Norfk...50 B8
West Newton Somset...16 J11
West Norwood Gt Lon...21 P8
West Norwood Crematorium Gt Lon...21 P8
Westoe S Tyne...77 T13
West Ogwell Devon...5 U6
Weston BaNES...17 T3
Weston Ches E...45 R3
Weston Devon...6 E5
Weston Devon...6 G6
Weston Dorset...7 S10
Weston Halton...55 M10
Weston Hants...9 U4
Weston Herefs...34 J9
Weston Herts...31 S6
Weston Lincs...49 L9
Weston N York...63 P10
Weston Nhants...37 Q11
Weston Notts...58 B13
Weston Shrops...35 M1
Weston Shrops...44 K9
Weston Staffs...46 B8
Weston W Berk...19 N6
Weston Beggard Herefs...35 N12
Westonbirt Gloucs...28 G10
Weston by Welland Nhants...37 U2
Weston Colley Hants...19 R13
Weston Colville Cambs...39 T10
Weston Corbett Hants...19 U11
Weston Coyney C Stke...46 C4
Weston Favell Nhants...37 U8
Weston Green Cambs...39 T9
Weston Heath Shrops...45 S11
Weston Hills Lincs...49 L9
Weston in Arden Warwks...37 L3
Westoning C Beds...31 N5
Weston-in-Gordano N Som...27 S13
Westoning Woodend C Beds...31 M5
Weston Jones Staffs...45 S9
Weston Longville Norfk...50 K10
Weston Lullingfields Shrops...44 K9
Weston-on-Avon Warwks...36 G10
Weston-on-the-Green Oxon...30 B9
Weston Park Staffs...45 T11
Weston Patrick Hants...19 U11
Weston Rhyn Shrops...44 G6
Weston-sub-Edge Gloucs...36 F12
Weston-super-Mare N Som...16 K4
Weston-super-Mare Crematorium N Som...17 L4
Weston Turville Bucks...30 J10
Weston-under-Lizard Staffs...45 T11
Weston under Penyard Herefs...28 B3
Weston-under-Redcastle Shrops...45 M7
Weston under Wetherley Warwks...37 L7
Weston Underwood Derbys...46 J5
Weston Underwood M Keyn...38 C10
Westonzoyland Somset...17 L10
West Orchard Dorset...7 U3
West Overton Wilts...18 H7
Westow N York...64 H6

West Raddon Devon...15 U12
West Rainton Dur...70 D3
West Rasen Lincs...58 J9
West Ravendale NE Lin...59 M7
Westray Airport Ork...106 t14
West Raynham Norfk...50 E9
West Retford Notts...57 U11
Westridge Green W Berk...19 S5
Westrigg W Loth...82 J5
West Road Crematorium N u Ty...77 Q12
Westrop Swindn...29 N10
West Rounton N York...70 F12
West Row Suffk...39 U5
West Rudham Norfk...50 D8
West Runton Norfk...51 L5
Westry Cambs...49 N14
West Saltoun E Loth...84 D5
West Sandford Devon...15 T12
West Sandwick Shet...106 u5
West Scrafton N York...63 L2
West Sleekburn Nthumb...77 R9
West Somerton Norfk...51 S10
West Stafford Dorset...7 T7
West Stockwith Notts...58 C8
West Stoke W Susx...10 C9
West Stonesdale N York...68 J12
West Stoughton Somset...17 M7
West Stour Dorset...17 T12
West Stourmouth Kent...13 Q3
West Stow Suffk...40 D6
West Stowell Wilts...18 H8
West Stratton Hants...19 S12
West Street Kent...12 H5
West Street Kent...13 Q2
West Street Medway...12 H2
West Street Suffk...40 G6
West Suffolk Crematorium Suffk...40 D7
West Tanfield N York...63 R3
West Taphouse Cnwll...4 E8
West Tarbert Ag & B...87 Q12
West Tarring W Susx...10 J10
West Thirston Nthumb...77 P6
West Thorney W Susx...10 B10
Westthorpe Derbys...57 Q11
West Thurrock Thurr...22 E12
West Tilbury Thurr...22 G12
West Tisted Hants...9 T3
West Torrington Lincs...58 K10
West Town BaNES...17 P4
West Town Hants...9 U9
West Town Herefs...35 L10
West Town N Som...17 M3
West Town Somset...17 Q7
West Tytherley Hants...8 K3
West Tytherton Wilts...18 E6
West Walton Norfk...49 Q11
West Walton Highway Norfk...49 Q11
Westward Cumb...67 M3
Westward Ho! Devon...14 K7
Westwell Kent...12 K6
Westwell Oxon...29 Q6
Westwell Leacon Kent...12 J6
West Wellow Hants...8 K5
West Wembury Devon...5 N11
West Wemyss Fife...91 M13
Westwick Cambs...39 P7
Westwick Dur...69 N9
West Wick N Som...17 L4
West Wickham Cambs...39 T11
West Wickham Gt Lon...21 Q9
West Williamston Pembks...24 H9
West Wiltshire Crematorium Wilts...18 D9
West Winch Norfk...49 U11
West Winterslow Wilts...8 J2
West Wittering W Susx...10 B11
West Witton N York...63 L1
Westwood Devon...6 D5
Westwood Kent...13 R2
Westwood Notts...47 N3
Westwood Wilts...18 B9
Westwood Heath Covtry...36 J5
West Woodburn Nthumb...76 H8
West Woodhay W Berk...19 N8
West Woodlands Somset...17 T8
Westwoodside N Linc...58 C6
West Worldham Hants...10 A3
West Worthing W Susx...10 J10
West Wratting Cambs...39 T10
West Wycombe Bucks...20 D4
West Wylam Nthumb...77 N13
West Yatton Wilts...18 C5
West Yoke Kent...22 E11
West Youlstone Cnwll...14 F9
Wetham Green Kent...12 H2
Wetheral Cumb...67 Q1
Wetherby Leeds...63 U10
Wetherby Services N York...63 U9
Wetherden Suffk...40 G8
Wetheringsett Suffk...40 K8
Wethersfield Essex...22 H1
Wethersta Shet...106 t7
Wetherup Street Suffk...40 K8
Wetley Rocks Staffs...46 C4
Wettenhall Ches E...45 P1
Wetton Staffs...46 F2
Wetwang E R Yk...65 L8
Wetwood Staffs...45 S7
Wexcombe Wilts...19 L9
Wexham Slough...20 G6
Wexham Street Bucks...20 G6
Weybourne Norfk...51 L5
Weybourne Surrey...20 E13
Weybread Suffk...41 M4
Weybridge Surrey...20 J10
Weycroft Devon...6 K5
Weydale Highld...112 E3
Weyhill Hants...19 M11
Weymouth Dorset...7 S9
Weymouth Crematorium Dorset...7 S9
Whaddon Bucks...30 H6
Whaddon Cambs...39 N11
Whaddon Gloucs...28 F4
Whaddon Wilts...8 H3
Whaddon Wilts...18 D8
Whale Cumb...67 R8
Whaley Derbys...57 R12
Whaley Bridge Derbys...56 F10
Whaley Thorns Derbys...57 R12
Whaligoe Highld...112 H7
Whalley Lancs...62 E12
Whalley Banks Lancs...62 E13
Whalsay Shet...106 v7
Whalton Nthumb...77 N8
Whaplode Lincs...49 M9
Whaplode Drove Lincs...49 M11
Wharf Warwks...37 P8
Wharfe N York...62 F6
Wharles Lancs...61 S13
Wharley End C Beds...30 K4
Wharncliffe Side Sheff...57 L7
Wharram-le-Street N York...64 K6
Wharton Ches W...55 Q14
Wharton Herefs...35 M9
Whashton N York...69 Q11
Whasset Cumb...61 U3
Whatcote Warwks...36 K12
Whateley Warwks...36 H2
Whatfield Suffk...40 H11
Whatley Somset...7 L3
Whatley Somset...17 T7
Whatlington E Susx...12 E12
Whatsole Street Kent...13 M7
Whatstandwell Derbys...46 K3
Whatton Notts...47 U6
Whauphill D & G...73 L9
Whaw N York...69 L12
Wheal Peevor Cnwll...2 H8
Wheal Rose Cnwll...2 H8
Wheatacre Norfk...41 R2
Wheatfield Oxon...19 U2
Wheathampstead Herts...31 Q10
Wheathill Shrops...35 N4
Wheathill Somset...17 Q10
Wheatley Calder...56 G1
Wheatley Hants...10 B2
Wheatley Oxon...30 C12
Wheatley Hill Dur...70 E5
Wheatley Hills Donc...57 S5
Wheatley Lane Lancs...62 G12
Wheaton Aston Staffs...45 T11
Wheatsheaf Wrexhm...44 H3
Wheddon Cross Somset...16 B10
Wheelbarrow Town Kent...13 M6
Wheeler End Bucks...20 D4
Wheeler's Street Kent...12 H6
Wheelerstreet Surrey...10 F2
Wheelock Ches E...45 S2
Wheelton Lancs...55 P2
Wheldale Wakefd...57 P2
Wheldrake N York...64 F11
Whelford Gloucs...29 N8
Whelpley Hill Bucks...31 L12
Whelpo Cumb...67 M5
Whelston Flints...54 F11
Whempstead Herts...31 U9

Whenby N York...64 E6
Whepstead Suffk...40 D9
Wherstead Suffk...41 L12
Wherwell Hants...19 N12
Wheston Derbys...56 H11
Whetsted Kent...12 C6
Whetstone Gt Lon...21 N4
Whetstone Leics...37 Q1
Wheyrigg Cumb...66 J3
Whicham Cumb...61 L3
Whichford Warwks...36 K13
Whickham Gatesd...77 Q13
Whiddon Devon...15 M11
Whiddon Down Devon...5 R2
Whigstreet Angus...91 N3
Whilton Nhants...37 R8
Whimble Devon...14 J12
Whimple Devon...6 D5
Whimpwell Green Norfk...51 Q8
Whinburgh Norfk...50 H12
Whin Lane End Lancs...61 R11
Whinnieliggate D & G...73 T8
Whinnow Cumb...66 K2
Whinnyfold Abers...105 T9
Whippingham IoW...9 Q10
Whipsnade C Beds...31 M9
Whipsnade Zoo ZSL C Beds...31 M9
Whipton Devon...6 B6
Whirlow Sheff...57 M9
Whisby Lincs...58 F13
Whissendine Rutlnd...48 B11
Whissonsett Norfk...50 F9
Whistlefield Ag & B...88 F7
Whistlefield Inn Ag & B...88 F6
Whistley Green Wokham...20 C8
Whiston Knows...55 L8
Whiston Nhants...38 B8
Whiston Rothm...57 P9
Whiston Staffs...45 U9
Whiston Staffs...46 E4
Whiston Cross Shrops...45 S13
Whiston Eaves Staffs...46 E4
Whitacre Fields Warwks...36 H3
Whitbeck Cumb...61 L3
Whitbourne Herefs...35 R9
Whitburn S Tyne...77 U13
Whitburn W Loth...82 H6
Whitby Ches W...54 J12
Whitby N York...71 Q10
Whitbyheath Ches W...54 J12
Whitchester Border...84 K8
Whitchurch BaNES...17 R3
Whitchurch Bucks...30 G8
Whitchurch Cardif...27 M12
Whitchurch Devon...5 M6
Whitchurch Hants...19 Q11
Whitchurch Herefs...27 V4
Whitchurch Pembks...24 D5
Whitchurch Shrops...45 M5
Whitchurch Canonicorum Dorset...7 L5
Whitchurch Hill Oxon...19 U5
Whitchurch-on-Thames Oxon...19 U5
Whitcombe Dorset...7 T7
Whitcot Shrops...34 J2
Whitcott Keysett Shrops...34 G4
Whiteacre Kent...13 M6
Whiteacre Heath Warwks...36 H3
White Ball Somset...16 F13
Whitebridge Highld...102 F10
Whitebrook Mons...27 U6
Whitecairns Abers...105 Q12
Whitechapel Lancs...61 U11
White Chapel Worcs...35 U8
Whitecliffe Gloucs...27 V6
White Colne Essex...23 L2
Whitecote Leeds...63 Q13
White Coppice Lancs...55 P3
Whitecraig E Loth...83 S4
Whitecroft Gloucs...28 B6
Whitecrook D & G...72 E8
White Cross Cnwll...2 H12
Whitecross Cnwll...3 N2
Whitecross Falk...82 H3
Whiteface Highld...109 N7
Whitefarland N Ayrs...79 R7
Whitefaulds S Ayrs...80 K11
Whitefield Bury...55 T5
Whitefield Devon...15 T6
Whitefield Somset...16 E11
Whitefield Lane End Knows...55 L9
Whiteford Abers...105 L10
Whitegate Ches W...55 P14
Whitehall Devon...16 G13
Whitehall Hants...20 B11
Whitehall Ork...106 v17
Whitehaven Cumb...66 E9
Whitehill and Bordon Hants...10 B4
Whitehills Abers...104 K2
Whitehouse Abers...104 K13
Whitehouse Common Birm...36 F2
White Kirkley Dur...69 M5
White Lackington Dorset...7 T5
Whitelackington Somset...17 L13
White Ladies Aston Worcs...36 B10
White Mill Carmth...25 S6
Whitemire Moray...103 Q5
Whitemoor C Nott...47 P5
Whitemoor Cnwll...3 N5
White Notley Essex...22 J4
Whiteoak Green Oxon...29 R5
White Pit Lincs...59 Q11
Whiterashes Abers...105 N11
Whiterow Highld...112 H7
Whiterow Moray...103 S4
Whiteshill Gloucs...28 F6
Whiteside Nthumb...76 D13
Whiteside W Loth...82 H5
Whitesmith E Susx...11 S8
Whitestaunton Somset...16 J13
Whitestone Devon...6 A6
Whitestone Cross Devon...6 A6
Whitestreet Green Suffk...40 G13
White Waltham W & M...20 D7
Whiteway Gloucs...28 G5
Whitewell Lancs...62 D11
Whiteworks Devon...5 Q7
Whitfield C Dund...91 P5
Whitfield Kent...13 R6
Whitfield Nhants...30 E5
Whitfield Nthumb...68 G2
Whitfield S Glos...28 C9
Whitfield Hall Nthumb...68 G2
Whitford Devon...6 J5
Whitford Flints...54 D11
Whitgift E R Yk...58 D2
Whitgreave Staffs...45 U8
Whithorn D & G...73 L10
Whiting Bay N Ayrs...79 S9
Whitkirk Leeds...63 S13
Whitland Carmth...25 L7
Whitlaw Border...76 C1
Whitletts S Ayrs...81 M8
Whitley N York...57 S1
Whitley Readg...20 B8
Whitley Sheff...57 M7
Whitley Wilts...18 C7
Whitley Bay N Tyne...77 S11
Whitley Bay Crematorium N Tyne...77 S11
Whitley Chapel Nthumb...76 J14
Whitley Heath Staffs...45 T8
Whitley Lower Kirk...56 K3
Whitley Row Kent...21 S12
Whitlock's End Solhll...36 F5
Whitminster Gloucs...28 E6
Whitmore Dorset...8 F7
Whitmore Staffs...45 T5
Whitnage Devon...16 E12
Whitnash Warwks...36 K8
Whitney-on-Wye Herefs...34 G11
Whitrigg Cumb...66 K2
Whitrigg Cumb...67 L1
Whitsbury Hants...8 G5
Whitsome Border...85 L8
Whitson Newpt...27 Q11
Whitstable Kent...13 M2
Whitstone Cnwll...14 G13
Whittingham Nthumb...77 L3
Whittingslow Shrops...34 K3
Whittington Derbys...57 N12
Whittington Gloucs...28 K3
Whittington Lancs...62 C5

Whittington Norfk...50 B14
Whittington Shrops...44 H7
Whittington Staffs...35 U3
Whittington Staffs...46 G12
Whittington Warwks...36 H3
Whittington Worcs...35 U10
Whittington Moor Derbys...57 N12
Whittlebury Nhants...30 E4
Whittlesey Cambs...39 L1
Whittlesford Cambs...39 Q11
Whittlestone Head Bl w D...55 R3
Whitton N Linc...58 F2
Whitton Nthumb...77 M5
Whitton Powys...34 G7
Whitton S on T...70 E9
Whitton Shrops...35 M6
Whitton Suffk...40 K11
Whittonditch Wilts...19 L6
Whittonstall Nthumb...77 N14
Whitway Hants...19 Q9
Whitwell Derbys...57 R11
Whitwell Herts...31 R8
Whitwell IoW...9 Q13
Whitwell N York...69 S13
Whitwell Rutlnd...48 D12
Whitwell-on-the-Hill N York...64 G6
Whitwell Street Norfk...50 K9
Whitwick Leics...47 M10
Whitwood Wakefd...57 P2
Whitworth Lancs...56 C3
Whixall Shrops...45 M6
Whixley N York...63 U8
Whorlton Dur...69 P9
Whorlton N York...70 G12
Whyle Herefs...35 N8
Whyteleafe Surrey...21 P11
Wibdon Gloucs...27 V8
Wibtoft Warwks...37 N3
Wichenford Worcs...35 S8
Wichling Kent...12 H4
Wick Bmouth...8 H10
Wick Devon...6 G4
Wick Highld...112 J6
Wick S Glos...28 D13
Wick Somset...16 K8
Wick Somset...17 L9
Wick V Glam...16 B2
Wick W Susx...10 G10
Wick Wilts...8 H4
Wick Worcs...36 C11
Wicken Cambs...39 S6
Wicken Nhants...30 F5
Wicken Bonhunt Essex...22 C1
Wickenby Lincs...58 J10
Wicken Green Village Norfk...50 E7
Wickersley Rothm...57 Q8
Wicker Street Green Suffk...40 G12
Wickford Essex...22 H9
Wickham Hants...9 R6
Wickham W Berk...19 N6
Wickham Bishops Essex...22 K5
Wickhambreaux Kent...13 P4
Wickhambrook Suffk...40 B10
Wickhamford Worcs...36 E12
Wickham Green Suffk...40 J7
Wickham Green W Berk...19 N6
Wickham Heath W Berk...19 P7
Wickham Market Suffk...41 P9
Wickhampton Norfk...51 R12
Wickham St Paul Essex...40 C13
Wickham Skeith Suffk...40 J7
Wickham Street Suffk...40 B10
Wickham Street Suffk...40 J7
Wick John o' Groats Airport Highld...112 J6
Wicklewood Norfk...50 J13
Wickmere Norfk...51 L7
Wick St Lawrence N Som...17 L3
Wickstreet E Susx...11 S9
Wickwar S Glos...28 D10
Widdington Essex...22 C1
Widdop Calder...62 J13
Widdrington Nthumb...77 Q6
Widdrington Station Nthumb...77 Q7
Widecombe in the Moor Devon...5 S6
Widegates Cnwll...4 H9
Widemouth Bay Cnwll...14 F12
Wide Open N Tyne...77 Q11
Widford Essex...22 G6
Widford Herts...22 B4
Widham Wilts...29 L10
Widmer End Bucks...20 E3
Widmerpool Notts...47 R7
Widmore Gt Lon...21 R9
Widnes Halton...55 M10
Widnes Crematorium Halton...55 M9
Widworthy Devon...6 H5
Wigan Wigan...55 N6
Wigan Crematorium Wigan...55 N6
Wigborough Somset...17 M13
Wiggaton Devon...6 F6
Wiggenhall St Germans Norfk...49 S11
Wiggenhall St Mary Magdalen Norfk...49 S11
Wiggenhall St Mary the Virgin Norfk...49 S11
Wiggens Green Essex...39 U12
Wigginton Herts...31 L11
Wigginton Oxon...29 T1
Wigginton Staffs...46 H12
Wigginton York...64 E8
Wigginton Bottom Herts...31 L11
Wigglesworth N York...62 G8
Wiggonby Cumb...66 K2
Wiggonholt W Susx...10 H7
Wighill N York...63 U10
Wighton Norfk...50 F6
Wigley Hants...8 K5
Wigmore Herefs...34 K7
Wigmore Medway...12 F3
Wigsley Notts...58 D12
Wigsthorpe Nhants...38 F4
Wigston Leics...37 R1
Wigston Fields Leics...37 R1
Wigston Parva Leics...37 N3
Wigthorpe Notts...57 S10
Wigtoft Lincs...49 L6
Wigton Cumb...66 K3
Wigtown D & G...73 L8
Wike Leeds...63 S11
Wilbarston Nhants...38 B3
Wilberfoss E R Yk...64 H9
Wilburton Cambs...39 Q5
Wilby Nhants...38 C8
Wilby Norfk...40 H3
Wilby Suffk...41 M6
Wilcot Wilts...18 H8
Wilcott Shrops...44 J10
Wilcrick Newpt...27 R10
Wilday Green Derbys...57 M12
Wildboarclough Ches E...56 E13
Wilden Bed...38 F9
Wilden Worcs...35 T6
Wildhern Hants...19 N10
Wildhill Herts...31 S11
Wildmanbridge S Lans...82 F8
Wildmoor Hants...19 U10
Wildmoor Worcs...36 C5
Wildsworth Lincs...58 D7
Wilford C Nott...47 Q6
Wilford Hill Crematorium Notts...47 Q6

Wilkesley Ches E...45 Q5
Wilkhaven Highld...109 S5
Wilkieston W Loth...83 M5
Wilksby Lincs...59 N14
Willand Devon...16 D13
Willand Somset...16 E13
Willards Hill E Susx...12 D11
Willaston Ches E...45 R3
Willaston Ches W...54 H12
Willen M Keyn...30 J5
Willenhall Covtry...37 L5
Willenhall Wolves...46 C14
Willerby E R Yk...65 N13
Willerby N York...65 M4
Willersey Gloucs...36 F13
Willersley Herefs...34 H11
Willesborough Kent...13 L7
Willesborough Lees Kent...13 L7
Willesden Gt Lon...21 M6
Willesleigh Devon...15 N6
Willesley Wilts...28 G10
Willett Somset...16 F10
Willey Shrops...35 P2
Willey Warwks...37 N4
Willey Green Surrey...20 F12
Williamscot Oxon...37 N11
Williamstown Rhondd...26 J9
Willian Herts...31 R6
Willicote Warwks...36 G11
Willingale Essex...22 E6
Willingdon E Susx...11 T10
Willingham Cambs...39 P6
Willingham by Stow Lincs...58 E10
Willingham Green Cambs...39 T10
Willington Bed...38 H10
Willington Derbys...46 J8
Willington Dur...69 Q5
Willington Kent...12 E5
Willington Warwks...36 J13
Willington Corner Ches W...55 M13
Willington Quay N Tyne...77 S12
Willitoft E R Yk...64 G13
Williton Somset...16 E8
Willoughby Lincs...59 S12
Willoughby Warwks...37 P7
Willoughby Hills Lincs...49 N4
Willoughby-on-the-Wolds Notts...47 R8
Willoughby Waterleys Leics...37 Q2
Willoughton Lincs...58 F9
Willow Green Ches W...55 P11
Willows Green Essex...22 H4
Willsbridge S Glos...17 S2
Willslock Staffs...46 D7
Wilmcote Warwks...36 G9
Wilmington BaNES...17 S4
Wilmington Devon...6 H5
Wilmington E Susx...11 S10
Wilmington Kent...22 E13
Wilmslow Ches E...55 T10
Wilnecote Staffs...46 H13
Wilpshire Lancs...62 D13
Wilsden C Brad...63 M12
Wilsford Lincs...48 F5
Wilsford Wilts...8 H1
Wilsford Wilts...18 H9
Wilsham Devon...15 R3
Wilshaw Kirk...56 H5
Wilsill N York...63 P7
Wilsley Green Kent...12 E8
Wilsley Pound Kent...12 E8
Wilson Herefs...28 A3
Wilson Leics...47 M8
Wilsontown S Lans...82 J7
Wilstead Bed...38 G11
Wilsthorpe Lincs...48 G11
Wilstone Herts...31 L10
Wilton Cumb...66 F10
Wilton Herefs...28 A3
Wilton N York...65 L3
Wilton R & Cl...70 K9
Wilton Wilts...8 F2
Wilton Wilts...19 L8
Wilton Dean Border...75 U2
Wimbish Essex...39 S13
Wimbish Green Essex...39 T13
Wimbledon Gt Lon...21 M8
Wimblington Cambs...39 P2
Wimboldsley Ches W...55 Q14
Wimborne Minster Dorset...8 E9
Wimborne St Giles Dorset...8 E6
Wimbotsham Norfk...49 T12
Wimpole Cambs...39 M10
Wimpstone Warwks...36 H11
Wincanton Somset...17 T11
Winceby Lincs...59 P13
Wincham Ches W...55 Q11
Winchburgh W Loth...83 L4
Winchcombe Gloucs...28 K2
Winchelsea E Susx...12 H12
Winchelsea Beach E Susx...12 H13
Winchester Hants...9 P3
Winchester Services Hants...19 R13
Winchet Hill Kent...12 D7
Winchfield Hants...20 C11
Winchmore Hill Bucks...20 F3
Winchmore Hill Gt Lon...21 P4
Wincle Ches E...56 E13
Wincobank Sheff...57 N8
Winder Cumb...66 F11
Windermere Cumb...67 P13
Windermere Jetty Steamboats & Museum Cumb...67 P13
Windhill Highld...102 F6
Windlehurst Stockp...56 E9
Windlesham Surrey...20 F10
Windmill Cnwll...3 M2
Windmill Derbys...56 J11
Windmill Hill E Susx...11 U9
Windmill Hill Somset...16 K13
Windsole Abers...104 G4
Windsor W & M...20 G7
Windsor Castle W & M...20 G7
Windsoredge Gloucs...28 F7
Windy Arbour Warwks...36 J6
Windygates Fife...91 M11
Windyharbour Ches E...55 T11
Windy Hill Wrexhm...44 H3
Wineham W Susx...11 L6
Winestead E R Yk...59 P1
Winewall Lancs...62 J11
Winfarthing Norfk...40 K3
Winford IoW...9 R12
Winford N Som...17 P4
Winforton Herefs...34 G11
Winfrith Newburgh Dorset...7 V8
Wing Bucks...30 J8
Wing Rutlnd...48 C13
Wingate Dur...70 E4
Wingates Bolton...55 Q5
Wingates Nthumb...77 N6
Wingerworth Derbys...57 M13
Wingfield C Beds...31 M7
Wingfield Suffk...41 M5
Wingfield Wilts...18 B9
Wingham Kent...13 P4
Wingmore Kent...13 N6
Wingrave Bucks...30 J9
Winkburn Notts...47 T2
Winkfield Br For...20 F8
Winkfield Row Br For...20 E8
Winkhill Staffs...46 E3
Winkhurst Green Kent...21 S13
Winkleigh Devon...15 P10
Winksley N York...63 R5
Winkton Dorset...8 H9
Winlaton Gatesd...77 P13
Winlaton Mill Gatesd...77 P13
Winless Highld...112 H6
Winmarleigh Lancs...61 T11
Winnall Hants...9 P2
Winnersh Wokham...20 C9
Winnington Ches W...55 P12
Winscales Cumb...66 F8
Winscombe N Som...17 M5
Winsford Ches W...55 Q14
Winsford Somset...16 B10
Winsham Devon...15 M5
Winsham Somset...7 L3
Winshill Staffs...46 J9
Winshwen Swans...26 B8
Winskill Cumb...67 R5
Winslade Hants...19 U11
Winsley Wilts...18 B8
Winslow Bucks...30 G7
Winsor Hants...9 L6
Winster Cumb...67 P13
Winster Derbys...46 J1
Winston Dur...69 P9
Winston Suffk...41 L8
Winstone Gloucs...28 H6
Winswell Devon...15 L9
Winterborne Came Dorset...7 T7
Winterborne Clenston Dorset...8 A8
Winterborne Herringston Dorset...7 S7
Winterborne Houghton Dorset...8 A8
Winterborne Kingston Dorset...8 B9
Winterborne Monkton Dorset...7 S7
Winterborne Stickland Dorset...8 A8
Winterborne Tomson Dorset...8 B9
Winterborne Whitechurch Dorset...8 A8
Winterborne Zelston Dorset...8 B9
Winterbourne S Glos...28 B11
Winterbourne W Berk...19 Q6
Winterbourne Abbas Dorset...7 R6
Winterbourne Bassett Wilts...18 G6
Winterbourne Dauntsey Wilts...8 H2
Winterbourne Earls Wilts...8 H2
Winterbourne Gunner Wilts...8 H2
Winterbourne Monkton Wilts...18 G6
Winterbourne Steepleton Dorset...7 R7
Winterbourne Stoke Wilts...18 G12

Winterbrook Oxon....19 T3
Winterburn N York....62 J8
Winteringham N Linc....58 F2
Winterley Ches E....45 R2
Winterset Wakefd....57 N3
Winterslow Wilts....8 J2
Winterton N Linc....58 F1
Winterton-on-Sea Norfk....51 S12
Winthorpe Lincs....59 U13
Winthorpe Notts....48 B2
Winton Bmouth....8 F10
Winton Cumb....68 G10
Winton E Susx....11 S10
Winton N York....70 F13
Wintringham N York....64 K5
Winwick Cambs....38 H4
Winwick Nhants....37 R6
Winwick Warrtn....55 P8
Wirksworth Derbys....46 J3
Wirral....54 G9
Wirswall Ches E....45 M5
Wisbech Cambs....49 Q12
Wisbech St Mary Cambs....49 P12
Wisborough Green
W Susx....10 H5
Wiseman's Bridge
Pembks....24 K9
Wiston Notts....58 B9
Wishanger Gloucs....28 H6
Wishaw N Lans....82 E7
Wishaw Warwks....36 G2
Wisley Surrey....20 J11
Wisley Garden RHS
Surrey....20 J11
Wispington Lincs....59 M12
Wissenden Kent....12 H7
Wissett Suffk....41 Q5
Wistanstow Shrops....35 L4
Wistanswick Shrops....45 Q8
Wistaston Ches E....45 Q3
Wistaston Green Ches E....45 Q3
Wisterfield Ches E....55 T12
Wiston Pembks....24 H7
Wiston S Lans....82 J11
Wiston W Susx....10 J8
Wistow Cambs....39 L4
Wistow Leics....37 R1
Wistow N York....64 D12
Wiswell Lancs....62 E12
Witcham Cambs....39 Q4
Witchampton Dorset....8 D8
Witchford Cambs....39 R5
Witcombe Somset....17 N12
Witham Essex....22 J6
Witham Friary Somset....17 T8
Witham St Hughs Lincs....48 C1
Withcall Lincs....59 N10
Withdean Br & H....11 N9
Witherenden Hill E Susx....12 D10
Witheridge Devon....15 T10
Witherley Leics....36 K1
Withern Lincs....59 R10
Withernsea E R Yk....65 U14
Withernwick E R Yk....65 R11
Withersdale Street Suffk....41 N4
Withersfield Suffk....39 U11
Witherslack Cumb....61 S3
Withiel Cnwll....3 P3
Withiel Florey Somset....16 C10
Withielgoose Cnwll....3 Q3
Withington Gloucs....28 K5
Withington Herefs....35 N12
Withington Manch....55 T8
Withington Shrops....45 N11
Withington Staffs....46 D6
Withington Green
Ches E....55 T12
Withington Marsh
Herefs....35 N12
Withleigh Devon....16 B2
Withnell Lancs....55 P2
Withybed Green Worcs....36 D6
Withybrook Warwks....37 N4
Withycombe Somset....16 D8
Withyham E Susx....11 S3
Withy Mills BaNES....17 S5
Withypool Somset....15 U6
Withywood Bristl....17 Q3
Witley Surrey....10 E3
Witnesham Suffk....41 L10
Witney Oxon....29 S5
Wittering C Pete....38 G13
Wittersham Kent....12 H10
Witton Birm....36 E2
Witton Norfk....51 P11
Witton Norfk....51 N7
Witton Gilbert Dur....69 R3
Witton Green Norfk....51 R13
Witton le Wear Dur....69 P6
Witton Park Dur....69 P6
Wiveliscombe Somset....16 E11
Wivelrod Hants....19 U13
Wivelsfield E Susx....11 N6
Wivelsfield Green E Susx....11 P7
Wivelsfield Station
E Susx....11 N7
Wivenhoe Essex....23 P3

Wivenhoe Cross Essex....23 P3
Wiveton Norfk....50 H5
Wix Essex....23 R2
Wixford Warwks....36 E10
Wix Green Essex....23 S2
Wixhill Shrops....45 N8
Wixoe Suffk....40 B12
Woburn C Beds....30 K6
Woburn Abbey C Beds....31 L6
Woburn Sands M Keyn....30 K6
Wokefield Park W Berk....19 U7
Woking Surrey....20 H11
Woking Crematorium
Surrey....20 G11
Wokingham Wokham....20 D9
Wolborough Devon....5 U6
Woldingham Surrey....21 Q11
Wold Newton E R Yk....65 N5
Wold Newton NE Lin....59 N7
Wolferlow Herefs....35 Q8
Wolferton Norfk....49 U9
Wolfhampcote Warwks....37 P7
Wolf Hills Nthumb....76 E14
Wolfhill P & K....90 J5
Wolf's Castle Pembks....24 F5
Wolfsdale Pembks....24 F6
Wollaston Dudley....35 U4
Wollaston Nhants....38 D8
Wollaston Shrops....44 H11
Wollaton C Nott....47 P6
Wollerton Shrops....45 P8
Wollescote Dudley....36 B4
Wolseley Bridge Staffs....46 C9
Wolsingham Dur....69 N5
Wolstanton Staffs....45 U4
Wolstenholme Rochdl....55 U4
Wolston Warwks....37 M5
Wolsty Cumb....66 H2
Wolvercote Oxon....29 U5
Wolverhampton Wolves....46 B14
Wolverley Shrops....45 L7
Wolverley Worcs....35 T5
Wolverton Hants....19 S9
Wolverton Kent....13 Q7
Wolverton M Keyn....30 H4
Wolverton Warwks....36 H8
Wolverton Wilts....17 U10
Wolverton Common
Hants....19 S9
Wolvesnewton Mons....27 T8
Wolvey Warwks....37 M3
Wolvey Heath Warwks....37 M3
Wolviston S on T....70 G7
Wombleton N York....64 F3
Wombourne Staffs....35 U2
Wombwell Barns....57 P6
Womenswold Kent....13 P5
Womersley N York....57 R3
Wonastow Mons....27 T4
Wonersh Surrey....20 H13
Wonford Devon....6 B6
Wonston Hants....19 Q13
Wooburn Bucks....20 F5
Wooburn Green Bucks....20 F5
Wooburn Moor Bucks....20 F5
Woodacott Devon....14 J11
Woodale N York....63 L4
Woodall Rothm....57 Q10
Woodall Services Rothm....57 Q10
Woodbank Ches W....54 J12
Woodbastwick Norfk....51 P10
Woodbeck Notts....58 C11
Woodborough Notts....47 R4
Woodborough Wilts....18 H9
Woodbridge Devon....6 F5
Woodbridge Suffk....41 N11
Wood Burcote Nhants....37 S11
Woodbury Devon....6 D7
Woodbury Salterton
Devon....6 D7
Woodchester Gloucs....28 F7
Woodchurch Kent....12 H9
Woodchurch Wirral....54 G9
Woodcombe Somset....16 C8
Woodcote Gt Lon....21 N10
Woodcote Oxon....19 T4
Woodcote Wrekin....45 S10
Woodcote Green Worcs....36 B6
Woodcott Hants....19 P10
Woodcroft Gloucs....27 U8
Woodcutts Dorset....8 D5
Wood Dalling Norfk....50 J9
Wooddtitton Cambs....39 U9
Woodeaton Oxon....30 B10
Wood Eaton Staffs....45 T10
Wooden Pembks....24 K9
Wood End Bed....38 F11
Wood End Bed....38 G8
Wood End Cambs....39 N5

Wood End Gt Lon....20 K6
Wood End Herts....31 T7
Wood End Highld....93 T6
Woodend Nhants....37 R11
Woodend Staffs....46 G8
Woodend W Loth....82 H5
Wood End W Susx....10 C9
Wood End Warwks....36 F6
Wood End Warwks....36 J3
Woodend Norfk....50 J10
Wood End Wolves....46 B13
Wood Enderby Lincs....59 N14
Woodend Green Essex....22 E2
Woodfalls Wilts....8 H4
Woodford Cnwll....14 F10
Woodford Devon....5 T10
Woodford Gloucs....28 C8
Woodford Gt Lon....21 R4
Woodford Nhants....38 E5
Woodford Stockp....56 C10
Woodford Bridge Gt Lon....21 R4
Woodford Halse Nhants....37 P10
Woodgate Birm....36 C4
Woodgate Devon....16 F13
Woodgate Norfk....50 H10
Woodgate Norfk....50 E10
Woodgate W Susx....10 F10
Woodgate Worcs....36 C7
Wood Green Gt Lon....21 P4
Woodgreen Hants....8 H5
Woodgreen Oxon....29 S5
Woodhall N York....62 K1
Woodhall Hill Leeds....63 Q12
Woodhall Spa Lincs....59 L14
Woodham Bucks....30 F9
Woodham Dur....69 S7
Woodham Surrey....20 H10
Woodham Ferrers Essex....22 J8
Woodham Mortimer
Essex....22 K7
Woodham Walter Essex....22 K6
Wood Hayes Wolves....46 B13
Woodhead Abers....105 M8
Woodhill Shrops....35 R4
Woodhill Somset....17 L11
Woodhorn Nthumb....77 R9
Woodhouse Demesne
Nthumb....77 S8
Woodhouse Leeds....63 R13
Woodhouse Leics....47 P11
Woodhouse Sheff....57 P10
Woodhouse Wakefd....57 N2
Woodhouse Eaves Leics....47 P11
Woodhouse Green Staffs....56 D14
Woodhouselee Mdloth....83 P6
Woodhouse Mill Sheff....57 P9
Woodhouses Cumb....67 M2
Woodhouses Oldham....56 D6
Woodhouses Staffs....46 E10
Woodhouses Staffs....46 F10
Woodhurst Cambs....39 L6
Woodingdean Br & H....11 P9
Woodkirk Leeds....57 L1
Woodland Devon....5 S8
Woodland Devon....5 R10
Woodland Dur....69 N7
Woodland Head Devon....15 S13
Woodlands Abers....99 P4
Woodlands Donc....57 R5
Woodlands Dorset....8 E7
Woodlands Hants....9 L7
Woodlands Kent....21 U10
Woodlands N York....63 S9
Woodlands Somset....16 G9
Woodlands (Coleshill)
Crematorium
Warwks....36 G3
Woodlands Park W & M....20 E7
Woodlands St Mary
W Berk....19 M5
Woodlands
(Scarborough)
Crematorium N York....65 N2
Woodlands
(Scunthorpe)
Crematorium N Linc....58 E4
Woodland Street Somset....17 Q9
Woodland View Sheff....57 M9
Wood Lane Shrops....44 K7
Wood Lane Staffs....45 T4
Woodleigh Devon....5 S11
Woodlesford Leeds....57 M1
Woodley Stockp....56 D8
Woodley Wokham....20 C8
Woodmancote Gloucs....28 E8
Woodmancote Gloucs....28 J2
Woodmancote Gloucs....28 K6
Woodmancote W Susx....9 S9
Woodmancote W Susx....11 L8
Woodmancott Hants....19 R12
Woodmancott Hants....19 R12
Woodmansey E R Yk....65 P12
Woodmansgreen W Susx....10 D5
Woodmansterne Surrey....21 N11

Woodmanton Devon....6 D7
Woodmarsh Wilts....18 C9
Woodmill Staffs....46 F9
Woodminton Wilts....8 E4
Woodnesborough Kent....13 R4
Woodnewton Nhants....38 F2
Woodnook Notts....47 N3
Wood Norton Norfk....50 H8
Woodplumpton Lancs....61 T13
Woodrising Norfk....50 G12
Wood's Corner E Susx....11 V7
Woodrow Worcs....35 U5
Wood's Eaves Herefs....34 G11
Woodseaves Shrops....45 Q7
Woodseaves Staffs....45 S8
Woodsend Wilts....18 K5
Woodsetts Rothm....57 R10
Woodsford Dorset....7 U6
Wood's Green E Susx....12 B9
Woodside Br For....20 F8
Woodside Cumb....66 F6
Woodside Essex....22 C7
Woodside Fife....91 P10
Woodside Gt Lon....21 P9
Woodside Hants....9 L9
Woodside Herts....31 R11
Woodside P & K....90 K4
Woodside Green Kent....12 H5
Woodstock Oxon....29 T4
Woodstock Pembks....24 H6
Wood Street Norfk....51 Q9
Wood Street Village
Surrey....20 G12
Woodthorpe Derbys....57 Q12
Woodthorpe Leics....47 P10
Woodthorpe Lincs....59 R10
Woodthorpe York....64 D10
Woodton Norfk....41 N2
Woodtown Devon....14 K8
Woodvale Sefton....54 H4
Woodville Derbys....46 K10
Woodwall Green Staffs....45 S7
Wood Walton Cambs....38 K4
Woodyates Dorset....8 E5
Woofferton Shrops....35 M7
Wookey Somset....17 P7
Wookey Hole Somset....17 P7
Wool Dorset....8 A11
Woolacombe Devon....14 L4
Woolage Green Kent....13 P6
Woolage Village Kent....13 P5
Woolaston Gloucs....28 A7
Woolavington Somset....16 K8
Woolbeding W Susx....10 D6
Woolcotts Somset....16 B10
Wooldale Kirk....56 J5
Wooler Nthumb....85 N13
Woolfardisworthy
Devon....14 H8
Woolfardisworthy
Devon....15 T11
Woolfold Bury....55 S5
Woolfords S Lans....82 K7
Woolhampton W Berk....19 S7
Woolhope Herefs....35 P13
Woolland Dorset....7 U3
Woolland BaNES....17 S5
Woollensbrook Herts....31 U11
Woolley BaNES....17 T3
Woolley Cambs....38 J6
Woolley Cnwll....14 G9
Woolley Derbys....47 L1
Woolley Wakefd....57 M4
Woolley Bridge Derbys....56 F8
Woolley Edge Services
Wakefd....57 M3
Woolmere Green Worcs....36 C8
Woolmer Green Herts....31 S10
Woolmerston Somset....16 J10
Woolminstone Somset....7 M3
Woolpack Kent....12 G8
Woolpit Suffk....40 G8
Woolpit Green Suffk....40 G8
Woolscott Warwks....37 P7
Woolsgrove Devon....15 S12
Woolsington N u Ty....77 P11
Woolstaston Shrops....35 L14
Woolsthorpe Lincs....48 B7
Woolsthorpe-by-
Colsterworth Lincs....48 D9
Woolston C Sotn....9 N6
Woolston Devon....5 S10
Woolston Devon....5 S12
Woolston Shrops....34 K3
Woolston Shrops....45 L8
Woolston Somset....16 E9
Woolston Somset....17 S11
Woolston Warrtn....55 P9
Woolstone Gloucs....28 H1
Woolstone M Keyn....30 J5
Woolstone Oxon....29 Q10
Woolston Green Devon....5 T7

Wotter Devon....5 P8
Wotton Surrey....20 K13
Wotton-under-Edge
Gloucs....28 E9
Wotton Underwood
Bucks....30 E9
Woughton on the Green
M Keyn....30 J5
Wouldham Kent....12 D3
Woundale Shrops....35 S2
Wrabness Essex....23 S1
Wrafton Devon....15 L5
Wragby Lincs....58 K11
Wragby Wakefd....57 N3
Wramplingham Norfk....50 K12
Wrangaton Devon....5 R9
Wrangbrook Wakefd....57 Q4
Wrangle Lincs....49 P2
Wrangle Common Lincs....49 P2
Wrangle Lowgate Lincs....49 P2
Wrangway Somset....16 F13
Wrantage Somset....16 K12
Wrawby N Linc....58 H5
Wraxall N Som....17 N2
Wraxall Somset....17 R10
Wraxall Somset....17 S10
Wray Lancs....62 C8
Wray Castle Cumb....67 N12
Wraysbury W & M....20 H8
Wrayton Lancs....62 C5
Wrea Green Lancs....61 S13
Wreaks End Cumb....61 N3
Wreay Cumb....67 N3
Wreay Cumb....67 P5
Wrecclesham Surrey....10 C2
Wrekenton Gatesd....77 R14
Wrelton N York....64 H2
Wrenbury Ches E....45 N4
Wrench Green N York....65 M2
Wreningham Norfk....51 L14
Wrentham Suffk....41 S4
Wrenthorpe Wakefd....57 M2
Wrentnall Shrops....44 K13
Wressle E R Yk....64 G13
Wressle N Linc....58 G5
Wrestlingworth C Beds....39 L11
Wretton Norfk....49 U13
Wrexham Wrexhm....44 H3
Wrexham Barns Norfk....41 N10
Wribbenhall Worcs....35 S5
Wrickton Shrops....35 P3
Wrightington Bar Lancs....55 M4
Wright's Green Essex....22 D4
Wrinehill Staffs....45 S4
Wrington N Som....17 N4
Writhlington BaNES....17 T5
Writtle Essex....22 G6
Wrockwardine Wrekin....45 P11
Wroot N Linc....58 C6
Wrose C Brad....63 P12
Wrotham Kent....12 B3
Wrotham Heath Kent....12 B3
Wrottesley Staffs....45 U13
Wroughton Swindn....18 H4
Wroxall IoW....9 R13
Wroxall Warwks....36 H6
Wroxeter Shrops....45 N12
Wroxham Norfk....51 P11
Wroxton Oxon....37 M12
Wyaston Derbys....46 G5
Wyatt's Green Essex....22 E8
Wyberton Lincs....49 M5
Wyboston Bed....38 J9
Wybunbury Ches E....45 R4
Wychbold Worcs....36 B8
Wych Cross E Susx....11 R3
Wychnor Staffs....46 G10
Wychnor Bridges Staffs....46 G10
Wyck Hants....10 B3
Wyck Rissington Gloucs....29 N4
Wycliffe Dur....69 P10
Wycoller Lancs....62 J12
Wycomb Leics....47 U9
Wycombe Marsh Bucks....20 E4
Wyddial Herts....31 T5
Wye Kent....13 L6
Wyesham Mons....27 U5
Wyfordby Leics....47 U10
Wyke Devon....5 U3
Wyke Devon....6 C4
Wyke Dorset....17 U11
Wyke Shrops....45 P13
Wyke Surrey....20 F12
Wyke Champflower
Somset....17 S10
Wyke Regis Dorset....7 S9
Wykey Shrops....44 J9
Wykeham N York....65 M3
Wykeham N York....64 K4
Wyken Covtry....37 L4
Wyken Shrops....35 S2
Wyke Regis Dorset....7 S9
Wykin Leics....37 M2
Wylam Nthumb....77 N13
Wylde Green Birm....36 F2
Wylye Wilts....18 F13
Wymeswold Leics....47 R9
Wymington Bed....38 E8
Wymondham Leics....48 B10
Wymondham Norfk....51 L13
Wyndham Brdgnd....26 H9
Wynford Eagle Dorset....7 Q5

Wynyard Park S on T....70 F7
Wynyard Village S on T....70 F7
Wyre Forest
Crematorium Worcs....35 T6
Wyre Piddle Worcs....36 C11
Wysall Notts....47 R8
Wyson Herefs....35 M7
Wythall Worcs....36 E5
Wytham Oxon....29 U6
Wythburn Cumb....67 M10
Wythenshawe Manch....55 T9
Wythop Mill Cumb....66 J7
Wyton Cambs....39 L6
Wyton E R Yk....65 R13
Wyverstone Suffk....40 H7
Wyverstone Street Suffk....40 H7
Wyville Lincs....48 C8

Y

Yaddlethorpe N Linc....58 E5
Yafford IoW....9 N12
Yafforth N York....70 D14
Yalberton Torbay....5 V9
Yalding Kent....12 C5
Yanley N Som....17 Q3
Yanwath Cumb....67 R7
Yanworth Gloucs....29 L5
Yapham E R Yk....64 H9
Yapton W Susx....10 F10
Yarborough N Som....17 L4
Yarbridge IoW....9 S12
Yarburgh Lincs....59 Q8
Yarcombe Devon....6 H3
Yard Devon....15 S8
Yardley Birm....36 F3
Yardley Crematorium
Birm....36 F4
Yardley Gobion Nhants....30 G4
Yardley Hastings Nhants....38 B9
Yardley Wood Birm....36 F5
Yardro Powys....34 F9
Yarkhill Herefs....35 N12
Yarlet Staffs....45 U8
Yarley Somset....17 P7
Yarlington Somset....17 S11
Yarm S on T....70 F10
Yarmouth IoW....9 M11
Yarnacott Devon....15 P6
Yarnbrook Wilts....18 C10
Yarner Devon....5 T5
Yarnfield Staffs....45 T7
Yarnscombe Devon....15 N8
Yarnton Oxon....29 U5
Yarpole Herefs....35 L8
Yarrow Border....83 S13
Yarrow Feus Border....83 R13
Yarrowford Border....83 T13
Yarsop Herefs....34 K11
Yarwell Nhants....38 G1
Yate S Glos....28 D11
Yateley Hants....20 D10
Yatesbury Wilts....18 G6
Yattendon W Berk....19 S6
Yatton Herefs....34 K8
Yatton Herefs....35 M9
Yatton N Som....17 M3
Yatton Keynell Wilts....18 B5
Yaverland IoW....9 S11
Yawl Devon....6 K6
Yawthorpe Lincs....58 E8
Yaxham Norfk....50 H11
Yaxley Cambs....38 J2
Yaxley Suffk....40 K6
Yazor Herefs....34 K11
Yeading Gt Lon....20 K6
Yeadon Leeds....63 Q11
Yealand Conyers Lancs....61 U4
Yealand Redmayne
Lancs....61 U4
Yealand Storrs Lancs....61 T4
Yealmbridge Devon....5 P10
Yealmpton Devon....5 P10
Yearby R & Cl....70 J8
Yearngill Cumb....66 H4
Yearsley N York....64 C5
Yeaton Shrops....44 K10
Yeaveley Derbys....46 G5
Yeavering Nthumb....85 N12
Yedingham N York....64 K4
Yelden Bed....38 F7
Yeldersley Derbys....46 H5
Yelford Oxon....29 S7
Yell Shet....106 u6
Yelland Devon....15 L6
Yelling Cambs....39 L8
Yelvertoft Nhants....37 Q5
Yelverton Devon....5 N7
Yelverton Norfk....51 N13
Yenston Somset....17 T12
Yeoford Devon....15 S13
Yeolmbridge Cnwll....4 J3
Yeo Mill Devon....15 T7
Yeo Vale Devon....14 K8
Yeovil Somset....7 Q13
Yeovil Crematorium
Somset....17 P13
Yeovil Marsh Somset....17 P12
Yeovilton Somset....17 P12
Yerbeston Pembks....24 J9

Yesnaby Ork....106 r18
Yetlington Nthumb....77 L4
Yetminster Dorset....7 Q2
Yetson Devon....5 U9
Yettington Devon....6 E7
Yetts o'Muckhart Clacks....90 F12
Yews Green C Brad....63 M13
Yew Tree Sandw....36 D1
Y Felinheli Gwynd....52 H9
Y Ferwig Cerdgn....32 C10
Y Ffor Gwynd....42 G6
Y Gyffylliog Denbgs....53 T11
Yieldshields S Lans....82 F8
Yiewsley Gt Lon....20 J6
Y Maerdy Conwy....53 U6
Y Nant Wrexhm....44 H3
Ynysboeth Rhondd....26 K8
Ynysddu Caerph....27 M8
Ynysforgan Swans....26 B8
Ynyshir Rhondd....26 J8
Ynyslas Cerdgn....33 M2
Ynysmaerdy Rhondd....26 J11
Ynysmeudwy Neath....26 C6
Ynystawe Swans....26 B7
Ynysybwl Rhondd....26 K8
Ynysymaengwyn Gwynd....43 M13
Yockenthwaite N York....62 J5
Yockleton Shrops....44 J11
Yokefleet E R Yk....58 C1
Yoker C Glas....89 M12
York C York....64 E9
York Lancs....62 E13
York City Crematorium
C York....64 D10
Yorkletts Kent....13 L3
Yorkley Gloucs....28 B6
York Minster C York....64 E8
Yorkshire Dales National
Park....62 H4
York Town Surrey....20 E10
Yorton Heath Shrops....45 M9
Youlgreave Derbys....56 K14
Youlthorpe E R Yk....64 G9
Youlton N York....63 U8
Youngsbury Herts....31 U9
Young's End Essex....22 H5
Yoxall Staffs....46 F10
Yoxford Suffk....41 Q7
Y Rhiw Gwynd....42 D8
Ysbyty Cynfyn Cerdgn....33 P6
Ysbyty Ifan Conwy....43 R4
Ysbyty Ystwyth Cerdgn....33 P6
Ysceifiog Flints....54 E12
Yspitty Carmth....25 T11
Ystalyfera Neath....26 C6
Ystrad Rhondd....26 J9
Ystrad Aeron Cerdgn....32 K9
Ystradfellte Powys....26 F5
Ystrad Ffin Carmth....33 Q11
Ystradgynlais Powys....26 D5
Ystrad Meurig Cerdgn....33 P7
Ystrad Mynach Caerph....27 L8
Ystradowen V Glam....26 J12
Ystumtuen Cerdgn....33 P6
Ythanbank Abers....105 Q9
Ythanwells Abers....104 J8
Ythsie Abers....105 P8

Z

Zeal Monachorum
Devon....15 R12
Zeals Wilts....17 U10
Zelah Cnwll....3 L6
Zennor Cnwll....2 C9
Zoar Cnwll....2 J14
Zouch Notts....47 P9
ZSL London Zoo Gt Lon....21 N6
ZSL Whipsnade Zoo
C Beds....31 M9

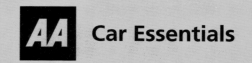